Models for Writers

Short Essays for Composition

ELEVENTH EDITION

Alfred Rosa
Paul Eschholz

University of Vermont

BEDFORD/ST. MARTIN'S

Boston ◆ *New York*

For Bedford/St. Martin's

Senior Developmental Editor: Martha Bustin
Senior Production Editor: Bridget Leahy
Senior Production Supervisor: Jennifer Peterson
Senior Marketing Manager: Molly Parke
Editorial Assistant: Mallory Moore
Production Assistant: Elise Keller
Copy Editor: Kathleen Lafferty
Indexer: Mary White
Photo Researcher: Connie Gardner
Permissions Manager: Kalina K. Ingham
Senior Art Director: Anna Palchik
Cover Design: Marine Bouvier Miller
Cover Photo: Folded paper crane © sozaijiten/Datacraft,
    Getty Images
Composition: Cenveo Publisher Services
Printing and Binding: RR Donnelley and Sons

President: Joan E. Feinberg
Editorial Director: Denise B. Wydra
Editor in Chief: Karen S. Henry
Director of Marketing: Karen R. Soeltz
Director of Production: Susan W. Brown
Associate Director, Editorial Production: Elise S. Kaiser
Managing Editor: Elizabeth M. Schaaf

Library of Congress Control Number: 2011941051

For information, write: Bedford/St. Martin's, 75 Arlington Street, Boston,
MA 02116   (617-399-4000)

ISBN: 978-0-312-55201-5   (Paperback)
ISBN: 978-0-312-55217-6   (High School edition)

Preface

Models for Writers, now in its eleventh edition, continues to offer students and instructors brief, accessible, high-interest models of rhetorical elements, principles, and patterns. As important as it is for students to read while they are learning to write college-level essays, *Models for Writers* offers more than a collection of essays. Through the abundant study materials that accompany each selection, students master the writing skills they will need for all their college classes. Writing activities and assignments give students the chance to stitch together the various rhetorical elements into coherent, forceful essays of their own. This approach, which has helped several million students since 1982 to become better writers, remains at the heart of the book.

In this eleventh edition, we continue to emphasize the classic features of *Models for Writers* that have won praise from teachers and students alike. In addition, we have strengthened the book by introducing new selections and new voices and by developing key new features that provide students with the tools they need to become better readers and writers.

■ FAVORITE FEATURES OF *MODELS FOR WRITERS*

• **Brief, Lively Readings that Provide Outstanding Models.** Most of the seventy-six selections in *Models for Writers* are comparable in length (two to three pages) to the essays students will write themselves, and each clearly illustrates a basic rhetorical element, principal, or pattern. Just as important, the essays deal with subjects that we know from our own teaching experience will spark the interest of most college students. The range of voices, cultural perspectives, and styles represented in the essays will resonate with today's students. They will enjoy and benefit from reading and writing about selections by many well-known authors, including Annie Dillard, Judith Ortiz Cofer, Stephen King, Anne Lamott, Brian Doyle, Diane Ackerman, Sandra Cisneros, Salman Rushdie, Martin Luther King Jr., and Steven Pinker.

• **Introductory Chapters on Reading and Writing.** Throughout the chapters in Part One, students review the writing process from fresh angles and use the essays they read to improve their own writing. Chapter 1, "The Writing Process," details the steps in the writing process and illustrates them with a student essay in progress. Chapter 2, "From Reading to Writing," shows students how to use the apparatus in the text, provides them with guidelines for critical reading, and demonstrates with four student essays (narrative, responsive, reflective, and argumentative) how they can generate their own writing from reading.

• **An Easy-to-Follow Rhetorical Organization.** Each of the twenty rhetorically based chapters in *Models for Writers* is devoted to a particular element or pattern important to college writing. Chapters 3 through 10 focus on the concepts of thesis, unity, organization, beginnings and endings, paragraphs, transitions, effective sentences, and writing with sources. Chapter 11 illustrates the importance of controlling diction and tone, and Chapter 12, the uses of figurative language. Chapters 13 through 21 explore the types of writing most often required of college students: illustration, narration, description, process analysis, definition, division and classification, comparison and contrast, cause and effect, and argument. The final chapter is a brief guide to writing a research paper.

• **Abundant Study Materials.** To help students use the readings to improve their writing, every essay is accompanied by ample study materials.

Reflecting on What You Know activities precede each reading and prompt students to explore their own ideas and experiences regarding the issues presented in the reading.

A *Thinking Critically about This Reading* question follows each essay. It encourages students to consider the writer's assumptions, make connections not readily apparent, or explore the broader implications of the selection.

Questions for Study and Discussion focus on the selection's content and on the author's purpose and the particular strategy used to achieve that purpose. To remind students that good writing is never one-dimensional, at least one question in each series focuses on a writing concern other than the one highlighted in the chapter.

Classroom Activities provide brief exercises enabling students to work (often in groups) on rhetorical elements, techniques, or patterns. These activities range from developing thesis statements to using strong action verbs and building argumentative evidence. These activities encourage students to apply concepts modeled in the readings to their own writing.

Suggested Writing Assignments provide at least two writing assignments for each essay, with one encouraging students to use the reading selection as a direct model and another asking them to respond to the content of the reading.

• **Concise and Interesting Chapter Introductions.** Writing instructors who use *Models for Writers* have continued to be generous in their praise for the brief, clear, practical, and student-friendly chapter introductions, which explain the various elements and patterns. In each introduction, students will find illuminating examples—many written by students—of the feature or principle under discussion.

• **Practical Instruction on Working with Sources.** One of the biggest challenges student writers face is incorporating supporting evidence from other writers into their essays. In Chapter 1, "The Writing Process," students find clear advice on developing strong thesis statements and marshaling evidence and support. Chapter 10 models strategies for taking effective notes from sources, using signal phrases to integrate quotations, summaries, and paraphrases smoothly, synthesizing sources, and avoiding plagiarism. Further reviewing the steps and skills involved in research and synthesis, Chapter 22, "A Brief Guide to Writing a Research Paper," also provides a full-length model student research paper. Students become more confident in joining academic conversations and in writing the kinds of essays that they will be called upon to write in their college courses.

• **Targeted Instruction on Sentence Grammar.** Chapter 1, "The Writing Process," addresses editing concerns that instructors across the country have identified as the most problematic for their students, such as run-on sentences, verb tense shifts, comma splices, sentence fragments, and dangling and misplaced modifiers. Brief explanations and hand-edited examples show students how to find and correct these common errors in their own writing.

• **Flexible Arrangement.** Each chapter is self-contained so that instructors can easily follow their own teaching sequences, omitting or emphasizing certain chapters according to the needs of their students or the requirements of the course.

• **Alternate Table of Contents Showing Thematic Clusters.** The alternate table of contents groups readings into twenty-five clusters, each with three to eight essays that share a common theme. Students and instructors attracted to the theme of one essay in *Models for*

Writers can consult this alternate table of contents to find other essays in the book that address the same topic or theme.

• **Glossary of Useful Terms.** Cross-referenced in many of the questions and writing assignments throughout the book, this list of key terms defines rhetorical and literary terms that student writers need to know. Terms that are explained in the Glossary are shown in boldface the first time they appear in the text.

■ NEW TO THE ELEVENTH EDITION OF *MODELS FOR WRITERS*

• **Engaging, Informative, and Diverse New Readings.** Twenty-seven of the book's seventy-six readings are new to this edition of *Models for Writers*—ideal models by both new and established writers. We selected these essays for their brevity and clarity, for their effectiveness as models, and for their potential to develop critical thinking and writing. Among the new readings are Tobias Wolff's "The Last Shot," Judith Ortiz Cofer's "Volar," Salman Rushdie's "The Taj Majal," Eduardo Porter's "What Happiness Is," and Tina McElroy Ansa's "The Center of the Universe."

• **Compelling New Examples of Argument.** The argument chapter now features a revised cluster on "Crime: What Constitutes an Effective Punishment?" and two brand-new clusters which examine "Advertising: How Does It Affect Our Lives?" and "Torture: Are We for or against It?" These three argument clusters are designed to spark lively debate, both in class discussions and in students' writing. Research-based writing suggestions accompany each selection.

• **New Chapter, "A Brief Guide to Writing a Research Paper."** A new Chapter 22 offers a documented research paper, "To Facebook or Not," written by a student using *Models for Writers* and applying the book's recommended strategies for academic writing. The chapter provides students with clear guidance on establishing a realistic schedule for a research project; conducting research on the Internet using directory and keyword searches; evaluating sources; analyzing sources; developing a working bibliography; taking useful notes; and using MLA citation style to fully document the paper. In combination with Chapter 10, "Writing with Sources," the new chapter gives students strategies and opportunities to build confidence in their academic writing skills.

• **New Visuals and a Portfolio of Advertisements for Discussion.** The biographical head notes that accompany each selection in *Models* now include engaging photographs of the writers — students now can see the person who wrote the essay they are reading. In the argument cluster on advertisement, we have included a collection of advertisements for discussion and written analysis and interpretation.

■ YOU GET MORE DIGITAL CHOICES FOR *MODELS FOR WRITERS*, ELEVENTH EDITION

Models for Writers does not stop with a book. Online, you will find both free and affordable premium resources to help students get even more out of the book and your course. You will also find convenient instructor resources, such as downloadable sample syllabi, classroom activities, and even a nationwide community of teachers with *Bits*. To learn more about or order any of the products below, contact your Bedford/St. Martin's sales representative, e-mail sales support (sales_support@bfwpub.com), or visit the Web site at bedfordstmartins.com.

Companion Web Site for *Models for Writers*
bedfordstmartins.com/models

Send students to free and open resources, choose flexible premium resources to supplement your print text, or upgrade to an expanding collection of innovative digital content.

• **Free and open resources for *Models for Writers*** provide students with easy-to-access reference materials, visual tutorials, and support for working with sources.

- Reading quizzes for readings in *Models for Writers* and access to more model documents
- Customized Learning Plan that provides additional practice with grammar and mechanics
- Three free tutorials from *ix visual exercises* by Cheryl Ball and Kristin Arola
- *TopLinks* with reliable online sources
- *The Bedford Bibliographer*: a tool for collecting source information and making a bibliography in MLA, APA, and *Chicago* styles

- *VideoCentral: English* is a growing collection of videos for the writing class that captures real-world, academic, and student writers talking about how and why they write. *VideoCentral* can be packaged for free with *Models for Writers*, Eleventh Edition. An activation code is required. To order *VideoCentral* packaged with the print book, use ISBN 13: 978-1-4576-1026-4.

- *Re:Writing Plus* gathers all of Bedford/St. Martin's' premium digital content for composition into one online collection. It includes hundreds of model documents, the first ever peer review game, and *VideoCentral*. *Re:Writing Plus* can be purchased separately or packaged with the print book at a significant discount. An activation code is required. To order *Re:Writing Plus* access card packaged with the print book, use ISBN 13: 978-1-4576-1027-1.

E-book Options

- **Assign an interactive e-book.** For the first time ever, *Models for Writers* is available in an e-book format. With all the content of the print book, the *Models for Writers e-Book* lets students easily search, highlight, and bookmark. Instructors can customize and rearrange chapters, add and share notes, and link to quizzes and activities. *Models for Writers e-Book* can be purchased standalone or packaged at a discount with the print book. To order the e-book packaged with the print book, use ISBN-13: 978-1-4576-1852-9.

- **Let students choose their format.** Students can purchase *Models for Writers* in other popular e-book formats for computers, tablets, and e-readers. For more details, visit bedfordstmartins.com/ebooks.

i-series

Add more value to your text by choosing one of the following tutorial series, free when packaged with *Models for Writers*, Eleventh Edition. This popular series presents multimedia tutorials in a flexible format—because there are things you can't do in a book. To learn more about package options or any of the products below, contact your Bedford/St. Martin's sales representative or visit bedfordstmartins.com.

- *ix visualizing composition 2.0* (available online) helps students put into practice key rhetorical and visual concepts. To order *ix visualizing composition* (free access card) packaged with the print book, use ISBN 13: 978-1-4576-1273-2.

- *i-claim: visualizing argument* (available on CD-ROM) offers a new way to see argument—with 6 tutorials, an illustrated glossary, and over 70 multimedia arguments. To order *i-claim: visualizing argument* (free CD-ROM) packaged with the print book, use ISBN 13: 978-1-4576-1028-8.

- *i-cite: visualizing sources* (available online as part of *Re:Writing Plus*) brings research to life through an animated introduction, four tutorials, and hands-on source practice. To order *i-cite: visualizing sources* (free CD-ROM) packaged with the print book, use ISBN 13: 978-1-4576-1029-5.

Instructor Resources

You have a lot to do in your course. Bedford/St. Martin's wants to make it easy for you to find the support you need—and to get it quickly.

- **The *Instructor's Manual for Models for Writers*,** Eleventh Edition, contains, for each reading, suggested answers for critical reading questions and study questions. The Instructor's Manual also includes essay analysis and discussion, tips to help students think critically about what they have read, and suggestions for classroom activities. The manual gives information on the rhetorical features of each essay as well as advice on how best to use the materials in class. This manual may be found in the *Instructor's Edition of Models for Writers*, Eleventh Edition, or it is available as a separate booklet or as downloadable PDFs from **bedfordstmartins.com/models/catalog**.

- *Teaching Central* (bedfordstmartins.com/teachingcentral) offers the entire list of Bedford/St. Martin's print and online professional resources in one place. You will find landmark reference works, sourcebooks on pedagogical issues, award-winning collections, and practical advice for the classroom—all free for instructors.

- *Bits* (bedfordbits.com) collects creative ideas for teaching a range of composition topics in an easily searchable blog. A community of teachers—leading scholars, authors, and editors—discuss revision, research, grammar and style, technology, peer review, and much more. Take, use, adapt, and pass the ideas around. Then, come back to the site to comment or share your own suggestion.

- **Bedford Course Packs** allow you to easily integrate our most popular content into your own course management systems. For details, visit bedfordstmartins.com/coursepacks.

ACKNOWLEDGMENTS

In response to the many thoughtful reviews from instructors who use this book, we have maintained the solid foundation of the previous edition of *Models for Writers* while adding fresh readings and writing topics to stimulate today's student writers.

We are indebted to many people for their advice as we prepared this eleventh edition. We are especially grateful to Matthew Allen, Purdue University; Mary Baken, Webster University; Shannon Blair, Central Piedmont Community College; Melana Cavenecia, English Butte College; April Childress, Greenville Technical College; Linda Cohen, Bridgewater State College; Robert De France, Long Beach City College; Jennifer DelVecchio, Sussex Community College; Lewis Disbrow, Los Medanos Community College; Kathleen Driscoll, Bristol Community College; Keri English, Berkeley College; Janice Fioravante, College of Staten Island; Lisa Goddard, Long Beach City College; Patricia Golder, Victor Valley College; Patricia Hironymous, Glendale Community College; Tom Howerton, Johnston Community College; Linda Jensen, UCLA; Carrie McWhorter, University of West Georgia; Kitty Nard, California State University, Northridge; Maria Rankin-Brown, Pacific Union College; William Rosenblatt, Glendale Community College; Gary Tessmer, University of Pittsburgh at Bradford; Jennifer Turner, The Citadel; Julie Vega, Ross State University; Andrew Virtue, University of Minnesota; Catherine S. Wolf, Dover Business College; Courtney Huse Wika, Black Hills State University; Jon Zonderman, University of Bridgeport.

It has been our good fortune to have the editorial guidance and good cheer of Martha Bustin, our developmental editor on this book, and Mallory Moore, editorial assistant. We have also benefited from the careful eye of Bridget Leahy, our production editor, the advice of Nancy Perry, our longtime friend and editor, and the rest of the excellent team at Bedford/St. Martin's—Joan Feinberg, Karen Henry, Denise Wydra, Erica Appel, Marcia Cohen, Steve Scipione, and Karita dos Santos—as we planned, developed, and wrote this new edition. Our special thanks go to the late Tom Broadbent—our mentor and original editor at St. Martin's Press—who helped us breathe life and soul into *Models for Writers* more than thirty years ago. The lessons that he shared with us during our fifteen-year partnership have stayed with us throughout our careers.

Thanks also to Sarah Federman, who authored the new material for the *Instructor's Manual*, and to Brian Kent, Cara Simone Bader, Tom Juvan, and Betsy Eschholz, who have shared their experiences using *Models for Writers* in the classroom. Our greatest debt is, as always, to our students—especially James Duffy, Trena Isley, Jake Jamieson, Zoe Ockenga, Jeffrey Olesky, and Cori Schmidtbauer, whose papers appear in this text—for all they have taught us over the years. Finally, we thank each other, partners in this writing and teaching venture for over four decades.

Alfred Rosa
Paul Eschholz

Contents

Preface   iii
Thematic Clusters   xxiii
Introduction for Students   1

part one **On Reading and Writing Well**

❙ The Writing Process   **7**

Prewriting   7

    Understand Your Assignment   8

    Choose a Subject Area, and Focus on a Topic   9

    Get Ideas and Collect Information   10

    Establish Your Thesis   12

    Know Your Audience   14

    Determine Your Method of Development   15

    Map Your Organization   17

Writing the First Draft   18

    Create a Title   19

    Focus on Beginnings and Endings   19

Revising   20

Editing   21

    Run-ons: Fused Sentences and Comma Splices   21

    Sentence Fragments   22

    Sentence-Verb Agreement   23

    Pronoun-Antecedent Agreement   24

    Verb Tense Shifts   25

Misplaced and Dangling Modifiers   26

Faulty Parallelism   27

Weak Nouns and Verbs   28

Academic Diction and Tone   28

ESL Concerns (Articles and Nouns)   30

Proofreading   32

Writing an Expository Essay: A Student Essay
in Progress   33

Jeffrey Olesky, Golf: A Character Builder (student essay)   38

2 From Reading to Writing   43

Getting the Most Out of Your Reading   43

Step 1: Prepare Yourself to Read the Selection   44

Step 2: Read the Selection   47

Step 3: Reread the Selection   47

Step 4: Annotate the Text with Marginal Notes   47

Step 5: Analyze the Text with Questions   48

An Example: Annotating Isaac Asimov's "Intelligence"   49

Isaac Asimov, Intelligence   49

Practice: Reading and Annotating Rachel Carson's
"Fable for Tomorrow"   51

Rachel Carson, Fable for Tomorrow   52

Using Your Reading in the Writing Process   57

Reading as a Writer   57

Writing from Reading: Four Sample Student Essays   59

A Narrative Essay: *Trena Isley*, On the Sidelines (student essay)   59

A Response Essay: *Zoe Ockenga*, The Excuse "Not To"
(student essay)   63

A Reflective Essay: *Jennifer Chu*, A Bowl of Noodles
(student essay)   68

An Argumentative Essay: *James Duffy*, One Dying Wish
(student essay)   73

part two **The Elements of the Essay**

3 Thesis 81

Helen Keller, The Most Important Day 84
The celebrated blind and deaf writer recalls her discovery of language.

Natalie Goldberg, Be Specific 90
The challenge and job of writing, says this writing guru, are in the details.

James Lincoln Collier, Anxiety: Challenge by Another Name 94
A writer asserts that we can "accomplish wonders" if we "accept anxiety as another name for challenge."

4 Unity 99

Thomas L. Friedman, My Favorite Teacher 103
A Pulitzer Prize–winning columnist describes the high school teacher who had the most influence on his career as a journalist.

Sandra Cisneros, My Name 109
A Chicana writer explores the many facets of her inherited name.

Gloria Naylor, The Meanings of a Word 113
In "meeting the word [nigger] head on," blacks have "rendered it impotent," according to a prominent African American novelist.

5 Organization 119

Cherokee Paul McDonald, A View from the Bridge 124
An encounter with a young fisherman teaches the author a lesson in what it means to see.

Audrey Schulman, Fahrenheit 59: What a Child's Fever Might Tell Us about Climate Change 131
A writer uses her young son's fever to explain the problem of global warming.

Sean Prentiss, Buying a House 137
A young writer embarks on his first house hunt and reflects on what the structure means for the rest of his life.

6 Beginnings and Endings

145

Michael T. Kaufman, Of My Friend Hector and My
Achilles Heel 154
*A journalist reveals his "prejudice and stupidity"
in this essay about his relationship with a childhood
friend.*

Richard Lederer, The Case for Short Words 160
*This English teacher and language expert argues that
"short words are as good as long ones."*

Carl T. Rowan, Unforgettable Miss Bessie 166
*A newspaper columnist remembers an influential teacher
in the segregated South.*

7 Paragraphs

172

William Zinsser, Simplicity 176
*"The secret of good writing," according to this expert,
"is to strip every sentence to its cleanest components."*

Mike Rose, "I Just Wanna Be Average" 183
*A former student pays tribute to a high school teacher who
inspired him and encouraged him to continue his studies.*

Tobias Wolff, The Last Shot 189
*An award-winning author takes issue with George Orwell's
assertion that it is "better still to die in your boots."*

8 Transitions

193

David Raymond, On Being 17, Bright, and Unable to Read 197
A dyslexic high school student describes his experiences.

Russell Baker, Becoming a Writer 203
*The author remembers his joy at the discovery that his
"words had the power to make people laugh."*

Nancy Gibbs, The Magic of the Family Meal 208
*An award-winning political writer reports on the
resurgence of the family dinnertime.*

9 Effective Sentences 217

Alice Walker, Childhood 222
> *This Pulitzer Prize–winning poet, novelist, and essayist shares her childhood memories of planting and harvesting, a love of which she passes to her daughter.*

Langston Hughes, Salvation 228
> *A famous poet remembers a church revival meeting at which he pretended to be "saved from sin."*

Judith Ortiz Cofer, Volar 233
> *A popular author focuses on the differences between island life in Puerto Rico and tenement living in New York.*

10 Writing with Sources 238

Sharon Begley, Praise the Humble Dung Beetle 255
> *A science writer argues that some less-cute species also deserve to be protected under the Endangered Species Act.*

Jake Jamieson, The English-Only Movement: Can America Proscribe Language with a Clear Conscience? 261
> *A student writer evaluates the merits of a movement in the United States that would require immigrants to learn English.*

Terry Tempest Williams, The Clan of One-Breasted Women 269
> *This popular author describes her family's struggles and ways of coping with hereditary breast cancer.*

part three **The Language of the Essay**

11 Diction and Tone 283

Dick Gregory, Shame 288
> *A civil rights advocate recalls a painful childhood incident.*

David Sedaris, Me Talk Pretty One Day   294
  *A popular American essayist recounts his experience
  of trying to learn French in Paris.*

Tina McElroy Ansa, The Center of the Universe   302
  *A novelist, filmmaker, and essayist reflects on her Southern
  upbringing and on how her experiences still influence
  her today.*

Brian Doyle, Irreconcilable Dissonance   308
  *The author discusses the idea that "every marriage is
  pregnant with divorce."*

12 Figurative Language   314

Robert Ramirez, The Barrio   316
  *A Hispanic writer paints a vivid and sensuous picture of
  the district called the barrio.*

Anne Lamott, Polaroids   323
  *This popular author equates writing to developing a
  Polaroid picture.*

Benjamin Percy, Invasion   329
  *A popular novelist tells two stories of invasion in his home
  state of Oregon.*

part four **Types of Essays**

13 Illustration   339

Barbara Huttmann, A Crime of Compassion   343
  *A nurse pleads for new legislation that would permit
  terminally ill patients to choose death with dignity.*

Gregory Pence, Let's Think Outside the Box of Bad Clichés   349
  *A professor points out that trite expressions often indicate a lack
  of clear, original thought.*

Verlyn Klinkenborg, Our Vanishing Night   355
  A writer and farmer discusses the often unnoticed negative effects of light pollution.

Steven Pinker, In Defense of Dangerous Ideas   361
  A celebrated academic prods us to consider some of the difficult moral questions we're afraid to ask because, he argues, "important ideas need to be aired."

14 Narration   **372**

Henry Louis Gates Jr., What's in a Name?   376
  A prominent African American scholar remembers a childhood encounter with racism.

Erin Murphy, White Lies   381
  This writer recalls a painful childhood memory of bullying, and questions the reliability of memory.

Maya Angelou, Momma, the Dentist, and Me   386
  A celebrated African American writer recounts how a toothache led to a confrontation with racism.

Kate Chopin, The Story of an Hour   395
  The short-story writer captures the truth of a marriage in the events of an hour.

15 Description   **400**

Eudora Welty, The Corner Store   402
  A novelist describes a cherished place from her childhood.

Joanne Lipman, And the Orchestra Played On   407
  A prize-winning journalist and author pays tribute to her childhood music teacher.

Kyoko Mori, Yarn   412
  A poet and novelist uses sensory detail to describe the process of knitting.

Salman Rushdie, The Taj Mahal   419
  The award-winning writer recounts the first time he saw the Taj Mahal.

16 Process Analysis   423

Paul W. Merrill, The Principles of Poor Writing   427
*In this classic essay, a scientist provides satirical
instructions he believes his colleagues must
follow when producing shoddy writing.*

Nicholson Baker, How to Make Chocolate Sauce   433
*This writer presents an unconventional
recipe for making chocolate sauce.*

Diane Ackerman, Why Leaves Turn Color in the Fall   438
*This noted nature writer explains the process
by which autumn leaves change color.*

17 Definition   444

Lawrence M. Friedman, What Is Crime?   447
*A law professor explains what it takes for
something to be considered criminal.*

Ellen Goodman, The Company Man   451
*A columnist denounces the workaholic lifestyle
with a disturbing example.*

Eduardo Porter, What Happiness Is   456
*A journalist explores many different perspectives
on the meaning of happiness.*

18 Division and Classification   461

Martin Luther King Jr., The Ways of Meeting Oppression   465
*In this classic essay, the civil rights leader
makes a case for nonviolent resistance.*

Marion Winik, What Are Friends For?   470
*This poet, essayist, and radio commentator places
her friends in different categories, among them
"Buddies," "Relative Friends," and "Friends
You Love to Hate."*

William Lutz, Doubts about Doublespeak   477
*A professor and language consultant discusses
"language that pretends to communicate but doesn't."*

19 Comparison and Contrast — 483

Mark Twain, Two Ways of Seeing a River — 488
*This popular American author makes his classic
observation that sometimes knowledge can be blinding.*

Bharati Mukherjee, Two Ways to Belong in America — 493
*An Indian American writer and professor recounts a
disagreement with her sister over the merits of citizenship.*

Suzanne Britt, That Lean and Hungry Look — 499
*An author uses humor and witty comparisons to examine
the perceived differences between fat and thin people.*

Amanda Ripley, Who Says a Woman Can't Be Einstein? — 505
*This author explores what research reveals about
the differences and similarities between the brains
of men and women.*

20 Cause and Effect — 517

Gita Mehta, The Famine of Bengal — 521
*A popular author recounts the series of events that led to the
starvation of 3,000,000 Indians just before her birth.*

Stephen King, Why We Crave Horror Movies — 524
*The king of macabre explains the appeal of horror
movies and why he thinks "we're all mentally ill."*

Myriam Marquez, Why and When We Speak Spanish in Public — 531
*A Hispanic columnist explains why she
speaks Spanish in public.*

Sanjay Gupta, Stuck on the Couch — 535
*A doctor examines Americans' unwillingness to
exercise despite the common knowledge that
regular exercise greatly improves overall health.*

21 Argument — 539

Thomas Jefferson, The Declaration of Independence — 547
*A country seeks to justify its action to its people
and the world in this classic argument.*

Martin Luther King Jr., I Have a Dream   553
*In this revered speech, the celebrated civil rights
leader imparts his vision of freedom and equality.*

Dave Zirin, What Pro Sports Owners Owe Us   560
*A sportswriter argues that the owners of professional
sports franchises need to start paying more attention
to the fans, and less attention to their own monetary
interests.*

Mary Sherry, In Praise of the F Word   564
*An educator argues that schools should consider using
the "trump card of failure" to motivate students.*

Crime: What Constitutes an Effective Punishment?

June Tangney, Condemn the Crime, Not the Person   569
*"Shame often makes a bad situation worse,"
suggests a psychology professor.*

Dan M. Kahan, Shame Is Worth a Try   574
*A law professor asserts that "shaming
punishments . . . are extraordinarily effective."*

Carl M. Cannon, Petty Crime, Outrageous Punishment   579
*A veteran journalist argues against the
"three strikes rule" for punishment.*

Advertising: How Does It Affect Our Lives?

Allen D. Kanner, The Piracy of Privacy: Why Marketers
Must Bare Our Souls   587
*A psychologist argues that the strategies and high-tech
tools used by marketers are having a negative effect
on their target audience's psychological health.*

Terry O'Reilly, Marketing Ate Our Culture—But
It Doesn't Have To   594
*A radio advertising expert argues that society has
an obligation to watch the advertisements
presented to them.*

Ruth La Ferla, Generation E. A.: Ethnically Ambiguous   602
   *This iconic fashion writer reports on the fairly recent trend of
   using models of indeterminate ethnic backgrounds or identities
   for fashion branding and advertising.*

Critical Thinking: Advertisements for Analysis

Hugh Rank, Intensify/Downplay   609

Torture: Are We For or Against It?

Charles Krauthammer, The Truth about Torture   616
   *This Pulitzer Prize–winning columnist argues in favor
   of the use of torture in especially dangerous situations.*

Andrew Sullivan, The Abolition of Torture   629
   *A journalist rebuts Charles Krauthammer's argument and supports
   the complete abolition of torture under any circumstances.*

22 A Brief Guide to Writing a Research Paper   642

Establishing a Realistic Schedule   643

Finding and Using Sources   644

Conducting Keyword Searches   645

Using Subject Directories to Define and Develop
   Your Research Topic   647

Evaluating Your Print and Online Sources   648

Analyzing Your Print and Online Sources   650

Developing a Working Bibliography for
   Your Sources   651

Taking Notes   653

Documenting Sources   654

An Annotated Student Research Paper: *Cori Schmidtbauer,*
   "To Facebook or Not" (student essay)   669

Glossary of Useful Terms   678
Index   697

Thematic Clusters

The thematic clusters of articles that follow focus on themes that students can pursue in their own compositions. The essays themselves provide ideas and information that will stimulate their thinking as well as provide source material for their writing. The clusters—the themes and the essays associated with them—are meant to be suggestive rather than comprehensive and fairly narrow in scope rather than far-ranging. Instructors and students are, of course, free to develop their own thematic groupings on which to base written work and are not limited by our groupings.

Teachers and Students

Isaac Asimov, Intelligence   49
Helen Keller, The Most Important Day   84
Carl T. Rowan, Unforgettable Miss Bessie   166
Thomas L. Friedman, My Favorite Teacher   103
Joanne Lipman, And the Orchestra Played On   407

Parenting

Alice Walker, Childhood   222
Erin Murphy, White Lies   381
Maya Angelou, Momma, the Dentist, and Me   386
Joanne Lipman, And the Orchestra Played On   407

Personal Dilemmas

James Lincoln Collier, Anxiety: Challenge by Another Name   94
Dick Gregory, Shame   288
Langston Hughes, Salvation   228
Brian Doyle, Irreconcilable Dissonance   308
Sanjay Gupta, Stuck on the Couch   535

Peer Pressure

Michael T. Kaufman, Of My Friend Hector and My Achilles Heel 154
Dick Gregory, Shame 288
Langston Hughes, Salvation 228
Amanda Ripley, Who Says a Woman Can't Be Einstein? 505

The Natural World

Rachel Carson, A Fable for Tomorrow 52
Audrey Schulman, Fahrenheit 59: What a Child's Fever Might Tell Us about Climate Change 131
Sharon Begley, Praise the Humble Dung Beetle 255
Terry Tempest Williams, The Clan of One-Breasted Women 269
Verlyn Klinkenborg, Our Vanishing Night 355
Diane Ackerman, Why Leaves Turn Color in the Fall 438

What's in a Name?

Sandra Cisneros, My Name 109
Gloria Naylor, The Meanings of a Word 113
Natalie Goldberg, Be Specific 90
Henry Louis Gates Jr., What's in a Name? 376

Power of Language

Jake Jamieson, The English-Only Movement: Can America Proscribe Language with a Clear Conscience? 261
William Lutz, Doubts about Doublespeak 477
Myriam Marquez, Why and When We Speak Spanish in Public 531
Hugh Rank, Intensify/Downplay 609

Punishment and Torture

Mary Sherry, In Praise of the F Word 564
June Tangney, Condemn the Crime, Not the Person 569
Dan M. Kahan, Is Shame Worth a Try? 574
Carl M. Cannon, Petty Crime, Outrageous Punishment 579
Charles Krauthammer, The Truth about Torture 616
Andrew Sullivan, The Abolition of Torture 629

Sensual World

Helen Keller, The Most Important Day 84
Judith Ortiz Cofer, Volar 233

Cherokee Paul McDonald, A View from the Bridge   124
Alice Walker, Childhood   222
Salman Rushdie, The Taj Mahal   419
Mark Twain, Two Ways of Seeing a River   488

People and Personalities

Eduardo Porter, What Happiness Is   456
Marion Winik, What Are Friends For?   470
Suzanne Britt, That Lean and Hungry Look   499
Amanda Ripley, Who Says a Woman Can't Be Einstein?   505

Medical Dilemmas

Terry Tempest Williams, The Clan of One-Breasted Women   269
Barbara Huttmann, A Crime of Compassion   343
Erin Murphy, White Lies   381
Maya Angelou, Momma, the Dentist, and Me   386
Gita Mehta, The Famine of Bengal   521

The World of Advertising

Allen D. Kanner, The Piracy of Privacy:
   Why Marketers Must Bare Our Souls   587
Terry O'Reilly, Marketing Ate Our Culture—But It Doesn't
   Have To   594
Ruth La Ferla, Generation E. A.: Ethnically Ambiguous   602
Hugh Rank, Intensify/Downplay   609

Writing about Writing

William Zinsser, Simplicity   176
Russell Baker, Becoming a Writer   203
Anne Lamott, Polaroids   323
Natalie Goldberg, Be Specific   90
Richard Lederer, The Case for Short Words   160
Gregory Pence, Let's Think Outside the Box of Bad Clichés   349
Paul W. Merrill, The Principles of Poor Writing   427

Life's Decisions

Bharati Mukherjee, Two Ways to Belong in America   493
Sean Prentiss, Buying a House   137
Ellen Goodman, The Company Man   451

Discoveries/Epiphanies

Helen Keller, The Most Important Day   84
James Lincoln Collier, Anxiety: Challenge by Another Name   94
Cherokee Paul McDonald, A View from the Bridge   124
Alice Walker, Childhood   222
Langston Hughes, Salvation   228

Moral Values

Martin Luther King Jr., The Ways of Meeting Oppression   465
Barbara Huttmann, A Crime of Compassion   343
Steven Pinker, In Defense of Dangerous Ideas   361
Gita Mehta, The Famine of Bengal   521

Pop Culture

Salman Rushdie, The Taj Mahal   419
Nicholson Baker, How to Make Chocolate Sauce   433
Stephen King, Why We Crave Horror Movies   524
Dave Zirin, What Pro Sports Owners Owe Us   560

The Immigrant Experience

Judith Ortiz Cofer, Volar   233
Bharati Mukherjee, Two Ways to Belong in America   493
David Sedaris, Me Talk Pretty One Day   294
Robert Ramirez, The Barrio   316
Myriam Marquez, Why and When We Speak Spanish
   in Public   531

Sense of Place

Sean Prentiss, Buying a House   137
Tina McElroy Ansa, The Center of the Universe   302
Benjamin Percy, Invasion   329
Robert Ramirez, The Barrio   316
Mark Twain, Two Ways of Seeing a River   488

The American Dream

Alice Walker, Childhood   222
Sean Prentiss, Buying a House   137
Amanda Ripley, Who Says a Woman Can't Be Einstein?   505

Thomas Jefferson, The Declaration of Independence   547
Martin Luther King Jr., I Have a Dream   553

Heroes/Role Models

Tobias Wolff, Last Shot   189
Carl Rowan, Unforgettable Miss Bessie   166
Mike Rose, "I Just Wanna Be Average"   183
Thomas L. Friedman, My Favorite Teacher   103
Joanne Lipman, And the Orchestra Played On   407

Consumerism

Eduardo Porter, What Happiness Is   456
Terry O'Reilly, Marketing Ate Our Culture—But It Doesn't
   Have To   594

Sense of Self

Michael T. Kaufman, Of My Friend Hector and My
   Achilles Heel   154
Erin Murphy, White Lies   381
Langston Hughes, Salvation   228
Dick Gregory, Shame   288
Kyoko Mori, Yarn   412
Eduardo Porter, What Happiness Is   456

Family and Friends

Nancy Gibbs, The Magic of the Family Meal   208
Kate Chopin, The Story of an Hour   395
Ellen Goodman, The Company Man   451
Marion Winik, What Are Friends For?   470

Race in America

Gloria Naylor, The Meanings of a Word   113
Bharati Mukherjee, Two Ways to Belong in America   493
Martin Luther King Jr., The Ways of Meeting Oppression   465
Dick Gregory, Shame   288
Henry Louis Gates Jr., What's in a Name?   376
Maya Angelou, Momma, the Dentist, and Me   386
Myriam Marquez, Why and When We Speak Spanish in Public   531
Martin Luther King Jr., I Have a Dream   553

Introduction for Students

Models for Writers is designed to help you learn to write by providing you with a collection of model essays — that is, essays that are examples of good writing. Good writing is direct and purposeful and communicates its message without confusing the reader. It doesn't wander from the topic, and it answers the reader's questions. Although good writing is well developed and detailed, it also accomplishes its task with the fewest possible words and with the simplest language appropriate to the writer's topic and thesis.

We know that one of the best ways to learn to write and to improve our writing is to read. By reading, we can see how other writers have communicated their experiences, ideas, thoughts, and feelings. We can study how they have used the various elements of the essay (words, sentences, paragraphs, organizational patterns, transitions, examples, evidence, and so forth) and thus learn how we might effectively do the same. When we see how a writer like James Lincoln Collier develops his essay "Anxiety: Challenge by Another Name" from a strong thesis statement, for example, we can better appreciate the importance of having a clear thesis statement in our own writing. When we see the way Russell Baker uses transitions in "Becoming a Writer" to link key phrases and important ideas so that readers can recognize how the parts of his essay fit together, we have a better idea of how to write coherently.

But we do not learn only by observing or by reading. We also learn by doing (that is, by writing), and in the best of all situations, we engage in these two activities in conjunction with each other. *Models for Writers* therefore encourages you to practice what you are learning and to move from reading to writing.

Part One of *Models for Writers* provides you with strategies to do just that. Chapter 1, The Writing Process, introduces you to the important steps of the writing process, gives you guidelines for writing, and illustrates the writing process with a student essay. Chapter 2, From Reading to Writing, shows you how to use the apparatus that accompanies each selection in this text, provides you with guidelines for critical reading, and demonstrates with four annotated student essays how you can generate your own writing from reading. You will soon see that an effective essay has a clear purpose, often provides useful information, has an effect on the reader's thoughts and feelings, and is usually a pleasure to read. The essays that you will read in *Models for Writers* were chosen because they are effective essays.

All well-written essays also share a number of structural and stylistic features that are illustrated by the various essays in *Models for Writers*. One good way to learn what these features are and how you can incorporate them into your own writing is to look at each of them in isolation. For this reason, we have divided the readings in *Models for Writers* into three major parts and, within these parts, into twenty chapters, each with its own particular focus and emphasis.

Part Two, The Elements of the Essay, includes eight chapters on the elements that are essential to a well-written essay, but because the concepts of thesis, unity, and organization underlie all the others, they come first in our sequence. Chapter 3, Thesis, shows how authors put forth or state the main ideas of their essays and how they use such statements to develop and control content. Chapter 4, Unity, shows how authors achieve a sense of wholeness in their essays, and Chapter 5, Organization, illustrates some important patterns that authors use to organize their thinking and writing. Chapter 6, Beginnings and Endings, offers advice on and models of ways to begin and conclude essays, while Chapter 7, Paragraphs, concentrates on the importance of well-developed paragraphs and what is necessary to achieve them. Chapter 8, Transitions, concerns various devices writers use to move from one idea or section of an essay to the next, and Chapter 9, Effective Sentences, focuses on techniques to make sentences powerful and to create stylistic variety. Finally, Chapter 10, Writing with Sources, provides you with proven strategies for taking effective notes from sources; for using signal phrases to integrate quotations, summaries, and paraphrases smoothly into the text of your papers; and for avoiding plagiarism.

Part Three, The Language of the Essay, starts with Chapter 11, Diction and Tone, which shows how writers carefully choose words either to convey exact meanings or to be purposely suggestive. In addition, this chapter shows how the words a writer uses can create a particular tone or relationship between the writer and reader—one of irony, humor, or seriousness, for example. This part also includes Chapter 12, Figurative Language, which concentrates on the usefulness of the special devices of language—such as simile, metaphor, and personification—that add richness and depth to writing.

Part Four of *Models for Writers*, Types of Essays, is made up of Chapters 13 to 22, which are on the types of writing that are most often required of college writing students—illustration (how to use examples to illustrate a point or idea), narration (how to tell a story or give an account of an event), description (how to present a verbal picture), process analysis (how to explain how something is done or happens), definition (how to explain what something is), division and classification (how to divide a subject into its parts and place items into appropriate categories), comparison and contrast (how to explain the similarities and differences between two or more items), cause and effect (how to explain the causes of an event or the effects of an action), argument (how to use reason and logic to persuade someone to your way of thinking), and the research paper. These types of writing are referred to as *organizational patterns* or *rhetorical modes*.

Studying and practicing the organizational patterns are important in any effort to broaden your writing skills. In *Models for Writers*, we look at each pattern separately because we believe that this is the simplest and most effective way to introduce them. However, it does not mean that the writer of a well-written essay necessarily chooses a single pattern and sticks to it exclusively and rigidly. Confining yourself to cause-and-effect analysis or definition throughout an entire essay, for example, might prove impractical and may yield an awkward or unnatural piece of writing. In fact, it is often best to use a single pattern to organize your essay and then to use other patterns as your material dictates. As you read the model essays in this text, you will find that a good many of them use one dominant pattern in combination with other patterns.

Combining organizational patterns is not something that you usually think about when you first tackle a writing assignment. Rather, such combinations of patterns develop naturally as you organize, draft, and revise your materials. Combinations of patterns also make your writing more interesting and effective. See Chapter 1 (pp. 15–17) for a discussion of combining patterns.

Chapters 3 to 21 are organized in the same way. Each opens with an explanation of the element or principle under discussion. These introductions are brief, clear, and practical and usually provide one or more short examples of the feature or principle being studied, including examples from students such as yourself. Following the chapter introduction, we present three or four model essays (Chapter 21, with thirteen essays, is an exception). Each essay has a brief introduction of its own, providing information about the author and directing your attention to the way the essay demonstrates the featured technique. A Reflecting on What You Know prompt precedes each reading and invites you to explore your own ideas and experiences regarding some issue presented in the reading. Each essay is followed by four kinds of study materials—Thinking Critically about This Reading, Questions for Study and Discussion, Classroom Activity, and Suggested Writing Assignments. Read Chapter 2, From Reading to Writing, for help on improving your writing by using the materials that accompany the readings.

Chapter 22, A Brief Guide to Writing a Research Paper, offers an annotated MLA-style student research paper, "To Facebook or Not." This chapter provides you clear guidance on establishing a realistic schedule for a research project, conducting research on the Internet using directory and keyword searches, evaluating sources, analyzing sources, developing a working bibliography, taking useful notes, and using MLA citation style to document your paper. This chapter, in combination with Chapter 10, Writing with Sources, helps you build confidence in your academic writing skills.

Models for Writers provides information, instruction, and practice in writing essays. By reading thoughtfully and by applying the writing strategies and techniques you observe other writers using, you will learn to write more expressively and effectively.

On Reading
and Writing Well

The Writing Process

The essays in this book will help you understand the elements of good writing and provide ample opportunity to practice writing in response to the model essays. As you write your own essays, pay attention to your writing process. This chapter focuses on the stages of the writing process—prewriting, writing the first draft, revising, editing, and proofreading. It concludes with a sample of one student's writing process that you can model your own writing after, from start to finish. The strategies suggested in this chapter for each stage of the writing process will help you overcome many of the problems you may face while writing your own essays.

■ PREWRITING

Writers rarely rely on inspiration alone to produce an effective piece of writing. Good writers prewrite or plan, write the first draft, revise, edit, and proofread. It is worth remembering, however, that the writing process is not as simple and as straightforward as this. Often the process is recursive, moving back and forth among the five stages. Moreover, writing is personal; no two people go about it exactly the same way. Still, it is possible to learn the steps in the process and thereby have a reassuring and reliable method for undertaking a writing task and producing a good composition.

Your reading can give you ideas and information, of course. But reading also helps expand your knowledge of the organizational patterns available to you, and, consequently, it can help direct all your prewriting activities. In *prewriting*, you select your subject and topic, gather ideas and information, and determine the thesis and organizational pattern or patterns you will use. Once you have worked through the prewriting process, you will be ready to start on your first draft. Let's explore how this works.

Understand Your Assignment

When you first receive an assignment, read it over several times. Focus on each word and each phrase to make sure you understand what you are being asked to do. Try restating the assignment in your own words to make sure you understand it. For example, consider the following assignments:

1. Narrate an experience that taught you that every situation has at least two sides.
2. Explain what is meant by *theoretical modeling* in the social sciences.
3. Write a persuasive essay in which you support or refute the following proposition: "Violence in the media is in large part responsible for an increase in violence in American society today."

Each of these assignments asks you to write in different ways. The first assignment asks you to tell the story of an event that showed you that every situation has more than one perspective. To complete the assignment, you might choose simply to narrate the event, or you might choose to analyze it in depth. In either case, you have to explain to your reader how you came to this new understanding of multiple perspectives and why it was important to you. The second assignment asks you to explain what theoretical modeling is and why it is used. To accomplish this assignment, you first need to read about the concept to gain a thorough understanding of it, and then you'll need to define it in your own words and explain its purpose and usefulness to your readers. You will also want to demonstrate the abstract concept with concrete examples to help your readers understand it. Finally, the third assignment asks you to take a position on a controversial issue for which there are many studies on both sides of the question. You will need to research the studies, consider the evidence they present, and then take a stand of your own. Your argument will necessarily have to draw on the sources and evidence you have researched, and you will need to refute the arguments and evidence presented by those experts who take an opposing position.

If, after reading the assignment several times, you are still unsure about what is being asked of you or about any additional requirements of the assignment, such as length or format, be sure to consult with your instructor. He or she should be willing to clear up any confusion before you start writing.

Choose a Subject Area, and Focus on a Topic

Although you will usually be given specific assignments in your writing course, you may sometimes have the freedom to write on any subject that interests you. In such a case, you may already have a specific idea in mind. For example, if you are interested in sports, you might argue against the use of performance-enhancing drugs by athletes. What happens, however, when you are free to choose your own subject and cannot think of anything to write about? If you find yourself in this situation, begin by determining a broad subject that you like to think about and might enjoy writing about — a general subject like virtual reality, medical ethics, amateur sports, or foreign travel. Also consider what you've recently read — essays in *Models for Writers*, for example — or your career ambitions when choosing a subject. Select several likely subjects, and let your mind explore their potential for interesting topics. Your goal is to arrive at an appropriately narrowed topic.

A topic is the specific part of a subject on which a writer focuses. Subjects such as the environment, literature, and sports are too broad to be dealt with adequately in a single essay. Entire books are written about these and other subjects. Start with your broad subject, and make it more specific. Thus if your subject is sports, you might choose as your topic rule violations in college recruiting, violence in ice hockey, types of fan behavior, the psychology of marathon runners, or the growth of sports medicine.

Suppose, for example, you select farming and advertising as possible subject areas. The examples on the following page illustrate how to narrow these broad subjects into manageable topics. Notice how each successive topic is more narrowed than the one before it. Moving from the general to the specific, the topics become appropriate for essay-length writing.

In moving from a broad subject to a particular topic, you should take into account any assigned constraints on length or format. You will also want to consider the amount of time you have to write. These practical considerations will affect the scope of your topic. For example, you couldn't adequately address subjects such as farming or

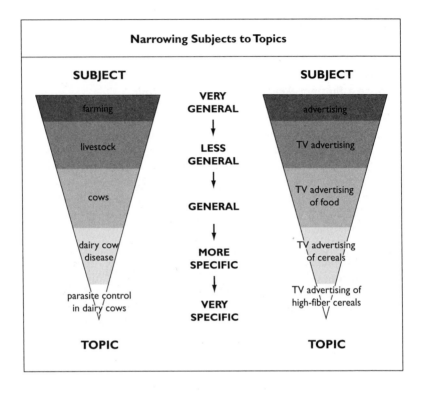

advertising in a five- to ten-page composition. These subjects are usually taken up in book-length publications.

Get Ideas and Collect Information

Once you have found your topic, you will need to determine what you want to say about it. The best way to do this is to gather information. Your ideas about a topic must be supported by information, such as facts and examples. The information you gather about a topic will influence your ideas about the topic and what you want to say. Here are some of the ways you can gather information:

1. *Ask questions about your topic.* If you were assigned the topic of theoretical modeling, for example, you could ask, what is *theoretical modeling*? Why, where, and by whom is theoretical

modeling used? What are the benefits of using it? Is it taught in school? Is it difficult to learn to use? Once the questioning starts, one question will lead to another, and the answers to these questions will be the stuff of your writing. Like a newspaper reporter going after a story, asking questions and getting answers are essential ways to understand a topic before trying to explain it to others.

2. *Brainstorm.* Jot down the things you know about a topic, freely associating ideas and information as a way to explore the topic and its possibilities. (See pp. 33–34 for an example.) Don't censor or edit your notes, and don't worry about spelling or punctuation. Don't write your notes in list form because such an organization will imply a hierarchy of ideas, which may hamper your creativity and the free flow of your thoughts. The objective of *brainstorming* is to free up your thinking before you start to write. You may want to set aside your notes and return to them over several days. Once you generate a substantial amount of brainstormed material, you will want to study the items, attempt to see relationships among them, or sort and group the entries by using different colored highlighters.

3. *Cluster.* Another strategy for stimulating your thinking about a topic is *clustering.* Place your topic in a circle, and draw lines from that circle to other circles in which you write related key words or phrases. Around each of these key words, generate more circles representing the various aspects of the key word that come to mind. (See p. 34 for an example.) The value of clustering over brainstorming is that you are generating ideas and organizing them at the same time. Both techniques work very well, but you may prefer one over the other or may find that one works better with one topic than another.

4. *Research.* You may want to add to what you already know about your topic with research. Research can take many forms beyond formal research carried out in your library. For example, firsthand observations and interviews with people knowledgeable about your topic can provide up-to-date information. Whatever your form of research, take careful notes so you can accurately paraphrase an author or quote an interviewee. Chapters 10 and 22 (see pp. 238–79 and 642–90) will help with all aspects of researching a topic.

5. *Think creatively.* To push an idea one step further, to make a connection not easily recognized by others, to step to one side of your topic and see it in a new light, to ask a question no one else would,

or to arrive at a fresh insight is to be creative. Don't be afraid to step outside conventional wisdom and ask a basic or unorthodox question. Take risks. Such bravery can add creativity to your writing.

Establish Your Thesis

Once you have generated ideas and information, you are ready to begin the important task of establishing a controlling idea, or *thesis*. The thesis of an essay is its main idea, the point the writer is trying to make. The thesis is often expressed in one or two sentences called a *thesis statement*. Here's an example:

> The so-called serious news programs are becoming too much like tabloid news shows in both their content and their presentation.

The thesis statement should not be confused with your purpose for writing. Whereas a thesis statement makes an assertion about your topic and actually appears in your essay as such, your purpose is what you are trying to do in the essay—to express, to explain, or to argue. For example, the purpose behind the preceding thesis statement might be expressed as follows:

> By comparing the transcripts of news shows like the *CBS Evening News* and tabloid shows like *Entertainment Tonight,* I will show troubling parallels in what the two genres of programs find "newsworthy."

This type of purpose statement should not appear in your essay. In other words, it's not a good idea to tell your readers what you are going to do in an essay. Just do it.

A thesis statement should be

- The most important point you make about a topic,
- More general than the ideas and facts used to support it, and
- Focused enough to be covered in the space allotted for the essay.

A thesis statement should not be a question but rather an assertion. If you find yourself writing a question for a thesis statement, answer the question first, and then write your statement.

How to Write a Thesis Statement

An effective method for developing a thesis statement is to begin by writing, "What I want to say is that . . ."

What I want to say is that unless language barriers between patients and healthcare providers are overcome, the lives of many patients in our more culturally diverse cities will be endangered.

Later, when you delete the formulaic opening, you will be left with a thesis statement:

Unless language barriers between patients and healthcare providers are overcome, many patients' lives in our more culturally diverse cities will be endangered.

A good way to determine whether your thesis is too general or too specific is to consider how easy it will be to present information and examples to support it. If you stray too far in either direction, your task will become much more difficult. A thesis statement that is too general will leave you overwhelmed by the number of issues you must address. For example, the statement, "Malls have ruined the fabric of American life" would lead to the question "How?" To answer it, you would probably have to include information about traffic patterns, urban decay, environmental damage, economic studies, and so on. You would obviously have to take shortcuts, and your paper would be ineffective. On the other hand, too specific a thesis statement will leave you with too little information to present. "The Big City Mall should not have been built because it reduced retail sales at the existing Big City stores by 21.4 percent" does not leave you with many options to develop an argument.

The thesis statement is usually set forth near the beginning of the essay, although writers sometimes begin with a few sentences that establish a context for the piece. One common strategy is to position the thesis as the final sentence of the first paragraph. In the opening paragraph of an essay on the harmful effects of quick weight-loss diets, student Marcie Turple builds a context for her thesis statement, which she presents in her last sentence:

Americans are obsessed with thinness—even at the risk of dying. In the 1930s, people took dinitrophenol, an industrial poison, to lose weight. It boosted metabolism but caused blindness and some deaths. Since then dieters have used hormone injections, amphetamines, liquid protein diets, and, more recently, the controversial fen-phen. What most dieters need to realize is that there is no magic way to lose weight—no pill, no crash diet plan. *The only way to permanent weight loss is through sensible eating and exercise.*

–Marcie Turple, student

Does Your Thesis Hold Water?

Once you have selected a possible thesis for an essay, ask yourself the following questions:

1. Does my thesis statement take a clear stance on an issue? If so, what is that stance?
2. Is my thesis too general?
3. Is my thesis too specific?
4. Does my thesis apply to a larger audience than myself? If so, who is that audience?

For a list of guidelines that will help you check the validity of your thesis, see the box above. For more on the various ways to build an effective thesis, see Chapter 3, Thesis (pp. 81–83).

Know Your Audience

Although it is not always possible to know who your readers are, you nevertheless need to consider your intended audience. Your attitude toward your topic, your tone, your sentence structure, and your choice of words are just some of the important considerations that rely on your awareness of audience. For a list of questions to help you determine your audience, see the box below.

Audience Questions

1. Who are my readers?
2. Is my audience specialized (for example, all those in my geology lab) or more general (college students)?
3. What do I know about my audience's age, gender, education, religious affiliation, socioeconomic status, and political attitudes?
4. What do my readers need to know that I can tell them?
5. Will my audience be interested, open-minded, resistant, objective, or hostile to what I am saying?
6. Is there any specialized language that my audience must have to understand my subject or that I should avoid?
7. What do I want my audience to do as a result of reading my essay?

Determine Your Method of Development

Part Four of *Models for Writers* includes chapters on the various types of writing most often required of college students. Often these types of writing are referred to as *methods of development, rhetorical patterns*, or *organizational patterns*.

Studying these organizational patterns and practicing the use of them are important in any effort to broaden your writing skills. In *Models for Writers*, we look at each pattern separately because we believe this is the most effective way to introduce them, but it does not necessarily mean that a well-written essay adheres exclusively and rigidly to a single pattern of development. Confining yourself exclusively to comparison and contrast throughout an entire essay, for instance, might prove impractical and result in a formulaic or stilted essay. In fact, it is often best to use a single pattern to organize and develop your essay and then use the other patterns as your material dictates. For a description of what each method of development involves, see the box below. As you read the model essays in this text, you will find that many of them use a combination of patterns to support the dominant pattern.

Methods of Development	
Illustration	Using examples to illustrate a point or idea
Narration	Telling a story or giving an account of an event
Description	Presenting a picture with words
Process Analysis	Explaining how something is done or happens
Definition	Explaining what something is
Division and Classification	Dividing a subject into its parts and placing them in appropriate categories
Comparison and Contrast	Demonstrating likenesses and differences
Cause and Effect	Explaining the causes of an event or the effects of an action
Argument	Using reason and logic to persuade someone to your way of thinking

Combining organizational patterns is probably not something you want to plan or even think about when you first tackle a writing assignment. Instead, let these patterns develop naturally as you organize, draft, and revise your materials. The combination of patterns will enhance the interest and effect of your writing.

If you're still undecided or concerned about combining patterns, try the following steps:

1. Summarize the point you want to make in a single phrase or sentence.
2. Restate the point as a question (in effect, the question your essay will answer).
3. Look closely at both the summary and the question for key words or concepts that suggest a particular pattern.
4. Consider other strategies that could support your primary pattern.

Here are some examples:

SUMMARY: Venus and Serena Williams are among the best female tennis players in the history of the game.

QUESTION: How do Venus and Serena Williams compare with other tennis players?

PATTERN: Comparison and contrast. The writer must compare the Williams sisters with other female players and provide evidence to support the claim that they are "among the best."

SUPPORTING PATTERNS: Illustration and description. Good evidence includes examples of the Williams sisters' superior ability and accomplishments and descriptions of their athletic feats.

SUMMARY: How to build a personal Web site.

QUESTION: How do you build a personal Web site?

PATTERN: Process analysis. The word *how,* especially in the phrase *how to,* implies a procedure that can be explained in steps or stages.

SUPPORTING PATTERNS: Description. It will be necessary to describe the Web site, especially the look and design of the site, at various points in the process.

SUMMARY: Petroleum and natural gas prices should be federally controlled.

QUESTION: What should be done about petroleum and natural gas prices?

PATTERN: Argument. The word *should* signals an argument, calling for evidence and reasoning in support of the conclusion.

SUPPORTING PATTERNS: Comparison and contrast and cause-and-effect analysis. The writer should present evidence from a comparison of federally controlled pricing with deregulated pricing as well as from a discussion of the effects of deregulation.

These are just a few examples showing how to decide on a pattern of development and supporting patterns that are suitable for your topic and what you want to say about it. In every case, your reading can guide you in recognizing the best plan to follow.

Map Your Organization

Once you decide what you want to write about and you come up with some ideas about what you might like to say, your next task is to jot down the main ideas for your essay in an order that seems both natural and logical to you. In other words, make a scratch outline. In constructing this outline, if you discover that one of the organizational patterns will help you in generating ideas, you might consider using that as your overall organizing principle.

Whether you write a formal outline, simply set down a rough sequence of the major points of your thesis, or take a middle ground between those two strategies, you need to think about the overall organization of your paper. Some writers make a detailed outline and fill it out point by point, whereas others follow a general plan and let the writing take them where it will, making any necessary adjustments to the plan when they revise.

Here are some major patterns of organization you may want to use for your outline:

- Chronological (oldest to newest, or the reverse)
- Spatial (top to bottom, left to right, inside to outside, and so forth)
- Least familiar to most familiar
- Easiest to most difficult to comprehend
- Easiest to most difficult to accept
- According to similarities or differences

Notice that some of these organizational patterns correspond to the rhetorical patterns in Part Four of this book. For example, a narrative essay generally follows a chronological organization. If you are having trouble developing or mapping an effective organization, refer to the introduction and readings in Chapter 5, Organization. Once you have settled on an organizational pattern, you are ready to write a first draft.

■ WRITING THE FIRST DRAFT

Your goal in writing a first draft is to get your ideas down on paper. Write quickly, and let the writing follow your thinking. Do not be overly concerned about spelling, word choice, or grammar because such concerns will break the flow of your ideas. After you have completed your first draft, you will go over your essay to revise and edit it.

As you write your draft, pay attention to your outline, but do not be a slave to it. It is there to help you, not restrict you. Often, when writing, you discover something new about your subject; if so, follow that idea freely. Wherever you deviate from your plan, place an X in the margin to remind yourself of the change. When you revise, you can return to that part of your writing and reconsider the change you made, either developing it further or abandoning it.

It may happen that while writing your first draft, you run into difficulty that prevents you from moving forward. For example, suppose you want to tell the story of something that happened to you, but you aren't certain whether you should be using the pronoun *I* so often. Turn to the essays in Chapters 11 and 14 to see how the authors use diction and tone and how other narrative essays handle this problem. You will find that the frequent use of *I* isn't necessarily a problem at all. For an account of a personal experience, it's perfectly acceptable to use *I* as often as you need to. Or suppose that after writing several pages describing someone who you think is quite a character, you find that your draft seems flat and doesn't express how lively and funny the person really is. If you read the introduction to Chapter 13, you will learn that descriptions need lots of factual, concrete detail; the selections in that chapter give further proof of this. You can use those guidelines to add details that are missing from your draft.

If you run into difficulties writing your first draft, don't worry or get upset. Even experienced writers run into problems at the beginning. Just try to keep going, and take the pressure off yourself. Think about your topic, and consider your details and what you want to say. You might even want to go back and look over the ideas and information you've gathered.

Create a Title

What makes a good title? There are no hard-and-fast rules, but most writers would agree that an effective title attracts attention and hooks the reader into reading the essay, either because the title is unusual or colorful and intrigues the reader or because it asks a question and the reader is curious to know the answer. A good title announces your subject and prepares your reader for the approach you take. You can create a title while writing your first draft or after you have seen how your ideas develop. Either way, the important thing is to brainstorm for titles and not simply use the first one that comes to mind. With at least a half dozen to choose from, preferably more, you will have a much better sense of how to pick an effective title, one that does important work explaining your subject to the reader and that is lively and inviting. Spend several minutes reviewing the titles of the essays in *Models for Writers* (see table of contents, pp. xii–xxii). You'll like some better than others, but reflecting on the effectiveness of each one will help you strengthen your own titles.

Focus on Beginnings and Endings

The beginning of your essay is vitally important to its success. Indeed, if your opening doesn't attract and hold your readers' attention, readers may be less than enthusiastic about proceeding.

Your ending is almost always as important as your beginning. An effective conclusion does more than end your essay. It wraps up your thoughts and leaves readers satisfied with the presentation of your ideas and information. Your ending should be a natural outgrowth of the development of your ideas. Avoid trick endings, mechanical summaries, and cutesy comments, and never introduce new concepts or information in the ending. Just as with the writing of titles, the writing of beginnings and endings is perhaps best done by generating several alternatives and then selecting from among them. Review the box on page 20 and Chapter 6 for more help developing your beginnings and endings.

Notes on Beginnings and Endings

Beginnings and endings are important to the effectiveness of an essay, but they can be difficult to write. Inexperienced writers often think that they must write their essays sequentially when, in fact, it is better to write both the beginning and the ending after you have completed most of the rest of your essay. Pay particular attention to both parts during revision. Ask yourself the following questions:

1. Does my introduction grab the reader's attention?
2. Is my introduction confusing in any way? How well does it relate to the rest of the essay?
3. If I state my thesis in the introduction, how effectively is it presented?
4. Does my essay come to a logical conclusion, or does it just stop short?
5. How well does the conclusion relate to the rest of the essay? Am I careful not to introduce new topics or issues that I did not address in the body of the essay?
6. Does the conclusion help underscore or illuminate important aspects of the body of the essay, or is it just another version of what I wrote earlier?

■ REVISING

Once you have completed a first draft, set it aside for a few hours or even until the next day. Removed from the process of drafting, you can approach the revision of your draft with a clear mind. When you revise, consider the most important elements of your draft first. You should focus on your thesis, purpose, content, organization, and paragraph structure. You will have a chance to look at grammar, punctuation, and mechanics after you revise. This way you will make sure that your essay is fundamentally solid and says what you want it to say before dealing with the task of editing.

It is helpful to have someone — your friend or member of your writing class — listen to your essay as you read it aloud. The process of reading aloud allows you to determine if your writing sounds clear and natural. If you have to strain your voice to provide emphasis, try rephrasing the idea to make it clearer. Whether you revise your work on your own or have someone assist you, the questions in the box below will help you focus on the largest, most important elements of your essay early in the revision process.

Questions for Revising

1. Have I focused on my topic?
2. Does my thesis make a clear statement about my topic?
3. Is the organizational pattern I have used the best one, given my purpose?
4. Does the topic sentence of each paragraph relate to my thesis? Does each paragraph support its topic sentence?
5. Do I have enough supporting details, and are my examples the best ones that I can develop?
6. How effective are my beginning and my ending? Can I improve them?
7. Do I have a good title? Does it indicate what my subject is and hint at my thesis?

■ EDITING

Once you are sure that the large elements of your essay are in place and that you have said what you intended, you are ready to begin editing your essay. At this stage, correct any mistakes in grammar, punctuation, mechanics, and spelling because a series of small errors can add up and distract readers. Such errors can cause readers to doubt the important points you are trying to make.

In this section we provide sound advice and solutions for the editing problems instructors have told us trouble their students most. For more guidance with these or other editing or grammar concerns, refer to your grammar handbook or ask your instructor for help. To practice finding and correcting these and many other problems, go to **bedfordstmartins.com/models** and click on "Exercise Central."

Run-ons: Fused Sentences and Comma Splices

Writers can become so absorbed in getting their ideas down on paper that they often combine two independent clauses (complete sentences that can stand alone when punctuated with a period) incorrectly, creating a *run-on sentence*. A run-on sentence fails to show where one thought ends and where another begins and can confuse readers. There are two types of run-on sentences: the fused sentence and the comma splice.

A *fused sentence* occurs when a writer combines two independent clauses with no punctuation at all. To correct a fused sentence, divide the independent clauses into separate sentences, or join them by adding words, punctuation, or both.

INCORRECT	Jen loves Harry Potter she was the first in line to buy the latest book.
EDITED	Jen loves Harry Potter <del>she</del> . She ^ was the first in line to buy the latest book.
EDITED	Jen loves Harry Potter she ; in fact, ^ was the first in line to buy the latest book.

A *comma splice* occurs when writers use only a comma to combine two independent clauses. To correct a comma splice, divide the independent clauses into separate sentences, or join them by adding words and/or punctuation.

INCORRECT	The e-mail looked like spam, Marty deleted it.
EDITED	The e-mail looked like spam, ; ^ Marty deleted it.
EDITED	The e-mail looked like spam, so ^ Marty deleted it.

Sentence Fragments

A *sentence fragment* is a word group that cannot stand alone as a complete sentence. Even if a word group begins with a capital letter and ends with punctuation, it is not a sentence unless it has a subject (the person, place, or thing the sentence is about) and a verb (a word that tells what the subject does) and expresses a complete thought. Word groups that do not express complete thoughts often begin with a subordinating conjunction such as *although, because, since,* or *unless.*

To correct a fragment, add a subject or a verb, or integrate the fragment into a nearby sentence to complete the thought.

INCORRECT	Divided my time between work and school last semester.
EDITED	^{I divided} ~~Divided~~ my time between work and school last semester.

INCORRECT	Terry's essay was really interesting. Because it brought up good points about energy conservation.
EDITED	Terry's essay was really interesting, ^{because} ~~Because~~ it brought up good points about energy conservation.

Creative use of intentional sentence fragments is occasionally acceptable—in narration essays, for example—when writers are trying to establish a particular mood or tone.

> I asked him about his recent trip. He asked me about work. Short questions. One-word answers. Then an awkward pause.
>
> –David P. Bardeen

Subject-Verb Agreement

Subjects and verbs must agree in number—that is, a singular subject (one person, place, or thing) must take a singular verb, and a plural subject (more than one person, place, or thing) must take a plural verb. Most native speakers of English use proper subject-verb agreement in their writing without conscious awareness. Even so, some sentence constructions can be troublesome.

When a prepositional phrase (a phrase that includes a preposition such as *on, of, in, at,* or *between*) falls between a subject and a verb, it can obscure their relationship. To make sure the subject agrees with its verb in a sentence with an intervening prepositional phrase, mentally cross out the phrase (*of basic training* in the following example) to isolate the subject and verb and determine if they agree.

INCORRECT   The first three weeks of basic training is the worst.

                                                     are
EDITED   The first three weeks of basic training ~~is~~ the worst.
                                                      ^

Writers often have difficulty with subject-verb agreement in sentences with compound subjects (two or more subjects joined together with the word *and*). As a general rule, compound subjects take plural verbs.

INCORRECT   My mother, sister, and cousin is visiting me next

             month.
                                               are
EDITED   My mother, sister, and cousin ~~is~~ visiting me next
                                            ^
             month.

However, in sentences with subjects joined by *either . . . or, neither . . . nor,* or *not only . . . but also,* the verb must agree with the subject closest to it.

INCORRECT   Neither the mechanics nor the salesperson know what's

             wrong with my car.
                                                      knows
EDITED   Neither the mechanics nor the salesperson ~~know~~ what's
                                                        ^
             wrong with my car.

While editing your essay, be sure to identify the subjects and verbs in your sentences and to check their agreement.

Pronoun-Antecedent Agreement

A *pronoun* is a word that takes the place of a noun in a sentence. To avoid repeating nouns in our speech and writing, we use pronouns as noun substitutes. The noun to which a pronoun refers is called its *antecedent.* A pronoun and its antecedent are said to *agree* when the relationship between them is clear. Pronouns must agree with their antecedents in both *person* and *number.*

There are three types of pronouns: first person (*I* and *we*), second person (*you*), and third person (*he, she, they,* and *it*). First-person pronouns refer to first-person antecedents, second-person pronouns refer to second-person antecedents, and third-person pronouns refer to third-person antecedents.

INCORRECT   House hunters should review their finances carefully

before you make an offer.

EDITED   House hunters should review their finances carefully
they
before ~~you~~ make an offer.
∧

A pronoun must agree in number with its antecedent; that is, a singular pronoun must refer to a singular antecedent, and a plural pronoun must refer to a plural antecedent. When two or more antecedents are joined by the word *and*, the pronoun must be plural.

INCORRECT   Gina, Kim, and Katie took her vacations in August.
their
EDITED   Gina, Kim, and Katie took ~~her~~ vacations in August.
∧

When the subject of a sentence is an indefinite pronoun such as *everyone, each, everybody, anyone, anybody, everything, either, one, neither, someone,* or *something,* use a singular pronoun to refer to it or recast the sentence to eliminate the agreement problem.

INCORRECT   Each of the women submitted their resumé.
her
EDITED   Each of the women submitted ~~their~~ resumé.
∧
Both   resumés
EDITED   ~~Each~~ of the women submitted their ~~resume.~~
∧   ∧

Verb Tense Shifts

A verb's tense indicates when an action takes place—sometime in the past, right now, or in the future. Using verb tense consistently helps your readers understand time changes in your writing. Inconsistent verb tenses, or *shifts,* within a sentence confuse readers and are especially noticeable in narration and process analysis writing, which are sequence and time oriented. Generally, you should write in the past or present tense and maintain that tense throughout your sentence.

INCORRECT	The painter studied the scene and pulls a fan brush decisively from her cup.
EDITED	The painter studied the scene and ~~pulls~~ pulled a fan brush decisively from her cup.

Misplaced and Dangling Modifiers

A *modifier* is a word or words that describe or give additional information about other words in a sentence. Always place modifiers as close as possible to the words you want to modify. An error in modifier placement could be unintentionally confusing (or amusing) to your reader. Two common problems arise with modifiers: the misplaced modifier and the dangling modifier.

A *misplaced modifier* unintentionally modifies the wrong word in a sentence because it is placed incorrectly.

INCORRECT	The waiter brought a steak to the man covered with onions.
EDITED	The waiter brought a steak covered with onions to the man ~~covered with onions.~~

A *dangling modifier* appears at the beginning or end of a sentence and modifies a word that does not appear in the sentence—often an unstated subject.

INCORRECT	Staring into the distance, large rain clouds form.
EDITED	Staring into the distance, Jon saw large rain clouds form.

While editing your essay, make sure you have positioned your modifiers as close as possible to the words you want to modify, and make sure each sentence has a clear subject that is modified correctly.

Faulty Parallelism

Parallelism means using similar grammatical forms to show that ideas in a sentence are of equal importance. Faulty parallelism can interrupt the flow of your writing and confuse your readers. Writers have trouble with parallelism in three kinds of sentence constructions.

In sentences that include items in a pair or series, make sure the elements of the pair or series are parallel in form. Delete any unnecessary or repeated words.

INCORRECT   Nina likes snowboarding, roller skating, and to hike.

EDITED   Nina likes snowboarding, roller skating, and ~~to hike.~~ hiking.

In sentences that include connecting words such as *both . . . and, either . . . or, neither . . . nor, rather . . . than,* and *not only . . . but also,* make sure the elements being connected are parallel in form. Delete any unnecessary or repeated words.

INCORRECT   The lecture was both enjoyable and it was a form

              of education.

EDITED   The lecture was both enjoyable and ~~it was a form of education.~~ educational.

In sentences that include the comparison word *as* or *than,* make sure the elements of the comparison are parallel in form. Delete any unnecessary or repeated words.

INCORRECT   It would be better to study now than waiting until the

              night before the exam.

EDITED   It would be better to study now than ~~waiting~~ to wait until the

              night before the exam.

Weak Nouns and Verbs

Inexperienced writers often believe that adjectives and adverbs are the stuff of effective writing. They're right in one sense, but not wholly so. Although strong adjectives and adverbs are crucial, good writing depends on well-chosen, strong nouns and verbs. The noun *vehicle* is not nearly as descriptive as *Jeep, snowmobile, pickup truck,* or *SUV,* for example. Why use the weak verb *look* when your meaning would be conveyed more precisely with *glance, stare, spy, gaze, peek, examine,* or *witness?* Instead of the weak verb *run,* use *fly, gallop, hustle, jog, race, rush, scamper, scoot, scramble,* or *trot.*

While editing your essay, look for instances of weak nouns and verbs. If you can't form a clear picture in your mind of what a noun looks like or what a verb's action is, your nouns and verbs are likely weak. The more specific and strong you make your nouns and verbs, the more lively and descriptive your writing will be.

WEAK	The flowers moved toward the bright light of the sun.
EDITED	The ~~flowers moved~~ toward the bright light of the sun.

(handwritten insertion above EDITED line: *tulips stretched* with caret ∧)

When you have difficulty thinking of strong, specific nouns and verbs, reach for a thesaurus—but only if you are sure you can identify the best word for your purpose. Thesauruses are available free online and in inexpensive paperback editions; most word processing programs include a thesaurus as well. A thesaurus will help you avoid redundancy in your writing and find specific words with just the right meaning.

Academic Diction and Tone

The language that you use in your college courses, known as *American Standard English,* is formal in diction and objective in tone. American Standard English is the language used by educators, civic leaders, the media, and professionals in all fields. Although the standard is fairly narrow in scope, it allows for individual differences in expression and voice so that your writing can retain its personality and appeal.

Tone is the distance that you establish between yourself and your audience and is created by your *diction* (the particular words you choose) and the complexity of your sentences. Formal writing creates a distance between yourself and your audience through the use of third-person pronouns (*he, she, it, they*) and provides the impression of objectivity. Formal writing values logic, evidence, and reason over opinion and bias. Informal writing, on the other hand, uses first-person pronouns (*I*, *we*); is usually found in narratives; and respects feelings, individual tastes, and personal preferences. Similarly, the second-person pronoun (*you*) is used to bring your reader close to you, as is done in this text, but it is too familiar for most academic writing and is best avoided if there is any question about its appropriateness.

INFORMAL	The experiment looked like it was going to be a bust.
FORMAL	After detecting a number of design flaws in the experiment, we concluded that it was going to be a failure.
SUBJECTIVE	The governor said that the shortfall in tax revenues was quite a bit bigger than anyone expected.
OBJECTIVE	The governor reported that tax revenues fell by 9 percent over last year.

When writing in a particular discipline, use discipline-specific language and conventions that reflect your understanding of the discipline. Key resources are your readings and the language you use with your instructors and classmates in each discipline. As you read, note how the writer uses technical language (*point of view* and *denouement*, for example, in literature; *mean distribution* in statistics; *derivatives* in financial analysis; *pan, tilt,* and *track* in film study; *exogamy* and *endogamy* in anthropology; and *polyphony* and *atonality* in music) to communicate difficult concepts, recognized phenomena in the discipline, and nuances that are characteristic of the discipline.

Discipline-Specific Prose (Psychology)

Shyness may be defined experientially as discomfort and/or inhibition in interpersonal situations that interferes with pursuing one's interpersonal or professional goals. It is a form of excessive self-focus, a preoccupation with one's thoughts, feelings, and physical reactions. It may vary from mild social awkwardness to totally inhibiting social phobia. Shyness may be chronic and dispositional, serving as a personality trait that is central in one's self-definition. Situational shyness involves experiencing the symptoms of shyness in specific social performance situations but not incorporating it into one's self-concept. Shyness reactions can occur at any or all of the following levels: cognitive, affective, physiological, and behavioral, and may be triggered by a wide variety of arousal cues. Among the most typical are: authorities, one-on-one opposite sex interactions, intimacy, strangers, having to take individuating action in a group setting, and initiating social actions in unstructured, spontaneous behavioral settings. Metaphorically, shyness is a shrinking back from life that weakens the bonds of human connection.

–"Shyness," Lynne Henderson and Philip Zimbardo

If you listen carefully and read closely, you will be able to discern the discipline-specific language cues that make a writer sound more like, say, a historian or an anthropologist than a psychologist. In turn, you will be able to use the language of your own discipline with greater ease and accuracy and achieve the subtleties of language that will allow you to carry out your research, draw sound conclusions, and write effectively and with authority.

ESL Concerns (Articles and Nouns)

Two areas of English grammar that can be especially problematic for nonnative speakers of English are articles and nouns. In English, correct use of articles and nouns is necessary for sentences to make sense.

There are two kinds of articles in English: *indefinite* (*a* and *an*) and *definite* (*the*). Use *a* before words beginning with a consonant sound and *an* before words beginning with a vowel sound. Note, too, that *a* is used before an *h* with a consonant sound (*happy*) and *an* is used before a silent *h* (*hour*).

There are two kinds of nouns in English: count and noncount. *Count nouns* name individual things or units that can be counted or separated out from a whole, such as *students* and *pencils*. *Noncount nouns* name things that cannot be counted because they are considered wholes in themselves and cannot be divided, such as *work* and *furniture*.

Use the indefinite article (*a* or *an*) before a singular count noun when you do not specify which one.

I would like to borrow *a* colored pencil.

Plural count nouns take *the*.

I would like to borrow *the* colored pencils.

If a plural count noun is used in a general sense, it does not take an article at all.

> I brought colored pencils to class today.

Noncount nouns are always singular and never take an indefinite article.

> We need new living room furniture.

The is sometimes used with noncount nouns to refer to a specific idea or thing.

> *The* furniture will be delivered tomorrow.

While editing your essay, be sure you have used articles and nouns correctly.

INCORRECT	I love an aroma of freshly baked cookies.
EDITED	I love a̶n̶ aroma of freshly baked cookies. *(the, ∧)*
INCORRECT	I have never had the chicken pox.
EDITED	I have never had t̶h̶e̶ chicken pox.

Questions for Editing Sentences

1. Do I include any fused sentences or comma splices?
2. Do I include any unintentional sentence fragments?
3. Do my verbs agree with their subjects?
4. Do my pronouns agree with their antecedents?
5. Do I make any unnecessary shifts in verb tense?
6. Do I have any misplaced or dangling modifiers?
7. Are my sentences parallel?
8. Do I use strong nouns and active verbs?
9. Do I pair articles and nouns correctly?

■ PROOFREADING

Do not assume that because you made edits and corrections to your essay electronically in your word processor that all your changes were saved or that your essay will print out correctly. Also do not assume that because you used your word processor's spell-check or grammar-check function you've found and corrected every spelling and grammatical error. In fact, such checkers often allow incorrect or misspelled words to pass while flagging correct grammatical constructions as incorrect. Although your word processor's spell-checker and grammar-checker are a good "first line of defense" against certain types of errors, there is no replacement for a human proofreader — you.

Print out your essay and carefully proofread it manually. Check to make sure you do not use *your* where you intend *you're, its* where you mean *it's,* or *to* where you want *too.* Spell-checkers *never* catch these types of errors. If you know you are prone to certain mistakes, go through your essay looking for those particular problems. For example, if you often have trouble with placing commas or other punctuation marks with quotations, proofread your essay for that specific problem.

Proofread a hard copy of your essay to make sure all your electronic changes appear on it and you have caught and corrected any grammatical problems. (Be sure to refer to the Questions for Editing Sentences box on p. 31 and to the Questions for Proofreading Essays box that follows.) Check to be certain you have followed your instructor's formatting guidelines. Above all, give your hard-copy essay one final read-through before submitting it to your instructor.

Questions for Proofreading Essays

1. Have I printed a hard copy of my essay for proofreading?
2. Have I misspelled or incorrectly typed any words? Has my spell-checker inadvertently approved commonly confused words like *its* and *it's,* or *their, there,* and *they're?*
3. Have I checked my essay for errors I make often?
4. Do all my edits and corrections appear in my hard copy?
5. Have I formatted my essay according to my instructor's directions?
6. Have I given the hard copy of my final draft a thorough review before turning it in?

■ WRITING AN EXPOSITORY ESSAY: A STUDENT ESSAY IN PROGRESS

While he was a student in a writing class at the University of Vermont, Jeffrey Olesky was asked to write an essay on any topic using a suitable method of development. After making a brief list of the subjects that interested him, he chose to write about golf. Golf had been a part of Olesky's life since he was a youngster, so he figured he would have enough material for an essay.

First, he needed to focus on a specific topic within the broad subject area of golf. Having considered a number of aspects of the game—how it's played, its popularity because of Tiger Woods, the controversies over the exclusion of women and minorities from private clubs—he kept coming back to how much golf meant to him. Focusing on his love of golf, he then established his tentative thesis: Golf has taught me a lot.

Olesky needed to develop a number of examples to support his thesis, so he brainstormed for ideas, examples, and anecdotes—anything that came to mind to help him develop his essay. These are his notes:

Brainstorming Notes

Golf is my life—I can't imagine being who I am without it.

I love to be out on the course early in the morning.

It's been embarrassing and stressful sometimes.

There's so much to know and remember about the game, even before you try to hit the ball.

The story about what my father taught me—felt badly and needed to apologize.

"You know better than that, Jeffrey."

I have pictures of me on the greens with a cut-down golf putter.

All kinds of character building goes on.

It's all about rules and playing fairly.

Wanted to be like my father.

The frustration is awesome, but you can learn to deal with it.

Golf is methodical.

I use golf to clear my head.

Golf teaches life's lessons.

Golf teaches you manners, to be respectful of others.

Golf teaches you to abide by the rules.

Golf is an internal tool.

When he thought that he had gathered enough information, he began to sort it out. He needed an organizational plan, some way to present his information that was not random but rather showed a logical progression. He realized that the character-building benefits of golf that he included in his brainstorming notes clustered around some key subtopics. He decided to do some clustering and drew circles that included his ideas about golf: the physical and mental demands of the game, the social values and morals it teaches, and the reflective benefits of golf. He then sorted out his related ideas and examples and added them, mapping their relationship in this diagram.

Clustering Diagram

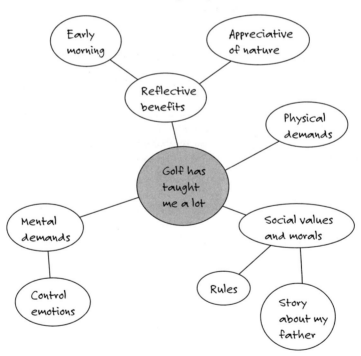

Before beginning to write the first draft of his paper, Olesky thought it would be a good idea to list in an informal outline the major points he wanted to make. Here is his informal outline:

Informal Outline

1. Brief introductory paragraph announcing the topic

2. An expansion of the introductory paragraph and the <u>thesis state-ment</u>: Golf has taught me a lot

3. A discussion of how, above all, golf teaches one to control one's emotions

4. A discussion of how much one needs to know and remember to play golf well

5. The values that golf teaches

6. A multiparagraph example illustrating a valuable lesson taught through golf

7. Golf provides an opportunity to reflect

8. Reflection, in turn, leads to a deeper appreciation of nature

With his outline before him, Olesky felt ready to try a rough draft of his paper. He wrote quickly, keeping his organizational plan in mind but striving to keep the writing going and get his thoughts down on paper. He knew that once he had a draft, he could determine how to improve it. Olesky wrote some fairly solid paragraphs, but he sensed that they were on different aspects of his topic and that the logical order of the points he was making was not quite right. He needed a stronger organizational plan, some way to present his information that was not random but rather showed a logical progression.

Reviewing his outline, Olesky could see that there was a natural progression from the physical lessons of the sport to the social and moral lessons to the psychological, emotional, and even spiritual benefits that one could derive. He decided therefore to move item 3 ("A discussion of how, above all, golf teaches one to control one's emotions") in his original organization and make it item 6 in the revision. Here is his reordered outline:

Reordered Outline

1. Brief introductory paragraph announcing the topic
2. An expansion of the introductory paragraph and the <u>thesis statement</u>: Golf has taught me a lot
3. A discussion of how much one needs to know and remember to play golf well
4. The social values that golf teaches
5. A multiparagraph example illustrating a valuable lesson taught through golf
6. A discussion of how, above all, golf teaches one to control one's emotions
7. Golf provides an opportunity to reflect
8. Reflection, in turn, leads to a deeper appreciation of nature

Olesky was satisfied that his essay now had a natural and logical organization: it moved from matters of lesser to greater importance to him personally. However, he now needed to revise his thesis to suit the argument he had established. He wanted his revised thesis to be focused and specific and to include the idea that the lessons and values golf taught him could not be learned as easily in other ways. Here is his revised thesis statement:

Revised Thesis Statement

In its simplicity, golf has taught me many lessons and values that other people have trouble learning elsewhere.

After revising the organization, he was now ready to edit his essay and to correct those smaller but equally important errors in word choice, wordiness, punctuation, and mechanics. He had put aside these errors to make sure his essay had the appropriate content.

Now he needed to make sure it was grammatically correct. Here are several sample paragraphs showing the editing Olesky did on his essay:

Edited Paragraphs

Addition for clarity

Ever since I was a little boy, no older than two or three, I have had a golf club in my hand. My mother has pictures of me ~~as a toddler~~

Elimination of unessential information

with my father on the putting green of the golf course. ~~that my father belonged to.~~ With a cut-down putter, the shaft ~~had been~~ reduced in length so that it would fit me, I would spend hours trying to place the small white ball into the little round hole. I'm

Change of period to colon to eliminate sentence fragment and introduce appositive phrase

sure at first that I took to the game to be like my father. ~~To~~ act like him, play like him, and hit the ball like him. However, it is not what I have learned about the mechanics of the golf swing or about all the facts ~~and figures~~ of the game that have caused golf to mean so much to me, but rather the things golf has taught me

Correction of it's to its

about everyday life. In it's simplicity, golf has taught me many lessons and values other people have trouble learning elsewhere.

Elimination of wordiness

Golf is a good teacher because ~~Along the same lines,~~ there are many variables and aspects to the game ~~of golf.~~ You ~~are~~ constantly having to think, analyze, and evaluate. ~~That is the difficulty of the game of golf.~~ Unlike many sports that rely on ~~once you~~ committing ~~the~~ actions to muscle memory, ~~there is no guarantee you will still perform well. There is~~ a phenomenal amount of information to think about and keys to remember. Legs shoulder-width apart, knees flexed, fingers interlocked, body loose . . . and you haven't even tried to hit the

Addition of specific information for clarity

ball yet. But having to go about things so methodically in golf has enabled me to apply the skills of patience and analysis ~~the methods of golf~~ to many other parts

Improved dicton

of my life. I don't believe I would have nearly the same
personality if golf had not played such an ~~intricate~~ integral role in
my development.

In addition to editing his revised paper, Olesky reexamined his title, "Character Builder." Olesky considered a half dozen alternatives. He finally settled on the use of "Golf" as a main title because it was such a key word for his topic and thesis; he used "A Character Builder" as his subtitle. He also thought about his conclusion, wondering whether it was forceful enough. After giving it considerable thought and seeking the advice of his classmates, Olesky decided to end with the low-key but meaningful final paragraphs he generated in his original draft. Here is the final version of his essay:

Final Essay

Golf: A Character Builder

Jeffrey Olesky

Title: suggests what the essay will be about

Golf is what I love. It is what I do, and it is who I am. In many respects, it has defined and shaped my character and personality. I couldn't possibly imagine my life without golf and what it has meant for me.

Beginning: effective opening paragraph sets the context for the essay

Ever since I was a little boy, no older than two or three, I have had a golf club in my hand. My mother has pictures of me as a toddler with my father on the putting green of the golf course. With a cut-down putter, the shaft reduced in length so that it would fit me, I would spend hours trying to place the small white ball in the little round hole. I'm sure at first that I took to the game to be like my father: to act like him, play like him, and hit the ball like him. However, it is not what I have learned about the mechanics of the golf swing or about the

Thesis statement: sets clear expectation in the reader's mind

facts of the game that have caused golf to mean so much to me, but rather it is the things golf has taught me about everyday life in general. In its simplicity, golf has taught me many lessons and values other people have trouble learning elsewhere.

Transition: discussion moves to how the game influences personality

Golf is a good teacher because there are many variables and aspects to the game. You constantly have to think, analyze, and evaluate your position and strategy. Unlike many sports that rely on committing actions to muscle memory, golf requires a phenomenal amount of information to think about and keys to remember. Legs shoulder-width apart, knees flexed, fingers interlocked, body loose . . . and you haven't even tried to hit the ball yet. But having to go about things so methodically in golf has enabled me to apply the skills of patience and analysis to many other parts of my life. I don't believe I would have nearly the same personality if golf had not played such an integral role in my development.

Golf requires lots of information, both physical and mental.

Golf teaches life lessons.

Golf has also changed and shaped my personality by repeatedly reinforcing many of the lessons of life. You know the ones I'm referring to, the rules you learn in kindergarten: treat others as you would like to be treated; respect other people and their property . . . the list goes on. Golf may not blare them out as obviously as my kindergarten teacher, but in its own subtle, respectful tone, golf has imbued me with many of the values and morals I have today. Simply by learning the rules of such a prestigious, honest, and respected game, you gradually learn the reasoning behind them and the ways that they relate to life.

Illustration: extended example in narrative of some lessons that golf teaches

A good example of such a life lesson comes from the first time my father ever took me out on an actual golf course. I had been waiting for this day for quite some time and was so excited when he finally gave me the chance. He had gone out to play with a few of his friends early one Saturday morning in one of the larger tournaments. I was caddying for my father. Although I was too young to actually carry his bag, I would clean his golf ball, rake the bunkers for him, and do the other minor tasks that caddies do. But the fact that I was actually out "with the big boys," watching them play golf, was enough to make me happy. Besides, none of the other gentlemen my father was playing with seemed to mind that I was along for the ride.

Narrative example continues.

    The lesson I learned that day appears rather simple now. It came on the putting green of the second hole. My father had finished putting out, and I was holding the flagstick off to the side of the green while the other players finished. Generally, my father would come stand next to me and give me a hand, but due to circumstances we ended up on opposite sides of the green. During the next player's putt, my father lowered his eyebrows at me and nodded his head to one side a few times. Curious as to what he wanted me to do, I almost let the question slip out of my mouth. But I knew better. I had already learned the rules of not talking or moving while other golfers were hitting. I quietly stood my ground until everyone was finished and then placed the flagstick back in the hole. While walking toward the next tee box, I neared my father. Regardless of what he had wanted me to do, I thought he would commend me for not talking or moving during the ordeal.

Dialogue: "shows rather than tells" and puts the reader in the scene

    "You know better than that, Jeffrey," he said.

    "What?" I asked curiously, disappointed that he had not praised me on a job well done.

    "You never stand so that your shadow is in someone's line."

    How could I be so stupid? He had reminded me a thousand times before. You never allow your shadow to fall in the line of someone's putt because it is distracting to the person putting. I rationalized to my father that maybe the man hadn't noticed or that it didn't bother him. Unfortunately, my father wasn't going to take that as an excuse. After explaining to me what I had done wrong, he suggested that I go over and apologize to the gentleman. I was still a young boy, and the figure of the older man was somewhat intimidating. This task was no easy chore because I was obviously very scared, and this is perhaps what made the lesson sink in a little deeper. I remember slowly approaching my father's friend and sheepishly looking back to my father for help. Once I realized I was on my own, I bashfully gave him my apologies and assured him that it wouldn't happen again. As you can probably guess, the repercussions were not as dramatic as I had envisioned them to be. Once my father had pointed out my mistake, I begged him to reconcile with the gentleman for me.

Transition: golf can also be a personal, internal tool.

However, in apologizing for myself, I learned a valuable lesson. Golf is important because it has taught me many social values such as this, but it can also be a personal, internal tool.

Golf has taught me how to deal with frustration and to control myself mentally in difficult and strenuous situations.

Organization continues to move from concrete practical concerns to those that are more abstract.

Golf is about mastering your emotions in stressful times and prevailing with a methodical, calm mind. I have dealt with the disappointment of missing a two-foot putt on the last hole to break eighty and the embarrassment of shanking my drive off the first hole in front of dozens of people. In dealing with these circumstances and continuing with my game, I have learned how to control my emotions. Granted, golf is not the most physically strenuous sport, but it is the mental challenge of complete and utter concentration that makes it difficult. People who are not able to control their temper or to take command of their emotions generally do not end up playing this game for very long.

Organization: Olesky moves to more philosophic influences.

Golf gives me the opportunity to be reflective — time to myself when I can debate and organize the thoughts in my head. There are few places where you can find the peace and tranquility like that of a golf course in the early morning or late afternoon. When I am playing by myself, which I make an effort to do when I need to "get away," I am able to reflect and work out some of the difficulties I am facing. I can think in complete quietness, but at the same time I have something to do while I am thinking. There are few places in the world offering this type of sanctuary that are easily accessible.

Organization: Olesky discusses golf's ability to bring him close to nature.

It is in these morning reflections that I also gain an appreciation of my surroundings. I often like to get up early on a Saturday or Sunday and be the first one on the course. There are many things I love about the scenery of a golf course during the morning hours. I love the smell of the freshly cut grass as the groundskeepers crisscross their patterns onto the fairways and greens. I love looking back on my progress toward the tee box on the first hole to witness my solitary foot tracks in the morning dew. I love the chirp of the yellow finches as they signal the break of dawn. All these conditions help to create the feeling of contentment as I walk down the first fairway. Thinking back to those days on the putting green with my father, I realize how dear golf is to me. Golf has created my values, taught me my lessons, and been my outlet. I love the game for all these reasons.

*Ending:
a quiet
but appro-
priate
conclusion*

From Reading to Writing

To move from reading to writing, you need to read actively, in a thoughtful spirit, and with an alert, inquiring mind. Reading actively means learning how to analyze what you read. You must be able to discover what is going on in an essay, to figure out the writer's reasons for shaping the essay in a particular way, to decide whether the result works well or poorly—and why. At first, such digging may seem odd, and for good reason. After all, we all know how to read. But do we know how to read *actively*?

Active reading is a skill that takes time to acquire. By becoming more familiar with different types of writing, you will sharpen your critical thinking skills and learn how good writers make decisions in their writing. After reading an essay, most people feel more confident talking about the content of the piece than about the writer's style. Content is more tangible than style, which always seems elusive. In large part, this discrepancy results from our schooling. Most of us have been taught to read for ideas. Not many of us, however, have been trained to read actively, to engage a writer and his or her writing, to ask why we like one piece of writing and not another. Similarly, most of us do not ask ourselves why one piece of writing is more convincing than another. When you learn to read actively, you begin to answer these important questions and come to appreciate the craftsmanship involved in writing. Active reading, then, is a skill you need if you are truly to engage and understand the content of a piece of writing as well as the craft that shapes the writer's ideas into a presentable form. Active reading will repay your efforts by helping you read more effectively and grow as a writer.

■ GETTING THE MOST OUT OF YOUR READING

Active reading requires, first of all, that you commit time and effort. Second, try to take a positive interest in what you are reading, even if the subject matter is not immediately appealing. Remember that you are not reading for content alone but also to understand a writer's methods—to see firsthand the kinds of choices writers make while they write.

To get the most out of your reading, follow the five steps of the reading process.

1. Prepare yourself to read the selection.
2. Read the selection.
3. Reread the selection.
4. Annotate the text with marginal notes.
5. Analyze the text with questions.

Step 1: Prepare Yourself to Read the Selection

Instead of diving right into any given selection in *Models for Writers* or any other book, there are a few things you can do that will prepare you to get the most out of what you will be reading. It's helpful, for example, to get a context for the reading: What's the essay about? What do you know about the writer's background and reputation? Where was the essay first published? Who was the intended audience for the essay? How much do you already know about the subject of the reading selection? We encourage you to review the materials that precede each selection in this book.

Each selection begins with a title, a headnote, and a writing prompt. From the *title,* you often discover the writer's position on an issue or attitude toward the topic. On occasion, the title provides clues about the intended audience and the writer's purpose in writing the piece. The *headnote* contains three essential elements: a *biographical note* about the author, *publication information,* and *rhetorical highlights* of the selection. In addition to information on the person's life and work, you'll find out something about his or her reputation and authority to write on the subject of the piece. The *publication information* tells you when the selection was published and in what book or magazine it appeared. This information gives you insights about the intended audience and the historical context. The *rhetorical highlights* direct your attention to one or more of the model features of the selection. Finally, the *writing prompt,* called "Reflecting on What You

Know," encourages you to collect your own thoughts and opinions about the topic or related subjects before you commence reading. This prompt makes it easy for you to keep a record of your own knowledge or thinking about a topic before you see what the writer has to offer in the essay.

To demonstrate how these context-building materials can work for you, carefully review the following materials that accompany Isaac Asimov's "Intelligence." The essay itself appears later in this chapter (pp. 49–51).

Intelligence

Title

■ **Isaac Asimov**

Headnote

1. Biographical note

Born in Russia, Isaac Asimov immigrated to the United States in 1923. His death in 1992 ended a long, prolific career as a science-fiction and nonfiction writer. Asimov was uniquely talented at making a diverse range of topics—from Shakespeare to atomic physics—comprehensible and entertaining to the general reader. Asimov earned three degrees at Columbia University and later taught biochemistry at Boston University. At the time of his death, he had published more than five hundred books. It's Been a Good Life, *published in 2002, was compiled from selections made from Asimov's three previous autobiographical volumes:* In Memory Yet Green *(1979),* In Joy Still Felt *(1980), and* I. Asimov: A Memoir *(1994). Edited by Janet Jeppson Asimov, the book also features "A Way of Thinking," Asimov's four hundredth essay for the* Magazine of Fantasy and Science Fiction.

In the following essay, which first appeared in Please Explain: The Myriad Mysteries of the Universe Revealed *(1973), Asimov, an intellectually gifted man, ponders the nature of intelligence. His academic brilliance, he concedes, would mean little*

2. Publication information

or nothing if like-minded intellectuals had not established the standards for intelligence in our society. Notice how he uses personal experience and the example of his auto mechanic to develop his definition of intelligence.

3. **Rhetorical highlights**

Reflecting on What You Know

Writing prompt

Our society defines the academically gifted as intelligent, but perhaps *book smart* would be a better term. IQ tests don't take into account common sense or experience, attributes that the academically gifted sometimes lack outside of a scholarly setting. Who's the smartest person you know? Is he or she academically gifted or smart in some way that would not be readily recognized as a form of intelligence?

From these preliminary materials, what expectations do you have for the selection itself? And how does this knowledge equip you to engage the selection before you read it? Asimov's title suggests the question "What is intelligence?" You can reasonably infer that Asimov will discuss the nature of intelligence. His purpose clearly seems to be to explore the subject with his readers. The short biographical note reveals that Asimov, a scientist, teacher, and prolific author, is no longer living, that he enjoyed a reputation as a renaissance man, and that he wrote with an ease and understanding that make difficult subjects readily accessible to the general public. This background material suggests that in the essay you'll get a thoughtful, easy-to-comprehend discussion of intelligence. The publication information indicates that this essay first appeared in a 1973 book in which Asimov explains popular "mysteries of the universe." The rhetorical highlights advise you to pay particular attention to how Asimov uses the examples of himself and his auto mechanic to think about the meaning of intelligence. Finally, the journal prompt asks you to consider how society defines the term *intelligence,* first by identifying the smartest person in your life and then by thinking about whether that person is more academically gifted (book smart) or experientially gifted (street smart). After reading the essay, you can compare your thoughts about the nature of intelligence with Asimov's.

Step 2: Read the Selection

Always read the selection at least twice, no matter how long it is. The first reading gives you a chance to get acquainted with the essay and to form your first impressions of it. With the first reading, you want to get an overall sense of what the writer is saying, keeping in mind the essay's title and the facts that you know about the writer from the essay's headnote. The essay will offer you information, ideas, and arguments—some you may have expected, some you may not have expected. As you read, you may find yourself modifying your sense of the writer's message and purpose. If there are any words that you do not recognize, circle them so that you can look them up later in a dictionary. Put question marks alongside any passages that are not immediately clear. You may, in fact, want to delay most of your annotating until a second reading so that your first reading can be fast and free.

Step 3: Reread the Selection

Your second reading should be quite different from the first. You will know what the essay is about, where it is going, and how it gets there. Now you can relate the parts of the essay more accurately to the whole. Use your second reading to test your first impressions against the words on the page, developing and deepening your sense of how the essay is written and how well. Because you now have a general understanding of the essay, you can pay special attention to the author's purpose and means of achieving that purpose. You can look for features of organization and style that you can learn from and adapt to your own work.

Step 4: Annotate the Text with Marginal Notes

When you annotate a text, you should do more than simply underline or highlight important points to remember. It is easy to underline so much that the notations become almost meaningless because you forget why you underlined the passages in the first place. Instead, as you read, write down your thoughts in the margins or on a separate piece of paper. (See pp. 49–51 for Asimov's "Intelligence" with student annotations.) Mark the selection's main point when you find it stated directly. Look for the pattern or patterns of development the author uses to explore and support that point, and jot the information down. If you disagree with a statement or conclusion, object in the margin: "No!" If you feel skeptical, indicate that response: "Why?" or "Explain." If you are impressed by an argument or turn of phrase, compliment the writer: "Good point!" Place vertical lines or stars in the margin to indicate important points.

What to Annotate in a Text

- Memorable statements of important points
- Key terms or concepts
- Central issues or themes
- Examples that support a main point
- Unfamiliar words
- Questions you have about a point or passage
- Your responses to a specific point or passage

Jot down whatever marginal notes come to mind. Most readers combine brief responses written in the margins with underlining, circling, highlighting, stars, or question marks. Here are some suggestions of elements you may want to mark to help you record your responses as you read:

Remember that there are no hard-and-fast rules for which elements you should annotate. Choose a method of annotation that works best for you and that will make sense when you go back to recollect your thoughts and responses to the essay. When annotating a text, don't be timid. Mark up your book as much as you like, or jot down as many responses in your notebook as you think will be helpful. Don't let annotating become burdensome. A word or phrase is usually as good as a sentence. One helpful way to focus your annotations is to ask yourself questions as you read the selection a second time.

Step 5: Analyze the Text with Questions

Questions to Ask Yourself as You Read
1. What does the writer want to say? What is the writer's main point or thesis?
2. Why does the writer want to make this point? What is the writer's purpose?
3. What pattern or patterns of development does the writer use?
4. How does the writer's pattern of development suit his or her subject and purpose?
5. What, if anything, is noteworthy about the writer's use of this pattern?
6. How effective is the essay? Does the writer make his or her points clearly?

As you read the essay a second time, probe for a deeper understanding of and appreciation for what the writer has done. Focus your attention by asking yourself some basic questions about its content and its form. Here are some questions you may find useful:

Each essay in *Models for Writers* is followed by study questions that are similar to the ones suggested here but specific to the essay. These questions help you analyze both the content of the essay and the writer's craft. As you read the essay a second time, look for details that will support your answers to these questions, and then answer the questions as fully as you can.

An Example: Annotating Isaac Asimov's "Intelligence"

Asks question central to the essay and relates army experience Notice how one of our students, guided by the six preceding questions, recorded her responses to Asimov's text with marginal notes.

What is intelligence, anyway? When I was in the army I received a kind of aptitude test that soldiers took and, against a norm of 100, scored 160. No one at the base had ever seen a figure like that, and for two hours they made a big fuss over me. (It didn't mean anything. The next day I was still a buck private with KP as my highest duty.)

Questions the meaning of high test scores. What do I think they mean?

All my life I've been registering scores like that, so that I have the complacent feeling that I'm highly intelligent, and I expect other people to think so, too. Actually, though, don't such scores simply mean that I am very good at answering the type of academic questions that are considered worthy of answers by the people who make up the intelligence tests—people with intellectual bents similar to mine?

Auto repair example. Any relationship between test scores and ability to fix cars?

For instance, I had an auto-repair man once, who, on these intelligence tests, could not possibly have scored more than 80, by my estimate. I always took it for granted that I was far more intelligent than he was. Yet, when anything went wrong with my car I hastened to him with it, watched him anxiously as he explored its vitals, and listened to his pronouncements as though they were divine oracles—and he always fixed my car.

Well, then, suppose my auto-repair man devised questions for an intelligence test. Or suppose a carpenter did, or a farmer, or, indeed, almost anyone but an academician. By every one of those tests, I'd prove myself a moron. And I'd *be* a moron, too. In a world where I could not use my academic training and my verbal talents but had to do something intricate or hard, working with my hands, I would do poorly. My intelligence, then, is not absolute but is a function of the society I live in and of the fact that a small subsection of that society has managed to foist itself on the rest as an arbiter of such matters.

Sees intelligence as function of roles in society. Good point!

Mechanic's joke about "deaf-and-dumb carpenter."

Consider my auto-repair man, again. He had a habit of telling me jokes whenever he saw me. One time he raised his head from under the automobile hood to say, "Doc, a deaf-and-dumb guy went into a hardware store to ask for some nails. He put two fingers together on the counter and made hammering motions with the other hand. The clerk brought him a hammer. He shook his head and pointed to the two fingers he was hammering. The clerk brought him nails. He picked out the sizes he wanted, and left. Well doc, the next guy who came in was a blind man.

Traps Asimov with question about blind customer.

He wanted scissors. How do you suppose he asked for them?"

What point did mechanic have?

Indulgently, I lifted my right hand and made scissoring motions with my first two fingers. Whereupon my auto-repair man laughed raucously and said, "Why you dumb jerk, he used his *voice* and asked for them." Then he said, smugly, "I've been trying that on all my customers today." "Did you catch many?" I asked. "Quite a few," he said, "but I knew for sure I'd catch *you*." "Why is that?" I asked. "Because you're so goddamned educated, doc, I *knew* you couldn't be very smart."

Brings up question, "Are all educated people smart?" Not in my experience!

And I have an uneasy feeling he had something there.

Practice: Reading and Annotating Rachel Carson's "Fable for Tomorrow"

Before you read the following essay, think about its title, the biographical and rhetorical information in the headnote, and the writing prompt. Make some marginal notes of your expectations for the essay, and write out a response to the prompt. Then, as you read the essay itself for the first time, try not to stop; take it all in as if in one breath. The second time, however, pause to annotate key points in the text, using the marginal fill-in lines provided alongside each paragraph. As you read, remember the six basic questions mentioned earlier:

1. What does Carson want to say? What is her main point or thesis?
2. Why does she want to make this point? What is her purpose?
3. What pattern or patterns of development does Carson use?
4. How does Carson's pattern of development suit her subject and purpose?
5. What, if anything, is noteworthy about Carson's use of this pattern?
6. How effective is Carson's essay? Does Carson make her points clearly?

Fable for Tomorrow

Title:

_____

_____

■ **Rachel Carson**

Headnote:

Naturalist Rachel Carson (1907–1964) majored in biology at the Pennsylvania College for Women (which later became Chatham College) in the mid-1920s and earned a master's degree in marine zoology from Johns Hopkins University. Later she worked as an aquatic biologist for the U.S.  *Bureau of Fisheries in Washington, D.C. She wrote* Under the Sea Wind *(1941),* The Sea around Us *(1951), and* The Edge of the Sea *(1955)—all sensitive investigations of marine life. But it was* Silent Spring *(1962), her study of herbicides and insecticides, that made Carson a controversial figure. Once denounced as an alarmist, she is now regarded as an early prophet of the ecology movement.*

In the following fable (a short tale teaching a moral) taken from Silent Spring, *Carson uses contrast to show her readers the devastating effects of the indiscriminate use of pesticides.*

1. Biographical note:

_____

_____

_____

_____

_____

_____

2. Publication information:

_____

_____

3. Rhetorical highlights:

_____

_____

Reflecting on What You Know

Hardly a week goes by that we don't hear a news story about the poisoning of the environment. Popular magazines have run cover stories about Americans' growing interest in organic foods. Where do you stand on the issue of using chemical fertilizers, herbicides, and pesticides to grow our nation's food? Do you seek out organic products when you shop? Why or why not?

Writing prompt:

_____

_____

_____

There was once a town in the heart of America where all life seemed to live in harmony with its surroundings. The town lay in the midst of a checkerboard of prosperous farms, with fields of grain and hillsides of orchards where, in spring, white clouds of bloom drifted above the green fields. In autumn, oak and maple and birch set up a blaze of color that flamed and flickered across a backdrop of pines. Then foxes barked in the hills and deer silently crossed the fields, half hidden in the mists of the fall mornings.

Along the roads, laurels, viburnum and alder, great ferns and wildflowers delighted the traveler's eye through much of the year. Even in winter the roadsides were places of beauty, where countless birds came to feed on the berries and on the seed heads of the dried weeds rising above the snow. The countryside was, in fact, famous for the abundance and variety of its bird life, and when the flood of migrants was pouring through in spring and fall people traveled from great distances to observe them. Others came to fish the streams, which flowed clear and cold out of the hills and contained shady pools where trout lay. So it had been from the days many years ago when the first settlers raised their houses, sank their wells, and built their barns.

Then a strange blight crept over the area and everything began to change. Some evil spell had settled on the community: mysterious maladies swept the flocks of chickens; the cattle and sheep sickened and died. Everywhere was a shadow of death. The farmers spoke of much illness among their families. In the town the doctors had become more and more puzzled by new kinds of sickness appearing among their patients. There had been several sudden and unexplained deaths, not only among adults but even among children, who would be stricken suddenly while at play and die within a few hours.

There was a strange stillness. The birds, for example—where had they gone? Many people spoke of them, puzzled and disturbed. The feeding stations

Annotations:

in the backyards were deserted. The few birds seen anywhere were moribund; they trembled violently and could not fly. It was a spring without voices. On the mornings that had once throbbed with the dawn chorus of robins, catbirds, doves, jays, wrens, and scores of other bird voices there was now no sound; only silence lay over the fields and woods and marsh.

5 On the farms the hens brooded, but no chicks hatched. The farmers complained that they were unable to raise any pigs—the litters were small and the young survived only a few days. The apple trees were coming into bloom but no bees droned among the blossoms, so there was no pollination and there would be no fruit.

6 The roadsides, once so attractive, were now lined with browned and withered vegetation as though swept by fire. These, too, were silent, deserted by all living things. Even the streams were now lifeless. Anglers no longer visited them, for all the fish had died.

7 In the gutters under the eaves and between the shingles of the roofs, a white granular powder still showed a few patches; some weeks before it had fallen like snow upon the roofs and the lawns, the fields and streams.

8 No witchcraft, no enemy action had silenced the rebirth of new life in this stricken world. The people had done it themselves.

9 This town does not actually exist, but it might easily have a thousand counterparts in America or elsewhere in the world. I know of no community that has experienced all the misfortunes I describe. Yet every one of these disasters has actually happened somewhere, and many real communities have already suffered a substantial number of them. A grim specter has crept upon us almost unnoticed, and this imagined tragedy may easily become a stark reality we all shall know.

Once you have read and reread Carson's essay and annotated the text, write your own answers to the six basic questions listed on page 51. Then compare your answers with the set of answers that follows.

1. *What does Carson want to say? What is her main point or thesis?* Carson wants to tell her readers a fable, a short narrative that makes an edifying or cautionary point. Carson draws the "moral" of her fable in the final paragraph. She believes that we have in our power the ability to upset the balance of nature, to turn what is an idyllic countryside into a wasteland. As she states in paragraph 8, "The people had done it [silenced the landscape] themselves." Human beings need to take heed and understand their role in environmental stewardship.

2. *Why does she want to make this point? What is her purpose?* Carson's purpose is to alert us to the clear danger of pesticides (the "white granular powder," paragraph 7) to the environment. Even though the composite environmental disaster she describes has not occurred yet, she feels compelled to inform her readers that each of the individual disasters has happened somewhere in a real community. Although Carson does not make specific recommendations for what each of us can do, her message is clear: to do nothing about pesticides is to invite environmental destruction.

3. *What pattern or patterns of development does Carson use?* Carson's dominant pattern of development is comparison and contrast. In paragraphs 1 and 2, she describes the mythical town before the blight ("all life seemed to live in harmony with its surroundings"); in paragraphs 3–7, she portrays the same town after the blight ("some evil spell had settled on the community"). Carson seems less interested in making specific contrasts than in drawing a total picture of the town before and after the blight. In this way, she makes the change dramatic and powerful. Carson enhances her contrast by using vivid descriptive details that appeal to our senses to paint her pictures of the town before and after the "strange blight." The countryside before the blight is full of life; the countryside after, barren and silent.

4. *How does Carson's pattern of development suit her subject and purpose?* Carson selects comparison and contrast as her method of development because she wants to shock her readers into seeing what happens when humans use pesticides indiscriminately. By

contrasting a mythical American town before the blight with the same town after the blight, Carson is able to *show* us the differences, not merely tell us about them. The descriptive details enhance this contrast: for example, "checkerboard of prosperous farms," "white clouds of bloom," "foxes barked," "seed heads of the dried weeds," "cattle and sheep sickened," "they trembled violently," "no bees droned," and "browned and withered vegetation." Perhaps the most striking detail is the "white granular powder" that "had fallen like snow upon the roofs and the lawns, the fields and streams" (7). The powder is the residue of the pervasive use of insecticides and herbicides in farming. Carson waits to introduce the powder for dramatic impact. Readers absorb the horror of the changing scene, wonder at its cause, and then suddenly realize it is not an unseen, uncontrollable force, but human beings who have caused the devastation.

5. *What, if anything, is noteworthy about Carson's use of this pattern?* In her final paragraph, Carson says, "A grim specter has crept upon us almost unnoticed." And this is exactly what happens in her essay. By starting with a two-paragraph description of "a town in the heart of America where all life seemed to live in harmony with its surroundings," Carson lulls her readers into thinking that all is well. But then at the beginning of paragraph 3, she introduces change: "a strange blight crept over the area." By opting to describe the preblight town in its entirety first and then to contrast it with the blighted town, she makes the change more dramatic and thus enhances its impact on readers.

6. *How effective is Carson's essay? Does Carson make her points clearly?* Instead of writing a strident argument against the indiscriminate use of pesticides, Carson chooses to engage her readers in a fable with an educational message. In reading her story of this American town, we witness what happens when farmers blanket the landscape with pesticides. When we learn in the last paragraph that "this town does not actually exist," we are given cause for hope. Even though "every one of these disasters has actually happened somewhere," we are led to believe that there is still time to act before "this imagined tragedy" becomes "a stark reality we all shall know." When she wrote *Silent Spring* in 1962 Carson was considered an alarmist, and now almost daily we read reports of water pollution, oil spills, hazardous waste removal, toxic waste dumps, and climate change. Her warning is as appropriate today as it was when she first wrote it five decades ago.

■ USING YOUR READING IN THE WRITING PROCESS

Reading and writing are the two sides of the same coin. Many people view writing as the making of reading, but the connection does not end there. Active reading is a means to help you become a better writer. We know that one of the best ways to learn to write and to improve our writing is to read. By reading we can begin to see how other writers have communicated their experiences, ideas, thoughts, and feelings in their writing. We can study how they have effectively used the various elements of the essay—thesis, unity, organization, beginnings and endings, paragraphs, transitions, effective sentences, diction and tone, and figurative language—to say what they wanted to say. By studying the style, technique, and rhetorical strategies of other writers, we learn how we might effectively do the same. The more we read and write, the more we begin to read as writers and, in turn, to write knowing what readers expect.

Reading as a Writer

What does it mean to read as a writer? As mentioned earlier, most of us have not been taught to read with a writer's eye, to ask why we like one piece of writing and not another. Similarly, most of us do not ask ourselves why one piece of writing is more convincing than another. When you learn to read with a writer's eye, you begin to answer these important questions. You read beyond the content to see how certain aspects of the writing itself affect you. You come to appreciate what is involved in selecting and focusing a subject as well as the craftsmanship involved in writing—how a writer selects descriptive details, uses an unobtrusive organizational pattern, opts for fresh and lively language, chooses representative and persuasive examples, and emphasizes important points with sentence variety. You come to see writing as a series of choices or decisions the writer makes.

On one level, reading stimulates your thinking by providing you with subjects to write about. For example, after reading Helen Keller's "The Most Important Day," you might take up your pen to write about a turning point in your life. Or by reading Mike Rose's "I Just Wanna Be Average,"Joanne Lipman's "And the Orchestra Played On," Carl T. Rowan's "Unforgettable Miss Bessie," and Thomas L. Friedman's "My Favorite Teacher," you might see how each of these writers creates a dominant impression of an influential person in his or her life and write about an influential person in your own life.

On a second level, reading provides you with information, ideas, and perspectives for developing your own paper. In this way, you respond to what you read, using material from what you've read in your essay. For example, after reading June Tangney's essay "Condemn the Crime, Not the Person," you might want to elaborate on what she has written and either agree with her examples or generate better ones of your own. You could also qualify her argument or take issue against it. Similarly, if you want to write about the effects of new technologies and engineering on our health and well-being, you will find Terry Tempest Williams's "The Clan of One-Breasted Women" and Verlyn Klinkenborg's "Our Vanishing Night" invaluable resources.

On a third level, active reading can increase your awareness of how others' writing affects you, thus making you more sensitive to how your own writing will affect your readers. For example, if you have ever been impressed by an author who uses convincing evidence to support each of his or her claims, you might be more likely to back up your own claims carefully. If you have been impressed by an apt turn of phrase or absorbed by a writer's new idea, you may be less inclined to feed your readers dull, worn-out, and trite phrases.

More to the point, however, the active reading that you are encouraged to do in *Models for Writers* will help you recognize and analyze the essential elements of the essay. When you see, for example, how a writer like Andrew Sullivan uses a strong thesis statement to control the parts of his essay on abolishing torture, you can better appreciate what a clear thesis statement is and see the importance of having one in your essay. When you see the way Nancy Gibbs uses transitions to link key phrases and important ideas so that readers can recognize clearly how the parts of her essay are meant to flow together, you have a better idea of how to achieve such coherence in your own writing. And when you see how Martin Luther King Jr. divides the ways in which people characteristically respond to oppression into three distinct categories, you witness a powerful way in which you too can organize an essay using division and classification.

Another important reason, then, to master the skills of active reading is that, for everything you write, you will be your own first reader and critic. How well you are able to scrutinize your own drafts will powerfully affect how well you revise them, and revising well is crucial to writing well. So reading others' writing with a critical eye is a useful and important practice; the more you read, the more practice you will have in sharpening your skills.

Remember that writing is the making of reading. The more sensitive you become to the content and style decisions made by the writers in *Models for Writers,* the more skilled you will be at seeing the rhetorical options available to you and making conscious choices in your own writing.

■ WRITING FROM READING: FOUR SAMPLE STUDENT ESSAYS

A Narrative Essay

Reading often triggers memories of pesonal experiences. After reading several narratives about growing up—David Raymond's "On Being 17, Bright, and Unable to Read" (p. 197) and Dick Gregory's "Shame" (p. 288), in particular—and discussing with her classmates how memorable events often signal significant changes in life, student Trena Isley decided to write a narrative about such a turning point in her own life. Trena focused on the day she told her father that she no longer wished to participate in sports. Recalling that event led her to reconsider her childhood experiences of running track. Trena welcomed the opportunity to write about this difficult period in her life. As she tried to make her dilemma clear to her classmates, she found that she clarified it for herself. She came to a deeper understanding of her own fears and feelings about striking out on her own and ultimately to a better appreciation of her difficult relationship with her father. What follows is the final draft of Trena's essay.

On the Sidelines

Trena Isley

Point of view: first person narrative　　It was a Monday afternoon, and I was finally home from track practice. The coach had just told me that I had a negative attitude and should contemplate why I was on the team. My father greeted me in the living room.

"Hi honey. How was practice?"

"Not good. Dad. Listen. I don't want to do this anymore. I hate the track team."

Opening: critical dialogue between writer and her father highlights conflict

"What do you mean *hate*?"

"This constant pressure is making me crazy."

"How so?"

"It's just not fun anymore."

"Well, I'll have to talk to Coach — "

"No! You're supposed to be my father, not my coach."

"I am your father, but I'm sure . . . "

"Just let me do what I want. You've had your turn."

He just let out a sigh and left the room. Later he told me that I was wasting my "God-given abilities." The funny part was that none of my father's anger hit me at first. All I knew was that I was free.

Flashback: writer returns to beginning of story and sets context

My troubles began the summer I was five years old. It was late June, and the sticky weather had already settled into the Champlain Valley. My father was yanking my hair into a ponytail in preparation for the first day of the summer track and field season.

As our truck pulled into the upper parking lot I could look down on the scene below. The other kids resembled ants against the massive black track, all of them parading around with no obvious purpose. I stepped out of the truck, never taking my eyes off the colony beneath me, and fell. As I stood there, both knees skinned and bleeding, the last thing I wanted to do was join the other kids. My father quickly hushed my sobs and escorted me down into the throng of children. Around the track we ran, each step stinging my knees as the tears in my eyes continued to rise. Through blurred vision I could see my father on the sidelines, holding his stopwatch in one hand and wearing a grin from ear to ear.

Echo of title
Organization: chronological sequence of events
Writer provides details of her track "career" and relationship with her father

For most of my childhood I was content to let my father make me a track star. As my collection of blue ribbons grew, I was perfect in my father's eyes. By the time I was ten, college coaches were joking with me about scholarships. So I continued to run. It was fun in the beginning, and Dad always had nice things to say about me. I can remember him talking to my grandmother over the holidays: "Trena's got a real shot at winning the 200 meters at the state meet this year, but she's got to train hard."

I began to alter my opinion of competition as I entered my teenage years. At this point I wasn't having fun anymore. My father took me to the gym for "training" sessions four days a week before school. I knew my friends weren't getting up at 5:00 A.M., so I didn't understand why I had to. At thirteen years old all I wanted was to be considered normal. I wanted to fit in with the other kids and do regular teenage stuff.

My father didn't understand my waning interest in track. He still looked forward to my competitions and practice every morning. When my alarm would go off, I would not jump out of bed, often claiming that I didn't feel well or pretending to oversleep. When I began not winning all or even most of my races, my father pushed me to work harder. He would talk incessantly about other competitors and how often they practiced. He never stopped trying to coax me into practicing by buying me breakfast or taking me out to lunch. He tried endlessly, but I just didn't care about track. I resented him more and more with each attempt. I needed to do something that I was truly interested in. And I needed to do it alone.

Dialogue: shows the disconnect between writer and her father

"Hey Dad, what do you think about me trying out for the school play this term? I was told I have a good shot at a part."

"I don't think you'd have time. Track practice is every day isn't it? I've been talking with the coach, and he says the team is looking strong this year. He tells me the state meet should be tough, though. Do you need new spikes?"

"No, Dad. The ones I have are fine, but I just thought . . . "

"Great, 'cause you'll need good spikes when you run on some of those dirt tracks."

So that was that. It got so bad that my father didn't hear me unless "track" was in the sentence. I was starving for my own identity. The mold "Trena the track star" that my father had created for me was crumbling rapidly. Sadly, he wasn't noticing; however, I knew I wanted to quit the track team, but I was afraid that if I gave up sports there would be nothing left for me to be good at. The worst thing someone could be in my family was average.

Writer returns to confrontation with father in opening scene.

When I finally did it — told my father the pressure was making me crazy and that I was quitting — I felt three times lighter. I came to find out, though, that this freedom did have its price. I got to sleep late, but Dad didn't ask me how my day was anymore. He didn't ask me much of anything except when I'd be home at night and with whom I was going out. He wasn't my coach anymore — he was my warden.

Every night I was grilled for details. He needed to know everyone I was with and what we were doing. When I'd tell him, he never seemed to believe me. My dreams of living on a farm and building my own house were laughed at. In the same conversation my younger sister could tell my parents that she was hoping to work for the United Nations, and she would be applauded. The shift had been made. I gained my personal and creative independence but lost a parent.

Organization: time reference "five years"

Ending: writer reflects on relationship with her father.

It has been five years since I retired from athletics and slipped out of my father's graces. Presently my father and I do speak, but it's all on the surface. I now realize that I didn't need the extra morning practices to be good at something. This transition was normal and healthy. It happened quickly, so quickly that I left my father holding the remains of our relationship. The problem was that neither of us bothered to reinvent one for our future as adults. It's not hard for me to understand why we still have a difficult time relating to each other. We really don't know each other very well.

Eventually we'll be able to talk about my quitting track as just that, a small incident that marked the turn of a page in both our lives. We both have unresolved feelings that are standing in the way of our friendship. I need to stop blaming him for my blemished self-image, and he needs to realize that I can succeed without his coaching. In the end we both have to forgive each other.

A Response Essay

For an assignment following James Lincoln Collier's essay "Anxiety: Challenge by Another Name" (p. 90), Zoe Ockenga tackled the topic of anxiety. In her first draft, she explored how anxious she felt the night before her first speech in a public speaking class and how in confronting that anxiety she benefited from the course. Ockenga read her paper aloud in class, and other students had an opportunity to ask her questions and to offer constructive criticism. Several students suggested that she might want to relate her experiences to those that Collier recounts in his essay. Another asked if she could include other examples to bolster the point she wanted to make. At this point in the discussion, Ockenga recalled a phone conversation she had had with her mother regarding her mother's indecision about accepting a new job. The thought of working outside the home for the first time in more than twenty years brought out her mother's worst fears and threatened to keep her from accepting the challenge. Armed with these valuable suggestions and ideas, Ockenga began revising. In subsequent drafts, she worked on the Collier connection, actually citing his essay on several occasions, and developed the example of the anxiety surrounding her mother's decision. What follows is the final draft of her essay, which incorporates the changes she made based on the peer evaluation of her first draft.

Title: indicates main idea of the essay

The Excuse "Not To"

Zoe Ockenga

Beginning: captures reader's attention with personal experience most college students can relate to

I cannot imagine anything worse than the nervous, anxious feeling I got the night before my first speech in public speaking class last spring semester. The knots in my stomach were so fierce that I racked my brain for an excuse to give the teacher so that I would not have to go through with the dreaded assignment. Once in bed, I lay awake thinking of all the mistakes that I might make while standing alone in front of my classmates. I spent the rest of the night tossing and turning, frustrated that now, on top of my panic, I would have to give my speech with huge bags under my eyes.

Anxiety is an intense emotion that can strike at any time or place, before a simple daily activity or a life-changing decision. For some people, anxiety is only a minor interference in the process of achieving a goal. For others, it can be a force that is impossible to overcome. In these instances, anxiety can prevent the accomplishment of lifelong hopes and dreams. Avoiding the causes of stress or fear can make us feel secure and safe. Avoiding anxiety, however, may mean forfeiting a once-in-a-lifetime opportunity. Confronting anxiety can make for a richer, more fulfilling existence.

Thesis

    The next day I trudged to class and sat on the edge of my seat until I could not stand the tension any longer. At this point, I forced myself to raise my hand to volunteer to go next simply to end my suffering. As I walked to the front of the room and assumed my position at the podium, the faces of the twenty-five classmates I had been sitting beside a minute ago suddenly seemed like fifty. I probably fumbled over a word or two as I discussed the harmful aspects of animal testing, but my mistakes were not nearly as severe as I had imagined the night before. Less than five minutes later the whole nightmare was over, and it had been much less painful than I had anticipated. As I sat down with a huge sigh of relief to listen to the next victim stumble repeatedly over how to milk dairy cows, I realized that I had not been half bad.

First example: continues story introduced in opening paragraph to support thesis

    Although I still dreaded giving the next series of speeches, I eventually became more accustomed to speaking in front of my peers. I would still have to force myself to volunteer, secretly hoping the teacher would forget about me, but the audience that once seemed large and forbidding eventually became much more human. A speech class is something that I would never have taken if it had not been a requirement, but I can honestly say that I am better off because of it. I was forced to grapple with my anxiety and in the process become a stronger, more self-confident individual. Before this class I had been able to hide out in large lectures, never offering any comments or insights. For the first time at college I was forced to participate, and I realized that I could speak effectively in front of strangers and, more important, that I had something to say.

Second example: cites essay from Models for Writers *to support thesis*

    The insomnia-inducing anticipation of giving a speech was a type of anxiety that I had to overcome to meet my distribution requirements for graduation. In the essay "Anxiety: Challenge by Another Name" by James Lincoln Collier, the author tells of his own struggles with anxiety. He tells of one particular event that happened between his sophomore and junior years in college when he was asked to spend a summer in Argentina with a good friend. He writes about how he felt after he made his decision not to go:

> I had turned down something I wanted to do because
> I was scared, and had ended up feeling depressed. I
> stayed that way for a long time. And it didn't help
> when I went back to college in the fall to discover
> that Ted and his friend had had a terrific time. (91)

The proposition of going to Argentina was an extremely difficult choice for Collier as it meant abandoning the comfortable routine of the past and venturing completely out of his element. Although the idea of the trip was exciting, the author could not bring himself to choose the summer in Argentina because of his uncertainties.

The summer abroad that Collier denied himself in his early twenties left him with such a feeling of regret that he vowed to change his approach to life. From then on, he faced challenges that made him uncomfortable and was able to accomplish feats he would never have dreamed possible — interviewing celebrities, traveling extensively throughout Europe, parachuting, and even learning to ski at age forty. Collier emphasizes that he was able to make his life fulfilling and exciting by adhering to his belief that anxiety cannot be stifled by avoidance; it can be stifled only by confrontation (92–93).

Third example: introduces mother's dilemma   Anxiety prevents many individuals from accepting life's challenges and changes. My own mother is currently struggling with such a dilemma. At age fifty-three, having never had a career outside the home, my mother has been recommended to manage a new art gallery. The River Gallery, as it will be called, will be opening in our town of Ipswich, Massachusetts, this spring. An avid collector and art lover as well as a budding potter, my mother would, I believe, be exceptional at this job.

Anticipating this new opportunity and responsibility has caused my mother great anxiety. Reentering the workforce after over twenty years is as frightening for my mother as the trip to Argentina was for Collier. When I recently discussed the job prospect with my mother, she was negative and full of doubt. "There's no way I could ever handle such a responsibility," she commented. "I have no business experience. I would look like a fool if I actually tried to pull something like this off. Besides, I'm sure the artists would never take me seriously." Just as my mother focused on all the possible negative aspects of the opportunity in front of her, Collier questioned the value of his opportunity to spend a summer abroad. He describes having second thoughts about just how exciting the trip would be:

Quotation: quotes Collier to help explain mother's indecision

> I had never been very far from New England, and I had been homesick my first few weeks at college. What would it be like in a strange country? What about the language? And besides, I had promised to teach my younger brother to sail that summer. (90–91)

Block quote in MLA style

Focusing on all the possible problems accompanying a new opportunity can arouse such a sense of fear that it can overpower the ability to take a risk. Both my mother and Collier found out that dwelling on possible negative outcomes allowed them to ignore the benefits of a new experience and thus maintain their safe current situations.

Currently my mother is using anxiety as an excuse "not to" act. To confront her anxiety and take an opportunity in which there is a possibility of failure as well as success is a true risk. Regardless of the outcome, to even contemplate a new challenge has changed her life. The summer forgone by Collier roused him to never again pass up an exciting opportunity and thus to live his life to the fullest. Just the thought of taking the gallery position has prompted my mother to contemplate taking evening classes so that if she refuses the offer she may be better prepared for a similar challenge in the future. Although her decision is unresolved, her anxiety has made her realize the possibilities that may be opening for her, whether or not she chooses to take them. If in the end her answer is no, I believe that a lingering "What if?" feeling will cause her to reevaluate her expectations and goals for the future.

Conclusion: includes strong statement about anxiety that echoes optimism of thesis

Anxiety can create confidence and optimism or depression, low self-esteem, and regret. The outcome of anxiety is entirely dependent on whether the individual runs from it or embraces it. Some forms of anxiety can be conquered merely by repeating the activity that causes them, such as giving speeches in a public speaking class. Anxiety brought on by unique opportunities or life-changing decisions, such as a summer in a foreign country or a new career, must be harnessed. Opportunities forgone due to anxiety and fear could be the chances of a lifetime. Although the unpleasant feelings that may accompany anxiety may make it initially easier to do nothing, the road not taken will never be forgotten. Anxiety is essentially a blessing in disguise. It is a physical and emotional trigger that tells us when and where there is an opportunity for us to grow and become stronger human beings.

MLA-style works cited list

Works Cited

Collier, James Lincoln. "Anxiety: Challenge by Another Name." *Models for Writers*. Ed. Alfred Rosa and Paul Eschholz. 11th ed. Boston: Bedford, 2012. 90–93. Print.

A Reflective Essay

Jennifer Chu wrote the following essay during her first year at the Massachusetts Institute of Technology. Her essay starts out simply enough as a personal narrative about making "real" Chinese noodles late at night on her birthday. Soon we learn that the significance of this activity is rooted in her family's long-standing tradition of making noodles as an integral part of celebrating a birthday. This simple celebration ignites Chu into reflecting about a number of Chinese holidays that she celebrated with her family. She interweaves her childhood memories of the foods and activities associated with each holiday with what she later discovers is the holiday's larger family and cultural significance. In reflecting on her own childhood, Chu is able to move beyond superficial descriptions of what happened and to question and explore the meaning and cultural significance of traditions and holidays for humans in general.

A Bowl of Noodles

Jennifer Chu

Opening: writer sets the scene for narrative—she's making noodles. Leaves readers wondering why?

It was 11:30 P.M. and I found myself hovering in front of the stove making a huge bowl of noodles. No, I wasn't just boiling water to make instant cup noodles; I was making genuine beef noodle soup with fresh, thick noodles, large chunks of real beef, and some chopped leafy vegetables in an MSG-free seasoned soup. And no, I was not making noodles because of a late-night hunger pang. Rather, I still felt the eight-inch sub I had eaten an hour ago and the slice of cake half an hour ago, and I loathed the thought of eating another bite. Yet I was still making noodles.

My mother had called me twenty minutes earlier, wishing me happy birthday, asking me how I was celebrating the night. I had gone out with my friends the night before, leaving me with an unbelievable amount of unfinished work to do, so I told her I was celebrating with my problem sets. She paused for a moment. I knew she did not get my joke and was trying to process what I meant literally, since she is an extremely seriously minded person. Then I could picture her frowning slightly as she finally replied, "Well . . . you have to celebrate in some fashion. You cannot just do work for your birthday. Have you eaten noodles today?" I hadn't. Eating noodles on birthdays is an old Chinese tradition that my mom and her mother adhere to adamantly. No matter what happens, my family always eats noodles in some manner on our birthdays.

Mother's phone call had reminded her that making "real" noodles on one's birthday is an old Chinese tradition in her family.

Sometimes, I would be shoved a mouthful of noodles at 6:28 in the morning, trying not to choke as I ran out the door for school. Now I am in college, two hundred miles away from my mom, but I still felt as if I was being force-fed birthday noodles. I had eaten a lunch of stir-fry he-fen, a dish made of inch-wide rice noodles. Yet this was unacceptable. According to my mom's standard of birthday noodles, I had to have real noodles: wheat noodles with soup, noodles that took more than boiling water and three minutes to make. So I was using forty-five precious homework minutes to cook noodles I was too full to eat.

Writer asks herself important question: Why "eat noodles on my birthday anyway?"

Why did I have to eat noodles on my birthday anyway? It is just some ancient tradition passed down to us. When I sit down to think about it, the noodle-eating is probably representative of longevity since noodles are very long, a way to wish the eater a long life. But that was definitely not what went through my mind as I got a messy tangle of noodles shoved into my mouth as a kid.

Question launches writer into exploration of historical significance of holidays and traditions.

There are so many traditions and holidays that I celebrate but don't understand the greater historical significance of. As a child, I loved these special days because of the food, the presents, and the days off from school. I wondered why I couldn't make up my own holidays and why the number of holidays never increased from year to year. Perhaps it is because of the increasing diversity of influences in people's lives today. It is simply too hard for one event to have enough impact on a significant portion of the population to justify its recognition as a national holiday.

Example 1: Chinese holiday Duan-Wu-Jie

I remember looking forward to the Chinese holiday Duan-Wu-Jie, set on the fifth day of the fifth lunar month. The day before the holiday, I would be in the kitchen all day helping my mom make sweet red bean or pork-filled zhongzis, triangular-shaped rice mounds wrapped in fragrant bamboo leaves. I would scrub the bamboo leaves clean in warm water, breathing in the calming aroma of the leaves. Then I would watch my mom skillfully wrap one zhongzi after another, waiting until she reached the last of the rice.

Immediately, I would jump up and tilt the rice pot for her so she could scoop the last straggling grain into the final zhongzi. I would stand next to her on tiptoes watching her tie the final knot and ask, "When can I eat one?" I always got the same answer: "When they are done cooking in three hours."

Writer provides detailed description of holiday.

While I waited anxiously in the living room for the zhongzi's to cook, my mouth watering from the delicious aroma, I would watch the Duan-Wu-Jie festival on TV. There were dragon boat races in gaily painted boats with the bow in the shapes of gracefully arching dragon heads. The rowers were dressed in bright yellow, green, and red costumes. Huge, six-feet wide, decorated drums would be cheering the rowers on, along with endless firecrackers. Sweet-scented decorative pouches would be handed out to children to wear around their necks, and many children had their faces painted. I would run to my mom asking for one of those pretty pouches and for her to paint my face.

Writer reflects on the historical significance on Duan-Wu-Jie.

As a result, my impression of Duan-Wu-Jie was simply a day of festivities and zhongzi making and eating. It was not until much later, in Chinese school, that I learned the solemn origin of the holiday. There was a patriotic and loyal official named Qu Yuan who lived in the Chu Kingdom during the Warring States Period. The weak-minded Chu emperor listened to the rumors of corrupt officials, who were hindered by Qu Yuan's reforms, and exiled him. As a result, the kingdom deteriorated and its lands were progressively taken over by the other warring states. Disheartened by the condition of his homeland, Qu Yuan tied a stone to his chest and plunged into the river. When the local fishermen found out about this, they rushed on their boats to search for the deeply respected Qu Yuan. When they could not find his body, they threw rice wrapped in bamboo leaves into the river so the fish wouldn't eat his body. This event eventually became the Duan-Wu-Jie festival of today, with the festive dragon boat races honoring the fishermen and the tossing of rice morphed into the modern zhongzi-eating tradition. The festival I associated with mouthwatering food and fun had actually originated as a

day to commemorate Qu Yuan and to remind people of their
patriotic duties.

*Example 2:
Harvest
Moon
Festival*

The Harvest Moon Festival is another major celebration my
family partakes in. We would buy a variety of different-flavored
mooncakes, ranging from the traditional lotus and red bean paste
ones to the trendier pineapple or lichee ones. My brother and I
would fight over the different flavored mooncakes, particularly the
pineapple ones, and then huddle around the window of my
parents' bedroom to gaze at the moon. We would compete to see
who could see the most interesting figures in the shadows of the
moon.

But most significant for me, the Moon Festival marked the
day that I received my first telescope. Noticing my interest in the
moon and the stars, my dad decided to buy me a real telescope that
allowed me to zoom close in to the dark spots of the moon and see
what it really looked like — a compilation of craters and ridges. On
the nights of the Moon Festivals with the full moon out, I would
study the moon and chase after the stars with my telescope for
hours while savoring the one pineapple mooncake I managed to
snatch from my brother.

Yet in truth, the Moon Festival is meant to be a day for
family gatherings and reunions. Family members, even those who
were abroad, would rush back to congregate that night. They would
sit together, enjoying each other's company, and gaze at the full
moon which had become whole just as the family had reunited as

*Insight: be-
moans fact
that tradi-
tional
holidays—
both
Chinese
and Ameri-
can—have
lost most of
their cul-
tural signifi-
cance*

a whole. Yet all these deeper sentiments have been lost for me.
With all the media influences and mass marketing of food and
festivities, the meaningful historical origins of the holidays have
been obscured and overlooked. For me, Duan-Wu-Jie is simply
zhongzi eating and dragon boat racing day; Harvest Moon Festival
is mooncake eating and telescope day; Chinese New Year's is red
envelope money day; Thanksgiving is turkey eating day; Labor Day
is shopping day; and all the other one-day holidays are homework
catch-up or relaxation days. Traditional holidays have lost their

cultural significance on me. Their original significance is being overlooked and replaced by personal associations and the experiences each of us has of the holidays.

Writer discusses first Chinese holiday alone at college, wondering if her own family is doing what she is.

During my second month of living at college away from home I had my first major Chinese holiday on my own. It was the Moon Festival, and I had gone out earlier that week to buy some mooncakes for myself, particularly a few pineapple ones. The night of the festival I pulled my chair next to the window, put my feet up on the windowsill, and sat back munching on my horde of mooncakes while I peered at the moon, my eyes squinting to see better, sorely missing my telescope in the basement back home. I finished my first pineapple mooncake and pondered carefully the choices of my second mooncake, my selection no longer limited by my brother's preferences. My gaze settled back onto the moon, and I wondered idly if my brother was still bothering to scope the moon for interesting figures without me there to compete with. Also, what were my parents up to? Were they also watching the same full moon right now just as I was? What kinds of mooncakes did they buy this year? Finally, I decided to call them up, asking my mom to save me a piece of mooncake in the freezer for the next time I come home from college.

Conclusion: writer seems to appreciate the meanings of holidays and settles down to enjoy her birthday noodles

The significance and the origins of the traditional holidays seems to be overlooked more and more today as people don't bother to understand them. However, perhaps the meanings to the holidays are not entirely lost to the people. Maybe it just takes some more years of living and growing for people to gain the experiences necessary to recognize and appreciate the sentiment behind the holidays.

After simmering for another eight minutes, my noodles were finally done. It overfilled my biggest bowl, towering high above the rim. I set it on my desk, watching the steam curl, tumble, and entwine together, and finally dissipate in the air. Then with a grin, I dug in. "Happy Birthday, Jennifer," I thought to myself.

An Argumentative Essay

James Duffy's assignment was to write a thesis-driven argument, and he was free to choose his own topic. He knew from past experience that to write a good essay he would have to write on a topic he cared about. He also knew that he should allow himself a reasonable amount of time to find a topic and to gather his ideas. A premedical student, James found himself reading the essays in *Models for Writers* with a scientific bent. He was particularly struck by Barbara Huttmann's essay, "A Crime of Compassion," because it dealt with the issues of the right to die and treating pain in terminally ill patients, issues that he would be confronting as a medical doctor.

James wrote this particular essay during the second half of the semester, after he had read a number of model arguments and had learned the importance of such matters as good paragraphing, unity, and transitions in his earlier papers. He began by brainstorming about his topic. He made lists of all the ideas, facts, issues, arguments, opposing arguments, and refutations that came to mind as a result of his own firsthand experiences with the topic while on an internship. Once he was confident that he had amassed enough information to begin writing, he made a rough outline of an organizational plan that he thought would work well for him. James then wrote a first draft of his essay. After conferencing with several peers as well as his instructor, James revised what he had written.

The final draft of James's essay illustrates that he had learned how the parts of a well-written essay fit together and how to make revisions that emulate some of the qualities in the model essays he had read and studied. The following is the final draft of James's essay.

One Dying Wish

James Duffy

Opening: context-setting story focuses attention on the central issue

It was an interesting summer. I spent most of my internship assisting postdoctoral students doing research in Cincinnati. One day I came across a file I will never forget. Within the thick file was the story of a fifty-something cancer patient. The man's cancer had metastasized and now was spread throughout his entire body. Over a period of two months he went under the knife seven times to repair and remove parts of his battle-weary body. He endured immeasurable pain. The final surgery on record was done in an effort to stop the pain — doctors intentionally severed the man's spinal cord.

Thesis: writer presents clear statement of position

Terminally ill patients experience intractable pain, and many lose the ability to live a life that has any real meaning to them. To force these people to stay alive when they are in pain and there is no hope for recovery is wrong. They should have the choice to let nature take its course. Forcing people to live in pain when only machines are keeping them alive is unjust.

Presentation of opposing argument: troublesome hospital policy

The hospital I was doing my internship in that summer had a policy that as long as someone was alive, they would do anything to keep him or her alive. The terminal cancer patient whose file I stumbled across fit into this category. He was on narcotics prescribed to alleviate his pain. The problem was that the doctors could not prescribe above a certain life-threatening dosage, a level far below what was necessary to manage the patient's pain. In such a situation, the doctors can't raise a dose because they risk sedating the patient to the point of heart failure.

Discussion of what writer believes is wrong with hospital policy

The hospital I was working at had fallen on hard times; the last thing they needed was to lose a large malpractice suit. If a doctor prescribes above the highest recommended dosage, his or her hospital is at risk if the patient dies. Keeping patients on life support at low dosages, however, is cruel. The doctors at many hospitals have their hands tied. They simply can't give dosages high enough to treat the pain without putting the hospital at risk, and the other option, stopping life support, is forbidden by many hospitals.

Evidence: writer uses example of his Aunt Eileen to show how patient choice and compassionate care should work

When I was fifteen, my Aunt Eileen, who was thirty-four, was diagnosed with a malignant skin cancer. The disease was caught late, and the cancer had metastasized throughout her body. At the time, Eileen had been married for eight years and had a four-year-old daughter and a six-year-old son. They were and are adorable children. When Eileen learned of the disease, she was devastated. She loved her husband and children very much and could not bear the thought of not being with them. Eileen fought the disease fiercely. She tried all the conventional treatments available. Her father and brother were both doctors, so she had access to the best possible care, but the disease did not succumb to the treatment. She tried unconventional and experimental treatments as well, but it was all for naught. The disease had an unshakable grip on her. She had wasted away to well below one hundred pounds; a tumor had grown to the size of a grapefruit on her stomach. It was the end, and everyone knew it. Luckily Eileen was able to get into a hospice center. While she was there, she was able to make peace with herself, her family, and God and die calmly without pain.

If Eileen had been forced to keep living, her pain undertreated and her body resuscitated again and again, the damage to her and her family would have been enormous. It would have been almost impossible to make peace with herself and God if she had been in pain so intense she couldn't think. The hospice personnel managed the pain and helped Eileen and her family avoid the anguish of a prolonged and painful death.

In "A Crime of Compassion," Barbara Huttmann, a registered nurse, recounts her hospital's disregard for a patient named Mac. Mac's story is one of a prolonged and painful death, without options. Mac came into the hospital with a persistent cough and walked out with a diagnosis of lung cancer. He battled the disease but lost ground fast. Over the course of six months, Mac lost "his youth . . . his hair, his bowel and bladder control, and his ability to do the slightest thing for himself" (344). Mac wasted away to a mere sixty pounds. He was in constant pain, which the hospital was unable to manage. His young wife now looked "haggard and beaten" (344). Mac went into arrest three times some days. Every time his wife broke down into tears. The nurses ordered "code blue" every time it happened, and the hospital staff resuscitated Mac. This situation repeated itself for over a month. During one month, Mac was resuscitated fifty-two

Evidence: writer introduces outside source to support his argument for patient choice

Writer summarizes Huttmann's story about her patient Mac, taking care to put any directly quoted material in quotation marks followed by in-text citation

times. Mac had long ago realized the battle was over. He pleaded with his doctors and nurses to let him die. The problem was that the hospital did not issue no-code orders. A no-code order meant that if Mac went into arrest again they would let him die. Days passed as Barbara Huttmann, his nurse, pleaded for a no-code order. Each time he went into arrest his wife, Maura, took another step toward becoming psychologically crippled. As Barbara worked to resuscitate Mac, she'd look into his eyes as he pleaded for her to stop. Finally, Barbara decided enough was enough. Mac went into arrest and she did not call the Code Blue until she was certain he could not be resuscitated. For granting Mac his dying wish, Barbara was charged with murder (343–46).

Writer uses anti-capital punishment argument to bolster his call for more humane treatment of the ter- minally ill

The situation of Mac illustrates the death many people are forced to endure. These situations constitute an irony in today's society. Many complain that executions are inhumane or cruel and unusual. A principle argument of these anti-capital punishment people is that the death is not pain free. People also think that regardless of the situation a patient should be allowed to die and should not be medicated to the point of death. Mac was forced to live on the brink of death for over a month, watching as his wife was also destroyed by his ordeal. The treatment Mac received can only be described as inhumane. To force a man to live in pain when there is no reasonable hope he will ever get better is truly cruel and unusual. Had Mac had the option of a peaceful and pain-free death, it would have saved himself and his wife the pain of being forced to live on the edge of death for such an extended period of time. Maura must have looked into Mac's tortured eyes and wondered why he had no choices concerning his life or death. Almost any choice would have been better than the treatment he received.

American society needs to follow the lead of countries like the Netherlands and Belgium or a state like Oregon with its Death with Dignity Act and reevaluate the right of the terminally ill to die. Keeping people in agonizing pain for a long period is uncivilized. Everyone would agree with that. Many people do not

Conclusion: Writer calls for action on the rights of the terminally ill.

understand, however, that prolonging the life of a terminally ill patient with unmanageable pain is the same thing. Laws need to be passed to protect doctors who accidently overmedicate a terminally ill patient in the interest of pain management. Patients also deserve the right to determine if they want to go off life support, no matter what hospital they are in. Until people demand that action be taken to resolve this issue, the terminally ill will continue to suffer.

Works Cited

Huttmann, Barbara. "A Crime of Compassion." *Models for Writers*. Ed. Alfred Rosa and Paul Eschholz. 11th ed. Boston: Bedford, 2012. 343–46. Print.

part ■ *two*

The Elements
of the Essay

Thesis

The **thesis** of an essay is its main or controlling idea, the point the writer is trying to make. The thesis is often expressed in a one- or two-sentence statement, although sometimes it is implied or suggested rather than stated directly. The thesis statement determines the content of the essay: everything the writer says must be logically related to the thesis statement.

Because everything you say in your composition must be logically related to your thesis, the thesis statement controls and directs the choices you make about the content of your essay. This does not mean that your thesis statement is a straitjacket. As your essay develops, you may want to modify your thesis statement to accommodate your new thinking. This urge is not only acceptable; it is normal.

One way to develop a working thesis is to determine a question that you are trying to answer in your essay. A one- or two-sentence answer to this question often produces a tentative thesis statement. For example, a student wanted to answer the following question in her essay:

Do men and women have different conversational speaking styles?

Her preliminary answer to this question was this:

Men and women appear to have different objectives when they converse.

After writing two drafts, she modified her thesis to better fit the examples she had gathered:

Very often, conversations between men and women become situations in which the man gives a mini-lecture and the woman unwittingly turns into a captive audience.

A thesis statement should be

- The most important point you make about your topic,
- More general than the ideas and facts used to support it, and
- Appropriately focused for the length of your paper.

A thesis statement is not a question but an assertion—a claim made about a debatable issue that can be supported with evidence.

Another effective strategy for developing a thesis statement is to begin by writing "What I want to say is that . . . "

> <u>What I want to say is that</u> unless the university administration enforces its strong anti-hazing policy, the well-being of many of its student-athletes will be endangered.

Later, when you delete the formulaic opening, you will be left with a thesis statement:

> Unless the university administration enforces its strong anti-hazing policy, the well-being of many of its student-athletes will be endangered.

Usually the thesis is presented early in the essay, sometimes in the first sentence. Here are some thesis statements that begin essays:

> One of the most potent elements in body language is eye behavior.
> —Flora Davis

> Americans can be divided into three groups—smokers, nonsmokers, and that expanding pack of us who have quit.
> —Franklin E. Zimring

> Over the past ten to fifteen years it has become apparent that eating disorders have reached epidemic proportions among adolescents.
> —Helen A. Guthrie

> Clutter is the disease of American writing. We are a society strangling in unnecessary words, circular constructions, pompous frills, and meaningless jargon.
> —William Zinsser

Each of these sentences does what a good thesis statement should do: it identifies the topic and makes an assertion about it.

Often writers prepare readers for the thesis statement with one or several sentences that establish a context. Notice in the following example how the author eases the reader into his thesis about television instead of presenting it abruptly in the first sentence:

> With the advent of television, for the first time in history, all aspects of animal and human life and death, of societal and individual behavior have been condensed on the average to a 19-inch diagonal screen and a 30-minute time slot. Television, a unique medium, claiming to be neither a reality nor art, has become reality for many of us, particularly for our children who are growing up in front of it.
>
> –Jerzy Kosinski

On occasion a writer may even purposely delay the presentation of a thesis until the middle or the end of an essay. If the thesis is controversial or needs extended discussion and illustration, the writer might present it later to make it easier for the reader to understand and accept it. Appearing near or at the end of an essay, a thesis also gains prominence. For example, after an involved discussion about why various groups put pressure on school libraries to ban books, a student ended an essay with her thesis:

> The effort to censor what our children are reading can turn into a potentially explosive situation and cause misunderstanding and hurt feelings within our schools and communities. If we can gain an understanding of why people have sought to censor children's books, we will be better prepared to respond in a sensitive and reasonable manner. More importantly, we will be able to provide the best edu- *Thesis* cational opportunity for our children through a sensible approach, one that neither overly restricts the range of their reading nor allows them to read all books, no matter how inappropriate.
>
> –Tara Ketch, student

Some kinds of writing do not need thesis statements. These include descriptions, narratives, and personal writing such as letters and diaries. But any essay that seeks to explain or prove a point has a thesis that is usually set forth in a formal thesis statement.

The Most Important Day

◼ Helen Keller

Helen Keller (1880–1968) was afflicted by a disease that left her blind and deaf at the age of eighteen months. With the aid of her teacher, Anne Mansfield Sullivan, she was able to overcome her severe handicaps, to graduate from Radcliffe College, and to lead a productive and challenging adult life. In the following selection from her autobiography, The Story of My Life *(1902), Keller tells of the day she first met Anne Sullivan, a day she regarded as the most important in her life.*

As you read, note that Keller states her thesis in the first paragraph and that the remaining paragraphs maintain unity by emphasizing the importance of the day her teacher arrived, even though they deal with the days and weeks following.

Reflecting on What You Know

Reflect on the events of what you consider "the most important day" of your life. Briefly describe what happened. Why was that particular day so significant?

The most important day I remember in all my life is the one on which my teacher, Anne Mansfield Sullivan, came to me. I am filled with wonder when I consider the immeasurable contrast between the two lives which it connects. It was the third of March, 1887, three months before I was seven years old.

On the afternoon of that eventful day, I stood on the porch, dumb,[1] expectant. I guessed vaguely from my mother's signs and from the hurrying to and fro in the house that something unusual was about to happen, so I went to the door and waited on the steps. The afternoon sun penetrated the mass of honeysuckle that covered the porch and fell on my upturned face. My fingers lingered almost unconsciously on the familiar leaves and blossoms which had just come forth to greet the

[1]*dumb*: unable to speak; mute.

sweet southern spring. I did not know what the future held of marvel or surprise for me. Anger and bitterness had preyed upon me continually for weeks and a deep languor[2] had succeeded this passionate struggle.

Have you ever been at sea in a dense fog, when it seemed as if a tangible white darkness shut you in, and the great ship, tense and anxious, groped her way toward the shore with plummet and sounding-line,[3] and you waited with beating heart for something to happen? I was like that ship before my education began, only I was without compass or sounding-line, and had no way of knowing how near the harbor was. "Light! Give me light!" was the wordless cry of my soul, and the light of love shone on me in that very hour.

3

I felt approaching footsteps. I stretched out my hand as I supposed to my mother. Someone took it, and I was caught up and held close in the arms of her who had come to reveal all things to me, and, more than all things else, to love me.

4

The morning after my teacher came she led me into her room and gave me a doll. The little blind children at the Perkins Institution[4] had sent it and Laura Bridgman[5] had dressed it; but I did not know this until afterward. When I had played with it a little while, Miss Sullivan slowly spelled into my hand the word "d-o-l-l." I was at once interested in this finger play and tried to imitate it. When I finally succeeded in making the letters correctly I was flushed with childish pleasure and pride. Running downstairs to my mother I held up my hand and made the letters for doll. I did not know that I was spelling a word or even that words existed; I was simply making my fingers go in monkeylike imitation. In the days that followed I learned to spell in this uncomprehending way a great many words, among them *pin, hat, cup* and a few verbs like *sit, stand,* and *walk.* But my teacher had been with me several weeks before I understood that everything has a name.

5

One day, while I was playing with my new doll, Miss Sullivan put my big rag doll into my lap also, spelled "d-o-l-l" and tried to make me understand that "d-o-l-l" applied to both. Earlier in the day we had had a tussle over the words "m-u-g" and "w-a-t-e-r." Miss Sullivan had tried to impress it upon me that "m-u-g" is *mug* and

6

---

[2]*languor:* sluggishness.
[3]*plummet . . . line:* a weight tied to a line that is used to measure the depth of the ocean.
[4]*Perkins Institution:* the first school for blind children in the United States, opened in 1832 and located in South Boston during her time there. The school moved to Watertown, Massachusetts, in 1912.
[5]*Laura Bridgman* (1829–1889): a deaf-blind girl who was educated at the Perkins Institution in the 1840s.

that "w-a-t-e-r" is *water,* but I persisted in confounding the two. In despair she had dropped the subject for the time, only to renew it at the first opportunity. I became impatient at her repeated attempts and, seizing the new doll, I dashed it upon the floor. I was keenly delighted when I felt the fragments of the broken doll at my feet. Neither sorrow nor regret followed my passionate outburst. I had not loved the doll. In the still, dark world in which I lived there was no strong sentiment or tenderness. I felt my teacher sweep the fragments to one side of the hearth, and I had a sense of satisfaction that the cause of my discomfort was removed. She brought me my hat, and I knew I was going out into the warm sunshine. This thought, if a wordless sensation may be called a thought, made me hop and skip with pleasure.

We walked down the path to the well-house, attracted by the fragrance of the honeysuckle with which it was covered. Someone was drawing water and my teacher placed my hand under the spout. As the cool stream gushed over one hand she spelled into the other the word *water,* first slowly, then rapidly. I stood still, my whole attention fixed upon the motions of her fingers. Suddenly I felt a misty consciousness as of something forgotten—a thrill of returning thought; and somehow the mystery of language was revealed to me. I knew then that "w-a-t-e-r" meant the wonderful cool something that was flowing over my hand. The living word awakened my soul, gave it light, hope, joy, set it free! There were barriers still, it is true, but barriers that could in time be swept away. 7

I left the well-house eager to learn. Everything had a name, and each name gave birth to a new thought. As we returned to the house every object which I touched seemed to quiver with life. That was because I saw everything with the strange, new sight that had come to me. On entering the door I remembered the doll I had broken. I felt my way to the hearth and picked up the pieces. I tried vainly to put them together. Then my eyes filled with tears; for I realized what I had done, and for the first time I felt repentance and sorrow. 8

I learned a great many new words that day. I do not remember what they all were; but I do know that *mother, father, sister, teacher* were among them—words that were to make the world blossom for me, "like Aaron's rod,[6] with flowers." It would have been difficult to find a happier child than I was as I lay in my crib at the close of that 9

---

[6]*Aaron's rod:* in Jewish and Christian traditions, a rod similar to Moses's staff that, in the high priest Aaron's hands, had miraculous power.

eventful day and lived over the joys it had brought me, and for the first time longed for a new day to come.

Thinking Critically about This Reading

Keller writes that "'Light! Give me light!' was the wordless cry of [her] soul" (paragraph 3). What was the "light" Keller longed for, and how did receiving it change her life?

Questions for Study and Discussion

1. What is Keller's thesis? What question do you think Keller is trying to answer? Does her thesis answer her question?
2. What is Keller's purpose? (Glossary: *Purpose*)
3. What was Keller's state of mind before Anne Sullivan arrived to help her? To what does she compare herself? (Glossary: *Analogy*) How effective is this comparison? Explain.
4. Why was the realization that everything has a name important to Keller?
5. How was the "mystery of language" (7) revealed to Keller? What were the consequences for her of this new understanding of the nature of language?
6. Keller narrates the events of the day Sullivan arrived (2–4), the morning after she arrived (5), and one day several weeks after her arrival (6–9). (Glossary: *Narration*) Describe what happens on each day, and explain how these separate incidents support Keller's thesis.

Classroom Activity Using Thesis

One effective way of focusing on your subject is to develop a list of specific questions about it at the start. This strategy has a number of advantages. Each question narrows the general subject area, suggesting a more manageable essay. Also, simply phrasing your topic as a question gives you a starting point; your work has focus and direction from the outset. Finally, a one- or two-sentence answer to your question often provides you with a preliminary thesis statement.

To test this strategy, develop a list of five questions about the subject "recycling paper waste on campus." To get you started, here is one possible question: should students be required to recycle paper waste?

1. _____
2. _____
3. _____
4. _____
5. _____

Now develop a preliminary thesis statement by answering one of your questions.

Suggested Writing Assignments

1. Think about an important day in your own life. Using the thesis statement "The most important day of my life was _____," write an essay in which you show the significance of that day by recounting and explaining the events that took place, as Keller does in her essay. Before you write, you might find it helpful to reflect on your journal entry for this reading.

2. For many people around the world, the life of Helen Keller symbolizes what a person can achieve despite seemingly insurmountable obstacles. Her achievements have inspired people with and without disabilities, leading them to believe they can accomplish more than they ever thought possible. Consider the role of people with disabilities in our society, develop an appropriate thesis, and write an essay on the topic.

3. Keller was visually and hearing impaired from the age of eighteen months, which meant she could neither read nor hear people speak. She was eventually able to read and write using braille, a system of "touchable symbols" invented by Louis Braille. In the photograph on page 89 taken at the Sorbonne in Paris, France, upon the one-hundredth anniversary of Braille's death, Keller demonstrates how to use the system. Write an essay in which you put forth the thesis that the invention of braille has liberated countless numbers of people who have shared Keller's impairment.

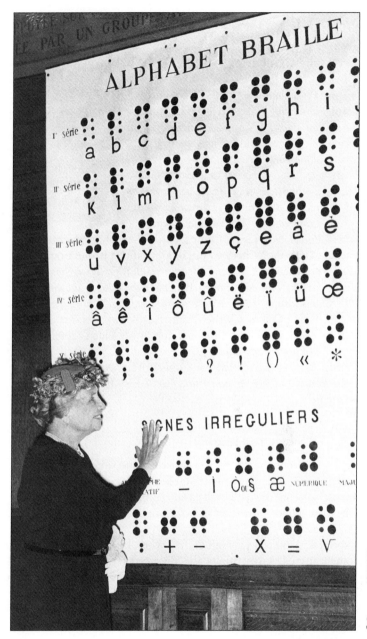

Be Specific

■ **Natalie Goldberg**

Born in 1948, Natalie Goldberg has made a
specialty of writing about writing. Her first and
best-known work, Writing Down the Bones:
Freeing the Writer Within, *was published in*
1986. Goldberg's advice to would-be writers is,
on the one hand, practical and pithy; on the
other, it is almost mystical in its call to know
and appreciate the world. Her other books
about writing include Wild Mind: Living the
Writer's Life *(1990),* Living Color *(1996),* Thunder and Lightning:
Cracking Open the Writer's Craft *(2000), and* Old Friend from Far
Away: The Practice of Writing Memoir *(2008). Goldberg has also*
written fiction. Her first novel, Banana Rose, *was published in*
1994. She is also a painter whose work is exhibited in Taos, New
Mexico. Living Color: A Writer Paints Her World *(1997) is about*
painting as her second art form, and Top of My Lungs *(2002) is a*
collection of poetry and paintings.

In "Be Specific," a chapter from Writing Down the Bones,
notice how Goldberg demonstrates her thesis about the need to
be specific.

Reflecting on What You Know

Suppose someone says to you, "I walked in the woods." What do
you envision? Write down what you see in your mind's eye. Now
suppose someone says, "I walked in the redwood forest." Again,
write what you see. How are the two descriptions different, and why?

Be specific. Don't say "fruit." Tell what kind of fruit—"It is a   1
pomegranate." Give things the dignity of their names. Just as
with human beings, it is rude to say, "Hey, girl, get in line." That
"girl" has a name. (As a matter of fact, if she's at least twenty years
old, she's a woman, not a "girl" at all.) Things, too, have names. It is
much better to say "the geranium in the window" than "the flower in
the window." "Geranium"—that one word gives us a much more

specific picture. It penetrates more deeply into the beingness of that flower. It immediately gives us the scene by the window—red petals, green circular leaves, all straining toward sunlight.

About ten years ago I decided I had to learn the names of plants 2
and flowers in my environment. I bought a book on them and walked down the tree-lined streets of Boulder,[1] examining leaf, bark, and seed, trying to match them up with their descriptions and names in the book. Maple, elm, oak, locust. I usually tried to cheat by asking people working in their yards the names of the flowers and trees growing there. I was amazed how few people had any idea of the names of the live beings inhabiting their little plot of land.

When we know the name of something, it brings us closer to the 3
ground. It takes the blur out of our mind; it connects us to the earth. If I walk down the street and see "dogwood," "forsythia," I feel more friendly toward the environment. I am noticing what is around me and can name it. It makes me more awake.

If you read the poems of William Carlos Williams,[2] you will see 4
how specific he is about plants, trees, flowers—chicory, daisy, locust, poplar, quince, primrose, black-eyed Susan, lilacs—each has its own integrity. Williams says, "Write what's in front of your nose." It's good for us to know what is in front of our nose. Not just "daisy," but how the flower is in the season we are looking at it— "The days-eye hugging the earth / in August . . . brownedged, / green and pointed scales / armor his yellow."* Continue to hone your awareness: to the name, to the month, to the day, and finally to the moment.

Williams also says: "No idea, but in things." Study what is "in 5
front of your nose." By saying "geranium" instead of "flower," you are penetrating more deeply into the present and being there. The closer we can get to what's in front of our nose, the more it can teach us everything. "To see the World in a Grain of Sand, and a heaven in a Wild Flower . . . "**

In writing groups and classes too, it is good to quickly learn the 6
names of all the other group members. It helps to ground you in the group and make you more attentive to each other's work.

---

[1]*Boulder:* a city in Colorado.
[2]*William Carlos Williams* (1883–1963): American poet.
*William Carlos Williams, "Daisy," in *The Collected Earlier Poems* (New York: New Directions, 1938). [Goldberg's note]
**William Blake, "The Auguries of Innocence." [Goldberg's note]

Learn the names of everything: birds, cheese, tractors, cars, build- 7
ings. A writer is all at once everything—an architect, French cook,
farmer—and at the same time, a writer is none of these things.

Thinking Critically about This Reading

What does Goldberg mean when she states, "Give things the dignity
of their names" (paragraph 1)? Why, according to Goldberg, should
writers refer to things by their specific names?

Questions for Study and Discussion

1. What is Goldberg's thesis and where does she state it?
2. How does Goldberg "specifically" follow the advice she gives
   writers in this essay?
3. Goldberg makes several lists of the names of things. What purpose do these lists serve? (Glossary: *Purpose*)
4. Throughout the essay, Goldberg instructs the reader to be specific and to be aware of the physical world. Of what besides
   names is the reader advised to be aware? Why?
5. In paragraphs 3, 5, and 6, Goldberg cites a number of advantages to be gained by knowing the names of things. What are
   these advantages? Do they ring true to you?
6. What specific audience does Goldberg address? (Glossary: *Audience*)
   How do you know?

Classroom Activity Using Thesis

A useful exercise in learning to be specific is to see the words we use
for people, places, things, and ideas as being positioned somewhere
on a "ladder of abstraction." In the following chart, notice how the
words progress from more general to more specific.

More General	General	Specific	More Specific
Organism	Plant	Flower	Alstrumaria
Vehicle	Car	Chevrolet	1958 Chevrolet Impala

Try to fill in the missing parts of the following ladder of abstraction:

More General	General	Specific	More Specific
Writing instrument	_____	Fountain pen	Waterman fountain pen
_____	Sandwich	Corned beef sandwich	Reuben
American	_____	Navaho	Laguna Pueblo
Book	Reference book	Dictionary	_____
School	High school	Technical high school	_____
Medicine	Oral medicine	Gel capsule	_____

Suggested Writing Assignments

1. Goldberg likes William Carlos Williams's statement, "No idea, but in things" (5). Using this line as both a title and a thesis, write your own argument for the use of the specific over the general in a certain field — news reporting, writing poetry, or making music, for example. (Glossary: *Argumentation*) Be sure to support your argument with specific examples.

2. Write a brief essay advising your readers of something they should do. Title your essay, as Goldberg does, with a directive ("Be Specific"). Tell your readers how they can improve their lives by taking your advice, and give strong examples of the behavior you are recommending.

Anxiety: Challenge
by Another Name

■ James Lincoln Collier

*James Lincoln Collier is a freelance writer with
more than six hundred articles to his credit. He
was born in New York in 1928 and graduated
from Hamilton College in 1950. Among his
published books are many works of fiction, including novels for young adults. His nonfiction
writing has often focused on American music.
His best-known book is* The Making of Jazz:
A Comprehensive History *(1978). With his
brother Christopher he has written a number of history books, including* A Century of Immigration: 1820–1924 *(2000),* The Civil
War *(2000),* The Changing Face of American Society: 1945–2000
*(2001), and a series of biographies for young readers covering
major figures in American history.*

As you read the following essay, which first appeared in Reader's
Digest *in 1986, pay attention to where Collier places his thesis. Note
also how his thesis statement identifies the topic (anxiety) and makes
an assertion about it (that it can have a positive effect on our lives).*

Reflecting on What You Know

Many people associate anxiety with stress and think of it as a
negative thing. Are there good kinds of anxiety, too? Provide an
example of anxiety that has been beneficial to you or to someone you know.

B etween my sophomore and junior years at college, a chance came 1
up for me to spend the summer vacation working on a ranch in
Argentina. My roommate's father was in the cattle business, and he
wanted Ted to see something of it. Ted said he would go if he could
take a friend, and he chose me.

The idea of spending two months on the fabled Argentine 2
Pampas[1] was exciting. Then I began having second thoughts. I had

---

[1]*Pampas:* a vast plain in central Argentina.

never been very far from New England, and I had been homesick my first few weeks at college. What would it be like in a strange country? What about the language? And besides, I had promised to teach my younger brother to sail that summer. The more I thought about it, the more the prospect daunted² me. I began waking up nights in a sweat.

In the end I turned down the proposition. As soon as Ted asked   3
somebody else to go, I began kicking myself. A couple of weeks later I went home to my old summer job, unpacking cartons at the local supermarket, feeling very low. I had turned down something I wanted to do because I was scared, and had ended up feeling depressed. I stayed that way for a long time. And it didn't help when I went back to college in the fall to discover that Ted and his friend had had a terrific time.

In the long run that unhappy summer taught me a valuable les-   4
son out of which I developed a rule for myself: *do what makes you anxious; don't do what makes you depressed.*

I am not, of course, talking about severe states of anxiety or   5
depression, which require medical attention. What I mean is that kind of anxiety we call stage fright, butterflies in the stomach, a case of nerves—the feelings we have at a job interview, when we're giving a big party, when we have to make an important presentation at the office. And the kind of depression I am referring to is that down-hearted feeling of the blues, when we don't seem to be interested in anything, when we can't get going and seem to have no energy.

I was confronted by this sort of situation toward the end of my   6
senior year. As graduation approached, I began to think about taking a crack at making my living as a writer. But one of my professors was urging me to apply to graduate school and aim at a teaching career.

I wavered. The idea of trying to live by writing was scary—a lot   7
more scary than spending a summer on the Pampas, I thought. Back and forth I went, making my decision, unmaking it. Suddenly, I realized that every time I gave up the idea of writing, that sinking feeling went through me; it gave me the blues.

The thought of graduate school wasn't what depressed me. It was   8
giving up on what deep in my gut I really wanted to do. Right then I learned another lesson. To avoid that kind of depression meant, inevitably, having to endure a certain amount of worry and concern.

The great Danish philosopher Søren Kierkegaard believed that   9
anxiety always arises when we confront the possibility of our own

---

²*daunted:* discouraged.

development. It seems to be a rule of life that you can't advance without getting that old, familiar, jittery feeling.

Even as children we discover this when we try to expand ourselves by, say, learning to ride a bike or going out for the school play. Later in life we get butterflies when we think about having that first child, or uprooting the family from the old hometown to find a better opportunity halfway across the country. Any time, it seems, that we set out aggressively to get something we want, we meet up with anxiety. And it's going to be our traveling companion, at least part of the way, into any new venture. 10

When I first began writing magazine articles, I was frequently required to interview big names—people like Richard Burton,[3] Joan Rivers,[4] sex authority William Masters, baseball-great Dizzy Dean. Before each interview I would get butterflies and my hands would shake. 11

At the time, I was doing some writing about music. And one person I particularly admired was the great composer Duke Ellington. Onstage and on television, he seemed the very model of the confident, sophisticated man of the world. Then I learned that Ellington still got stage fright. If the highly honored Duke Ellington, who had appeared on the bandstand some 10,000 times over thirty years, had anxiety attacks, who was I to think I could avoid them? 12

I went on doing those frightening interviews, and one day, as I was getting onto a plane for Washington to interview columnist Joseph Alsop, I suddenly realized to my astonishment that I was looking forward to the meeting. What had happened to those butterflies? 13

Well, in truth, they were still there, but there were fewer of them. I had benefited, I discovered, from a process psychologists call "extinction." If you put an individual in an anxiety-provoking situation often enough, he will eventually learn that there isn't anything to be worried about. 14

Which brings us to a corollary[5] to my basic rule: *you'll never eliminate anxiety by avoiding the things that caused it.* I remember how my son Jeff was when I first began to teach him to swim at the lake cottage where we spent our summer vacations. He resisted, and when I got him into the water he sank and sputtered and wanted to 15

---

[3]*Richard Burton* (1925–1984): a well-known British stage and Hollywood movie actor.
[4]*Joan Rivers* (b. 1933): a stand-up comedian and talk-show host.
[5]*corollary:* a proposition that follows with little or no proof required.

quit. But I was insistent. And by summer's end he was splashing around like a puppy. He had "extinguished" his anxiety the only way he could—by confronting it.

The problem, of course, is that it is one thing to urge somebody   16 else to take on those anxiety-producing challenges; it is quite another to get ourselves to do it.

Some years ago I was offered a writing assignment that would   17 require three months of travel through Europe. I had been abroad a couple of times on the usual "If it's Tuesday this must be Belgium" trips, but I hardly could claim to know my way around the continent. Moreover, my knowledge of foreign languages was limited to a little college French.

I hesitated. How would I, unable to speak the language, totally   18 unfamiliar with local geography or transportation systems, set up interviews and do research? It seemed impossible, and with considerable regret I sat down to write a letter begging off. Halfway through, a thought—which I subsequently made into another corollary to my basic rule—ran through my mind: *you can't learn if you don't try.* So I accepted the assignment.

There were some bad moments. But by the time I had finished   19 the trip I was an experienced traveler. And ever since, I have never hesitated to head for even the most exotic of places, without guides or even advanced bookings, confident that somehow I will manage.

The point is that the new, the different, is almost by definition   20 scary. But each time you try something, you learn, and as the learning piles up, the world opens to you.

I've made parachute jumps, learned to ski at forty, flown up the   21 Rhine[6] in a balloon. And I know I'm going to go on doing such things. It's not because I'm braver or more daring than others. I'm not. But I don't let the butterflies stop me from doing what I want. Accept anxiety as another name for challenge and you can accomplish wonders.

Thinking Critically about This Reading

Collier writes that "Kierkegaard believed that anxiety always arises when we confront the possibility of our own development" (paragraph 9). How do Collier's own experiences and growth substantiate Kierkegaard's belief in the value of anxiety?

---

[6]*Rhine:* a major river and waterway of western Europe.

Questions for Study and Discussion

1. What is Collier's thesis? Based on your own experiences, do you think Collier's thesis is valid? Explain.
2. What is the process known to psychologists as "extinction"?
3. What causes Collier to come up with his basic rule for himself: "Do what makes you anxious; don't do what makes you depressed" (4)? (Glossary: *Cause and Effect*) How does he develop the two corollaries to his basic rule? How do the basic rule and the two corollaries prepare you for his thesis?
4. What is Collier's purpose? (Glossary: *Purpose*)
5. What function do paragraphs 17–19 serve in Collier's essay?

Classroom Activity Using Thesis

A good thesis statement identifies the topic and makes an assertion about it. Evaluate each of the following sentences, and explain why each one either works or doesn't work as a thesis statement.

1. Americans are suffering from overwork.
2. Life is indeed precious, and I believe the death penalty helps to affirm this fact.
3. Birthday parties are loads of fun.
4. New York is a city of sounds: muted sounds and shrill sounds, shattering sounds and soothing sounds, urgent sounds and aimless sounds.
5. Everyone is talking about the level of violence in American society.

Suggested Writing Assignments

1. Building on your own experiences and the reading you have done, write an essay in which you use as your thesis either Collier's basic rule or one of his corollaries to that basic rule.
2. Write an essay using any one of the following as your thesis:

    Good manners are a thing of the past.
    We need rituals in our lives.
    To tell a joke well is an art.
    We are a drug-dependent society.
    Regular exercise offers many benefits.

Unity

Unity is an essential quality in a well-written essay. The principle of unity requires that every element in a piece of writing—whether a paragraph or an essay—be related to the main idea. Sentences that stray from the subject, even though they might be related to it or provide additional information, can weaken an otherwise strong piece of writing. Notice how the italicized segments in the following paragraph undermine its unity and divert our attention from its main idea:

> When I was growing up, one of the places I enjoyed most was the cherry tree in the backyard. *Behind the yard was an alley and then more houses.* Every summer when the cherries began to ripen, I used to spend hours high up in the tree, picking and eating the sweet, sun-warmed cherries. *My mother always worried about my falling out of the tree, but I never did.* But I had some competition for the cherries—flocks of birds that enjoyed them as much as I did would perch all over the tree, devouring the fruit whenever I wasn't there. I used to wonder why the grown-ups never ate any of the cherries—*my father loved all kinds of fruit*—but actually, when the birds and I had finished, there weren't many left.
>
> –Betty Burns, student

When the italicized sentences are eliminated, the paragraph is unified and reads smoothly.

Now consider another paragraph, this one from an essay about family photographs and how they allow the author to learn about her past and to stay connected with her family in the present:

> Photographs have taken me to places I have never been and have shown me people alive before I was born. I can visit my grandmother's childhood home in Vienna, Austria, and walk down the high-ceilinged, iron staircase by looking through the small,

white album my grandma treasures. I also know of the tomboy she once was, wearing lederhosen instead of the dirndls worn by her friends. And I have seen her as a beautiful young woman who traveled with the Red Cross during the war, uncertain of her future. The photograph that rests in a red leather frame on my grandma's nightstand has allowed me to meet the man she would later marry. He died before I was born. I have been told that I would have loved his calm manner, and I can see for myself his gentle smile and tranquil expression.

–Carrie White, student

Did you notice that the first sentence gives focus and direction to the paragraph and that all of the subsequent sentences are directly related to it?

A well-written essay should be unified both within and between paragraphs; that is, everything in it should be related to its **thesis,** the main idea of the essay. The first requirement for unity is that the thesis itself be clear, either through a direct statement, called the *thesis statement,* or by implication. The second requirement is that there be no digressions—no discussion or information that is not shown to be logically related to the thesis. A unified essay stays within the limits of its thesis.

Here, for example, is a short essay by Stuart Chase about the dangers of making generalizations. As you read, notice how carefully Chase sticks to his point.

Overgeneralizing

One swallow does not make a summer, nor can two or three cases often support a dependable generalization. Yet all of us, including the most polished eggheads, are constantly falling into this mental peopletrap. It is the most common, probably the most seductive, and potentially the most dangerous, of all the fallacies.

You drive through a town and see a drunken man on the sidewalk. A few blocks further on you see another. You turn to your companion: "Nothing but drunks in this town!" Soon you are out in the country, bowling along at fifty. A car passes you as if you were parked. On a curve a second whizzes by. Your companion turns to you: "All the drivers in this state are crazy!" Two thumping generalizations, each built on two cases. If we stop to think, we usually recognize the exaggeration and the unfairness of such generalizations. Trouble comes when we do not stop to think—or when we build them on a prejudice.

This kind of reasoning has been around for a long time. Aristotle was aware of its dangers and called it "reasoning by example," meaning too few examples. What it boils down to is failing to count your swallows before announcing that summer is here. Driving from my home to New Haven the other day, a distance of about forty miles, I caught myself saying: "Every time I look around I see a new ranch-type house going up." So on the return trip I counted them; there were exactly five under construction. And how many times had I "looked around"? I suppose I had glanced to right and left—as one must at side roads and so forth in driving—several hundred times.

In this fallacy, we do not make the error of neglecting facts altogether and rushing immediately to the level of opinion. We start at the fact level properly enough, but *we do not stay there.* A case of two and up we go to a rousing oversimplification about drunks, speeders, ranch-style houses—or, more seriously, about foreigners, African Americans, labor leaders, teenagers.

Why do we overgeneralize so often and sometimes so disastrously? One reason is that the human mind is a generalizing machine. We would not be people without this power. The old academic crack: "All generalizations are false, including this one," is only a play on words. We *must* generalize to communicate and to live. But we should beware of beating the gun; of not waiting until enough facts are in to say something useful. Meanwhile it is a plain waste of time to listen to arguments based on a few handpicked examples.

–Stuart Chase

Everything in the essay relates to Chase's thesis statement, which is included in the essay's first sentence: "nor can two or three cases often support a dependable generalization." Paragraphs 2 and 3 document the thesis with examples; paragraph 4 explains how overgeneralizing occurs; paragraph 5 analyzes why people overgeneralize; and, for a conclusion, Chase restates his thesis in different words. An essay may be longer, more complex, and more wide-ranging than this one, but to be effective it must also avoid digressions and remain close to the author's main idea.

A good way to check that your essay is indeed unified is to underline your thesis and then to explain to yourself how each paragraph in your essay is related to the thesis. If you find a paragraph that does not appear to be logically connected, you can revise it so that the relationship is clear. Similarly, it is useful to make sure that each sentence in a paragraph is related to the topic sentence. (See pp. 172–75 for a discussion of topic sentences.)

My Favorite Teacher

■ Thomas L. Friedman

New York Times *foreign affairs columnist*  *Thomas L. Friedman was born in Minneapolis, Minnesota, in 1953. He graduated from Brandeis University in 1975 and received a Marshall Scholarship to study modern Middle East studies at St. Antony's College, Oxford University, where he earned a master's degree. He has worked for the* New York Times *since 1981, first in Lebanon, then in Israel, and since 1989 in Washington, D.C. He has won three Pulitzer Prizes. His 1989 bestseller,* From Beirut to Jerusalem, *received the National Book Award for nonfiction. Friedman's most recent books include* The World Is Flat: A Brief History of the Twenty-First Century *(2005),* Hot, Flat, and Crowded: Why We Need a Green Revolution—and How It Can Renew America *(2008), and* That Used to Be Us: How America Fell Behind in the World It Invented and How We Can Come Back *(2011), co-written with Michael Mandelbaum.*

In the following essay, which first appeared in the New York Times *on January 9, 2001, Friedman pays tribute to his tenth-grade journalism teacher. As you read Friedman's profile of Hattie M. Steinberg, note the descriptive detail he selects to create a unified, dominant impression of "a woman of clarity in an age of uncertainty."*

Reflecting on What You Know

If you had to name your three favorite teachers to date, who would be on your list? Why do you consider each of the teachers a favorite? Which one, if any, are you likely to remember twenty-five years from now? Why?

Last Sunday's *New York Times Magazine* published its annual review 1 of people who died last year who left a particular mark on the world. I am sure all readers have their own such list. I certainly do.

Indeed, someone who made the most important difference in my life died last year—my high school journalism teacher, Hattie M. Steinberg.

I grew up in a small suburb of Minneapolis, and Hattie was the legendary journalism teacher at St. Louis Park High School, Room 313. I took her intro to journalism course in 10th grade, back in 1969, and have never needed, or taken, another course in journalism since. She was that good.

2

Hattie was a woman who believed that the secret for success in life was getting the fundamentals right. And boy, she pounded the fundamentals of journalism into her students—not simply how to write a lead or accurately transcribe a quote, but, more important, how to comport yourself in a professional way and to always do quality work. To this day, when I forget to wear a tie on assignment, I think of Hattie scolding me. I once interviewed an ad exec for our high school paper who used a four-letter word. We debated whether to run it. Hattie ruled yes. That ad man almost lost his job when it appeared. She wanted to teach us about consequences.

3

Hattie was the toughest teacher I ever had. After you took her journalism course in 10th grade, you tried out for the paper, *The Echo,* which she supervised. Competition was fierce. In 11th grade, I didn't quite come up to her writing standards, so she made me business manager, selling ads to the local pizza parlors. That year, though, she let me write one story. It was about an Israeli general who had been a hero in the Six-Day War,[1] who was giving a lecture at the University of Minnesota. I covered his lecture and interviewed him briefly. His name was Ariel Sharon.[2] First story I ever got published.

4

Those of us on the paper, and the yearbook that she also supervised, lived in Hattie's classroom. We hung out there before and after school. Now, you have to understand, Hattie was a single woman, nearing 60 at the time, and this was the 1960s. She was the polar opposite of "cool," but we hung around her classroom like it was a malt shop and she was Wolfman Jack.[3] None of us could have articulated it then, but it was because we enjoyed being harangued[4] by her,

5

---

[1]*Six-Day War:* the short but pivotal war in June 1967 between Israel and the allied countries of Egypt, Syria, and Jordan.

[2]*Ariel Sharon* (b. 1928): Israeli general and politician, elected prime minister of Israel in 2001.

[3]*Wolfman Jack:* pseudonym of Robert Weston Smith (1938–1995), a famous American rock-and-roll radio disc jockey.

[4]*harangued:* given a long, scolding lecture.

disciplined by her, and taught by her. She was a woman of clarity in an age of uncertainty.

We remained friends for 30 years, and she followed, bragged   6
about, and critiqued every twist in my career. After she died, her friends sent me a pile of my stories that she had saved over the years. Indeed, her students were her family—only closer. Judy Harrington, one of Hattie's former students, remarked about other friends who were on Hattie's newspapers and yearbooks: "We all graduated 41 years ago; and yet nearly each day in our lives something comes up—some mental image, some admonition[5] that makes us think of Hattie."

Judy also told the story of one of Hattie's last birthday parties, when   7
one man said he had to leave early to take his daughter somewhere. "Sit down," said Hattie. "You're not leaving yet. She can just be a little late."

That was my teacher! I sit up straight just thinkin' about her.   8

Among the fundamentals Hattie introduced me to was *The New*   9
York Times. Every morning it was delivered to Room 313. I had never seen it before then. Real journalists, she taught us, start their day by reading *The Times* and columnists like Anthony Lewis and James Reston.

I have been thinking about Hattie a lot this year, not just because she   10
died on July 31, but because the lessons she imparted seem so relevant now. We've just gone through this huge dot-com-Internet-globalization bubble—during which a lot of smart people got carried away and forgot the fundamentals of how you build a profitable company, a lasting portfolio, a nation state, or a thriving student. It turns out that the real secret of success in the information age is what it always was: fundamentals—reading, writing, and arithmetic; church, synagogue, and mosque; the rule of law; and good governance.

The Internet can make you smarter, but it can't make you smart.   11
It can extend your reach, but it will never tell you what to say at a P.T.A. meeting. These fundamentals cannot be downloaded. You can only upload them, the old-fashioned way, one by one, in places like Room 313 at St. Louis Park High. I only regret that I didn't write this column when the woman who taught me all that was still alive.

Thinking Critically about This Reading

What do you think Friedman means when he states, "The Internet can make you smarter, but it can't make you smart" (paragraph 11)?

---

[5]*admonition:* a cautionary advice or warning.

Questions for Study and Discussion

1. Friedman claims that his high school journalism teacher, Hattie M. Steinberg, was "someone who made the most important difference in my life" (1). What descriptive details does Friedman use to support this thesis? (Glossary: *Thesis*)

2. Hattie M. Steinberg taught her students the fundamentals of journalism — "not simply how to write a lead or accurately transcribe a quote, but, more important, how to comport yourself in a professional way and to always do quality work" (3). According to Friedman, what other fundamentals did she introduce to her students? Why do you think he values these fundamentals so much?

3. Friedman punctuates his description of Steinberg's teaching with short, pithy sentences. For example, he ends paragraph 2 with the sentence "She was that good" and paragraph 3 with "She wanted to teach us about consequences." Identify several other short sentences Friedman uses. What do these sentences have in common? How do short sentences like these affect you as a reader? Explain.

4. Why do you think Friedman tells us three times that Hattie's classroom was number 313 at St. Louis Park High School?

5. What details in Friedman's portrait of his teacher stand out for you? Why do you suppose Friedman chose the details that he did? What dominant impression of Hattie M. Steinberg do they collectively create? (Glossary: *Dominant Impression*)

6. According to Friedman, what went wrong when the "huge dot-com-Internet-globalization bubble" (10) of the late 1990s burst? Do you agree?

Classroom Activity Using Unity

Mark Wanner, a student, wrote the following paragraphs for an essay using this thesis statement:

> In order to provide a good learning environment in school, the teachers and administrators need to be strong leaders.

Unfortunately, some of the sentences disrupt the unity of the essay. Find these sentences, eliminate them, and reread the essay.

Strong School Leaders

School administrators and teachers must do more than simply 1
supply students with information and a school building. They must
also provide students with an atmosphere that allows them to focus
on learning within the walls of the school. Whether the walls are
brick, steel, or cement, they are only walls, and they do not help to
create an appropriate atmosphere. Strong leadership both inside and
outside the classroom yields a school in which students are able to
excel in their studies because they know how to conduct themselves
in their relationships with their teachers and fellow students.

A recent change in the administration of Eastside High School 2
demonstrated how important strong leadership is to learning. Under
the previous administration, parents and students complained that
not enough emphasis was placed on studies. Most of the students
lived in an impoverished neighborhood that had only one park for
several thousand residents. Students were allowed to leave school at
any time of the day, and little was done to curb the growing substance abuse problem. "What's the point of trying to teach algebra to
students who are just going to get jobs as part-time sales clerks, anyway?" Vice Principal Iggy Norant said when questioned about his
school's poor academic standards. Mr. Norant was known to students as Twiggy Iggy because of his tall, thin frame. Standardized test
scores at the school lagged well behind the state average, and only
16% of the graduates attended college within two years.

Five years ago, the school board hired Mary Peña, former chair 3
of the state educational standards committee, as principal. A cheer-
leader in college, Ms. Peña got her B.A. in recreation science before
getting her masters in education. She immediately emphasized the importance of learning, replacing any faculty members who did not
share her high expectations of the students. Among those she fired
was Mr. Norant; she also replaced two social studies teachers, one
math teacher, four English teachers, and a lab instructor who let students play Gameboy in lab. She also established a code of conduct,
which clearly stated the rules all students had to follow. Students
were allowed second chances, but those who continued to conduct
themselves in a way that interfered with the other students' ability to
learn were dealt with quickly and severely. "The attitude at Eastside
has changed so much since Mary Peña arrived," said math teacher
Jeremy Rifkin after Peña's second year. "Students come to class much

more relaxed and ready to learn. I feel like I can teach again." Test scores at Eastside are now well above state averages, and 68% of the most recent graduating class went straight to college.

–Mark Wanner, student

Suggested Writing Assignments

1. Friedman believes that "the real secret of success in the information age is what it always was: fundamentals—reading, writing, and arithmetic; church, synagogue, and mosque; the rule of law; and good governance" (10). Do you agree? What are the fundamentals that you value most? Write a unified essay in which you discuss what you believe to be the secret of success today.

2. Who are your favorite teachers? What important differences did these people make in your life? What characteristics do these teachers share with Hattie M. Steinberg in this essay, Miss Bessie in Carl T. Rowan's "Unforgettable Miss Bessie" (pp. 166–71), Anne Mansfield Sullivan in Helen Keller's "The Most Important Day" (pp. 84–89), or Jerry Kupchynsky in Joanne Lipman's "And the Orchestra Played On" (pp. 407–10)? Using examples from your own school experience as well as from one or more of the essays above, write an essay in which you explore what makes a great teacher. Be sure to choose examples that clearly illustrate each of your points.

My Name

■ **Sandra Cisneros**

Sandra Cisneros was born in Chicago in 1954, the only daughter in a family of seven children. After graduating from Loyola University in Chicago in 1976 with a degree in English and the Iowa Writers' Workshop in 1978, she moved to the Southwest and now lives in San Antonio, Texas. Cisneros has had numerous occupations within the fields of education and the arts and has been a visiting writer at various universities, including the University of California, Berkeley, and the University of Michigan. Although she has written two well-received books of poetry, My Wicked, Wicked Ways *(1987) and* Loose Woman *(1994), she is better known for the autobiographical fiction of* The House on Mango Street *(1984)—from which the following selection is taken—and for* Woman Hollering Creek and Other Stories *(1991). In 1995, she was awarded a grant from the prestigious MacArthur Foundation. In 2002, she published a novel,* Caramelo. *She is currently working on a collection of fiction titled* Infinito, *a children's book* Bravo, Bruno, *and a book about writing tentatively titled* Writing in My Pajamas.

As you read "My Name," pay attention to how tightly Cisneros unifies her paragraphs by intertwining the meanings of her name (originally Esperanza) and her feelings about the great-grandmother with whom she shares that name.

Reflecting on What You Know

Who chose your name, and why was it given to you? Does your name have a special meaning for the person who gave it to you? Are you happy with your name?

I n English my name means hope. In Spanish it means too many letters. It means sadness, it means waiting. It is like the number nine. A muddy color. It is the Mexican records my father plays on Sunday mornings when he is shaving, songs like sobbing.   1

It was my great-grandmother's name and now it is mine. She was   2
a horse woman too, born like me in the Chinese year of the
horse—which is supposed to be bad luck if you're born female—but
I think this is a Chinese lie because the Chinese, like the Mexicans,
don't like their women strong.

My great-grandmother. I would've liked to have known her, a wild   3
horse of a woman, so wild she wouldn't marry until my great-
grandfather threw a sack over her head and carried her off. Just like
that, as if she were a fancy chandelier. That's the way he did it.

And the story goes she never forgave him. She looked out the win-   4
dow all her life, the way so many women sit their sadness on an elbow. I
wonder if she made the best with what she got or was she sorry because
she couldn't be all the things she wanted to be. Esperanza. I have
inherited her name, but I don't want to inherit her place by the window.

At school they say my name funny as if the syllables were made   5
out of tin and hurt the roof of your mouth. But in Spanish my name is
made out of a softer something like silver, not quite as thick as my sister's name Magdalena which is uglier than mine. Magdalena who at
least can come home and become Nenny. But I am always Esperanza.

I would like to baptize[1] myself under a new name, a name more   6
like the real me, the one nobody sees. Esperanza as Lisandra or Maritza
or Zeze the X. Yes. Something like Zeze the X will do.

Thinking Critically about This Reading

What does Cisneros mean when she says of her great-grandmother, "I
have inherited her name, but I don't want to inherit her place by the
window" (paragraph 4)? What about her great-grandmother does
she admire and respect?

Questions for Study and Discussion

1. What is Cisneros's thesis? (Glossary: *Thesis*)
2. Are there any digressions, discussions, or information in this essay
   that do not logically connect to Cisneros's thesis? (Glossary: *Thesis*)
   Explain how each paragraph in the essay relates to her thesis.
3. What is Cisneros's purpose? (Glossary: *Purpose*)

---

[1]*baptize:* to initiate into Christianity; to give a first or Christian name to.

4. In what way do you think a name can be "like the number nine"? Like "a muddy color" (1)? What is your impression of the author's name, based on these similes? (Glossary: *Figure of Speech*)

5. What is Cisneros's tone? (Glossary: *Tone*) How does she establish the tone? What does it tell the reader about how she feels about her name?

6. Why do you think Cisneros waits until the end of paragraph 4 to reveal her given name?

7. Why do you think Cisneros chose "Zeze the X" as a name that better represents her inner self?

Classroom Activity Using Unity

Carefully read the following five-paragraph sequence, paying special attention to how each paragraph relates to the writer's thesis. Identify the paragraph that disrupts the unity of the sequence, and explain why it doesn't belong.

How to Build a Fire in a Fireplace

Though "experts" differ as to the best technique to follow when building a fire, one generally accepted method consists of first laying a generous amount of crumpled newspaper on the hearth between the andirons. Kindling wood is then spread generously over this layer of newspaper and one of the thickest logs is placed across the back of the andirons. This should be as close to the back of the fireplace as possible, but not quite touching it. A second log is then placed an inch or so in front of this, and a few additional sticks of kindling are laid across these two. A third log is then placed on top to form a sort of pyramid with air space between all logs so that flames can lick freely up between them. 1

Roaring fireplace fires are particularly welcome during the winter months, especially after hearty outdoor activities. To avoid any mid-winter tragedies, care should be taken to have a professional inspect and clean the chimney before starting to use the fireplace in the fall. Also, be sure to clean out the fireplace after each use. 2

A mistake frequently made is building the fire too far forward so that the rear wall of the fireplace does not get properly heated. A 3 heated back wall helps increase the draft and tends to suck smoke and flames rearward with less chance of sparks or smoke spurting out into the room.

Another common mistake often made by the inexperienced fire-   4 tender is to try to build a fire with only one or two logs, instead of using at least three. A single log is difficult to ignite properly, and even two logs do not provide an efficient bed with adequate fuel-burning capacity.

Use of too many logs, on the other hand, is also a common fault   5 and can prove hazardous. Building too big a fire can create more smoke and draft than the chimney can safely handle, increasing the possibility of sparks or smoke being thrown out into the room. For best results, the homeowner should start with three medium-size logs as described above, then add additional logs as needed if the fire is to be kept burning.

The five paragraphs on "How to Build a Fire in a Fireplace" are taken from Bernard Gladstone's book *The New York Times Complete Manual of Home Repair.*

Suggested Writing Assignments

1. If you, like Cisneros, wished to choose a different name for your-self, what would it be? Write a unified essay that reveals your choice of a new name and explains why you like it or why it might be particularly appropriate for you. Make sure every para-graph directly supports your name choice.

2. Choose a grandparent or other relative at least two generations older than you about whom you know an interesting story. What effect has the relative, or the stories about him or her, had on your life? Write a unified narrative essay about the relative and what is interesting about him or her. (Glossary: *Narration*)

The Meanings of a Word

■ Gloria Naylor

American novelist, essayist, and screenwriter Gloria Naylor was born in 1950 in New York City, where she lives today. She worked first as a missionary for the Jehovah's Witnesses from 1967 to 1975 and then as a telephone operator until 1981. That year she graduated from Brooklyn College of the City University of New York. She also holds a graduate degree in African American studies  *from Yale University. Naylor has taught writing and literature at George Washington University, New York University, and Cornell University, in addition to publishing several novels:* The Women of Brewster Place *(1982),* Linden Hills *(1985),* Mama Day *(1988),* Bailey's Cafe *(1992), and* The Men of Brewster Place *(1998). Naylor's most recent novel is* 1996 *(2005), a book that has been described as a "fictionalized memoir."*

The following essay first appeared in the New York Times *in 1986. In it Naylor examines the ways in which words can take on meaning, depending on who uses them and for what purpose. Notice how the paragraphs describing her experiences with the word* nigger *relate back to a clearly stated thesis at the end of paragraph 2.*

Reflecting on What You Know

Have you ever been called a derogatory name? What was the name, and how did you feel about it?

L anguage is the subject. It is the written form with which I've managed to keep the wolf away from the door and, in diaries, to keep my sanity. In spite of this, I consider the written word inferior to the spoken, and much of the frustration experienced by novelists is the awareness that whatever we manage to capture in even the most transcendent[1] passages falls far short of the richness of life. Dialogue

---

[1]*transcendent:* preeminent; above all others.

achieves its power in the dynamics of a fleeting moment of sight, sound, smell, and touch.

I'm not going to enter the debate here about whether it is language that shapes reality or vice versa. That battle is doomed to be waged whenever we seek intermittent reprieve from the chicken and egg dispute. I will simply take the position that the spoken word, like the written word, amounts to a nonsensical arrangement of sounds or letters without a consensus that assigns "meaning." And building from the meanings of what we hear, we order reality. Words themselves are innocuous;[2] it is the consensus that gives them true power.   2

I remember the first time I heard the word *nigger*.[3] In my third-grade class, our math tests were being passed down the rows, and as I handed the papers to a little boy in back of me, I remarked that once again he had received a much lower mark than I did. He snatched his test from me and spit out that word. Had he called me a nymphomaniac or a necrophiliac, I couldn't have been more puzzled. I didn't know what a nigger was, but I knew that whatever it meant, it was something he shouldn't have called me. This was verified when I raised my hand, and in a loud voice repeated what he had said and watched the teacher scold him for using a "bad" word. I was later to go home and ask the inevitable question that every black parent must face — "Mommy, what does *nigger* mean?"   3

And what exactly did it mean? Thinking back, I realize that this could not have been the first time the word was used in my presence. I was part of a large extended family that had migrated from the rural South after World War II and formed a close-knit network that gravitated around my maternal grandparents. Their ground-floor apartment in one of the buildings they owned in Harlem[4] was a weekend mecca for my immediate family, along with countless aunts, uncles, and cousins who brought along assorted friends. It was a bustling and open house with assorted neighbors and tenants popping in and out to exchange bits of gossip, pick up an old quarrel, or referee the ongoing checkers game in which my grandmother cheated shamelessly. They were all there to let down their hair and put up their feet after a week of labor in the factories, laundries, and shipyards of New York.   4

---

[2]*innocuous:* harmless; lacking significance or effect.
[3]"The use of the word 'nigger' is reprehensible in today's society. This essay speaks to a specific time and place when that word was utilized to empower African-Americans; today it is used to degrade them even if spoken from their own mouths."–Gloria Naylor
[4]*Harlem:* a predominantly African American neighborhood located in New York City.

Amid the clamor, which could reach deafening proportions—   5
two or three conversations going on simultaneously, punctuated by
the sound of a baby's crying somewhere in the back rooms or out
on the street—there was still a rigid set of rules about what was
said and how. Older children were sent out of the living room when
it was time to get into the juicy details about "you-know-who" up
on the third floor who had gone and gotten herself "p-r-e-g-n-a-
n-t!" But my parents, knowing that I could spell well beyond my
years, always demanded that I follow the others out to play. Beyond
sexual misconduct and death, everything else was considered harmless for our young ears. And so among the anecdotes[5] of the tri-
umphs and disappointments in the various workings of their lives,
the word *nigger* was used in my presence, but it was set within contexts and inflections[6] that caused it to register in my mind as something else.

In the singular, the word was always applied to a man who had   6
distinguished himself in some situation that brought their approval
for his strength, intelligence, or drive:

"Did Johnny *really* do that?"   7

"I'm telling you, that nigger pulled in $6,000 of overtime last   8
year. Said he got enough for a down payment on a house."

When used with a possessive adjective by a woman—"my nig-   9
ger"—it became a term of endearment for her husband or boyfriend.
But it could be more than just a term applied to a man. In their mouths it
became the pure essence of manhood—a disembodied force that chan-
neled their past history of struggle and present survival against the odds
into a victorious statement of being: "Yeah, that old foreman found out
quick enough—you don't mess with a nigger."

In the plural, it became a description of some group within the   10
community that had overstepped the bounds of decency as my family
defined it. Parents who neglected their children, a drunken couple
who fought in public, people who simply refused to look for work,
those with excessively dirty mouths or unkempt households were all
"trifling niggers." This particular circle could forgive hard times, un-
employment, the occasional bout of depression—they had gone
through all of that themselves—but the unforgivable sin was a lack
of self-respect.

---

[5]*anecdotes:* short accounts or stories of life experiences.
[6]*inflections:* alterations in pitch or tone of voice.

A woman could never be a "nigger" in the singular, with its con- 11
notation of confirming worth. The noun *girl* was its closest equivalent in that sense, but only when used in direct address and regardless
of the gender doing the addressing. *Girl* was a token of respect for a
woman. The one-syllable word was drawn out to sound like three in
recognition of the extra ounce of wit, nerve, or daring that the
woman had shown in the situation under discussion.

"G-i-r-l, stop. You mean you said that to his face?" 12

But if the word was used in a third-person reference or shortened 13
so that it almost snapped out of the mouth, it always involved some
element of communal disapproval. And age became an important factor in these exchanges. It was only between individuals of the same
generation, or from any older person to a younger (but never the
other way around), that *girl* would be considered a compliment.

I don't agree with the argument that use of the word *nigger* at this 14
social stratum of the black community was an internalization of racism.
The dynamics were the exact opposite: the people in my grandmother's
living room took a word that whites used to signify worthlessness or
degradation and rendered it impotent.[7] Gathering there together, they
transformed *nigger* to signify the varied and complex human beings
they knew themselves to be. If the word was to disappear totally from
the mouths of even the most liberal of white society, no one in that
room was naive enough to believe it would disappear from white minds.
Meeting the word head-on, they proved it had absolutely nothing to do
with the way they were determined to live their lives.

So there must have been dozens of times that *nigger* was spoken 15
in front of me before I reached the third grade. But I didn't "hear" it
until it was said by a small pair of lips that had already learned it
could be a way to humiliate me. That was the word I went home and
asked my mother about. And since she knew that I had to grow up in
America, she took me in her lap and explained.

Thinking Critically about This Reading

What does Naylor mean when she states that "words themselves are
innocuous; it is the consensus that gives them true power" (paragraph
2)? How does she use the two meanings of the word *nigger* to illustrate her point?

---

[7]*impotent:* weak; powerless.

Questions for Study and Discussion

1. Naylor states her thesis in the last sentence of paragraph 2. (Glossary: *Thesis*) How does what she says in the first two paragraphs build unity by connecting to her thesis statement?

2. What are the two meanings of the word *nigger* as Naylor uses it in her essay? Where is the clearest definition of each use of the word presented? (Glossary: *Definition*)

3. Naylor says she must have heard the word *nigger* many times while she was growing up, yet she "heard" it for the first time when she was in the third grade. How does she explain this seeming contradiction?

4. Naylor gives a detailed narration of her family and its lifestyle in paragraphs 4 and 5. (Glossary: *Narration*) What kinds of details does she include in her brief story? (Glossary: *Details*) How does this narration contribute to your understanding of the word *nigger* as used by her family? Why do you suppose she offers so little in the way of a definition of the other use of the word *nigger*? (Glossary: *Definition*) Explain.

5. Would you characterize Naylor's tone as angry, objective, cynical, or something else? (Glossary: *Tone*) Cite examples of her diction to support your answer. (Glossary: *Diction*)

6. What is the meaning of Naylor's last sentence? How well does it work as an ending for her essay? (Glossary: *Beginnings and Endings*)

Classroom Activity Using Unity

Take a paragraph from a draft of an essay you have been working on, and test it for unity. Be prepared to read the paragraph in class and explain why it is unified, or, if it is not, what you need to do to make it unified.

Suggested Writing Assignments

1. Naylor disagrees with the notion that use of the word *nigger* in the African American community can be taken as an "internalization of racism" (14). Reexamine her essay, and discuss in what ways her definition of the word *nigger* affirms or denies her

position. (Glossary: *Definition*) Draw on your own experiences, observations, and reading to support your answer.

2. Write a short essay in which you define a word—for example, *wife, macho, liberal, success,* or *marriage*—that has more than one meaning, depending on one's point of view.

Organization

In an essay, ideas and information cannot be presented all at once; they have to be arranged in some order. That order is the essay's **organization.**

The pattern of organization in an essay should be suited to the writer's subject and **purpose.** For example, if you are writing about your experience working in a fast-food restaurant and your purpose is to tell about the activities of a typical day, you might present those activities in chronological order. If, on the other hand, you wish to argue that working in a bank is an ideal summer job, you might proceed from the least rewarding to the most rewarding aspect of this job; this is called *climactic order.*

Some common patterns of organization are time order, space order, and logical order. Time order, or chronological order, is used to present a sequence of events as they occurred. A personal narrative, a report of a campus incident, or an account of a historical event can be most naturally and easily related in chronological order. In the following paragraph, the author uses chronological order to recount a disturbing childhood memory:

> I clearly remember my sixth birthday because Dad was in the hospital with pneumonia. He was working so hard he paid very little attention to his health. As a result, he spent almost the entire summer before I entered the first grade in the hospital. Mom visited him nightly. On my birthday I was allowed to see him. I have memories of sitting happily in the lobby of the hospital talking to the nurses, telling them with a big smile that I was going to see my dad because it was my birthday. I couldn't wait to see him because children under twelve were not allowed to visit patients, so I had not seen him in a long time. When I entered the hospital room, I saw tubes inserted into his nose and needles stuck in his arm. He was very, very thin. I was frightened and wanted to cry, but I was determined to

have a good visit. So I stayed for a while, and he wished me a happy birthday. When it was time to go, I kissed him good-bye and waited until I left his room to cry.

–Grace Ming-Yee Wai

Of course, the order of events can sometimes be rearranged for special effect. For example, an account of an auto accident may begin with the collision itself and then flash back in time to the events leading up to it. The description of a process—such as framing a poster, constructing a bookcase with cinder blocks and boards, or serving a tennis ball—almost always calls for a chronological organization.

When analyzing a causally related series of events, writers often use a chronological organization to clarify for readers the exact sequence of events. In the following example, the writer examines sequentially the series of malfunctions that led to the near disaster at the Three Mile Island nuclear facility in Harrisburg, Pennsylvania, showing clearly how each one led to the next:

On March 28, 1979, at 3:53 A.M., a pump at the Harrisburg plant failed. Because the pump failed, the reactor's heat was not drawn off in the heat exchanger and the very hot water in the primary loop overheated. The pressure in the loop increased, opening a release valve that was supposed to counteract such an event. But the valve stuck open and the primary loop system lost so much water (which ended up as a highly radioactive pool, six feet deep, on the floor of the reactor building) that it was unable to carry off all the heat generated within the reactor core. Under these circumstances, the intense heat held within the reactor could, in theory, melt its fuel rods, and the resulting "meltdown" could then carry a hugely radioactive mass through the floor of the reactor. The reactor's emergency cooling system, which is designed to prevent this disaster, was then automatically activated, but when it was, apparently, turned off too soon, some of the fuel rods overheated. This produced a bubble of hydrogen gas at the top of the reactor. (The hydrogen is dissolved in the water in order to react with oxygen that is produced when the intense reactor radiation splits water molecules into their atomic constituents. When heated, the dissolved hydrogen bubbles out of the solution.) This bubble blocked the flow of cooling water so that despite the action of the emergency cooling system the reactor core was again in danger of melting down. Another danger was that the gas might contain enough oxygen to cause an explosion that could rupture the huge containers that surround the reactor and release a deadly cloud of radioactive material into the surrounding country-side. Working desperately, technicians were able to gradually reduce the size of the gas bubble using a special apparatus brought in from the atomic laboratory at Oak Ridge, Tennessee, and the danger of a catastrophic release of radioactive materials subsided. But the sealed-off plant was now so radioactive that no one could enter it for many months—or, according to some observers, for years—without being exposed to a lethal dose of radiation.

–Barry Commoner

Space order is used when describing a person, place, or thing. This organizational pattern begins at a particular point and moves in some direction, such as left to right, top to bottom, east to west, outside to inside, front to back, near to far, around, or over. In describing a house, for example, a writer could move from top to bottom, from outside to inside, or in a circle around the outside.

In the following paragraph, the subject is a baseball, and the writer describes it from the inside out, moving from its "composition-cork nucleus" to the print on its stitched cowhide cover:

It weighs just over five ounces and measures between 2.86 and 2.94 inches in diameter. It is made of a composition-cork nucleus encased in two thin layers of rubber, one black and one red, sur-rounded by 121 yards of tightly wrapped blue-gray wool yarn, 45 yards of white wool yarn, 54 more yards of blue-gray wool yarn, 150 yards of fine cotton yarn, a coat of rubber cement, and a cowhide (formerly horsehide) exterior, which is held together with 216 slightly raised red cotton stitches. Printed certifications, endorse-ments, and outdoor advertising spherically attest to its authenticity.

–Roger Angell

Logical order can take many forms, depending on the writer's pur-pose. Often-used patterns include general to specific, most familiar to least familiar, and smallest to biggest. Perhaps the most common type of logical order is order of importance. Notice how the writer uses this order in the following paragraph:

The Egyptians have taught us many things. They were excellent farmers. They knew all about irrigation. They built temples which were afterwards copied by the Greeks and which served as the earliest models for the churches in which we worship nowadays. They in-vented a calendar which proved such a useful instrument for the purpose of measuring time that it has survived with few changes until today. But most important of all, the Egyptians learned how to preserve speech for the benefit of future generations. They invented the art of writing.

–Hendrick Willem Van Loon

By organizing the material according to the order of increasing importance, the writer places special emphasis on the final sentence.

A student essay on outdoor education provides another example of logical order. In the paragraph that follows, the writer describes some of the special problems students have during the traditionally difficult high school years. She then explains the benefits of involving such students in an outdoor education curriculum as a possible remedy, offers a quotation from a noteworthy text on outdoor education to support her views, and presents her thesis statement in the final sentence of the paragraph—all logical steps in her writing.

For many students, the normally difficult time of high school is especially troublesome. These students may have learning disabilities, emotional-behavioral disorders, or low self-esteem, or they may be labeled "at-risk" because of socioeconomic background, delinquency, or drug and alcohol abuse. Any combination of these factors contributes negatively to students' success in school. Often the traditional public or private high school may not be the ideal environment in which these students can thrive and live up to their highest potential. Outdoor Education can benefit these high schoolers and provide them with the means necessary to overcome their personal issues and develop skills, knowledge, and self-esteem that will enable them to become successful, self-aware, emotionally stable, and functional adults. In their book *Outdoor Education,* authors Smith, Carlson, Donaldson, and Masters state poignantly that outdoor education "can be one of the most effective forces in the community to prevent human erosion as well as land erosion; it can be one of the means of saving youngsters from the education scrap heap" (49). Outdoor education builds a relationship between students and the natural environment that might not be formed otherwise and gives students a respect for the world in which they live.

Statement of the problem

A possible remedy is offered and explained.

Authorities are quoted to support the suggested solution.

The thesis is given after a preliminary discussion to increase its acceptability.

Aspects of outdoor education should be implemented
in the curriculums of high schools in order to achieve
these results in all students.

–Jinsie Ward, student

Although logical order can take many different forms, the exact
rationale always depends on the topic of the writing. For example, in
writing a descriptive essay about a place you visited, you can move
from the least striking to the most striking detail to keep your readers
interested and involved in the description. In an essay explaining how
to pick individual stocks for investment, you can start with the point
that readers will find least difficult to understand and move on to the
most difficult. (That's how teachers organize many courses.) Or in
writing an essay arguing for more internships and service learning
courses, you can move from your least controversial point to the
most controversial, preparing your reader gradually to accept your
argument.

A simple way to check the organization of an essay is to outline it
once you have a draft. Does the outline represent the organizational
pattern—chronological, spatial, or logical—that you set out to use?
Problems in outlining will naturally indicate sections that you need to
revise.

A View from the Bridge

■ **Cherokee Paul McDonald**

A fiction writer, memoirist, and journalist, Cherokee Paul McDonald was raised and schooled in Fort Lauderdale, Florida. In 1970, he returned home from a tour of duty in Vietnam and joined the Fort Lauderdale Police Department, where he rose to the rank of sergeant. In 1980, after receiving a degree in criminal science from Broward Community College, McDonald left the po-
lice *department to become a writer. He worked a number of odd jobs before publishing his first book,* The Patch, *in 1986. In 1991, he published* Blue Truth, *a memoir. His novel,* Summer's Reason, *was released in 1994, and his most recent book, a memoir of the Vietnam War titled* Into the Green: A Reconnaissance by Fire, *was published in 2001.*

"A View from the Bridge" was originally published in Sunshine *magazine in 1990. As you read, notice how McDonald organizes his narrative. He tells us what the narrator and the boy are doing, but he also relies heavily on their dialogue to structure his story, which unfolds as the two talk. McDonald makes the story come alive by showing us, rather than by simply telling us, what happens.*

Reflecting on What You Know

Make a list of your interests, focusing on those to which you devote a significant amount of time. Do you share any of these interests with people you know? What does a shared interest do for a relationship between two people?

I was coming up on the little bridge in the Rio Vista neighborhood of   1
Fort Lauderdale, deepening my stride and my breathing to negotiate the slight incline without altering my pace. And then, as I neared the crest, I saw the kid.

He was a lumpy little guy with baggy shorts, a faded T-shirt and   2
heavy sweat socks falling down over old sneakers.

Partially covering his shaggy blond hair was one of those blue 3
baseball caps with gold braid on the bill and a sailfish patch sewn
onto the peak. Covering his eyes and part of his face was a pair of
those stupid-looking '50s-style wrap-around sunglasses.

He was fumbling with a beat-up rod and reel, and he had a little 4
bait bucket by his feet. I puffed on by, glancing down into the empty
bucket as I passed.

"Hey mister! Would you help me, please?" 5

The shrill voice penetrated my jogger's concentration, and I was 6
determined to ignore it. But for some reason, I stopped.

With my hands on my hips and the sweat dripping from my nose 7
I asked, "What do you want, kid?"

"Would you please help me find my shrimp? It's my last one and I've 8
been getting bites and I know I can catch a fish if I can just find that
shrimp. He jumped outta my hand as I was getting him from the bucket."

Exasperated, I walked slowly back to the kid, and pointed. 9

"There's the damn shrimp by your left foot. You stopped me for 10
that?"

As I said it, the kid reached down and trapped the shrimp. 11

"Thanks a lot, mister," he said. 12

I watched as the kid dropped the baited hook down into the 13
canal. Then I turned to start back down the bridge.

That's when the kid let out a "Hey! Hey!" and the prettiest tar- 14
pon[1] I'd ever seen came almost six feet out of the water, twisting and
turning as he fell through the air.

"I got one!" the kid yelled as the fish hit the water with a loud 15
splash and took off down the canal.

I watched the line being burned off the reel at an alarming rate. 16
The kid's left hand held the crank while the extended fingers felt for
the drag setting.

"No, kid!" I shouted. "Leave the drag alone . . . just keep that 17
damn rod tip up!"

Then I glanced at the reel and saw there were just a few loops of 18
line left on the spool.

"Why don't you get yourself some decent equipment?" I said, but 19
before the kid could answer I saw the line go slack.

"Ohhh, I lost him," the kid said. I saw the flash of silver as the 20
fish turned.

---

[1]*tarpon:* a large, silvery fish.

"Crank, kid, crank! You didn't lose him. He's coming back toward   21
you. Bring in the slack!"

The kid cranked like mad, and a beautiful grin spread across   22
his face.

"He's heading in for the pilings,"[2] I said. "Keep him out of those   23
pilings!"

The kid played it perfectly. When the fish made its play for the   24
pilings, he kept just enough pressure on to force the fish out. When
the water exploded and the silver missile hurled into the air, the kid
kept the rod tip up and the line tight.

As the fish came to the surface and began a slow circle in the   25
middle of the canal, I said, "Whooee, is that a nice fish or what?"

The kid didn't say anything, so I said, "Okay, move to the edge   26
of the bridge and I'll climb down to the seawall and pull him out."

When I reached the seawall I pulled in the leader, leaving the fish   27
lying on its side in the water.

"How's that?" I said.   28

"Hey, mister, tell me what it looks like."   29

"Look down here and check him out," I said. "He's beautiful."   30

But then I looked up into those stupid-looking sunglasses and it   31
hit me. The kid was blind.

"Could you tell me what he looks like, mister?" he said again.   32

"Well, he's just under three, uh, he's about as long as one of   33
your arms," I said. "I'd guess he goes about 15, 20 pounds. He's
mostly silver, but the silver is somehow made up of *all* the colors, if
you know what I mean." I stopped. "Do you know what I mean by
colors?"

The kid nodded.   34

"Okay. He has all these big scales, like armor all over his body.   35
They're silver too, and when he moves they sparkle. He has a strong
body and a large powerful tail. He has big round eyes, bigger than a
quarter, and a lower jaw that sticks out past the upper one and is very
tough. His belly is almost white and his back is a gunmetal gray.
When he jumped he came out of the water about six feet, and his
scales caught the sun and flashed it all over the place."

By now the fish had righted itself, and I could see the bright-red   36
gills as the gill plates opened and closed. I explained this to the kid,
and then said, more to myself, "He's a beauty."

----

[2]*pilings:* support columns driven vertically into the ground or ocean floor.

"Can you get him off the hook?" the kid asked. "I don't want to kill him." 37

I watched as the tarpon began to slowly swim away, tired but still alive. 38

By the time I got back up to the top of the bridge the kid had his line secured and his bait bucket in one hand. 39

He grinned and said, "Just in time. My mom drops me off here, and she'll be back to pick me up any minute." 40

He used the back of one hand to wipe his nose. 41

"Thanks for helping me catch that tarpon," he said, "and for helping me to see it." 42

I looked at him, shook my head, and said, "No, my friend, thank you for letting *me* see that fish." 43

I took off, but before I got far the kid yelled again. 44

"Hey, mister!" 45

I stopped. 46

"Someday I'm gonna catch a sailfish and a blue marlin and a giant tuna and *all* those big sportfish!" 47

As I looked into those sunglasses I knew he probably would. I wished I could be there when it happened. 48

Thinking Critically about This Reading

Near the end of the story, why does the narrator say to the boy, "No, my friend, thank you for letting *me* see that fish" (paragraph 43)? What happens to the narrator's attitude as a result of his encounter with the boy? What lesson do you think the narrator learns?

Questions for Study and Discussion

1. How does McDonald organize his essay? What period of time would you estimate is covered in this essay?

2. What clues lead up to the revelation that the boy is blind? Why does it take McDonald so long to realize it?

3. Notice the way McDonald chooses and adjusts some of the words he uses to describe the fish to the boy in paragraphs 33–36. Why does he do this? How does he organize his description of the fish so that the boy can visualize it better?

4. By the end of the essay, we know much more about the boy beyond that he is blind, but after the initial description, McDonald characterizes him only indirectly. As the essay unfolds, what do we learn about the boy, and how does the author convey this knowledge?

5. McDonald tells much of his experience through dialogue. (Glossary: *Dialogue*) What does this dialogue add to the narration? (Glossary: *Narration*) What would have been lost had McDonald not used dialogue?

6. What is the connotation of the word *view* in the title? (Glossary: *Connotation/Denotation*) Of the word *bridge?*

Classroom Activity Using Organization

Consider the ways in which you might organize a discussion of the seven states listed below. For each state, we have provided some basic information: the date it entered the Union, population (2010 census), land area, and number of electoral votes in a presidential election.

ALASKA
January 3, 1959
710,231 people
570,374 square miles
3 electoral votes

MISSOURI
August 10, 1821
5,988,927 people
69,709 square miles
10 electoral votes

ARIZONA
February 14, 1912
6,392,017 people
113,642 square miles
11 electoral votes

MONTANA
November 8, 1889
989,415 people
145,556 square miles
3 electoral votes

FLORIDA
March 3, 1845
18,801,310 people
53,937 square miles
29 electoral votes

OREGON
February 14, 1859
3,831,074 people
98,386 square miles
7 electoral votes

MAINE
March 15, 1820
1,328,361 people
30,865 square miles
4 electoral votes

Suggested Writing Assignments

1. In groups of two or three, take turns describing a specific beautiful or remarkable thing to the others as if they were blind. You may want to actually bring an object to observe while your classmates cover their eyes. Help each other find the best words to create a vivid verbal picture. Using McDonald's paragraphs 33–36 as a model, write a brief description of your object, retaining the informal style of your speaking voice.

2. Recall a time when you and one other person held a conversation that helped you see something more clearly—visually, in terms of understanding, or both. Using McDonald's narrative as an organizational model, tell the story of that moment, re-creating the dialogue exactly as you remember it.

3. McDonald's "A View from the Bridge" and the *Calvin and Hobbes* cartoon on page 130 are just two "fish stories" in the long and rich tradition of that genre. In their own ways, both the essay and the cartoon play on the ironic notion that fishing is a quiet sport but one in which participants come to expect the unexpected. (Glossary: *Irony*) For the narrator in McDonald's story, there is a lesson in not merely looking but truly seeing, in describing the fish so that the blind boy can "see" it. For Calvin, there is the story of "latchin' on to the big one." It is interesting that a sport in which "nothing happens" can be the source of so much storytelling. Write an essay in which you tell a "fish story" of your own, one that reveals a larger, significant truth or life lesson. Pay particular attention to the pattern of organization you choose, and be sure to revise your essay to tighten up your use of that pattern. If possible, incorporate some elements of surprise as well.

Fahrenheit 59: What a Child's Fever Might Tell Us about Climate Change

■ **Audrey Schulman**

Novelist Audrey Schulman was born in Montreal, Quebec, Canada, in 1963. She attended Sarah Lawrence College from 1981 to 1983 and graduated from Barnard College in 1985. Schulman has worked as a scriptwriter, a computer consultant, and an Internet Web site designer while developing her skills as a writer. In her first novel, The Cage *(1995), Schulman tells the story of a young female photographer who is sent to the wilds of northern Canada to study polar bears. She followed this with* Swimming with Jonah *(1999),* A House Named Brazil *(2000),* The Third Way *(2009), and* Three Weeks in December *(2010). Her articles on global climate change and severe climatic events have appeared in* E Magazine, Conservation Matters, Ms., *and* Grist.

In "Fahrenheit 59," first published in the January–February 2007 issue of Orion *magazine, Schulman explores the inner workings of climate change. As you read, pay attention to how she organizes a vivid analogy (her son's body and its ability to deal with temperature changes and illness) to explain how the earth deals with the complexities of climate change.*

Reflecting on What You Know

How concerned are you about climate changes or global warming? What, if anything, do you think needs to be done? Have you personally made any lifestyle changes as a result of your concerns? If so, describe what you have done.

Yesterday afternoon, my six-year-old son practiced swimming with me. Delighted with the water and my attention, Corey stayed in for forty minutes. Despite the water's chill, I knew if I took his temperature it would be close to 98.6° Fahrenheit. For an hour afterward he ran through the humid July heat, playing tag with his cousins, his hair damp with sweat. Still, a reading would have shown his body to be within a degree or two of 98.6°.

This stability is a product of homeostasis. A holy word for biologists, *homeostasis* refers to an organism's ability to maintain its ideal temperature and chemistry. 2

Each species has its own preferred level of warmth, but among most mammals the possible range is surprisingly narrow, generally between 97° and 103°F. Each body's temperature works to optimize the function of its enzymes, which are critical to its every chemical interaction. Too cold, and these catalysts slow down. Too hot, and they break down entirely. 3

Such homeostatic regulation depends on a mechanism known as negative feedback: a response that maintains a system's balance. Yesterday, for example, when Corey ran in the hot sun, his cheeks got rosy as more blood moved to the surface, maximizing heat loss off his skin. No, his body said to his increasing temperature. 4

It turns out that our bodies' homeostasis can provide an analogy with which to understand the complexities of climate change—and the human response to it. Over geological time, the biosphere uses negative feedbacks in a way that maintains a stable global average temperature. When the earth's oceans heat up past a certain point, for example, hurricanes (which thrive only on warm water) increase their intensity, leaving a trail of stirred-up nutrients. The food creates a massive bloom of phytoplankton, which suck in enough of the greenhouse gas carbon dioxide to start cooling the global climate. 5

Conversely, when temperatures fall too low, vast quantities of methane are released into the atmosphere, possibly in part because ice sheets build up, lowering sea levels and exposing coastal methane hydrates. As a greenhouse gas twenty times more powerful than carbon dioxide, the methane warms the biosphere quickly. 6

Through a large array of negative feedbacks like these, the biosphere has managed to maintain a relatively stable temperature, despite massive volcanic eruptions of greenhouse gasses and orbital and solar irregularities. To earth-based organisms, the fluctuations may have seemed severe, allowing ice sheets to roll in or crocodiles to paddle across the Arctic. But through its self-corrections, the biosphere has remained habitable. 7

According to New York University biology professor Tyler Volk, the sun's temperature has increased 30 percent over the course of earth's 8 history, which would have increased temperatures about one hundred degrees were it not for the cooling effect of phytoplankton and other life. And scientists calculate that the earth would be a frigid fifty to sixty degrees colder without any greenhouse gases. Over the last million years, the biosphere has remained within about eighteen degrees of 59°F.

Humanity's intemperate carbon emissions, however, have severely   9
tested these negative feedbacks. Since 1900 alone, the earth has warmed more than a full degree—one-fifth the entire temperature range over the past ten thousand years. The earth is now within two degrees of its warmest levels in one million years.

The increased heat dries up the soil faster and pumps water vapor   10
into the clouds, exaggerating the severity of drought, then rain. Gentle summer days turn into baking onslaughts, temperate-zone drizzles become tropical monsoons, tropical diseases and pests have whole new latitudes to conquer, and temperate-zone animals and plants are flee-ing toward the poles. The increased heat has also warmed the oceans, causing hurricanes to grow in intensity.

And when a situation becomes extreme enough, biological sys-   11
tems can abandon their attempts at moderation. Corey crawled into bed with me in the middle of last night, saying his head hurt. His hands and face felt hot. Touching his ribs I could feel his heart rac-ing. Ill with the flu, his body no longer fought to maintain its normal temperature. Instead it was using positive feedbacks, reactions that amplify a change, to create a fever. Holding him close in bed, I could feel his muscles violently shivering, creating heat and more heat. Within an hour of the first symptoms, his temperature was 102°.

Positive feedbacks can also shift the earth's climate quickly, with   12
the kind of results seen in the latest global warming news. As ice sheets melt near the poles, for example, the water slips through the crevasses to the rock below. At some point the water pools up enough to raise the glacier just a fraction, greasing its slide into the ocean. James Hansen of the Goddard Institute, whose science has been un-cannily accurate since he alerted Congress in 1988 to signs of human-induced climate change, points out that this phenomenon can cause millennia-old ice sheets to disappear with an explosive splash. At that point, white ice no longer reflects sunlight into space. Instead, dark water draws the sunlight in as heat, accelerating the rise in the earth's temperature. Yes, the water says, yes.

The thaw of the Siberian permafrost may provide another ex-   13
ample of a positive feedback. Roughly 400,000 megatons of dead

plant matter that has never finished decaying because it has been frozen, the permafrost is now thawing more rapidly than expected, according to recent reports. Because all this plant flesh is wet—under snow that's now melting—the decay is engineered by anaerobic bacteria, which metabolize the plants straight into methane, that muscular greenhouse gas. Once truly underway, this release of methane would dwarf any effect humans have on climate change. There'd be no more discussion of Energy Star appliances or raising the emission standards of cars. The rising temperatures would effectively no longer be powered by us, or subject to our influences. The system would take over.

As medical researchers have discovered in the past decade, our bodies give us fevers for a specific reason: certain antibodies and other infection-fighting agents function optimally at 100°F or higher. When Corey's body detected the presence of overly aggressive microbes, it turned its thermostat up high. His hypothalamus made his muscles shiver, minimized the blood flow to his skin, conserved heat in his gut. For a little while, his body could withstand a high temperature while the immune system brought out its heavy artillery. Overall this strategy tends to work well: Corey slept straight through the day, and, late in the afternoon, he sat up, skinnier and ferociously thirsty, but healthy again. Research shows, however, that while the feverish response may preserve the human organism as a whole, some of the immune system's agents have side effects: their activity can kill many "innocent" nonaggressive cells.

We should take note. It may seem a poetic stretch to say the earth itself ever sickens or has a fever. Seen from a distance, the earth itself does not become more or less "healthy"—just more or less populated with life. But as seen from the ground, the view is rather different. If our planet's feedback systems switch over from negative to positive and the biosphere heats up fast, the earth will certainly seem feverishly ill to a number of species, many of which will not survive.

In terms of our planetary climate, it's easy to guess which species is playing the role of overly aggressive microbe. But we do have a choice. Some human cultures, through their agriculture and hunting, have respected and adapted to ecological limits. We have the ability to shape our destiny—to be microbial attackers, or humble cells inside a living body.

Thinking Critically about This Reading

In her final paragraph, Schulman says that "it's easy to guess which species is playing the role of the overly aggressive microbe." In terms of her analogy, in what ways can human beings be considered "overly aggressive microbes"? Does this analogy help you explain what is happening to our planetary climate? Explain.

Questions for Study and Discussion

1. How does Schulman's organizational pattern help her develop the analogy she builds between her son's illness and the earth's climate changes? Would her essay work as well if she changed the order of her discussion? Why or why not?

2. Why does Schulman begin with what happens to her son Corey before moving to a discussion of what is happening to the earth's climate and the relationship between the two subjects?

3. What is homeostasis? How does it work in humans? Why is it an important concept to understand? Why does Schulman need to explain it early in her essay?

4. What is negative feedback? How does the author use her son to explain this concept?

5. According to Schulman, how has the biosphere used negative feedback to maintain a relatively constant temperature over time?

6. How does Schulman use her son's fever to explain what is happening to the earth's climate today? Does her analogy help you understand climate change? Explain.

Classroom Activity Using Organization

The best ways to conserve energy in a home might be organized according to space, time, and logic, as follows:

1. From the basement to the attic
2. From the least expensive to the most expensive
3. From the inside of the home to the outside
4. From the simplest to the most difficult
5. From the quickest to the longest

6. From the longest payback to the quickest payback
7. From the easiest to the most difficult
8. From the most general to the most specific
9. From the first to the last
10. From what you can do to what you need help with

How might you organize an essay on one of the following topics using space, time, and logical patterns?

1. What to do when a tornado threatens
2. What we can do about the homeless
3. What we mean by freedom of speech
4. A description of a painting
5. How a digital camera works
6. Why we need a flat income tax
7. What happened at your friend's birthday party
8. Why we can't let languages become extinct
9. The case for the legalization of drugs

Suggested Writing Assignments

1. Write an essay in which you develop an analogy of your own, or use Schulman's essay as a model. Be sure to develop a clear organizational plan and pattern so that your essay is easy to follow. Keep in mind that the purpose for using an analogy is to help explain a complex idea or concept.
2. Schulman concludes: "Some human cultures, through their agriculture and hunting, have respected and adapted to ecological limits. We have the ability to shape our destiny—to be microbial attackers, or humble cells inside a living body" (16). Which choice do you think Schulman recommends? Write an essay in which you propose measures that could be taken on your college campus to make it more climate-friendly. What energy-saving measures are already being taken? What can be done to control carbon dioxide emissions? What measures do you think would have the greatest effect? You may find it helpful to review your response to the Reflecting on What You Know prompt for this selection before you start writing.

Buying a House

■ Sean Prentiss

Although Sean Prentiss was born on Long Island, New York, he was raised on the banks of Pennsylvania's Delaware River and calls that landscape, the Poconos, his only childhood home. He received his BA in business administration in 1994 and his MFA in creative nonfiction from the University of Idaho in May 2005. Currently, Prentiss is an assistant professor of creative writing at Grand Valley State University in Allendale, Michigan. He has published nonfiction, poetry, and fiction in literary journals such as Pacific Review, Ascent, Sycamore Review, River Styx, Nimrod, High Desert, *and* ISLE. *He has been recognized for his nonfiction by the* Atlantic Monthly *and has twice been nominated for a Pushcart Prize. He is now at work on a nonfiction book about the celebrated naturalist Edward Abbey as well as a book on the craft of creative nonfiction. A former Peace Corps volunteer who served in Jamaica, Prentiss works building trails in the Pacific Northwest and the desert Southwest and spends his summers in Colorado working on his cabin in the mountains.*

"Buying a House" was originally published in the Spring 2010 issue of Sou'wester. *In response to the question of what advice he would give students, Prentiss said, in part: "As I write, I think about music, the ups and downs, the way a lyric would sound. I want my piece to have a flow. I think about where I want my piece — like a song — to be hushed and where I want it loud, the guitars wailing, the singer screaming." About his readers, he offered these words: "Without the reader I have no one to read my work. So I need to offer clarity. The reader needs to understand what I am talking about and why these ideas matter. So the reader is always in the back of my mind, saying, 'Tell me more. Give me a better detail. Yank me in. Make me sit up and listen.'"*

Reflecting on What You Know

If you own your own home or dream of purchasing a home, what does that home represent for you? Do you see it as a lasting purchase or just one of a number of real estate purchases you might make in your lifetime? In what ways do you see that home as merely a place of shelter or alternatively as itself a way of life, a place where you will raise a family, entertain relatives and friends, carry out life's significant milestones—graduations, engagements, marriages, anniversaries—and perhaps even spend your final years?

A s Chad the Realtor slows his car onto quiet Lockwood Avenue, he says, *This is 626 Lockwood. Tell me what you think.*

Chad and I are searching for my first home to buy. I've just got a new job as tenure-track professor in western Michigan. I guess I'm ready to settle down. I guess after a life moving town to town, fifteen states in the last twenty years, it's time to plant roots.

We're on the fifth house today. The first house we checked had a huge front porch and sat in an upscale neighborhood. *You can make fifty grand off this house*, Chad said. Inside, the house had a gutted kitchen, sagging floors, ruined sheetrock. *A fixer-upper, for sure*, Chad said. I thought of the time needed to put the house back together, how I'd rather write or travel than drywall and spackle. We moved on.

The second and third houses had moldy basements and cracked foundations. Chad just nodded back toward the front door. We left without seeing the upstairs. The fourth house had such a cute kitchen that it felt as if I'd need a trophy wife and a cooing baby before I moved into the house to live happily ever after. . . .

As we stop at this Lockwood house, the first thing (the very first thing) I notice is the front porch. Chad must know what I'm thinking because he says, *Look at that screened-in porch.* I'm a sucker for sitting outside. For watching the world go by.

I walk onto the porch, turn around, listen to the screen door slap shut, and stare back at the quiet street. A basketball net on rollers. A beat-up pickup. A tricycle tipped over on the sidewalk. Chalk drawings in front of a neighbor's house.

I imagine early autumn, my feet up on a table, a Pabst. Maybe grading student essays in the afternoon sun or reading a book of poetry. (Hugo. No, no, Wright! *Suddenly I realize / that if I stepped out of my body I would break / into blossom.*) I think, *This could be my street. My porch. Mine.*

Then the scene changes and I am no longer reading James Wright. 8 Instead, my next lover (a girl I have yet to meet—but I can see her perfectly—rounded cheeks, face in a grin, thin lips, long brown hair, curly) is standing on this porch. It is our first date (a date we laughed through, at a restaurant, later the long walk home) and it is latest dusk—nearing dark. Lockwood is quiet. The air cold (nearly freezing). The air still. Standing on my porch, I lean toward her.

Chad unlocks the front door and holds it open. I walk into a tiny 9 foyer as Chad says, *Nineteen hundred square feet. A house to grow into.*

I barely hear Chad. Instead I see my father visiting from three 10 states away. As he walks in the front door, I reach for his leather coat. As I see my dad's future visit, I think about how most of my adult years, I've felt like I wasn't living up to what my father expected. I felt that I wasn't being successful (though he's always been supportive of every one of my harebrained ideas). But I have always felt that, sure, I was skiing and traveling and even earning my terminal degree, but I wasn't successful in the ways that I thought he'd care about. But now I'm tenure-track. A real job. A real life.

Standing in the foyer, I almost mumble those words, *A real job. A* 11 *real life.*

I imagine my father talking to his friends over glasses of merlot, 12 saying, *My youngest son, Sean—remember him?—just got a tenure-track job in Michigan. Teaching creative writing. He's buying a house in Michigan. An old Craftsman.*

As Chad leads me into an older kitchen, he says, *This kitchen* 13 *needs work, but it's an easy redo.*

I think about how I'll never redo the kitchen. No stainless steel 14 appliances. No tile floors. No fresh paint on the walls. I'll just put a wooden table—old and worn and scratched and found in a house I rented in Idaho—in the corner. I'll buy two thrift store chairs.

As Chad points out the dishwasher, the gas stove, the cabinets, I 15 find myself in the future—god, this house has a way of transporting me—to nights eating alone, crockpots simmering during long weekends, the smell of stew blanketing the house. I'll read a magazine while eating a quick meal. The second chair at the table unmoved for weeks (months?)—waiting.

Waiting for that next lover (Or has she already left?). I'll wash   16
the few dishes, leaving the kitchen as clean as I find it today.

In the master bedroom (whenever I hear *master bedroom* I imag-   17
ine a canopied bed, pink walls, doilies on the bureaus), Chad pulls up the blinds. The afternoon sun blinds me with its dazzling light, illuminating the dust in the air. I twist from the sun as Chad moves to the living room—giving me time. Time. I need time.

With the bedroom empty of furniture, I turn a slow circle, arms   18
outstretched—touching empty space. Empty space. *Empty space.*

I imagine this bedroom after I move in. A single bed with poorly   19
fitted sheets (They come undone every night I toss and turn.), a nightstand for my book of the week (a mediocre collection of essays, later a novel by Abbey), a dresser full of wrinkled clothes. What else? What else? My cell phone. What else? House keys. What else? Sneakers and dress shirts in the closet. What else? Nothing. What else? Nothing. A room to fill with nothing.

But maybe in a year (or in two, or three), my next lover—the   20
one I kissed on the porch—will move in. In another year, she'll become my wife. And I question (alone in this bedroom) how is it possible that after twenty years of not getting married (dodging three marriage proposals) that now I can no longer stop thinking about marriage. It's not that I want to get married. It's just friends married. Family expecting me married. My mother asking, *Have you met any nice girls in Michigan.*

Not yet, Mom, not yet.   21

I think to my future lover and how once she becomes my wife,   22
the small bed will be replaced with a queen. She will hang new blinds on these windows (though we'll never shut them—let the sun flood us). The old furniture moved out, donated. And my keys, they'll end up in a clay dish that my wife will buy at a flea market (just for my keys). When I toss my keys in the dish, the clanging will remind me of something—though I'll never figure out exactly what.

In the living room, I run my hands along hardwood floors. Chad   23
says, *Oak. I have the same wood in my house.*

In five years (Or ten, fifteen?) if I buy this house (this very house)   24
will these floors only feel the slow steps of my feet quietly moving

room to room? The lonely steps of me coming home day after day from work at the university? Or will—some distant year—there be the patter of a child (A daughter? A little girl in pigtails?) running over these slick floors (her giggles bouncing off the walls)?

I've never wanted kids (or a wife, or even in these last few years a   25
serious girlfriend). But now I'm studying the creaking of these floors (like an Indian in a 1960s Western with his ear pressed to the tracks listening for the sound of a coming train) for the pattering of a child's steps. I don't want 4 a.m. wakeups. I don't want to change diapers. I don't want to have her burp on my shoulder. I don't want to teach her to throw (Okay, okay, maybe I want to teach her to throw—first an awkward sidearm throw, later a laser. *Good job, girl!*).

But in this living room—warm with its yellow walls—it feels   26
that if I buy this house (this very house, this Lockwood house), I'll need a child. Not just because I'll own the house, but because if I own the house, this house will need a child (Is this just me telling lies? Trying to pretend it's not my wants?)—her voice bouncing off walls, her cries from her bedroom calling to me—to me (only me) during middle of her nights (she has such cute nightmares). *Monsters in the closet. A dream where she couldn't find me.*

As I envision all of this, I cannot find her mother. I cannot find   27
her at all. I grow desperate. Where is she? The yellow walls blind me, it seems.

Chad asks, *Do you need more time?*   28

I want to say, *Just a minute. One minute* (though I mean a life-   29
time or two).

I want to say, *I can see all the world.*   30

I want to say, *Hold me. Someone. Please?*   31

I want to say, *Every story is true and every story is a lie.*   32

Instead I nod. Chad moves to the front porch. I hear the clicking   33
of the door.

In the living room, I stare at the ceiling until it is forty years into   34
the future (the mortgage paid off, the water heater and furnace twice replaced). I am seventy-seven with a beard of gray. I lie in the queen bed as a chest-rattling cough runs through my body. Then another: In a hallucination, I call to that future wife, wanting her by my side (holding my hand through this)—never realizing (this is for the best, the best) that she's been gone years and years (maybe exactly a thousand years). The divorce papers in a filing cabinet in the basement

(mildewed, brittle). Or did she die young, cancer? *Such a sad story*, the neighbors will whisper as they watch my daughter play on the sidewalk.

When the coughing subsides, a live-in nurse (or is it my daughter, 35 home for her father) feeds me ice chips, takes my pulse. When the days (now the minutes) are done and it is latest dusk (the same time of day as when I first kissed that girl), I use my last energy to lift my arm. The nurse, the girl?, hurriedly stands from her seat. She rests her hand on my forehead, but she struggles to understand this final moment. Am I calling to her? Am I pointing to a western sun?

This house echoes, *Stay down, champion, stay down.* 36

As Chad locks the front door tight— 37

—as the sun sets over 626 Lockwood, as the trees stand bare 38 (still earliest spring), as the grass lays down (from long winter), as a grandfather wheels in his grandson's basketball net, as three children play army (*Bang, bang, bang, you're dead.*)—

—I stand on the front porch and think, *I can own this house. I* 39 *can own it all.*

Thinking Critically about This Reading

Might it help us in thinking about Prentiss's essay to remember the distinction that is often made between a house and home? What is that distinction? Is there something to the idea that Prentiss is looking at a house but prefiguring it as a home? Explain.

Questions for Study and Discussion

1. How does Prentiss organize the narration of his experience with the real estate agent in attempting to buy a house?

2. What is the significance of the italicized passages spread throughout the narrative? What organizational pattern do they represent?

3. Are Prentiss's problems with the house he contemplates buying with his own psychological state at the time, or are they with both the house and his state of mind? Explain.

4. What is the significance of the front porch of the house for the narrator? Does the front porch rise to the level of a symbol for

him? Is the whole house a symbol for him? If so, what does it
symbolize? (Glossary: *Symbol*)

5. How effective is Prentiss's ending? Is it a happy ending? A sad
one? Something else? Explain. (Glossary: *Beginnings and Endings*)

6. Do you think Prentiss will buy the house? Why or why not?

Classroom Activity Using Organization

While cleaning out the center drawer of his desk, a student found the
following items:

3 no. 2 pencils	2 pairs of scissors
2 rubber bands	1 book mailing bag
1 roll of adhesive tape	1 mechanical pencil
1 plastic comb	3 first-class postage stamps
25 3- × 5-inch cards	5 postcards
3 ballpoint pens	2 clasps
1 eraser	2 8- × 10-inch manila envelopes
6 paper clips	7 thumbtacks
1 nail clipper	1 bottle of correction fluid
1 highlighting marker	1 nail file
1 bottle of glue	1 toothbrush
3 business envelopes	1 felt-tip pen
6 postcard stamps	2 airmail stamps

To organize the student's drawer, into what categories would you
divide these items? Explain which items you would place in each category, and suggest an order you might use to discuss the categories in
an essay. (Glossary: *Division and Classification*)

Suggested Writing Assignments

1. Write an essay about a residence that you have lived in and know
well and what that place means to you. Think about the various
organizational patterns along which you might organize your
essay. You might move from the quietest room for you to the
room where most of your family's important events took place,
or from the least interesting to most vibrant either in terms of its
décor, noise level, or usual occupants, or according to principles

of your own choosing. Remember that your essay should have a thesis or main point. Also remember that your organizational pattern should not be the main attraction of your essay but rather should help you develop your thesis clearly and effectively.

2. Even though we all know, or should know, that our physical world has no feelings, we also know that it can be responsible for some powerful emotions. For example, beautiful landscapes, people, art, nature, symbols, and buildings can move us deeply. Write an essay that is modeled after Prentiss's in which you alternate observations on the physical aspects of your subject and the powerful emotions and contemplations that grow from its physical and objective reality. You may chose to use the organizational technique that Prentiss employs in showing the difference between the objective and subjective worlds of your subject through the use of italics.

Beginnings and Endings

"Begin at the beginning and go on till you come to the end: then stop," advised the King of Hearts in *Alice in Wonderland.* "Good advice, but more easily said than done," you might be tempted to reply. Certainly, no part of writing essays can be more daunting than coming up with effective **beginnings and endings.** In fact, many writers believe that beginnings and endings are the most important parts of any piece of writing regardless of its length. Even before coming to your introduction, your readers will usually know something about your intentions from your title. Titles such as "The Case against Euthanasia," "How to Buy a Used Car," and "What Is a Migraine Headache?" indicate both your subject and approach and prepare your readers for what follows.

■ BEGINNINGS

What makes for an effective beginning? Not unlike a personal greeting, a good beginning should catch a reader's interest and then hold it. The experienced writer realizes that many readers would rather do almost anything than make a commitment to read, so the opening or *lead,* as journalists refer to it, requires a lot of thought and much revising to make it right and to keep the reader's attention from straying. The inexperienced writer, on the other hand, knows that the beginning is important but tries to write it first and to perfect it before moving on to the rest of the essay. Although there are no "rules" for writing introductions, we can offer one bit of general advice: Wait until the writing process is well under way or almost completed before focusing on your lead. Following this advice will keep you from spending too much time on an introduction that you will undoubtedly revise. More important, once you actually see how your essay develops, you will know better how to introduce it to your reader.

In addition to capturing your reader's attention, a good beginning usually introduces your thesis and either suggests or actually reveals the structure of the composition. Keep in mind that the best beginning is not necessarily the most catchy or the most shocking but the one most appropriate for the job you are trying to do.

There are many effective ways of beginning an essay. Consider using one of the following.

Anecdote

Introducing your essay with an anecdote—a brief narrative drawn from current news events, history, or your personal experience—can be an effective way to capture your reader's interest. In the following example, the writer introduces an essay on becoming a man by recounting an encounter he witnessed between two boys.

> Two nine-year-old boys, neighbors and friends, were walking home from school. The one in the bright blue windbreaker was laughing and swinging a heavy-looking book bag toward the head of his friend, who kept ducking and stepping back. "What's the matter?" asked the kid with the bag, whooshing it over his head. "You chicken?"
>
> His friend stopped, stood still, and braced himself. The bag slammed into the side of his face, the thump audible all the way across the street where I stood watching. The impact knocked him to the ground, where he lay mildly stunned for a second. Then he struggled up, rubbing the side of his head. "See?" he said proudly. "I'm no chicken."
>
> No. A chicken would probably have had the sense to get out of the way. This boy was already well on the road to becoming a *man*, having learned one of the central ethics of his gender: experience pain rather than show fear.
>
> –Jon Katz

Analogy and Comparison

An analogy or comparison can be useful in getting readers to contemplate a topic they might otherwise reject as unfamiliar or uninteresting. In the following multiparagraph example, Roger Garrison introduces a subject few would consider engrossing—writing—with an analogy to stone wall building. By pairing these two seemingly unrelated concepts, he both introduces and vividly illustrates the idea he will develop in his essay: that writing is a difficult, demanding craft with specific skills to be learned.

> In northern New England, where I live, stone walls mark boundaries, border meadows, and march through the woods that grew up around them long ago. Flank-high, the walls are made of granite rocks stripped from fields when pastures were cleared and are used to fence in cattle. These are dry walls, made without mortar, and the stones in them, all shapes and sizes, are fitted to one another with such care that a wall, built a hundred years ago, still runs as straight and solid as it did when people cleared the land.
>
> Writing is much like wall building. The writer fits together separate chunks of meaning to make an understandable statement. Like the old Yankee wall builders, anyone who wants to write well must learn some basic skills, one at a time, to build soundly. This [essay] describes these skills and shows you how to develop them and put them together. You can learn them.
>
> Building a stone wall is not easy: It is gut-wrenching labor. Writing is not easy either. It is a complex skill, mainly because it demands a commitment of our own complicated selves. But it is worth learning how to do well—something true of any skill. Solid walls do get built, and good writing does get done. We will clear away some underbrush and get at the job.
>
> –Roger Garrison

Dialogue/Quotation

Although relying heavily on the ideas of others can weaken an effective introduction, opening your essay with a quotation or a brief dialogue can attract a reader's attention and can succinctly illustrate a particular attitude or point that you want to discuss. In the following example, the writer introduces an essay about the three main types of stress in our lives by recounting a brief dialogue with one of her roommates.

> My roommate, Megan, pushes open the front door, throws her keys on the counter, and flops down on the couch.
>
> "Hey, Megan, how are you?" I yell from the kitchen.
>
> "I don't know what's wrong with me. I sleep all the time, but I'm still tired. No matter what I do, I just don't feel well."
>
> "What did the doctor say?"
>
> "She said it sounds like chronic fatigue syndrome."
>
> "Do you think it might be caused by stress?" I ask.
>
> "Nah, stress doesn't affect me very much. I like keeping busy and running around. This must be something else."

> Like most Americans, Megan doesn't recognize the numerous factors in her life that cause her stress.
>
> –Sarah Federman

Facts and Statistics

For the most part, you should use facts and statistics to support your argument rather than let them speak for you, but presenting brief and startling facts or statistics can be an effective way to engage readers in your essay.

> One out of every five new recruits in the United States military is female.
>
> The Marines gave the Combat Action Ribbon for service in the Persian Gulf to twenty-three women.
>
> Two female soldiers were killed in the bombing of the USS *Cole*.
>
> The Selective Service registers for the draft all male citizens between the ages of eighteen and twenty-five.
>
> What's wrong with this picture?
>
> –Anna Quindlen

Irony or Humor

It is often effective to introduce an essay with irony or humor. Humor signals to the reader that your essay will be entertaining to read, and irony can indicate an unexpected approach to a topic. In his essay "Shooting an Elephant," George Orwell begins by simultaneously establishing a wry tone and indicating to the reader that he, the narrator, occupies the position of outsider in the events he is about to relate.

> In Moulmein, in lower Burma, I was hated by large numbers of people—the only time in my life that I have been important enough for this to happen to me.
>
> –George Orwell

In his essay "I Led the Pigeons to the Flag," language commentator William Safire uses humorous examples to introduce his discussion of what happens when we creatively reproduce what we think we hear.

> The most saluted man in America is Richard Stans. Legions of schoolchildren place their hands over their hearts to pledge allegiance to the flag, "and to the republic for Richard Stans."
>
> With all due patriotic fervor, the same kids salute "one nation, under guard." Some begin with "I pledge a legion to the flag," others with "I led the pigeons to the flag."

This is not a new phenomenon. When they come to "one nation, indivisible," this generation is likely to say, "One naked individual," as a previous generation was to murmur, "One nation in a dirigible," or "One nation and a vegetable."

–William Safire

There are several other good ways to begin an essay; the following opening paragraphs illustrate each approach.

Short Generalization

Washington is a wonderful city. The scale seems right, more humane than other places. I like all the white marble and green trees, the ideals celebrated by the great monuments and memorials. I like the climate, the slow shift of the seasons here. Spring, so southern in feeling, comes early, and the long, sweet autumns can last into December. Summers are murder, equatorial—no question; the compensation is that Congress adjourns, the city empties out, eases off. Winter evenings in Georgetown with the snow falling and the lights just coming on are as beautiful as any I've known.

–David McCullough

Startling Claim

I've finally figured out the difference between neat and sloppy people. The distinction is, as always, moral. Neat people are lazier and meaner than sloppy people.

–Suzanne Britt

Strong Proposition

Everyone agrees that we've got to improve academic achievement in America's public schools. So why is it that districts distract students from core academics with a barrage of activities—everything from field hockey to music, drama, debating, and chess teams? And there's more: Drug education and fundraising eat away at classroom time. All manner of holidays, including Valentine's Day, get celebrated during the school day, as well as children's birthdays. These diversions are costly. They consume money and time.

Here's a bold proposition: privatize school sports and other extracurricular activities, and remove all but basic academic studies from the classroom. Sound like sacrilege? Look at what these extras really cost.

–Etta Kralovec

Rhetorical Questions

> *"Doesn't he realize this presentation is a waste of time?*
> *Why doesn't he just tell us what matters and get it over with?"*
> How many times have you heard (or muttered) that? How many
> of us have been frustrated at seeing too many presentations
> where PowerPoint or other visual aids obscure rather than en-
> hance the point? After one too many bad presentations at a
> meeting in January 2000, I decided to see if I could *do* some-
> thing about it.
>
> –Peter Norvig

Following are some examples of how *not* to begin an essay. You
should always *avoid* using beginnings such as these in your writing.

Beginnings to Avoid

Apology
I am a college student and do not consider myself an expert on
intellectual property, but I think file sharing and MP3 downloads
should be legal.

Complaint
I'd rather write about a topic of my own choice than the one that is
assigned, but here goes.

Webster's Dictionary
Webster's New Collegiate Dictionary defines the verb *to snore* as
follows: "to breathe during sleep with a rough hoarse noise due to
vibration of the soft palate."

Platitude
America is the land of opportunity, and no one knows that better than
Martha Stewart.

Reference to Title
As you can see from my title, this essay is about why we should continue to experiment with embryonic stem cells.

■ ENDINGS

An effective ending does more than simply indicate where the writer stopped writing. A conclusion may summarize; may inspire the reader to further thought or even action; may return to the beginning by repeating key words, phrases, or ideas; or may surprise the reader by providing a particularly convincing example to support a thesis. Indeed, there are many ways to write a conclusion, but the effectiveness of any choice must be measured by how appropriately it fits what comes before it. You might consider concluding with a restatement of your thesis, with a prediction, or with a recommendation.

In an essay contrasting the traditional Hispanic understanding of the word *macho* with the meaning it has developed in mainstream American culture, Rose Del Castillo Guilbault begins her essay with a succinct, two-sentence paragraph offering her thesis:

> What is macho? That depends which side of the border you come from.

She concludes her essay by restating her thesis, but in a manner that reflects the detailed examination she has given the concept of macho in her essay:

> The impact of language in our society is undeniable. And the misuse of macho hints at a deeper cultural misunderstanding that extends beyond mere word definitions.
>
> –Rose Del Castillo Guilbault

In the following conclusion to a long chapter on weasel words, a form of deceptive advertising language, the writer summarizes the points that he has made, ending with a recommendation to the reader:

> A weasel word is a word that's used to imply a meaning that cannot be truthfully stated. Some weasels imply meanings that are not the same as their actual definition, such as "help," "like," or "fortified." They can act as qualifiers and/or comparatives. Other weasels, such as "taste" and "flavor," have no definite meanings, and are simply subjective opinions offered by the manufacturer. A weasel of omission is one that implies a claim so strongly that it forces you to supply the bogus fact. Adjectives are weasels used to convey feelings and emotions to a greater extent than the product itself can.

In dealing with weasels, you must strip away the innuendos and try to ascertain the facts, if any. To do this, you need to ask questions such as: How? Why? How many? How much? Stick to basic definitions of words. Look them up if you have to. Then, apply the strict definition to the text of the advertisement or commercial. "Like" means similar to, but not the same as. "Virtually" means the same in essence, but not in fact.

Above all, never underestimate the devious qualities of a weasel. Weasels twist and turn and hide in dark shadows. You must come to grips with them, or advertising will rule you forever.

My advice to you is: Beware of weasels. They are nasty and untrainable, and they attack pocketbooks.

–Paul Stevens

In the following conclusion to a composition titled "Title IX Just Makes Sense," the writer offers an overview of her argument and concludes by predicting the outcome of the solution she advocates:

There have undeniably been major improvements in the treatment of female college athletes since the enactment of Title IX. But most colleges and universities still don't measure up to the actual regulation standards, and many have quite a ways to go. The Title IX fight for equality is not a radical feminist movement, nor is it intended to take away the privileges of male athletes. It is, rather, a demand for fairness, for women to receive the same opportunities that men have always had. When colleges and universities stop viewing Title IX budget requirements as an inconvenience and start complying with the spirit and not merely the letter of the law, collegiate female athletes will finally reach the parity they deserve.

–Jen Jarjosa, student

If you are having trouble with your conclusion—which is not an uncommon occurrence—it may be because of problems with your essay itself. Frequently, writers do not know when to end because they are not sure about their overall purpose. For example, if you are taking a trip and your purpose is to go to Chicago, you'll know when you get there and will stop. But if you don't really know where you are going, it's very difficult to know when to stop.

It's usually a good idea in your conclusion to avoid such overworked expressions as "In conclusion," "In summary," "I hope I have shown," or "Finally." Your conclusion should also do more than simply repeat what you've said in your opening paragraph. The most satisfying essays are those in which the conclusion provides an interesting way of wrapping up ideas introduced in the beginning and developed throughout so that your reader has the feeling of coming full circle.

You might find it revealing as your course progresses to read with special attention the beginnings and endings of the essays throughout *Models for Writers*. Take special note of the varieties of beginnings and endings, the possible relationship between a beginning and an ending, and the general appropriateness of these elements to the writer's subject and purpose.

Of My Friend Hector and My Achilles Heel

■ Michael T. Kaufman

Michael T. Kaufman (1938–2010) was born in Paris and grew up in the United States. He studied at the Bronx High School of Science, and shortly after graduating from City College of New York in 1959, he began working with the New York Times, *first as a reporter and later as a foreign cor-*  *respondent and columnist. He chronicled despotic regimes in Europe and Africa, the fall of Communism, and the ever-changing American scene. For his work in Africa in the late 1970s, Kaufman was the recipient of the George Polk Award for International Reporting. He retired from the* Times *in 1999. Kaufman wrote seven books and authored thousands of articles. In 1973, he published two books that captured urban life in the United States:* Rooftops & Alleys: Adventures with a City Kid *and* In Their Own Good Times. *Kaufman's experiences as bureau chief in Warsaw, Poland, during the early 1980s pro-vided the material for* Mad Dreams, Saving Graces *(1989). Together with Bernard Gwertzman, Kaufman broke the news about the downfall of the Soviet Union in* The Collapse of Communism *(1991) and* The Decline and Fall of the Soviet Empire *(1992). His most recent books are* Soros: The Life and Times of a Messianic Billionaire *(2002), an authorized biography of investor George Soros, and* 1968 *(2009), an in-depth analysis of that tumultuous year in U.S. history.*

In the following selection, which appeared in the New York Times *in 1992, Kaufman uses the story of his childhood friend Hector Elizondo to reflect on his own "prejudice and stupidity." Notice how the two brief sentences at the begin-ning establish the chronological and narrative structure of what follows.*

Reflecting on What You Know

Many schools "track" students by intellectual ability into such categories as "honors," "college bound," "vocational," "remedial," or "terminal." Did you go to a high school that tracked its students? How did you feel about your placement? What did you think about classmates who were on tracks higher or lower than yours? Looking back on your high school experience, do you think the tracking system worked for you?

This story is about prejudice and stupidity. My own.   1

It begins in 1945 when I was a 7-year-old living on the fifth floor of   2
a tenement walkup on 107th Street between Columbus and Manhattan Avenues in New York City. The block was almost entirely Irish and Italian, and I believe my family was the only Jewish one around.

One day a Spanish-speaking family moved into one of the four   3
apartments on our landing. They were the first Puerto Ricans I had met. They had a son who was about my age named Hector, and the two of us became friends. We played with toy soldiers and I particularly remember how, using rubber bands and wood from orange crates, we made toy pistols that shot off little squares we cut from old linoleum.

We visited each other's homes and I know that at the time I liked   4
Hector and I think he liked me. I may even have eaten my first avocado at his house.

About a year after we met, my family moved to another part of   5
Manhattan's West Side and I did not see Hector again until I entered Booker T. Washington Junior High School as an 11-year-old.

The Special Class

The class I was in was called 7SP-1; the SP was for special. Earlier, I   6
recall, I had been in the IGC class, for "intellectually gifted children." The SP class was to complete the seventh, eighth, and ninth grades in two years and almost all of us would then go to schools like Bronx Science, Stuyvesant, or Music and Art, where admission was based on competitive exams. I knew I was in the SP class and the IGC class. I guess I also knew that other people were not.

Hector was not. He was in some other class, maybe even 7-2, the   7
class that was held to be the next-brightest, or maybe 7-8. I remember

I was happy to see him whenever we would meet, and sometimes we played punchball during lunch period. Mostly, of course, I stayed with my own classmates, with other Intellectually Gifted Children.

Sometimes children from other classes, those presumably not so intellectually gifted, would tease and taunt us. At such times I was particularly proud to have Hector as a friend. I assumed that he was tougher than I and my classmates and I guess I thought that if necessary he would come to my defense.   8

Different High Schools

For high school, I went uptown to Bronx Science. Hector, I think, went downtown to Commerce. Sometimes I would see him in Riverside Park, where I played basketball and he worked out on the parallel bars. We would acknowledge each other, but by this time the conversations we held were perfunctory[1] — sports, families, weather.   9

After I finished college, I would see him around the neighborhood pushing a baby carriage. He was the first of my contemporaries to marry and to have a child.   10

A few years later, in the 60s, married and with children of my own, I was once more living on the West Side, working until late at night as a reporter. Some nights as I took the train home I would see Hector in the car. A few times we exchanged nods, but more often I would pretend that I didn't see him, and maybe he also pretended he didn't see me. Usually he would be wearing a knitted watch cap, and from that I deduced that he was probably working on the docks as a longshoreman.   11

I remember quite distinctly how I would sit on the train and think about how strange and unfair fate had been with regard to the two of us who had once been playmates. Just because I had become an intellectually gifted adult or whatever and he had become a longshoreman or whatever, was that any reason for us to have been left with nothing to say to each other? I thought it was wrong and unfair, but I also thought that conversation would be a chore or a burden. That is pretty much what I thought about Hector, if I thought about him at all, until one Sunday in the mid-70s, when I read in the   12

---

[1]*perfunctory:* a routine act done with little interest or care.

drama section of this newspaper that my childhood friend, Hector Elizondo, was replacing Peter Falk[2] in the leading role in *The Prisoner of Second Avenue*.[3]

Since then, every time I have seen this versatile and acclaimed 13 actor in movies or on television I have blushed for my assumptions. I have replayed the subway rides in my head and tried to fathom why my thoughts had led me where they did.

In retrospect it seems far more logical that the man I saw on the 14 train, the man who had been my friend as a boy, was coming home from an Off Broadway theater or perhaps from a job as a waiter while taking acting classes. So why did I think he was a longshoreman? Was it just the cap? Could it be that his being Puerto Rican had something to do with it? Maybe that reinforced the stereotype I concocted, but it wasn't the root of it.

When It Got Started

No, the foundation was laid when I was 11, when I was in 7SP-1 and 15 he was not, when I was in the IGC class and he was not.

I have not seen him since I recognized how I had idiotically kept 16 tracking him for years and decades after the school system had tracked both of us. I wonder now if my experience was that unusual, whether social categories conveyed and absorbed before puberty do not generally tend to linger beyond middle age. And I wonder, too, that if they affected the behavior of someone like myself who had been placed on the upper track, how much more damaging it must have been for someone consigned to the lower.

I have at times thought of calling him, but kept from doing it 17 because how exactly does one apologize for thoughts that were never expressed? And there was still the problem of what to say. "What have you been up to for the last 40 years?" Or "Wow, was I wrong about you!" Or maybe just, "Want to come over and help me make a linoleum gun?"

---

[2]*Peter Falk* (1927–2011): a well-known stage, television, and movie actor who starred as the rumpled television detective Columbo.
[3]*The Prisoner of Second Avenue*: a play by Neil Simon, which premiered at the Eugene O'Neill Theatre in New York City in 1971. The Broadway hit was made into a movie released in 1975.

Thinking Critically about This Reading

What "thoughts that were never expressed" (paragraph 17) does Kaufman feel the need to apologize for? In retrospect, how do you suppose Kaufman feels about his treatment of Hector?

Questions for Study and Discussion

1. How do Kaufman's first two sentences affect how the reader views the rest of the essay? Did they catch your attention? Why or why not?
2. If you are unfamiliar with the Greek myth of Hector and Achilles, look it up online or in a book on mythology. Why does Kaufman allude to Hector and Achilles in his title? (Glossary: *Allusion*)
3. How does Kaufman organize his essay? (Glossary: *Organization*)
4. What is Kaufman's purpose? (Glossary: *Purpose*) How does his organization help him express his purpose?
5. Why did Kaufman ignore Hector after graduating from college? What does that tell Kaufman about society in general?
6. Why is Kaufman's ending effective? What point does he emphasize with his ending?

Classroom Activity Using Beginnings and Endings

Carefully read the following three possible beginnings for an essay on the world's most famous practical joker, Hugh Troy. What are the advantages and disadvantages of each? Which one would you select as an opening paragraph? Why?

> Whether questioning the values of American society or simply relieving the monotony of daily life, Hugh Troy always managed to put a little of himself into each of his stunts. One day he attached a plaster hand to his shirt sleeve and took a trip through the Holland Tunnel. As he approached the tollbooth, with his toll ticket between the fingers of the artificial hand, Troy left both ticket and hand in the grasp of the stunned tollbooth attendant and sped away.

> Nothing seemed unusual. In fact, it was a rather common occurrence in New York City. Five men dressed in overalls roped off a section of busy Fifth Avenue in front of the old Rockefeller

residence, hung out MEN WORKING signs, and began ripping up the pavement. By the time they stopped for lunch, they had dug quite a hole in the street. This crew was different, however, from all the others that had descended upon the streets of the city. It was led by Hugh Troy—the world's greatest practical joker.

Hugh Troy was born in Ithaca, New York, where his father was a professor at Cornell University. After graduating from Cornell, Troy left for New York City, where he became a successful illustrator of children's books. When World War II broke out, he went into the army and eventually became a captain in the 21st Bomber Command, 20th Air Force, under General Curtis LeMay. After the war he made his home in Garrison, New York, for a short while before finally settling in Washington, D.C., where he lived until his death.

Suggested Writing Assignments

1. Kaufman's essay is a deeply personal one. Use it as a model to write an essay about a time or an action in your life that you are not proud of. What happened? Why did it happen? What would you do differently if you could? Be sure to catch the reader's attention in the beginning and to end your essay with a thought-provoking conclusion.

2. We all have childhood friends that we either have lost track of or don't communicate with as often as we would like. Choose an old friend whom you have lost track of and would like to see again. Write an essay about your relationship. What made your friend special to you as a child? Why did you lose touch? What does the future hold? Organize your essay chronologically.

The Case for Short Words

■ **Richard Lederer**

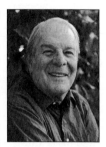

Born in 1938, Richard Lederer holds degrees from Haverford College, Harvard University, and the University of New Hampshire. He has been a prolific and popular writer about language. A high school English and media teacher for 27 years at St. Paul's School in New Hampshire, he is now vice president of SPELL, the Society for the Preservation of English Language and Literature. Lederer has written more than 30 books about how Americans use language, including Anguished English *(1987),* Crazy English: The Ultimate Joy Ride through Our Language *(1989),* The Play of Words *(1990),* The Miracle of Language *(1991),* More Anguished English *(1993),* Adventures of a Verbivore *(1994),* Fractured English *(1996), and* A Man of My Words: Reflections on the English Language *(2003). In addition to writing books, Lederer pens a weekly column called "Looking at Language" for newspapers and magazines across the United States. He is also the Grammar Grappler for* Writer's Digest, *the language commentator for National Public Radio, and an award-winning public speaker who makes approximately two hundred appearances each year.*

In the following essay, taken from The Miracle of Language, *pay attention to the different ways Lederer uses examples to illustrate his central point. Notice also that Lederer's diction demonstrates the versatility and strength of everyday words, thus helping him make the case for short words.*

Reflecting on What You Know

We all carry with us a vocabulary of short, simple-looking words that possess a special personal meaning. For example, to some the word *rose* represents not just a flower but a whole array of gardens, ceremonies, and romantic occasions. What little words have special meaning for you? What images do they bring to mind?

When you speak and write, there is no law that says you have   1
to use big words. Short words are as good as long ones,
and short, old words—like *sun* and *grass* and *home*—are best of
all. A lot of small words, more than you might think, can meet
your needs with a strength, grace, and charm that large words do
not have.

Big words can make the way dark for those who read what you   2
write and hear what you say. Small words cast their clear light on big
things—night and day, love and hate, war and peace, and life and
death. Big words at times seem strange to the eye and the ear and the
mind and the heart. Small words are the ones we seem to have known
from the time we were born, like the hearth fire that warms the
home.

Short words are bright like sparks that glow in the night, prompt   3
like the dawn that greets the day, sharp like the blade of a knife, hot
like salt tears that scald the cheek, quick like moths that flit from
flame to flame, and terse like the dart and sting of a bee.

Here is a sound rule: Use small, old words where you can. If a   4
long word says just what you want to say, do not fear to use it. But
know that our tongue is rich in crisp, brisk, swift, short words. Make
them the spine and the heart of what you speak and write. Short
words are like fast friends. They will not let you down.

The title of this [essay] and the four paragraphs that you have   5
just read are wrought entirely of words of one syllable. In setting myself this task, I did not feel especially cabined, cribbed, or confined. In
fact, the structure helped me to focus on the power of the message I
was trying to put across.

One study shows that twenty words account for twenty-five per-   6
cent of all spoken English words, and all twenty are monosyllabic. In
order of frequency they are: *I, you, the, a, to, is, it, that, of, and, in,
what, he, this, have, do, she, not, on,* and *they.* Other studies indicate
that the fifty most common words in written English are each made of a
single syllable.

For centuries our finest poets and orators have recognized and   7
employed the power of small words to make a straight point between
two minds. A great many of our proverbs punch home their points with
pithy monosyllables: "Where there's a will, there's a way," "A stitch in
time saves nine," "Spare the rod and spoil the child," "A bird in the
hand is worth two in the bush."

Nobody used the short word more skillfully than William Shake-   8
speare, whose dying King Lear laments:

> And my poor fool is hang'd! No, no, no life!
> Why should a dog, a horse, a rat have life,
> And thou no breath at all? . . .
> Do you see this? Look on her, look, her lips.
> Look there, look there!

Shakespeare's contemporaries made the King James Bible a center-   9
piece of short words—"And God said, Let there be light: and there
was light. And God saw the light, that it was good." The descendants
of such mighty lines live on in the twentieth century. When asked to
explain his policy to Parliament, Winston Churchill[1] responded with
these ringing monosyllables: "I will say: it is to wage war, by sea, land,
and air, with all our might and with all the strength that God can give
us." In his "Death of the Hired Man" Robert Frost[2] observes that
"Home is the place where, when you have to go there, / They have to
take you in." And William H. Johnson[3] uses ten two-letter words to
explain his secret of success: "If it is to be, / It is up to me."

You don't have to be a great author, statesman, or philosopher   10
to tap the energy and eloquence of small words. Each winter I ask
my ninth graders at St. Paul's School to write a composition composed entirely of one-syllable words. My students greet my request
with obligatory moans and groans, but, when they return to class
with their essays, most feel that, with the pressure to produce high-
sounding polysyllables relieved, they have created some of their most
powerful and luminous prose. Here are submissions from two of my
ninth graders:

> What can you say to a boy who has left home? You can say
> that he has done wrong, but he does not care. He has left home so
> that he will not have to deal with what you say. He wants to go as
> far as he can. He will do what he wants to do.
>   This boy does not want to be forced to go to church, to comb
> his hair, or to be on time. A good time for this boy does not lie in
> your reach, for what you have he does not want. He dreams of
> ripped jeans, shorts with no starch, and old socks.
>   So now this boy is on a bus to a place he dreams of, a place
> with no rules. This boy now walks a strange street, his long hair

---

[1] *Winston Churchill* (1874–1965): British orator, author, and statesman.
[2] *Robert Frost* (1874–1963): American poet.
[3] *William H. Johnson* (1771–1834): associate justice of the U.S. Supreme Court, 1804–1834.

blown back by the wind. He wears no coat or tie, just jeans and an old shirt. He hates your world, and he has left it.

–Charles Shaffer

For a long time we cruised by the coast and at last came to a wide bay past the curve of a hill, at the end of which lay a small town. Our long boat ride at an end, we all stretched and stood up to watch as the boat nosed its way in.

The town climbed up the hill that rose from the shore, a space in front of it left bare for the port. Each house was a clean white with sky blue or gray trim; in front of each one was a small yard, edged by a white stone wall strewn with green vines.

As the town basked in the heat of noon, not a thing stirred in the streets or by the shore. The sun beat down on the sea, the land, and the back of our necks, so that, in spite of the breeze that made the vines sway, we all wished we could hide from the glare in a cool, white house. But, as there was no one to help dock the boat, we had to stand and wait.

At last the head of the crew leaped from the side and strode to a large house on the right. He shoved the door wide, poked his head through the gloom, and roared with a fierce voice. Five or six men came out, and soon the port was loud with the clank of chains and creak of planks as the men caught ropes thrown by the crew, pulled them taut, and tied them to posts. Then they set up a rough plank so we could cross from the deck to the shore. We all made for the large house while the crew watched, glad to be rid of us.

–Celia Wren

You too can tap into the vitality and vigor of compact expression. Take a suggestion from the highway department. At the boundaries of your speech and prose place a sign that reads "Caution: Small Words at Work."   11

Thinking Critically about This Reading

In his opening paragraph, Lederer states that "short, old words—like *sun* and *grass* and *home*—are best of all." What attributes make these words the "best"? Does this claim surprise you by running counter to what we've always heard about "big words" and a large vocabulary?

Questions for Study and Discussion

1. In this essay, written to encourage the use of short words, Lederer himself employs many polysyllabic words, especially in

paragraphs 5–9. What is his purpose in doing so? (Glossary: *Purpose*)

2. Lederer quotes a variety of passages to illustrate the effectiveness of short words. For example, he quotes from famous, universally familiar sources such as Shakespeare and the King James Bible, and from unknown contemporary sources such as his own ninth-grade students. How does the variety of his illustrations serve to inform his readers? How does each example gain impact from the inclusion of the others?

3. To make clear to the reader why short words are effective, Lederer relies heavily on metaphors and similes, especially in the first four paragraphs. (Glossary: *Figure of Speech*) Choose at least one metaphor and one simile from these paragraphs, and explain the comparison implicit in each.

4. In paragraph 10, Lederer refers to the relief his students feel when released from "the pressure to produce high-sounding poly-syllables." Where does this pressure come from? How does it re-late to the central purpose of this essay?

5. How does the final paragraph serve to close the essay effectively? (Glossary: *Beginnings and Endings*)

6. This essay abounds with examples of striking sentences and pas-sages consisting entirely of words of one syllable. Choose four of the single-sentence examples or a section of several sentences from one of the longer examples, and rewrite them, using pri-marily words of two or more syllables. Notice how the revision differs from the original.

Classroom Activity Using Beginnings and Endings

Choose one of the essays you have been writing for your course, and write at least two different beginnings for it. If you are having trouble coming up with two new beginnings, check to see whether one of the paragraphs in the body of your essay would be appropri-ate, or consult the list of effective beginnings in the introduction to this chapter. After you have finished, have several classmates read your beginnings and select their favorite. Do any of your new begin-nings suggest ways that you can improve the focus, the organiza-tion, or the ending of your essay? Explain these revision possibilities to your partners.

Suggested Writing Assignments

1. Follow the assignment Lederer gives his own students, and write a composition composed entirely of one-syllable words. Make your piece about the length of his student examples or of his own four-paragraph opening.

2. A chief strength of Lederer's essay is his use of a broad variety of examples to illustrate his thesis that short words are the most effective words. Choose a subject you are knowledgeable about, and find as wide a range of examples as you can to illustrate its appeal. For example, if you are enthusiastic about water sports and activities, you could explore the relative attractions of rivers, ponds, lakes, and oceans; if you are a music lover, you might consider why Bach or the Beatles remain popular today.

Unforgettable Miss Bessie

■ **Carl T. Rowan**

In addition to being a popular syndicated newspaper columnist, Carl T. Rowan (1925–2000) was an ambassador to Finland and director of the U.S. Information Agency. Born in Ravenscroft, Tennessee, he received degrees from Oberlin College and the University of Minnesota. He worked as a columnist for the Minneapolis Tribune *and the* Chicago Sun-Times *before moving to Washington, D.C. In 1996, Washington College awarded Rowan an honorary doctor of letters degree in recognition of his achievements as a writer and his contributions to minority youth, most notably through the organization he founded in 1987, Project Excellence. In 1991, Rowan published* Breaking Barriers: A Memoir. *He is also the author of two biographies, one of baseball great Jackie Robinson and the other of former Supreme Court Justice Thurgood Marshall. His last book,* The Coming Race War in America, *was published in 1996.*

In the following essay, first published in the March 1985 issue of Reader's Digest, *Rowan describes one of his high school teachers whose lessons went far beyond the subjects she taught. Through telling details about Miss Bessie's background, behavior, and appearance, Rowan creates a dominant impression of her—the one he wants to leave readers with. Notice how he begins with some factual information about Miss Bessie and concludes by showing why she was "so vital to the minds, hearts, and souls" of her students.*

Reflecting on What You Know

Perhaps you have at some time taught a friend or younger brother or sister how to do something—tie a shoe, hit a ball, read, solve a puzzle, drive a car—but you never thought of yourself as a teacher. Did you enjoy the experience of sharing what you know with someone else? Would you consider becoming a teacher someday?

She was only about five feet tall and probably never weighed more 1
than 110 pounds, but Miss Bessie was a towering presence in the
classroom. She was the only woman tough enough to make me read
Beowulf[1] and think for a few foolish days that I liked it. From 1938
to 1942, when I attended Bernard High School in McMinnville,
Tennessee, she taught me English, history, civics—and a lot more than
I realized.

I shall never forget the day she scolded me into reading *Beowulf*. 2

"But Miss Bessie," I complained, "I ain't much interested in it." 3

Her large brown eyes became daggerish slits. "Boy," she said, "how 4
dare you say 'ain't' to me! I've taught you better than that."

"Miss Bessie," I pleaded, "I'm trying to make first-string end on the 5
football team, and if I go around saying 'it isn't' and 'they aren't,' the
guys are gonna laugh me off the squad."

"Boy," she responded, "you'll play football because you have 6
guts. But do you know what *really* takes guts? Refusing to lower your
standards to those of the crowd. It takes guts to say you've got to live
and be somebody fifty years after all the football games are over."

I started saying "it isn't" and "they aren't," and I still made first- 7
string end—and class valedictorian—without losing my buddies'
respect.

During her remarkable 44-year career, Mrs. Bessie Taylor Gwynn 8
taught hundreds of economically deprived black youngsters—including my mother, my brother, my sisters, and me. I remember her now
with gratitude and affection—especially in this era when Americans
are so wrought-up about a "rising tide of mediocrity"[2] in public education and the problems of finding competent, caring teachers. Miss
Bessie was an example of an informed, dedicated teacher, a blessing to
children, and an asset to the nation.

Born in 1895, in poverty, she grew up in Athens, Alabama, where 9
there was no public school for blacks. She attended Trinity School, a
private institution for blacks run by the American Missionary Association,
and in 1911 graduated from the Normal School (a "super" high school)
at Fisk University in Nashville. Mrs. Gwynn, the essence of pride and
privacy, never talked about her years in Athens; only in the months
before her death did she reveal that she had never attended Fisk
University itself because she could not afford the four-year course.

---

[1]*Beowulf*: an epic poem written in Old English by an anonymous author in the early
eighth century.
[2]*mediocrity*: state of being second-rate; not outstanding.

At Normal School she learned a lot about Shakespeare, but most   10
of all about the profound importance of education—especially, for a
people trying to move up from slavery. "What you put in your head,
boy," she once said, "can never be pulled out by the Ku Klux Klan,[3]
the Congress, or anybody."

Miss Bessie's bearing of dignity told anyone who met her that she   11
was "educated" in the best sense of the word. There was never a discipline problem in her classes. We didn't dare mess with a woman who
knew about the Battle of Hastings, the Magna Carta, and the Bill of
Rights—and who could also play the piano.

This frail-looking woman could make sense of Shakespeare,   12
Milton, Voltaire, and bring to life Booker T. Washington and
W. E. B. Du Bois. Believing that it was important to know who the
officials were that spent taxpayers' money and made public policy,
she made us memorize the names of everyone on the Supreme Court
and in the President's Cabinet. It could be embarrassing to be unpre-
pared when Miss Bessie said, "Get up and tell the class who Frances
Perkins[4] is and what you think about her."

Miss Bessie knew that my family, like so many others during the   13
Depression,[5] couldn't afford to subscribe to a newspaper. She knew
we didn't even own a radio. Still, she prodded me to "look out for
your future and find some way to keep up with what's going on in
the world." So I became a delivery boy for the Chattanooga *Times*. I
rarely made a dollar a week, but I got to read a newspaper every day.

Miss Bessie noticed things that had nothing to do with schoolwork,   14
but were vital to a youngster's development. Once a few classmates
made fun of my frayed, hand-me-down overcoat, calling me
"Strings." As I was leaving school, Miss Bessie patted me on the back
of that old overcoat and said, "Carl, never fret about what you *don't*
have. Just make the most of what you *do* have—a brain."

Among the things that I did not have was electricity in the little   15
frame house that my father had built for $400 with his World War I

---

[3]*Ku Klux Klan:* a secret organization in the United States hostile toward African
Americans (eventually other groups as well), founded in 1915 and continuing to the
present.
[4]*Frances Perkins* (1882–1965): U.S. secretary of labor during the presidency of
Franklin D. Roosevelt and the first woman appointed to a cabinet post.
[5]*Depression:* the longest and most severe modern economic slump in North America,
Europe, and other industrialized areas of the world so far; it began in 1929 and ended
around 1939. Also called the *Great Depression.*

bonus. But because of her inspiration, I spent many hours squinting beside a kerosene lamp reading Shakespeare and Thoreau, Samuel Pepys and William Cullen Bryant.

No one in my family had ever graduated from high school, so 16 there was no tradition of commitment to learning for me to lean on. Like millions of youngsters in today's ghettos and barrios, I needed the push and stimulation of a teacher who truly cared. Miss Bessie gave plenty of both, as she immersed me in a wonderful world of similes, metaphors and even onomatopoeia. She led me to believe that I could write sonnets as well as Shakespeare, or iambic-pentameter verse to put Alexander Pope to shame.

In those days the McMinnville school system was rigidly "Jim 17 Crow,"[6] and poor black children had to struggle to put anything in their heads. Our high school was only slightly larger than the once-typical little red schoolhouse, and its library was outrageously inadequate — so small, I like to say, that if two students were in it and one wanted to turn a page, the other one had to step outside.

Negroes, as we were called then, were not allowed in the town 18 library, except to mop floors or dust tables. But through one of those secret Old South arrangements between whites of conscience and blacks of stature, Miss Bessie kept getting books smuggled out of the white library. That is how she introduced me to the Brontës, Byron, Coleridge, Keats and Tennyson. "If you don't read, you can't write, and if you can't write, you might as well stop dreaming," Miss Bessie once told me.

So I read whatever Miss Bessie told me to, and tried to remember 19 the things she insisted that I store away. Forty-five years later, I can still recite her "truths to live by," such as Henry Wadsworth Longfellow's lines from "The Ladder of St. Augustine":

The heights by great men reached and kept
Were not attained by sudden flight.
But they, while their companions slept,
Were toiling upward in the night.

Years later, her inspiration, prodding, anger, cajoling, and almost 20 osmotic infusion of learning finally led to that lovely day when Miss Bessie dropped me a note saying, "I'm so proud to read your column in the Nashville *Tennessean.*"

---

[6] *"Jim Crow":* a term referring to the racial segregation laws in the U.S. South between the late 1800s and the mid-1900s.

Miss Bessie was a spry 80 when I went back to McMinnville and 21 visited her in a senior citizens' apartment building. Pointing out proudly that her building was racially integrated, she reached for two glasses and a pint of bourbon. I was momentarily shocked, because it would have been scandalous in the 1930s and '40s for word to get out that a teacher drank, and nobody had ever raised a rumor that Miss Bessie did.

I felt a new sense of equality as she lifted her glass to mine. Then she 22 revealed a softness and compassion that I had never known as a student.

"I've never forgotten that examination day," she said, "when Buster 23 Martin held up seven fingers, obviously asking you for help with question number seven, 'Name a common carrier.' I can still picture you looking at your exam paper and humming a few bars of 'Chattanooga Choo Choo.' I was so tickled, I couldn't punish either of you."

Miss Bessie was telling me, with bourbon-laced grace, that I never 24 fooled her for a moment.

When Miss Bessie died in 1980, at age 85, hundreds of her 25 former students mourned. They knew the measure of a great teacher: love and motivation. Her wisdom and influence had rippled out across generations.

Some of her students who might normally have been doomed to 26 poverty went on to become doctors, dentists, and college professors. Many, guided by Miss Bessie's example, became public-school teachers.

"The memory of Miss Bessie and how she conducted her class- 27 room did more for me than anything I learned in college," recalls Gladys Wood of Knoxville, Tennessee, a highly respected English teacher who spent 43 years in the state's school system. "So many times, when I faced a difficult classroom problem, I asked myself, *How would Miss Bessie deal with this?* And I'd remember that she would handle it with laughter and love."

No child can get all the necessary support at home, and millions 28 of poor children get *no* support at all. This is what makes a wise, educated, warm-hearted teacher like Miss Bessie so vital to the minds, hearts, and souls of this country's children.

Thinking Critically about This Reading

Rowan states that Miss Bessie "taught me English, history, civics— and a lot more than I realized" (paragraph 1). Aside from the standard school subjects, what did Miss Bessie teach Rowan? What role did she play in his life?

Questions for Study and Discussion

1. Do you think Rowan's first few paragraphs make for an effective introduction? Explain.

2. At what point in the essay does Rowan give us the details of Miss Bessie's background? Why do you suppose he delays giving us this important information?

3. Throughout the essay Rowan offers details of Miss Bessie's physical appearance. What specific details does he give, and in what context does he give them? (Glossary: *Details*) Do Miss Bessie's physical characteristics match the quality of her character? Explain.

4. Does Miss Bessie's drinking influence your opinion of her? Why or why not? Why do you think Rowan includes this part of her behavior in his essay?

5. How does dialogue serve Rowan's purpose? (Glossary: *Dialogue; Purpose*)

6. How would you sum up the character of Miss Bessie? Make a list of the key words that Rowan uses that you believe best describe her.

Classroom Activity Using Beginnings and Endings

Rowan uses a series of facts about his teacher, the "unforgettable" Miss Bessie, to begin his essay. Pick two from among the eight other methods for beginning essays discussed in the introduction to this chapter, and use them to write alternative openings for Rowan's essay. Share your beginnings with others in the class, and discuss their effectiveness.

Suggested Writing Assignments

1. In paragraph 18, Rowan writes the following: "'If you don't read, you can't write, and if you can't write, you might as well stop dreaming,' Miss Bessie once told me." Write an essay in which you explore this theme (which, in essence, is also the theme of *Models for Writers*).

2. Think of all the teachers you have had, and then write a description of the one who has had the greatest influence on you. (Glossary: *Description*) Remember to give some consideration to the balance you want to achieve between physical attributes and personality traits.

Paragraphs

Within an essay, the **paragraph** is the most important unit of thought. Like the essay, it has its own main idea, often stated directly in a topic sentence. Like a good essay, a good paragraph is unified: it avoids digressions and develops its main idea. Paragraphs use many of the rhetorical strategies that essays use—strategies like classification, comparison and contrast, and cause and effect. As you read the following three paragraphs, notice how each writer develops his or her topic sentence with explanations, concrete details and statistics, or vivid examples. The topic sentence in each paragraph is italicized.

> *I've learned from experience that good friendships are based on a delicate balance.* When friends are on a par, professionally and personally, it's easier for them to root for one another. It's taken me a long time to realize that not all my "friends" wish me well. Someone who wants what you have may not be able to handle your good fortune: If you find yourself apologizing for your hard-earned raise or soft-pedaling your long-awaited promotion, it's a sure sign that the friendship is off balance. Real friends are secure enough in their own lives to share each other's successes—not begrudge them.
>
> –Stephanie Mansfield

> The problem of substance abuse is far more complex and far more pervasive than any of us really knows or is willing to admit. *Most stories of illegal drugs overshadow Americans' struggles with alcohol, tobacco, food, and nonprescription drugs—our so-called legal addictions.* In 2000, for example, 17,000 deaths were attributed to cocaine and heroin. In that same year, 435,000 deaths were attributed to tobacco and 85,000 to alcohol. It's not surprising, then, that many sociologists believe we are a nation of substance abusers—drinkers, smokers, overeaters, and pill poppers. Although the statistics are alarming, they do not begin to suggest the heavy

toll of substance abuse on Americans and their families. Loved ones die, relationships are fractured, children are abandoned, job productivity falters, and the dreams of young people are extinguished.

–Alfred Rosa and Paul Eschholz

Photographs have let me know my parents before I was born, as the carefree college students they were, in love and awaiting the rest of their lives. I have seen the light blue Volkswagen van my dad used to take surfing down the coast of California and the silver dress my mom wore to her senior prom. Through pictures I was able to witness their wedding, which showed me that there is much in their relationship that goes beyond their children. I saw the look in their eyes as they held their first, newborn daughter, as well as the jealous expressions of my sister when I was born a few years later. There is something almost magical about viewing images of yourself and your family that you were too young to remember.

–Carrie White, student

Many writers find it helpful to think of the paragraph as a very small, compact essay. Here is a paragraph from an essay on testing:

Multiple-choice questions distort the purposes of education. Picking one answer among four is very different from thinking a question through to an answer of one's own, and far less useful in life. Recognition of vocabulary and isolated facts makes the best kind of multiple-choice questions, so these dominate the tests, rather than questions that test the use of knowledge. Because schools want their children to perform well, they are often tempted to teach the limited sorts of knowledge most useful on the tests.

This paragraph, like all well-written paragraphs, has several distinguishing characteristics. It is unified, coherent, and adequately developed. It is unified in that every sentence and every idea relates to the main idea, stated in the topic sentence, "Multiple-choice questions distort the purposes of education." It is coherent in that the sentences and ideas are arranged logically and the relationships among them are made clear by the use of effective transitions. Finally, the paragraph is adequately developed in that it presents a short but persuasive argument supporting its main idea.

How much development is "adequate" development? The answer depends on many things—how complicated or controversial the main idea is, what readers already know and believe, how much space the writer is permitted. Nearly everyone agrees that the earth circles around the sun; a single sentence would be enough to make that point. A writer arguing that affirmative action has outlived its usefulness, however, would need many sentences—indeed, many paragraphs—to develop that idea convincingly.

Here is another model of an effective paragraph. As you read this paragraph about the resourcefulness of pigeons in evading attempts to control them, pay attention to its main idea, unity, development, and coherence.

> Pigeons (and their human friends) have proved remarkably resourceful in evading nearly all the controls, from birth-control pellets to carbide shells to pigeon apartment complexes, that pigeon-haters have devised. One of New York's leading museums once put large black rubber owls on its wide ledges to discourage the large number of pigeons that roosted there. Within the day the pigeons had gotten over their fear of owls and were back perched on the owls' heads. A few years ago San Francisco put a sticky coating on the ledges of some public buildings, but the pigeons got used to the goop and came back to roost. The city then tried trapping, using electric owls, and periodically exploding carbide shells outside a city building, hoping the noise would scare the pigeons away. It did, but not for long, and the program was abandoned. More frequent explosions probably would have distressed the humans in the area more than the birds. Philadelphia tried a feed that makes pigeons vomit, and then, they hoped, go away. A New York firm claimed it had a feed that made a pigeon's nervous system send "danger signals" to the other members of its flock.

The main idea is stated at the beginning in a topic sentence. Other sentences in the paragraph support this idea with examples. Because all the separate examples illustrate how pigeons have evaded attempts to control them, the paragraph is unified. Because there are enough examples to convince the reader of the truth of the topic statement, the paragraph is adequately developed. Finally, the regular use of transitional words and phrases like *once, within the day, a few years ago,* and *then* lends the paragraph coherence.

How long should a paragraph be? In modern essays, most paragraphs range from 50 to 250 words, but some run a full printed page or more, and others may be only a few words long. The best answer is that a paragraph should be long enough to develop its main idea adequately. When some writers find a paragraph running very long, they break it into two or more paragraphs so that readers can pause and catch their breath. Other writers forge ahead, relying on the unity and coherence of their paragraph to keep their readers from getting lost.

Articles and essays that appear in magazines and newspapers often have relatively short paragraphs, some of only one or two sentences. Short paragraphs are a convention in journalism because of the narrow columns, which make paragraphs of average length appear very long. But often you will find that these journalistic "paragraphs" could be joined together into a few longer paragraphs. Longer, adequately developed paragraphs are the kind you should use in all but journalistic writing.

Simplicity

■ **William Zinsser**

William Zinsser was born in New York City in 1922. After graduating from Princeton University, he worked for the New York Herald Tribune, *first as a feature writer and later as its drama editor and film critic. During the 1970s he taught writing at Yale University. A former executive editor of the* Book-of-the-Month Club, *Zinsser has also served on the Usage Panel of the* American Heritage Dictionary. *Currently, he is the series editor for the Writer's Craft Series, which publishes talks by writers, and teaches writing at the New School University in New York. Zinsser's own published works cover many aspects of contemporary American culture, but he is best known as the author of lucid and accessible books about writing, including* Writing to Learn *(1988),* Inventing the Truth: The Art and Craft of Memoir *(1998, with Russell Baker and Jill Ker Conway),* Writing about Your Life: A Journey into the Past *(2005), and* On Writing Well, *a perennial favorite for college writing courses, published in a thirtieth anniversary edition in 2006.* Writing Places: The Life Journey of a Writer and Teacher *(2009) is his latest book about writing.*

In the following piece from On Writing Well, *Zinsser reminds us, as did Henry David Thoreau before him, to "simplify, simplify." As you read each paragraph, notice the clarity with which Zinsser presents its main idea, and observe how he develops that idea with adequate and logically related supporting information. You should also notice that he follows his own advice about simplicity.*

Reflecting on What You Know

Sometimes we get so caught up in what's going on around us that we start to feel frantic, and we lose sight of what is really important or meaningful to us. At such times, it's a good idea to take stock of what we are doing and to simplify our lives by dropping activities that are no longer rewarding. Write about a time when you've felt the need to simplify your life.

Clutter is the disease of American writing. We are a society stran- 1
gling in unnecessary words, circular constructions, pompous frills,
and meaningless jargon.

Who can understand the clotted language of everyday American 2
commerce: the memo, the corporation report, the business letter, the
notice from the bank explaining its latest "simplified" statement?
What member of an insurance or medical plan can decipher the brochure explaining his costs and benefits? What father or mother can
put together a child's toy from the instructions on the box? Our
national tendency is to inflate and thereby sound important. The
airline pilot who announces that he is presently anticipating experiencing considerable precipitation wouldn't think of saying it may rain.
The sentence is too simple — there must be something wrong with it.

But the secret of good writing is to strip every sentence to its clean- 3
est components. Every word that serves no function, every long word
that could be a short word, every adverb that carries the same meaning
that's already in the verb, every passive construction that leaves the
reader unsure of who is doing what—these are the thousand and one
adulterants[1] that weaken the strength of a sentence. And they usually
occur in proportion to education and rank.

During the 1960s the president of my university wrote a letter to 4
mollify[2] the alumni after a spell of campus unrest. "You are probably
aware," he began, "that we have been experiencing very considerable
potentially explosive expressions of dissatisfaction on issues only partially related." He meant the students had been hassling them about
different things. I was far more upset by the president's English than
by the students' potentially explosive expressions of dissatisfaction. I
would have preferred the presidential approach taken by Franklin D.
Roosevelt when he tried to convert into English his own government's
memos, such as this blackout order of 1942:

> Such preparations shall be made as will completely obscure
> all Federal buildings and non-Federal buildings occupied by the
> Federal government during an air raid for any period of time from
> visibility by reason of internal or external illumination.

"Tell them," Roosevelt said, "that in buildings where they have 5
to keep the work going to put something across the windows."

---

[1]*adulterants:* unnecessary ingredients that taint the purity of something.
[2]*mollify:* to soothe in temper; appease.

Simplify, simplify. Thoreau[3] said it, as we are so often reminded, 6
and no American writer more consistently practiced what he preached.
Open *Walden* to any page and you will find a man saying in a plain and
orderly way what is on his mind:

> I went to the woods because I wished to live deliberately, to
> front only the essential facts of life, and see if I could not learn
> what it had to teach, and not, when I came to die, discover that I
> had not lived.

How can the rest of us achieve such enviable freedom from 7
clutter? The answer is to clear our heads of clutter. Clear thinking becomes clear writing; one can't exist without the other. It's impossible
for a muddy thinker to write good English. He may get away with it
for a paragraph or two, but soon the reader will be lost, and there's
no sin so grave, for the reader will not easily be lured back.

Who is this elusive creature, the reader? The reader is someone 8
with an attention span of about 30 seconds—a person assailed by
many forces competing for attention. At one time those forces were
relatively few: newspapers, magazines, radio, spouse, children, pets.
Today they also include a galaxy of electronic devices for receiving
entertainment and information—television, VCRs, DVDs, CDs, video
games, the Internet, e-mail, cell phones, BlackBerries, iPods—as well
as a fitness program, a pool, a lawn, and that most potent of competitors, sleep. The man or woman snoozing in a chair with a magazine or
a book is a person who was being given too much unnecessary trouble
by the writer.

It won't do to say that the reader is too dumb or too lazy to keep 9
pace with the train of thought. If the reader is lost, it's usually because
the writer hasn't been careful enough. The carelessness can take any
number of forms. Perhaps a sentence is so excessively cluttered that the
reader, hacking through the verbiage, simply doesn't know what it
means. Perhaps a sentence has been so shoddily constructed that the
reader could read it in several ways. Perhaps the writer has switched
pronouns in midsentence, or has switched tenses, so the reader loses
track of who is talking or when the action took place. Perhaps
Sentence B is not a logical sequel to Sentence A; the writer, in whose

---

[3]*Henry David Thoreau* (1817–1862): American essayist, poet, and philosopher
activist. *Walden*, his masterwork, was published in 1854.

head the connection is clear, hasn't bothered to provide the missing link. Perhaps the writer has used a word incorrectly by not taking the trouble to look it up.

Faced with such obstacles, readers are at first tenacious. They blame themselves—they obviously missed something, and they go back over the mystifying sentence, or over the whole paragraph, piecing it out like an ancient rune, making guesses and moving on. But they won't do that for long. The writer is making them work too hard, and they will look for one who is better at the craft.   10

Writers must therefore constantly ask: what am I trying to say? Surprisingly often they don't know. Then they must look at what they have written and ask: have I said it? Is it clear to someone encountering the subject for the first time? If it's not, some fuzz has worked its way into the machinery. The clear writer is someone clearheaded enough to see this stuff for what it is: fuzz.   11

I don't mean that some people are born clearheaded and are therefore natural writers, whereas others are naturally fuzzy and will never write well. Thinking clearly is a conscious act that writers must force on themselves, as if they were working on any other project that requires logic: making a shopping list or doing an algebra problem. Good writing doesn't come naturally, though most people seem to think it does. Professional writers are constantly bearded[4] by people who say they'd like to "try a little writing sometime"—meaning when they retire from their real profession, like insurance or real estate, which is hard. Or they say, "I could write a book about that." I doubt it.   12

Writing is hard work. A clear sentence is no accident. Very few sentences come out right the first time, or even the third time. Remember this in moments of despair. If you find that writing is hard, it's because it *is* hard.   13

Thinking Critically about This Reading

How does Zinsser support his claim that "we are a society strangling in unnecessary words, circular constructions, pompous frills, and meaningless jargon" (paragraph 1)? What are the implications of his claim for writers in general and for you in particular?

---

[4]*bearded:* confronted boldly.

Questions for Study and Discussion

1. What exactly does Zinsser mean by "clutter" (1)? How does he believe we can free ourselves of clutter?
2. Identify the main idea in each of the thirteen paragraphs. How is each paragraph related to Zinsser's topic and purpose?
3. In what ways do paragraphs 4–6 serve to illustrate the main idea of paragraph 3? (Glossary: *Illustration*)
4. In paragraph 11, Zinsser says that writers must constantly ask themselves some questions. What are these questions, and why are they important?
5. How do Zinsser's first and last paragraphs serve to introduce and conclude his essay? (Glossary: *Beginnings and Endings*)
6. What is the relationship between thinking and writing for Zinsser?

Classroom Activity Using Paragraphs

Below you will find a passage from Zinsser's final manuscript of this chapter from the first edition of *On Writing Well*. Zinsser has included these manuscript pages showing his editing for clutter in every edition of his book because he believes they are instructive. He says, "Although they look like a first draft, they had already been rewritten and retyped—like almost every other page—four or five times. With each rewrite I try to make what I have written tighter, stronger, and more precise, eliminating every element that's not doing useful work. Then I go over it once more, reading it aloud, and am always amazed at how much clutter can still be cut. (In later editions I eliminated the sexist pronoun 'he' denoting 'the writer' and 'the reader.')"

Carefully study these manuscript pages and Zinsser's editing, and be prepared to discuss how the changes enhance his paragraphs' unity, coherence, and logical development.

```
is too dumb or too lazy to keep pace with the ~~writer's~~ train
of thought. My sympathies are ~~entirely~~ with him. ~~He's not~~
~~so dumb.~~ If the reader is lost, it is generally because the
writer ~~of the article~~ has not been careful enough to keep
him on the ~~proper~~ path.
```

This carelessness can take any number of ~~different~~ forms. Perhaps a sentence is so excessively ~~long and~~ cluttered that the reader, hacking his way through ~~all~~ the verbiage, simply doesn't know what *it* ~~the writer~~ means. Perhaps a sentence has been so shoddily constructed that the reader could read it in any of *several* ~~two or three different~~ ways. ~~He thinks he knows what the writer is trying to say, but he's not sure.~~ Perhaps the writer has switched pronouns in midsentence, or ~~perhaps he~~ has switched tenses, so the reader loses track of who is talking ~~to whom~~ or ~~exactly~~ when the action took place. Perhaps Sentence B is not a logical sequel to Sentence A -- the writer, in whose head the connection is ~~perfectly~~ clear, has not *bothered to provide* ~~given enough thought to providing~~ the missing link. Perhaps the writer has used an important word incorrectly by not taking the trouble to look it up~~, and make sure.~~ He may think that "sanguine" and "sanguinary" mean the same thing, but ~~I can assure you that~~ the difference is a bloody big one~~, to the reader.~~ *The reader* ~~He~~ can only ~~try to~~ infer ~~xxxx~~ (speaking of big differences) what the writer is trying to imply.

Faced with *these* ~~such a variety of~~ obstacles, the reader is at first a remarkably tenacious bird. He ~~tends to~~ blame*s* himself. ~~He~~ *He* obviously missed something, ~~he thinks,~~ and he goes back over the mystifying sentence, or over the whole paragraph, piecing it out like an ancient rune, making guesses and moving on. But he won't do this for long. ~~He will soon run out of patience.~~ The writer is making him work too hard, ~~harder than he should have to work --~~ and the reader will look for *one* ~~a writer~~ who is better at his craft.

The writer must therefore constantly ask himself: What am I trying to say? ~~in this sentence?~~ Surprisingly often, he doesn't know. ~~And~~ Then he must look at what he has ~~just~~ written and ask: Have I said it? Is it clear to someone *encountering* ~~who is coming upon~~ the subject for the first time? If it's not, ~~clear,~~ it is because some fuzz has worked its way into the machinery. The clear writer is a person ~~who is~~ clear-headed enough to see this stuff for what it is: fuzz.

I don't mean ~~to suggest~~ that some people are born
clear-headed and are therefore natural writers, whereas
others
^~~other people~~ are naturally fuzzy and will ~~therefore~~ never write
                                                    a
well. Thinking clearly is ^~~an entirely~~ conscious act that the
                    force
writer must ^~~keep forcing~~ upon himself, just as if he were
embarking   requires
^~~starting out~~ on any other ~~kind of~~ project that ^~~calls for~~ logic:
adding up a laundry list or doing an algebra problem ~~, or playing~~
~~chess.~~ Good writing doesn't ~~just~~ come naturally, though most
                          it does.
people obviously think ^~~it's as easy as walking.~~

Suggested Writing Assignments

1. If what Zinsser writes about clutter is an accurate assessment, we
   should easily be able to find numerous examples of clutter all
   around us. During the next few days, look for clutter in the written materials you come across. Choose one example that you
   find—an article, an essay, a form letter, or a section from a
   textbook, for example—and write an extended analysis explaining how it might have been written more simply. Develop your
   paragraphs well, make sure they are coherent, and try not to
   "clutter" your own writing.

2. Using some of the ideas you explored in your journal entry for
   this selection, write a brief essay analyzing your need to simplify
   some aspect of your life. For example, are you involved in too
   many extracurricular activities, taking too many courses, working too many hours at a job, or not making sensible choices with
   regard to your social life?

"I Just Wanna Be Average"

■ Mike Rose

Born in Altoona, Pennsylvania, in 1944 to Italian American parents, Mike Rose moved to California in the early 1950s. A graduate of Loyola University in Los Angeles, Rose is now a professor at the UCLA Graduate School of Education and Information Studies. He has written a number of books and articles on language and literacy. His best-known book, Lives on the Boundary: The Struggles and Achievements of America's Underprepared, *was recognized by the National Council of Teachers of English with its highest award in 1989. More recently, he published* Possible Lives: The Promise of Public Education *(1995),* The Mind at Work: Valuing the Intelligence of the American Worker *(2004),* An Open Language: Selected Writing on Literacy, Learning, and Opportunity *(2006), and* Why School? *(2009).*

In the following selection from Lives on the Boundary, *Rose explains how a high school English teacher, Jack MacFarland, picked him up out of the doldrums of "scholastic indifference." As you read, notice that although his paragraphs are fairly lengthy, Rose never digresses from the main point of each.*

Reflecting on What You Know

Often our desire to get more out of high school and to go on to college can be traced back to the influence of a single teacher. Which teacher most encouraged you to learn? Describe what that person did to stimulate change in you.

Jack MacFarland couldn't have come into my life at a better time. My   1
father was dead, and I had logged up too many years of scholastic indifference. Mr. MacFarland had a master's degree from Columbia and decided, at twenty-six, to find a little school and teach his heart out. He never took any credentialing courses, couldn't bear to, he said, so he had to find employment in a private system. He ended up at Our

Lady of Mercy teaching five sections of senior English. He was a beatnik[1] who was born too late. His teeth were stained, he tucked his sorry tie in between the third and fourth buttons of his shirt, and his pants were chronically wrinkled. At first, we couldn't believe this guy, thought he slept in his car. But within no time, he had us so startled with work that we didn't much worry about where he slept or if he slept at all. We wrote three or four essays a month. We read a book every two to three weeks, starting with the *Iliad*[2] and ending up with Hemingway. He gave us a quiz on the reading every other day. He brought a prep school curriculum to Mercy High.

　MacFarland's lectures were crafted, and as he delivered them he would pace the room jiggling a piece of chalk in his cupped hand, using it to scribble on the board the names of all the writers and philosophers and plays and novels he was weaving into his discussion. He asked questions often, raised everything from Zeno's paradox to the repeated last line of Frost's "Stopping by Woods on a Snowy Evening." He slowly and carefully built up our knowledge of Western intellectual history—with facts, with connections, with speculations. We learned about Greek philosophy, about Dante, the Elizabethan world view, the Age of Reason, existentialism. He analyzed poems with us, had us reading sections from John Ciardi's *How Does a Poem Mean?*, making a potentially difficult book accessible with his own explanations. We gave oral reports on poems Ciardi didn't cover. We imitated the styles of Conrad, Hemingway, and *Time* magazine. We wrote and talked, wrote and talked. The man immersed us in language. 2

　Even MacFarland's barbs were literary. If Jim Fitzsimmons, hung over and irritable, tried to smart-ass him, he'd rejoin[3] with a flourish that would spark the indomitable[4] Skip Madison—who'd lost his front teeth in a hapless tackle—to flick his tongue through the gap and opine, "good chop," drawing out the single "o" in stinging indictment. Jack MacFarland, this tobacco-stained intellectual, brandished linguistic weapons of a kind I hadn't encountered before. Here was this *egghead,* for God's sake, keeping some pretty difficult people in line. And from what I heard, Mike Dweetz and Steve Fusco and all the notorious Voc. Ed.[5] crowd settled down as well when MacFarland took the podium. 3

---

[1]*beatnik:* a person whose behavior, views, and style of dress are unconventional.
[2]*Iliad:* an ancient Greek epic poem attributed to Homer.
[3]*rejoin:* respond sharply; counterattack.
[4]*indomitable:* impossible to subdue.
[5]*Voc. Ed.:* vocational education, training for a specific industry or trade.

Though a lot of guys groused in the schoolyard, it just seemed that giving trouble to this particular teacher was a silly thing to do. Tomfoolery, not to mention assault, had no place in the world he was trying to create for us, and instinctively everyone knew that. If nothing else, we all recognized MacFarland's considerable intelligence and respected the hours he put into his work. It came to this: The troublemaker would look foolish rather than daring. Even Jim Fitzsimmons was reading *On the Road* and turning his incipient[6] alcoholism to literary ends.

There were some lives that were already beyond Jack MacFarland's   4
ministrations,[7] but mine was not. I started reading again as I hadn't since elementary school. I would go into our gloomy little bedroom or sit at the dinner table while, on the television, Danny McShane was paralyzing Mr. Moto with the atomic drop, and work slowly back through *Heart of Darkness,* trying to catch the words in Conrad's sentences. I certainly was not MacFarland's best student; most of the other guys in College Prep, even my fellow slackers, had better backgrounds than I did. But I worked very hard, for MacFarland had hooked me. He tapped my old interest in reading and creating stories. He gave me a way to feel special by using my mind. And he provided a role model that wasn't shaped on physical prowess alone, and something inside me that I wasn't quite aware of responded to that. Jack MacFarland established a literacy club, to borrow a phrase of Frank Smith's, and invited me—invited all of us—to join.

There's been a good deal of research and speculation suggesting   5
that the acknowledgment of school performance with extrinsic rewards—smiling faces, stars, numbers, grades—diminishes the intrinsic satisfaction children experience by engaging in reading or writing or problem solving. While it's certainly true that we've created an educational system that encourages our best and brightest to become cynical grade collectors and, in general, have developed an obsession with evaluation and assessment, I must tell you that venal[8] though it may have been, I loved getting good grades from MacFarland. I now know how subjective grades can be, but then they came tucked in the back of essays like bits of scientific data, some sort of spectroscopic readout that said, objectively and publicly, that I had made something of value. I suppose I'd been

---

[6]*incipient:* developing; starting to appear.
[7]*ministrations:* help; service.
[8]*venal:* unprincipled.

mediocre for too long and enjoyed a public redefinition. And I suppose the workings of my mind, such as they were, had been private for too long. My linguistic play moved into the world; like the intergalactic stories I told years before on Frank's berry-splattered truck bed, these papers with their circled, red B-pluses and A-minuses linked my mind to something outside it. I carried them around like a club emblem.

One day in the December of my senior year, Mr. MacFarland   6
asked me where I was going to go to college. I hadn't thought much about it. Many of the students I teach today spent their last year in high school with a physics text in one hand and the Stanford catalog in the other, but I wasn't even aware of what "entrance requirements" were. My folks would say that they wanted me to go to college and be a doctor, but I don't know how seriously I ever took that; it seemed a sweet thing to say, a bit of supportive family chatter, like telling a gangly[9] daughter she's graceful. The reality of higher education wasn't in my scheme of things: No one in the family had gone to college; only two of my uncles had completed high school. I figured I'd get a night job and go to the local junior college because I knew that Snyder and Company were going there to play ball. But I hadn't even prepared for that. When I finally said, "I don't know," MacFarland looked down at me—I was seated in his office—and said, "Listen, you can write."

My grades stank. I had As in biology and a handful of Bs in a   7
few English and social science classes. All the rest were Cs—or worse. MacFarland said I would do well in his class and laid down the law about doing well in the others. Still, the record for my first three years wouldn't have been acceptable to any four-year school. To nobody's surprise, I was turned down flat by USC and UCLA. But Jack MacFarland was on the case. He had received his bachelor's degree from Loyola University, so he made calls to old professors and talked to somebody in admissions and wrote me a strong letter. Loyola finally accepted me as a probationary student. I would be on trial for the first year, and if I did okay, I would be granted regular status. MacFarland also intervened to get me a loan, for I could never have afforded a private college without it. Four more years of religion classes and four more years of boys at one school, girls at another. But at least I was going to college. Amazing.

---

[9]*gangly:* ungracefully tall and thin.

Thinking Critically about This Reading

Rose writes, "While it's certainly true that we've created an educational system that encourages our best and brightest to become cynical grade collectors and, in general, have developed an obsession with evaluation and assessment, I must tell you that venal though it may have been, I loved getting good grades from MacFarland" (paragraph 5). Why did Rose love getting good grades from his English teacher? Why did those grades mean something different coming from MacFarland?

Questions for Study and Discussion

1. Why do you think Rose chose the title "I Just Wanna Be Average"? (Glossary: *Title*) How does it relate to the essay?
2. Describe Jack MacFarland. How does his appearance contrast with his ability as a teacher?
3. Rose's paragraphs are long and full of information, but they are very coherent. Summarize the topic of each of the seven paragraphs in separate sentences.
4. How does Rose organize paragraph 2? How does he prepare the reader for the concluding sentence: "The man [MacFarland] immersed us in language"?
5. Analyze the transitions between paragraphs 2 and 3 and between paragraphs 3 and 4. (Glossary: *Transition*) What techniques does Rose use to smoothly introduce the reader to different aspects of his relationship with MacFarland?
6. Rose introduces the reader to some of his classmates, quickly establishes their personalities, and names them in full: Jim Fitzsimmons, Skip Madison, Mike Dweetz, Steve Fusco (3). Why does he do this? How does it help him describe MacFarland?
7. Why does Rose have difficulty getting into college? How does he finally make it?

Classroom Activity Using Paragraphs

Write a unified, coherent, and adequately developed paragraph using one of the following topic sentences. Be sure to select details that clearly demonstrate or support the general statement you choose. In a classroom discussion students should compare and discuss those paragraphs developed from the same topic sentences as a way to understand the potential for variety in developing a topic sentence.

1. It was the noisiest place I had ever visited.
2. I was terribly frightened.
3. Signs of the sanitation strike were evident everywhere.
4. It was the best meal I've ever eaten.
5. Even though we lost, our team earned an "A" for effort.

Suggested Writing Assignments

1. Describe how one of your teachers has influenced your life. Write an essay about the teacher using Rose's essay as a model. Make sure that each paragraph accomplishes a specific purpose and is coherent enough to be readily summarized.

2. Write an essay about the process you went through to get into college. Did you visit different schools? Did a parent or relative pressure you to go to college? Had you always wanted to go, or did you make the decision in high school, like Rose, or after high school? Did a particular teacher help you? Make sure to develop your paragraphs fully and to include effective transitions between paragraphs.

The Last Shot

■ Tobias Wolff

Born in Birmingham, Alabama, in 1945, Tobias Wolff graduated from Hertford College, Oxford, England, in 1972 and then earned his M.A. from Stanford University, where he is now the Ward B. and Priscilla B. Woods Professor in the School of Humanities and Sciences. He has written two novels, Ugly Rumors *(1975) and* Old School *(2003), but his reputation rests mainly on his work in two genres: the short story and the memoir. His collections of short stories include* The Night in Question *(1997),* In the Garden of the North American Martyrs *(1981),* Back in the World *(1989), and* Our Story Begins: New and Collected Short Stories *(2008). Wolff's memoirs include* The Boy's Life *(1989) and* In Pharaoh's Army: Memoirs of the Lost War *(1994). Wyatt Mason wrote in the* London Review of Books, *"Typically, his protagonists face an acute moral dilemma, unable to reconcile what they know to be true with what they feel to be true. Duplicity is their great failing and Wolff's main theme." Wolff often contributes to a variety of literary journals and popular magazines, among them* The New Yorker, The Atlantic, *and* Harper's.*

In the following essay, taken from In Pharaoh's Army: Memoirs of the Lost War *(1994), Wolff recounts how he responded to a quotation he encountered while his son was writing a paper on the great English novelist and essayist George Orwell. As you read, pay particular attention to the way Wolff has developed his paragraphs.*

Reflecting on What You Know

Do you sometimes wonder what might have been the experiences of someone you know who was dear to you but who died? Do you ever feel guilty that you have continued on in life and are unable to share both the joys and troubled times you have known since that friend or relative has left you? How have you learned to cope with the situation?

George Orwell wrote an essay called "How the Poor Die" about his experience in the public ward of a Paris hospital during his lean years. I happened to read it not long ago because one of my sons was writing a paper on Orwell, and I wanted to be able to talk with him about it. The essay was new to me. I liked it for its gallows humor and cool watchfulness. Orwell had me in the palm of his hand until I came to this line: "It is a great thing to die in your own bed, though it is better still to die in your boots." 1

It stopped me cold. Figure of speech or not, he meant it, and anyway the words could not be separated from their martial beat and the rhetoric that promotes dying young as some kind of good deal. They affected me like an insult. I was so angry I had to get up and walk it off. Later I looked up the date of the essay and found that Orwell had written it before Spain and World War II, before he'd had the chance to see what dying in your boots actually means. (The truth is, many of those who "die in their boots" are literally blown right out of them.) 2

Several men I knew were killed in Vietnam. Most of them I didn't know well, and haven't thought much about since. But my friend Hugh Pierce was a different case. We were very close, and would have gone on being close, as I am with my other good friends from those years. He would have been one of them, another godfather for my children, another big-hearted man for them to admire and stay up late listening to. An old friend, someone I couldn't fool, who would hold me to the best dreams of my youth as I would hold him to his. 3

Instead of remembering Hugh as I knew him, I too often think of him in terms of what he never had a chance to be. The things the rest of us know, he will not know. He will not know what it is to make a life with someone else. To have a child slip in beside him as he lies reading on a Sunday morning. To work at, and then look back on, a labor of years. Watch the decline of his parents, and attend their dissolution. Lose faith. Pray anyway. Persist. We are made to persist, to complete the whole tour. That's how we find out who we are. 4

I know it's wrong to think of Hugh as an absence, a thwarted shadow. It's my awareness of his absence that I'm describing, and 5 maybe something else, some embarrassment, kept hidden even from myself, that I went on without him. To think of Hugh like this is to make selfish use of him. So, of course, is making him a character in a book. Let me at least remember him as he was.

He loved to jump. He was the one who started the "My Girl" business, singing and doing the Stroll to the door of the plane. I always take the position behind him, hand on his back, according to the drill we've been taught. I do not love to jump, to tell the truth, but I feel better about it when I'm connected to Hugh. Men are disappearing out the door ahead of us, the sound of the engine is getting louder. Hugh is singing in falsetto, doing a goofy routine with his hands. Just before he reaches the door he looks back and says something to me. I can't hear him for the wind. What? I say. He yells, *Are we having fun?* He laughs at the look on my face, then turns and takes his place in the door, and jumps, and is gone.

6

Thinking Critically about This Reading

Should Americans allow the branches of the armed forces to use advertisements that encourage our young men and women to put themselves in harm's way? Should recruitment ads emphasize world travel, adventure, education, service, patriotism, and comradeship while deemphasizing the very real dangers that military service might entail?

Questions for Study and Discussion

1. What is Wolff's thesis in this essay? (Glossary: *Thesis*)
2. What upsets Wolff about George Orwell's statement in paragraph 1?
3. Choose any two of Wolff's paragraphs, and examine each one for paragraph integrity by asking the following questions (consult the Glossary for definitions of any unfamiliar terms):

   • Does the paragraph have a clear topic sentence?
   • Does the author develop the paragraph clearly and effectively?
   • Is the paragraph unified?
   • Is the paragraph coherent?

   Be prepared to discuss your evaluation of the two paragraphs.

4. Explain how Wolff uses transitions to move from one paragraph to the next in his essay. Are the transitions always smooth? Explain. (Glossary: *Transition*)

5. Why do you think that Wolff begins paragraph 6 in the past tense and then switches to the present tense?

6. What is the last shot Wolff refers to in his title? (Glossary: *Title*)

Classroom Activity Using Paragraphs

Rearrange the sentences listed below to create an effective paragraph. Be ready to explain why you chose that particular order.

1. PGA golfer Fred Divot learned the hard way what overtraining could do.

2. Divot's case is typical, and most researchers believe that too much repetition makes it difficult for the athlete to reduce left-hemisphere brain activity.

3. Athletes who overtrain find it very difficult to get in the flow.

4. "Two weeks later, all I could think about was mechanics, and I couldn't hit a fairway to save my life."

5. Athletes think about mechanics (left hemisphere) rather than feel (right hemisphere), and they lose the ability to achieve peak performance.

6. "I was playing well, so I thought with a bit more practice, I could start winning on tour," Divot recalled.

Suggested Writing Assignments

1. Many readers think that the "last shot" in Wolff's title refers to the memory of the last time Wolf saw Hugh Pierce. Write an essay in which you recall the last time you saw someone who meant a lot to you. What was special about that person in that time and place? Be sure to construct paragraphs that have strong topic sentences, are unified, and are well developed.

2. The idea for Wolff's essay is triggered by his reading of a George Orwell statement that took him off-guard and made him angry. Write an essay that is similarly triggered by a statement you have read to which you have a strong negative reaction. Pay particular attention to your topic sentences, paragraph development, and the transitions that tie your paragraphs together.

Transitions

A **transition** is a word or phrase used to signal the relationships among ideas in an essay and to join the various parts of an essay together. Writers use transitions to relate ideas within sentences, between sentences, and between paragraphs. Perhaps the most common type of transition is the so-called transitional expression. Following is a list of transitional expressions categorized according to their functions.

Transitional Expressions
Addition
and, again, too, also, in addition, further, furthermore, moreover, besides
Cause and Effect
therefore, consequently, thus, accordingly, as a result, hence, then, so
Comparison
similarly, likewise, by comparison
Concession
to be sure, granted, of course, it is true, to tell the truth, certainly, with the exception of, although this may be true, even though, naturally
Contrast
but, however, in contrast, on the contrary, on the other hand, yet, nevertheless, after all, in spite of
Example
for example, for instance

Place
elsewhere, here, above, below, farther on, there, beyond, nearby, opposite to, around

Restatement
that is, as I have said, in other words, in simpler terms, to put it differently, simply stated

Sequence
first, second, third, next, finally

Summary
in conclusion, to conclude, to summarize, in brief, in short

Time
afterward, later, earlier, subsequently, at the same time, simultaneously, immediately, this time, until now, before, meanwhile, shortly, soon, currently, when, lately, in the meantime, formerly

Besides transitional expressions, there are two other important ways to make transitions: by using pronoun references and by repeating key words, phrases, and ideas. This paragraph begins with the phrase "Besides transitional expressions," which contains the transitional word *besides* and also repeats wording from the last sentence of the previous paragraph. Thus the reader knows that this discussion is moving toward a new but related idea. Repetition can also give a word or idea emphasis: "Foreigners look to America as a land of freedom. Freedom, however, is not something all Americans enjoy."

Pronoun references avoid monotonous repetition of nouns and phrases. Without pronouns, these two sentences are wordy and tiring to read: "Jim went to the concert, where he heard Beethoven's Ninth Symphony. Afterward, Jim bought a recording of the Ninth Symphony." A more graceful and readable passage results if two pronouns are substituted in the second sentence: "Afterward, he bought a recording of it." The second version has another advantage in that it is now more tightly related to the first sentence. The transition between the two sentences is smoother.

In the following example, notice how Rachel Carson uses transitional expressions, repetition of words and ideas, and pronoun references:

Under primitive agricultural conditions the farmer had few insect problems. *These* arose with the intensification of agriculture—the devotion of immense acreages to a single crop. *Such a system* set the stage for explosive increases in specific insect populations. Single-crop farming does not take advantage of the principles by which nature works; *it* is agriculture as an engineer might conceive it to be. Nature has introduced great variety into the landscape, but man has displayed a passion for simplifying *it. Thus he* undoes the built-in checks and balances by which nature holds the species within bounds. One important natural *check* is a limit on the amount of suitable habitat for each species. *Obviously then,* an insect that lives on wheat can build up its population to much higher levels on a farm devoted to wheat than on one in which wheat is intermingled with other crops to which the insect is not adapted.

> *Pronoun reference*

> *Repeated key idea*

> *Pronoun reference*

> *Pronoun reference*

> *Repeated key word*

> *Pronoun reference*

> *Transitional expression; pronoun reference*

> *Transitional expression*

The same thing happens in other situations. A generation or more ago, the towns of large areas of the United States lined their streets with the noble elm tree. *Now* the beauty *they* hopefully created is threatened with complete destruction as disease sweeps through the elms, carried by a beetle that would have only limited chance to build up large populations and to spread from tree to tree if the elms were only occasional trees in a richly diversified planting.

> *Repeated key idea*

> *Transitional expression; pronoun reference*

–Rachel Carson

Carson's transitions in this passage enhance its **coherence**—that quality of good writing that results when all sentences and paragraphs of an essay are effectively and naturally connected.

In the following four-paragraph sequence about a vegetarian's ordeal with her family at Thanksgiving each year, the writer uses transitions effectively to link one paragraph to another.

The holiday that I dread the most is fast approaching. The relatives will gather to gossip and bicker, the house will be filled with the smells of turkey, onions, giblets, and allspice, and I will be pursuing trivial conversations in the hope of avoiding any commentaries upon the state of my plate.

Reference to key idea in previous paragraph

Do not misunderstand me: I am not a scrooge. I enjoy the idea of Thanksgiving—the giving of thanks for blessings received in the past year and the opportunity to share an unhurried day with family and friends. The problem for me is that I am one of those freaky, misunderstood people who—as my family jokingly reminds me—eats "rabbit food." Because all traditional Western holidays revolve around food and more specifically around ham, turkey, lamb, or roast beef and their respective starchy accompaniments, it is no picnic for us vegetarians.

Repeated key word

The mention of the word *vegetarian* has, at various family get-togethers, caused my Great-Aunt Bertha to rant and rave for what seems like hours about those "liberal conspirators." Other relations cough or groan or simply stare, change the subject or reminisce about somebody they used to know who was "into that," and some proceed either to demand that I defend my position or try to talk me out of it. That is why I try to avoid the subject, but especially during the holidays.

Transitional time reference

In years past I have had about as many *successes as failures in steering comments about my food toward other topics.* Politics and religion are the easiest outs, guaranteed to immerse the family in a heated debate lasting until the loudest shouter has been abandoned amidst empty pie plates, wine corks, and rumpled linen napkins. I prefer, however, to use this tactic as a last resort. Holidays are supposed to be for relaxing.

Repeated key idea

–Mundy Wilson-Libby, student

On Being 17, Bright, and Unable to Read

■ **David Raymond**

David Raymond was born in 1959 in Connecticut. When the following article appeared in the New York Times *in 1976, Raymond was a junior in high school. In 1981, Raymond graduated from Curry College outside of Boston, one of the few colleges with learning-disability programs at the time. He and his family now live in Fairfield, Connecticut, where he works as a builder.*

    In his essay, Raymond poignantly discusses the great difficulties he had with reading because of his dyslexia and the many problems he experienced in school as a result. As you read, pay attention to the simple and unassuming quality of the words he uses to convey his ideas and the way that naturalness of diction contributes to the essay's informal yet sincere tone. Notice how he transitions from one paragraph to the next with repeated words, repeated key ideas, and pronoun references.

Reflecting on What You Know

One of the fundamental skills that we are supposed to learn in school is how to read. How would you rate yourself as a reader? Would you like to be able to read better? How important is reading in your everyday life?

One day a substitute teacher picked me to read aloud from the textbook. When I told her "No, thank you," she came unhinged. She thought I was acting smart, and told me so. I kept calm, and that got her madder and madder. We must have spent 10 minutes trying to solve the problem, and finally she got so red in the face I thought she'd blow up. She told me she'd see me after class.

Maybe someone like me was a new thing for that teacher. But she wasn't new to me. I've been through scenes like that all my life. You see,

197

even though I'm 17 and a junior in high school, I can't read because I have dyslexia.[1] I'm told I read "at a fourth-grade level," but from where I sit, that's not reading. You can't know what that means unless you've been there. It's not easy to tell how it feels when you can't read your homework assignments or the newspaper or a menu in a restaurant or even notes from your own friends.

3 My family began to suspect I was having problems almost from the first day I started school. My father says my early years in school were the worst years of his life. They weren't so good for me, either. As I look back on it now, I can't find the words to express how bad it really was. I wanted to die. I'd come home from school screaming, "I'm dumb. I'm dumb—I wish I were dead!"

4 I guess I couldn't read anything at all then—not even my own name—and they tell me I didn't talk as good as other kids. But what I remember about those days is that I couldn't throw a ball where it was supposed to go, I couldn't learn to swim, and I wouldn't learn to ride a bike, because no matter what anyone told me, I knew I'd fail.

5 Sometimes my teachers would try to be encouraging. When I couldn't read the words on the board they'd say, "Come on, David, you know that word." Only I didn't. And it was embarrassing. I just felt dumb. And dumb was how the kids treated me. They'd make fun of me every chance they got, asking me to spell "cat" or something like that. Even if I knew how to spell it, I wouldn't; they'd only give me another word. Anyway, it was awful, because more than anything I wanted friends. On my birthday when I blew out the candles I didn't wish I could learn to read; what I wished for was that the kids would like me.

6 With the bad reports coming from school, and with me moaning about wanting to die and how everybody hated me, my parents began looking for help. That's when the testing started. The school tested me, the child guidance center tested me, private psychiatrists tested me. Everybody knew something was wrong—especially me.

7 It didn't help much when they stuck a fancy name onto it. I couldn't pronounce it then—I was only in second grade—and I was ashamed to talk about it. Now it rolls off my tongue, because I've been living with it for a lot of years—dyslexia.

8 All through elementary school it wasn't easy. I was always having to do things that were "different," things the other kids didn't have to do. I had to go to a child psychiatrist, for instance.

---

[1]*dyslexia:* a learning disorder that impairs the ability to read.

One summer my family forced me to go to a camp for children 9 with reading problems. I hated the idea, but the camp turned out pretty good, and I had a good time. I met a lot of kids who couldn't read and somehow that helped. The director of the camp said I had a higher I.Q. than 90 percent of the population. I didn't believe him.

About the worst thing I had to do in fifth and sixth grade was go 10 to a special education class in another school in our town. A bus picked me up, and I didn't like that at all. The bus also picked up emotionally disturbed kids and retarded kids. It was like going to a school for the retarded. I always worried that someone I knew would see me on that bus. It was a relief to go to the regular junior high school.

Life began to change a little for me then, because I began to feel 11 better about myself. I found the teachers cared; they had meetings about me and I worked harder for them for a while. I began to work on the potter's wheel, making vases and pots that the teachers said were pretty good. Also, I got a letter for being on the track team. I could always run pretty fast.

At high school the teachers are good and everyone is trying to help 12 me. I've gotten honors some marking periods and I've won a letter on the cross-country team. Next quarter I think the school might hold a show of my pottery. I've got some friends. But there are still some embarrassing times. For instance, every time there is writing in the class, I get up and go to the special education room. Kids ask me where I go all the time. Sometimes I say, "to Mars."

Homework is a real problem. During free periods in school I go 13 into the special ed room and staff members read assignments to me. When I get home my mother reads to me. Sometimes she reads an assignment into a tape recorder, and then I go into my room and listen to it. If we have a novel or something like that to read, she reads it out loud to me. Then I sit down with her and we do the assignment. She'll write, while I talk my answers to her. Lately I've taken to dictating into a tape recorder, and then someone—my father, a private tutor, or my mother—types up what I've dictated. Whatever homework I do takes someone else's time, too. That makes me feel bad.

We had a big meeting in school the other day—eight of us, four 14 from the guidance department, my private tutor, my parents, and me. The subject was me. I said I wanted to go to college, and they told me about colleges that have facilities and staff to handle people like me. That's nice to hear.

As for what happens after college, I don't know and I'm worried   15
about that. How can I make a living if I can't read? Who will hire me?
How will I fill out the application form? The only thing that gives me
any courage is the fact that I've learned about well-known people who
couldn't read or had other problems and still made it. Like Albert
Einstein,[2] who didn't talk until he was 4 and flunked math. Like
Leonardo da Vinci,[3] who everyone seems to think had dyslexia.

I've told this story because maybe some teacher will read it and go   16
easy on a kid in the classroom who has what I've got. Or maybe some
parent will stop nagging his kid, and stop calling him lazy. Maybe he's
not lazy or dumb. Maybe he just can't read and doesn't know what's
wrong. Maybe he's scared, like I was.

Thinking Critically about This Reading

Raymond writes about having to take a bus to another school in his
town in order to attend special education classes: "I always worried that
someone I knew would see me on that bus" (paragraph 10). Why doesn't
Raymond want his classmates to know that he attends special education
classes? What does he do to keep his learning disability a secret?

Questions for Study and Discussion

1. Writers often use repeated words and phrases, transitional expressions, pronouns that refer to a specific antecedent, and repeated
   key ideas to connect one paragraph to another. What types of
   transitional devices does Raymond use in his essay? Cite specific
   examples.

2. Raymond uses many colloquial and idiomatic expressions, such
   as "she came unhinged" and "she got so red in the face I thought
   she'd blow up" (1). (Glossary: *Colloquial Expression*) Identify
   other examples of such diction, and tell how they affect your reaction to the essay.

3. How would you describe Raymond's tone?

---

[2]*Albert Einstein* (1879–1955): German-American physicist.
[3]*Leonardo da Vinci* (1452–1519): Italian painter, draftsman, sculptor, architect, and
engineer.

4. What is dyslexia? Is it essential for an understanding of the essay that we know more about dyslexia than Raymond tells us? Explain.

5. What is Raymond's purpose? (Glossary: *Purpose*)

6. What does Raymond's story tell us about the importance of our early childhood experiences?

Classroom Activity Using Transitions

In *The New York Times Complete Manual of Home Repair,* Bernard Gladstone gives directions for applying blacktop sealer to a driveway. His directions appear below in scrambled order. First, read all Gladstone's twelve sentences carefully. Next, arrange the sentences in what seems to you to be the logical sequence. Finally, identify places where Gladstone has used transitional expressions, the repetition of words and ideas, and pronoun reference to give coherence to his paragraph.

1. A long-handled pushbroom or roofing brush is used to spread the coating evenly over the entire area.

2. Care should be taken to make certain the entire surface is uniformly wet, though puddles should be swept away if water collects in low spots.

3. Greasy areas and oil slicks should be scraped up, then scrubbed thoroughly with a detergent solution.

4. With most brands there are just three steps to follow.

5. In most cases one coat of sealer will be sufficient.

6. The application of blacktop sealer is best done on a day when the weather is dry and warm, preferably while the sun is shining on the surface.

7. This should not be applied until the first coat is completely dry.

8. First sweep the surface absolutely clean to remove all dust, dirt, and foreign material.

9. To simplify spreading and to ensure a good bond, the surface of the driveway should be wet down thoroughly by sprinkling with a hose.

10. However, for surfaces in poor condition a second coat may be required.

11. The blacktop sealer is next stirred thoroughly and poured on while the surface is still damp.

12. The sealer should be allowed to dry overnight (or longer if recommended by the manufacturer) before normal traffic is resumed.

Suggested Writing Assignments

1. After explaining his learning disability and how he plans to deal with it in college, Raymond goes on to say, "As for what happens after college, I don't know and I'm worried about that" (15). Write an essay in which you explain what worries you about life after college. Are you concerned about finding a job, paying off student loans, or moving away from friends and family, for example? Are you looking forward to living in "the real world," as so many college students call the postgraduation world? Why or why not?

2. Imagine that you and your friends have plans to go to a concert next weekend. However, you will not be able to attend because you have a research paper due the following Monday and you haven't even chosen a topic yet. Write an e-mail in which you apologize to your friends and explain how you procrastinated. Make sure your e-mail is coherent and flows well by using transitional expressions to help readers follow what you did instead of working on your paper.

Becoming a Writer

■ **Russell Baker**

Russell Baker has had a long and distin-guished career as a newspaper reporter and columnist. He was born in Morrisonville, Virginia, in 1925 and graduated from Johns Hopkins University in 1947. *He got his first newspaper job with the* Baltimore Sun *and moved to the* New York Times *in 1954, where he wrote the "Observer" column from 1962 to 1998. His columns have been collected in numerous books over the years. In 1979, he was awarded the Pulitzer Prize, journalism's highest award, as well as the George Polk Award for commentary.* Baker's *memoir,* Growing Up *(1983), also received a Pulitzer. His autobiographical follow-up,* The Good Times, *appeared in 1989. His other works include* Russell Baker's Book of American Humor *(1993);* Inventing the Truth: The Art and Craft of Memoir *(1998, with William Zinsser and Jill Ker Conway); and* Looking Back *(2002), a collection of his essays for the* New York Review of Books. *From 1992 to 2004, he hosted the PBS television series* Exxon-Mobil Masterpiece Theater. *Baker now lives in Leesburg, Virginia.*

The following selection is from Growing Up. *As you read Baker's account of how he discovered his abilities as a writer, no-tice how effectively he uses repetition of key words and ideas to achieve coherence and to emphasize his emotional responses to the events he describes.*

Reflecting on What You Know

Life is full of moments that change us, for better or worse, in major and minor ways. We decide what hobbies we like and dislike, whom we want to date and perhaps eventually marry, what we want to study in school, what career we eventually pursue. Identify an event that changed your life or helped you make an important decision. How did it clarify your situation? How might your life be different if the event had never happened?

The notion of becoming a writer had flickered off and on in my   1
head . . . but it wasn't until my third year in high school that the
possibility took hold. Until then I'd been bored by everything associated with English courses. I found English grammar dull and baffling. I
hated the assignments to turn out "compositions," and went at them
like heavy labor, turning out leaden, lackluster paragraphs that were
agonies for teachers to read and for me to write. The classics thrust on
me to read seemed as deadening as chloroform.[1]

When our class was assigned to Mr. Fleagle for third-year English   2
I anticipated another grim year in that dreariest of subjects. Mr. Fleagle
was notorious among City students for dullness and inability to inspire. He was said to be stuffy, dull, and hopelessly out of date. To me
he looked to be sixty or seventy and prim to a fault. He wore primly
severe eyeglasses, his wavy hair was primly cut and primly combed.
He wore prim vested suits with neckties blocked primly against the
collar buttons of his primly starched white shirts. He had a primly
pointed jaw, a primly straight nose, and a prim manner of speaking
that was so correct, so gentlemanly, that he seemed a comic antique.

I anticipated a listless, unfruitful year with Mr. Fleagle and for a   3
long time was not disappointed. We read *Macbeth*. Mr. Fleagle loved
Macbeth and wanted us to love it too, but he lacked the gift of infecting
others with his own passion. He tried to convey the murderous ferocity
of Lady Macbeth one day by reading aloud the passage that concludes

> . . . I have given suck, and know
> How tender 'tis to love the babe that milks me.
> I would, while it was smiling in my face,
> Have plucked my nipple from his boneless gums . . .

The idea of prim Mr. Fleagle plucking his nipple from boneless gums
was too much for the class. We burst into gasps of irrepressible[2] snick-
ering. Mr. Fleagle stopped.

"There is nothing funny, boys, about giving suck to a babe. It is   4
the — the very essence of motherhood, don't you see."

He constantly sprinkled his sentences with "don't you see." It   5
wasn't a question but an exclamation of mild surprise at our ignorance.
"Your pronoun needs an antecedent, don't you see," he would say,

---

[1]*chloroform:* a chemical that puts one to sleep.
[2]*irrepressible:* unable to be restrained or controlled.

very primly. "The purpose of the Porter's scene, boys, is to provide comic relief from the horror, don't you see."

Late in the year we tackled the informal essay. "The essay, don't you see, is the . . ." My mind went numb. Of all forms of writing, none seemed so boring as the essay. Naturally we would have to write informal essays. Mr. Fleagle distributed a homework sheet offering us a choice of topics. None was quite so simpleminded as "What I Did on My Summer Vacation," but most seemed to be almost as dull. I took the list home and dawdled until the night before the essay was due. Sprawled on the sofa, I finally faced up to the grim task, took the list out of my notebook, and scanned it. The topic on which my eye stopped was "The Art of Eating Spaghetti." 6

This title produced an extraordinary sequence of mental images. Surging up from the depths of memory came a vivid recollection of a night in Belleville when all of us were seated around the supper table— Uncle Allen, my mother, Uncle Charlie, Doris, Uncle Hal—and Aunt Pat served spaghetti for supper. Spaghetti was an exotic treat in those days. Neither Doris nor I had ever eaten spaghetti, and none of the adults had enough experience to be good at it. All the good humor of Uncle Allen's house reawoke in my mind as I recalled the laughing arguments we had that night about the socially respectable method for moving spaghetti from plate to mouth. 7

Suddenly I wanted to write about that, about the warmth and good feeling of it, but I wanted to put it down simply for my own joy, not for Mr. Fleagle. It was a moment I wanted to recapture and hold for myself. I wanted to relive the pleasure of an evening at New Street. To write it as I wanted, however, would violate all the rules of formal composition I'd learned in school, and Mr. Fleagle would surely give it a failing grade. Never mind. I would write something else for Mr. Fleagle after I had written this thing for myself. 8

When I finished it the night was half gone and there was no time left to compose a proper, respectable essay for Mr. Fleagle. There was no choice next morning but to turn in my private reminiscence of Belleville. Two days passed before Mr. Fleagle returned the graded papers, and he returned everyone's but mine. I was bracing myself for a command to report to Mr. Fleagle immediately after school for discipline when I saw him lift my paper from his desk and rap for the class's attention. 9

"Now, boys," he said, "I want to read you an essay. This is titled 'The Art of Eating Spaghetti.'" 10

And he started to read. My words! He was reading *my words* out 11
loud to the entire class. What's more, the entire class was listening.
Listening attentively. Then somebody laughed, then the entire class was
laughing, and not in contempt and ridicule, but with open-hearted
enjoyment. Even Mr. Fleagle stopped two or three times to repress a
small prim smile.

I did my best to avoid showing pleasure, but what I was feeling 12
was pure ecstasy at this startling demonstration that my words had
the power to make people laugh. In the eleventh grade, at the eleventh
hour as it were, I had discovered a calling. It was the happiest moment
of my entire school career. When Mr. Fleagle finished he put the final
seal on my happiness by saying, "Now that, boys, is an essay, don't you
see. It's—don't you see—it's of the very essence of the essay, don't
you see. Congratulations, Mr. Baker."

For the first time, light shone on a possibility. It wasn't a very heart- 13
ening possibility, to be sure. Writing couldn't lead to a job after high
school, and it was hardly honest work, but Mr. Fleagle had opened a
door for me. After that I ranked Mr. Fleagle among the finest teachers
in the school.

Thinking Critically about This Reading

In paragraph 11 Baker states, "And he started to read. My words! He
was reading *my words* out loud to the entire class. What's more, the
entire class was listening. Listening attentively." Why was this episode
so key to Baker's decision to become a writer? Why did it lead him to
rank "Mr. Fleagle among the finest teachers in the school" (13)?

Questions for Study and Discussion

1. Baker makes good use of transitional expressions, repetition of
   words and ideas, and pronoun references in paragraphs 1 and 2.
   Carefully reread the paragraphs, and identify where he employs
   these techniques.
2. Examine the transitions Baker uses between paragraphs from
   paragraph 4 to the end of the essay. Explain how these transitions work to make the paragraphs flow from one to another.
3. How does Baker describe his English teacher, Mr. Fleagle, in the
   second paragraph? (Glossary: *Description*) Why does he repeat the

word *prim* throughout the paragraph? Why is the vivid description important to the essay as a whole?

4. What does Baker write about in his informal essay for Mr. Fleagle? Why does he write about this subject? Why doesn't he want to turn the essay in?

5. What door does Mr. Fleagle open for Baker? Why is Baker reluctant to pursue the opportunity?

Classroom Activity Using Transitions

Read the following three paragraphs. Provide transitions between paragraphs so that the narrative flows smoothly.

> In the late 1950s, I got lost on a camping trip in the Canadian wilderness. My only thought was to head south, toward warmth and civilization. My perilous journey was exhausting: the cold sapped my strength, and there were few places to find shelter and rest.
>
> There I found friendly faces and a warm fire. As I built my strength, I tried to communicate with the villagers, but they did not understand me. I came to the conclusion that I could stay in the village and wait—perhaps forever—for help to come, or I could strike out on my own again.
>
> I heard a gurgling sound. It was running water. Running water! Spring was here at last. Perhaps I would survive after all. I picked up my pack, squared my shoulders, and marched, the afternoon sun a beautiful sight, still ahead, but starting to drift to my right.

Suggested Writing Assignments

1. Using as a model Baker's effort to write about eating spaghetti, write something from your own experience that you would like to record for yourself, not necessarily for the teacher. Don't worry about writing a formal essay. Simply use language with which you are comfortable to convey why the event or experience is important to you.

2. Write an essay in which you describe how your perception of someone important in your life changed. How did you feel about the person at first? How do you feel now? What brought about the change? What effect did the transition have on you? Make sure that your essay is coherent and flows well: use transitional expressions to help the reader follow the story of *your* transition.

The Magic of the Family Meal

■ **Nancy Gibbs**

Born in 1960 in New York City, Nancy Gibbs graduated with honors in history from Yale University in 1982. She continued her studies at Oxford University as a Marshall scholar, earning a master's degree in politics and philosophy in 1984. She went to work at Time *magazine in 1985 and became a feature writer in 1988. In 1991, she was named a senior editor and later became chief political writer. In that capacity, she wrote more than 20 cover stories about the 1996 and 2000 presidential campaigns and elections. In 2002,* Time *appointed her editor-at-large. In her years at* Time, *she has authored more than 130 cover stories, including the one for September 11, 2001, for which she received the National Magazine Award in 2002, and another entitled "Faith, God, and the Oval Office" about the role of religion in the 2004 George W. Bush–John Kerry presidential campaign. Gibbs also coauthored* Preacher and the Presidents: Billy Graham in the White House *(2007) with Michael Duffy. She lives in Westchester, New York, with her husband and two daughters.*

In "The Magic of the Family Meal," an essay first published in the June 12, 2006, issue of Time, *Gibbs reports on the current status of family dining in the United States and the ways that this dying tradition has shown a resurgence in recent years. Because research shows that children who eat with their parents are healthier, happier, and better students than children who don't, Gibbs advises that families should "make meals together a priority." As you read Gibbs's essay, notice how she achieves unity and coherence by using repeated words and phrases, transitional expressions, pronouns with specific antecedents, and repeated key ideas to connect one paragraph to another.*

Reflecting on What You Know

What was dinnertime like in your house while you were growing up? How many times a week did you eat dinner with your family? What activities and obligations made it difficult to eat together as a family? For you, what is the value of the so-called family meal?

Close your eyes and picture Family Dinner. June Cleaver is in an apron and pearls, Ward[1] in a sweater and tie. The napkins are linen, the children are scrubbed, steam rises from the greenbean casserole, and even the dog listens intently to what is being said. This is where the tribe comes to transmit wisdom, embed expectations, confess, conspire, forgive, repair. The idealized version is as close to a regular worship service, with its litanies and lessons and blessings, as a family gets outside a sanctuary.

That ideal runs so strong and so deep in our culture and psyche that when experts talk about the value of family dinners, they may leave aside the clutter of contradictions. Just because we eat together does not mean we eat right: Domino's alone delivers a million pizzas on an average day. Just because we are sitting together doesn't mean we have anything to say: children bicker and fidget and daydream; parents stew over the remains of the day. Often the richest conversations, the moments of genuine intimacy, take place somewhere else, in the car, say, on the way back from soccer at dusk, when the low light and lack of eye contact allow secrets to surface.

Yet for all that, there is something about a shared meal—not some holiday blowout, not once in a while but regularly, reliably—that anchors a family even on nights when the food is fast and the talk cheap and everyone has someplace else they'd rather be. And on those evenings when the mood is right and the family lingers, caught up in an idea or an argument explored in a shared safe place where no one is stupid or shy or ashamed, you get a glimpse of the power of this habit and why social scientists say such communion acts as a kind of vaccine, protecting kids from all manner of harm.

In fact, it's the experts in adolescent development who wax most emphatic about the value of family meals, for it's in the teenage years that this daily investment pays some of its biggest dividends. Studies show that the more often families eat together, the less likely kids are

----

[1]*June and Ward Cleaver:* the parents in the classic family sitcom *Leave It to Beaver,* which aired from 1957 to 1963.

to smoke, drink, do drugs, get depressed, develop eating disorders, and consider suicide, and the more likely they are to do well in school, delay having sex, eat their vegetables, learn big words, and know which fork to use. "If it were just about food, we would squirt it into their mouths with a tube," says Robin Fox, an anthropologist who teaches at Rutgers University in New Jersey, about the mysterious way that family dinner engraves our souls. "A meal is about civilizing children. It's about teaching them to be a member of their culture."

The most probing study of family eating patterns was published last year by the National Center on Addiction and Substance Abuse (CASA) at Columbia University and reflects nearly a decade's worth of data gathering. The researchers found essentially that family dinner gets better with practice; the less often a family eats together, the worse the experience is likely to be, the less healthy the food, and the more meager the talk. Among those who eat together three or fewer times a week, 45 percent say the TV is on during meals (as opposed to 37 percent of all households), and nearly one-third say there isn't much conversation. Such kids are also more than twice as likely as those who have frequent family meals to say there is a great deal of tension among family members, and they are much less likely to think their parents are proud of them.

The older that kids are, the more they may need this protected time together, but the less likely they are to get it. Although a majority of twelve-year-olds in the CASA study said they had dinner with a parent seven nights a week, only a quarter of seventeen-year-olds did. Researchers have found all kinds of intriguing educational and ethnic patterns. The families with the least educated parents, for example, eat together the most; parents with less than a high school education share more meals with their kids than do parents with high school diplomas or college degrees. That may end up acting as a generational corrective; kids who eat most often with their parents are 40 percent more likely to say they get mainly As and Bs in school than kids who have two or fewer family dinners a week. Foreign-born kids are much more likely to eat with their parents. When researchers looked at ethnic and racial breakdowns, they found that more than half of Hispanic teens ate with a parent at least six times a week, in contrast to 40 percent of black teens and 39 percent of whites.

Back in the really olden days, dinner was seldom a ceremonial event for U.S. families. Only the very wealthy had a separate dining room. For most, meals were informal, a kind of rolling refueling; often only the men sat down. Not until the mid-nineteenth century did the day acquire its middle-class rhythms and rituals; a proper dining room became a Victorian aspiration. When children were eight or nine, they were allowed to join the adults at the table for instruction in proper etiquette. By the turn of the century, restaurants had appeared to cater to clerical workers, and in time, eating out became a recreational sport. Family dinner in the Norman Rockwell mode had taken hold by the 1950s: Mom cooked, Dad carved, son cleared, daughter did the dishes.

All kinds of social and economic and technological factors then 8 conspired to shred that tidy picture to the point that the frequency of family dining fell about a third over the next thirty years. With both parents working and the kids shuttling between sports practices or attached to their screens at home, finding a time for everyone to sit around the same table, eating the same food and listening to one another, became a quaint kind of luxury. Meanwhile, the message embedded in the microwave was that time spent standing in front of a stove was time wasted.

But something precious was lost, anthropologist Fox argues, when 9 cooking came to be cast as drudgery and meals as discretionary. "Making food is a sacred event," he says. "It's so absolutely central—far more central than sex. You can keep a population going by having sex once a year, but you have to eat three times a day." Food comes so easily to us now, he says, that we have lost a sense of its significance. When we had to grow the corn and fight off predators, meals included a serving of gratitude. "It's like the American Indians. When they killed a deer, they said a prayer over it," says Fox. "That is civilization. It is an act of politeness over food. Fast food has killed this. We have reduced eating to sitting alone and shoveling it in. There is no ceremony in it."

Or at least there wasn't for many families until researchers in the 10 1980s began looking at the data and doing all kinds of regression analyses that showed how a shared pot roast could contribute to kids' success and health. What the studies could not prove was what is cause and what is effect. Researchers speculate that maybe kids who eat a lot of family meals have less unsupervised time and thus less chance to get into trouble. Families who make meals a priority also tend to spend more time on reading for pleasure and homework. A whole basket of values and habits, of which a common mealtime is only one, may work together to ground kids. But it's a bellwether, and baby boomers who won't listen to their instincts will often listen to the experts: the 2005 CASA study found that the number of adolescents eating with their family most nights has increased 23 percent since 1998.

That rise may also reflect a deliberate public-education campaign,   11
including public-service announcements on TV Land and Nick at Nite
that are designed to convince families that it's worth some inconvenience or compromise to make meals together a priority. The enemies
here are laziness and leniency: "We're talking about a contemporary
style of parenting, particularly in the middle class, that is overindulgent
of children," argues William Doherty, a professor of family social science at the University of Minnesota at Minneapolis and author of *The
Intentional Family: Simple Rituals to Strengthen Family Ties.* "It treats
them as customers who need to be pleased." By that, he means the willingness of parents to let dinner be an individual improvisation—no routine, no rules, leave the television on, everyone eats what they want,
teenagers take a plate to their room so they can keep IMing their friends.

The food-court mentality—Johnny eats a burrito, Dad has a   12
burger, and Mom picks pasta—comes at a cost. Little humans often
resist new tastes; they need some nudging away from the salt and fat
and toward the fruits and fiber. A study in the *Archives of Family
Medicine* found that more family meals tends to mean less soda and
fried food and far more fruits and vegetables.

Beyond promoting balance and variety in kids' diets, meals   13
together send the message that citizenship in a family entails certain
standards beyond individual whims. This is where a family builds its
identity and culture. Legends are passed down, jokes rendered, eventually the wider world examined through the lens of a family's values. In
addition, younger kids pick up vocabulary and a sense of how conversation is structured. They hear how a problem is solved, learn to listen
to other people's concerns, and respect their tastes. "A meal is about
sharing," says Doherty. "I see this trend where parents are preparing
different meals for each kid, and it takes away from that. The sharing
is the compromise. Not everyone gets their ideal menu every night."

Doherty heard from a YMCA camp counselor about the number   14
of kids who arrive with a list of foods they won't eat and who require
basic instruction from counselors on how to share a meal. "They have
to teach them how to pass food around and serve each other. The kids
have to learn how to eat what's there. And they have to learn how to
remain seated until everyone else is done." The University of Kansas
and Michigan State offer students coaching on how to handle a business lunch, including what to do about food they don't like ("Eat it
anyway") and how to pass the salt and pepper ("They're married.
They never take separate vacations").

When parents say their older kids are too busy or resistant to   15
come to the table the way they did when they were seven, the dinner
evangelists produce evidence to the contrary. The CASA study found
that a majority of teens who ate three or fewer meals a week with
their families wished they did so more often. Parents sometimes seem
a little too eager to be rejected by their teenage sons and daughters,
suggests Miriam Weinstein, a freelance journalist who wrote *The
Surprising Power of Family Meals*. "We've sold ourselves on the idea
that teenagers are obviously sick of their families, that they're bonded
to their peer group," she says. "We've taken it to an extreme. We've
taken it to mean that a teenager has no need for his family. And that's
just not true." She scolds parents who blame their kids for undermin-
ing mealtime when the adults are coconspirators. "It's become a badge
of honor to say, 'I have no time. I am so busy,'" she says. "But we make
a lot of choices, and we have a lot more discretion than we give ourselves credit for," she says. Parents may be undervaluing themselves
when they conclude that sending kids off to every conceivable
extracurricular activity is a better use of time than an hour spent
around a table, just talking to Mom and Dad.

The family-meal crusaders offer lots of advice to parents seeking   16
to recenter their household on the dinner table. Groups like Ready, Set,
Relax!, based in Ridgewood, New Jersey, have dispensed hundreds of
kits to towns from Kentucky to California, coaching communities on
how to fight overscheduling and carve out family downtime. More
schools are offering basic cooking instruction. It turns out that when
kids help prepare a meal, they are much more likely to eat it, and it's a
useful skill that seems to build self-esteem. Research on family meals
does not explore whether it makes a difference if dinner is with two
parents or one or even whether the meal needs to be dinner. For families whose schedules make evenings together a challenge, breakfast or
lunch may have the same value. So pull up some chairs. Lose the TV.
Let the phone go unanswered. And see where the moment takes you.

Thinking Critically about This Reading

In paragraph 6, Gibbs states that "researchers have found [that] all
kinds of intriguing educational and ethnic patterns" surround family
dining. Did any of the statistical patterns cited in that paragraph surprise
you? How well do these statistical findings fit your own experiences
and observations? What conclusions, if any, can you draw from them?

Questions for Study and Discussion

1. According to Gibbs, what happens at the "idealized" family dinner? What do you think she means when she says, "The idealized version is as close to a regular worship service, with its litanies and lessons and blessings, as a family gets outside a sanctuary" (paragraph 1)?

2. What are the dividends for teenagers who grow up in a family that eats together? In what ways do family dinners act "as a kind of vaccine, protecting kids from all manner of harm" (3)?

3. Do you agree with Gibbs when she says, "The older that kids are, the more they may need this protected time [family meals] together" (6)? Explain why or why not.

4. Gibbs cites a number of surveys, studies, and experts in her essay to both explain and support the points she makes. Which information did you find most interesting? Most convincing?

5. Identify the strategies Gibbs uses to transition between paragraphs 1 and 2, 7 and 8, 8 and 9, 10 and 11, 11 and 12, and 12 and 13. How does each strategy work? Explain.

6. What cultural factors during the 1960s, 1970s, and 1980s undermined and helped destroy the ritual of family dining? According to Gibbs, what has happened since then to reinvigorate the idea of family meals?

7. According to Robin Fox, with the advent of fast food "we have reduced eating to sitting alone and shoveling it in. There is no ceremony in it" (9). What nutritional, social, and family values does a "shared pot roast" offer children? Do you think that "it's worth some inconvenience or compromise to make meals together a priority" (11)? Explain.

Classroom Activity Using Transitions

The following sentences, which make up the first paragraph of E. B. White's essay "Once More to the Lake," have been rearranged. Place the sentences in what seems to you to be a coherent sequence by relying on language signals like transitions, repeated words, pronouns, and temporal references. Be prepared to explain your reasons for the placement of each sentence.

1. I have since become a salt-water man, but sometimes in summer there are days when the restlessness of the tides and the fearful cold of the sea water and the incessant wind which blows across the afternoon and into the evening make me wish for the placidity of a lake in the woods.

2. We all got ringworm from some kittens and had to rub Pond's Extract on our arms and legs night and morning, and my father rolled over in a canoe with all his clothes on; but outside of that the vacation was a success and from then on none of us ever thought there was any place in the world like that lake in Maine.

3. A few weeks ago this feeling got so strong I bought myself a couple of bass hooks and a spinner and returned to the lake where we used to go for a week's fishing and to revisit old haunts.

4. One summer, along about 1904, my father rented a camp on a lake in Maine and took us all there for the month of August.

5. We returned there summer after summer—always on August 1st for one month.

Suggested Writing Assignments

1. In paragraph 4, Gibbs quotes anthropologist Robin Fox: "A meal is about civilizing children. It's about teaching them to be a member of their culture." What exactly is Fox claiming here? What do children learn from eating meals with their family on a regular basis? Write an essay in which you agree or disagree with Fox's claim. Be sure to use examples from your own family experiences or observations of other families to illustrate and support your position.

2. Looking back on your own childhood and adolescence, how would you assess your family's mealtime experiences? Was mealtime in your house a family time, or did a "food-court mentality" (12) prevail? Was mealtime a place where your family built "its identity and culture" (13)? What did your parents do really well? What could they have done better? Based on your own experiences and observations, write an essay in which you offer advice to today's young parents. What insights can you offer parents to help them "recenter their household on the dinner table" (16)?

3. From February 20 to March 13, 1943, during the height of World War II, the *Saturday Evening Post* published Norman

Rockwell's now famous "The Four Freedoms" series of paintings, which were inspired by President Franklin D. Roosevelt's speech of the same name. When Gibbs states that "family dinner in the Norman Rockwell mode had taken hold by the 1950s" (7), she's undoubtedly referring to Rockwell's *Freedom from Want* painting, also popularly known as *Thanksgiving Dinner,* which captured the standard for family dining in the postwar era. After viewing Rockwell's painting online (search "Freedom from Want"), consider the following photograph by Michael Elins that accompanied Gibbs's essay in *Time* magazine. What were your first impressions of each picture? What feelings or ideas about family meals do you think that Rockwell and Elins are trying to convey to viewers? Do these two pictures evoke feelings of a past era for you, or do you think that they have something to offer us today? Write an essay in which you compare and contrast Rockwell's painting with Elin's photograph and discuss any insights into the value of family meals you gain from them.

© Michael Elins/Corbis.

Effective Sentences

Each of the following paragraphs describes the Canadian city of Vancouver, British Columbia. Although the content of both paragraphs is essentially the same, the first paragraph is written in sentences of nearly the same length and pattern, and the second paragraph in sentences of varying length and pattern.

Unvaried Sentences

Water surrounds Vancouver on three sides. The snow-crowned Coast Mountains ring the city on the northeast. Vancouver has a floating quality of natural loveliness. There is a curved beach at English Bay. This beach is in the shape of a half moon. Residential high-rises stand behind the beach. They are in pale tones of beige, blue, and ice-cream pink. Turn-of-the-century houses of painted wood frown upward at the glitter of office towers. Any urban glare is softened by folds of green lawns, flowers, fountains, and trees. Such landscaping appears to be unplanned. It links Vancouver to her ultimate treasure of greenness. That treasure is thousand-acre Stanley Park. Surrounding stretches of water dominate. They have image-evoking names like False Creek and Lost Lagoon. Sailboats and pleasure craft skim blithely across Burrard Inlet. Foreign freighters are out in English Bay. They await their turn to take on cargoes of grain.

Varied Sentences

Surrounded by water on three sides and ringed to the northeast by the snow-crowned Coast Mountains, Vancouver has a floating quality of natural loveliness. At English Bay, the half-moon curve of beach is backed by high-rises in pale tones of beige, blue, and ice-cream pink. Turn-of-the-century houses of painted wood frown upward at the glitter of office towers. Yet any urban glare is quickly softened by folds of green lawns, flowers, fountains, and trees that in a seemingly unplanned fashion link Vancouver to her ultimate treasure of greenness—thousand-acre Stanley Park. And always it is the surrounding stretches of water that dominate, with their image-evoking names like False Creek and Lost Lagoon. Sailboats and pleasure craft skim blithely across Burrard Inlet, while out in English Bay foreign freighters await their turn to take on cargoes of grain.

The difference between these two paragraphs is dramatic. The first is monotonous because of the sameness of the sentences and because the ideas are not related to one another in a meaningful way. The second paragraph is much more interesting and readable; its sentences vary in length and are structured to clarify the relationships among the ideas. Sentence variety, an important aspect of all good writing, should not be used for its own sake but should express ideas precisely and emphasize the most important ideas within each sentence. Sentence variety includes the use of subordination, periodic and loose sentences, dramatically short sentences, active and passive voice, coordination, and parallelism.

■ SENTENCE VARIETY

Subordination

Subordination, the process of giving one idea less emphasis than another in a sentence, is one of the most important characteristics of an effective sentence and a mature prose style. Writers subordinate ideas by introducing them either with subordinating conjunctions (*because, if, as though, while, when, after*) or with relative pronouns (*that, which, who, whomever, what*). Subordination not only deemphasizes some ideas, but also highlights others that the writer believes are more important.

There is nothing about an idea—*any* idea—that automatically makes it primary or secondary in importance. The writer decides what to emphasize, and he or she may choose to emphasize the less profound or noteworthy of two ideas. Consider, for example, the following sentence: "Melissa was reading a detective story while the national election results were televised." Everyone, including the author of the sentence, knows that the national election is a more noteworthy event than that Melissa was reading a detective story. But the sentence concerns Melissa, not the election, and so her reading is stated in the main clause, while the election news is subordinated in a dependent clause.

Generally, writers place the ideas they consider important in main clauses, and other ideas go into dependent clauses. For example:

> When she was thirty years old, she made her first solo flight across the Atlantic.

> When she made her first solo flight across the Atlantic, she was thirty years old.

The first sentence emphasizes the solo flight; in the second, the emphasis is on the pilot's age.

Periodic and Loose Sentences

Another way to achieve emphasis is to place the most important words, phrases, and clauses at the beginning or end of a sentence. The ending is the most emphatic part of a sentence, the beginning is less emphatic, and the middle is the least emphatic of all. The two sentences above about the thirty-year-old pilot put the main clause at the end, achieving special emphasis. The same thing occurs in a much longer kind of sentence, called a *periodic sentence,* in which the main idea is placed at the end, closest to the period. Here is an example:

> On the afternoon of the first day of spring, when the gutters were still heaped high with Monday's snow but the sky itself had been swept clean, we put on our galoshes and walked up the sunny side of Fifth Avenue to Central Park.
>
> –John Updike

By holding the main clause back, Updike keeps his readers in suspense and so puts the most emphasis possible on his main idea.

A *loose sentence,* on the other hand, states its main idea at the beginning and then adds details in subsequent phrases and clauses. Rewritten as a loose sentence, Updike's sentence might read like this:

> We put on our galoshes and walked up the sunny side of Fifth Avenue to Central Park on the afternoon of the first day of spring, when the gutters were still heaped high with Monday's snow but the sky itself had been swept clean.

The main idea still gets plenty of emphasis, since it is contained in a main clause at the beginning of the sentence. A loose sentence resembles the way people talk: it flows naturally and is easy to understand.

Dramatically Short Sentences

Another way to create emphasis is to use a *dramatically short sentence*. Especially following a long and involved sentence, a short declarative sentence helps drive a point home. Here are two examples:

> The qualities that Barbie promotes (slimness, youth, and beauty) allow no tolerance of gray hair, wrinkles, sloping posture, or failing eyesight and hearing. Barbie's perfect body is eternal.
>
> –Danielle Kuykendall, student

> The executive suite on the thirty-fifth floor of the Columbia Broadcasting System skyscraper in Manhattan is a tasteful blend of dark wood paneling, expensive abstract paintings, thick carpets, and pleasing colors. It has the quiet look of power.
>
> –David Wise

Active and Passive Voice

Finally, since the subject of a sentence is automatically emphasized, writers may choose to use the *active voice* when they want to emphasize the doer of an action and the *passive voice* when they want to downplay or omit the doer completely. Here are two examples:

> High winds pushed our sailboat onto the rocks, where the force of the waves tore it to pieces.

> Our sailboat was pushed by high winds onto the rocks, where it was torn to pieces by the force of the waves.
>
> –Liz Coughlan, student

The first sentence emphasizes the natural forces that destroyed the boat, while the second sentence focuses attention on the boat itself. The passive voice may be useful in placing emphasis, but it has important disadvantages. As the examples show, and as the terms suggest, active-voice verbs are more vigorous and vivid than the same verbs in the passive voice. Then, too, some writers use the passive voice to hide or evade responsibility. "It has been decided" conceals who did the deciding, whereas "I have decided" makes all clear. So the passive voice should be used only when necessary, as it is in this sentence.

■ SENTENCE EMPHASIS

Coordination

Often a writer wants to place equal emphasis on several facts or ideas. One way to do so is to give each its own sentence. For example, consider these three sentences about golfer Lorena Ochoa.

> Lorena Ochoa selected her club. She lined up her shot. She chipped the ball to within a foot of the pin.

But a long series of short, simple sentences quickly becomes tedious. Many writers would combine these three sentences by using **coordination**. The coordinating conjunctions *and, but, or, nor, for, so,* and *yet* connect words, phrases, and clauses of equal importance:

> Lorena Ochoa selected her club, lined up her shot, *and* chipped the ball to within a foot of the pin.
>
> –Will Briggs, student

By coordinating three sentences into one, the writer makes the same words easier to read and also shows that Ochoa's three actions are equally important parts of a single process.

Parallelism

When parts of a sentence are not only coordinated but also grammatically the same, they are parallel. **Parallelism** in a sentence is created by balancing a word with a word, a phrase with a phrase, or a clause with a clause. Here is a humorous example from the beginning of Mark Twain's *Adventures of Huckleberry Finn:*

> Persons attempting to find a motive in this narrative will be prosecuted; persons attempting to find a moral in it will be banished; persons attempting to find a plot in it will be shot.
>
> –Mark Twain

Parallelism is also often found in speeches. For example, in the last sentence of the Gettysburg Address, Lincoln proclaims his hope that "government of the people, by the people, for the people, shall not perish from the earth."

Childhood

■ **Alice Walker**

Alice Walker is a prolific writer of poetry, essays, and fiction and won the Pulitzer Prize for her novel The Color Purple. *She was born in Georgia in 1944, the youngest of eight children in a sharecropping family. She escaped a life of poverty and servitude by attending Spelman College in Georgia and then graduating from Sarah Lawrence College in New York. An African American activist and feminist, Walker has dealt with controversial subjects in her novels,* The Color Purple *(1982) and* Possessing the Secret of Joy *(1992), and in the nonfiction* Warrior Marks *(1993). Other widely acclaimed works by Walker include her collected poems,* Her Blue Body Everything We Know: Earthling Poems, 1965–1990 *(1991); a memoir entitled* The Same River Twice: Honoring the Difficult *(1996); a collection of essays,* Anything We Love Can Be Saved: A Writer's Activism *(1997); and a collection of stories,* The Way Forward Is with a Broken Heart *(2000). Walker's most recent work includes* Sent by Earth: A Message from the Grandmother Spirit after the Bombing of the World Trade Center and the Pentagon *(2001),* Absolute Trust in the Goodness of the Earth: New Poems *(2003), and* Hard Times Require Furious Dancing: New Poems *(2010).*

In the following essay, Walker uses her considerable craft to build sentences about how she was introduced to the wonders of planting and harvesting when she was a little girl and how she passed on her love of the earth and her people to her daughter.

Reflecting on What You Know

Think about your childhood memories. Which pleasant memory recurs often and leads you to believe that it has a significance greater than your other memories? What might be the significance of that memory?

One evening my daughter came to pick me up from the country; I had been expecting her for several hours. Almost as soon as she came through the door I asked if she knew how potatoes look before they are dug out of the ground. She wasn't sure. Then I will show you in the morning before we head back to the city, I told her.

I had begun to harvest my potato crop the day before. In the spring I planted five varieties: my favorite, Yellow Finn; Yukon Gold; Peruvian Purple; Irish white; and red new. Even though the summer had been chilly and there was morning shade from the large oak at the front of the garden, the potatoes came up quickly and developed into healthy plants. Jose, who helps me in the garden, had shoveled an extra collar of humus around each plant, and I was delighted as each of them began to bloom. It had been years since I planted potatoes. I planted them in the garden I'd previously devoted to corn, because I have a schedule that often means I am far away from my garden at just the time my corn becomes ripe. Having sped home to my garden three years in a row to a plot of overmatured, tasteless corn, I decided to plant potatoes instead, thinking the worst that could happen, if I was delayed elsewhere, would be a handful of potatoes nibbled by gophers or moles.

I had been dreading going back to the city, where I had more things to do than I cared to think about; I sat in the swing on the deck thinking hard about what would be my last supper in the country. I had bought some green peas from the roadside stand a few miles from my house, chard and kale were flourishing a few steps from my door, and I had brought up corn from a small hopeful planting in a lower garden. Tasting the corn, however, I discovered it had, as I'd feared, given up its sweetness and turned into starch. Then I remembered my potatoes! Grabbing a shovel, I went out to the garden and began to dig. The experience I had had digging the potatoes, before turning them into half of a delicious meal, was one I wanted my daughter to know.

After boiling, I ate my newly dug potatoes, several small Yellow Finns and two larger Peruvian Purples, with only a dressing of butter. Organic butter with a dash of sea salt—that reminded me of the butter my mother and grandmother used to make. As I ate the mouth-watering meal, I remembered them sitting patiently beside the brown or creamy white churn, moving the dasher up and down in a steady rhythmic motion until flecks of butter appeared at the top of the milk. These flecks grew until eventually there was enough butter to make a small mound. We owned a beautiful handcrafted butter press. It was sometimes my job to press its wooden carving of flowers into the hardening butter, making a cheerful and elegant design.

In the morning, just before packing the car for the ride to the city, I harvested an abundance of Chardonnay grapes, greenish silver and refreshingly sweet, a bucket of glistening eggplants, an armful of collards and chard and kale, some dark green and snake-like cucumbers, plus a small sack of figs and half a dozen late-summer peaches. Then I took my daughter out to the neat rows of potatoes, all beginning to turn brown. Using the shovel to scrape aside the dirt, I began to reveal, very slowly and carefully, the golden and purple potatoes that rested just beneath the plants. She was enchanted. It's just like . . . it's just like . . . she said. It's just like finding gold, I completed her thought. Yes! she said, her eyes wide.

Though my daughter is now thirty-one, her enthusiasm reminded me of my own when I was probably no more than three. My parents, exemplary farmers and producers of fine produce in garden and field, had enchanted me early in just this same way. As I scraped dirt aside from another potato plant and watched as my daughter began to fill her skirt with our treasure, I was taken back to a time when I was very young, perhaps too young even to speak. The very first memory I have is certainly preverbal; I was lifted up by my father or an older brother, very large and dark and shining men, and encouraged to pick red plums from a heavily bearing tree. The next is of going with my parents, in a farm wagon, to a watermelon patch that in memory seems to have been planted underneath pine trees. A farmer myself now, I realize this couldn't have been true. It is likely that to get to the watermelon patch we had to go through the pines. In any case, and perhaps this was preverbal as well, I remember the absolute wonder of rolling along in a creaky wooden wagon that was pulled by obedient if indifferent mules, arriving at a vast field, and being taken down and placed out of the way as my brothers and parents began to find watermelon after watermelon and to bring them back, apparently, as gifts for me! In a short time the wagon was filled with large green watermelons. And there were still dozens more left to grow larger, in the field! How had this happened? What miracle was this?

As soon as they finished filling the wagon, my father broke open a gigantic melon right on the spot. The "spot" being a handy boulder as broad as a table that happened to reside there, underneath the shady pines, beside the field. We were all given pieces of its delicious red and thirst-quenching heart. He then carefully, from my piece, removed all the glossy black seeds. If you eat one of these, he joked, poking at my protruding tummy, a watermelon just like this will grow inside you.

It will? My eyes were probably enormous. I must have looked 8
shocked.

Everyone laughed. 9

If you put the seed into the ground, it will grow, said an older 10
brother, who could never bear to see me deceived. That's how all of these watermelons came to be here. We planted them.

It seemed too wonderful for words. *Too incredible to be believed.* 11
One thing seemed as astonishing as another. That a watermelon could grow inside me if I ate a seed, and that watermelons grew from seeds put in the ground!

When I think of my childhood at its best, it is of this magic that I 12
think. Of having a family that daily worked with nature to produce the extraordinary, and yet they were all so casual about it, and never failed to find my wonderment amusing. Years later I would write poems and essays about the way growing up in the country seemed the best of all possible worlds, regardless of the hardships that made getting by year to year, especially for a family of color in the South half a century ago, a heroic affair.

Thinking Critically about This Reading

Walker places a lot of value on the "magic" of growing up in the country, particularly the ability of her family to "produce the extra-ordinary" (paragraph 12) and do it casually. If you grew up in the country, do you agree with Walker? If you grew up in a city or sub-urb, what form of magic did you encounter?

Questions for Study and Discussion

1. What is Walker's thesis in this essay? (Glossary: *Thesis*) Where does she give her thesis statement?

2. Analyze the sentences in the first four paragraphs. How would you describe Walker's use of sentence variety? Identify her very short sentences—those with eight or fewer words. What does each contribute to the essay?

3. Walker uses a very long sentence to begin paragraph 5. How effective is that sentence? Is it difficult to read? Explain.

4. Reread paragraph 12, noting Walker's sentence constructions. In what way does their construction reinforce Walker's content? Explain.

5. Why did Walker want to share with her daughter the experience of harvesting potatoes?

6. What does the similarity of Walker's and her daughter's responses to digging potatoes reveal about the significance of that activity for them?

7. How does Walker reveal that she is an experienced farmer?

Classroom Activity Using Effective Sentences

Rewrite the following paragraph, presenting the information in any order you choose. Use sentence variety and subordination, as discussed in the chapter introduction, to make the paragraph more interesting to read.

> When Billy saw the crime, he was in a grocery store buying hot dog buns for the barbecue he had scheduled for the next weekend. The crime was a burglary, and the criminal was someone you would never expect to see commit a crime. His basketball shoes squeaked as he ran away, and he looked no more than 15 years old with a fresh, eager face that was the picture of innocence. Billy watched the youth steal a purse right off a woman's shoulder, and the bright sun reflected off the thief's forehead as he ran away, although the weather was quite chilly and had been for a week. The police officer who caught the thief tripped him and handcuffed him as Billy paid for the hot dog buns, got in his car, and drove away.

Suggested Writing Assignments

1. Alice Walker shares with her daughter the surprise and joy of harvesting the potatoes she has planted. The experience is a dual sharing—of each other's company and of nature's bounty through the harvest. In addition, the act of writing also allows Walker to share her experiences with readers. Write an essay about a similar experience—whether with a friend, a sibling, an aunt or uncle, or a parent—that brought you some new awareness or insight and also taught you something about the friendship and guidance offered to you. Perhaps someone taught you to swim, read to you,

brought you to a special sporting event, consoled you, or celebrated one of your achievements. Think about the quality of your sentences as you draft your essay, and pay attention to their effectiveness and variety when you revise and edit.

2. Write a brief essay using one of the following sentences to focus and control the descriptive details you select. Place the sentence in the essay wherever it will have the greatest emphasis.

a. I couldn't believe what I had just seen.
b. The music stopped.
c. It was broken glass.
d. I started to sweat.
e. She had convinced me.
f. It was my turn to step forward.
g. Now I understand.

Salvation

■ **Langston Hughes**

Born in Joplin, Missouri, Langston Hughes
*(1902–1967) became an important figure in
the African American cultural movement of
the 1920s known as the Harlem Renaissance.
He wrote poetry, fiction, and plays and contributed columns to the* New York Post *and
an African American weekly, the* Chicago
Defender. *He is best known for* The Weary
Blues *(1926) and other books of poetry that
express his racial pride, his familiarity with African American traditions, and his understanding of blues and jazz rhythms. In his
memory, New York City designated his residence at 20 East
127th Street in Harlem as a landmark, and his street was renamed
"Langston Hughes Place."*

In the following selection from his autobiography, The Big
Sea *(1940), notice how, for the sake of emphasis, Hughes varies
the length and types of sentences he uses. The effect of the dramatically short sentence in paragraph 12, for instance, derives
from the variety of sentences preceding it.*

Reflecting on What You Know

What role does religion play in your family? Do you consider yourself a religious person? Have you ever felt pressure from others to
participate in religious activities? How did that make you feel?

I was saved from sin when I was going on thirteen. But not really   1
saved. It happened like this. There was a big revival at my Auntie
Reed's church. Every night for weeks there had been much preaching,
singing, praying, and shouting, and some very hardened sinners had
been brought to Christ, and the membership of the church had grown
by leaps and bounds. Then just before the revival ended, they held a
special meeting for children, "to bring the young lambs to the fold."
My aunt spoke of it for days ahead. That night I was escorted to the

front row and placed on the mourners' bench with all the other young sinners, who had not yet been brought to Jesus.

My aunt told me that when you were saved you saw a light, and   2
something happened to you inside! And Jesus came into your life! And God was with you from then on! She said you could see and hear and feel Jesus in your soul. I believed her. I had heard a great many old people say the same thing and it seemed to me they ought to know. So I sat there calmly in the hot, crowded church, waiting for Jesus to come to me.

The preacher preached a wonderful rhythmical sermon, all moans   3
and shouts and lonely cries and dire pictures of hell, and then he sang a song about the ninety and nine safe in the fold, but one little lamb was left out in the cold. Then he said: "Won't you come? Won't you come to Jesus? Young lambs, won't you come?" And he held out his arms to all us young sinners there on the mourners' bench. And the little girls cried. And some of them jumped up and went to Jesus right away. But most of us just sat there.

A great many old people came and knelt around us and prayed,   4
old women with jet-black faces and braided hair, old men with work-gnarled hands. And the church sang a song about the lower lights are burning, some poor sinners to be saved. And the whole building rocked with prayer and song.

Still I kept waiting to *see* Jesus.   5

Finally all the young people had gone to the altar and were saved,   6
but one boy and me. He was a rounder's son named Westley. Westley and I were surrounded by sisters and deacons praying. It was very hot in the church, and getting late now. Finally Westley said to me in a whisper: "God damn! I'm tired o' sitting here. Let's get up and be saved." So he got up and was saved.

Then I was left all alone on the mourners' bench. My aunt came   7
and knelt at my knees and cried, while prayers and songs swirled all around me in the little church. The whole congregation prayed for me alone, in a mighty wail of moans and voices. And I kept waiting serenely for Jesus, waiting, waiting—but he didn't come. I wanted to see him, but nothing happened to me. Nothing! I wanted something to happen to me, but nothing happened.

I heard the songs and the minister saying: "Why don't you come?   8
My dear child, why don't you come to Jesus? Jesus is waiting for you. He wants you. Why don't you come? Sister Reed, what is this child's name?"

"Langston," my aunt sobbed. 9

"Langston, why don't you come? Why don't you come and be 10 saved? Oh, Lamb of God! Why don't you come?"

Now it was really getting late. I began to be ashamed of myself, 11 holding everything up so long. I began to wonder what God thought about Westley, who certainly hadn't seen Jesus either, but who was now sitting proudly on the platform, swinging his knickerbockered legs and grinning down at me, surrounded by deacons and old women on their knees praying. God had not struck Westley dead for taking his name in vain or for lying in the temple. So I decided that maybe to save further trouble, I'd better lie, too, and say that Jesus had come, and get up and be saved.

So I got up. 12

Suddenly the whole room broke into a sea of shouting, as they 13 saw me rise. Waves of rejoicing swept the place. Women leaped in the air. My aunt threw her arms around me. The minister took me by the hand and led me to the platform.

When things quieted down, in a hushed silence, punctuated by a 14 few ecstatic "Amens," all the new young lambs were blessed in the name of God. Then joyous singing filled the room.

That night, for the last time in my life but one—for I was a big 15 boy twelve years old—I cried. I cried, in bed alone, and couldn't stop. I buried my head under the quilts, but my aunt heard me. She woke up and told my uncle I was crying because the Holy Ghost had come into my life, and because I had seen Jesus. But I was really crying because I couldn't bear to tell her that I had lied, that I had deceived everybody in the church, that I hadn't seen Jesus, and that now I didn't believe there was a Jesus any more, since he didn't come to help me.

Thinking Critically about This Reading

Why does Hughes cry on the night of his being "saved"? What makes the story of his being saved so ironic?

Questions for Study and Discussion

1. What is salvation? Is it important to young Hughes that he be saved? Why does he expect to be saved at the revival meeting?

2. Hughes varies the length and structure of his sentences through-out the essay. How does this variety capture and reinforce the rhythms and drama of the evening's events? Explain.

3. What would be gained or lost if the essay began with the first two sentences combined as follows: "I was saved from sin when I was going on thirteen, but I was not really saved"?

4. Identify the coordinating conjunctions in paragraph 3. (Glossary: *Coordination*) Rewrite the paragraph without them. Compare your paragraph with the original, and explain what Hughes gains by using coordinating conjunctions.

5. Identify the subordinating conjunctions in paragraph 15. (Glossary: *Subordination*) What is it about the ideas in this last paragraph that makes it necessary for Hughes to use subordinating conjunctions?

6. How does Hughes's choice of words, or diction, help establish a realistic atmosphere for a religious revival meeting? (Glossary: *Diction*)

Classroom Activity Using Effective Sentences

Using coordination or subordination, rewrite each set of short sentences as a single sentence. Here is an example:

ORIGINAL: This snow is good for Colorado's economy. Tourists are now flocking to ski resorts.

REVISED: This snow is good for Colorado's economy because tourists are now flocking to ski resorts.

1. I can take the 6:30 express train. I can catch the 7:00 bus.

2. Miriam worked on her research paper. She interviewed five people for the paper. She worked all weekend. She was tired.

3. Juan's new job kept him busy every day. He did not have time to work out at the gym for more than a month.

4. The Statue of Liberty welcomes newcomers to the United States. It was a gift of the French government. It was completely restored for the nation's two hundredth birthday. It is more than 120 years old.

5. Carla is tall. She is strong. She is a team player. She was the starting center on the basketball team.

6. Betsy loves Bach's music. She also likes Scott Joplin.

Suggested Writing Assignments

1. Like the young Hughes, we sometimes find ourselves in situations in which, for the sake of conformity, we do things we do not believe in. Consider one such experience you have had, and write an essay about it. What in human nature makes us act occasionally in ways that contradict our inner feelings? As you write, pay attention to your sentence variety.

2. Reread the introduction to this chapter. Then review one of the essays that you have written, paying attention to sentence structure. Recast sentences as necessary to make your writing more interesting and effective.

Volar

■ Judith Ortiz Cofer

Poet, novelist, and educator Judith Ortiz Cofer was born in Hormigueros, Puerto Rico, in 1952, and her family immigrated to the United States in 1954. She grew up in New Jersey and then moved south to continue her education, receiving her M.A. in English from Florida Atlantic University in 1977, and is now Franklin Professor of English and Creative Writing at the University of  *Georgia. Her published works include a novel,* The Line of the Sun *(1989), which was nominated for the Pulitzer Prize, two collections of poetry, and several other titles that collect and combine her essays, stories, and poetry. One of these,* Silent Dancing, *a collection of essays and poetry, was awarded a Pushcart Prize for nonfiction in 1990. Cofer also received an O. Henry Prize for short stories in 1994, and* An Island Like You: Stories of the Barrio *(1995), her collection of young adult short stories, was named a Best Book of the Year by the American Library Association. Her most recent books include* The Meaning of Consuelo: A Novel *(2003) and* First Person Fiction: Call Me Maria *(2004). In the* New York Times Book Review, *reviewer Roberto Marquez called Cofer "a prose writer of evocatively lyrical authority."*

Although much of Cofer's writing focuses on Hispanic issues and the culture clashes that occur between Anglo and Hispanic communities, she departs from that theme in the following selection to focus on the differences between island life in Puerto Rico and tenement living in the United States. "Volar" first appeared in The Year of Our Revolution: New and Selected Stories and Poems *(1998).*

Reflecting on What You Know

Do you remember fantasizing about being able to perform superhuman feats when you were a child? Do you think most children have such fantasies? Why do you think that we develop such fantasies? What purposes, if any, do you think that they serve?

At twelve I was an avid consumer of comic books—*Supergirl* being my favorite. I spent my allowance of a quarter a day on two twelve-cent comic books or a double issue for twenty-five. I had a stack of *Legion of Super Heroes* and *Supergirl* comic books in my bedroom closet that was as tall as I. I had a recurring dream in those days: that I had long blond hair and could fly. In my dream I climbed the stairs to the top of our apartment building as myself, but as I went up each flight, changes would be taking place. Step by step I would fill out: my legs would grow long, my arms harden into steel, and my hair would magically go straight and turn a golden color. Of course I would add the bonus of breasts, but not too large; Supergirl had to be aerodynamic. Sleek and hard as a supersonic missile. Once on the roof, my parents safely asleep in their beds, I would get on tip-toe, arms outstretched in the position for flight and jump out my fifty-story-high window into the black lake of the sky. From up there, over the rooftops, I could see everything, even beyond the few blocks of our barrio; with my X-ray vision I could look inside the homes of people who interested me. Once I saw our landlord, whom I knew my parents feared, sitting in a treasure room dressed in an ermine coat and a large gold crown. He sat on the floor counting his dollar bills. I played a trick on him. Going up to his building's chimney, I blew a little puff of my super-breath into his fireplace, scattering his stacks of money so that he had to start counting all over again. I could more or less program my Supergirl dreams in those days by focusing on the object of my current obsession. This way I "saw" into the private lives of my neighbors, my teachers, and in the last days of my childish fantasy and the beginning of adolescence, into the secret room of the boys I liked. In the mornings I'd wake up in my tiny bedroom with the incongruous—at least in our tiny apartment—white "princess" furniture my mother had chosen for me, and find myself back in my body: my tight curls still clinging to my head, skinny arms and legs and flat chest unchanged.

In the kitchen my mother and father would be talking softly over a café con leche. She would come "wake me" exactly forty-five minutes after they had gotten up. It was their time together at the beginning of each day and even at an early age I could feel their disappointment if I interrupted them by getting up too early. So I would stay in my bed recalling my dreams of flight, perhaps planning my next flight. In the kitchen they would be discussing events in the barrio. Actually, he would be carrying that part of the conversation; when it was her turn to speak she would, more often than not, try shifting the topic toward her desire to see her *familia* on the Island: *How about a vacation in Puerto Rico together this year, Querido? We could rent a car, go to the beach. We could . . .* And he would answer patiently, gently, *Mi amor, do you know how much it would cost for the all of us to fly there? It is not possible for me to take the time off . . . Mi vida, please understand. . . .* And I knew that soon she would rise from the table. Not abruptly. She would light a cigarette and look out the kitchen window. The view was of a dismal alley that was littered with refuse thrown from windows. The space was too narrow for anyone larger than a skinny child to enter safely, so it was never cleaned. My mother would check the time on the clock over her sink, the one with a prayer for patience and grace written in Spanish. A birthday gift. She would see that it was time to wake me. She'd sigh deeply and say the same thing the view from her kitchen window always inspired her to say: *Ay, si yo pudiera volar.*

Thinking Critically about This Reading

By focusing in her essay on the theme of isolation that she and her family experienced in tenement living, Cofer only hints at the many other differences between life in Puerto Rico and the United States that they must have experienced once they moved. Imagine for a few minutes what the other differences might have been for them. In what ways might those differences be the same for all people who leave their native country and settle elsewhere?

Questions for Study and Discussion

1. What does the title mean? To whom does it refer? Why is it an appropriate one for Cofer's essay? (Glossary: *Title*)
2. What does the desire to fly represent both for her mother and for the young Cofer?
3. Analyze the sentences in this essay. How would you describe Cofer's use of sentence variety? Identify her very short sentences — those with eight or fewer words. What does each contribute to the essay?

4. Cofer uses a very long sentence at the end of paragraph 1. How effective is that sentence? Is it difficult to read? Explain.

5. In this essay, Cofer uses dashes (often found in informal writing), as well as semicolons and colons (often found in academic writing). Analyze the way she uses them and assess their effectiveness.

6. Identify several sentence fragments Cofer uses. Are they effective? Why or why not?

Classroom Activity Using Effective Sentences

Rewrite the following sets of sentences to combine short, simple sentences and to reduce repetition wherever possible. Here is an example:

ORIGINAL: Angelo's team won the championship. He pitched a two-hitter. He struck out ten batters. He hit a home run.

REVISED: Angelo's team won the championship because he pitched a two-hitter, struck out ten batters, and hit a home run.

1. Bonnie wore shorts. The shorts were red. The shorts had pockets.

2. The deer hunter awoke at 5 a.m. He ate a quick breakfast. The breakfast consisted of coffee, juice, and cereal. He was in the woods before the sun came up.

3. My grandparents played golf every weekend for years. Last year they stopped playing. They miss the game now.

4. Fly over any major city. Look out the airplane's window. You will be appalled at the number of tall smokestacks you will see.

5. It did not rain for more than three months. Most crops in the region failed. Some farmers were on the brink of declaring bankruptcy.

6. Every weekday I go to work. I exercise. I shower and relax. I eat a light, low-fat dinner.

Suggested Writing Assignments

1. Most writers have a particular place in their homes where they write. It's usually a quiet spot that is away from normal household activities and is comfortable enough to allow them to think, create, and do their best work. That place might be a dining

room table, an alcove under a stairway, a room over a garage, or a bedroom. For these artists, trying to write in another location simply doesn't work. If you have a certain place where you usually write, describe and share with your readers why it works best for you. If you don't presently have an ideal place for writing, describe your dream location and the conditions that might lead to maximum creativity and output for you. Have a clear purpose for your description, and use a variety of sentences to make your writing lively.

2. Have you ever dreamed of something only to be disappointed when your dream came true? For example, have you ever fantasized about taking a trip someplace only to be disappointed when you actually visited that place? Perhaps you hoped of attending a particular college or university and it turned out to not be what you expected it to be. Write an essay about an experience in which reality falls short of a dream. Be sure to use a variety of sentence structures—active and passive, subordinated and coordinated, loose and periodic—as well as sentences demonstrating parallelism to create an essay with a lively and varied style.

Writing with Sources

Some of the writing you do in college will be experiential (that is, based on your personal experiences), but many of your college assignments will ask you to do some research—to write with sources. Although most of us can do basic research—locate and evaluate print and on-line sources, take notes from those sources, and document those sources—we have not learned how to integrate these sources effectively and purposefully into our papers. (For more information on basic research and documentation practices, see Chapter 22, A Brief Guide to Writing a Research Paper.) Your purpose in writing with sources is not to present quotations that report what others have said about your topic. Your goal is to take ownership of your topic by analyzing, evaluating, and synthesizing the materials you have researched. By learning how to view the results of research from your own perspective, you can arrive at an informed opinion of your topic. In short, you become a participant in a conversation with your sources about your topic.

To help you on your way, this chapter provides advice on (1) summarizing, paraphrasing, and quoting sources; (2) integrating summaries, paraphrases, and quotations into the text of your paper using signal phrases; (3) synthesizing sources; and (4) avoiding plagiarism when writing with sources. In addition, one student paper and two professional essays model different ways of engaging meaningfully with outside sources and of reflecting that engagement in writing.

■ USE OUTSIDE SOURCES IN YOUR WRITING

Each time you introduce an outside source into your paper, be sure that you are using that source in a purposeful way. Outside sources can be used to

- support your thesis,
- support your points with statements from noted authorities,

- offer memorable wording of key terms or ideas,
- extend your ideas by introducing new information, and
- articulate opposing positions for you to argue against.

Consider Lily Huang's use of an outside source in the following paragraph from her essay entitled "The Case of the Disappearing Rabbit," published in the July 25, 2009, issue of *Newsweek*.

> What sets the Crown [of the Continent] apart from every other ecosystem on earth is its ecological schizophrenia. Straddling the Continental Divide, it is besieged by disparate climates from the fertile west, the open prairie to the east, and the cold north; even its rivers, issuing from Triple Divide Peak, flow in all four compass directions into the Pacific, the Atlantic, and the Arctic oceans. In all this, the mountains are the agents of volatility: They toss the wind and snow to different sides of the Divide and wildly apportion sunlight to different slopes; historically, their dramatic nightly cooling has produced some of the coldest temperatures ever recorded below the Arctic. The convergence of these forces is what packs into the Crown the widest range of life on the continent, a diversity as distinctive as the tight profusion of Madagascar or the sweeping wealth of the Serengeti. "We have this incredible mix of microclimates," says University of Montana climate expert Steve Running, who shared the Nobel Peace Prize in 2007 with the Intergovernmental Panel on Climate Change, "which then allows an incredible mix of microhabitats for animals."

Here Huang quotes Steve Running, a university professor, Nobel laureate, and climatologist specializing in climate change, to support her main point that the Crown is a unique ecosystem with "the widest range of life on the continent."

The following passage comes from the article "How Marijuana Got Mainstreamed" that appeared in the November 11, 2010, issue of *Time* magazine. Here writer Andrew Ferguson uses two representative quotations from consumers to substantiate his claim that "Robinson's muffins and Rice Krispies squares are getting rave reviews."

> Jenelise Robinson is all business—a consummate tradeswoman. In the past 16 months she has found a way to combine her passions for food and pot and make the combination pay, as founder, owner and head baker of Nancy B's Edible Medicine, one of the most successful startups in Colorado's newest "industry": medical marijuana.

Robinson's muffins and Rice Krispies squares are getting rave reviews. "I have a very high tolerance," said one food critic in the *Denver Chronicle*, a medical-marijuana blog, "and a 2-dose lemon bar will put me on my ass." "I loved the buzz, which lasted 8 hours," wrote another. "Very functional and social." The growth of Robinson's business has come with the explosion in the number of Colorado's medical-marijuana dispensaries, or centers.

Sometimes source material is too long and detailed to be quoted directly in its entirety. In such cases, a writer will choose to summarize or paraphrase the material in his or her own words before introducing it in an essay. For example, notice how Judith Newman summarizes two lengthy sleep studies for use in her essay "What's Really Going On Inside Your Teen's Head" that appeared in the November 28, 2010, issue of *Parade* magazine.

In a pair of related studies published in 1993 and 1997 by Mary Carskadon, a professor of psychiatry at Brown University and director of the Sleep Research program at Bradley Hospital in Rhode Island, Carskadon and colleagues found that more physically mature girls preferred activities later in the day than did less-mature girls and that the sleep-promoting hormone melatonin rises later in teenagers than in children and adults. Translation: Teenagers are physically programmed to stay up later and sleep later.

Here Newman introduces her summary by citing Carskadon's name and giving her academic credentials and concludes with a pointed statement of the researchers' conclusion.

Finally, in the following passage from "*The Way We Really Are: Coming to Terms with America's Changing Families* (1998)," Stephanie Coontz uses outside sources to present the position that she will argue against.

The fallback position for those in denial about the socioeconomic transformation we are experiencing is to admit that many families are in economic stress but to blame their plight on divorce and unwed motherhood. Lawrence Mead of New York University argues that economic inequalities stemming from differences in wages and employment patterns "are now trivial in comparison to those stemming from family structure." David Blankenhorn claims that the "primary fault line" dividing privileged and nonprivileged Americans is no longer "race, religion, class, education, or gender" but family structure. Every major newspaper in the country has published editorials and opinion pieces along these lines. This "new consensus" produces a delightfully simple, inexpensive solution to the economic ills of America's families. From Republican Dan Quayle to the Democratic Party's Progressive Policy Institute, we hear the same words: "Marriage is the best anti-poverty program for children."

Now I am as horrified as anyone by irresponsible parents who yield to the temptations of our winner-take-all society and abandon their family obligations. But we are kidding ourselves if we think the solution to the economic difficulties of America's children lies in getting their parents back together. Single-parent families, it is true, are five to six times more likely to be poor than two-parent ones. But correlations are not the same as causes. The association between poverty and single parenthood has several different sources, suggesting that the battle to end child poverty needs to be fought on a number of different fronts.

By letting the opposition articulate its own position, Coontz reduces the possibility of being criticized for misrepresenting her opponents while setting herself up to give strong voice to her thesis.

■ LEARN TO SUMMARIZE, PARAPHRASE, AND QUOTE FROM YOUR SOURCES

When taking notes from your sources, you must decide whether to summarize, paraphrase, or quote directly. The approach you take is largely determined by the content of the source passage and the way that you envision using it in your paper. Each technique—summarizing, paraphrasing, and quoting—will help you incorporate source material into your essays. Making use of all three of these techniques rather than relying on only one or two will keep your text varied and interesting. All the examples and page numbers in the following discussion are taken from essays in *Models for Writers* unless otherwise noted.

Summary

When you *summarize* material from one of your sources, you capture in condensed form the essential idea of a passage, an article, or an entire chapter. Summaries are particularly useful when you are working with lengthy, detailed arguments or long passages of narrative or descriptive background information in which the details are not germane to the overall thrust of your paper. You simply want to capture the essence of the passage because you are confident that your readers will readily understand the point being made or do not need to be convinced of its validity. Because you are distilling information, a summary is always shorter than the original; often a chapter or more can be reduced to a paragraph, or several paragraphs to a sentence or two. Remember, in writing a summary you should use your own words.

Consider the following paragraphs, in which Richard Lederer compares big words with small words in some detail:

> When you speak and write, there is no law that says you have to use big words. Short words are as good as long ones, and short, old words—like *sun* and *grass* and *home*—are best of all. A lot of small words, more than you might think, can meet your needs with a strength, grace, and charm that large words do not have.
>
> Big words can make the way dark for those who read what you write and hear what you say. Small words cast their clear light on big things—night and day, love and hate, war and peace, and life and death. Big words at times seem strange to the eye and ear and the mind and the heart. Small words are the ones we seem to have known from the time we were born, like the hearth fire that warms the home.
>
> –Richard Lederer, "The Case for Short Words," page 161

A student wishing to capture the gist of Lederer's point without repeating his detailed contrast created the accompanying summary note card.

Summary Note Card

Short Words

Lederer favors short words for their clarity, familiarity, durability, and overall usefulness.

Lederer, "The Case for Short Words," 161

Paraphrase

When you *paraphrase* material from a source, you restate the information in your own words instead of quoting directly. Unlike a summary, which gives a brief overview of the essential information in the original, a paraphrase seeks to maintain the same level of detail as the original to aid readers in understanding or believing the information presented. A paraphrase presents the original information in approximately the same number of words but with different wording. To put it another way, your paraphrase should closely parallel the presentation of ideas in the original, but it should not use the same words or sentence structure as the original. Even though you are using your own words in a paraphrase, it's important to remember that you are borrowing ideas and therefore must acknowledge the source of these ideas with a citation.

How would you paraphrase the following passage from "The Ways of Meeting Oppression" by Martin Luther King Jr.?

> If the American Negro and other victims of oppression succumb to the temptation of using violence in the struggle for freedom, future generations will be the recipients of a desolate night of bitterness, and our chief legacy to them will be an endless reign of meaningless chaos. Violence is not the way.
>
> –Martin Luther King Jr., "The Ways of Meeting Oppression," page 465

See the accompanying note card for an example of how one student paraphrased the passage.

Paraphrase Note Card

Non-Violence

African Americans and other oppressed peoples must not resort to taking up arms against their oppressors because to do so would lead the country into an era of turmoil and confusion. Confrontation will not yield the desired results.

Martin Luther King Jr.,
"The Ways of Meeting Oppression," 465

In most cases, it is best to summarize or paraphrase material—which by definition means using your own words—instead of quoting verbatim (word for word). Capturing an idea in your own words demonstrates that you have thought about and understood what your source is saying.

Direct Quotation

When you *quote* a source directly, you copy the words of your source exactly, putting all quoted material in quotation marks. When you make a quotation note card, check the passage carefully for accuracy, including punctuation and capitalization. Be selective about what you choose to quote. Reserve direct quotation for important ideas stated memorably, for especially clear explanations by authorities, and for arguments by proponents of a particular position in their own words.

Consider the accompanying direct quotation note card. It quotes a passage from William Zinsser's "Simplicity," on page 177 in this text, emphasizing the importance—and rarity—of clear, concise writing.

Direct Quotation Note Card

Wordiness

"Clutter is the disease of American writing. We are a society strangling in unnecessary words, circular constructions, pompous frills, and meaningless jargon."

William Zinsser, "Simplicity," 177

On occasion you'll find a long, useful passage with some memorable wording in it. Avoid the temptation to quote the whole passage; instead, try combining summary or paraphrase with direct quotation. Consider the following paragraph from Abe Whaley's essay "Once Unique, Soon a Place Like Any Other" which appeared on page 13 of the November 14, 2005, issue of *Newsweek*:

Though native Appalachians like me are gradually being outnumbered by newcomers, we remain tied to the land in a way outsiders will never understand. It provides for us physically, socially,
spiritually, and emotionally. Without it, we lose our cultural identity and, ultimately, ourselves. This is not a new fight; it has raged
in these mountains for generations as our land has been exploited
again and again. For too long, we have suffered the effects of clear-
cutting, strip mining, and unscrupulous land grabs by timber companies, coal companies, and even the federal government. Developers
are simply the latest to try their hand at making a buck.

–Abe Whaley

In the accompanying quotation and summary note card, notice how
the student is careful to put quotation marks around all words borrowed directly.

Quotation and Summary Note Card

Sense of Place and Personal Identity

Even though outsiders have flooded in, "we remain tied to the
land in a way outsiders will never understand. It provides for us
physically, socially, spiritually, and emotionally. Without it, we lose
our cultural identity and, ultimately, ourselves." Over the years
greedy business types have ravaged our land, leaving us and the
once beautiful mountains scarred forever.

Abe Whaley, "Once Unique, Soon a Place Like Any Other," 13

Notes from Internet Sources

Working from the computer screen or from a printout, you can take
notes from the Internet just as you would from print sources. You will
need to decide whether to summarize, paraphrase, or quote directly the
information you wish to borrow. Copy the material into a separate
document by highlighting the portion of the text you want to save and
then using the Copy and Paste features to add it to your research notes.

■ INTEGRATE BORROWED MATERIAL INTO YOUR TEXT

Whenever you want to use borrowed material (such as a quotation, a paraphrase, or summary), your goal is to integrate these sources smoothly and logically and not disrupt the flow of your paper or confuse your readers. It is best to introduce borrowed material with a *signal phrase*, which alerts readers that borrowed information is about to be presented.

A signal phrase consists of at least the author's name and a verb (such as "Stephen King contends"). Signal phrases help readers follow your train of thought. When you integrate a quote, paraphrase, or summary into your paper, vary your signal phrases and choose verbs for the signal phrases that accurately convey the tone and intent of the writer you are citing. If a writer is arguing, use the verb *argues* (or *asserts, claims,* or *contends*); if a writer is contesting a particular position or fact, use the verb *contests* (or *denies, disputes, refutes,* or *rejects*). Verbs that are specific to the situation in your paper will bring your readers into the intellectual debate (and avoid the monotony of all-purpose verbs like *says* or *writes*). The following examples show how you can vary signal phrases to add precision to your paper:

Ellen Goodman asserts that . . .

To summarize Audrey Schulman's observations about climate change, . . .

Social activist and nutrition guru Dick Gregory demonstrates that . . .

Mary Sherry explains . . .

Terry Tempest Williams rejects the widely held belief that . . .

Bharati Mukherjee exposes . . .

Other verbs to keep in mind when constructing signal phrases include the following:

acknowledges	compares	grants	reasons
adds	confirms	implies	reports
admits	declares	insists	responds
believes	endorses	points out	suggests

Well-chosen signal phrases help you integrate quotations, paraphrases, and summaries into the flow of your paper. Besides, signal phrases let your reader know who is speaking and, in the case of summaries and paraphrases, exactly where your ideas end and someone else's begin. Never confuse your reader with a quotation that appears suddenly without introduction. Unannounced quotations leave your reader wondering how the quoted material relates to the point you are trying to make. Look at the following student example. The quotation is from Ruth Russell's "The Wounds That Can't Be Stitched Up," which appeared on page 11 of the December 20, 1999, issue of *Newsweek*.

Unannounced Quotation

America has a problem with drinking and driving. In 2004 drunk drivers killed almost 17,000 people and injured 500,000 others. While many are quick to condemn drinking and driving, they are also quick to defend or offer excuses for such behavior, especially when the offender is a friend. "Many local people who know the driver are surprised when they hear about the accident, and they are quick to defend him. They tell me he was a war hero. His parents aren't well. He's an alcoholic. Or my favorite: 'He's a good guy when he doesn't drink'" (Russell 11). When are we going to get tough with drunk drivers?

In the following revision, the student integrates the quotation into the text by means of a signal phrase and in a number of other ways as well. By giving the name of the writer being quoted, referring to her authority on the subject, and noting that the writer is speaking from experience, the student provides more context so that the reader can better understand how this quotation fits into the discussion.

Integrated Quotation

America has a problem with drinking and driving. In 2004 drunk drivers killed almost 17,000 people and injured 500,000 others. While many are quick to condemn drinking and driving, they are also quick to defend or offer excuses for such behavior, especially when the offender is a friend. Ruth Russell, whose family was shattered by a drunk driver, recalls that "many local people who know the driver are surprised when they hear about the accident, and they are quick to defend him. They tell me he was a war hero. His parents aren't well. He's an alcoholic. Or my favorite: 'He's a good guy when he doesn't drink'" (11). When are we going to get tough with drunk drivers?

■ SYNTHESIZE SEVERAL SOURCES TO DEEPEN YOUR DISCUSSION

Synthesis enables you to weave together your own ideas with the ideas of others—the sources you have researched for your essay—in the same paragraph so as to deepen your discussion or to arrive at a new interpretation or conclusion. By learning how to synthesize the results of your research from your own perspective, you can arrive at an informed opinion of your topic.

When you synthesize several sources in your writing, you get your sources to "talk" with one another; you literally create a conversation in which you take an active role. Some times you will find yourself discussing two or three sources together to show a range of views regarding a particular topic or issue—this is called **informational** or **explanatory synthesis**. At other times, you will have opportunities to play off your sources against one another so as to delineate the opposing positions—this is called **persuasive** or **argument synthesis**.

In the following example from her essay "The Qualities of Good Teachers," student Marah Britto uses informational synthesis to combine her own thoughts about good teachers with the thoughts of three other writers whose essays appear in *Models for Writers* (parenthetical citations refer to pages in this text). In doing so, she explains the range of attributes that distinguish good teachers from their peers.

> We have all experienced a teacher who in some way stands out from all the others we have had, a teacher who has made an important difference in each of our lives. While most of us can agree on some of the character traits — dedication, love for students, patience, passion for his/her subject — that such teachers have in common, we cannot agree on that special something that sets them apart, that distinguishes them from the crowd. For me, it was my sixth-grade teacher Mrs. Engstrom, a teacher who motivated with her example. She never asked me to do anything that she was not willing to do herself. How many teachers show their love of ornithology by taking a student out for a bird walk at 5:30 in the morning, on a school day no less? For Thomas L. Friedman, it was his high school journalism teacher, Hattie M. Steinberg. In "My Favorite Teacher," he relates how her insistence upon the importance of "fundamentals" (104) made a life-long impression on him, so much so that he never had to take another journalism course. For Carl Rowan, it was his high school English, history, and civics teacher, Miss Bessie Taylor Gwynn, whose influence he captures in

"Unforgettable Miss Bessie." Miss Bessie taught Rowan to hold himself to high standards, to refuse "to lower [his] standards to those of the crowd" (167). And for Joanne Lipman, it was Mr. Jerry Kupchynsky, her childhood music teacher. She remembers how tough and demanding he was on his students, how he made his students "better than we had any right to be." Ironically, Lipman muses, "I doubt any of us realized how much we loved him for it" (408). Interestingly, isn't it mutual respect and love that is at the heart of any memorable student-teacher bond?

This second example is taken from student Bonnie Sherman's essay "Should Shame Be Used as Punishment?" Here she uses argument synthesis deftly to combine Hawthorne's use of shame in *The Scarlet Letter* with two opposing essays about shame as punishment, both of which appear in this text. Notice how Sherman uses her own reading of *The Scarlet Letter* as evidence to side ultimately with Professor Kahan's position.

Shame has long been used as an alternative punishment to more traditional sentences of corporeal punishment, jail time, or community service. American colonists used the stocks to publically humiliate citizens for their transgressions. In *The Scarlet Letter,* for example, Nathaniel Hawthorne recounts the story of how the community of Boston punished Hester Prynne for her adulterous affair by having her wear a scarlet letter "A" on her breast as a badge of shame. Such punishments were controversial then and continue to spark heated debate in the world of criminal justice today. Like June Tangney, psychology professor at George Mason University, many believe that shaming punishments — designed to humiliate offenders — are unusually cruel and should be abandoned. In her article "Condemn the Crime, Not the Person," she argues that "shame serves to escalate the very destructive patterns of behavior we aim to curb" (571). Interestingly, Hester Prynne's post-punishment life of community service and charitable work does not seem to bear out Tangney's claim. In contrast, Yale Law School professor Dan M. Kahan believes that Tangney's "anxieties about shame . . . seem overstated," and he persuasively supports this position in his essay "Shame Is Worth a Try" by citing a study showing that the threat of public humiliation generates more compliance than does the threat of jail time (574).

Instead of simply presenting your sources with a quotation here and a summary there in your essay, look for opportunities to use synthesis, to go beyond an individual source by relating several of your sources to one another and to your own thesis. Use the following checklist to help you with synthesis in your writing.

Checklist for Writing a Synthesis

1. Start by writing a brief summary of each source that you will be referring to in your synthesis.
2. Explain in your own words how your sources are related to one another and to your own ideas. For example, what assumptions do your sources share? Do your sources present opposing views? Do your sources illustrate a range or diversity of opinions? Do your sources support or challenge your ideas?
3. Have a clear idea or topic sentence for your paragraph before starting to write.
4. Combine information from two or more sources with your own ideas to support or illustrate your main idea.
5. Use signal phrases and parenthetical citations to show your readers the source of your borrowed materials.
6. Have fresh interpretations or conclusions as a goal each time you synthesize sources.

■ AVOID PLAGIARISM

Honesty and accuracy with sources are essential. Any material that you have borrowed word for word must be placed within quotation marks and be properly cited. Any idea, explanation, or argument that you have paraphrased or summarized must be documented, and you must show clearly where the paraphrased or summarized material begins and ends. In short, to use someone else's idea—whether in its original form or in an altered form—without proper acknowledgment is to be guilty of *plagiarism.*

You must acknowledge and document the source of your information whenever you do any of the following:

- quote a source word for word;
- refer to information and ideas from another source that you present in your own words as either a paraphrase or summary; or
- cite statistics, tables, charts, graphs, or other visuals.

You do not need to document the following types of information:

- your own observations, experiences, ideas, and opinions;
- factual information available in many sources (information known as *common knowledge*); or
- proverbs, sayings, or familiar quotations.

For a discussion of MLA style for in-text documentation practices, see pages 655–56 of Chapter 22.

The Council of Writing Program Administrators offers the following helpful definition of *plagiarism* in academic settings for administrators, faculty, and students: "In an instructional setting, plagiarism occurs when a writer deliberately uses someone else's language, ideas, or other (not common knowledge) material without acknowledging its source." Accusations of plagiarism can be substantiated even if plagiarism is accidental. A little attention and effort at the note-taking stage can go a long way toward eliminating inadvertent plagiarism. Check all direct quotations against the wording of the original, and double-check your paraphrases to be sure that you have not used the writer's wording or sentence structure. It is easy to forget to put quotation marks around material taken verbatim or to use the same sentence structure and most of the same words—substituting a synonym here and there—and treat it as a paraphrase. In working closely with the ideas and words of others, intellectual honesty demands that we distinguish between what we borrow—acknowledging it in a citation—and what is our own.

While writing, be careful whenever you incorporate one of your notes into your paper. Make sure that you put quotation marks around material taken verbatim, and double-check your text against your note card—or, better yet, against the original if you have it on hand—to make sure that your quotation is accurate. When paraphrasing or summarizing, make sure you do not inadvertently borrow key words or sentence structures from the original.

For additional guidance, go to the St. Martin's Tutorial on Avoiding Plagiarism at **bedfordstmartins.com/plagiarismtutorial.**

Using Quotation Marks for Language Borrowed Directly

When you use another person's exact words or sentences, you must enclose the borrowed language in quotation marks. Without quotation marks, you give your reader the impression that the wording is your own. Even if you cite the source, you are guilty of plagiarism if you fail to use quotation marks. The following examples demonstrate both plagiarism and a correct citation for a direct quotation.

Original Source

So Grant and Lee were in complete contrast, representing two diametrically opposed elements in American life. Grant was the modern man emerging; beyond him, ready to come on the stage, was the great age of steel and machinery, of crowded cities and a restless burgeoning vitality.

–Bruce Catton, "Grant and Lee: A Study in Contrasts," in *The American Story*, p. 204

Plagiarism

So Grant and Lee were in complete contrast, according to Civil War historian Bruce Catton, representing two diametrically opposed elements in American life. Grant was the modern man emerging; beyond him, ready to come on the stage, was the great age of steel and machinery, of crowded cities and a restless burgeoning vitality (204).

Correct Citation of Borrowed Words in Quotation Marks

"So Grant and Lee were in complete contrast," according to Civil War historian Bruce Catton, "representing two diametrically opposed elements in American life. Grant was the modern man emerging; beyond him, ready to come on the stage, was the great age of steel and machinery, of crowded cities and a restless burgeoning vitality" (204).

Using Your Own Words and Word Order
When Summarizing and Paraphrasing

When summarizing or paraphrasing a source, you must use your own language. Pay attention to word choice and word order, especially if you are paraphrasing. Remember that it is not enough simply to use a synonym here or there and think that you have paraphrased the source; you *must* restate the original idea in your own words, using your own style and sentence structure. In the following examples, notice how plagiarism can occur when care is not taken in the wording or sentence structure of a paraphrase. Notice that in the acceptable paraphrase, the student writer uses her own language and sentence structure.

Original Source

Stereotypes are a kind of gossip about the world, a gossip that makes us prejudice people before we ever lay eyes upon them. Hence it is not surprising that stereotypes have something to do with the dark world of prejudice. Explore most prejudices (note that the word means prejudgment) and you will find a cruel stereotype at the core of each one.

–Robert L. Heilbroner, "Don't Let Stereotypes Warp Your Judgments," p. 254

Unacceptably Close Wording

According to Heilbroner, we prejudge other people even before we have seen them when we think in stereotypes. That stereotypes are related to the ugly world of prejudice should not surprise anyone. If you explore the heart of most prejudices, beliefs that literally prejudge, you will discover a mean stereotype lurking (254).

Unacceptably Close Sentence Structure

Heilbroner believes that stereotypes are images of people, images that enable people to prejudge other people before they have seen them. Therefore, no one should find it surprising that stereotypes are somehow related to the ugly world of prejudice. Examine most prejudices (the word literally means prejudgment) and you will uncover a vicious stereotype at the center of each (254).

Acceptable Paraphrase

Heilbroner believes that there is a link between stereotypes and the hurtful practice of prejudice. Stereotypes make for easy conversation, a kind of shorthand that enables us to find fault with people before ever meeting them. If you were to dissect most human prejudices, you would likely discover an ugly stereotype lurking somewhere inside them (254).

Review the following Avoiding Plagiarism box as you proofread your final draft and check your citations one last time. If at any time while you are taking notes or writing your paper you have a question about plagiarism, consult your instructor for clarification and guidance before proceeding.

Avoiding Plagiarism

Questions to Ask about Direct Quotations
- Do quotation marks clearly indicate the language that I borrowed verbatim?
- Is the language of the quotation accurate, with no missing or misquoted words or phrases?
- Do the brackets or ellipsis marks clearly indicate any changes or omissions I have introduced?
- Does a signal phrase naming the author introduce each quotation?
- Does the verb in the signal phrase help establish a context for each quotation?
- Does a parenthetical page citation follow each quotation?

Questions to Ask about Summaries and Paraphrases
- Is each summary or paraphrase written in my own words and style?
- Does each summary or paraphrase accurately represent the opinion, position, or reasoning of the original writer?
- Does each summary or paraphrase start with a signal phrase so that readers know where my borrowed material begins?
- Does each summary or paraphrase conclude with a parenthetical page citation?

Questions to Ask about Facts and Statistics
- Do I use a signal phrase or some other marker to introduce each fact or statistic that is not common knowledge so that readers know where the borrowed material begins?
- Is each fact or statistic that is not common knowledge clearly documented with a parenthetical page citation?

Praise the Humble Dung Beetle

■ Sharon Begley

Award-winning science journalist Sharon Begley was born in Englewood, New Jersey, in 1956. After graduating from Yale University in 1977, she became an editorial assistant in science at Newsweek *and was named senior science editor at the magazine in 1996. Her many cover stories on a variety of cutting-edge science topics have demonstrated her ability to write about complex scientific ideas, theories, and laboratory studies in clear, accessible prose. Begley teamed up with Collette Dowling and Anne Marie Cunningham to write* The Techno/ Peasant Survival Manual *(1980), a book that describes new technologies, explains the principles behind them, and speculates on the effect their use could have on society. In 2002, Begley published* The Mind and the Brain *with psychiatrist Jeffrey Schwartz. She had regularly served as a science consultant for radio and television shows like* Imus in the Morning, Today Weekend, CBS's The Early Show, *and* The Charlie Rose Show. *Since 2002, Begley has been science editor at the* Wall Street Journal, *where her column "Science Journal" appears every Friday.*

In "Praise the Humble Dung Beetle," an essay first published in the June 9, 2008, issue of Newsweek, *Begley champions the cause of bugs and other creepy-crawly invertebrates that should be protected by the Endangered Species Act. As you read, pay attention to how Begley integrates her sources into the discussion smoothly with clear signal phrases.*

Reflecting on What You Know

Make a list of any endangered wildlife that you've heard about. Are any of these plants and animals from your region of the country? How did you first hear about the endangered species on your list?

Nothing against polar bears, which Sacha Spector loves as much 1
as the next biologist, but to really get him going you need to ask
about beetles. Specifically, dung beetles, whose disappearance would
undoubtedly leave less of a void in our collective heart than the polar
bear's but would rip a bigger hole in the web of life. Without the dung
beetles that roam America's rangelands and pastures, animal droppings
would not get rolled up and buried. Seeds in the droppings would not
get dispersed. Populations of parasites and disease-carrying pest species
such as flies, to which the raw droppings on the ground are like condos
with MOVE RIGHT IN! signs, would explode. Nutrients in the waste
would be washed away rather than returned to the ground. Spector, who
runs the invertebrate program at the Center for Biodiversity and
Conservation at the American Museum of Natural History, could go
on, but you can tell from his voice that he knows he's fighting a losing
battle. Getting people to care about the 238 species of spiders, clams,
moths, snails, isopods, and other invertebrates on the list of endangered species is about as likely as a magazine putting a photo of a dung
beetle rather than a polar bear on its cover.

Of all creatures great and small, it is the charismatic megafauna— 2
tigers and rhinos and gorillas and pandas and other soulful-eyed, warm,
and fuzzy animals—that personify endangered species. That's both a
shame and a dangerous bias. "Plants and invertebrates are the silent majority which feed the entire planet, stabilize the soil, and make all life
possible," says Kiernan Suckling, cofounder of the Center for Biological
Diversity. They pollinate crops and decompose carcasses, filter water,
and, lacking weapons like teeth and claws, brew up molecules to defend
themselves that turn out to be remarkably potent medicines: the breast-
cancer compound taxol comes from a yew tree, and a leukemia drug
from the rosy periwinkle. Those are tricks that, Suckling dryly notes,
"polar bears and blue whales haven't mastered yet."

Since the lesser beasts of the field can't just muscle their way to 3
survival, they tend to have talents that higher ones—with more
brains as well as brawn to draw on—don't. As a result, they're loaded
with gizmos that human engineers are tapping for inspiration. The
Namibian beetle, for instance, has tips on the bumpy scales of its wings
that pull water from fog, a design that has inspired a fog-harvesting net
(it's used in cooling towers, industrial condensers, and dry farming
regions). The spiral in mollusk shells, which fluids flow through especially smoothly and efficiently, has inspired a rotor that draws up to
85 percent less energy than standard fans and is finding its way into
computers and air conditioners. Biologists are cloning mussel proteins

to produce an epoxy, mimicking the bivalves' ability to stick to rocks, that is expected to rival any superglue on the market. The American burying beetle, which feeds on carrion, can smell death from afar. "It can find a dead mouse [which it eats and feeds, regurgitated, to its off-spring] within an hour of its demise from two miles away," says Quentin Wheeler, director of the International Institute for Species Exploration at Arizona State University. "Think of the potential if we could mimic that for finding earthquake victims."

Biologists draw an analogy between ecosystems and airplanes. 4
The latter can fly without some of their rivets, and the former can survive without some of their species. But in neither case can you tell how many, or which ones, are dispensable until the thing crashes. "Some 99.99 percent of species that ever existed have disappeared, and nature moves on," notes Wheeler. "But you can never predict what the consequences will be in the short term, especially for humans who rely on the services that invertebrates provide." But after a species' numbers plummet, the effects haven't been pretty. For instance, as freshwater mussels have declined (70 percent of their species are threatened or endangered), taking with them their filtration services, water quality in streams, rivers, and lakes has deteriorated badly. In the Chesapeake Bay, each adult oyster once filtered 60 gallons of water a day, packaging sediment and pollutants into blobs that fell harmlessly to the bay floor. Before the population crashed in the 1990s, oysters filtered 19 trillion gallons—an entire bay's worth—once a week. The survivors struggle to do that in a year. The result is cloudy, more polluted water, and a loss of fisheries and baymen's livelihoods.

The value of creepy-crawlies is not reflected in which creatures 5
are protected by the Endangered Species Act, and this one isn't the Bush administration's fault. Like the rest of us, scientists gravitate toward the huggable. The upshot is that much less is known about invertebrates, including whether they're in danger of extinction, than about mammals. "With 57 insect species on the endangered list, out of 90,000 in the United States, either there's something unbelievably resilient about insects or we're off by an order of magnitude in how many are in trouble," says Spector.

If Earth's species are a living library, then polar bears and other 6
cuddly mammals are the best-selling beach reads. Everything else is the volumes of history and literature and other scholarship, written in the alphabet of DNA: 99 percent of all animals are invertebrates. To understand the history and the majesty of life requires reading, and thus preserving, those volumes.

Thinking Critically about This Reading

What is Begley's purpose in this essay? (Glossary: *Purpose*) Does she simply want to inform us about beetles and other invertebrates? Is she arguing that more plants and invertebrates should be included on the list of endangered species? Is she asking us to become better informed about invertebrates, which account for 99 percent of all animals? Or all three? Explain.

Questions for Study and Discussion

1. According to Begley, what would happen to "the web of life" (paragraph 1) if the dung beetle were to become extinct? How does Begley use Sacha Spector's expertise and perspective to help her make this point?

2. Begley acknowledges that "it is the charismatic megafauna . . . that personify endangered species" (2). In what ways is this "both a shame and a dangerous bias"? How does Begley use the opinions of Kiernan Suckling of the Center for Biological Diversity to answer this question?

3. Identify the signal phrases Begley uses to introduce her sources. How do these signal phrases help you as a reader? Besides giving the name of each source, what other information does Begley provide?

4. Begley claims that lesser beasts are "loaded with gizmos that human engineers are tapping for inspiration" (3). What examples does she use to support this claim? To what end does she quote Quentin Wheeler in paragraph 3? Explain.

5. Explain the analogy "between ecosystems and airplanes" (4) that biologists use. How does it inform Begley's discussion of unappreciated invertebrates?

6. What point does Begley make with her "if Earth's species are a living library" analogy in the final paragraph?

Classroom Activity Using Writing with Sources

Use the examples of signal phrases and parenthetical citations on pages 246–47 as models for integrating the quotation into the flow of the discussion in each of the following two paragraphs. The quotation in the first example comes from page 100 of William L. Rathje's article entitled "Rubbish!" in the December 1989 issue of the *Atlantic*

Monthly. Rathje teaches at the University of Arizona, where he directs the Garbage Project.

> Most Americans think that we are producing more trash per person than ever, that plastic is a huge problem, and that paper biodegrades quickly in landfills. "The biggest challenge we will face is to recognize that the conventional wisdom about garbage is often wrong."

The quotation in the second example comes from page 99 of Rita Dove's essay "Loose Ends" from her 1995 book *The Poet's World.* Dove is a former poet laureate of the United States and teaches at the University of Virginia.

> Television, it could be argued, presents life in tidy almost predictable thirty- and sixty-minute packages. As any episode of *Friends, House,* or *Law and Order* demonstrates, life on television, though exciting, is relatively easy to follow. Humor, simultaneous action, and special effects cannot overshadow the fact that each show has a beginning, a middle, and an end. "Life . . . is ragged. Loose ends rule." For many Americans, television provides an escape from their disjointed day-to-day lives.

Compare your signal phrases with those of your classmates, and discuss how smoothly each integrates the quotation into the passage.

Suggested Writing Assignments

1. Visit the U.S. Fish and Wildlife Service Web site at www.fws.gov/ Endangered to learn about its Endangered Species Program and the Endangered Species Act. Find the Service's list of endangered vertebrate and invertebrate animals and flowering and nonflowering plants in the United States. From these lists, adopt an endangered species that is found in your region of the country, and write a report about it. In your report, include a description of your plant or "critter," an explanation of where it is found and what it does, and an argument for why it should be protected.

2. Begley says that "getting people to care about the 238 species of spiders, clams, moths, snails, isopods, and other invertebrates on the list of endangered species is about as likely as a magazine putting a photo of a dung beetle rather than a polar bear on its cover" (1). Consider the pair of photographs—one of the dung beetle and the other, a polar bear—on page 260. Were you drawn to the picture of the polar bear? Why or why not? Write an essay in which you argue that because lowly bugs, spiders, and

© Mark Moffett/Minden Pictures/Getty Images, Inc.

Photo by Alfred Rosa.

mollusks are more critical to ecology than larger, more glamorous mammals are, we all should learn more about unglamorous invertebrates instead of focusing our attention and dollars on cuddly and huggable mammals.

The English-Only Movement: Can America Proscribe Language with a Clear Conscience?

■ Jake Jamieson

An eighth-generation Vermonter, Jake Jamieson was born in Berlin, Vermont, and grew up in nearby Waterbury. He graduated from the University of Vermont in 1996 with a degree in elementary education and a focus in English. After graduation, he "bounced around" California and Colorado before landing in the Boston area, where he directs the product innovation and training department at iProspect, a search-engine marketing company.

Jamieson wrote the following essay while he was a student at the University of Vermont and has updated it for inclusion in this book. As a believer in the old axiom "If it isn't broken, don't fix it," Jamieson thinks that the official-English crowd wants to fix a system that seems to be working just fine. In this essay, he tackles the issue of legislating English as the official language of the United States. As you read, notice how he uses outside sources to present various pieces of the English-only position. He then tries to undercut that position by using his own thinking and examples as well as the opinions of experts who support him. Throughout his essay, Jamieson uses MLA style for his in-text citations and his list of works cited.

Reflecting on What You Know

It is now possible to visit many countries and be understood in English, regardless of other languages that are spoken in the host country. If you were to emigrate, how hard would you work to learn the predominant language of your chosen country? What advantages would you gain by learning that language, even if you could get by in English? How would you feel if the country had a law that required you to use its language in its schools and businesses? Write down your thoughts about these questions.

Many people think of the United States as a giant cultural "melting pot" where people from other countries come together and bathe in the warm waters of assimilation. In this scenario, the newly arrived immigrants readily adopt American cultural ways and learn to speak English. For others, however, this serene picture of the melting pot analogy does not ring true. These people see the melting pot as a giant cauldron into which immigrants are tossed; here their cultures, values, and backgrounds are boiled away in the scalding waters of discrimination. At the center of the discussion about immigrants and assimilation is language: should immigrants be required to learn English, or should accommodations be made so they can continue to use their native languages? 1

Those who argue that the melting pot analogy is valid believe that immigrants who come to America do so willingly and should be expected to become a part of its culture instead of hanging on to their past. For them, the expectation that immigrants will celebrate this country's holidays, dress as Americans dress, embrace American values, and most importantly speak English is not unreasonable. They believe that assimilation offers the only way for everyone in this country to live together in harmony and the only way to dissipate the tensions that inevitably arise when cultures clash. A major problem with this argument, however, is that there is no agreement on what exactly constitutes the "American way" of doing things. 2

Not everyone in America is of the same religious persuasion or has the same set of values, and different people affect vastly different styles of dress. There are so many sets of variables that it would be hard to defend the argument that there is only one culture in the United States. Currently, the one common denominator in America is that the majority of us speak English, and because of this a major movement is being staged in favor of making English the country's "official" language while it is still the country's national and common language. Making English America's "official" language would change the ground rules and expectations surrounding immigrant assimilation. According to the columnist and social commentator Charles Krauthammer, making English the "official" language has important implications: 3

> "Official" means the language of the government and its institu-
> tions. "Official" makes clear our expectations of acculturation.
> "Official" means that every citizen, upon entering America's most
> sacred political space, the voting booth, should minimally be able

to identify the words *president* and *vice president* and *county commissioner* and *judge*. The immigrant, of course, has the right to speak whatever he wants. But he must understand that when he comes to the United States, swears allegiance, and accepts its bounty, he undertakes to join its civic culture. In English. (112)

Many reasons are given to support the notion that making English the official language of the land is a good idea and that it is exactly what this country needs, especially in the face of the growing diversity of languages in metropolitan areas. Indeed, in a recent survey one Los Angeles school reported sixty different languages spoken in the homes of its students (National Education Association, par. 4).

Supporters of English-only contend that all government communi-   4
cation must be in English. Because communication is absolutely necessary for democracy to survive, they believe that the only way to ensure the existence of our nation is to make sure a common language exists. Making English official would ensure that all government business, from ballots to official forms to judicial hearings, would have to be conducted in English. According to former senator and presidential candidate Bob Dole, "Promoting English as our national language is not an act of hostility but a welcoming act of inclusion." He goes on to state that while immigrants are encouraged to continue speaking their native languages, "thousands of children [are] failing to learn the language, English, that is the ticket to the 'American Dream'" (qtd. in Donegan 51). Political and cultural commentator Greg Lewis echoes Dole's sentiments when he boldly states, "To succeed in America . . . it's important to speak, read, and understand English as most Americans speak it. There's nothing cruel or unfair in that; it's just the way it is" (par. 5).

For those who do not subscribe to this way of thinking, however,   5
this type of legislation is anything but the "welcoming act of inclusion" that it is described to be. Many of them, like Myriam Marquez, readily acknowledge the importance of English but fear that "talking in Spanish—or any other language, for that matter—is some sort of litmus test used to gauge American patriotism" ("Why and When" 512). Others suggest that anyone attempting to regulate language is treading dangerously close to the First Amendment and must have a hidden agenda of some type. Why, it is asked, make a language official when it is already firmly entrenched and widely used in this country without legislation to mandate it? According to language diversity advocate James Crawford, the answer is plain and simple: "discrimination." He

states that "it is certainly more respectable to discriminate by language than by race" or ethnicity. He points out that "most people are not sensitive to language discrimination in this nation, so it is easy to argue that you're doing someone a favor by making them speak English" (qtd. in Donegan 51). English-only legislation has been criticized as bigoted, anti-immigrant, mean-spirited, and steeped in nativism by those who oppose it, and some go so far as to say that this type of legislation will not foster better communication, as is the claim, but will instead encourage a "fear of being subsumed by a growing 'foreignness' in our midst" (Underwood 65).

For example, when a judge in Texas ruled that a mother was abusing her five-year-old girl by speaking to her only in Spanish, an uproar ensued. This ruling was accompanied by the statement that by talking to her daughter in a language other than English, the mother was "abusing that child and . . . relegating her to the position of house maid." The National Association for Bilingual Education (NABE) condemned this statement for "labeling the Spanish language as abuse." The judge, Samuel C. Kiser, subsequently apologized to the housekeepers of the country, adding that he held them "in the highest esteem," but stood firm on his ruling (qtd. in Donegan 51). One might notice that he went out of his way to apologize to the housekeepers he might have offended but saw no need to apologize to the millions of Spanish speakers whose language had just been belittled in a nationally publicized case. 6

This tendency of official-English proponents to put down other languages is one that shows up again and again, even though they maintain that they have nothing against other languages or the people who speak them. If there is no malice intended toward other languages, why is the use of any language other than English tantamount to lunacy according to an almost constant barrage of literature and editorial opinion? In a recent listing of the "New Year's Resolutions" of various conservative organizations, a group called U.S. English, Inc., stated that the U.S. government was not doing its job of convincing immigrants that they "must learn English to succeed in this country." Instead, according to Stephen Moore and his associates, "in a bewildering display of irrationality, the U.S. government makes it possible to vote, file a tax return, get married, obtain a driver's license, and become a U.S. citizen in many languages" (46). 7

Now, according to this mindset, not only is speaking any language other than English abusive, but it is also irrational and bewildering. What is this world coming to when people want to speak and make transactions in their native language? Why do they refuse to change 8 and become more like us? Why can't immigrants see that speaking English is quite simply the right way to go? These and many other questions like them are implied by official-English proponents when they discuss the issue.

Conservative attorney David Price argues that official-English 9 legislation is a good idea because most English-speaking Americans prefer "out of pride and convenience to speak their native language on the job" (A13). This statement implies not only that the pride and convenience of non-English-speaking Americans is unimportant but that their native tongues are not as important as English. The scariest prospect of all is that this opinion is quickly gaining popularity all around the country. It appears to be most prevalent in areas with high concentrations of Spanish-speaking residents.

To date, a number of official-English bills and one amendment to 10 the Constitution have been proposed in the House and Senate. There are more than twenty-seven states—including Missouri, North Dakota, Florida, Massachusetts, California, Virginia, and New Hampshire—that have made English their official language, and more are debating the issue every day. An especially disturbing fact about this debate—and it was front and center in 2007 during the discussions and protests about what to do with America's 12.5 million illegal immigrants—is that official-English laws always seem to be linked to anti-immigration legislation, such as proposals to limit immigration or to restrict government benefits to immigrants.

Although official-English proponents maintain that their bid for 11 language legislation is in the best interest of immigrants, the facts tend to show otherwise. University of Texas Professor Robert D. King strongly believes that "language does not threaten American unity." He recommends that "we relax and luxuriate in our linguistic richness and our traditional tolerance of language differences" (64). A decision has to be made in this country about what kind of message we will send to the rest of the world. Do we plan to allow everyone in this country the freedom of speech that we profess to cherish, or will we decide to reserve it only for those who speak English? Will we hold firm to our belief that everyone is deserving of life, liberty, and the pursuit of happiness in this country? Or will we show the world that we believe in these things only when they pertain to ourselves and people like us? "The irony," as Hispanic columnist Myriam Marquez observes, "is that English-only laws directed at government have done little to change the inevitable multicultural flavor of America" ("English-Only Laws" A10).

Works Cited

Donegan, Craig. "Debate over Bilingualism: Should English Be the Nation's Official Language?" *CQ Researcher* 19 Jan. 1996: 51–71. Print.

King, Robert D. "Should English Be the Law?" *Atlantic Monthly* Apr. 1997: 55–64. Print.

Krauthammer, Charles. "In Plain English: Let's Make It Official." *Time* 12 June 2006: 112. Print.

Lewis, Greg. "An Open Letter to Diversity's Victims." *WashingtonDispatch .com*. N.P. 12 Aug. 2003. Web. 15 Nov. 2011.

Marquez, Myriam. "English-Only Laws Serve to Appease Those Who Fear the Inevitable." *Orlando Sentinel* 10 July 2000: A10. Print.

---. "Why and When We Speak Spanish in Public." *Models for Writers.* 11th ed. Ed. Alfred Rosa and Paul Eschholz. Boston: Bedford, 2012. 531–34. Print.

Moore, Stephen, et al. "New Year's Resolutions." *National Review* 29 Jan. 1996: 46–48. Print.

National Education Association. "NEA Statement on the Debate over English Only." Teacher's College, U of Nebraska, Lincoln. 27 Sept. 1999. Web. 15 Nov. 2011.

Price, David. "English-Only Rules: EEOC Has Gone Too Far." *USA Today* 28 Mar. 1996, final ed.: A13. Print.

Underwood, Robert L. "At Issue: Should English Be the Official Language of the United States?" *CQ Researcher* 19 Jan. 1996: 65. Print.

Thinking Critically about This Reading

Jamieson claims that "there are so many sets of variables that it would be hard to defend the argument that there is only one culture in the United States" (paragraph 3). Do you agree with him, or do you see a dominant American culture with many regional variations? Explain.

Questions for Study and Discussion

1. What question does Jamieson seek to answer in his essay? How does he answer this question?

2. How does Jamieson respond to the people who argue that the melting pot analogy is valid? Do you agree with his counterargument?

3. Former senator Bob Dole believes that English "is the ticket to the 'American Dream'" (4). In what ways can it be considered the ticket?

4. For what purpose does Jamieson quote Greg Lewis in paragraph 4? What would have been lost had he dropped the Lewis quotation? Explain.

5. James Crawford believes that official-English legislation is motivated by "discrimination" (5). What do you think he means? Do you think that Crawford would consider Bob Dole's remarks in paragraph 4 discriminatory? Explain.

6. In paragraph 6, Jamieson presents the example of the Texas judge who ruled that speaking to a child only in Spanish constituted abuse. What point does this example help Jamieson make?

7. Jamieson is careful to use signal phrases to introduce each of his quotations and paraphrases. How do these signal phrases help readers follow the flow of the argument in his essay?

8. In his concluding paragraph, Jamieson leaves his readers with three important questions. How do you think that he would answer each one? How would you answer them?

Classroom Activity Using Writing with Sources

Using the examples on pages 246–47 as a model, write a paraphrase for each of the following paragraphs — that is, restate the original ideas in your own words, using your own style and sentence structure.

> Punctuation, one is taught, has a point: to keep up law and order. Punctuation marks are the road signs placed along the highway of our communications — to control speeds, provide directions, and prevent head-on collisions. A period has the unblinking finality of a red light; the comma is a flashing yellow light that asks us only to slow down; and the semicolon is a stop sign that tells us to ease gradually to a halt, before gradually starting up again.
>
> –Pico Iyer, "In Praise of the Humble Comma"

> The history of a nation is more often the result of the unexpected than of the planned. In many cases it turns on momentous events. In 1968, American history was determined by a garbage men's strike. As Martin Luther King Jr. and the members of the SCLC commenced planning the Poor Peoples' March on Washington, the garbage men of Memphis, Tennessee, were embroiled in a wage dispute with Mayor Henry Loeb. On February 12th, the garbage men, most of whom were black, went on strike. What began as a simple dispute over wages soon developed into a full-fledged racial battle between the predominantly black union, local 1733, and the white power structure of the City of Memphis.
>
> –Robert L. Walsh and Leon F. Burrell, *The Other America*

Compare your paraphrases with those of your classmates.

Suggested Writing Assignments

1. It's no secret that English is the common language of the United States, but few of us know that the country has been cautious about promoting a government-mandated official language. Why do you suppose the federal government has chosen to take a hands-off position on the language issue? If it has not been necessary to mandate English in the past, why do you think that people now feel a need to declare English the "official language" of the United States? Do you think that this need is real? Write an essay in which you articulate your position on the English-only issue. Support your position with your own experiences and observations as well as several outside sources.

2. Before writing an essay about assimilating non-English-speaking immigrants into American society, consider the following three statements:

   a. At this time, it is highly unlikely that Congress will pass a law saying that English is the official language of the United States.

   b. Immigrants should learn English as quickly as possible after arriving in the United States.

   c. The culture and languages of immigrants should be respected and valued to reduce bitterness and resentment as immigrants are assimilated into American society.

   In your opinion, what is the best way to assimilate non-English-speaking immigrants into our society? Write an essay in which you propose how the United States, as a nation, can make statements (b) and (c) above a reality without resorting to an English-only solution. How can we help immigrants become Americans without provoking ill will?

3. Is the English-only debate a political issue, a social issue, an economic issue, or some combination of the three? In this context, what do you see as the relationship between language and power? Write an essay in which you explore the relationship between language and power as it pertains to the non-English-speaking immigrants living and functioning within an English-speaking culture.

The Clan of One-Breasted Women

■ **Terry Tempest Williams**

American author, naturalist, conservationist, and activist Terry Tempest Williams was born in Corona, California, in 1955, and grew up in Utah, where she is descended from six genera- tions of Mormon pioneers. Williams received a degree in English and biology in 1978 and an M.S. in environmental education in 1984 from the University of Utah. After graduation, she taught on a Navajo reservation in Montezuma Creek, Utah; she has also been naturalist-in-residence at the Utah Museum of Natural History. A prolific writer, her essays have appeared in the New Yorker, *the* Nation, Orion, *the* New York Times, *and* The Best American Essays *(2000). Williams is best known for her award-winning* Refuge: An Unnatural History of Family and Place *(1991), a book that interweaves memoir with a chronicle of the flooding of the Bear River Migratory Bird Refuge in 1983. Williams's other books include* Pieces of White Shell: A Journey to Navajoland *(1984),* An Unspoken Hunger *(1994),* Desert Quartet: An Erotic Landscape *(1995),* Red: Patience and Passion in the Desert *(2001),* The Open Space of Democracy *(2004), and* Finding Beauty in a Broken World *(2008). She has also written two books for children,* The Secret Language of Snow *(1984) and* Cattails *(1985). In 2009, Williams was featured in Ken Burns's PBS series* The National Parks: America's Best Idea. *Currently, she teaches English and environmental humanities at the University of Utah.*

"The Clan of One-Breasted Women" first appeared as the epilogue to her acclaimed Refuge. *This essay has since been pub- lished worldwide. In it, Williams explores the connection between radioactive fallout from aboveground nuclear testing on the Nevada desert during the 1950s and early 1960s and the high inci- dence of cancer occurring not only in her own family but in other Utah families as well.*

Reflecting on What You Know

Today people are much more aware of the health risks caused by radiation and chemicals lurking in our environment than they were, say, 50 or 60 years ago. What exactly do you know about the potential dangers of nuclear energy facilities, chemical fertilizers and pesticides, exhaust from the cars we drive, and preservatives and other additives in the foods we eat? Are you aware of any environmental contamination issues in the area where you grew up? Explain.

I belong to a Clan of One-breasted Women. My mother, my grand- 1
mothers, and six aunts have all had mastectomies. Seven are dead. The two who survive have just completed rounds of chemotherapy and radiation.

I've had my own problems: two biopsies for breast cancer and a 2
small tumor between my ribs diagnosed as "a border-line malignancy."

This is my family history. 3

Most statistics tell us breast cancer is genetic, hereditary, with ris- 4
ing percentages attached to fatty diets, childlessness, or becoming pregnant after thirty. What they don't say is living in Utah may be the greatest hazard of all.

We are a Mormon family with roots in Utah since 1847. The 5
word-of-wisdom, a religious doctrine of health, kept the women in my family aligned with good foods: no coffee, no tea, tobacco, or alcohol. For the most part, these women were finished having their babies by the time they were thirty. And only one faced breast cancer prior to 1960. Traditionally, as a group of people, Mormons have a low rate of cancer.

Is our family a cultural anomaly? The truth is we didn't think about 6
it. Those who did, usually the men, simply said, "bad genes." The women's attitude was stoic. Cancer was part of life. On February 16, 1971, the eve before my mother's surgery, I accidently picked up the telephone and overheard her ask my grandmother what she could expect.

"Diane, it is one of the most spiritual experiences you will ever 7
encounter."

I quietly put down the receiver. 8

Two days later, my father took my three brothers and me to the 9
hospital to visit her. She met us in the lobby in a wheelchair. No

bandages were visible. I'll never forget her radiance, the way she held herself in a purple velour robe and how she gathered us around her.

"Children, I am fine. I want you to know I felt the arms of God   10 around me."

We believed her. My father cried. Our mother, his wife, was   11 thirty-eight years old.

Two years ago, after my mother's death from cancer, my father   12 and I were having dinner together. He had just returned from St. George where his construction company was putting in natural gas lines for towns in southern Utah. He spoke of his love for the country: the sandstoned landscape, bare-boned and beautiful. He had just finished hiking the Kolob trail in Zion National Park. We got caught up in reminiscing, recalling with fondness our walk up Angel's Landing on his fiftieth birthday and the years our family had vacationed there. This was a remembered landscape where we had been raised.

Over dessert, I shared a recurring dream of mine. I told my father   13 that for years, as long as I could remember, I saw this flash of light in the night in the desert. That this image had so permeated my being, I could not venture south without seeing it again, on the horizon, illuminating buttes and mesas.

"You did see it," he said.   14

"Saw what?" I asked, a bit tentative.   15

"The bomb. The cloud. We were driving home from Riverside,   16 California. You were sitting on your mother's lap. She was pregnant. In fact, I remember the date, September 7, 1957. We had just gotten out of the Service. We were driving north, past Las Vegas. It was an hour or so before dawn, when this explosion went off. We not only heard it, but felt it. I thought the oil tanker in front of us had blown up. We pulled over and suddenly, rising from the desert floor, we saw it, clearly, this golden-stemmed cloud, the mushroom. The sky seemed to vibrate with an eerie pink glow. Within a few minutes, a light ash was raining on the car."

I stared at my father. This was new information to me.   17

"I thought you knew that," my father said. "It was a common   18 occurrence in the fifties."

It was at this moment I realized the deceit I had been living under.   19 Children growing up in the American Southwest, drinking contaminated milk from contaminated cows, even from the contaminated breasts of their mother, my mother—members, years later, of the Clan of One-breasted Women.

It is a well-known story in the Desert West, "The Day We 20 Bombed Utah," or perhaps, "The Years We Bombed Utah."[1] Above ground atomic testing in Nevada took place from January 27, 1951, through July 11, 1962. Not only were the winds blowing north, covering "low use segments of the population" with fallout and leaving sheep dead in their tracks, but the climate was right. The United States of the 1950s was red, white, and blue. The Korean War was raging. McCarthyism was rampant. Ike was it and the Cold War was hot. If you were against nuclear testing, you were for a Communist regime.

Much has been written about this "American nuclear tragedy." 21 Public health was secondary to national security. The Atomic Energy Commissioner, Thomas Murray said, "Gentlemen, we must not let anything interfere with this series of tests, nothing."[2]

Again and again, the American public was told by its govern- 22 ment, in spite of burns, blisters, and nausea, "It has been found that the tests may be conducted with adequate assurance of safety under conditions prevailing at the bombing reservations."[3] Assuaging public fears was simply a matter of public relations. "Your best action," an Atomic Energy Commission booklet read, "is not to be worried about fallout." A news release typical of the times stated, "We find no basis for concluding that harm to any individual has resulted from radioactive fallout."[4]

On August 30, 1979, during Jimmy Carter's presidency, a suit 23 was filed entitled "Irene Allen vs. the United States of America." Mrs. Allen was the first to be alphabetically listed with twenty-four test cases, representative of nearly 1200 plaintiffs seeking compensation from the United States government for cancers caused from nuclear testing in Nevada.

Irene Allen lived in Hurricane, Utah. She was the mother of five 24 children and had been widowed twice. Her first husband with their two oldest boys had watched the tests from the roof of the local high school. He died of leukemia in 1956. Her second husband died of pancreatic cancer in 1978.

---

[1]John G. Fuller, *The Day We Bombed Utah* (New York: New American Library, 1984). [All notes are Williams's.]
[2]Ferenc M. Szasz, "Downwind from the Bomb," *Nevada Historical Society Quarterly*, Fall 1987 Vol. XXX, No. 3, p. 185.
[3]Philip L. Fradkin, *Fallout* (Tucson: University of Arizona Press, 1989), 98.
[4]Ibid., 109.

In a town meeting conducted by Utah Senator Orrin Hatch, 25
shortly before the suit was filed, Mrs. Allen said, "I am not blaming
the government, I want you to know that, Senator Hatch. But I
thought if my testimony could help in any way so this wouldn't happen again to any of the generations coming up after us . . . I am really
happy to be here this day to bear testimony of this."[5]

God-fearing people. This is just one story in an anthology of 26
thousands.

On May 10, 1984, Judge Bruce S. Jenkins handed down his opin- 27
ion. Ten of the plaintiffs were awarded damages. It was the first time
a federal court had determined that nuclear tests had been the cause
of cancers. For the remaining fourteen test cases, the proof of causation was not sufficient. In spite of the split decision, it was considered
a landmark ruling.[6] It was not to remain so for long.

In April, 1987, the 10th Circuit Court of Appeals overturned 28
Judge Jenkins' ruling on the basis that the United States was protected from suit by the legal doctrine of sovereign immunity, the cen-
turies-old idea from England in the days of absolute monarchs.[7]

In January, 1988, the Supreme Court refused to review the 29
Appeals Court decision. To our court system, it does not matter
whether the United States government was irresponsible, whether it
lied to its citizens or even that citizens died from the fallout of nuclear
testing. What matters is that our government is immune. "The King
can do no wrong."

In Mormon culture, authority is respected, obedience is revered, 30
and independent thinking is not. I was taught as a young girl not to
"make waves" or "rock the boat."

"Just let it go —" my mother would say. "You know how you 31
feel, that's what counts."

For many years, I did just that — listened, observed, and quietly 32
formed my own opinions within a culture that rarely asked questions
because they had all the answers. But one by one, I watched the
women in my family die common, heroic deaths. We sat in waiting
rooms hoping for good news, always receiving the bad. I cared for
them, bathed their scarred bodies and kept their secrets. I watched

---

[5]Town meeting held by Senator Orrin Hatch in St. George, Utah, April 17, 1979,
transcript, 26–28.
[6]Fradkin, Op. cit., 228.
[7]U.S. vs. Allen, 816 Federal Reporter, 2d/1417 (10th Circuit Court 1987), cert. denied,
108 S. Ct. 694 (1988).

beautiful women become bald as cytoxan, cisplatin, and adriamycin were injected into their veins. I held their foreheads as they vomited green-black bile and I shot them with morphine when the pain became inhuman. In the end, I witnessed their last peaceful breaths, becoming a midwife to the rebirth of their souls. But the price of obedience became too high.

The fear and inability to question authority that ultimately killed   33 rural communities in Utah during atmospheric testing of atomic weapons was the same fear I saw being held in my mother's body. Sheep. Dead sheep. The evidence is buried.

I cannot prove that my mother, Diane Dixon Tempest, or my   34 grandmothers, Lettie Romney Dixon and Kathryn Blackett Tempest, along with my aunts contracted cancer from nuclear fallout in Utah. But I can't prove they didn't.

My father's memory was correct, the September blast we drove   35 through in 1957 was part of Operation Plumbbob, one of the most intensive series of bomb tests to be initiated. The flash of light in the night in the desert I had always thought was a dream developed into a family nightmare. It took fourteen years, from 1957 to 1971, for cancer to show up in my mother—the same time, Howard L. Andrews, an authority on radioactive fallout at the National Institutes of Health, says radiation cancer requires to become evident.[8] The more I learn about what it means to be a "downwinder," the more questions I drown in.

What I do know, however, is that as a Mormon woman of the   36 fifth generation of "Latter-Day-Saints," I must question everything, even if it means losing my faith, even if it means becoming a member of a border tribe among my own people. Tolerating blind obedience in the name of patriotism or religion ultimately takes our lives.

When the Atomic Energy Commission described the country   37 north of the Nevada Test Site as "virtually uninhabited desert terrain," my family members were some of the "virtual uninhabitants."

One night, I dreamed women from all over the world circling a   38 blazing fire in the desert. They spoke of change, of how they hold the moon in their bellies and wax and wane with its phases. They mocked at the presumption of even-tempered beings and made promises that they would never fear the witch inside themselves. The women

---

[8]Fradkin, Op. cit., 116.

danced wildly as sparks broke away from the flames and entered the night sky as stars.

And they sang a song given to them by Shoshone grandmothers: 39

Ah ne nah, nah
nin nah nah—
Ah ne nah, nah
nin nah nah—
Nyaga mutzi
oh ne nay—
Nyaga mutzi
oh ne nay—[9]

The women danced and drummed and sang for weeks, preparing   40
themselves for what was to come. They would reclaim the desert for the sake of their children, for the sake of the land.

A few miles downwind from the fire circle, bombs were being   41
tested. Rabbits felt the tremors. Their soft leather pads on paws and feet recognized the shaking sands while the roots of mesquite and sage were smoldering. Rocks were hot from the inside out and dust devils hummed unnaturally. And each time there was another nuclear test, ravens watched the desert heave. Stretch marks appeared. The land was losing its muscle.

The women couldn't bear it any longer. They were mothers. They   42
had suffered labor pains but always under the promise of birth. The red hot pains beneath the desert promised death only as each bomb became a stillborn. A contract had been broken between human be-ings and the land. A new contract was being drawn by the women who understood the fate of the earth as their own.

Under the cover of darkness, ten women slipped under the barbed   43
wire fence and entered the contaminated country. They were trespass-ing. The walked toward the town of Mercury in moonlight, taking their cues from coyote, kit fox, antelope squirrel, and quail. They moved quietly and deliberately through the maze of Joshua trees. When a hint of daylight appeared they rested, drinking tea and

---

[9]This song was sung by the Western Shoshone women as they crossed the line at the Nevada Test Site on March 18, 1988, as part of their "Reclaim the Land" action. The translation they gave was: "Consider the rabbits how gently they walk on the earth. Consider the rabbits how gently they walk on the earth. We remember them. We can walk gently also. We remember them. We can walk gently also."

sharing their rations of food. The women closed their eyes. The time had come to protest with the heart, that to deny one's genealogy with the earth was to commit treason against one's soul.

At dawn, the women draped themselves in mylar, wrapping long 44 streamers of silver plastic around their arms to blow in the breeze. They wore clear masks that became the faces of humanity. And when they arrived on the edge of Mercury, they carried all the butterflies of a summer day in their wombs. They paused to allow their courage to settle.

The town which forbids pregnant women and children to enter 45 because of radiation risks to their health was asleep. The women moved through the streets as winged messengers, twirling around each other in slow motion, peeking inside homes and watching the easy sleep of men and women. They were astonished by such stillness and periodically would utter a shrill note or low cry just to verify life.

The residents finally awoke to what appeared as strange appari- 46 tions. Some simply stared. Others called authorities, and in time, the women were apprehended by wary soldiers dressed in desert fatigues. They were taken to a white, square building on the other edge of Mercury. When asked who they were and why they were there, the women replied, "We are mothers and we have come to reclaim the desert for our children."

The soldiers arrested them. As the ten women were blindfolded 47 and handcuffed, they began singing:

> *You can't forbid us everything*
> *You can't forbid us to think —*
> *You can't forbid our tears to flow*
> *And you can't stop the songs that we sing.*

The women continued to sing louder and louder, until they heard 48 the voices of their sisters moving across the mesa.

> *Ah ne nah, nah*
> *nin nah nah —*
> *Ah ne nah, nah*
> *nin nah nah —*
> *Nyaga mutzi*
> *oh ne nay —*
> *Nyaga mutzi*
> *oh ne nay —*

"Call for re-enforcement," one soldier said.   49

"We have," interrupted one woman. "We have—and you have   50
no idea of our numbers."

On March 18, 1988, I crossed the line at the Nevada Test Site and   51
was arrested with nine other Utahns for trespassing on military lands.
They are still conducting nuclear tests in the desert. Ours was an act
of civil disobedience. But as I walked toward the town of Mercury, it
was more than a gesture of peace. It was a gesture on behalf of the
Clan of One-breasted Women.

As one officer cinched the handcuffs around my wrists, another   52
frisked my body. She found a pen and a pad of paper tucked inside
my left boot.

"And these?" she asked sternly.   53

"Weapons," I replied.   54

Our eyes met. I smiled. She pulled the leg of my trousers back   55
over my boot.

"Step forward, please," she said as she took my arm.   56

We were booked under an afternoon sun and bussed to Tonapah,   57
Nevada. It was a two-hour ride. This was familiar country to me.
The Joshua trees standing their ground had been named by my ancestors who believed they looked like prophets pointing west to the
promised land. These were the same trees that bloomed each spring,
flowers appearing like white flames in the Mojave. And I recalled a
full moon in May when my mother and I had walked among them,
flushing out mourning doves and owls.

The bus stopped short of town. We were released. The officials   58
thought it was a cruel joke to leave us stranded in the desert with no
way to get home. What they didn't realize is that we were home, soul-
centered and strong, women who recognized the sweet smell of sage
as fuel for our spirits.

Thinking Critically about This Reading

In paragraph 20, Williams tells us that "the United States of the
1950s was red, white, and blue. The Korean War was raging.
McCarthyism was rampant. Ike was it and the Cold War was hot. If
you were against nuclear testing, you were for a Communist regime." Why do you think that Williams thought it was important
for readers to know what the United States was like during these
years? Explain.

Questions for Study and Discussion

1. How did you respond to Williams's opening three paragraphs? Together, did they work well as a beginning for you? Explain why or why not.

2. What "new information" (paragraph 17) does Williams learn while talking with her father over dinner shortly after her mother had died from cancer? Of what importance is this new information?

3. How does Williams use outside sources to support the idea that "public health was secondary to national security" (21)?

4. In paragraph 35, Williams paraphrases Howard L. Andrews. How does Williams signal where the paraphrase begins and ends? For what purpose does Williams bring Andrews into the discussion at this point?

5. Why did Williams remain silent about her suspicions about the nuclear testing for so long? What ultimately convinced her that she should speak out?

6. Williams has organized her essay into three sections—paragraphs 1–19, 20–29, and 30–58. How are the three sections related? Why do you think Williams ordered her essay in this way? (Glossary: *Organization*)

7. Why did the Shoshone women cross the line at the Nevada Test Site and enter the "contaminated country"? Why did Williams join them? What did Williams mean when she told the soldier frisking her that her pen and pad of paper were "weapons" (54)?

Classroom Activity Using Writing with Sources

For each of the following quotations, write an acceptable paraphrase and then a paraphrase including a partial quotation that avoids plagiarism (see pp. 251–54). Pay attention to the word choice and sentence structure of the original.

> The sperm whale is the largest of the toothed whales. Moby Dick was a sperm whale. Generally, male toothed whales are larger than the females. Female sperm whales may grow thirty-five to forty feet in length, while the males may reach sixty feet.
>
> –Richard Hendrick, *The Voyage of the Mimi*

Astronauts from over twenty nations have gone into space, and
they all come back, amazingly enough, saying the very same thing:
the earth is a small, blue place of profound beauty that we must
take care of. For each, the journey into space, whatever its original
intents and purposes, became above all a spiritual one.

–Al Reinhert, *For All Mankind*

One of the usual things about education in mathematics in the
United States is its relatively impoverished vocabulary. Whereas the
student completing elementary school will already have a vocabulary for most disciplines of many hundreds, even thousands of
words, the typical student will have a mathematics vocabulary of
only a couple of dozen words.

–Marvin Minsky, *The Society of Mind*

Suggested Writing Assignments

1. In paragraph 36, Williams emphatically states, "Tolerating blind
   obedience in the name of patriotism or religion ultimately takes
   our lives." Using examples from your own experience, observation, and reading, write an essay in which you agree or disagree
   with Williams's position.

2. Poet and environmentalist Wendell Berry has said that "it is impossible to care more or differently for each other than we care
   for the land." What do you think that he means? Like the
   Western Shoshone women who crossed the government line at
   the Nevada Test Site as part of their "Reclaim the Land" action,
   we are all stewards of the earth. What responsibilities do you
   think we have toward the land? Toward one another? How can
   humans work in partnership with the land? Using your own experiences as well as research in your library and on the Internet,
   write an argumentative essay that answers these questions.

3. In 1962, Rachel Carson charged, in her landmark book *Silent
   Spring*, that "we have put poisonous and biologically potent
   chemicals indiscriminately into the hands of persons largely or
   wholly ignorant of their potential for harm." The validity of her
   charge is everywhere evident today. Write an essay about chemical and nuclear abuses using specific examples that have been
   brought to the public's attention since *Silent Spring* first appeared.

part ■ *three*

The Language
of the Essay

Diction and Tone

◼ DICTION

Diction refers to a writer's choice and use of words. Good diction is precise and appropriate: The words mean exactly what the writer intends, and the words are well suited to the writer's subject, purpose, and intended audience.

Careful writers do not merely come close to saying what they want to say; they select words that convey their exact meaning. Perhaps Mark Twain put this idea best when he said, "The difference between the right word and the almost right word is the difference between lightning and the lightning bug." Inaccurate, imprecise, or inappropriate diction fails to convey the writer's intended meaning and also may cause confusion and misunderstanding for the reader.

Connotation and Denotation

Both **connotation** and **denotation** refer to the meanings of words. Denotation is the dictionary meaning of a word, the literal meaning. Connotative meanings are the associations or emotional overtones that words have acquired. For example, the word *home* denotes a place where someone lives, but it connotes warmth, security, family, comfort, affection, and other more private thoughts and images. The word *residence* also denotes a place where someone lives, but its connotations are colder and more formal.

Many words in English have synonyms, words with very similar denotations—for example, *mob, crowd, multitude,* and *bunch.* Deciding which to use depends largely on the connotations that each synonym has and the context in which the word is to be used. For example, you might say, "There was a crowd at the lecture," but not "There was a mob at the lecture." Good writers are sensitive to both the denotations and the connotations of words.

Abstract and Concrete Words

Abstract words name ideas, conditions, emotions—things nobody can touch, see, or hear. Some abstract words are *love, wisdom, cowardice, beauty, fear,* and *liberty.* People often disagree about abstract things. You may find a forest beautiful, while someone else might find it frightening, and neither of you would be wrong. Beauty and fear are ideas; they exist in your mind, not in the forest along with the trees and the owls. **Concrete** words refer to things we can touch, see, hear, smell, and taste, such as *sandpaper, soda, birch tree, smog, cow, sailboat, rocking chair,* and *pancake.* If you disagree with someone on a concrete issue—say, you claim that the forest is mostly birch trees, while the other person says that it is mostly pine—only one of you can be right, and both of you can be wrong; the kinds of trees that grow in the forest is a concrete fact, not an abstract idea.

Good writing balances ideas and facts, and it also balances abstract and concrete diction. If the writing is too abstract and has too few concrete facts and details, it will be unconvincing and tiresome. If the writing is too concrete and is devoid of abstract ideas and emotions, it can seem mundane and dry.

General and Specific Words

General and **specific** do not necessarily refer to opposites. The same word can often be either general or specific, depending on the context: *Dessert* is more specific than *food* but more general than *chocolate cream pie.* Being specific is like being concrete: Chocolate cream pie is something you can see and taste. Being general, on the other hand, is like being abstract. Food, dessert, and even pie are large classes of things that bring to mind only general tastes or images.

Good writing moves back and forth from the general to the specific. Without specific words, generalities can be unconvincing and even confusing: the writer's idea of "good food" may be very different from the reader's. But writing that does not relate specifics to each other by generalization often lacks focus and direction.

Clichés

A word, phrase, or expression that has become trite through overuse is called a **cliché.** Let's assume your roommate has just returned from an evening out. You ask her, "How was the concert?" She responds, "The concert was okay, but they had us *packed in* there *like sardines.*

How was your evening?" And you reply, "Well, I finished my term paper, but the noise here is enough to *drive me crazy*. The dorm is a real *zoo*." At one time the italicized expressions were vivid and colorful, but through constant use they have grown stale and ineffective. Experienced writers always try to avoid such clichés as *believe it or not, doomed to failure, hit the spot, let's face it, sneaking suspicion, step in the right direction*, and *went to great lengths*. They strive to use fresh language.

Jargon

Jargon, or technical language, is the special vocabulary of a trade or profession. Writers use jargon with an awareness of their audience. If their audience is a group of coworkers or professionals, jargon may be used freely. If the audience is general, jargon should be used sparingly and carefully so that readers can understand it. Jargon becomes inappropriate when it is overused, used out of context, or used pretentiously. For example, computer terms like *input, output,* and *feedback* are sometimes used in place of *contribution, result,* and *response* in other fields, especially in business. If you think about it, these terms suggest that people are machines that receive and process information according to a program imposed by someone else.

Formal and Informal Diction

Diction is appropriate when it suits the occasion for which it is intended. If the situation is informal—a friendly letter, for example—the writing may be colloquial; that is, its words may be chosen to suggest the way people talk with each other. If, on the other hand, the situation is formal—an academic paper or a research report, for example—the words should reflect this formality. Informal writing tends to be characterized by slang, contractions, references to the reader, and concrete nouns. Formal writing tends to be impersonal, abstract, and free of contractions and references to the reader. Formal writing and informal writing are the extremes. Most writing falls between these two extremes and is a blend of those formal and informal elements that best fit the context.

■ TONE

Tone is the attitude a writer takes toward the subject and the audience. The tone may be friendly or hostile, serious or humorous, intimate or distant, enthusiastic or skeptical.

As you read the following paragraphs, notice how each writer creates a different tone and how that tone is supported by the diction — the writer's particular choice and use of words.

Nostalgic

When I was six years old, I thought I knew a lot. How to jump rope, how to skip a rock across a pond, and how to color and stay between the lines — these were all things I took great pride in. Nothing was difficult, and my days were carefree. That is, until the summer when everything became complicated and I suddenly realized I didn't know that much.

–Heather C. Blue, student

Angry

Cans. Beer cans. Glinting on the verges of a million miles of roadways, lying in scrub, grass, dirt, leaves, sand, mud, but never hidden. Piels, Rheingold, Ballantine, Schaefer, Schlitz, shining in the sun or picked by moon or the beams of headlights at night; washed by rain or flattened by wheels, but never dulled, never buried, never destroyed. Here is the mark of savages, the testament of wasters, the stain of prosperity.

–Marya Mannes

Humorous

In perpetrating a revolution, there are two requirements: someone or something to revolt against and someone to actually show up and do the revolting. Dress is usually casual and both parties may be flexible about time and place, but if either faction fails to attend the whole enterprise is likely to come off badly. In the Chinese Revolution of 1650 neither party showed up and the deposit on the hall was forfeited.

–Woody Allen

Resigned

I make my living humping cargo for Seaboard World Airlines, one of the big international airlines at Kennedy Airport. They handle strictly all cargo. I was once told that one of the Rockefellers is the major stockholder for the airline, but I don't really think about that too much. I don't get paid to think. The big thing is to beat that race with the time clock every morning of your life so the airline will be happy. The worst thing a man could ever do is to make suggestions about building a better airline. They pay people $40,000 a year to come up with better ideas. It doesn't matter that these ideas never work; it's just that they get nervous when a guy from South Brooklyn or Ozone Park acts like he has a brain.

–Patrick Fenton

Ironic

Once upon a time there was a small, beautiful, green and graceful country called Vietnam. It needed to be saved. (In later years no one could remember exactly what it needed to be saved from, but that is another story.) For many years Vietnam was in the process of being saved by France, but the French eventually tired of their labors and left. Then America took on the job. America was well equipped for country saving. It was the richest and most powerful nation on earth. It had, for example, nuclear explosives on hand and ready to use equal to six tons of TNT for every man, woman, and child in the world. It had huge and very efficient factories, brilliant and dedicated scientists, and most (but not everybody) would agree, it had good intentions. Sadly, America had one fatal flaw—its inhabitants were in love with technology and thought it could do no wrong. A visitor to America during the time of this story would probably have guessed its outcome after seeing how its inhabitants were treating their own country. The air was mostly foul, the water putrid, and most of the land was either covered with concrete or garbage. But Americans were never much on introspection, and they didn't foresee the result of their loving embrace on the small country. They set out to save Vietnam with the same enthusiasm and determination their forefathers had displayed in conquering the frontier.

–The Sierra Club

The diction and tone of an essay are subtle forces, but they exert a tremendous influence on readers. They are instrumental in determining how we will feel while reading the essay and what attitude we will have toward its argument or the points it makes. Readers react in a variety of ways. An essay written informally but with a largely angry tone may make one reader defensive and unsympathetic; another may believe that the author is being unusually honest and courageous and may admire these qualities and feel moved by them. Either way, the diction and tone of the piece have made a strong emotional impression. As you read the essays in this chapter and throughout this book, see if you can analyze how the diction and tone shape your reactions.

Shame

■ Dick Gregory

*Dick Gregory, activist, comedian, and nutri-
tion expert, was born in St. Louis, Missouri,
in 1932. While attending Southern Illinois
University on an athletic scholarship, Gregory
excelled in track, winning the university's
Outstanding Athlete Award in 1953. In
1954, he was drafted into the army. After his
discharge, he immediately became active in
the civil rights movement led by Martin
Luther King Jr. In the 1960s, Gregory was an outspoken critic
of U.S. involvement in Vietnam, which in turn led to his run for
the presidency in 1968 as a write-in candidate for the Freedom
and Peace Party. Two of his books from this era are* No More
Lies: The Myth and Reality of American History *(1971) and*
Dick Gregory's Political Primer *(1972). Throughout his life he
has crusaded for economic reforms, antidrug issues, and minority rights. In 2000, he published* Callus on My Soul, *the second
volume of his autobiography. In recent years, Gregory has been
active in the diet and health food industry.*

    In the following episode from Nigger *(1964), the first volume
of his autobiography, Gregory narrates the story of a childhood
experience that taught him the meaning of shame. Through his use
of dialogue, he dramatically re-creates the experience for readers.
Notice how he uses concrete nouns and strong action verbs to describe his experiences and his intense emotional responses to them.*

Reflecting on What You Know

We all learn many things in school beyond the lessons we study
formally. Some of the extracurricular truths we learn stay with us
for the rest of our lives. Write about something you learned in
school—something that has made life easier or more understandable for you—that you still find useful.

I never learned hate at home, or shame. I had to go to school for that. 1
I was about seven years old when I got my first big lesson. I was in
love with a little girl named Helene Tucker, a light-complexioned little
girl with pigtails and nice manners. She was always clean and she was
smart in school. I think I went to school then mostly to look at her. I
brushed my hair and even got me a little old handkerchief. It was a
lady's handkerchief, but I didn't want Helene to see me wipe my nose
on my hand. The pipes were frozen again, there was no water in the
house, but I washed my socks and shirt every night. I'd get a pot, and
go over to Mister Ben's grocery store, and stick my pot down into his
soda machine. Scoop out some chopped ice. By evening the ice melted
to water for washing. I got sick a lot that winter because the fire
would go out at night before the clothes were dry. In the morning I'd
put them on, wet or dry, because they were the only clothes I had.

Everybody's got a Helene Tucker, a symbol of everything you 2
want. I loved her for her goodness, her cleanness, her popularity. She'd
walk down my street and my brothers and sisters would yell, "Here
comes Helene," and I'd rub my tennis sneakers on the back of my
pants and wish my hair wasn't so nappy[1] and the white folks' shirt fit
me better. I'd run out on the street. If I knew my place and didn't come
too close, she'd wink at me and say hello. That was a good feeling.
Sometimes I'd follow her all the way home, and shovel the snow off
her walk and try to make friends with her Momma and her aunts. I'd
drop money on her stoop late at night on my way back from shining
shoes in the taverns. And she had a Daddy, and he had a good job. He
was a paper hanger.

I guess I would have gotten over Helene by summertime, but 3
something happened in that classroom that made her face hang in
front of me for the next twenty-two years. When I played the drums in
high school it was for Helene and when I broke track records in college
it was for Helene and when I started standing behind microphones
and heard applause I wished Helene could hear it, too. It wasn't until
I was twenty-nine years old and married and making money that I
finally got her out of my system. Helene was sitting in that classroom
when I learned to be ashamed of myself.

It was on a Thursday. I was sitting in the back of the room, in a seat 4
with a chalk circle drawn around it. The idiot's seat, the troublemaker's
seat.

---

[1] *nappy:* shaggy or fuzzy.

The teacher thought I was stupid. Couldn't spell, couldn't read, ⁵ couldn't do arithmetic. Just stupid. Teachers were never interested in finding out that you couldn't concentrate because you were so hungry, because you hadn't had any breakfast. All you could think about was noontime, would it ever come? Maybe you could sneak into the cloakroom and steal a bite of some kid's lunch out of a coat pocket. A bite of something. Paste. You can't really make a meal of paste, or put it on bread for a sandwich, but sometimes I'd scoop a few spoonfuls out of the paste jar in the back of the room. Pregnant people get strange tastes. I was pregnant with poverty. Pregnant with dirt and pregnant with smells that made people turn away, pregnant with cold and pregnant with shoes that were never bought for me, pregnant with five other people in my bed and no Daddy in the next room, and pregnant with hunger. Paste doesn't taste too bad when you're hungry.

The teacher thought I was a troublemaker. All she saw from the ⁶ front of the room was a little black boy who squirmed in his idiot's seat and made noises and poked the kids around him. I guess she couldn't see a kid who made noises because he wanted someone to know he was there.

It was on a Thursday, the day before the Negro payday. The eagle ⁷ always flew on Friday. The teacher was asking each student how much his father would give to the Community Chest. On Friday night, each kid would get the money from his father, and on Monday he would bring it to the school. I decided I was going to buy me a Daddy right then. I had money in my pocket from shining shoes and selling papers, and whatever Helene Tucker pledged for her Daddy I was going to top it. And I'd hand the money right in. I wasn't going to wait until Monday to buy me a Daddy.

I was shaking, scared to death. The teacher opened her book and ⁸ started calling out names alphabetically.

"Helene Tucker?" ⁹

"My daddy said he'd give two dollars and fifty cents." ¹⁰

"That's very nice, Helene. Very, very nice indeed." ¹¹

That made me feel pretty good. It wouldn't take too much to top ¹² that. I had almost three dollars in dimes and quarters in my pocket. I stuck my hand in my pocket and held onto the money, waiting for her to call my name. But the teacher closed her book after she called everybody else in the class.

I stood up and raised my hand. ¹³

"What is it now?" ¹⁴

"You forgot me."　15

She turned toward the blackboard. "I don't have time to be play-　16
ing with you, Richard."

"My Daddy said he'd . . ."　17

"Sit down, Richard, you're disturbing the class."　18

"My Daddy said he'd give . . . fifteen dollars."　19

She turned around and looked mad. "We are collecting this　20
money for you and your kind, Richard Gregory. If your Daddy can
give fifteen dollars you have no business being on relief."

"I got it right now, I got it right now, my Daddy gave it to me to　21
turn in today, my Daddy said . . ."

"And furthermore," she said, looking right at me, her nostrils　22
getting big and her lips getting thin and her eyes opening wide, "we
know you don't have a Daddy."

Helene Tucker turned around, her eyes full of tears. She felt sorry　23
for me. Then I couldn't see her too well because I was crying, too.

"Sit down, Richard."　24

And I always thought the teacher kind of liked me. She always　25
picked me to wash the blackboard on Friday, after school. That was a
big thrill, it made me feel important. If I didn't wash it, come Monday
the school might not function right.

"Where are you going, Richard?"　26

I walked out of school that day, and for a long time I didn't go　27
back very often. There was shame there.

Now there was shame everywhere. It seemed like the whole world　28
had been inside that classroom, everyone had heard what the teacher
had said, everyone had turned around and felt sorry for me. There was
shame in going to the Worthy Boys Annual Christmas Dinner for you
and your kind, because everybody knew what a worthy boy was. Why
couldn't they just call it the Boys Annual Dinner; why'd they have to
give it a name? There was shame in wearing the brown and orange and
white plaid mackinaw[2] the welfare gave to three thousand boys. Why'd
it have to be the same for everybody so when you walked down the
street the people could see you were on relief? It was a nice warm mackinaw and it had a hood, and my Momma beat me and called me a little
rat when she found out I stuffed it in the bottom of a pail full of garbage
way over on Cottage Street. There was shame in running over to Mister
Ben's at the end of the day and asking for his rotten peaches, there was

---

[2]*mackinaw:* a short, double-breasted wool coat.

shame in asking Mrs. Simmons for a spoonful of sugar, there was shame in running out to meet the relief truck. I hated that truck, full of food for you and your kind. I ran into the house and hid when it came. And then I started to sneak through alleys, to take the long way home so the people going into White's Eat Shop wouldn't see me. Yeah, the whole world heard the teacher that day, we all know you don't have a Daddy.

Thinking Critically about This Reading

In paragraph 28, Gregory states, "Now there was shame everywhere. It seemed like the whole world had been inside that classroom, everyone had heard what the teacher had said, everyone had turned around and felt sorry for me." What did Gregory's teacher say, and why did it hurt him so greatly?

Questions for Study and Discussion

1. How do the first three paragraphs of the essay help establish a context for the narrative that follows? (Glossary: *Narration*)
2. What does Gregory mean by "shame"? What precisely was he ashamed of, and what in particular did he learn from the incident? (Glossary: *Definition*)
3. In a word or phrase, how would you describe Gregory's tone? What specific words or phrases in his essay lead you to this conclusion?
4. What is the teacher's attitude toward Gregory? In arriving at your answer, consider her own words and actions as well as Gregory's opinion.
5. What role does money play in Gregory's experience? How does money relate to his sense of shame?
6. Specific details can enhance the reader's understanding and appreciation of a subject. (Glossary: *Details*) Gregory's description of Helene Tucker's manners or the plaid of his mackinaw, for example, makes his account vivid and interesting. Cite several other specific details he gives, and consider how the essay would be different without them.
7. Reread this essay's first and last paragraphs, and compare how much each one emphasizes shame. (Glossary: *Beginnings and Endings*) Which emotion other than shame does Gregory reveal

in the first paragraph, and does it play a role in the last one? Is the last paragraph an effective ending? Explain.

Classroom Activity Using Diction and Tone

Good writers rely on strong verbs—verbs that contribute significantly to what is being said. Because they must repeatedly describe similar situations, sportswriters, for example, are acutely aware of the need for strong action verbs. It is not enough for them to say that a team wins or loses; they must describe the type of win or loss more precisely. As a result, such verbs as *beat, bury, edge, shock,* and *trounce* are common in sports headlines. In addition to describing the act of winning, each of these verbs makes a statement about the quality of the victory. Like sportswriters, we all write about actions that are performed daily. If we were restricted only to the verbs *eat, drink, sleep,* and *work* for each of these activities, our writing would be repetitious, monotonous, and most likely wordy. List as many verbs as you can that you could use in place of these four. What connotative differences do you find in your lists of alternatives? What is the importance of these connotative differences for you as a writer?

Suggested Writing Assignments

1. Using Gregory's essay as a model, write an essay narrating an experience that made you feel especially afraid, angry, surprised, embarrassed, or proud. Include details that allow your readers to know exactly what happened. Pay attention to how you use your first and last paragraphs to present the emotion your essay focuses on.

2. Most of us grow up with some sense of the socioeconomic class that our family belongs to, and often we are aware of how we are, or believe we are, different from people of other classes. Write an essay in which you describe a possession or activity that you thought revealed your socioeconomic standing and made you self-conscious about how you were different from others. Be sure to recount an experience that seemed to confirm your belief, and discuss why it did. Pay attention to your essay's first and last paragraphs so that they serve your purpose.

Me Talk Pretty One Day

■ David Sedaris

David Sedaris was born in 1956 in Binghamton, New York, and grew up in Raleigh, North Carolina. He briefly attended Western Carolina University and Kent State University but ultimately graduated from the Art Institute of Chicago in 1987. Before becoming a writer, Sedaris worked as a mover, an office temp, a housekeeper, and an elf in a department store Christmas display, an experience he wrote about in his celebrated essay "Santaland Diaries." *He is a regular contributor to National Public Radio,* Harper's, Details, *the* New Yorker, *and* Esquire *and has won several awards, including the James Thurber Prize for American Humor. Sedaris often writes about his quirky Greek family and his travels with his partner, Hugh Hamrick, with whom he currently lives in London. His essays and stories have been collected in several best-selling books, including* Barrel Fever *(1994),* Holidays on Ice *(1997),* Naked *(1997),* Dress Your Family in Corduroy and Denim *(2004),* When You Are Engulfed in Flames *(2008), and most recently* Squirrel Seeks Chipmunk: A Modest Bestiary *(2010).*

The following essay about taking French language lessons in Paris first appeared in Esquire *in March 1999 and later became the title piece for Sedaris's fourth book,* Me Talk Pretty One Day *(2000). As you read, pay attention to how he uses his words to play with the ideas of language, understanding, and belonging.*

Reflecting on What You Know

Have you ever been in a situation where you did not speak the prevalent language—for example, in a foreign country, a language class, or a group of people who spoke a language other than yours? How did you feel about not being able to communicate? How, if at all, did you get your thoughts across to others?

At the age of forty-one, I am returning to school and having to   1
think of myself as what my French textbook calls "a true debu-
tant." After paying my tuition, I was issued a student ID, which allows
me a discounted entry fee at movie theaters, puppet shows, and
Festyland, a far-flung amusement park that advertises with billboards
picturing a cartoon stegosaurus sitting in a canoe and eating what appears to be a ham sandwich.

I've moved to Paris in order to learn the language. My school is   2
the Alliance Française, and on the first day of class, I arrived early,
watching as the returning students greeted one another in the school
lobby. Vacations were recounted, and questions were raised concerning mutual friends with names like Kang and Vlatnya. Regardless of
their nationalities, everyone spoke what sounded to me like excellent
French. Some accents were better than others, but the students exhibited an ease and confidence I found intimidating. As an added discomfort, they were all young, attractive, and well dressed, causing me
to feel not unlike Pa Kettle[1] trapped backstage after a fashion show.

I remind myself that I am now a full-grown man. No one will ever   3
again card me for a drink or demand that I weave a floor mat out of
newspapers. At my age, a reasonable person should have completed his
sentence in the prison of the nervous and the insecure—isn't that the
great promise of adulthood? I can't help but think that, somewhere
along the way, I made a wrong turn. My fears have not vanished.
Rather, they have seasoned and multiplied with age. I am now twice as
frightened as I was when, at the age of twenty, I allowed a failed nursing student to inject me with a horse tranquilizer, and eight times more
anxious than I was the day my kindergarten teacher pried my fingers
off my mother's ankle and led me screaming toward my desk. "You'll
get used to it," the woman had said.

I'm still waiting.   4

The first day of class was nerve-racking because I knew I'd be   5
expected to perform. That's the way they do it here—everyone into the
language pool, sink or swim. The teacher marched in, deeply tanned
from a recent vacation, and rattled off a series of administrative
announcements. I've spent some time in Normandy,[2] and I took a
monthlong French class last summer in New York. I'm not completely
in the dark, yet I understood only half of what this teacher was saying.

---

[1]*Pa Kettle:* someone who is simple or unsophisticated; the name of a character in a
series of comic movies popular in the 1950s.
[2]*Normandy:* a province in northwestern France.

"If you have not *meismslsxp* by this time, you should not be in 6 this room. Has everybody *apzkiubjxow*? Everyone? Good, we shall proceed." She spread out her lesson plan and sighed, saying, "All right, then, who knows the alphabet?"

It was startling because a) I hadn't been asked that question in a 7 while, and b) I realized, while laughing, that I myself did not know the alphabet. They're the same letters, but they're pronounced differently.

"Ahh." The teacher went to the board and sketched the letter *A*. "Do 8 we have anyone in the room whose first name commences with an ahh?"

Two Polish Annas raised their hands, and the teacher instructed 9 them to present themselves, giving their names, nationalities, occupations, and a list of things they liked and disliked in this world. The first Anna hailed from an industrial town outside of Warsaw and had front teeth the size of tombstones. She worked as a seamstress, enjoyed quiet times with friends, and hated the mosquito.

"Oh, really," the teacher said. "How very interesting. I thought 10 that everyone loved the mosquito, but here, in front of all the world, you claim to detest him. How is it that we've been blessed with someone as unique and original as you? Tell us, please."

The seamstress did not understand what was being said, but she 11 knew that this was an occasion for shame. Her rabbity mouth huffed for breath, and she stared down at her lap as though the appropriate comeback were stitched somewhere alongside the zipper of her slacks.

The second Anna learned from the first and claimed to love sun- 12 shine and detest lies. It sounded like a translation of one of those Playmate of the Month data sheets, the answers always written in the same loopy handwriting: "Turn-ons: Mom's famous five-alarm chili! Turnoffs: Insincerity and guys who come on too strong!!!"

The two Polish women surely had clear notions of what they 13 liked and disliked, but, like the rest of us, they were limited in terms of vocabulary, and this made them appear less than sophisticated. The teacher forged on, and we learned that Carlos, the Argentine bandoneon[3] player, loved wine, music, and, in his words, "Making sex with the women of the world." Next came a beautiful young Yugoslavian who identified herself as an optimist, saying that she loved everything life had to offer.

The teacher licked her lips, revealing a hint of the sadist[4] we would 14 later come to know. She crouched low for her attack, placed her hands

---

[3] *bandoneon:* a small accordion popular in South America.
[4] *sadist:* one who finds pleasure in being cruel to others.

on the young woman's desk, and said, "Oh, yeah? And do you love your little war?"[5]

While the optimist struggled to defend herself, I scrambled to   15
think of an answer to what had obviously become a trick question. How often are you asked what you love in this world? More important, how often are you asked and then publicly ridiculed for your answer? I recalled my mother, flushed with wine, pounding the table late one night, saying, "Love? I love a good steak cooked rare. I love my cat, and I love . . ." My sisters and I leaned forward, waiting to hear our names. "Tums," our mother said. "I love Tums." The teacher killed some time accusing the Yugoslavian girl of masterminding a program of genocide, and I jotted frantic notes in the margins of my pad. While I can honestly say that I love leafing through medical textbooks devoted to severe dermatological conditions, it is beyond the reach of my French vocabulary, and acting it out would only have invited unwanted attention.

When called upon, I delivered an effortless list of things I detest: 16
blood sausage, intestinal paté, brain pudding. I'd learned these words the hard way. Having given it some thought, I then declared my love for IBM typewriters, the French word for "bruise," and my electric floor waxer. It was a short list, but still I managed to mispronounce IBM and afford the wrong gender to both the floor waxer and the typewriter. Her reaction led me to believe that these mistakes were capital crimes in the country of France.

"Were you always this *palicmkrexjs*?" she asked. "Even a *fiu-*   17
scrzsws tociwegixp knows that a typewriter is feminine."

I absorbed as much of her abuse as I could understand, thinking,   18
but not saying, that I find it ridiculous to assign a gender to an inanimate object incapable of disrobing and making an occasional fool of itself. Why refer to Lady Flesh Wound or Good Sir Dishrag when these things could never deliver in the sack?

The teacher proceeded to belittle everyone from German Eva,   19
who hated laziness, to Japanese Yukari, who loved paintbrushes and soap. Italian, Thai, Dutch, Korean, Chinese—we all left class foolishly believing that the worst was over. We didn't know it then, but the coming months would teach us what it is like to spend time in the presence of a wild animal. We soon learned to dodge chalk and to cover our heads and stomachs whenever she approached us with a

---

[5] "*. . . your little war*": the Balkan War (1991–2001), armed conflict and genocide in the territory of the former Yugoslavia.

question. She hadn't yet punched anyone, but it seemed wise to prepare ourselves against the inevitable.

Though we were forbidden to speak anything but French, the teacher would occasionally use us to practice any of her five fluent languages. [20]

"I hate you," she said to me one afternoon. Her English was flawless. "I really, really hate you." Call me sensitive, but I couldn't help taking it personally. [21]

Learning French is a lot like joining a gang in that it involves a long and intensive period of hazing. And it wasn't just my teacher; the entire population seemed to be in on it. Following brutal encounters with my local butcher and the concierge[6] of my building, I'd head off to class, where the teacher would hold my corrected paperwork high above her head, shouting, "Here's proof that *David* is an ignorant and uninspired *ensigiejsokhjx*." [22]

Refusing to stand convicted on the teacher's charges of laziness, I'd spend four hours a night on my homework, working even longer whenever we were assigned an essay. I suppose I could have gotten by with less, but I was determined to create some sort of an identity for myself. We'd have one of those "complete the sentence" exercises, and I'd fool with the thing for hours, invariably settling on something like, "A quick run around the lake? I'd love to. Just give me a minute to strap on my wooden leg." The teacher, through word and action, conveyed the message that, if this was my idea of an identity, she wanted nothing to do with it. [23]

My fear and discomfort crept beyond the borders of my classroom and accompanied me out onto the wide boulevards, where, no matter how hard I tried, there was no escaping the feeling of terror I felt whenever anyone asked me a question. I was safe in any kind of a store, as, at least in my neighborhood, one can stand beside the cash register for hours on end without being asked something so trivial as, "May I help you?" or "How would you like to pay for that?" [24]

My only comfort was the knowledge that I was not alone. Huddled in the smoky hallways and making the most of our pathetic French, my fellow students and I engaged in the sort of conversation commonly overheard in refugee camps. [25]

"Sometimes me cry alone at night." [26]

"That is common for me also, but be more strong, you. Much work, and someday you talk pretty. People stop hate you soon. Maybe tomorrow, okay?" [27]

---

[6]*concierge:* a doorman in a French apartment building.

Unlike other classes I have taken, here there was no sense of com- 28
petition. When the teacher poked a shy Korean woman in the eyelid
with a freshly sharpened pencil, we took no comfort in the fact that,
unlike Hyeyoon Cho, we all knew the irregular past tense of the verb
"to defeat." In all fairness, the teacher hadn't meant to hurt the woman,
but neither did she spend much time apologizing, saying only, "Well,
you should have been paying more attention."

Over time, it became impossible to believe that any of us would 29
ever improve. Fall arrived, and it rained every day. It was mid-October
when the teacher singled me out, saying, "Every day spent with you
is like having a cesarean section." And it struck me that, for the first
time since arriving in France, I could understand every word that
someone was saying.

Understanding doesn't mean that you can suddenly speak the 30
language. Far from it. It's a small step, nothing more, yet its rewards
are intoxicating and deceptive. The teacher continued her diatribe,
and I settled back, bathing in the subtle beauty of each new curse and
insult.

"You exhaust me with your foolishness and reward my efforts 31
with nothing but pain, do you understand me?"

The world opened up, and it was with great joy that I responded, 32
"I know the thing what you speak exact now. Talk me more, plus,
please, plus."

Thinking Critically about This Reading

Sedaris's French teacher tells him that "every day spent with you is
like having a cesarean section" (paragraph 29). Why is Sedaris's ability
to recount this insult significant? What does the teacher's "cesarean
section" metaphor mean?

Questions for Study and Discussion

1. Sedaris's tone is humorous. (Glossary: *Tone*) What words in particular help him create this tone? Did you find yourself smiling or
   laughing out loud as you read his essay? If so, what specific passages affected you this way?
2. What is your impression of Sedaris and his classmates? What
   words and phrases does he use to describe himself and them?

3. Why do you think Sedaris uses nonsense jumbles of letters—
   meismslsxp and *palicmkrexjs,* for example—in several places?
   How would his essay be different had he used the real words
   instead?

4. What does Sedaris realize in the final three paragraphs? What
   evidence does he provide of his realization?

Classroom Activity Using Diction and Tone

Many restaurant menus use connotative language in an attempt to
persuade patrons that they are about to have an exceptional dining
experience: "skillfully seasoned," "festive and spicy," "fresh from the
garden," "grilled to perfection," "freshly ground." Imagine that you are
charged with the task of creating such a menu. Use connotative language to describe the following basic foods, making them sound as
attractive and inviting as possible.

tomato juice	peas	pasta
onion soup	potatoes	ice cream
ground beef	salad	tea
chicken	bread and butter	cake

Suggested Writing Assignments

1. Write a narrative essay recounting a humorous incident in your
   life. (Glossary: *Narration*) Use the following questions to start
   thinking about the incident: Where were you? What happened?
   Who witnessed the incident? Did you think it was humorous at
   the time? Do you view it differently now? Why or why not? Choose
   words and phrases for your narrative that convey a humorous tone.
   (Glossary: *Tone*)

2. "Refusing to stand convicted on the teacher's charges of laziness,"
   Sedaris explains, "I'd spend four hours a night on my homework,
   working even longer whenever we were assigned an essay" (23).
   Write an essay in which you evaluate Sedaris's teacher. Given that
   she inspired Sedaris to apply himself to his work, do you think
   she was an effective teacher? Would her methods have the same
   effect on you? Why or why not? (Glossary: *Cause and Effect*)

3. As Sedaris's essay and the following cartoon illustrate, fitting in often depends on our ability to communicate with authenticity — using the appropriate pronunciation, terminology, or slang — to a particular audience. (Glossary: *Audience; Slang*) Have you ever felt alienated by a group because you didn't use its lingo appropriately, or have you ever alienated someone else for the same reason? Write a narrative essay in which you recount one such event. (Glossary: *Narration*) Be sure to use diction and tone creatively to convey your meaning. Before you begin, you might find it helpful to refer to your response to the prereading prompt for this selection.

The Center of the Universe

■ Tina McElroy Ansa

Novelist, filmmaker, teacher, and essayist, Tina McElroy Ansa was born in 1949 in Macon, Georgia, and grew up in its historic African American Pleasant Hill neighborhood. After graduating from Spelman College in Atlanta in 1971, Ansa worked as an editor and reporter at the Atlanta Constitution *and later at the* Charlotte Observer *in North Carolina before launching her career as a freelance writer in 1982. Her essays have appeared in various periodicals, including the* Los Angeles Times, Newsday, *and the* Atlanta Journal-Constitution, *and she has contributed the essays "Postcards from Georgia" to* CBS News Sunday Morning. *Ansa has taught writing at Spelman College, Brunswick College, and Emory University. Her first four novels—*Baby of the Family *(1989),* Ugly Ways *(1993),* The Hand I Fan With *(1996), and* You Know Better *(2002)—present the stories of black women in the modern American South interwoven with an interesting touch of traditional folklore and the supernatural. In 2007, she launched DownSouth, an independent publishing company focused on African American fiction and nonfiction. Her fifth novel,* Taking After Mudear, *was the lead title on her new press's fall 2007 list. Ansa and her husband collaborate on making movies and actively promote the arts on St. Simons Island, Georgia, where they live. Currently, they are adapting the award-winning* Baby of the Family *for the screen.*

The following essay first appeared in Dream Me Home Safely *(2003), a collection of essays edited by Susan Richards Shreve in which 34 American writers share memories of their formative years. Ansa's straightforward, almost conversational, tone engages readers at once and draws them into her reflections about growing up in the segregated South in the 1950s and how her experiences with family continue to influence her today.*

Reflecting on What You Know

Where did grow up? What are some of your strongest childhood memories of that place? To what extent do you identify with your hometown or area of the country?

On the way home from school one day when I was seven or eight years old—a black child growing up in Macon, Georgia, in the 1950s—my father, Walter McElroy, took me to a huge fountain in a city park. At the edge of the fountain, he pointed to the water and said very seriously, "That is the exact center of Georgia." 1

It was a momentous revelation for me. Since that instant, I have always thought of myself being at the center of my universe, enveloped in the world around me. From that day, I have imagined myself standing at that fountain surrounded by my African American community of Pleasant Hill, in my hometown of Macon, in middle Georgia, with the muddy Ocmulgee River running nearby, with the entire state of Georgia around me, then all of the southeastern section of the continental United States, then the country, the Western Hemisphere, then the world. 2

The image has always made me feel safe. Sheltered by my surroundings, enveloped in the arms of "family" of one kind or another, mostly southern family. That is how I see myself, a southerner. 3

For some folks, my discussing my southernness makes them downright uncomfortable. I mean really, the very idea, a black person, an African American over the age of thirty-five, going on and on about the South and her place in it as if she weren't aware of the region, its past, and all it stands for. 4

Doesn't she know history? she seems to think. And she's a writer, too. It's almost embarrassing. 5

As if a black person does not belong in the South, to the South. In a couple of decades of moving up and down the United States' eastern seaboard, I found there was no place else I *did belong*. 6

Of course I know the region's history, I want to tell folks looking askance at me. I know it because I am a part of the history. My parents were part of that history. And their parents were part of it. 7

My father's people came from Wrightsville, in the south-central part of the state. They were farming people, like most black people at the turn of the twentieth century. At that time, black folks owned nearly twenty million acres of farmland in the United States. When 8 my father's father, Frank, left the farm nearly one hundred years ago for the city of Macon and work on the M-D-S—the Macon-Dublin-Savannah train line, which connected those three Georgia cities—his brother Isadore (whom we called "Uncle Sunshine") and his family remained there on the farm. As a child, when my parents, two older brothers and two older sisters, and I piled into our green woodie station wagon and left the "city" for a few days in summer to visit the "country," it was to Uncle Sunshine's farm we went.

My mother's people—the Lees—were also from middle Georgia.   9 But they were "city people," they were not farmers. They were schoolteachers and tradespeople and semiprofessionals. Everyone in town knew my great-grandfather as "Pat, the barber." All I have to do now is say that name to make my mother smile with nostalgia and begin telling me stories surrounding the antique red leather barbershop chair that sat on my great-aunt's back porch for decades. Patrick Lee's maiden daughter, Elizabeth, not only took over her father's barbershop when he died in the 1930s. She also taught folks in middle Georgia from the cradle to the grave. During the day, she led her own private kindergarten class. During the evenings, she taught illiterate adults to read. "All I want to do is learn to read the Bible," they would tell her. She always chuckled: "Lord, some of the most difficult words and concepts in the world are in the Bible."

In childhood, I always thought of her as just a stern religious old   10 maid who didn't even drink Coca-Colas or take aspirin because they were "dope" or let you sleep in any bed in her house past sunup lest you get "the big head." I thank the Holy Spirit that she and I both lived long enough for me to see her for the extraordinary African American woman that she was. She was one of the reasons my mother loved reading and passed that love on to her children.

Today, every word I write, I write on a computer atop the old   11 pedal-motored Singer sewing machine console that once sat in Auntie's bedroom.

It is no wonder that in my childhood family house—a big old   12 brick two-story house with an attic and basement—there were books everywhere: in the bedrooms, the bathroom, the living room, and the kitchen. When I was a child, the joke in our family was to shove a copy of the tiny Macon telephone book under the door of the bathroom when someone hollered out for some new reading material. Whenever that happened to me, I happily sat there with my legs dangling off the toilet and amused myself by reading that phone book, looking up my friends' numbers and addresses, coming upon interesting names, making up stories about the people and streets I encountered there.

When I was growing up, I thought the entire world was made up 13
of stories. My mother gossiping on the phone was to my ear my mother weaving stories. The tales of love and woe that I overheard from the customers at my father's juke joints and liquor store down on Broadway and Mulberry Street, as I sat at the end of the bar in my Catholic school uniform doing my homework, were to me stories. My grandfather Walter McElroy's ghost stories of cats wearing diamond rings sticking their hands into blazing campfires. My Baptist great-auntie Elizabeth Lee relating how she always wanted to go to the Holy Land but had no intention of crossing any water to get there. My mother telling me over and over as she whipped up batter for one of her light-as-air, sweet-as-mother's-love desserts how she made her first cake when she was only seven.

I draw sustenance from these stories, in the same way I draw 14
nourishment from knowing that my father's people farmed land right up the road in Wrightsville, Georgia. In my southern mind, I can see Uncle Sunshine drawing his bony mule under the hot shade of a tall Georgia pine and wiping his brow when I gaze at the pine trees around my house. I never cross a railroad track without recalling my grandfather's years with the M-D-S line and the first time my father put me on the famed "Nancy Hanks" train for a trip to Savannah by myself. After my father handed me over to the care of the train's porters, they asked, pointing to my father's retreating back, "Who was that boy?" I replied indignantly, "That's no boy! That's my daddy!" The black men looked at each other and just beamed. Then proceeded to getting me cold Coca-Colas and sneaking me sandwiches from the whites-only dining car. For the rest of the four-hour trip, they treated me like a princess, heaping on me the loving attention usually thought of as the preserve of little white girls traveling on the southern train system. In fact, they treated me better. They treated me like family.

Family. As a writer, a novelist, it is all that I write about. My first 15
novel, *Baby of the Family,* is not just about my retaining that special place of the last born in my household. It is also about the ties, the connections, the stories, the food, the rituals, the seasons, the minutiae that go into forming the family unit.

Like all of us, I carry my childhood with me. 16

No matter where I go or in what time zone I find myself, at 17
eleven o'clock Eastern Standard Time Sunday mornings, I think of St.

Peter Claver Church sitting at the top of Pleasant Hill and the sacrament of the Eucharist being celebrated there. Sunday morning mass in my childhood parish is still the quintessential Sunday morning to me. Just as that fountain in the middle of Tatnall Square Park is the primary bellwether for my place in the universe.

When I write, I still envision myself standing at that fountain surrounded by my family, my community, my hometown, my state, my country, and the world.   18

From time to time, my mother will wistfully remind some old friend of hers who asks about me, "Tina doesn't live in Macon anymore."   19

My Mama is right. I *don't* live in Macon anymore.   20

Macon lives in me.   21

Thinking Critically about This Reading

Ansa concedes that "for some folks, my discussing my southernness makes them downright uncomfortable" (paragraph 4). Why do you suppose some people might find her "going on and on about the South" embarrassing? Why is Ansa proud to call herself a "southerner," to admit that "there was no place else I *did belong* (6)"? Explain.

Questions for Study and Discussion

1. When Ansa was a child, her father told her that the fountain in the local city park was "the exact center of Georgia" (1). Why was that a "momentous revelation" (2) for Ansa?

2. How does Ansa organize her essay? (Glossary: *Organization*) You may find it helpful to outline the essay before answering.

3. How would you describe Ansa's tone in this essay—informal, nostalgic, conversational, light-hearted, reflective, or serious? In what ways is her tone appropriate for her subject? Explain.

4. Why does Ansa consider her great-auntie Elizabeth Lee so important in her life? In what ways did Elizabeth influence or shape Ansa's life?

5. Ansa shares that "the joke in our family was to shove a copy of the tiny Macon telephone book under the door of the bathroom when someone hollered out for some new reading material" (12). What did Ansa do when that happened to her? In what ways is a telephone book useful for an aspiring writer? Explain.

6. Ansa observes that, as a child, "I thought the entire world was made up of stories" (13). Why are these family stories so important to Ansa? Which of the stories recounted in paragraphs 13 and 14 affect you the most? Explain why.

7. How effective did you find the way Ansa concluded her essay in paragraphs 18–21? (Glossary: *Beginnings and Endings*) In what ways does her ending complete the story started in her opening paragraphs?

Classroom Activity Using Diction and Tone

Writers create and control tone in their writing in part through the words they choose. For example, the words *laugh, cheery, dance,* and *melody* help create a tone of celebration. Make a list of the words that come to mind for each of the following tones:

humorous	authoritative	tentative
angry	triumphant	repentant

Compare your lists of words with those of others in the class. What generalizations can you make about the connotations associated with each of these tones?

Suggested Writing Assignments

1. In paragraph 16, Ansa confesses that, as an adult, "I carry my childhood with me." To what extent do you carry your childhood with you? Which family members most influenced who you are today? What events are strongly etched in your memory? Using Ansa's essay as a model, write an essay about your own childhood, including as much family history as you think necessary.

2. In what ways has your hometown changed since you were a child? Many people argue that the United States is becoming homogenized and that everywhere is beginning to look like everywhere else. Cities and towns throughout the United States are beginning to look alike because of an influx of malls and chain stores with similar appearance. Do you want to live in a country that is dotted with large cities surrounded by suburbs and towns that are interchangeable? Write an essay in which you argue against such homogenization as a threat to regional, cultural, and individual identities. Build your essay on a strong thesis, and be sure to use examples from your own experiences, observations, and reading.

Irreconcilable Dissonance

■ Brian Doyle

Born in New York City in 1956, Brian Doyle, son of a newspaper editor and a gifted teacher, grew up in a large Irish Catholic family on Long Island near Jones Beach. After graduating from Notre Dame University in 1978, he worked as a newspaper and magazine journalist in Boston, Chicago, and, most recently, Portland, Oregon, where he edits Portland *magazine, the University of Portland's alumni magazine. No "fluff and grab" magazine, it is annually ranked among the top ten best university magazines, publishing the work of such popular writers as Barry Lopez, Terry Tempest Williams, Bill McKibben, and Cynthia Ozick. Doyle is an award-winning essayist and author in his own right. His essays have appeared in the* Atlantic Monthly, Orion, Georgia Review, *and* Harper's, *and several have been reprinted in the* Best American Essays *anthologies. Doyle has written ten books, including* Leaping: Revelations & Epiphanies *(2003), a collection of essays with spirituality as the common thread;* Thirsty for Joy: Australian & American Voices *(2007), a collection of poems;* The Grail: A Year of Ambling and Shambling Through an Oregon Vineyard in Pursuit of the Best Pinot Noir Wine in the Whole Wild World *(2006), a work of nonfiction best described by its subtitle; and* Mink River *(2010), a novel of small-town life in coastal Oregon. He is currently working on a collection of short stories to be titled* Bin Laden's Bald Spot & Other Stories.

The following essay first appeared in the summer 2009 issue of Oregon Humanities. *In this candid look at marriage and divorce, Doyle explores a variety of reasons people give for getting divorced, arriving at the conclusion that "every marriage is pregnant with divorce, every day, every hour, every minute." Perhaps it is this ever-present threat of divorce that just might be the glue of marriage itself. As you read Doyle's essay, pay particular attention to his relatively simple choice of words and his sometimes complex sentence structures and how they combine to create a tone reflective of what Doyle calls the "shagginess" of our daily lives.*

Reflecting on What You Know

From your own reading and observations, what do you think about marriage and divorce? Why do you think that people get divorced? In your opinion, do people put enough into making a marriage work? Is marriage in your own plans sometime in the future?

I have been married once to the woman to whom I am still married, so far, and one thing I have noticed about being married is that it makes you a lot more attentive to divorce, which used to seem like something that happened to other people, but doesn't anymore, because of course every marriage is pregnant with divorce, and also now I know a lot of people who are divorced, or are about to be, or are somewhere in between those poles, for which shadowy status there should be words like mivorced or darried or sleeperated or schleperated, but there aren't, so far.

People seem to get divorced for all sorts of reasons, and I find myself taking notes, probably defensively, but also out of sheer amazement at the chaotic wilderness of human nature. For example, I read recently about one man who got divorced so he could watch all sixty episodes of *The Wire* in chronological order. Another man got divorced after thirty years so he could, he said, fart in peace. Another man got divorced in part because he told his wife he had an affair, but he didn't have an affair, he just couldn't think of any other good excuse to get divorced, and he didn't want to have an affair, or be with anyone else other than his wife, because he liked his wife, and rather enjoyed her company as a rule, he said, but he just didn't want to be married to her every day anymore, he preferred to be married to her every second or third day, but she did not find that a workable arrangement, and so they parted company, confused.

Another man I read about didn't want to get divorced, he said, but when his wife kept insisting that they get divorced because she had fallen in love with another guy, he, the husband, finally agreed to get divorced, and soon after he found himself dating the other guy's first wife; as the first guy said, who could invent such a story?

I read about a woman who divorced her husband because he picked his nose. I read about a woman who got divorced because her husband never remembered to pay their property taxes and finally, she said, it was just too much. Is it so very much to ask, she asked, that the person who shares responsibility for your life remembers to pay your joint taxes? Does this have to be a crisis every year? She seemed sort of embarrassed to say what she said, but she said it.

It seems to me that the reasons people divorce are hardly ever for 5 the dramatic reasons that we assume are the reasons people get divorced, like snorting cocaine for breakfast or discovering that the minister named Bernard who you married ten years ago is actually a former convict named Ezzard with a wife in Wisconsin, according to the young detective who sat down in your office at the accounting firm one morning and sounded embarrassed about some things he had come to tell you that you should know.

I read about a couple who got divorced because of "irresolute 6 differences," a phrase that addled me for weeks. Another couple filed for divorce on the grounds of irreconcilable dissonance, which seemed like one of those few times in life when the exact right words are applied to the exact right reason for those words. I read about another woman who divorced her husband because one time they were walking down the street, the husband on the curb side in accordance with the ancient courteous male custom of being on that side so as to receive the splatter of mud or worse from the street and keep such splatter from the pristine acreage of his beloved, and as they approached a fire hydrant he lifted his leg, puppylike, as a joke, and she marched right to their lawyer's office and instituted divorce proceedings. That particular woman refused to speak to reporters about the reasons for divorce, but you wonder what the iceberg was under that surface, you know?

The first divorce I saw up close, like the first car crash you see up 7 close, is imprinted on the inside of my eyelids, and I still think about it, not because it happened, but because years after it happened it seems so fated to have happened. How could it be that two people who really liked each other, and who took a brave crazy leap on not just living together, which lots of mammals do, but swearing fealty and respect in front of a huge crowd, and filing taxes as a joint entity, and spawning a child, and cosigning mortgages and car loans, how could they end up signing settlement papers on the dining room table and then wandering out into the muddy garden to cry? How could that be?

The saddest word I've heard wrapped around divorce like a 8 tattered blanket is tired, as in "We were both just tired," because being tired seems so utterly normal to me, so much the rug always bunching in that one spot no matter what you do, the slightly worn dish rack, the belt with extra holes punched with an ice pick that you borrowed from your cousin for exactly this purpose, the flashlight in the pantry that has never had batteries and never will, that the thought of tired being both your daily bread and also grounds for divorce gives me the willies. The shagginess of things, the way they never quite work out as planned and break down every other Tuesday, necessitating wine and foul language and duct tape and the wrong-size screw quietly hammered into place with the bottom of the garden gnome, seems to me the very essence of marriage; so if what makes a marriage work (the constant shifting of expectations and eternal parade of small surprises) is also what causes marriages to dissolve, where is it safe to stand?

Nowhere, of course. Every marriage is pregnant with divorce, 9 every day, every hour, every minute. The second you finish reading this essay, your spouse could close the refrigerator, after miraculously finding a way to wedge the juice carton behind the milk jug, and call it quits, and the odd truth of the matter is that because she might end your marriage in a moment, and you might end hers, you're still married. The instant there is no chance of death is the moment of death.

Thinking Critically about This Reading

What do you think Doyle means when he says, "the thought of tired being both your daily bread and also grounds for divorce gives me the willies" (paragraph 8)? How would you answer his question, "If what makes a marriage work (the constant shifting of expectations and eternal parade of small surprises) is also what causes marriages to dissolve, where is it safe to stand?" How does Doyle, himself, answer his own question? Do you agree? Why or why not?

Questions for Study and Discussion

1. Doyle's opening paragraph is a single sentence. Did you find it an effective beginning? (Glossary: *Beginnings and Endings*) In what ways is it related to his concluding paragraph?
2. What are some reasons Doyle discovered for people getting divorced? In what ways do these reasons illustrate "the chaotic wilderness of human nature" (2)? (Glossary: *Example*)

3. In paragraph 7, Doyle discusses the "first divorce I saw up close." What about this divorce is so memorable as to make Doyle "still think about it"?

4. What fascinates Doyle about the phrases "irresolute differences" and "irreconcilable dissonance" (6) as grounds for divorce?

5. How would you describe Doyle's tone in this essay—serious, humorous, formal, informal, flip, bemused, reflective? What does his use of made-up words such as *mivorced, darried, sleeperated,* and *schleperated* contribute to this tone? Point to other examples of his choice of words that helped him create the tone. Did you find Doyle's tone appropriate for both his subject and his audience?

6. How would you describe Doyle's attitude toward marriage and divorce?

Classroom Activity Using Diction and Tone

When asked what advice he had for aspiring writers who are still in college, Doyle responded as follows. As you read his answer, determine what you think the tone of the piece is. What about his choice of words and sentence structure help create this tone?

> Never sit down to write Literature. Never sit down to write anything with a label—Essay, Poem, etc. Just sit down and start telling a story. Let the piece take its own shape. Write every day at least half an hour. Listen to everyone else. Stop writing about yourself and ask questions and pay attention, and the world will hand you more amazing stories that will rattle and amaze you than you can ever write. Type fast. Carry two pens and scraps of paper. Live the moment, but make notes fast and then go mill your notes with your keyboard. Don't comment. Don't think about style or beauty of your prose. Don't worry about structure. Catch the jazz and then shape it—the shaping is the craft of the writing, the jazz is the elusive itch where all good writing is born. Tell no lies except whoppers. Everyone is cooler than you are, roll with it, accept it, enjoy it. Cut grimly where necessary. When you are sure you are notes done, get the piece the hell off your desk and onto an editor's [or teacher's] or else it isn't finished. Be wary of poetry's self-indulgence. The essay is the greatest form because it's the most naked and direct of our voices. But readers love novels best because they can live in them. Read your brains out. Read E. B. White and Annie Dillard and Mark Twain's angry essays.

How did you respond to Doyle's advice? In what ways did his diction and tone affect your response? Explain.

Suggested Writing Assignments

1. In his final paragraph, Doyle argues that the ever-present threat of divorce is actually good for a marriage, "that because she might end your marriage in a moment, and you might end hers, you're still married. The instant there is no chance of death is the moment of death." Do you agree with his position? Why or why not? Write an essay in which you clearly present your position.

2. The cover of the November 29, 2010, issue of *Time* magazine flashed the question "Who needs marriage?" In an age when marriage is sometimes perceived as a moral duty, too little praised, and not shown to be a meaningful lifestyle, this question is interesting. Indeed, today we hear much about marriages that have gone awry and little, it seems, about marriages that endure and flourish. Write an essay in which you argue on behalf of marriage as a religious and social institution. Do as much research as you deem appropriate, but also be sure to reflect on your own experiences and observations as well as those of your relatives and friends.

Figurative Language

Figurative language is language used in an imaginative rather than a literal sense. Although it is most often associated with poetry, figurative language is used widely in our daily speech and in our writing. Prose writers have long known that figurative language brings freshness and color to writing and also helps clarify ideas. For example, when asked by his teacher to explain the concept of brainstorming, one student replied, "Well, brainstorming is like having a tornado in your head." This figurative language helps others imagine the whirl of ideas in this young writer's head as he brainstorms a topic for writing.

The two most common **figures of speech** are the simile and the metaphor. A **simile** compares two essentially different ideas or things and uses the word *like* or *as* to link them.

> Canada geese sweep across the hills and valleys like a formation of strategic bombers.
>
> –Benjamin B. Bachman

> I walked toward her and hailed her as a visitor to the moon might salute a survivor of a previous expedition.
>
> –John Updike

A **metaphor** compares dissimilar ideas or things without using *like* or *as*.

> She was very old and small and she walked slowly in the dark pine shadows, moving a little from side to side in her steps, with the balanced heaviness and lightness of a pendulum in a grandfather clock.
>
> –Eudora Welty

> Charm is the ultimate weapon, the supreme seduction, against which there are few defenses.
>
> –Laurie Lee

To expand the richness of a particular comparison, writers sometimes use several sentences or even a whole paragraph to develop a metaphor. Such a comparison is called an *extended metaphor*.

> The point is that you have to strip down your writing before you can build it back up. You must know what the essential tools are and what job they were designed to do. If I may belabor the metaphor on carpentry, it is first necessary to be able to saw wood neatly and to drive nails. Later you can bevel the edges or add elegant finials, if that is your taste. But you can never forget that you are practicing a craft that is based on certain principles. If the nails are weak, your house will collapse. If your verbs are weak and your syntax is rickety, your sentences will fall apart.
>
> –William Zinsser

Another frequently used figure of speech is **personification**. In personification, the writer attributes human qualities to ideas or objects.

> The moon bathed the valley in a soft, golden light.
>
> –Corey Davis, student

> Blond October comes striding over the hills wearing a crimson shirt and faded green trousers.
>
> –Hal Borland

> Indeed, haste can be the assassin of elegance.
>
> –T. H. White

In all the preceding examples, notice how the writers' use of figurative language enlivens their prose and emphasizes their ideas. Each vividly communicates an idea or the essence of an object by comparing it to something concrete and familiar. In each case, too, the figurative language grows out of the writer's thinking, reflecting the way he or she sees the material. Be similarly honest in your use of figurative language, keeping in mind that figures of speech should never be used merely to "dress up" writing. Above all, use them to develop your ideas and clarify your meaning for the reader.

The Barrio

■ **Robert Ramirez**

Robert Ramirez was born in Edinburg, Texas, in 1949. After graduating from the University of Texas–Pan American, he taught writing and worked as a cameraman, reporter, anchor, and producer for the local news on KGBT-TV, the CBS affiliate in Harlingen, Texas. He cur-
rently works as an alumni fundraiser for the University of Texas–Pan American.
    The following essay first appeared in Pain and Promise: The Chicano Today *(1972), edited by Edward Simmens. Notice how Ramirez uses figurative language, particularly metaphors, to awaken the reader's senses to the sights, sounds, and smells that are the essence of the barrio.*

Reflecting on What You Know

Where did you grow up? What do you remember most about your childhood neighborhood? How did it feel as a young person to live in this world? Do you still call this neighborhood "home"? Explain.

The train, its metal wheels squealing as they spin along the silvery   1
tracks, rolls slower now. Through the gaps between the cars blinks a streetlamp, and this pulsing light on a barrio streetcorner beats slower, like a weary heartbeat, until the train shudders to a halt, the light goes out, and the barrio is deep asleep.

Throughout Aztlán[1] (the Nahuatl term meaning "land to the   2
north"), trains grumble along the edges of a sleeping people. From Lower California, through the blistering Southwest, down the Rio Grande[2] to the muddy Gulf, the darkness and mystery of dreams engulf communities fenced off by railroads, canals, and expressways.

---

[1]*Aztlán:* the mythical place of origin of the Aztec peoples.
[2]*Rio Grande:* a river flowing from southwest Colorado to Texas and Mexico and into the Gulf of Mexico.

Paradoxical[3] communities, isolated from the rest of the town by concrete columned monuments of progress, and yet stranded in the past.
They are surrounded by change. It eludes their reach, in their own
backyards, and the people, unable and unwilling to see the future, or
even touch the present, perpetuate the past.

Leaning from the expressway or jolting across the tracks, one   3
enters a different physical world permeated by a different attitude. The
physical dimensions are impressive. It is a large section of town which
extends for fifteen blocks north and south along the tracks, and then
advances eastward, thinning into nothingness beyond the city limits.
Within the invisible (yet sensible) walls of the barrio are many, many
people living in too few houses. The homes, however, are much more
numerous than on the outside.

Members of the barrio describe the entire area as their home. It is a   4
home, but it is more than this. The barrio is a refuge from the harshness
and the coldness of the Anglo world. It is a forced refuge. The leprous
people are isolated from the rest of the community and contained in
their section of town. The stoical pariahs of the barrio accept their fate,
and from the angry seeds of rejection grow the flowers of closeness between outcasts, not the thorns of bitterness and the mad desire to flee.
There is no want to escape, for the feeling of the barrio is known only
to its inhabitants, and the material needs of life can also be found here.

The *tortillería* [tortilla factory] fires up its machinery three times   5
a day, producing steaming, round, flat slices of barrio bread. In the
winter, the warmth of the tortilla factory is a wool *sarape* [blanket] in
the chilly morning hours, but in the summer, it unbearably toasts every
noontime customer.

The *panadería* [bakery] sends its sweet messenger aroma down   6
the dimly lit street, announcing the arrival of fresh, hot sugary *pan
dulce* [sweet rolls].

The small corner grocery serves the meal-to-meal needs of cus-   7
tomers, and the owner, a part of the neighborhood, willingly gives credit
to people unable to pay cash for foodstuffs.

The barbershop is a living room with hydraulic chairs, radio, and   8
television, where old friends meet and speak of life as their salted hair
falls aimlessly about them.

The pool hall is a junior level country club where '*chucos* [young   9
men], strangers in their own land, get together to shoot pool and rap,

---

[3]*paradoxical:* seemingly contradictory.

while veterans, unaware of the cracking, popping balls on the green felt, complacently play dominoes beneath rudely hung *Playboy* foldouts.

The *cantina* [canteen or snackbar] is the night spot of the barrio. 10 It is the country club and the den where the rites of puberty are enacted. Here the young become men. It is in the taverns that a young dude shows his *machismo* through the quantity of beer he can hold, the stories of *rucas* [women] he has had, and his willingness and ability to defend his image against hardened and scarred old lions.

No, there is no frantic wish to flee. It would be absurd to leave 11 the familiar and nervously step into the strange and cold Anglo community when the needs of the Chicano[4] can be met in the barrio.

The barrio is closeness. From the family living unit, familial rela- 12 tionships stretch out to immediate neighbors, down the block, around the corner, and to all parts of the barrio. The feeling of family, a rare and treasurable sentiment, pervades and accounts for the inability of the people to leave. The barrio is this attitude manifested on the countenances[5] of the people, on the faces of their homes, and in the gaiety of their gardens.

The color-splashed homes arrest your eyes, arouse your curiosity, 13 and make you wonder what life scenes are being played out in them. The flimsy, brightly colored, wood-frame houses ignore no neon-brilliant color. Houses trimmed in orange, chartreuse, lime-green, yellow, and mixtures of these and other hues beckon the beholder to reflect on the peculiarity of each home. Passing through this land is refreshing like Brubeck,[6] not narcoticizing like revolting rows of similar houses, which neither offend nor please.

In the evenings, the porches and front yards are occupied with 14 men calmly talking over the noise of children playing baseball in the unpaved extension of the living room, while the women cook supper or gossip with female neighbors as they water the *jardines* [gardens]. The gardens mutely echo the expressive verses of the colorful houses. The denseness of multicolored plants and trees gives the house the appearance of an oasis or a tropical island hideaway, sheltered from the rest of the world.

Fences are common in the barrio, but they are fences and not the 15 walls of the Anglo community. On the western side of town, the high

---

[4]*Chicano:* an American of Mexican descent.
[5]*countenances:* facial expressions that indicate mood or character.
[6]*Dave Brubeck* (b. 1920): pianist, composer, and conductor of "cool" modern jazz.

wooden fences between houses are thick, impenetrable walls, built to keep the neighbors at bay. In the barrio, the fences may be rusty, wire contraptions or thick green shrubs. In either case you can see through them and feel no sense of intrusion when you cross them.

Many lower-income families of the barrio manage to maintain a 16 comfortable standard of living through the communal action of family members who contribute their wages to the head of the family. Economic need creates interdependence and closeness. Small bare-footed boys sell papers on cool, dark Sunday mornings, deny themselves pleasantries, and give their earnings to *mamá.* The older the child, the greater the responsibility to help the head of the household provide for the rest of the family.

There are those, too, who for a number of reasons have not 17 achieved a relative sense of financial security. Perhaps it results from too many children too soon, but it is the homes of these people and their situation that numbs rather than charms. Their houses, aged and bent, oozing children, are fissures[7] in the horn of plenty. Their wooden homes may have brick-pattern asbestos tile on the outer walls, but the tile is not convincing.

Unable to pay city taxes or incapable of influencing the city to live 18 up to its duty to serve all the citizens, the poorer barrio families remain trapped in the nineteenth century and survive as best they can. The back-yards have well-worn paths to the outhouses, which sit near the alley. Running water is considered a luxury in some parts of the barrio. Decent drainage is usually unknown, and when it rains, the water stands for days, an incubator of health hazards and an avoidable nuisance. Streets, costly to pave, remain rough, rocky trails. Tires do not last long, and the constant rattling and shaking grind away a car's life and spread dust through screen windows.

The houses and their *jardines,* the jollity of the people in an adverse 19 world, the brightly feathered alarm clock pecking away at supper and cautiously eyeing the children playing nearby, produce a mystifying sensation at finding the noble savage[8] alive in the twentieth century. It is easy to look at the positive qualities of life in the barrio, and look at them with a distantly envious feeling. One wishes to experience the feelings of the barrio and not the hardships. Remembering the illness, the hunger, the feeling of time running out on you, the walls, both

---

[7]*fissures:* narrow openings or cracks.
[8]*noble savage:* in literature, an idealized concept of uncivilized man.

real and imagined, reflecting on living in the past, one finds his envy becoming more elusive, until it has vanished altogether.

Back now beyond the tracks, the train creaks and groans, the cars 20 jostle each other down the track, and as the light begins its pulsing, the barrio, with all its meanings, greets a new dawn with yawns and restless stretchings.

Thinking Critically about This Reading

What evidence does Ramirez give to support the following claim: "Members of the barrio describe the entire area as their home. It is a home, but it is more than this" (paragraph 4)?

Questions for Study and Discussion

1. What is the barrio? Where is it? What does Ramirez mean when he states, "There is no want to escape, for the feeling of the barrio is known only to its inhabitants, and the material needs of life can also be found here" (4)?

2. Ramirez uses Spanish phrases throughout his essay. Why do you suppose he uses them? What is their effect on the reader? He also uses the words *home, refuge, family,* and *closeness.* What do they connote in the context of this essay? (Glossary: *Connotation/Denotation*) In what ways, if any, are they essential to the writer's purpose? (Glossary: *Purpose*)

3. Identify several metaphors and similes Ramirez uses in his essay, and explain why they are particularly appropriate.

4. In paragraph 6, Ramirez uses personification when he calls the aroma of freshly baked sweet rolls a "messenger" who announces the arrival of the baked goods. Cite other words or phrases Ramirez uses to give human characteristics to the barrio.

5. Explain Ramirez's use of the imagery of walls and fences to describe a sense of cultural isolation. What might this imagery symbolize? (Glossary: *Symbol*)

6. Ramirez begins with a relatively positive picture of the barrio, but ends on a more disheartening note. (Glossary: *Beginnings and Endings*) Why does he organize his essay in this way? What might the effect have been had he reversed these images?

Classroom Activity Using Figurative Language

Create a metaphor or simile that would be helpful in describing each item in the following list. To illustrate the process, the first one has been completed for you.

1. Skyscraper: The skyscraper sparkled like a huge glass needle.
2. Sound of an explosion
3. Intelligent student
4. Crowded bus
5. Slow-moving car
6. Pillow
7. Narrow alley
8. Greasy french fries
9. Hot sun
10. Dull knife

Compare your metaphors and similes with those written by other members of your class. Which metaphors and similes for each item on the list seem to work best? Why? Do any seem tired or clichéd?

Suggested Writing Assignments

1. In paragraph 19, Ramirez states, "One wishes to experience the feelings of the barrio and not the hardships." Explore his meaning in light of what you have just read and of other experience or knowledge you may have of "ghetto" living. In what way can it be said that the hardships of such living are a necessary part of its "feelings"? How might barrio life change, for better or for worse, if the city were to "live up to its duty to serve all the citizens" (18)?
2. Write a brief essay in which you describe your own neighborhood. (Glossary: *Description*) You may find it helpful to review what you wrote in response to the prereading prompt for this selection.
3. The following photograph shows a Hispanic woman in San Diego, California, carrying her groceries past a striking mural honoring Hispanic heroes and revolutionaries. Prominently featured are such figures as Cesar Chavez, an American who led migrant farmworkers' protests against poor working conditions in California in the 1950s to 1970s, and Che Guevara, a Cuban

revolutionary leader who helped Fidel Castro come to power in the late 1950s. What details about the San Diego community can you glean from the mural? Which details tell you about the neighborhood? About the socioeconomic struggles of the barrio? Write an essay about life in the barrio as it is depicted in the mural, incorporating the visual details you see and inferences you draw from them. Be creative, and use as many figures of speech as you can in your essay.

© Peter Menzel/Stock Boston, Inc.

Polaroids

■ **Anne Lamott**

Born in San Francisco in 1954, Anne Lamott is a graduate of Goucher College in Baltimore and the author of seven novels; Imperfect Birds *(2010) is the most recent of them. She has also written a food-review column for* California *magazine and a book-review column for* Mademoiselle. *In 1993, she published* Operating Instructions: A Journal of My Son's First Year, *in which she describes her own adventures as a single parent. Lamott has also written three books about her thoughts on faith:* Traveling Mercies: Some Thoughts on Faith *(1999);* Plan B: Further Thoughts on Faith *(2005); and* Grace (Eventually): Thoughts on Faith.

The following selection is a chapter from Lamott's popular book about writing, Bird by Bird *(1994). The entire essay is built around the metaphor of a developing Polaroid photograph. Notice how effectively Lamott weaves in references to the Polaroid to clarify points she wishes to make about the process of writing.*

Reflecting on What You Know

Do you or does someone in your family enjoy taking photographs? Do the pictures always come out just the way you expected (or hoped) they would, or do they sometimes contain surprises? Perhaps they made you laugh, or disappointed you, or revealed something of value—some new insight into a familiar person, scene, or relationship. Describe a photograph or photographs that literally developed into something unexpected.

Writing a first draft is very much like watching a Polaroid   1
develop. You can't—and, in fact, you're not supposed to—know exactly what the picture is going to look like until it has finished developing. First you just point at what has your attention and take the picture. In the last chapter, for instance, what had my attention

were the contents of my lunch bag. But as the picture developed, I found I had a really clear image of the boy against the fence. Or maybe *your* Polaroid was supposed to be a picture of that boy against the fence, and you didn't notice until the last minute that a family was standing a few feet away from him. Now, maybe it's his family, or the family of one of the kids in his class, but at any rate these people are going to be in the photograph, too. Then the film emerges from the camera with a grayish green murkiness that gradually becomes clearer and clearer, and finally you see the husband and wife holding their baby with two children standing beside them. And at first it all seems very sweet, but then the shadows begin to appear, and then you start to see the animal tragedy, the baboons baring their teeth. And then you see a flash of bright red flowers in the bottom left quadrant that you didn't even know were in the picture when you took it, and these flowers evoke a time or a memory that moves you mysteriously. And finally, as the portrait comes into focus, you begin to notice all the props surrounding these people, and you begin to understand how props define us and comfort us, and show us what we value and what we need, and who we think we are.

You couldn't have had any way of knowing what this piece of work 2 would look like when you first started. You just knew that there was something about these people that compelled you, and you stayed with that something long enough for it to show you what it was about.

Watch this Polaroid develop: 3

Six or seven years ago I was asked to write an article on the 4 Special Olympics. I had been going to the local event for years, partly because a couple of friends of mine compete. Also, I love sports, and I love to watch athletes, special or otherwise. So I showed up this time with a great deal of interest but no real sense of what the finished article might look like.

Things tend to go very, very slowly at the Special Olympics. It is 5 not like trying to cover the Preakness. Still, it has its own exhilaration, and I cheered and took notes all morning.

The last track-and-field event before lunch was a twenty-five-yard 6 race run by some unusually handicapped runners and walkers, many of whom seemed completely confused. They lumped and careened along, one man making a snail-slow break for the stands, one heading out toward the steps where the winners receive their medals; both of them were shepherded back. The race took just about forever. And here it was nearly noon and we were all so hungry. Finally, though, everyone crossed over the line, and those of us in the stands got up to go — when we noticed that way down the track, four or five yards from the starting line, was another runner.

She was a girl of about sixteen with a normal-looking face above 7 a wracked and emaciated body. She was on metal crutches, and she was just plugging along, one tiny step after another, moving one crutch forward two or three inches, then moving a leg, then moving the other crutch two or three inches, then moving the other leg. It was just excruciating. Plus, I was starving to death. Inside I was going, Come on, come on, come on, swabbing at my forehead with anxiety, while she kept taking these two- or three-inch steps forward. What felt like four hours later, she crossed the finish line, and you could see that she was absolutely stoked, in a shy, girlish way.

A tall African American man with no front teeth fell into step 8 with me as I left the bleachers to go look for some lunch. He tugged on the sleeve of my sweater, and I looked up at him, and he handed me a Polaroid someone had taken of him and his friends that day. "Look at us," he said. His speech was difficult to understand, thick and slow as a warped record. His two friends in the picture had Down's syndrome. All three of them looked extremely pleased with themselves. I admired the picture and then handed it back to him. He stopped, so I stopped, too. He pointed to his own image. "That," he said, "is one cool man."

And this was the image from which an article began forming, 9 although I could not have told you exactly what the piece would end up being about. I just knew that something had started to emerge.

After lunch I wandered over to the auditorium, where it turned 10 out a men's basketball game was in progress. The African American man with no front teeth was the star of the game. You could tell that he was because even though no one had made a basket yet, his teammates almost always passed him the ball. Even the people on the *other* team passed him the ball a lot. In lieu of any scoring, the men stampeded in slow motion up and down the court, dribbling the ball thunderously. I had never heard such a loud game. It was all sort of crazily beautiful. I imagined describing the game for my article and then for my students: the loudness, the joy. I kept replaying the scene of the girl on crutches making her way up the track to the finish line — and all of a sudden my article began to appear out of the grayish green murk. And I could see that it was about tragedy transformed over the years into joy. It was about the beauty of sheer effort.

I could see it almost as clearly as I could the photograph of that one cool man and his two friends.

The auditorium bleachers were packed. Then a few minutes later, 11
still with no score on the board, the tall black man dribbled slowly from one end of the court to the other, and heaved the ball up into the air, and it dropped into the basket. The crowd roared, and all the men on both teams looked up wide-eyed at the hoop, as if it had just burst into flames.

You would have loved it, I tell my students. You would have felt 12
like you could write all day.

Thinking Critically about This Reading

In what way does the African American man's perception of himself in the Polaroid picture help Lamott with her writing assignment?

Questions for Study and Discussion

1. This entire essay is based on an extended metaphor or analogy. (Glossary: *Analogy*) What is the metaphor? How does it serve to clarify Lamott's central idea?

2. Besides the extended metaphor, Lamott uses several figures of speech in this essay. Find at least one metaphor and one simile. How does each contribute to the effect of the piece on the reader?

3. Lamott uses the phrase "grayish green murkiness" in the first paragraph and refers again to "grayish green murk" near the end of the essay, in paragraph 10. Why does she repeat these words? What does this phrase mean to a photographer? To a writer? For which of them does it function as a metaphor?

4. In paragraph 1, Lamott identifies four elements in "*your* Polaroid" that you didn't expect to find. What are they? Why does she include them?

5. Although the diction of this essay is simple and informal (Glossary: *Diction*), the structure is quite complicated. It is almost like an essay within an essay. What purpose is served by the long embedded narrative about the Special Olympics? (Glossary: *Example*) How does Lamott succeed in achieving unity? (Glossary: *Unity*)

Classroom Activity Using Figurative Language

Carefully read the following descriptions of October. Identify the figures of speech that each writer uses. Did you find one description more effective than the other? Why, or why not? Compare your reactions with those of others in the class.

The Fading Season

October's lyrics are spilled in scarlet syllables on shadowed paths that bend with the wind as they wander through field and forest to heights where foliate hills commune with azure skies in the last golden moments of the autumns of our days.

Where a wisp of the wind tingles with the cidery essences of vagrant apples, fluttering leaflets bear bittersweet messages of another season's passing and warnings of harsh moments yet to be. Caught for a breath of a moment in the fingers of slim sunbeams, they glisten and gleam in a saffron splendor before they settle gently into the dappled pattern on the forest floor.

Walk slowly in October and you can savor the scents of cedar and pine, the musky odor of the earth before it dozes off for another winter, and the crackling leaves beneath your feet will snap and echo in the silences that only woods contain. Stop for a moment and you will sense scurryings in the underbrush where squirrels dash to and fro in a frenetic race to hoard as much as they can before winter sets in. A whirr of sudden wings will tell you that you have invaded the partridge's exclusive territory.

In the dusk of an October day when the sun's last crimson embers have slipped behind the hills, the crisp chill in the air signals fall's coming surrender to the approaching winter's legions.

–Burlington Free Press

October

Blond October comes striding over the hills wearing a crimson shirt and faded green trousers. His morning breath is the mist in the valleys, and at evening there are stars in his eyes, a waxing moon over his shoulder, and the cool whisper of a valley breeze in his voice. He comes this way to light the fires of autumn in the maple groves, to put a final polish on the late winesaps, to whistle a farewell to summer and set the foxes to barking and tell the owls that now they can ask their eternal questions.

October might be called a god of travel, if we were to fashion a new mythology; for now come the perfect days to get out and wander the hills and valleys of these latitudes. The scene changes from day to day, as though all the color in the spectrum were being spilled across the landscape—radiant blue of the sky and the lakes and ponds reflecting it, green of every tone in the conifers and in the reluctant oaks, yellows verging from the sun simmer to moon orange in the elms, the beeches, the maples, and reds that range to purplish browns, sumac and dogwood and maple and oak and sour gum and sassafras and viburnum. There is the indigo of fox grapes, if you know where to find them.

October is colorful, it is exuberant, it is full of lively spirit. Spring fever can't hold a candle to October fever, when it comes to inner restlessness. The birds are on the wing, the leaves are footloose and eager for a breeze, the horizon is a challenge that amounts to an insidious summons. Listen closely and you can hear October, that fellow in the crimson shirt, whistling a soft melody that is as old as autumn upon this earth.

–Hal Borland, *New York Times*

Suggested Writing Assignments

1. With sudden insight, Lamott understands what the Special Olympics meant to her: "It was about tragedy transformed over the years into joy. It was about the beauty of sheer effort" (10). Everyone has experiences in life that take on special meaning. Look back on a significant event you have witnessed or in which you took part, one that has come to represent to you some important truth about life. Write a narrative essay describing the event. Wait until you are at or approaching the end of your narrative to reveal explicitly your insight into its meaning.

2. When we think about our daily activities, we often clarify our understanding of some aspect of them by seeing one activity in terms of another. Not everyone's perceptions will be the same: A good horseback rider, for example, might come back from a relaxing day on the trail thinking, "Riding a horse is a form of meditation," while the novice bumping around in the saddle thinks, "Riding a horse is a form of torture." A computer expert finds that surfing the Web is like traveling on a magic carpet, while someone else might find it more like being lost in a labyrinth. Choose an activity in your daily life that suggests such a simile or metaphor. Write an essay about the activity that begins with a figure of speech and explores its implications.

Invasion

■ **Benjamin Percy**

Benjamin Percy was born in 1979 in Eugene, Oregon, and then lived briefly in Hawaii. He later returned to Oregon and then went to Brown University, where he earned his undergraduate degree studying archaeology. After deciding against a career as an archae-ologist, Percy enrolled at Southern Illinois University, where he earned an MFA in cre-ative writing. He first taught at the University of Wisconsin–Stevens and then moved to Marquette University. He is currently assistant professor of creative writing (fiction and nonfiction) in the MFA program at Iowa State University. Percy is the author of two novels, Red Moon *(forthcoming) and* The Wilding *(2010); two books of short stories,* The Language of Elk *(2006) and* Refresh, Refresh *(2007); and numerous articles and stories in a variety of publications including* Esquire, Men's Journal, Slate, Paris Review, Wall Street Journal, *and* Fugue.

The following essay first appeared in 2010 in the 20th anni-versary issue of Fugue, *which had as its theme the changing West. In this essay, Percy employs unusual figures of speech to compare an invasion of Pandora moths to other equally undesir-able newcomers who settle in the Bend, Oregon, area, where their numbers continue to increase and annoy the natives.*

Reflecting on What You Know

How well do you know the zoning laws in the area where you live? How easy is it for developers to build housing subdivisions in your town? Has real estate development in your area always been in the best interests of the community in providing jobs and housing and also preserving its natural environment?

The soil in Central Oregon is acidic, sandy, coarse, high in pumice, 1
low in humus. You would think nothing could grow here, nothing but cheat grass, sagebrush, rabbit brush, juniper trees, ponderosas,

lodgepoles. But hundreds of miles of canals provide water for tens of thousands of acres. Boys in Wrangler jeans trudge through the fields all day, appearing like trapeze artists as they carry long wobbly irrigation pipes, locking them in place, sending silvery arcs of water through the air to keep the alfalfa green, to fight the blighted yellow found naturally here.

Other things grow, too, given the right conditions. Into this 2 soil—this dry, unforgiving soil—the larvae of the Pandora moth drops like a seed. And begins to pupate.

In the late 1980s, the population of Bend was 18,000. There are 3 now, in the metro area, more than 200,000 people. Some of them come from places like Portland and Seattle—but most of them come from California.

The men wear Izod golf shirts and Ecco leather shoes with no 4 socks. They part their hair and stink of cologne and smile white toothy smiles when talking about how fast the greens are at Widgi Creek golf course. The women wear white pants and bright blouses and carry small black purses from which they are constantly withdrawing pink cell phones. Their brightly blond hair appears flattened out of gold. All of them drive Saabs, Audis, Volvos, BMWs, Land Rovers that have never left pavement.

Pandora epidemics occur every twenty to thirty years. Sometimes 5 chipmunks dig up the pupae—sometimes the soil is too hot—sometimes birds and insects and parasites feast of the young larvae.

But sometimes the larvae grow undisturbed. Sometimes the 6 Pandora break through the soil and probe the air and shake off the pumice that dusts their bodies and begin to feast.

My friends and I wore tight jeans, big belt buckles, sharp- 7 pointed boots. We would tear around on dirt bikes, four-wheelers. We would listen to Alan Jackson and Garth Brooks and Tim McGraw. We would move irrigation pipe and clean out horse stalls and mend barbed-wire fences for money to go to the movies, buy Coca Cola and baseball cards. Our families drove pickups. Our fathers had skin as brown and creased as an old work-glove, and during hunting season, we would follow them into the woods—and we would emerge with bucks draped over our shoulders and bleeding down our backs. From the trees in our front yards we would hang the gutted carcasses to skin, and they would shift in the breeze like strange ornaments.

Our governor once said, "We welcome you to visit our state, but   8
please don't plan to move here." Billboards along the Interstate said
the same. Our parents didn't like the Californians, so we didn't either.
Our clothes and our cars didn't match theirs. They brought with
them wine shops, clothing boutiques, white-linen restaurants that
served sushi and arugula salads that cost too much. Golf courses
spread into the desert like green oil slicks. Expensive housing developments rose up overnight with names like Brasada Ranch and
Broken Top.

The caterpillars—at first small and black-bodied and bristling   9
with hairs—grow as fat and long as shotgun shells. Their color fades
to a yellowish green and sharp spines rise along their backs. They
gnaw the needles of pine trees down to stubble—chew the terminal
buds off—so that great swaths of forest appear burned-out, skeletal.

They pulsed along trunks and branches, fell all around us like   10
some poisonous fruit. Certain sections of road grew slick with their
burst bodies and cars would lose their traction, spin out. I remember
racing along a bike path with a buddy, maneuvering the bike constantly, not to avoid the caterpillars that littered the asphalt, instead
seeking them out, splattering them beneath my wheels so that their
guts decorated my legs.

We shoved bananas up the tailpipes of Land Rovers. We dragged   11
rocks along the side of BMWs. We used a metal saw to hack the hood
ornaments off the noses of Mercedes. We hauled a port-a-potty three
miles in the bed of a pickup and dropped it off on the porch of a
sprawling hillside home.

We started with M80s—then upgraded to quarter-sticks of dy-   12
namite bought off the Warm Springs Indian Reservation. We would
drive into the rich neighborhoods at night and we would light the
quarter-stick fuses and shove them in mailboxes and sprint away and
breathlessly watch the explosion, the twisted snarl of metal. And then
we would go tearing off into the night, laughing.

One time we shoved a plastic mailbox full of paper and lit it on   13
fire and stood around watching as it melted, as the mouth of it closed
like a dying trout.

The caterpillars became moths, and the moths were wine-   14
colored and as big as two hands brought together at the thumbs.
They fluttered through forests, through city streets, thousands of

them. We would chase them down with tennis rackets and swat them from the air. We would hit them with our cars, and their feathery antennae and powdery wings and yellowish guts would smear our grills and windshields.

One time, during one of my baseball games, a night game, the 15
moths swarmed the spotlights and threw their black swirling color across the diamond. They lighted on our gloves and our helmets, flexing their wings. We couldn't see the ball—and when my friend was struck in the mouth by a pitch, the umpire called off the game on account of moths.

When I go back to Bend now, I don't recognize it. I get lost driv- 16
ing around. There are roads where there were none before. There are roundabouts where there were once intersections. Acres of sagebrush have given way to big box stores. The sawmill my grandfather designed is long gone. So is a ratty baseball diamond I used to play on. Property values have skyrocketed—and the tax base has risen—and many have been forced to move, to make way for those who can afford to live here. The Old Mill district—once exactly that, a rotten collection of abandoned buildings—is now crowded with million-dollar condos, an REI, a sixteen-screen cineplex. The golf courses are legion.

The last time I was there, January, I trudged into a coffee shop 17
to warm up. Ahead of me in line stood a teenager. He was wearing sunglasses, designer aviators. His hair was bleached, gelled up in a fauxhawk. His jeans looked European and his North Face parka might have cost as much as my monthly mortgage. He was part of the new Bend—he was the kind of guy my buddies and I might have shoved, tripped, yanked an ear, bloodied a lip.

He ordered a bubble tea. I do not know what bubble tea is, but 18
that is what he ordered. The girl behind the counter said, "I'm so sorry—we're out of bubbles." He sighed heavily and then shoved his way out the door and into the cold.

Later, when I drove through downtown, I saw him crossing the 19
road ahead of me. His parka was fat and segmented and the way he strolled along so lazily gave him the appearance of a caterpillar. For one wild moment, for old time's sake, I thought about slamming my boot on the accelerator, splattering him beneath my tires. Then I realized that this was no longer my town, but his. That I was in fact the intruder—that I no longer knew this place—a town founded by millers and ranchers, where coyotes howled all night and jacked-up

pickup trucks growled all day. The mountains and the rivers were still here, but the very essence of the place had otherwise been smeared away as easily as the dust off a moth's wing.

Thinking Critically about This Reading

Percy laments that new residents have settled in Bend and have altered the nature of that place as he knew it. In some measure, he conveys a sense of ownership in his essay, until the last paragraph where he experiences an epiphany or sudden awareness of another way of seeing things. How do you think Percy would relate to a statement attributed to Chief Seattle, Chief of the Suquamish Indians, as excerpted from a letter he wrote to the U.S. government in the nineteenth century: "This we know: the earth does not belong to man, man belongs to the earth. All things are connected like the blood that unites us all. Man did not weave the web of life, he is merely a strand in it. Whatever he does to the web, he does to himself."

Questions for Study and Discussion

1. What is the dominant impression of Percy's description of Bend, Oregon? (Glossary: *Dominant Impression*)
2. What is Percy's purpose in this essay? (Glossary: *Purpose*) Does he expect anything of his readers as a result of reading his work? Explain.
3. Identify examples of where Percy has used figurative language in this essay. What kinds of figures has he used? Why do you think he has used them?
4. Percy has used an extended metaphor or analogy in this essay, and it is central to his purpose and the way he structures his essay. How does the extended metaphor work? Do you find it effective in helping him get his point across? Explain.
5. Review the essay, and identify several instances where Percy abandons his poetic style for a more objective, straightforward style. What effect do those instances have on the reader? Explain.
6. Discuss the realization that Percy comes to in his final paragraph. How does that realization grow out of his metaphor between the Pandora moths and the new residents of Bend?

Classroom Activity Using Figurative Language

What is the most unusual event you have witnessed? Using the figures of speech you have learned (simile, metaphor, and personification), write a half dozen sentences that describe the event so that your readers can appreciate it. First state what the event was, and then present your sentences in either a connected paragraph or a series of separate sentences. Share your description with your classmates to determine how effectively you have conveyed the dominant impression you wished to create.

Suggested Writing Assignments

1. When you are asked to use more figures of speech in your writing, you may respond in any of the following ways:

   - I really can't see that figures of speech add very much to my writing.
   - It's too much work to think of better ways to say something.
   - I usually don't have the time to think of clever ways of expressing myself.
   - I've never been very imaginative, so I try to keep things simple.

   Everyday speech is actually filled with similes, metaphors, and personifications. Indeed, it's difficult to talk without using them. For example, when we say that "She was as cute as a button," "The path runs around the pond," or "His caress took my breath away," we're using simile, metaphor, and personification. The goal is to find fresh ways to describe, share experiences, and make our writing vibrant and memorable. Review one of your essays, and find opportunities to sharpen your language with figures of speech. Make sure that the figures of speech are fresh and not simply clichés. (Glossary: *Cliché*)

2. Percy argues against the "invasion" of Californians into the Bend, Oregon, area. One problem that arises in such cases is that the United States is becoming homogenized and that everywhere is beginning to look like everywhere else. The following photograph, for example, shows the kind of new construction that dots our once-remote mountaintops and that needs to be regulated and zoned to control aggressive development. Write an

essay in which you argue against land exploitation and reckless development and for the preservation of a ruggedly beautiful natural landscape. What are the costs to a community when farmland disappears and mountaintops are developed recklessly? How can developers earn reasonable profits while also being sensitive to the needs of the people they are trying to serve? Use an appropriate number of figures of speech to stress the nature of the problem as well as the solution you propose. Also use an extended metaphor such as the one between the Pandora moths and the people who flocked to Bend, Oregon, if you think that it will help your argument. Be careful not to stretch any metaphor you use, however, or your argument will lose some of its credibility.

p a r t ■ *f o u r*

Types of Essays

Illustration

Illustration is the use of **examples**—facts, opinions, samples, and anecdotes or stories—to make ideas more concrete and to make generalizations more specific and detailed. Examples enable writers not just to tell but also to show what they mean. The more specific the example, the more effective it is. For instance, in an essay about alternative sources of energy, a writer might offer an example of how a local architecture firm designed a home heated by solar collectors instead of by a conventional oil, gas, or electric system.

A writer uses examples to clarify or support the thesis in an essay and the main ideas in paragraphs. Sometimes a single striking example suffices; at other times a whole series of related examples is necessary. The following paragraph presents a single extended example—an anecdote that illustrates the writer's point about cultural differences:

> Whenever there is a great cultural distance between two people, there are bound to be problems arising from differences in behavior and expectations. An example is the American couple who consulted a psychiatrist about their marital problems. The husband was from New England and had been brought up by reserved parents who taught him to control his emotions and to respect the need for privacy. His wife was from an Italian family and had been brought up in close contact with all the members of her large family, who were extremely warm, volatile, and demonstrative. When the husband came home after a hard day at the office, dragging his feet and longing for peace and quiet, his wife would rush to him and smother him. Clasping his hands, rubbing his brow, crooning over his weary head, she never left him alone. But when the wife was upset or anxious about her day, the husband's response was to withdraw completely and leave her alone. No comforting, no affectionate embrace, no attention—just solitude. The woman became convinced her husband didn't love her and, in desperation,

she consulted a psychiatrist. Their problem wasn't basically psychological but cultural.

–Edward T. Hall

This single example is effective because it is *representative*—that is,
essentially similar to other such problems Hall might have described
and familiar to many readers. Hall tells the story with enough detail
that readers can understand the couple's feelings and so better understand the point he is trying to make.

In contrast, another writer supports his topic sentence about superstitions with ten examples:

> In the folklore of the country, numerous superstitions relate to
> winter weather. Back-country farmers examine their corn husks—
> the thicker the husk, the colder the winter. They watch the acorn
> crop—the more acorns, the more severe the season. They observe
> where white-faced hornets place their paper nests—the higher they
> are, the deeper will be the snow. They examine the size and shape
> and color of the spleens of butchered hogs for clues to the severity
> of the season. They keep track of the blooming of dogwood in the
> spring—the more abundant the blooms, the more bitter the cold in
> January. When chipmunks carry their tails high and squirrels have
> heavier fur and mice come into country houses early in the fall, the
> superstitious gird themselves for a long, hard winter. Without any
> scientific basis, a wider-than-usual black band on a woolly-bear
> caterpillar is accepted as a sign that winter will arrive early and stay
> late. Even the way a cat sits beside the stove carries its message to
> the credulous. According to a belief once widely held in the Ozarks,
> a cat sitting with its tail to the fire indicates very cold weather is on
> the way.

–Edwin Way Teale

Teale uses numerous examples because he is writing about various
superstitions. Also, putting all those strange beliefs side by side in a
kind of catalog makes the paragraph fun to read as well as convincing and informative.

To use illustration effectively, begin by thinking of ideas and generalizations about your topic that you can make clearer and more
persuasive by illustrating them with facts, anecdotes, or specific details.
You should focus primarily on your main point, the central generalization that you will develop in your essay. Also be alert for other

Illustration **341**

statements or references that may benefit from illustration. Points that are already clear and uncontroversial and that your readers will understand and immediately agree with can stand on their own as you pass along quickly to your next idea; belaboring the obvious wastes your time and energy, as well as your reader's. Often, however, you will find that examples add clarity, color, and weight to what you say.

Consider the following generalization:

> Americans are a pain-conscious people who would rather get rid of pain than seek and cure its root causes.

This assertion is broad and general; it raises the following questions: How so? What does this mean exactly? Why does the writer think so? The statement could be the topic sentence of a paragraph or perhaps even the thesis of an essay or of an entire book. As a writer, you could make the generalization stronger and more meaningful through illustrations. You might support this statement by citing specific situations or specific cases in which Americans have gone to the drugstore instead of to a doctor, as well as by supplying sales figures per capita of painkillers in the United States as compared with other countries.

Illustration is so useful and versatile a strategy that it is found in all kinds of writing. It is essential, for example, in writing a successful argument essay. In an essay arguing that non-English-speaking students starting school in the United States should be taught English as a second language, one writer supports her argument with the following illustration, drawn from her own experience as a Spanish-speaking child in an English-only school:

> Without the use of Spanish, unable to communicate with the teacher or students, for six long weeks we guessed at everything we did. When we lined up to go anywhere, neither my sister nor I knew what to expect. Once, the teacher took the class on a bathroom break, and I mistakenly thought we were on our way to the cafeteria for lunch. Before we left, I grabbed our lunch money, and one of the girls in line began sneering and pointing. Somehow she figured out my mistake before I did. When I realized why she was laughing, I became embarrassed and threw the money into my sister's desk as we walked out of the classroom.
>
> –Hilda Alvarado, student

Alvarado could have summarized her point in the preceding paragraph in fewer words:

> Not only are non-English-speaking students in English-only schools unable to understand the information they are supposed to be learning, but they are also subject to frequent embarrassment and teasing from their classmates.

By offering an illustration, however, Alvarado makes her point more vividly and effectively.

A Crime of Compassion

■ **Barbara Huttmann**

Barbara Huttmann was born in Oakland in 1935 and now lives in the San Francisco Bay area. She received her nursing degree in 1976. After obtaining a master's degree in nursing administration, she cofounded a healthcare consulting firm for hospitals, nursing organizations, and consumers. Her interest in patients' rights is clearly evident in her two books, The Patient's Advocate *(1981) and* Code Blue: A Nurse's True Life Story *(1982).*

In the following essay, which first appeared in Newsweek *in 1983, Huttmann narrates the final months of the life of Mac, one of her favorite patients. By using emotional and graphic details, Huttmann hopes that Mac's example will convince her audience of the need for new legislation that would permit terminally ill patients to choose to die rather than suffer great pain and indignity. As you read about Mac, consider the degree to which his experience seems representative of what patients often endure because medical technology is now able to keep them alive longer than they would be able to survive on their own.*

Reflecting on What You Know

For most people, being sick is at best an unpleasant experience. Reflect on an illness you have had, whether a simple common cold or an affliction that required you to be hospitalized. What were your concerns and fears? For what were you most thankful?

"**M**urderer," a man shouted. "God help patients who get *you* for a   1
nurse."

"What gives you the right to play God?" another one asked.   2

It was the *Phil Donahue Show*[1] where the guest is a fatted calf   3
and the audience a 200-strong flock of vultures hungering to pick at
the bones. I had told them about Mac, one of my favorite cancer

---

[1]*Phil Donahue Show:* the first daytime TV talk show that involved the audience. It
aired from 1970 to 1996.

patients. "We resuscitated him fifty-two times in just one month. I refused to resuscitate him again. I simply sat there and held his hand while he died."

There wasn't time to explain that Mac was a young, witty, macho cop who walked into the hospital with thirty-two pounds of attack equipment, looking as if he could single-handedly protect the whole city, if not the entire state. "Can't get rid of this cough," he said. Otherwise, he felt great.   4

Before the day was over, tests confirmed that he had lung cancer. And before the year was over, I loved him, his wife, Maura, and their three kids as if they were my own. All the nurses loved him. And we all battled his disease for six months without ever giving death a thought. Six months isn't such a long time in the whole scheme of things, but it was long enough to see him lose his youth, his wit, his macho, his hair, his bowel and bladder control, his sense of taste and smell, and his ability to do the slightest thing for himself. It was also long enough to watch Maura's transformation from a young woman into a haggard, beaten old lady.   5

When Mac had wasted away to a sixty-pound skeleton kept alive by liquid food we poured down a tube, IV solutions we dripped into his veins, and oxygen we piped to a mask on his face, he begged us: "Mercy . . . for God's sake, please just let me go."   6

The first time he stopped breathing, the nurse pushed the button that calls a "code blue" throughout the hospital and sends a team rushing to resuscitate the patient. Each time he stopped breathing, sometimes two or three times in one day, the code team came again. The doctors and technicians worked their miracles and walked away. The nurses stayed to wipe the saliva that drooled from his mouth, irrigate the big craters of bedsores that covered his hips, suction the lung fluids that threatened to drown him, clean the feces that burned his skin like lye,[2] pour the liquid food down the tube attached to his stomach, put pillows between his knees to ease the bone-on-bone pain, turn him every hour to keep the bedsores from getting worse, and change his gown and linen every two hours to keep him from being soaked in perspiration.   7

At night I went home and tried to scrub away the smell of decaying flesh that seemed woven into the fabric of my uniform. It was in my hair, the upholstery of my car—there was no washing it away.   8

---

[2]*lye:* a chemical that is used in cleaning products and that can burn skin.

And every night I prayed that Mac would die, that his agonized eyes would never again plead with me to let him die.

Every morning I asked his doctor for a "no-code" order. Without 9 that order, we had to resuscitate every patient who stopped breathing. His doctor was one of several who believe we must extend life as long as we have the means and knowledge to do it. To not do it is to be liable for negligence, at least in the eyes of many people, including some nurses. I thought about what it would be like to stand before a judge, accused of murder, if Mac stopped breathing and I didn't call a code.

And after the fifty-second code, when Mac was still lucid enough 10 to beg for death again, and Maura was crumbled in my arms again, and when no amount of pain medication stilled his moaning and agony, I wondered about a spiritual judge. Was all this misery and suffering supposed to be building character or infusing us all with the sense of humility that comes from impotence?

Had we, the whole medical community, become so arrogant that 11 we believed in the illusion of salvation through science? Had we become so self-righteous that we thought meddling in God's work was our duty, our moral imperative, and our legal obligation? Did we really believe that we had the right to force "life" on a suffering man who had begged for the right to die?

Such questions haunted me more than ever early one morning 12 when Maura went home to change her clothes and I was bathing Mac. He had been still for so long, I thought he at last had the blessed relief of coma. Then he opened his eyes and moaned, "Pain . . . no more . . . Barbara . . . do something . . . God, let me go."

The desperation in his eyes and voice riddled me with guilt. "I'll 13 stop," I told him as I injected the pain medication.

I sat on the bed and held Mac's hands in mine. He pressed his 14 bony fingers against my hand and muttered, "Thanks." Then there was one soft sigh and I felt his hands go cold in mine. "Mac?" I whispered, as I waited for his chest to rise and fall again.

A clutch of panic banded my chest, drew my finger to the code 15 button, urged me to do something, anything . . . but sit there alone with death. I kept one finger on the button, without pressing it, as a waxen pallor[3] slowly transformed his face from person to empty shell. Nothing I've ever done in my forty-seven years has taken so much effort as it took *not* to press that code button.

---

[3]*pallor:* extreme paleness.

Eventually, when I was as sure as I could be that the code team   16
would fail to bring him back, I entered the legal twilight zone and
pushed the button. The team tried. And while they were trying,
Maura walked into the room and shrieked, "No . . . don't let them do
this to him . . . for God's sake . . . please, no more."

Cradling her in my arms was like cradling myself, Mac, and all   17
those patients and nurses who had been in this place before, who do
the best they can in a death-denying society.

So a TV audience accused me of murder. Perhaps I am guilty. If a   18
doctor had written a no-code order, which is the only *legal* alternative, would he have felt any less guilty? Until there is legislation making it a criminal act to code a patient who has requested the right to
die, we will all of us risk the same fate as Mac. For whatever reason,
we developed the means to prolong life, and now we are forced to use
it. We do not have the right to die.

Thinking Critically about This Reading

In the rhetorical question "Did we really believe that we had the right
to force 'life' on a suffering man who had begged for the right to
die?" (paragraph 11), why do you think Huttmann places the word
life in quotation marks?

Questions for Study and Discussion

1. Why do people in the audience of the *Phil Donahue Show* call
   Huttmann a "murderer"? Is their accusation justified? In what
   ways do you think Huttmann might agree with them?

2. In paragraph 15, Huttmann states, "Nothing I've ever done in my
   forty-seven years has taken so much effort as it took *not* to press
   that code button." How effectively does she describe her struggle
   against pressing the button? What steps led to her ultimate decision not to press the code button?

3. What, according to Huttmann, is "the only *legal* alternative" (18)
   to her action? What does she find hypocritical about that choice?

4. Huttmann makes a powerfully emotional appeal for a patient's
   right to die. Some readers might find some of her story shocking
   or offensive. Cite examples of some of the graphic scenes Huttmann

describes, and discuss their impact on you as a reader. (Glossary: *Example*) Do they help persuade you to Huttmann's point of view, or do you find them overly unnerving? What would have been gained or lost had she left them out?

5. Huttmann's story covers a period of six months. In paragraphs 4–6, she describes the first five months of Mac's illness; in paragraphs 7–10, the sixth month; and in paragraphs 12–17, the final morning. What important point about narration does her use of time in this sequence demonstrate? (Glossary: *Narration*)

6. Huttmann concludes her essay with the statement "We do not have the right to die" (18). What does she mean by this? In your opinion, is she exaggerating or simply stating the facts? Does her example of Mac adequately illustrate her concluding point? Explain.

Classroom Activity Using Illustration

Huttmann illustrates her thesis by using the single example of Mac's experience in the hospital. Using the first statement and example as a model, find a single example that might be used to best illustrate each of the following potential thesis statements:

MODEL: Seat belts save lives. (*Possible example:* an automobile accident in which a relative's life was saved because she was wearing her seat belt)

Friends can be very handy.

Having good study skills can improve a student's grades.

Loud music can damage your hearing.

Reading the directions for a new product you have just purchased can save time and aggravation.

Humor can often make a bad situation more tolerable.

U.S. manufacturers can make their products safer.

Suggested Writing Assignments

1. Write a letter to the editor of *Newsweek* in response to Huttmann's essay. Are you for or against legislation that would give terminally

ill patients the right to die? Give examples from your personal experience or from your reading to support your opinion. You may find it helpful to read the student paper on pages 73–77, an argument for the rights of the terminally ill to die, before starting to write your letter.

2. Using one of the following sentences as your thesis statement, write an essay giving examples from your personal experience or from your reading to support your opinion.

• Consumers have more power than they realize.

• Most products do (or do not) measure up to the claims of their advertisements.

• Religion is (or is not) alive and well in the United States.

• The U.S. government works far better than its critics claim.

• Being able to write well is more than a basic skill.

• The seasons for professional sports are too long.

• Today's college students are (or are not) serious-minded when it comes to academics.

Let's Think Outside the Box
of Bad Clichés

■ **Gregory Pence**

*Born in 1949, Gregory Pence is an internationally known expert
in the field of bioethics. He is a cum laude graduate of the
College of William and Mary and earned his doctorate in philos-
ophy at New York University, writing his dissertation under the
direction of Australian bioethicist Peter Singer. A longtime pro-
fessor of philosophy at the Medical School of the University of
Alabama at Birmingham, Pence has published a number of
books in the field of cloning and medical ethics, including* Classic
Works in Medical Ethics *(1995),* Who's Afraid of Human
Cloning? *(1998),* Flesh of My Flesh: The Ethics of Human
Cloning *(1998),* Re-Creating Medicine: Ethical Issues at the
Frontiers of Medicine *(2000),* Designer Food: Mutant Harvest or
Breadbasket of the World? *(2001),* The Ethics of Food: A Reader
for the Twenty-first Century *(2002),* The Elements of Bioethics
(2007), and Medical Ethics: Accounts of Ground-Breaking Cases
in Medical Ethics *(6th ed., 2010). An award-winning teacher,
Pence coached the University of Alabama at Birmingham team
to the national championships* Ethics Bowl *in 2010.*

In the following essay, first published in Newsweek *on
August 6, 2007, Pence argues that sloppy writing leads to
sloppy thinking. Notice how he uses examples of trite expressions and inaccurate phrases from his students' papers to prove
his point.*

Reflecting on What You Know

Make a list of six or more clichés that you hear used around
you. Why do you think writing instructors discourage their students from using clichés in their writing? What do you think is
bad about clichés?

As a professor of bioethics, I strive to teach my students that clear   1
writing fosters clear thinking. But as I was grading a stack of blue
books today, I discovered so many clichés that I couldn't help writing

them down. Before I knew it, I had spent the afternoon not grading essays but cataloging the many trite or inaccurate phrases my students rely on to express themselves.

When I grade written work by students, one of the phrases I hate   2
most is "It goes without saying," in response to which I scribble on their essays, "Then why write it?" Another favorite of undergraduates is "It's not for me to say," to which I jot in their blue books, "Then why continue writing?"

I also despise the phrase "Who can say?" to which I reply, "You!   3
That's who! That's the point of writing an essay!"

In teaching bioethics, I constantly hear about "playing God," as   4
in "To allow couples to choose X is to play God." Undergraduates use the phrase constantly as a rhetorical hammer, as if saying it ends all discussion. And I don't even want to get into "opening Pandora's box" or "sliding down the slippery slope."

Sometimes the clichés are simply redundant, as when my students   5
write of a "mass exodus." Can there be a "small" exodus? "Exodus" implies a mass of people.

Other times the expressions defy the rules of logic. A student in a   6
philosophy class writes that philosophy "bores me to tears." But if something brings him to tears, it's certainly not boring.

I also fear that most students don't know what they are saying   7
when they write that a question "boggles the mind." Does every problem in bioethics really boggle the mind? What does this mean?

My students aren't the only ones guilty of cliché abuse. The lan-   8
guage of medicine confuses patients' families when physicians write, "On Tuesday the patient was declared brain dead, and on Wednesday life support was removed." So when did the patient really die? Can people die in two ways, once when they are declared brain dead and second when their respirators are removed? Better to write, "Physicians declared the patient dead by neurological criteria and the next day removed his respirator."

All of us repeat trite expressions without thinking. My TV weather-   9
man sometimes says, "It's raining cats and dogs." Should I call the Humane Society? Where did this silly expression come from?

Another common mistake involves "literally." I often hear people   10
on election night say, "He literally won by a landslide." If so, should geologists help us understand how?

Then, of course, there's the criminal who was caught in "broad   11
daylight." I guess he could not have been caught in "narrow" daylight.

And are we sure that the sun shone on the day he was caught? I some-times read about a "bone of contention." I imagine two animals fight-ing over a bone from a carcass (and not, as students write, from "a dead carcass"). But do writers want to convey that image?

And how can we forget about the "foreseeable future" (versus 12 the "unforeseeable future"?) and the "foregone conclusion" (versus the "non-foregone conclusion"?).

Spare me jargon from sports, such as being "on the bubble" for 13 something. I'd also rather do without other jargon, such as "pushing the [edge of the] envelope." And has writing that we should "think outside the box" become such a cliché that it's now inside the box?

Some of the worst phrases come from the business world. Because 14 of my profession, I read a lot of essays on medicine, ethics, and money. So I must endure endless strings of nouns acting as adjectival phrases, such as "health care finance administration official business." Even authors of textbooks on business and hospital administration use such phrases; no wonder that students use them, too.

And in these fields and others, can we do away with "take a lead- 15 ership role"? These days, can't anyone just lead?

Can we also hear more about the short arm of the law (versus its 16 "long" one), about things that sell well besides "hotcakes," and about a quick tour other than a "whirlwind" one?

Beyond the shadow of a doubt, I'd like to leave no stone unturned 17 in grinding such writing to a halt, saving each and every student's essay in the nick of time. But I have a sneaking suspicion that, from time immemorial, that has been an errand of mercy and easier said than done.

Thinking Critically about This Reading

In his well-known essay "Politics and the English Language," George Orwell argues that writers should avoid using meaningless language. He writes, "Prose consists less and less of words chosen for the sake of their meaning, and more and more of phrases tacked together like the sections of a prefabricated henhouse." Would Pence agree with Orwell?

Questions for Study and Discussion

1. What is Pence's thesis in this essay? How well does he make his case as far as you are concerned?

2. What types of clichés does Pence discuss? Are they equally bad, or are some more annoying than others? Are there good clichés? Explain.

3. In paragraph 8, Pence gives an example of confusing medical language. Explain how the example he uses contains clichés that are in conflict with each other. Does his rewrite of the example solve the problem that he sees? Explain.

4. Pence does not offer any suggestions for avoiding clichés in writing. How do you avoid such usage? How would you advise others to avoid clichés?

5. How effective did you find Pence's conclusion? (Glossary: *Beginnings and Endings*) How else could he have ended his essay? Explain.

Classroom Activity Using Illustration

One way to determine whether an expression is a cliché is to take part of the expression and see if the missing part comes readily to mind. For example, how would you complete the following incomplete expressions?

when push comes to _____   paying lip _____

fall between _____ _____   put the _____ before the _____

scratch the _____   patience of a _____

If you correctly filled in each of the above examples, you have a good sense of what constitutes a cliché and will be able to detect and eliminate them in your own writing.

Suggested Writing Assignments

1. Pence claims "Some of the worst phrases come from the business world" (14). To test his statement, find a recent article in a business magazine such as *Forbes, Fortune, Money,* or *Harvard Business Review* and/or three or four print advertisements, and look for clichés, empty or inaccurate phrases, and unnecessary jargon. Write a report of your findings. Is Pence's statement justified in your opinion?

2. The following cartoon by Goddard depicts a frightened patient begging his doctor for a truthful diagnosis. What is your reaction to the cartoon? What insights, if any, does the cartoon give you into Pence's essay about the nature of clichés and how we use them? Write an essay in which you explore the presence of clichés in the language of sports figures, doctors, educators, lawyers, or fashion designers. You may find it helpful to think about the following questions before beginning to write. What are the most common clichés used by the people in the area you chose? Why do you think that these people use so many clichés? What is actually being communicated when people use these clichés? What do you think would happen if clichés were no longer used? Use as support examples from Pence's essay and Goddard's cartoon, as well as your own experiences and observations.

3. Following up on the Thinking Critically about This Reading exercise on p. 351, write an essay on George Orwell's own essay "Politics and the English Language." What is the thesis of his essay and what prompted him to write it? What additional writing advice does he offer his readers? Is his advice pertinent today? Why or why not? Be sure to comment on the connection Orwell makes between politics and the English language. In what ways are his observations about that connection even more timely today than when they were first published in 1946? Would you add any additional warnings to Orwell's list based on the ways you see language being used today?

Our Vanishing Night

■ Verlyn Klinkenborg

Born in 1952 in Meeker, Colorado, Verlyn Klinkenborg grew up on farms in Iowa and Minnesota, where he developed his keen observation skills and love for life in rural America. After graduating from Pomona College and receiving a PhD from Princeton University, he embarked on a career as a writer and farmer. His first book, Making Hay *(1986), reflects Klinkenborg's fascination with small family farms.* The Last Fine Time *(1991) is a history of immigrant life in Buffalo, New York, where his father-in-law owned a neighborhood bar. Since 1997, his column "The Rural Life" has appeared regularly on the editorial pages of the* New York Times, *and in 2003 these essays were published in the collection* The Rural Life. *His most recent book is* Timothy; Or, Notes of an Abject Reptile *(2006). Klinkenborg's essays have also appeared in* Harper's, Smithsonian, Audubon, National Geographic, *and the* New Yorker. *He has taught literature and creative writing at Fordham University, St. Olaf College, Bennington College, and Harvard University, and currently is working on a book about the 18th-century radical and farmer William Cobbett.*

The following essay first appeared in the November 2008 issue of National Geographic. *Notice how Klinkenborg supports his thesis about the often unnoticed negative effects of light pollution with striking examples from the natural world and everyday life.*

Reflecting on What You Know

As a child, did you ever go outside on a clear night to look at the stars? Do you remember the names of some of the constellations and planets—like Orion, the Big Dipper, or Venus—that you were able to identify? When you find yourself outside walking now, do you look up at the evening sky? Are the heavens still as you remember them as a child? If not, what's changed?

If humans were truly at home under the light of the moon and stars, we would go in darkness happily, the midnight world as visible to us as it is to the vast number of nocturnal species on this planet. Instead, we are diurnal creatures, with eyes adapted to living in the sun's light. This is a basic evolutionary fact, even though most of us don't think of ourselves as diurnal beings any more than we think of ourselves as primates or mammals or Earthlings. Yet it's the only way to explain what we've done to the night: We've engineered it to receive us by filling it with light.

1

This kind of engineering is no different than damming a river. Its benefits come with consequences—called light pollution—whose effects scientists are only now beginning to study. Light pollution is largely the result of bad lighting design, which allows artificial light to shine outward and upward into the sky, where it's not wanted, instead of focusing it downward, where it is. Ill-designed lighting washes out the darkness of night and radically alters the light levels—and light rhythms—to which many forms of life, including ourselves, have adapted. Wherever human light spills into the natural world, some aspect of life—migration, reproduction, feeding—is affected.

2

For most of human history, the phrase "light pollution" would have made no sense. Imagine walking toward London on a moonlit night around 1800, when it was Earth's most populous city. Nearly a million people lived there, making do, as they always had, with candles and rushlights and torches and lanterns. Only a few houses were lit by gas, and there would be no public gaslights in the streets or squares for another seven years. From a few miles away, you would have been as likely to *smell* London as to see its dim collective glow.

3

Now most of humanity lives under intersecting domes of reflected, refracted light, of scattering rays from overlit cities and suburbs, from light-flooded highways and factories. Nearly all of nighttime Europe is a nebula of light, as is most of the United States and all of Japan. In the south Atlantic the glow from a single fishing fleet—squid fishermen luring their prey with metal halide lamps—can be seen from space, burning brighter, in fact, than Buenos Aires or Rio de Janeiro.

4

In most cities the sky looks as though it has been emptied of stars, leaving behind a vacant haze that mirrors our fear of the dark and resembles the urban glow of dystopian science fiction. We've grown so used to this pervasive orange haze that the original glory of an unlit night—dark enough for the planet Venus to throw shadows

5

on Earth—is wholly beyond our experience, beyond memory almost. And yet above the city's pale ceiling lies the rest of the universe, utterly undiminished by the light we waste—a bright shoal of stars and planets and galaxies, shining in seemingly infinite darkness.

We've lit up the night as if it were an unoccupied country, when ⁶ nothing could be further from the truth. Among mammals alone, the number of nocturnal species is astonishing. Light is a powerful biological force, and on many species it acts as a magnet, a process being studied by researchers such as Travis Longeore and Catherine Rich, co-founders of the Los Angeles–based Urban Wildlands Group. The effect is so powerful that scientists speak of songbirds and seabirds being "captured" by searchlights on land or by the light from gas flares on marine oil platforms, circling and circling in the thousands until they drop. Migrating at night, birds are apt to collide with brightly lit tall buildings; immature birds on their first journey suffer disproportionately.

Insects, of course, cluster around streetlights, and feeding at ⁷ those insect clusters is now ingrained in the lives of many bat species. In some Swiss valleys the European lesser horseshoe bat began to vanish after streetlights were installed, perhaps because those valleys were suddenly filled with light-feeding pipistrelle bats. Other nocturnal mammals—including desert rodents, fruit bats, opossums, and badgers—forage more cautiously under the permanent full moon of light pollution because they've become easier targets for predators.

Some birds—blackbirds and nightingales, among others—sing ⁸ at unnatural hours in the presence of artificial light. Scientists have determined that long artificial days—and artificially short nights—induce early breeding in a wide range of birds. And because a longer day allows for longer feeding, it can also affect migration schedules. One population of Bewick's swans wintering in England put on fat more rapidly than usual, priming them to begin their Siberian migration early. The problem, of course, is that migration, like most other aspects of bird behavior, is a precisely timed biological behavior. Leaving early may mean arriving too soon for nesting conditions to be right.

Nesting sea turtles, which show a natural predisposition for ⁹ dark beaches, find fewer and fewer of them to nest on. Their hatchlings, which gravitate toward the brighter, more reflective sea horizon, find themselves confused by artificial lighting behind the beach. In Florida alone, hatchling losses number in the hundreds of thousands every year. Frogs and toads living near brightly lit high-ways suffer nocturnal light levels that are as much as a million times brighter than normal, throwing nearly every aspect of their behavior out of joint, including their nighttime breeding choruses.

Of all the pollutions we face, light pollution is perhaps the most 10 easily remedied. Simple changes in lighting design and installation yield immediate changes in the amount of light spilled into the atmosphere and, often, immediate energy savings.

It was once thought that light pollution only affected astrono- 11 mers, who need to see the night sky in all its glorious clarity. And, in fact, some of the earliest civic efforts to control light pollution—in Flagstaff, Arizona, half a century ago—were made to protect the view from Lowell Observatory, which sits high above that city. Flagstaff has tightened its regulations since then, and in 2001 it was declared the first International Dark Sky City. By now the effort to control light pollution has spread around the globe. More and more cities and even entire countries, such as the Czech Republic, have committed themselves to reducing unwanted glare.

Unlike astronomers, most of us may not need an undiminished 12 view of the night sky for our work, but like most other creatures we do need darkness. Darkness is as essential to our biological welfare, to our internal clockwork, as light itself. The regular oscillation of waking and sleep in our lives—one of our circadian rhythms—is nothing less than a biological expression of the regular oscillation of light on Earth. So fundamental are these rhythms to our being that altering them is like altering gravity.

For the past century or so, we've been performing an open- 13 ended experiment on ourselves, extending the day, shortening the night, and short-circuiting the human body's sensitive response to light. The consequences of our bright new world are more readily perceptible in less adaptable creatures living in the peripheral glow of our prosperity. But for humans, too, light pollution may take a biological toll. At least one new study has suggested a direct correlation between higher rates of breast cancer in women and the nighttime brightness of their neighborhoods.

In the end, humans are no less trapped by light pollution than 14 the frogs in a pond near a brightly lit highway. Living in a glare of our own making, we have cut ourselves off from our evolutionary and cultural patrimony—the light of the stars and the rhythms of day and night. In a very real sense, light pollution causes us to lose sight of our true place in the universe, to forget the scale of our being, which is best measured against the dimensions of a deep night with the Milky Way—the edge of our galaxy—arching overhead.

Thinking Critically about This Reading

According to Klinkenborg, are there any benefits to lighting up the night? What are the consequences? (Glossary: *Cause and Effect*) For you, do the benefits outweigh the consequences? Explain.

Questions for Study and Discussion

1. What is Klinkenborg's thesis, and where does he present it? (Glossary: *Thesis*)
2. What examples does Klinkenborg use to support and illustrate his thesis? Which of his examples had the greatest effect on you? Explain why.
3. What does Klinkenborg mean when he says that "we are diurnal creatures" (paragraph 1)?
4. In what ways is light "a powerful biological force" (6)?
5. What can be done to remedy the problem of light pollution?
6. Klinkenborg claims that "light pollution causes us to lose sight of our true place in the universe" (14). What do you think that he means? Do you agree or disagree with his conclusion? Why?

Classroom Activity Using Illustration

Linton Weeks begins his essay "Burdens of the Modern Beast" (*Washington Post*, February 8, 2006) by contrasting the people in two old photographs with people of today. Carefully consider how Weeks uses examples in these opening five paragraphs to enhance the contrast and to introduce the central point of his essay.

> Slogging around with a backpack, a notebook, and a bottle of water, you stop for a while and stare at the historic black-and-white photographs in the National Museum of American History. You know, the ones depicting Americans going about their everyday lives: folks waiting for District trolley cars circa 1900, for instance, or people crisscrossing Pennsylvania Avenue in 1905.

Notice something missing? That's right: stuff.

The people—all ages, all colors, all genders—are not carrying any backpacks or water bottles. They are not schlepping cell phones, cradling coffee cups, or lugging laptops. They have no bags—shopping, tote, or diaper. Besides a small purse here or a walking cane or umbrella there, they are unburdened: footloose and fingers free.

Now walk outside and take a look around. People on the same city streets are loaded down. They are laden with books, newspapers, Gatorade jugs, personal stereos, knapsacks, briefcases, and canvas totes with high-heel shoes inside. They have iPods strapped to upper arms, fanny packs buckled around waists, and house keys Velcroed to shoelaces.

Perhaps it's because we are multitaskers. Or because we're insecure. Maybe we are becoming more independent. Whatever the reasons, we are more and more burdened by our own belongings.

What is your reaction to Weeks's examples? What would have been lost had he relied on generalizations to make his point? Identify any examples you would consider "more specific" than some of the other examples. Why do you suppose Weeks did not make all his examples as specific as he could have? Explain.

Suggested Writing Assignments

1. What examples of light pollution can you identify on campus or in town? Some things you might look for include overilluminated parking lots, walkways, and streets; lights not properly shielded; and lighting left on in buildings after closing. How might the light pollution you identify be corrected? Write a letter to the building and grounds administrator at your school or to your town manager in which you argue to have the light pollution reduced or eliminated.

2. Klinkenborg claims, "Wherever human light spills into the natural world, some aspect of life—migration, reproduction, feeding—is affected" (2). Do some research in your library or on the Internet about how human light affects the migration and feeding patterns of certain migratory birds or the reproduction of sea turtles, for example. Write an essay in which you report your findings.

In Defense of Dangerous Ideas

■ **Steven Pinker**

Internationally recognized language and cognition scholar and researcher Steven Pinker was born in Montreal, Quebec, Canada, in 1954. He immigrated to the United States shortly after receiving his BA from McGill University in 1976. After earning a doctorate from Harvard University in 1979, Pinker taught psychology at Stanford University and the Massachusetts Institute of Technology, where he directed the Center for Cognitive Neuroscience. Currently, he is the Johnstone Family Professor of Psychology at Harvard University. Pinker has written extensively on language development in children, starting with* Language Learnability and Language Development *(1984). He has what one critic writing in the* New York Times Book Review *calls "that facility, so rare among scientists, of making the most difficult material . . . accessible to the average reader." Pinker's books* The Language Instinct *(1994),* How the Mind Works *(1997),* Words and Rules: The Ingredients of Language *(1999),* The Blank Slate: The Modern Denial of Human Nature *(2002), and* The Stuff of Thought: Language as a Window into Human Nature *(2007) all attest to the public's interest in human language and the world of ideas.*

The following article was first published as the preface to What Is Your Dangerous Idea? Today's Leading Thinkers on the Unthinkable *(2006, edited by John Brockman) and later posted at* Edge *(www.edge.com). In this essay, Steven Pinker explores what makes an idea "dangerous" and argues that "important ideas need to be aired," especially in academia, no matter how discomfiting people find them. Notice how Pinker uses a number of examples from a wide range of academic disciplines to illustrate his points about dangerous ideas and the need to discuss them.*

Reflecting on What You Know

What did you think when you first read the title to Pinker's essay? For you, what would make an idea dangerous? Do any issues or questions make you uncomfortable or unwilling to discuss them? Explain.

In every age, taboo questions raise our blood pressure and threaten   1
moral panic. But we cannot be afraid to answer them.

Do women, on average, have a different profile of aptitudes and   2
emotions than men?

Were the events in the Bible fictitious—not just the miracles, but   3
those involving kings and empires?

Has the state of the environment improved in the last fifty years?   4

Do most victims of sexual abuse suffer no lifelong damage?   5

Did Native Americans engage in genocide and despoil the   6
landscape?

Do men have an innate tendency to rape?   7

Did the crime rate go down in the 1990s because two decades   8
earlier poor women aborted children who would have been prone to
violence?

Are suicide terrorists well-educated, mentally healthy, and morally   9
driven?

Would the incidence of rape go down if prostitution were legalized?   10

Do African American men have higher levels of testosterone, on   11
average, than white men?

Is morality just a product of the evolution of our brains, with no   12
inherent reality?

Would society be better off if heroin and cocaine were legalized?   13

Is homosexuality the symptom of an infectious disease?   14

Would it be consistent with our moral principles to give parents   15
the option of euthanizing newborns with birth defects that would con-
sign them to a life of pain and disability?

Do parents have any effect on the character or intelligence of   16
their children?

Have religions killed a greater proportion of people than Nazism?   17

Would damage from terrorism be reduced if the police could   18
torture suspects in special circumstances?

Would Africa have a better chance of rising out of poverty if it   19
hosted more polluting industries or accepted Europe's nuclear waste?

Is the average intelligence of Western nations declining because   20
duller people are having more children than smarter people?

Would unwanted children be better off if there were a market in   21
adoption rights, with babies going to the highest bidder?

Would lives be saved if we instituted a free market in organs for   22
transplantation?

Should people have the right to clone themselves, or enhance the   23
genetic traits of their children?

Perhaps you can feel your blood pressure rise as you read these   24
questions. Perhaps you are appalled that people can so much as think
such things. Perhaps you think less of me for bringing them up. These
are dangerous ideas—ideas that are denounced not because they are
self-evidently false, nor because they advocate harmful action, but because they are thought to corrode the prevailing moral order.

Think about It

By "dangerous ideas" I don't have in mind harmful technologies, like   25
those behind weapons of mass destruction, or evil ideologies, like those
of racist, fascist, or other fanatical cults. I have in mind statements of
fact or policy that are defended with evidence and argument by serious
scientists and thinkers but which are felt to challenge the collective
decency of an age. The ideas listed above, and the moral panic that each
one of them has incited during the past quarter century, are examples.
Writers who have raised ideas like these have been vilified, censored,
fired, threatened, and in some cases physically assaulted.

Every era has its dangerous ideas. For millennia, the monotheistic   26
religions have persecuted countless heresies, together with nuisances
from science such as geocentrism, biblical archeology, and the theory
of evolution. We can be thankful that the punishments have changed
from torture and mutilation to the canceling of grants and the writing
of vituperative reviews. But intellectual intimidation, whether by sword
or by pen, inevitably shapes the ideas that are taken seriously in a given
era, and the rear-view mirror of history presents us with a warning.

Time and again, people have invested factual claims with ethical   27
implications that today look ludicrous. The fear that the structure of
our solar system has grave moral consequences is a venerable
example, and the foisting of "intelligent design" on biology students
is a contemporary one. These travesties should lead us to ask whether
the contemporary intellectual mainstream might be entertaining

similar moral delusions. Are we enraged by our own infidels and heretics whom history may some day vindicate?

Unsettling Possibilities

Dangerous ideas are likely to confront us at an increasing rate, and we are ill-equipped to deal with them. When done right, science (together with other truth-seeking institutions, such as history and journalism) characterizes the world as it is, without regard to whose feelings get hurt. Science in particular has always been a source of heresy, and today the galloping advances in touchy areas like genetics, evolution, and the environment sciences are bound to throw unsettling possibilities at us. Moreover, the rise of globalization and the Internet are allowing heretics to find one another and work around the barriers of traditional media and academic journals. I also suspect that a change in generational sensibilities will hasten the process. The term "political correctness" captures the 1960s conception of moral rectitude that we baby boomers brought with us as we took over academia, journalism, and government. In my experience, today's students—black and white, male and female—are bewildered by the idea, common among their parents, that certain scientific opinions are immoral or certain questions too hot to handle. 28

What makes an idea "dangerous"? One factor is an imaginable train of events in which acceptance of the idea could lead to an outcome recognized as harmful. In religious societies, the fear is that if people ever stopped believing in the literal truth of the Bible they would also stop believing in the authority of its moral commandments. That is, if today people dismiss the part about God creating the earth in six days, tomorrow they'll dismiss the part about "Thou shalt not kill." In progressive circles, the fear is that if people ever were to acknowledge any differences between races, sexes, or individuals, they would feel justified in discrimination or oppression. Other dangerous ideas set off fears that people will neglect or abuse their children, become indifferent to the environment, devalue human life, accept violence, and prematurely resign themselves to social problems that could be solved with sufficient commitment and optimism. 29

All these outcomes, needless to say, would be deplorable. But none of them actually follows from the supposedly dangerous idea. Even if it turns out, for instance, that groups of people are different in their averages, the overlap is certainly so great that it would be irrational and unfair to discriminate against individuals on that basis. Likewise, even if it turns out that parents don't have the power to shape their children's 30 personalities, it would be wrong on grounds of simple human decency to abuse or neglect one's children. And if currently popular ideas about how to improve the environment are shown to be ineffective, it only highlights the need to know what would be effective.

Another contributor to the perception of dangerousness is the intellectual blinkers that humans tend to don when they split into factions. People have a nasty habit of clustering in coalitions, professing certain beliefs as badges of their commitment to the coalition and treating rival coalitions as intellectually unfit and morally depraved. Debates between members of the coalitions can make things even worse, because when the other side fails to capitulate to one's devastating arguments, it only proves they are immune to reason. In this regard, it's disconcerting to see the two institutions that ought to have the greatest stake in ascertaining the truth—academia and government—often blinkered by morally tinged ideologies. One ideology is that humans are blank slates and that social problems can be handled only through government programs that especially redress the perfidy[1] of European males. Its opposite number is that morality inheres in patriotism and Christian faith and that social problems may be handled only by government policies that punish the sins of individual evildoers. New ideas, nuanced ideas, hybrid ideas—and sometimes dangerous ideas—often have trouble getting a hearing against these group-bonding convictions.

The conviction that honest opinions can be dangerous may even arise from a feature of human nature. Philip Tetlock and Alan Fiske have argued that certain human relationships are constituted on a basis of unshakable convictions. We love our children and parents, are faithful to our spouses, stand by our friends, contribute to our communities, and are loyal to our coalitions not because we continually question and evaluate the merits of these commitments but because we feel them in our bones. A person who spends too much time pondering whether logic and fact really justify a commitment to one of these relationships is seen as just not "getting it." Decent people don't carefully weigh the advantages and disadvantages of selling their children or selling out their friends or their spouses or their colleagues or their country. They reject these possibilities outright; they "don't go there." So the taboo on questioning sacred values makes sense in the context of personal relationships. It makes far less sense in the context of discovering how the world works or running a country.

---

[1]*Perfidy:* disloyalty, infidelity, or unfaithfulness.

Explore All Relevant Ideas

Should we treat some ideas as dangerous? Let's exclude outright lies, 33 deceptive propaganda, incendiary conspiracy theories from malevolent crackpots, and technological recipes for wanton destruction. Consider only ideas about the truth of empirical claims or the effectiveness of policies that, if they turned out to be true, would require a significant rethinking of our moral sensibilities. And consider ideas that, if they turn out to be false, could lead to harm if people believed them to be true. In either case, we don't know whether they are true or false a priori[2], so only by examining and debating them can we find out. Finally, let's assume that we're not talking about burning people at the stake or cutting out their tongues but about discouraging their research and giving their ideas as little publicity as possible. There is a good case for exploring all ideas relevant to our current concerns, no matter where they lead. The idea that ideas should be discouraged a priori is inherently self-refuting. Indeed, it is the ultimate arrogance, as it assumes that one can be so certain about the goodness and truth of one's own ideas that one is entitled to discourage other people's opinions from even being examined.

Also, it's hard to imagine any aspect of public life where igno- 34 rance or delusion is better than an awareness of the truth, even an unpleasant one. Only children and madmen engage in "magical thinking," the fallacy that good things can come true by believing in them or bad things will disappear by ignoring them or wishing them away. Rational adults want to know the truth, because any action based on false premises will not have the effects they desire. Worse, logicians tell us that a system of ideas containing a contradiction can be used to deduce any statement whatsoever, no matter how absurd. Since ideas are connected to other ideas, sometimes in circuitous and unpredictable ways, choosing to believe something that may not be true, or even maintaining walls of ignorance around some topic, can corrupt all of intellectual life, proliferating error far and wide. In our everyday lives, would we want to be lied to, or kept in the dark by paternalistic "protectors," when it comes to our health or finances or even the weather? In public life, imagine someone saying that we should not do research into global warming or energy shortages because if it found that they were serious the consequences for the economy would be extremely unpleasant. Today's leaders who tacitly take this position

---

[2]*a priori:* beforehand.

are rightly condemned by intellectually responsible people. But why should other unpleasant ideas be treated differently?

There is another argument against treating ideas as dangerous. 35 Many of our moral and political policies are designed to preempt what we know to be the worst features of human nature. The checks and balances in a democracy, for instance, were invented in explicit recognition of the fact that human leaders will always be tempted to arrogate power to themselves. Likewise, our sensitivity to racism comes from an awareness that groups of humans, left to their own devices, are apt to discriminate and oppress other groups, often in ugly ways. History also tells us that a desire to enforce dogma and suppress heretics is a recurring human weakness, one that has led to recurring waves of gruesome oppression and violence. A recognition that there is a bit of Torquemada[3] in everyone should make us wary of any attempt to enforce a consensus or demonize those who challenge it.

"Sunlight is the best disinfectant," according to Justice Louis 36 Brandeis's famous case for freedom of thought and expression. If an idea really is false, only by examining it openly can we determine that it is false. At that point we will be in a better position to convince others that it is false than if we had let it fester in private, since our very avoidance of the issue serves as a tacit acknowledgment that it may be true. And if an idea is true, we had better accommodate our moral sensibilities to it, since no good can come from sanctifying a delusion. This might even be easier than the ideaphobes fear. The moral order did not collapse when the earth was shown not to be at the center of the solar system, and so it will survive other revisions of our understanding of how the world works.

Dangerous to Air Dangerous Ideas?

In the best Talmudic[4] tradition of arguing a position as forcefully as 37 possible and then switching sides, let me now present the case for discouraging certain lines of intellectual inquiry. . . . [Alison] Gopnik and [W. Daniel] Hillis offer as their "dangerous idea" the exact opposite of [Daniel] Gilbert's: they say that it's a dangerous idea for thinkers to air their dangerous ideas. How might such an argument play out?

First, one can remind people that we are all responsible for the 38 foreseeable consequences of our actions, and that includes the

---

[3]*Torquemada:* Tomás de Torquemada (1420–1498), Spanish grand inquisitor.
[4]*Talmudic:* Jewish or Hebrew.

consequences of our public statements. Freedom of inquiry may be an important value, according to this argument, but it is not an absolute value, one that overrides all others. We know that the world is full of malevolent and callous people who will use any pretext to justify their bigotry or destructiveness. We must expect that they will seize on the broaching of a topic that seems in sympathy with their beliefs as a vindication of their agenda.

Not only can the imprimatur of scientific debate add legitimacy to   39
toxic ideas, but the mere act of making an idea common knowledge can change its effects. Individuals, for instance, may harbor a private opinion on differences between genders or among ethnic groups but keep it to themselves because of its opprobrium. But once the opinion is aired in public, they may be emboldened to act on their prejudice—not just because it has been publicly ratified but because they must anticipate that everyone else will act on the information. Some people, for example, might discriminate against the members of an ethnic group despite having no pejorative opinion about them, in the expectation that their customers or colleagues will have such opinions and that defying them would be costly. And then there are the effects of these debates on the confidence of the members of the stigmatized groups themselves.

Of course, academics can warn against these abuses, but the qual-   40
ifications and nitpicking they do for a living may not catch up with the simpler formulations that run on swifter legs. Even if they did, their qualifications might be lost on the masses. We shouldn't count on ordinary people to engage in the clear thinking—some would say the hair-splitting—that would be needed to accept a dangerous idea but not its terrible consequence. Our overriding precept, in intellectual life as in medicine, should be "First, do no harm."

We must be especially suspicious when the danger in a dangerous   41
idea is to someone other than its advocate. Scientists, scholars, and writers are members of a privileged elite. They may have an interest in promulgating ideas that justify their privileges, that blame or make light of society's victims, or that earn them attention for cleverness and iconoclasm. Even if one has little sympathy for the cynical Marxist argument that ideas are always advanced to serve the interest of the ruling class, the ordinary skepticism of a tough-minded intellectual should make one wary of "dangerous" hypotheses that are no skin off the nose of their hypothesizers. (The mindset that leads us to blind review, open debate, and statements of possible conflicts of interest.)

But don't the demands of rationality always compel us to seek the   42
complete truth? Not necessarily. Rational agents often choose to be

ignorant. They may decide not to be in a position where they can receive a threat or be exposed to a sensitive secret. They may choose to
avoid being asked an incriminating question, where one answer is
damaging, another is dishonest, and a failure to answer is grounds for
the questioner to assume the worst (hence the Fifth Amendment protection against being forced to testify against oneself). Scientists test
drugs in double-blind studies in which they keep themselves from
knowing who got the drug and who got the placebo, and they referee
manuscripts anonymously for the same reason. Many people rationally choose not to know the gender of their unborn child, or whether
they carry a gene for Huntington's disease, or whether their nominal
father is genetically related to them. Perhaps a similar logic would call
for keeping socially harmful information out of the public sphere.

Intolerance of Unpopular Ideas

As for restrictions on inquiry, every scientist already lives with them.　43
They accede, for example, to the decisions of committees for the protection of human subjects and to policies on the confidentiality of personal information. In 1975, biologists imposed a moratorium on
research on recombinant DNA pending the development of safeguards
against the release of dangerous microorganisms. The notion that intellectuals have carte blanche in conducting their inquiry is a myth.

Though I am more sympathetic to the argument that important　44
ideas be aired than to the argument that they should sometimes be sup-
pressed, I think it is a debate we need to have. Whether we like it or
not, science has a habit of turning up discomfiting thoughts, and the
Internet has a habit of blowing their cover.

Tragically, there are few signs that the debates will happen in the　45
place where we might most expect it: academia. Though academics
owe the extraordinary perquisite of tenure to the ideal of encouraging
free inquiry and the evaluation of unpopular ideas, all too often academics are the first to try to quash them. The most famous recent
example is the outburst of fury and disinformation that resulted when
Harvard president Lawrence Summers gave a measured analysis of the
multiple causes of women's underrepresentation in science and math
departments in elite universities and tentatively broached the possibility that discrimination and hidden barriers were not the only cause.

But intolerance of unpopular ideas among academics is an old　46
story. Books like Morton Hunt's *The New Know-Nothings* and Alan

Kors and Harvey Silverglate's *The Shadow University* have depressingly shown that universities cannot be counted on to defend the rights of their own heretics and that it's often the court system or the press that has to drag them into policies of tolerance. In government, the intolerance is even more frightening, because the ideas considered there are not just matters of intellectual sport but have immediate and sweeping consequences. Chris Mooney, in *The Republican War on Science,* joins Hunt in showing how corrupt and demagogic legislators are increasingly stifling research findings they find inconvenient to their interests.

Thinking Critically about This Reading

What do you think is Pinker's purpose in defending dangerous ideas? What does he want his readers to do after reading this essay? Did he achieve his purpose with you? Explain.

Questions for Study and Discussion

1. Pinker starts his essay with a list of twenty-two questions, each an example of a dangerous idea. What were you thinking as you read Pinker's list? Which questions touched a sensitive nerve for you? Explain.

2. How does Pinker define "dangerous idea"? Do you agree with his definition?

3. According to Pinker, fear is one of the main factors that contributes to the perception of dangerousness. What examples of fears does Pinker use to illustrate this claim? What other factors contribute to the perception of dangerousness?

4. Do you believe that "the taboo on questioning sacred values makes sense in the context of personal relationships" (paragraph 32)? Why or why not? Why do you think that Pinker believes his statement, "It makes far less sense in the context of discovering how the world works or running a country" (32)?

5. What does Pinker mean when he says, "The idea that ideas should be discouraged a priori is inherently self-refuting" (33)?

6. According to Pinker, what is the "case for discouraging certain lines of intellectual inquiry" (37)? What evidence does he present to support this side of the issue?

7. How does Pinker support his claim that "intolerance of unpopular ideas among academics is an old story" (46)?

Classroom Activity Using Illustration

Consider the following paragraph from the rough draft of a student paper on Americans' obsession with losing weight. The student writer wanted to show the extreme actions people sometimes take to improve their appearance.

> Americans have long been obsessed with thinness—even at the risk of dying. In the 1930s, people took di-nitrophenol, an industrial poison, to lose weight. It boosted metabolism but caused blindness and some deaths. Since that time, dieters have experimented with any number of bizarre schemes that seem to work wonders in the short term but often end in disappointment or disaster in the long term. Some weight-loss strategies have even led to life-threatening eating disorders.

Try your hand at revising this paragraph, supplying specific examples of "bizarre schemes" or "weight-loss strategies" you have tried, observed, or read about. Share your examples with others in your class. Which examples best illustrate and support the central idea contained in the writer's topic sentence?

Suggested Writing Assignments

1. Reread the list of twenty-two questions at the beginning of Pinker's essay. After giving them some thought, select one to use as a central example in an essay about the need to debate important ideas no matter how uncomfortable those ideas might make us. Before you start writing, consider the following questions: What about the question I've chosen makes me or others uncomfortable? What are some of the idea's implications if we find it to be true? False? What would happen if we simply ignore this question?

2. In a case involving freedom of thought and expression, Justice Louis Brandeis said, "Sunlight is the best disinfectant" (36). What do you think that he meant? How do you think that Justice Brandeis would respond to the proposition that "it's a dangerous idea for thinkers to air their dangerous ideas" (37)? How do you respond to this proposition? Write an essay in which you present your position, and support that position with clear examples from your own experiences or reading.

Narration

To *narrate* is to tell a story or to recount a series of events. Whenever you relate an incident or use an **anecdote** (a very brief story) to make a point, you use narration. In its broadest sense, **narration** is any account of any event or series of events. We all love to hear stories; some people believe that sharing stories is a part of what defines us as human beings. Good stories are interesting, sometimes suspenseful, and always instructive because they give us insights into the human condition. Although most often associated with fiction, narration is effective and useful in all kinds of writing. For example, in "A Crime of Compassion," (pp. 343–46) nurse Barbara Huttmann tells how she brought one of her patient's long suffering to an end as she argues against repeatedly using extraordinary measures to revive dying patients against their wishes.

Good narration has five essential features — a clear context; well-chosen and thoughtfully emphasized details; a logical, often chronological organization; an appropriate and consistent point of view; and a meaningful point or purpose. Consider, for example, the following narrative, titled "Is Your Jar Full?"

> One day, an expert in time management was speaking to a group of business students and, to drive home a point, used an illustration those students will never forget. As he stood in front of the group of high-powered overachievers he said, "Okay, time for a quiz," and he pulled out a one-gallon mason jar and set it on the table in front of him. He also produced about a dozen fist-sized rocks and carefully placed them, one at a time, into the jar. When the jar was filled to the top and no more rocks would fit inside, he asked, "Is this jar full?"
>
> Everyone in the class yelled, "Yes."
>
> The time management expert replied, "Really?" He reached under the table and pulled out a bucket of gravel. He dumped some

gravel in and shook the jar causing pieces of gravel to work themselves down into the spaces between the big rocks. He then asked
the group once more, "Is the jar full?" By this time the class was on
to him.

"Probably not," one of them answered.

"Good!" he replied. He reached under the table and brought
out a bucket of sand. He started dumping the sand in the jar and
it went into all of the spaces left between the rocks and the gravel.

Once more he asked the question, "Is this jar full?"

"No!" the class shouted.

Once again he said, "Good." Then he grabbed a pitcher of
water and began to pour it in until the jar was filled to the brim.
Then he looked at the class and asked, "What is the point of this
illustration?"

One eager beaver raised his hand and said, "The point is, no
matter how full your schedule is, if you try really hard you can
always fit some more things in it!"

"No," the speaker replied, "that's not the point. The truth this
illustration teaches us is: If you don't put the big rocks in first, you'll
never get them in at all. What are the 'big rocks' in your life—time
with your loved ones, your faith, your education, your dreams, a
worthy cause, teaching or mentoring others? Remember to put these
BIG ROCKS in first or you'll never get them in at all."

So, tonight, or in the morning, when you are reflecting on this
short story, ask yourself this question: What are the "big rocks" in
my life? Then, put those in your jar first.

This story contains all the elements of good narration. The writer
begins by establishing a clear context for her narrative by telling
when, where, and to whom the action happened. She has chosen details well, including enough details so that we know what is happening but not so many that we become overwhelmed, confused, or
bored. The writer organizes her narration logically with a beginning
that sets the scene, a middle that relates the exchange between the
time-management expert and the students, and an end that makes her
point, all arranged chronologically. She tells the story from the third-
person point of view. Finally, she reveals the point of her narration:
people need to think about what's important in their lives and put
these activities first.

The writer could have told her story from the first-person point of
view. In this point of view, the narrator is a participant in the action
and uses the pronoun *I*. In the following example, Willie Morris tells a

story of how the comfortably well-off respond coolly to the tragedies of the ghetto. We experience the event directly through the writer's eyes and ears, as if we too had been on the scene of the action.

> One afternoon in late August, as the summer's sun streamed into the [railroad] car and made little jumping shadows on the windows, I sat gazing out at the tenement dwellers, who were themselves looking out of their windows from the gray crumbling buildings along the tracks of upper Manhattan. As we crossed into the Bronx, the train unexpectedly slowed down for a few miles. Suddenly from out of my window I saw a large crowd near the tracks, held back by two policemen. Then, on the other side from my window, I saw a sight I would never be able to forget: a little boy almost severed in halves, lying at an incredible angle near the track. The ground was covered with blood, and the boy's eyes were opened wide, strained and disbelieving in his sudden oblivion. A policeman stood next to him, his arms folded, staring straight ahead at the windows of our train. In the orange glow of late afternoon the policemen, the crowd, the corpse of the boy were for a brief moment immobile, motionless, a small tableau to violence and death in the city. Behind me, in the next row of seats, there was a game of bridge. I heard one of the four men say as he looked out at the sight, "God, that's horrible." Another said, in a whisper, "Terrible, terrible." There was a momentary silence, punctuated only by the clicking of the wheels on the track. Then, after the pause, I heard the first man say: "Two hearts."
>
> –Willie Morris

As you begin to write your own narration, take time to ask yourself why you are telling your story. Your purpose in writing will influence which events and details you include and which you leave out. You should include enough details about the action and its context so that your readers can understand what's going on. You should not get so carried away with details that your readers become confused or bored by an excess of information, however. In good storytelling, deciding what to leave out is as important as deciding what to include.

Be sure to give some thought to the organization of your narrative. Chronological organization is natural in narration because it is a reconstruction of the original order of events, but it is not always the most interesting. To add interest to your storytelling, try using a technique common in the movies and theater called *flashback*. Begin your narration midway through the story with an important or exciting event, and then use flashback to fill in what happened earlier. Notice how one student uses this very technique. She disrupts the chronological organization of her narrative by beginning in the recent past and then uses a flashback to take us back to when she was a youngster:

It was a Monday afternoon, and I was finally home from track practice. The coach had just told me that I had a negative attitude and should contemplate why I was on the team. My father greeted me in the living room. *Essay opens in recent past*

"Hi, honey. How was practice?"

"Not good, Dad. Listen, I don't want to do this anymore. I hate the track team." *Dialogue creates historical present*

"What do you mean *hate?*"

"The constant pressure is making me crazy."

"How so?"

"It's just not fun anymore."

"Well, I'll have to talk to the coach—"

"No! You're supposed to be my father, not my coach."

"I am your father, but I'm sure . . ."

"Just let me do what I want. You've had your turn."

He just let out a sigh and left the room. Later he told me that I was wasting my "God-given abilities." The funny part was that none of my father's anger hit me at first. All I knew was that I was free. *Essay returns in time to when troubles began*

My troubles began the summer I was five years old. It was late June. . . .

–Trena Isley, student

What's in a Name?

■ **Henry Louis Gates Jr.**

The preeminent African American scholar of our time, Henry Louis Gates Jr. is the Alphonse Fletcher University Professor and director of the W. E. B. Du Bois Institute for African and African American Research at Harvard University. Among his impressive list of publications are Figures in Black: Words, Signs, and the "Racial" Self *(1987),* The Signifying Monkey: A Theory of Afro-American Literary Criticism *(1988),* Loose Canons: Notes on Culture Wars *(1992),* The Future of the Race *(1997),* Thirteen Ways of Looking at a Black Man *(1999),* Mr. Jefferson and Miss Wheatley *(2003), and* Finding Oprah's Roots: Finding Your Own *(2007). In 2010, Gates published* Faces of America: How 12 Extraordinary Americans Reclaimed Their Pasts. *His* Colored People: A Memoir *(1994) recollects in a wonderful prose style his youth growing up in Piedmont, West Virginia, and his emerging sexual and racial awareness. Gates first enrolled at Potomac State College and later transferred to Yale University, where he studied history. With the assistance of an Andrew W. Mellon Foundation Fellowship and a Ford Foundation Fellowship, he pursued advanced degrees in English at Clare College at the University of Cambridge. He has been honored with a MacArthur Foundation Fellowship, inclusion on* Time *magazine's "25 Most Influential Americans" list, a National Humanities Medal, and election to the American Academy of Arts and Letters.*

In this essay, excerpted from a longer article published in the fall 1989 issue of Dissent *magazine, Gates tells the story of an early encounter with the language of prejudice. In learning how one of the "bynames" used by white people to define African Americans robs them of their identity, he feels the sting of racism first hand. Notice how Gates's use of dialogue gives immediacy and poignancy to his narration.*

Reflecting on What You Know

Reflect on the use of racially charged language. For example, has anyone ever used a racial epithet or name to refer to you? When did you first become aware that such names existed? How do you feel about being characterized by your race? If you yourself have ever used such names, what was your intent in using them? What was the response of others?

The question of color takes up much space in these pages, but the question of color, especially in this country, operates to hide the graver questions of the self.
–James Baldwin, 1961

. . . blood, darky, Tar Baby, Kaffir, shine . . . moor, blackamoor, Jim Crow, spook . . . quadroon, meriney, red bone, high yellow . . . Mammy, porch monkey, home, homeboy, George . . . spearchucker, schwarze, Leroy, Smokey . . . mouli, buck, Ethiopian, brother, sistah. . . .
–Trey Ellis, 1989

had forgotten the incident completely, until I read Trey Ellis's essay, "Remember My Name," in a recent issue of the *Village Voice*[1] (June 13, 1989). But there, in the middle of an extended italicized list of the bynames of "the race" ("the race" or "our people" being the terms my parents used in polite or reverential discourse, "jigaboo" or "nigger" more commonly used in anger, jest, or pure disgust), it was: "George." Now the events of that very brief exchange return to mind so vividly that I wonder why I had forgotten it.

My father and I were walking home at dusk from his second job. He "moonlighted" as a janitor in the evenings for the telephone company. Every day but Saturday, he would come home at 3:30 from his regular job at the paper mill, wash up, eat supper, then at 4:30 head downtown to his second job. He used to make jokes frequently about a union official who moonlighted. I never got the joke, but he and his friends thought it was hilarious. All I knew was that my family always ate well, that my brother and I had new clothes to wear, and that all of the white people in Piedmont, West Virginia, treated my parents with an odd mixture of resentment and respect that even we understood at the time had something directly to do with a small but certain measure of financial security.

---

[1]*Village Voice:* a nationally distributed weekly newspaper published in New York City.

He had left a little early that evening because I was with him and   3
I had to be in bed early. I could not have been more than five or six,
and we had stopped off at the Cut-Rate Drug Store (where no black
person in town but my father could sit down to eat, and eat off real
plates with real silverware) so that I could buy some caramel ice cream,
two scoops in a wafer cone, please, which I was busy licking when
Mr. Wilson walked by.

Mr. Wilson was a very quiet man, whose stony, brooding, silent   4
manner seemed designed to scare off any overtures of friendship,
even from white people. He was Irish, as was one-third of our village
(another third being Italian), the more affluent among whom sent
their children to "Catholic School" across the bridge in Maryland.
He had white straight hair, like my Uncle Joe, whom he uncannily
resembled, and he carried a black worn metal lunch pail, the kind
that Riley[2] carried on the television show. My father always spoke to
him, and for reasons that we never did understand, he always spoke
to my father.

"Hello, Mr. Wilson," I heard my father say.   5

"Hello, George."   6

I stopped licking my ice cream cone, and asked my Dad in a loud   7
voice why Mr. Wilson had called him "George."

"Doesn't he know your name, Daddy? Why don't you tell him   8
your name? Your name isn't George."

For a moment I tried to think of who Mr. Wilson was mixing Pop   9
up with. But we didn't have any Georges among the colored people in
Piedmont; nor were there colored Georges living in the neighboring
towns and working at the mill.

"Tell him your name, Daddy."   10

"He knows my name, boy," my father said after a long pause.   11
"He calls all colored people George."

A long silence ensued. It was "one of those things," as my Mom   12
would put it. Even then, that early, I knew when I was in the presence
of "one of those things," one of those things that provided a glimpse,
through a rent[3] curtain, at another world that we could not affect but
that affected us. There would be a painful moment of silence, and

---

[2]*Riley:* Chester A. Riley, the lead character on the U.S. television show *The Life of Riley*, a blue-collar, ethnic sitcom popular in the 1950s.

[3]*rent:* torn.

you would wait for it to give way to a discussion of a black superstar such as Sugar Ray[4] or Jackie Robinson.[5]

    "Nobody hits better in a clutch than Jackie Robinson."   13

    "That's right. Nobody."   14

    I never again looked Mr. Wilson in the eye.   15

Thinking Critically about This Reading

What is "one of those things," as Gates's mom put it (paragraph 12)? In what ways is "one of those things" really Gates's purpose in telling this story?

Questions for Study and Discussion

1. Gates prefaces his essay with two quotations. What is the meaning of each quotation? Why do you suppose Gates uses both quotations? How does each relate to his purpose? (Glossary: *Purpose*)

2. Gates begins by explaining where he got the idea for his essay. How well does this approach work? Is it an approach you could see yourself using often? Explain.

3. In his first paragraph, Gates sets the context for his narrative. He also reveals that his parents used terms of racial abuse among themselves. Why does Gates make so much of Mr. Wilson's use of *George* when his own parents used words so much more obviously offensive?

4. Gates describes and provides some background information about Mr. Wilson in paragraph 4. (Glossary: *Description*) What is Gates's purpose in providing this information? (Glossary: *Purpose*)

Classroom Activity Using Narration

Beginning at the beginning and ending at the end is not the only way to tell a story. Think of the events in a story that you would like to tell. Don't write the story, but simply list the events that need to be included. Be sure to include at least ten major events in your story.

---

[4]*Sugar Ray:* Walker Smith Jr. (1921–1989), American professional boxer and six-time world champion.

[5]*Jackie Robinson:* Jack Roosevelt Robinson (1919–1972), the first black baseball player in the major leagues in the modern era.

Now play with the arrangement of those events so as to avoid the chronological sequencing of them that would naturally come to mind. Try to develop as many patterns as you can, but be careful that you have a purpose in developing each sequence and that you create nothing that might confuse a listener or reader. Discuss your results with your classmates.

Suggested Writing Assignments

1. Using Gates's essay as a model, identify something that you have recently read that triggers in you a story from the past. Perhaps a newspaper article about how local high school students helped the community reminds you of a community project you and your classmates were involved in. Or perhaps reading about some act of heroism reminds you of a situation in which you performed (or failed to perform) a similar deed. Make sure that you have a purpose in telling the story, that you establish a clear context for it, and that you have enough supporting details to enrich your story. (Glossary: *Purpose; Details*) Also think about how to begin and end your story and which narrative sequence you will use. (Glossary: *Beginnings and Endings*)

2. How do you feel about your name? Do you like it? Does it sound pleasant? Do you think that your name shapes your self-identity in a positive or negative way, or do you think that it has no effect on your sense of who you are? Write an essay about your name and the way it helps or fails to help you present yourself to the world. Be sure to develop your essay using narration by including several anecdotes or a longer story involving your name. (Glossary: *Anecdote*)

White Lies

■ **Erin Murphy**

Erin Murphy was born in New Britain, Connecticut, in 1968 and grew up in Richmond, Virginia. She earned a BA in English from Washington University in 1990 and an MFA in English and poetry from the University of Massachusetts in 1993. Murphy is author of three collections of po-etry: Science of Desire *(2004), a finalist for the Paterson Poetry Prize;* Dislocation and Other Theories *(2008); and* Too Much of this World *(2008), winner of the Anthony Piccione Poetry Prize. Other awards in-clude the National Writers' Union Poetry Award judged by Donald Hall; a Dorothy Sargent Rosenberg Poetry Prize; the Foley Poetry Award; and fellowships from the Pennsylvania Council on the Arts, the Maryland State Arts Council, and the Virginia Center for the Creative Arts. Her poems have appeared in dozens of journals and several anthologies, including* 180 More: Extraordinary Poems for Every Day *edited by Billy Collins. She is on the faculty at Pennsylvania State University's Altoona College, where she teaches English and creative writing.*

First published in 2010 in Brevity, *the following essay has been nominated for a Pushcart Prize. Murphy comments on her writing of the narrative and how she feels about it now: "This is a story that I carried with me for thirty years before I wrote about it. Now that I am a mother, I have a heightened aware-ness of the kind of bullying that is all too common in schools. When my own children came home with stories about class-mates being ostracized, I thought of Connie and her candy. For decades, I've felt sympathy for Connie; from my current per-spective, I also feel tremendous sympathy for her mother."*

Reflecting on What You Know

At what point do repeated mocking comments directed at our classmates and school friends cross the line into bullying? Have you engaged in such mocking comments? Have you been bullied? Have you come to anyone's rescue who was being bullied? Explain.

Arpi, a Lebanese girl who pronounced *ask* as *ax* no matter how 1
many times the teacher corrected her, must have been delighted by the arrival of Connie, the new girl in our fifth grade class. Connie was albino, exceptionally white even by the ultra-Caucasian standards of our southern suburb. Only her eyelids had color: mouse-nose pink, framed by moth-white lashes and brows.

We had been taught that there was no comparative or superlative 2 for *different*. Things were either different or the same, the teacher said. Likewise for *perfect*—something was either perfect or not. But surely Arpi thought of Connie as *more different* than herself. Arpi may have had a name that sounded all too close to Alpo, a brand of dog food, but at least she had a family whose skin and hair and eyes looked like hers. Connie, by comparison, was alone in her difference. She was, perhaps, *most different. Differentest.*

This was confirmed by the ridicule, which was immediate and 3 unrelenting: *Casper, Chalk Face, Q-Tip.* Connie, whose shoulders hunched in a permanent parenthesis, pretended not to hear the names or the taunting questions: *What'd ya do, take a bath in bleach? Who's your boyfriend—Frosty the Snowman?* She sat in the front of the classroom, and if she felt the boys plucking white hairs from her scalp, she didn't react. The teacher, who was serving the last nine months of a thirty-year sentence in the public school system, spent the bulk of each day perusing magazines and L.L. Bean catalogs in the back of the room. As far as I know, she never intervened.

All of this changed in mid-October when Connie's father got a 4 job at a candy factory, news Connie announced tentatively one rainy day during indoor recess,

Can he get us candy? 5

Yes. 6

Any kind? As much as we want? For free? 7

Yes, yes, yes. 8

And so the daily ritual began. Kids placed orders for Reese's 9 Cups, Baby Ruth bars, Hubba-Bubba bubble gum. Connie kept a log of the requests in a pocket-sized notebook. The next day, she would tote a box full of candy into the classroom and distribute the promised sweets to eager hands. Overnight, Connie became the center of attention. Girls—even Marcia Miller, the first in our class to wear mascara—would beg to sit by Connie at lunch so they could update their orders.

And what about me? What was my role? Did I request my 10 favorites—Three Musketeers and coconut-centered Mounds bars? Or did I, as I have told myself and others in the years since, refuse to contribute to such cruelty? Or, in a more likely scenario, did I dump out my loot triumphantly at home one afternoon, only to be scolded by my mother? I don't remember, my memory obscured, I'm sure, by the wishful image of myself as a precocious champion of social justice. And I don't remember if I actually witnessed—or just imagined—Connie and her mother at the 7-Eleven one day after school. They were in the candy aisle. Her mother was filling a cardboard box. And Connie, bathed in unflinching fluorescence, was curved over her notebook making small, careful check marks.

Thinking Critically about This Reading

In her essay, Murphy introduces an interesting technique for an essay writer. Murphy explains:

> This essay hinges on the use of what the writer Lisa Knopp calls "perhapsing." Sometimes when we're writing, we can't recall the exact details of our experiences. In this case, we can "perhaps" or speculate about what actually happened. In the final paragraph of "White Lies," I speculate about whether I saw or dreamt about Connie and her mother in the convenience store. The result of this rhetorical strategy is two-fold: it establishes me as a reliable narrator and allows me to question my own motives in "re-membering" (as in the opposite of "dismembering") the past.

How well does this strategy work for Murphy in her final paragraph? Explain.

Questions for Study and Discussion

1. Murphy's story is brief, but how well does she satisfy the five essential features of good narration—a clear context; well-chosen details; a logical, often chronological organization; an appropriate

and consistent point of view; and a meaningful point or purpose? Explain.

2. What point does Murphy make about the lack of comparative and superlative forms for some adjectives? Does reality support the grammatical rule? Explain.

3. Explain Murphy's ending. Do you think that you know what Murphy's "role" was? On what evidence do you base your opinion?

4. What is Murphy's attitude toward Connie's classroom teacher? Why does she include information about her? (Glossary: *Attitude*)

5. What is the point of Murphy's story?

6. Is Connie's mother a hero, or is she someone whose actions are ethically questionable, even wrong? Explain.

7. What motivates Connie's mother's actions? If you were Connie's mother, what would you do in her situation?

Classroom Activity Using Narration

In a classroom discussion, consider how "perhapsing" might be helpful in essays that you and your classmates have written. Select a passage in one of your essays that might benefit from the insertion of some conjecture. Be prepared to discuss the value of the "perhapsing" strategy in the particular example you have chosen to discuss. Here are some questions to help you prepare for your classroom discussions:

1. Are there points in my essay where I need information that I can't recall accurately?

2. Why might I have lost or forgotten the missing information?

3. How have I worked around the problem of missing information?

4. How can I use "perhapsing" to supply information that makes my writing richer and more interesting and me a more reliable narrator?

Writing Suggestions

1. In a short narrative, retell the story of "White Lies" from either Connie's or her mother's point of view, or tell of a similar situation drawn from your own experiences as a schoolchild. What

information do you need to tell your story? What information might you have to supply by using the "perhapsing" strategy Murphy includes in her essay and discusses? Murphy's theme is one of prejudice and marginalization, so you might want to base your narrative on similar situations in which you felt isolated and powerless. Perhaps you were responsible for making someone else feel like an outsider. Perhaps, like Murphy, you regarded the solution to such a problem as less than adequate because it raised yet more ethical dilemmas.

2. Narrate a brief story in which one or both of your parents came to your rescue at a time when you thought yourself to be in a tight spot. Did they answer your request for help, or did they simply see that you were in need? How did the "rescue" work out? Was there a solution? Were you thankful for your parents' involvement? Or, did the solution make the situation worse and cause you to regret their involvement? Think about the usual demands of narration but especially the requirement that your story have some meaningful point or purpose.

Momma, the Dentist, and Me

■ **Maya Angelou**

Best-selling author and poet Maya Angelou was born in 1928. She is an educator, historian, actress, playwright, civil rights activist, producer, and director. She is best known as the author of I Know Why the Caged Bird Sings *(1970), the first book in a series that constitutes her complete autobiography, and for "On the Pulse of the Morning," a characteristically optimistic poem on the need for personal and national renewal that she read at President Bill Clinton's inauguration in 1993. Starting with her beginnings in St. Louis in 1928, Angelou's autobiography presents a life of joyful triumph over hardships that test her courage and threaten her spirit. It includes the titles* All God's Children Need Traveling Shoes *(1986),* Wouldn't Take Nothing for My Journey Now *(1993), and* Heart of a Woman *(1997). The sixth and final book in the series,* A Song Flung Up to Heaven, *was published in 2002. Several volumes of her poetry were collected in* Complete Collected Poems of Maya Angelou *in 1994. Angelou is Reynolds Professor of American Studies at Wake Forest University and has received more than 30 honorary degrees.*

In the following excerpt from I Know Why the Caged Bird Sings, *Angelou narrates what happened, and what might have happened, when her grandmother, the "Momma" of the story, took her to the local dentist. As you read, consider how vital first-person narration is to the essay's success, particularly as you gauge the effect of the italicized paragraphs.*

Reflecting on What You Know

When you were growing up, were you ever present when one or both of your parents were arguing with another adult about a matter concerning you? What were the circumstances? Narrate the events that brought about the controversy, and show how it was resolved. Were you embarrassed by your parents' actions, or were you happy that they stood up for you?

The angel of the candy counter had found me out at last, and was 1
exacting excruciating penance for all the stolen Milky Ways,
Mounds, Mr. Goodbars, and Hersheys with Almonds. I had two cavi-
ties that were rotten to the gums. The pain was beyond the bailiwick[1]
of crushed aspirins or oil of cloves. Only one thing could help me, so I
prayed earnestly that I'd be allowed to sit under the house and have
the building collapse on my left jaw. Since there was no Negro dentist
in Stamps, nor doctor either, for that matter, Momma had dealt with
previous toothaches by pulling them out (a string tied to the tooth
with the other end looped over her fist), pain killers, and prayer. In this
particular instance the medicine had proved ineffective; there wasn't
enough enamel left to hook a string on, and the prayers were being
ignored because the Balancing Angel was blocking their passage.

I lived a few days and nights in blinding pain, not so much toying 2
with as seriously considering the idea of jumping in the well, and
Momma decided I had to be taken to a dentist. The nearest Negro
dentist was in Texarkana, twenty-five miles away, and I was certain
that I'd be dead long before we reached half the distance. Momma
said we'd go to Dr. Lincoln, right in Stamps, and he'd take care of
me. She said he owed her a favor.

I knew there were a number of whitefolks in town that owed her 3
favors. Bailey and I had seen the books which showed how she had
lent money to Blacks and whites alike during the Depression, and most
still owed her. But I couldn't aptly remember seeing Dr. Lincoln's name,
nor had I ever heard of a Negro's going to him as a patient. However,
Momma said we were going, and put water on the stove for our
baths. I had never been to a doctor, so she told me that after the bath
(which would make my mouth feel better) I had to put on freshly
starched and ironed underclothes from inside out. The ache failed to
respond to the bath, and I knew then that the pain was more serious
than that which anyone had ever suffered.

Before we left the Store, she ordered me to brush my teeth and 4
then wash my mouth with Listerine. The idea of even opening my
clamped jaws increased the pain, but upon her explanation that when
you go to a doctor you have to clean yourself all over, but most especially the part that's to be examined, I screwed up my courage and un-
locked my teeth. The cool air in my mouth and the jarring of my molars
dislodged what little remained of my reason. I had frozen to the pain,

---

[1]*bailiwick:* a specific area of interest, skill, or authority.

my family nearly had to tie me down to take the toothbrush away. It was no small effort to get me started on the road to the dentist. Momma spoke to all the passers-by, but didn't stop to chat. She explained over her shoulder that we were going to the doctor and she'd "pass the time of day" on our way home.

Until we reached the pond the pain was my world, an aura that haloed me for three feet around. Crossing the bridge into whitefolks' country, pieces of sanity pushed themselves forward. I had to stop moaning and start walking straight. The white towel, which was drawn under my chin and tied over my head, had to be arranged. If one was dying, it had to be done in style if the dying took place in whitefolks' part of town.

On the other side of the bridge the ache seemed to lessen as if a whitebreeze blew off the whitefolks and cushioned everything in their neighborhood—including my jaw. The gravel road was smoother, the stones smaller, and the tree branches hung down around the path and nearly covered us. If the pain didn't diminish then, the familiar yet strange sights hypnotized me into believing that it had.

But my head continued to throb with the measured insistence of a bass drum, and how could a toothache pass the calaboose,[2] hear the songs of the prisoners, their blues and laughter, and not be changed? How could one or two or even a mouthful of angry tooth roots meet a wagonload of powhitetrash children, endure their idiotic snobbery, and not feel less important?

Behind the building which housed the dentist's office ran a small path used by servants and those tradespeople who catered to the butcher and Stamps's one restaurant. Momma and I followed that lane to the backstairs of Dentist Lincoln's office. The sun was bright and gave the day a hard reality as we climbed up the steps to the second floor.

Momma knocked on the back door and a young white girl opened it to show surprise at seeing us there. Momma said she wanted to see Dentist Lincoln and to tell him Annie was there. The girl closed the door firmly. Now the humiliation of hearing Momma describe herself as if she had no last name to the young white girl was equal to the physical pain. It seemed terribly unfair to have a toothache and a headache and have to bear at the same time the heavy burden of Blackness.

_____

[2]*calaboose:* a jail.

It was always possible that the teeth would quiet down and 10
maybe drop out of their own accord. Momma said we would wait.
We leaned in the harsh sunlight on the shaky railings of the dentist's
back porch for over an hour.

He opened the door and looked at Momma. "Well, Annie, what 11
can I do for you?"

He didn't see the towel around my jaw or notice my swollen face. 12

Momma said, "Dentist Lincoln. It's my grandbaby here. She got 13
two rotten teeth that's giving her a fit."

She waited for him to acknowledge the truth of her statement. 14
He made no comment, orally or facially.

"She had this toothache purt' near four days now, and today I 15
said, 'Young lady, you going to the Dentist.'"

"Annie?" 16

"Yes, sir, Dentist Lincoln." 17

He was choosing words the way people hunt for shells. "Annie, 18
you know I don't treat nigra, colored people."

"I know, Dentist Lincoln. But this here is just my little grand- 19
baby, and she ain't gone be no trouble to you . . ."

"Annie, everybody has a policy. In this world you have to have a 20
policy. Now, my policy is I don't treat colored people."

The sun had baked the oil out of Momma's skin and melted the 21
Vaseline in her hair. She shone greasily as she leaned out of the dentist's shadow.

"Seem like to me, Dentist Lincoln, you might look after her, she 22
ain't nothing but a little mite.[3] And seems like maybe you owe me a
favor or two."

He reddened slightly. "Favor or no favor. The money has all been 23
repaid to you and that's the end of it. Sorry, Annie." He had his hand
on the doorknob. "Sorry." His voice was a bit kinder on the second
"Sorry," as if he really was.

Momma said, "I wouldn't press on you like this for myself but I 24
can't take No. Not for my grandbaby. When you come to borrow my
money you didn't have to beg. You asked me, and I lent it. Now, it
wasn't my policy. I ain't no moneylender, but you stood to lose this
building and I tried to help you out."

"It's been paid, and raising your voice won't make me change my 25
mind. My policy . . ." He let go of the door and stepped nearer Momma.

---

[3]*mite:* a very small creature.

The three of us were crowded on the small landing. "Annie, my policy is I'd rather stick my hand in a dog's mouth than in a nigger's."

He had never once looked at me. He turned his back and went 26
through the door into the cool beyond. Momma backed up inside herself for a few minutes. I forgot everything except her face which was almost a new one to me. She leaned over and took the doorknob, and in her everyday soft voice she said, "Sister, go on downstairs. Wait for me. I'll be there directly."

Under the most common of circumstances I knew it did no good 27
to argue with Momma. So I walked down the steep stairs, afraid to look back and afraid not to do so. I turned as the door slammed, and she was gone.

Momma walked in that room as if she owned it. She shoved 28
that silly nurse aside with one hand and strode into the dentist's
office. He was sitting in his chair, sharpening his mean instruments
and putting extra sting into his medicines. Her eyes were blazing
like live coals and her arms had doubled themselves in length. He
looked up at her just before she caught him by the collar of his
white jacket.

"Stand up when you see a lady, you contemptuous scoundrel." 29
Her tongue had thinned and the words rolled off well enunciated.
Enunciated and sharp like little claps of thunder.

The dentist had no choice but to stand at R.O.T.C.[4] *attention.* 30
His head dropped after a minute and his voice was humble. "Yes,
ma'am, Mrs. Henderson."

"You knave, do you think you acted like a gentleman, speaking 31
to me like that in front of my granddaughter?" She didn't shake him,
although she had the power. She simply held him upright.

"No, ma'am, Mrs. Henderson." 32

"No, ma'am, Mrs. Henderson, what?" Then she did give him the 33
tiniest of shakes, but because of her strength the action set his head
and arms to shaking loose on the ends of his body. He stuttered much
worse than Uncle Willie. "No, ma'am, Mrs. Henderson, I'm sorry."

With just an edge of her disgust showing, Momma slung him back 34
in his dentist's chair. "Sorry is as sorry does, and you're about the sorriest
dentist I ever laid my eyes on." (She could afford to slip into the ver-
nacular[5] *because she had such eloquent command of English.)*

---

[4]*R.O.T.C.:* Reserve Officers Training Corps of the U.S. military.
[5]*vernacular:* the everyday language spoken by people of a particular country or region.

"*I didn't ask you to apologize in front of Marguerite, because I don't want her to know my power, but I order you, now and herewith. Leave Stamps by sundown.*"   35

"*Mrs. Henderson, I can't get my equipment . . .*" He was shaking terribly now.   36

"*Now, that brings me to my second order. You will never again practice dentistry. Never! When you get settled in your next place, you will be a veterinarian caring for dogs with the mange, cats with the cholera, and cows with the epizootic. Is that clear?*"   37

The saliva ran down his chin and his eyes filled with tears. "*Yes, ma'am. Thank you for not killing me. Thank you, Mrs. Henderson.*"   38

Momma pulled herself back from being ten feet tall with eight-foot arms and said, "*You're welcome for nothing, you varlet,*[6] *I wouldn't waste a killing on the likes of you.*"   39

On her way out she waved her handkerchief at the nurse and turned her into a crocus sack of chicken feed.   40

Momma looked tired when she came down the stairs, but who wouldn't be tired if they had gone through what she had. She came close to me and adjusted the towel under my jaw (I had forgotten the toothache; I only knew that she made her hands gentle in order not to awaken the pain). She took my hand. Her voice never changed. "Come on, Sister."   41

I reckoned we were going home where she would concoct a brew to eliminate the pain and maybe give me new teeth too. New teeth that would grow overnight out of my gums. She led me toward the drugstore, which was in the opposite direction from the Store. "I'm taking you to Dentist Baker in Texarkana."   42

I was glad after all that I had bathed and put on Mum[7] and Cashmere Bouquet talcum powder. It was a wonderful surprise. My toothache had quieted to solemn pain, Momma had obliterated the evil white man, and we were going on a trip to Texarkana, just the two of us.   43

On the Greyhound she took an inside seat in the back, and I sat beside her. I was so proud of being her granddaughter and sure that some of her magic must have come down to me. She asked if I was scared. I only shook my head and leaned over on her cool brown upper arm. There was no chance that a dentist, especially a Negro   44

---

[6]*varlet:* a rascal; lowlife.
[7]*Mum:* a brand of deodorant.

dentist, would dare hurt me then. Not with Momma there. The trip was uneventful, except that she put her arm around me, which was very unusual for Momma to do.

The dentist showed me the medicine and the needle before he 45 deadened my gums, but if he hadn't I wouldn't have worried. Momma stood right behind him. Her arms were folded and she checked on everything he did. The teeth were extracted and she bought me an ice cream cone from the side window of a drug counter. The trip back to Stamps was quiet, except that I had to spit into a very small empty snuff can which she had gotten for me and it was difficult with the bus humping and jerking on our country roads.

At home, I was given a warm salt solution, and when I washed 46 out my mouth I showed Bailey the empty holes, where the clotted blood sat like filling in a pie crust. He said I was quite brave, and that was my cue to reveal our confrontation with the peckerwood dentist and Momma's incredible powers.

I had to admit that I didn't hear the conversation, but what 47 else could she have said than what I said she said? What else done? He agreed with my analysis in a lukewarm way, and I happily (after all, I'd been sick) flounced into the Store. Momma was preparing our evening meal and Uncle Willie leaned on the door sill. She gave her version.

"Dentist Lincoln got right uppity. Said he'd rather put his hand 48 in a dog's mouth. And when I reminded him of the favor, he brushed it off like a piece of lint. Well, I sent Sister downstairs and went inside. I hadn't never been in his office before, but I found the door to where he takes out teeth, and him and the nurse was in there thick as thieves. I just stood there till he caught sight of me." Crash bang the pots on the stove. "He jumped just like he was sitting on a pin. He said, 'Annie, I done tole you, I ain't gonna mess around in no niggah's mouth.' I said, 'Somebody's got to do it then,' and he said, 'Take her to Texarkana to the colored dentist' and that's when I said, 'If you paid me my money I could afford to take her.' He said, 'It's all been paid.' I tole him everything but the interest been paid. He said, ''Twasn't no interest.' I said, ''Tis now. I'll take ten dollars as payment in full.' You know, Willie, it wasn't no right thing to do, 'cause I lent that money without thinking about it.

"He tole that little snippety nurse of his'n to give me ten dollars 49 and make me sign a 'paid in full' receipt. She gave it to me and I signed the papers. Even though by rights he was paid up before, I figger, he gonna be that kind of nasty, he gonna have to pay for it."

Momma and her son laughed and laughed over the white man's 50 evilness and her retributive[8] sin.

I preferred, much preferred, my version. 51

Thinking Critically about This Reading

What does Angelou mean when she states, "On the other side of the bridge the ache seemed to lessen as if a whitebreeze blew off the white-folks and cushioned everything in their neighborhood—including my jaw" (paragraph 6)? How long did Angelou's pain relief last? Why?

Questions for Study and Discussion

1. What is Angelou's purpose? (Glossary: *Purpose*)
2. Compare and contrast the content and style of the interaction between Momma and the dentist that is given in italics with the one given at the end of the narrative. (Glossary: *Comparison and Contrast*)
3. Angelou tells her story chronologically and in the first person. (Glossary: *Point of View*) What are the advantages of first-person narration?
4. Identify three similes Angelou uses in her narrative. (Glossary: *Figure of Speech*) Explain how each simile serves her purpose. (Glossary: *Purpose*)
5. Why do you suppose Angelou says she prefers her own version of the episode to that of her grandmother?
6. This is a story of pain—and not just the pain of a toothache. How does Angelou describe the pain of the toothache? What other pain does she tell of in this autobiographical piece?

Classroom Activity Using Narration

One of Angelou's themes in "Momma, the Dentist, and Me" is that cruelty, whether racial, social, professional, or personal, is difficult to

---

[8]*retributive:* demanding something in repayment, especially punishment.

endure and leaves a lasting impression on a person. As a way of practicing chronological order, consider a situation in which an unthinking or insensitive person made you feel inferior. Rather than write a draft of an essay at this point, simply list the sequence of events that occurred, in chronological order. Once you have completed this step, consider whether there is a more dramatic order you might use if you were actually to write an essay.

Suggested Writing Assignments

1. Using Angelou's essay as a model, give two versions of an actual event—one the way you thought or wished it had happened and the other the way events actually took place. You may want to refer to your answers to the prereading reflections for this selection before you begin writing.

2. Every person who tells a story puts his or her signature on it in some way—by the sequencing of events, the amount and type of details used, and the tone the teller of the story employs. (Glossary: *Tone*) Consider a time when you and a relative or friend experienced the same interesting sequence of events, and try telling the story of those events from your unique perspective. (Glossary: *Point of View*) Once you have done so, try telling the story from what you imagine the other person's perspective to be. Perhaps you even heard the other person actually tell the story. What is the same in both versions? How do the renditions differ?

The Story of an Hour

■ Kate Chopin

Kate Chopin (1851–1904) was born in St. Louis of Creole Irish descent. After becoming married, she lived in Louisiana, where she acquired the intimate knowledge of Creole Cajun culture that provided the impetus for much of her work and earned her a reputation as a writer who captured the ambience of the bayou region. When her first novel, The Awakening *(1899), was published, however, it generated scorn and outrage for its explicit depiction of a southern woman's sexual awakening. Only recently has Chopin been recognized for her literary talent and originality. Besides* The Awakening, *her works include two collections of short fiction,* Bayou Folk *(1894) and* A Night in Acadie *(1897). In 1969,* The Complete Works of Kate Chopin *was published by Louisiana State University Press, and the Library of America published* Kate Chopin: Complete Novels and Stories *in 2002.*

As you read the following story, first published as "The Dream of an Hour" in Vogue *magazine in 1894, try to gauge how your reactions to Mrs. Mallard are influenced by Chopin's use of third-person narration.*

Reflecting on What You Know

How do you react to the idea of marriage—committing to someone for life? What are the advantages of such a union? What are the disadvantages?

Knowing that Mrs. Mallard was afflicted with a heart trouble, great care was taken to break to her as gently as possible the news of her husband's death. 1

It was her sister Josephine who told her, in broken sentences; veiled hints that revealed in half concealing. Her husband's friend Richards was there, too, near her. It was he who had been in the 2 newspaper office when intelligence of the railroad disaster was received, with Brently Mallard's name leading the list of "killed." He had only taken the time to assure himself of its truth by a second telegram, and had hastened to forestall any less careful, less tender friend in bearing the sad message.

She did not hear the story as many women have heard the same, 3 with a paralyzed inability to accept its significance. She wept at once, with sudden, wild abandonment, in her sister's arms. When the storm of grief had spent itself she went away to her room alone. She would have no one follow her.

There stood, facing the open window, a comfortable, roomy arm- 4 chair. Into this she sank, pressed down by a physical exhaustion that haunted her body and seemed to reach into her soul.

She could see in the open square before her house the tops of trees 5 that were all aquiver with the new spring life. The delicious breath of rain was in the air. In the street below a peddler was crying his wares. The notes of a distant song which someone was singing reached her faintly, and countless sparrows were twittering in the eaves.

There were patches of blue sky showing here and there through 6 the clouds that had met and piled one above the other in the west facing her window.

She sat with her head thrown back upon the cushion of the chair, 7 quite motionless, except when a sob came up into her throat and shook her, as a child who has cried itself to sleep continues to sob in its dreams.

She was young, with a fair, calm face, whose lines bespoke re- 8 pression and even a certain strength. But now there was a dull stare in her eyes, whose gaze was fixed away off yonder on one of those patches of blue sky. It was not a glance of reflection, but rather indicated a suspension of intelligent thought.

There was something coming to her and she was waiting for it, 9 fearfully. What was it? She did not know; it was too subtle and elusive to name. But she felt it, creeping out of the sky, reaching toward her through the sounds, the scents, the color that filled the air.

Now her bosom rose and fell tumultuously. She was beginning to 10 recognize this thing that was approaching to possess her, and she was striving to beat it back with her will—as powerless as her two white slender hands would have been.

When she abandoned herself a little whispered word escaped her 11 slightly parted lips. She said it over and over under her breath: "free,

free, free!" The vacant stare and the look of terror that had followed it went from her eyes. They stayed keen and bright. Her pulses beat fast, and the coursing blood warmed and relaxed every inch of her body.

She did not stop to ask if it were or were not a monstrous joy that held her. A clear and exalted perception enabled her to dismiss the suggestion as trivial. 12

She knew that she would weep again when she saw the kind, tender hands folded in death; the face that had never looked save with love upon her, fixed and gray and dead. But she saw beyond that bitter moment a long procession of years to come that would belong to her absolutely. And she opened and spread her arms out to them in welcome. 13

There would be no one to live for her during those coming years; she would live for herself. There would be no powerful will bending hers in that blind persistence with which men and women believe they have a right to impose a private will upon a fellow-creature. A kind intention or a cruel intention made the act seem no less a crime as she looked upon it in that brief moment of illumination. 14

And yet she had loved him—sometimes. Often she had not. What did it matter! What could love, the unsolved mystery, count for in face of this possession of self-assertion which she suddenly recognized as the strongest impulse of her being! 15

"Free! Body and soul free!" she kept whispering. 16

Josephine was kneeling before the closed door with her lips to the keyhole, imploring for admission. "Louise, open the door! I beg; open the door—you will make yourself ill. What are you doing, Louise? For heaven's sake open the door." 17

"Go away. I am not making myself ill." No; she was drinking in a very elixir of life through that open window. 18

Her fancy was running riot along those days ahead of her. Spring days, and summer days, and all sorts of days that would be her own. She breathed a quick prayer that life might be long. It was only yesterday she had thought with a shudder that life might be long. 19

She arose at length and opened the door to her sister's importunities.[1] There was a feverish triumph in her eyes, and she carried herself unwittingly like a goddess of Victory. She clasped her sister's waist, and together they descended the stairs. Richards stood waiting for them at the bottom. 20

---

[1]*importunities:* urgent requests or demands.

Some one was opening the front door with a latchkey. It was   21
Brently Mallard who entered, a little travel-stained, composedly carrying his grip-sack and umbrella. He had been far from the scene of the
accident, and did not even know there had been one. He stood
amazed at Josephine's piercing cry; at Richards' quick motion to
screen him from the view of his wife.

But Richards was too late.   22

When the doctors came they said she had died of heart disease—   23
of joy that kills.

Thinking Critically about This Reading

Chopin describes Mrs. Mallard as "beginning to recognize this thing
that was approaching to possess her, and she was striving to beat it
back with her will—as powerless as her two white slender hands
would have been" (paragraph 10). Why does Mrs. Mallard fight her
feeling of freedom, however briefly? How does she come to accept it?

Questions for Study and Discussion

1. What assumptions do Mrs. Mallard's relatives and friends make
   about her feelings toward her husband? What are her true feelings?
2. Reread paragraphs 5–9. What is Chopin's purpose in this section? (Glossary: *Purpose*) Do these paragraphs add to the story's
   effectiveness? Explain.
3. All the events of Chopin's story take place in an hour. Would the
   story be as poignant if they had taken place over the course of a
   day or even several days? Explain. Why do you suppose the author
   selected the time frame as a title for her story? (Glossary: *Title*)
4. Chopin could have written an essay detailing the oppression of
   women in marriage, but she chose instead to write a fictional
   narrative. This allows her to show readers the type of situation
   that can arise in an outwardly happy marriage rather than tell
   them about it. Why else do you think that she chose to write a
   fictional narrative? What other advantages does it give her over
   nonfiction?
5. Why do you think Chopin narrates her story in the third person?
   (Glossary: *Point of View*)

Classroom Activity Using Narration

Using cues in the following sentences, rearrange them in chronological order.

1. The sky was gray and gloomy for as far as she could see, and sleet hissed off the glass.
2. "Oh, hi. I'm glad you called," she said happily, but her smile dimmed when she looked outside.
3. As Betty crossed the room, her phone rang, startling her.
4. "No, the weather's awful, so I don't think I'll get out to visit you today," she sighed.
5. "Hello," she said, and she wandered over to the window.

Write five sentences of your own that cover a progression of events. Try to include dialogue. (Glossary: *Dialogue*) Then scramble them, and see if a classmate can put them back in the correct order.

Suggested Writing Assignments

1. Using Chopin's story as a model, write a short piece of narrative fiction in which your main character reacts to a specific, dramatic event. Portray the character's emotional response, as well as how the character perceives his or her surroundings. What does the character see, hear, touch? How are these senses affected by the situation?

2. Write a narrative essay in which you describe your reaction to a piece of news you once received—good or bad—that provoked a strong emotional response. What were your emotions? What did you do in the couple of hours after you received the news? How did your perceptions of the world around you change? What made the experience memorable?

Description

To describe is to create a verbal picture. A person, a place, a thing—even an idea or a state of mind—can be made vividly concrete through **description.** Here, for example, is a brief description of a delicatessen:

> It was a narrow room, with a rather high ceiling, and crowded from floor to ceiling with goodies. There were rows and rows of hams and sausages of all shapes and colors—white, yellow, red, and black; fat and lean and round and long—rows of canned preserves, cocoa and tea, bright translucent glass bottles of honey, marmalade, and jam; round bottles and slender bottles, filled with liqueurs and punch—all these things crowded every inch of the shelves from top to bottom.
>
> –Thomas Mann

Writing any description requires, first of all, that the writer gather many details about a subject, relying not only on what the eyes see but on the other sense impressions—touch, taste, smell, hearing—as well. From this catalog of details, the writer selects those that will most effectively create a **dominant impression**—the single quality, mood, or atmosphere the writer wishes to emphasize. Consider, for example, the details Mary McCarthy uses to evoke the dominant impression in the following passage, and contrast them with those in the subsequent example by student Dan Bubany:

> Whenever we children came to stay at my grandmother's house, we were put to sleep in the sewing room, a bleak, shabby, utilitarian rectangle, more office than bedroom, more attic than office, that played to the hierarchy of chambers the role of poor relation. It was a room without pride: the old sewing machine, some cast-off chairs, a shadeless lamp, rolls of wrapping paper, piles of cardboard

boxes that might someday come in handy, papers of pins, and remnants of a material united with the iron folding cots put out for our use and the bare floor boards to give an impression of intense and ruthless temporality. Thin white spreads, of the kind used in hospitals and charity institutions, and naked blinds at the windows reminded us of our orphaned condition and of the ephemeral character of our visit; there was nothing here to encourage us to consider this our home.

–Mary McCarthy

For this particular Thursday game against Stanford, Fleming wears white gloves, a maroon sport coat with brass buttons, and gray slacks. Shiny silver-framed bifocals match the whistle pressed between the lips on his slightly wrinkled face, and he wears freshly polished black shoes so glossy that they reflect the grass he stands on. He is not fat, but his coat neatly conceals a small, round pot belly.

–Dan Bubany, student

The dominant impression that McCarthy creates is one of clutter, bleakness, and shabbiness. There is nothing in the sewing room that suggests permanence or warmth. Bubany, on the other hand, creates a dominant impression of a neat, polished, kindly man.

Writers must also carefully plan the order in which to present their descriptive details. The pattern of organization must fit the subject of the description logically and naturally and must be easy to follow. For example, visual details can be arranged spatially—from left to right, top to bottom, near to far—or in any other logical order. Other patterns include smallest to largest, softest to loudest, least significant to most significant, most unusual to least unusual. McCarthy, for example, suggests a jumble of junk not only by her choice of details but by the apparently random order in which she presents them.

How much detail is enough? There is no fixed answer. A good description includes enough vivid details to create a dominant impression and to bring a scene to life but not so many that readers are distracted, confused, or bored. In an essay that is purely descriptive, there is room for much detail. Usually, however, writers use description to create the setting for a story, to illustrate ideas, to help clarify a definition or a comparison, or to make the complexities of a process more understandable. Such descriptions should be kept short and should include just enough detail to make them clear and helpful.

The Corner Store

■ Eudora Welty

*One of the most honored and respected writ-
ers of the twentieth century, Eudora Welty
was born in 1909 in Jackson, Mississippi,
where she lived most of her life and where she
died in 2001.* Her first book, A Curtain of
Green *(1941), is a collection of short stories.
Although she went on to become a successful
writer of novels, essays, and book reviews,
among other genres (as well as a published*

*photographer), she is most often remembered as a master of
the short story. In 1980, Welty was awarded the prestigious
Presidential Medal of Freedom.* The Collected Stories of Eudora
Welty *was published in 1982. Her other best-known works include a collection of essays,* The Eye of the Story *(1975); her autobiography,* One Writer's Beginnings *(1984); and a collection of
book reviews and essays,* The Writer's Eye *(1994). Welty's novel*
The Optimist's Daughter *won the Pulitzer Prize for Fiction in
1973, and in 1999 the Library of Congress published two collections of her work:* Welty: Collected Novels *and* Welty: Collected
Essays and Memoirs.

*Welty's description of the corner store, taken from an essay
in* The Eye of the Story *about growing up in Jackson, recalls for
many readers the neighborhood store in the town or city where
they grew up. As you read, pay attention to the effect Welty's
spatial arrangement of descriptive details has on the dominant
impression of the store.*

Reflecting on What You Know

Write about a store you frequented as a child. Maybe it was the
local supermarket, the hardware store, or the corner convenience
store. Using your five senses (sight, smell, taste, touch, and
hearing), describe what you remember about the place.

Our Little Store rose right up from the sidewalk; standing in a street 1
of family houses, it alone hadn't any yard in front, any tree or
flower bed. It was a plain frame building covered over with brick. Above
the door, a little railed porch ran across on an upstairs level and four
windows with shades were looking out. But I didn't catch on to those.

Running in out of the sun, you met what seemed total obscurity 2
inside. There were almost tangible smells—licorice recently sucked in a
child's cheek, dill pickle brine[1] that had leaked through a paper sack in
a fresh trail across the wooden floor, ammonia-loaded ice that had been
hoisted from wet croker sacks[2] and slammed into the icebox[3] with its
sweet butter at the door, and perhaps the smell of still untrapped mice.

Then through the motes of cracker dust, cornmeal dust, the Gold 3
Dust of the Gold Dust Twins that the floor had been swept out with,
the realities emerged. Shelves climbed to high reach all the way
around, set out with not too much of any one thing but a lot of
things—lard, molasses, vinegar, starch, matches, kerosene, Octagon
soap (about a year's worth of octagon-shaped coupons cut out and
saved brought a signet ring[4] addressed to you in the mail). It was up
to you to remember what you came for, while your eye traveled from
cans of sardines to tin whistles to ice-cream salt to harmonicas to fly-
paper (over your head, batting around on a thread beneath the blades
of the ceiling fan, stuck with its testimonial catch).

Its confusion may have been in the eye of its beholder. Enchantment 4
is cast upon you by all those things you weren't supposed to have need
for, to lure you close to wooden tops you'd outgrown, boys' marbles
and agates in little net pouches, small rubber balls that wouldn't bounce
straight, frail, frazzly kite string, clay bubble pipes that would snap
off in your teeth, the stiffest scissors. You could contemplate those
long narrow boxes of sparklers gathering dust while you waited for it
to be the Fourth of July or Christmas, and noisemakers in the shape
of tin frogs for somebody's birthday party you hadn't been invited to
yet, and see that they were all marvelous.

You might not have even looked for Mr. Sessions when he came 5
around his store cheese (as big as a doll's house) and in front of the
counter looking for you. When you'd finally asked him for, and

---

[1]*brine:* salty water used to preserve or pickle food.
[2]*croker sacks:* sacks or bags made of burlap, a coarse, woven fabric.
[3]*icebox:* a wooden box or cupboard that held ice in a lower compartment to cool a
second compartment above it, which was used for storing perishable food.
[4]*signet ring:* a ring bearing an official-looking seal.

received from him in its paper bag, whatever single thing it was that you had been sent for, the nickel that was left over was yours to spend.

Down at a child's eye level, inside those glass jars with mouths in their sides through which the grocer could run his scoop or a child's hand might be invited to reach for a choice, were wineballs, all-day suckers, gumdrops, peppermints. Making a row under the glass of a counter were the Tootsie Rolls, Hershey bars, Goo Goo Clusters, Baby Ruths. And whatever was the name of those pastilles that came stacked in a cardboard cylinder with a cardboard lid? They were thin and dry, about the size of tiddledy-winks,⁵ and in the shape of twisted rosettes. A kind of chocolate dust came out with them when you shook them out in your hand. Were they chocolate? I'd say, rather, they were brown. They didn't taste of anything at all, unless it was wood. Their attraction was the number you got for a nickel.

6

Making up your mind, you circled the store around and around, around the pickle barrel, around the tower of Crackerjack boxes; Mr. Sessions had built it for us himself on top of a packing case like a house of cards.

7

If it seemed too hot for Crackerjacks, I might get a cold drink. Mr. Sessions might have already stationed himself by the cold-drinks barrel, like a mind reader. Deep in ice water that looked black as ink, murky shapes—that would come up as Coca-Colas, Orange Crushes, and various flavors of pop—were all swimming around together. When you gave the word, Mr. Sessions plunged his bare arm in to the elbow and fished out your choice, first try. I favored a locally bottled concoction called Lake's Celery. (What else could it be called? It was made by a Mr. Lake out of celery. It was a popular drink here for years but was not known universally, as I found out when I arrived in New York and ordered one in the Astor bar.) You drank on the premises, with feet set wide apart to miss the drip, and gave him back his bottle and your nickel.

8

But he didn't hurry you off. A standing scale was by the door, with a stack of iron weights and a brass slide on the balance arm, that would weigh you up to three hundred pounds. Mr. Sessions, whose hands were gentle and smelled of carbolic,⁶ would lift you up and set your feet on the platform, hold your loaf of bread for you, and taking his time while you stood still for him, he would make

9

---

⁵*tiddledy-winks:* playing pieces from the game Tiddledy-Winks, flat and round in shape, the size of quarters (tiddledies) and dimes (winks).
⁶*carbolic:* a sweet, musky-smelling chemical once used in soap.

certain of what you weighed today. He could even remember what you weighed the last time, so you could subtract and announce how much you'd gained. That was goodbye.

Thinking Critically about This Reading

What does Mr. Sessions himself contribute to the overall experience of Welty's store? What does Welty's store contribute to the community?

Questions for Study and Discussion

1. Which of the three patterns of organization does Welty use in this essay—chronological, spatial, or logical? If she uses more than one, where precisely does she use each type?
2. In paragraph 2, Welty describes the smells that a person encountered when entering the corner store. Why do you think she presents these smells before giving any visual details of the inside of the store?
3. What dominant impression does Welty create in her description of the corner store? (Glossary: *Dominant Impression*) How does she create this dominant impression?
4. What impression of Mr. Sessions does Welty create? What details contribute to this impression? (Glossary: *Details*)
5. Why does Welty place certain pieces of information in parentheses? What, if anything, does this information add to your understanding of the corner store? Might this information be left out? Explain.
6. Comment on Welty's ending. (Glossary: *Beginnings and Endings*) Is it too abrupt? Why or why not?

Classroom Activity Using Description

Make a long list of the objects and people in your classroom as well as the physical features of the room—desks, windows, chalkboard, students, professor, dirty walls, burned-out lightbulb, a clock that is always ten minutes fast, and so on. Determine a dominant impression that you would like to create in describing the classroom. Now choose from your list those items that would best illustrate the dominant impression you have chosen. Your instructor may wish to have students compare their responses.

Suggested Writing Assignments

1. Using Welty's essay as a model, describe your neighborhood store or supermarket. Gather a large quantity of detailed information from memory and from an actual visit to the store if that is still possible. You may find it helpful to reread what you wrote in response to the prereading prompt. Once you have gathered your information, try to select those details that will help you create a dominant impression of the store. Finally, organize your examples and illustrations according to some clear organizational pattern.

2. Consider the following photograph of historic London Paddington Station, a major National Rail and London Underground station complex near central London, England. What is your dominant impression of Paddington Station? (Glossary: *Dominant Impression*) What details in the photograph come together to create this dominant impression for you? Using Welty's essay as a model, write a description of Paddington Station that captures the dominant impression you identified above.

Photo by Alfred Rosa.

And the Orchestra Played On

■ **Joanne Lipman**

Prize-winning journalist and editor Joanne  *Lipman was born in 1961 in New Brunswick, New Jersey. She graduated from Yale University in 1983 with a major in history. An internship at the* Wall Street Journal *while she was a student at Yale landed her a job as a staff reporter after graduation. At the* Journal, *Lipman worked her way through the ranks, first as a reporter covering insurance, real estate, and advertising, then as a page one editor, and later as the editor-in-chief of the popular* Weekend Journal. *In 2000, she was named a deputy managing editor, the first woman to serve in that capacity at the newspaper. In 2005, Lipman went to Condé Nast, where she became the founding editor-in-chief of* Condé Nast Portfolio *and* Portfolio.com, *a business magazine and Web site. She appears regularly on CNN, CNBC, and CBS, commenting on business issue and trends. She also contributes to the* New York Times.*

In the following essay, which first appeared in the New York Times *on February 28, 2010, Lipman pays tribute to her childhood music teacher, Jerry Kupchynsky. As you read Lipman's tribute to Kupchynsky, notice the descriptive details she selects to create the dominant impression of the man and his legacy to the students of East Brunswick, New Jersey.*

Reflecting on What You Know

Did you participate in the music program at your elementary or high school? If so, in what capacity—did you sing or play an instrument? Has music been a valuable part of your education to date? If so, explain how. If you didn't participate, what are your impressions or memories of the program and those who participated in it?

The other day, I found myself rummaging through a closet, search- 1
ing for my old viola. This wasn't how I'd planned to spend the
afternoon. I hadn't given a thought to the instrument in years. I
barely remembered where it was, much less how to play it. But I had
just gotten word that my childhood music teacher, Jerry Kupchynsky—
"Mr. K." to his students—had died.

In East Brunswick, N.J., where I grew up, nobody was feared 2
more than Mr. K. He ran the town's music department with a ferocity
never before seen in our quiet corner of suburbia. In his impenetrably
thick Ukrainian accent, he would berate us for being out of tune, our
elbows in the wrong position, our counting out of sync.

"Cellos sound like hippopotamus rising from bottom of river," 3
he would yell during orchestra rehearsals. Wayward violinists played
"like mahnyiak," while hapless gum chewers "look like cow chewing
cud." He would rehearse us until our fingers were callused, then interrupt us with "Stop that cheekin plocking!"

Mr. K. pushed us harder than our parents, harder than our other 4
teachers, and through sheer force of will made us better than we had
any right to be. He scared the daylight out of us.

I doubt any of us realized how much we loved him for it. 5

Which is why, decades later, I was frantically searching for an 6
instrument whose case still bore the address of my college dorm.
After almost a half-century of teaching, at the age of 81, Mr. K. had
died of Parkinson's disease. And across the generations, through
Facebook and e-mail messages and Web sites, came the call: it was
time for one last concert for Mr. K.—performed by us, his old students and friends.

Now, I used to be a serious student. I played for years in a 7
string quartet with Mr. K.'s violin-prodigy daughters, Melanie and
Stephanie. One of my first stories as a *Wall Street Journal* reporter
was a first-person account of being a street musician.

But I had given it up 20 years ago. Work and motherhood inter- 8
vened; with two children and long hours as an editor, there wasn't
time for music any more. It seemed kind of frivolous. Besides, I
wasn't even sure I would know how.

The hinges creaked when I opened the decrepit case. I was 9
greeted by a cascade of loose horsehair—my bow a victim of mites,
the repairman later explained. It was pure agony to twist my fingers
into position. But to my astonishment and that of my teenage children—who had never heard me play—I could still manage a sound.

It turned out, a few days later, that there were 100 people just   10
like me. When I showed up at a local school for rehearsal, there they
were: five decades worth of former students. There were doctors and
accountants, engineers and college professors. There were people
who hadn't played in decades, sitting alongside professionals like Mr.
K.'s daughter Melanie, now a violinist with the Chicago Symphony
Orchestra. There were generations of music teachers.

They flew in from California and Oregon, from Virginia and   11
Boston. They came with siblings and children; our old quartet's cel-
list, Miriam, took her seat with 13 other family members.

They came because Mr. K. understood better than anyone the   12
bond music creates among people who play it together. Behind his
bluster—and behind his wicked sense of humor and taste for Black
Russians—that was his lesson all along.

He certainly learned it the hard way. As a teenager during World   13
War II, he endured two years in a German internment camp. His wife
died after a long battle with multiple sclerosis. All those years while
we whined that he was riding us too hard, he was raising his daughters and caring for his sick wife on his own. Then his younger daughter Stephanie, a violin teacher, was murdered. After she vanished in
1991, he spent seven years searching for her, never giving up hope
until the day her remains were found.

Yet the legacy he had left behind was pure joy. You could see it   14
in the faces of the audience when the curtain rose for the performance
that afternoon. You could hear it as his older daughter Melanie, her
husband and their violinist children performed as a family. You could
feel it when the full orchestra, led by one of Mr. K.'s protégés, poured
itself into Tchaikovsky and Bach. It powered us through the lost
years, the lack of rehearsal time—less than two hours—and the stray
notes from us rustier alums.

Afterward, Melanie took the stage to describe the proud father   15
who waved like a maniac from a balcony in Carnegie Hall the first
time she played there. At the end of his life, when he was too ill to
talk, she would bring her violin to his bedside and play for hours, letting the melodies speak for them both. The bonds of music were as
strong as ever.

In a way, this was Mr. K.'s most enduring lesson—and one he   16
had been teaching us since we were children. Back when we were in
high school, Mr. K. had arranged for Melanie and our quartet to play
at the funeral of a classmate killed in a horrific car crash. The boy

had doted on his little sister, a violinist. We were a reminder of how much he loved to listen to her play.

As the far-flung orchestra members arrived for Mr. K.'s final concert, suddenly we saw her, that little girl, now grown, a professional musician herself. She had never stopped thinking about her brother's funeral, she told me, and when she heard about this concert, she flew from Denver in the hope that she might find the musicians who played in his honor. For 30 years, she had just wanted the chance to say, "Thank you." 17

As did we all. 18

Thinking Critically about This Reading

Although Lipman never tells us directly that Mr. K. was a great teacher, it is clear that she believes that he was. How does Lipman show us how she feels about her beloved teacher? Did she convince you that he was a teacher to be remembered? Why or why not?

Questions for Study and Discussion

1. What dominant impression of Mr. K. did Lipman give you? What descriptive details helped create this impression?

2. In paragraph 3, Lipman provides several examples of Mr. K. berating his students during orchestra rehearsals. What would have been lost had she not quoted him directly? Explain.

3. Why do you suppose Lipman chose to make paragraph 5 a one-sentence paragraph? What do think would have been lost had she simply added it to the end of paragraph 4?

4. In paragraphs 10 and 11, we learn of the occupations of some of Kupchynsky's former students and the distances they traveled to be at the memorial concert. Why do you suppose Lipman gives us this information? What does this information tell us about Mr. K.?

5. According to Lipman, what was Mr. K.'s "most enduring lesson" (paragraph 16)?

6. What's the point of Lipman's story about the little girl in paragraphs 16 and 17?

7. How effective did you find Lipman's ending? In what ways is it tied to her opening paragraph? (Glossary: *Beginnings and Endings*)

Classroom Activity Using Description

One of the best ways to make a description of a person memorable is to use a simile (making a comparison using *like* or *as,* such as "Her feet floated like a feather in a breeze") or a metaphor (making a comparison without the use of *like* or *as,* such as "His fists were iron"). Think of a time when you were one of a group of people assembled to do something most or all of you didn't really want to do. People in such a situation behave in various ways, showing their discomfort. One might stare steadily at the ground, for example. A writer describing the scene could use a metaphor to make it more vivid for the reader: "With his gaze he drilled a hole in the ground between his feet." Other people in an uncomfortable situation might fidget, lace their fingers together, breathe rapidly, squirm, or tap an object, such as a pen or key. Create a simile or a metaphor to describe each of these behaviors. Compare your metaphors and similes with those of your classmates. Discuss which ones work best for each behavior.

Suggested Writing Assignments

1. In paragraph 4, Lipman reveals that "Mr. K. pushed us harder than our parents, harder than our other teachers, and through sheer force of will made us better than we had any right to be." He was a teacher who had higher expectations for his students than they had for themselves. Have you ever had any teachers or coaches like that? If so, how did you respond to this type of teacher? If not, would you have liked to have such a teacher? What happens when a teacher or coach has higher expectations for you than you have for yourself? Write an essay in which you describe your experiences with just such a teacher or coach, or an essay about why you would have or not have liked such a teacher.

2. Like Lipman, we often do not take the opportunity to thank people who have made a difference in our lives while they are still alive. Think of several people who have made a difference in your life, and then write a letter to one of them in which you explain just how much that person has meant to you. After sharing your letter with your teacher and classmates, send your letter to the person who made a difference for you. You may find it helpful to read Thomas L. Friedman's essay "My Favorite Teacher" on pages 103–105 before starting to write your letter.

Yarn

■ **Kyoko Mori**

Kyoko Mori was born in Kobe, Japan, in 1957. Under the tutelage of her mother and grandfather, she began to write at an early age. "These two people in my family," Mori remembers, "gave me the idea that writing was something we did every day or even every week with enjoyment." After high school, she moved to the United States for her college education. She graduated from Rockford College in Illinois and later received a master's degree and PhD from the University of Wisconsin. Mori is an accomplished poet, novelist, and nonfiction writer. Her first book, Shizuko's Daughter, *a novel for young adults, appeared in 1993. It was followed by* Fallout *(1994), a collection of poems;* The Dream of Water *(1995), a memoir; and* One Bird *(1995), a second novel for young adults. In 1998, she published* Polite Lies, *a collection of essays about her life in the Midwest, and in 2000,* Stone Field, True Arrow, *a novel for adults, appeared. In 2005, she joined the MFA faculty at George Mason University to teach creative nonfiction.*

The following selection first appeared in the Harvard Review *in the Spring 2003 issue. It later appeared as part of* Yarn: Remembering the Way Home *(2009), a memoir that one reviewer called both "a personal history of knitting and a story of strength and survival." As you read Mori's essay, notice how she uses the senses of sight, hearing, and touch to enhance her description of yarn and knitting.*

Reflecting on What You Know

As a child, did you ever undertake any "creative" projects like baking a cake or pie, sewing your own clothing, building a birdhouse or model airplane, painting pictures, or writing poems? What do you remember about the first time you tried doing it? Was it difficult? Were you self-conscious? Did anyone help or coach you? How did you feel about what you created?

The yellow mittens I made in seventh-grade home economics proved that I dreamed in color. For the unit on knitting, we were supposed to turn in a pair of mittens. The two hands had to be precisely the same size so that when we held them together, palm to palm, no extra stitches would stick out from the thumb, the tip of the fingers, or the cuff. Somewhere between making the fourth and the fifth mitten to fulfill this requirement, I dreamed that the ball of yellow yarn in my bag had turned green. Chartreuse, leaf, Granny Smith, lime, neon, acid green. The brightness was electric. I woke up knowing that I was, once again, doomed for a D in home ec.

I don't remember what possessed me to choose yellow yarn for that assignment. Yellow was a color I never liked; perhaps I was conceding defeat before I started. Mittens, as it turns out, are just about the worst project possible for a beginner. Each hand has to be knitted as a very small tube, with the stitches divided among four pointed needles that twist and slip unless you are holding them with practiced confidence. The pair won't be the same size if you drop or pick up extra stitches along the way, skip a couple of decreases in shaping the top, or knit too tightly in your nervousness and then let up in relief as you approach the end. You might inadvertently make two right mittens or two lefts because you forgot that the thumb has to be started in a different position for each hand. I ended up with two right hands of roughly the same size and three left hands that could have been illustrations for a fairytale. *Once upon a time, there lived three brothers, each with only one hand — large, medium, and very small — and, even though the villagers laughed at them and called them unkind names, the brothers could do anything when they put their three left hands together . . .*

I didn't knit again until graduate school when I met a woman from Germany with a closet full of beautiful sweaters. Sabina came to our seminar wearing a soft angora cardigan one week, a sturdy fisherman's pullover the next.

"I make all my sweaters," she said. "I can teach you."

I told her about my mitten fiasco.

"Knitting is easy," Sabina insisted. "A sweater's bigger than a mitten but much simpler."

"The patterns will confuse me."

"You don't need patterns. You can make things up as you go."

Sabina took me to a local yarn store, where I bought skeins of red cotton yarn. Following her instructions, I first knit the body of the sweater: two flat pieces, front and back, with a few simple decreases to shape the shoulders and the neck. The pieces were surprisingly easy to sew together. Sabina showed me how to pick up the stitches along the arm opening, connect the new yarn, and knit the sleeves, going from the shoulder to the wrist. I finished the sweater in a month. The result was slightly lopsided—one sleeve was half an inch wider than the other around the elbow—but the arms looked more or less even once I put the sweater on. The small mistakes in a knitted garment disappear when the garment is on the body, where it belongs. That might have been the most important thing I learned from my first sweater.

In the twenty years since then, I've made sweaters, vests, hats, 10 bedspreads, lap blankets, shawls, scarves, socks, and mittens. Like most people who knit, I have bags of yarn stashed in my closet for future projects. The bags are a record of the cities where I've wandered into yarn stores: Madison, Portland, Cambridge, New Orleans, Evanston, Washington, D.C. Like hair salons, yarn stores have slightly witty names: Woolgathering, Woolworks, Woolcotts, the Knitting Tree, the Quarter Stitch (New Orleans), Fiber Space. Inside each store, the walls are lined with plastic crates bursting with color. My friend Yenkuei took up knitting because she fell in love with the fuchsia sleeveless sweater in the window of Woolcotts in Harvard Square, floating, she thought, and beckoning to her. Another friend, who doesn't knit, comes along just to touch. She goes from shelf to shelf fingering the rayon chenilles, angoras, alpacas, and silk/cotton blends, while I'm trying to figure out how much yarn I need. When I was five, in kindergarten, I was horrified to see other kids stick their fingers in the library paste, scoop up the pale glob, and put it in their mouths, but I tried to eat the raspberry-colored crayon on my teacher's desk because it looked so delicious. Knitting is about that same hunger for color. I never again picked up yellow yarn. . . .

In my first ten years of knitting, I took full advantage of the forgiv- 11 ing quality of yarn and made hats and scarves from patterns that had only five- to ten-sentence directions. For sweaters, I made three tubes (one big tube for the body, two smaller tubes for the sleeves) and then knitted them together at the yoke and shoulders so I didn't have to sew the pieces together at the end. If, half way through the body or the sleeve, I noticed the piece getting wider faster than I'd expected, I simply stopped increasing stitches; if the piece looked too small, I increased more. It was just as Sabina had told me: I could make things up as I went along.

My favorite project was a hat from a pattern I found in a yarn　12
store on a visit to Portland, Oregon. I bought the thick mohair yarn
and extra needles so I could start knitting the first one in my hotel
room. The hat, which I finished on the flight home the next day,
looked more like a lamp shade; the brim came down to my shoulders.
At home, I threw this enormous hat in the washer, set it on hot wash
and cold rinse, and ran the cycle twice. Just as the pattern promised,
the hat came out shrunk and "felted": the stitches had contracted till
they were invisible, leaving a dense, fuzzy nap. I reshaped the hat on
a mixing bowl about the size of my head, and by the time it dried, it
looked like a professionally made bowler.

The washing-machine hat became a staple of my gift-giving. A　13
few years later, I visited an antique mall with a couple who had fallen
in love with an oak dresser they thought was too expensive. Every
weekend for two months, they brought a different friend to look at
the dresser, to ooh and aah over it, and help them work up the nerve
to spend the money. The antique mall was a huge place out in the
country and we had to walk what felt like three city blocks crammed
with furniture and knick-knacks. When we finally got to the right
section, I failed my friends completely by not noticing the dresser because to the right of it, on a small table, was a wooden hat form. To
an untrained eye, the hat form looks like a wooden head, but I knew
what it was. Tired of reshaping hats over a bowl, I had been trying to
order one (except all the modern hat forms were made of styrofoam
and I didn't think I could stand the squeaky noise they would make).
I grabbed the wooden head and walked around with it tightly
clutched under my arm while my friends showed me all the other oak
dressers, every one of them inferior to the one they wanted. At the
counter, I paid twelve dollars for my find.

This fall, I brought the wooden head with me to Wisconsin be-　14
cause I still make those hats for gifts. But in the last five years, I've
graduated to more complicated patterns. I had gotten tired of the
rugged look of the make-it-as-you-go kind of sweater, but more than
that, my reasons for knitting have changed. In my twenties and
thirties, I wanted everything I did to express what I considered my
essential nature: casual, relaxed, and intuitively creative, rather than
formal, precise, and meticulous. That's why I chose knitting over
sewing, running and cycling over tennis or golf. Now, in my mid-
forties, I look instead for balance. If following step-by-step instructions doesn't come naturally to me, that is all the more reason for me

to try it. I would rather knit from a complicated pattern and make a few mistakes than execute an easier one flawlessly.

The folklore among knitters is that everything handmade should   15
have at least one mistake so an evil spirit will not become trapped in the maze of perfect stitches. A missed increase or decrease, a crooked seam, a place where the tension is uneven—the mistake is a crack left open to let in the light. The evil spirit I want to usher out of my knitting and my life is at once a spirit of laziness and of over-achieving. It's that little voice in my head that says, I won't even try this because it doesn't come naturally to me and I won't be very good at it.

Thinking Critically about This Reading

In her opening two paragraphs, Mori describes her seventh-grade home economics "mitten" project. What does her telling of this experience reveal about Mori herself? Why do you think knitting is such an important part of her life after this unfortunate initial experience?

Questions for Study and Discussion

1. According to Mori, why are mittens "just about the worst project possible for a beginner" (paragraph 2)? In what ways are sweaters "simpler" than mittens? Explain.

2. After her disastrous experience in seventh grade, Mori didn't knit again until she was in graduate school. What important lesson about knitting and sweaters does Mori learn from the German graduate student, Sabina? What does Mori gain by letting her readers hear Sabina speak in paragraphs 4 through 8? (Glossary: *Dialogue*)

3. In paragraph 10, Mori describes the collection of yarns in her closet in terms of the yarn stores she has visited while traveling around the United States. How does she describe the inside of a yarn store? What dominant impression of a yarn store does she create?

4. Identify several similes Mori uses in her essay. (Glossary: *Figure of Speech*) What does each simile add to what Mori is describing?

5. What does Mori mean when she talks about "the forgiving quality of yarn" (11)?

6. Why do you think Mori considers her "washing-machine hat" (13), her favorite knitting project? Why did Mori eventually graduate to more complicated knitting projects?

7. Comment on the way Mori ends her essay. (Glossary: *Beginnings and Endings*) In what ways does her final paragraph relate to her opening two paragraphs? Explain.

Classroom Activity Using Description

Important advice for writing well is to show rather than tell. Let's assume your task is to reveal a person's character. What activities might you show the person doing to give your readers the correct impression of his or her character? For example, to indicate that someone is concerned about current events without coming out and saying so, you might show her reading the morning newspaper. Or you might show a character's degree of formality by including his typical greeting: *How ya doing?* In other words, the things a person says and does are often important indicators of personality. Choose one of the following traits, and make a list of at least four ways to show that someone possesses that trait. Share your list with the class, and discuss the "show-not-tell" strategies you have used.

simple but good	thoughtful	independent
reckless	politically involved	quick-witted
sensitive to the arts	irresponsible	public spirited
a sports lover		

Suggested Writing Assignments

1. Using Mori's essay as a model, describe a familiar inanimate object in a way that brings out its character and meaning and that makes it interesting to the reader. First, determine your purpose in describing the object. Suppose, for example, your family has had the same dining table for as long as you can remember. Think of what that table has been a part of over the years—the birthday parties, the fights, the holiday meals, the long hours of studying and doing homework. A description of such a table would give your reader a sense of the history of your family. Next, make an exhaustive list of the object's physical features,

and include in your descriptive essay the features that contribute to your dominant impression and support your purpose.

2. Most descriptive writing is primarily visual; that is, it appeals to our sense of sight. Good description, however, often goes beyond the visual; it appeals to one or more of the other senses—hearing, smell, taste, and touch. One way to heighten your awareness of these other senses is to purposefully deemphasize the visual impressions you receive. For example, while standing on a busy street corner, sitting in a small Chinese restaurant, or walking into a movie theater after the show has started, carefully note what you hear, smell, taste, and feel. (It may help if you close your eyes to eliminate visual distractions as you carry out this experiment.) Use these sense impressions to write a brief description of the street corner, the Chinese restaurant, the movie theater, or another spot of your own choosing.

The Taj Mahal

■ Salman Rushdie

Novelist and essayist Salman Rushdie was born in Bombay (now known as Mumbai), India, in 1947. He grew up in Mumbai, where he attended Cathedral and John Cannon School, and later graduated from King's College, Cambridge, with a degree in history. Rushdie first worked as an advertising copywriter and only became a full-time writer after the publication of his second novel, Midnight's Children, *in 1981. He is the author of nine other novels, including* Shame *(1983),* The Moor's Last Sigh *(1995),* Fury *(2001),* Shalimar the Clown *(2005), and* Luka and the Fire of Life *(2010); several collections of short stories including* East, West *(1994); and five volumes of nonfiction, including* The Jaguar Smile: A Nicaraguan Journey *(1987) and* Imaginary Homelands: Essays and Criticism, 1981– 1991 *(1992). Rushdie is perhaps best known for the controversy that swirled around the publication of* The Satanic Verses *in 1988. The book rocked the Islamic world with violence and death threats against Rushdie for what was perceived as a blasphemous depiction of the prophet Muhammad. In 2007, Queen Elizabeth II knighted Rushdie for his services to literature, and later that same year he was appointed the Distinguished Writer in Residence at Emory University in Atlanta. He is currently working on his memoirs.*

The following essay was written in 1999 for a National Geographic *survey of the great marvels of the world and was later published in* Step Across This Line: Collected Nonfiction 1992– 2002 *(2002). As you read Rushdie's description of his own personal response to seeing the Taj Mahal for the first time, relish the thought that real buildings and landmarks possess the power to overwhelm and inspire even in our image-saturated world of "counterfeits."*

Reflecting on What You Know

What do you know about the Taj Mahal? Where is it located? Would you recognize a picture of it if you saw it?

The trouble with the Taj Mahal is that it has become so overlaid with accumulated meanings as to be almost impossible to see. A billion chocolate-box images and tourist guidebooks order us to "read" the Mughal emperor Shah Jehan's marble mausoleum for his wife Mumtaz Mahal, known as Taj Bibi, as the World's Greatest Monument to Love. It sits at the top of the West's short list of images of the Exotic (and also Timeless) Orient. Like the *Mona Lisa*, like Andy Warhol's screenprinted Elvis, Marilyn, and Mao, mass reproduction has all but sterilized the Taj. 1

Nor is this by any means a simple case of the West's appropriation or "colonization" of an Indian masterwork. In the first place, the Taj, which in the mid-nineteenth century had been all but abandoned, and had fallen into a severe state of disrepair, would probably not be standing today were it not for the diligent conservationist efforts of the colonial British. In the second place, India is perfectly capable of over-merchandising itself. 2

When you arrive at the outer walls of the gardens in which the Taj is set, it's as if every hustler and hawker in Agra is waiting for you to make the familiarity-breeds-contempt problem worse, peddling imitation Taj Mahals of every size and price. This leads to a certain amount of shoulder-shrugging disenchantment. Recently, a British friend who was about to make his first trip to India told me that he had decided to leave the Taj off his itinerary because of its over-exposure. If I urged him not to, it was because of my own vivid memory of pushing my way for the first time through the jostling crowd, not only of imitation-vendors but also of prescribed readings, past all the myriad hawkers of meaning and interpretation, and into the presence of the *thing-in-itself*, which utterly overwhelmed me and made all my notions about its devaluation feel totally and completely redundant. 3

I had been skeptical about the visit. One of the legends of the Taj is that the hands of the master masons who built it were cut off by the emperor, so that they could never build anything lovelier. Another is that the mausoleum was constructed in secrecy behind high walls, and a man who tried to sneak a preview was blinded for his interest in architecture. My personal imagined Taj was somewhat tarnished by these cruel tales. 4

The building itself left my skepticism in shreds, however. Announcing itself as itself, insisting with absolute force on its sovereign authority, it simply obliterated the million million counterfeits of it and glowingly filled, once and forever, the place in the mind previously occupied by its simulacra. 5

And this, finally, is why the Taj Mahal must be seen: to remind 6
us that the world is real, that the sound is truer than the echo, the
original more forceful than its image in a mirror. The beauty of beautiful things is still able, in these image-saturated times, to transcend
imitations. And the Taj Mahal is, beyond the power of words to say
it, a lovely thing, perhaps the loveliest of things.

Thinking Critically about This Reading

What difficulties face a writer trying to describe a landmark that "has
become so overlaid with accumulated meanings as to be almost impossible to see" (paragraph 1)? How successful do you think Rushdie has
been in overcoming these difficulties? Explain.

Questions for Study and Discussion

1. What does Rushdie mean when he says that "mass reproduction
   has all but sterilized the Taj" (1)?
2. What awaits visitors at the outer walls of the gardens surrounding the Taj Mahal? What do you think Rushdie means by "the
   familiarity-breeds-contempt problem" (3)?
3. What does Rushdie remember about his first visit to the Taj Mahal?
   Why do you think he italicized the phrase "*thing-in-itself*" (3)? Why
   does Rushdie believe that people must see the Taj Mahal in person?
4. How do the "cruel tales" recounted in paragraph 4 function in
   the context of Rushdie's description? Explain.
5. Comment on Rushdie's use of transitions to achieve coherence in
   moving smoothly from one paragraph to the next. (Glossary:
   Transition)
6. What dominant impression of the Taj Mahal does Rushdie create?
   Why do you think he gives readers almost no physical details of its
   appearance? Explain. (Glossary: *Dominant Impression*)

Classroom Activity Using Description

The verbs you use in writing a description can themselves convey much
descriptive information. Take, for example, the verb *walk*. This word
actually tells us little more than "to move on foot," in the most
general sense. Using more precise and descriptive alternatives—*hike,
slink, saunter, stalk, step, stride, stroll, tramp, wander*—enhances your
descriptive powers and enlivens your writing. For each of the following

verbs, make a list of at least four descriptive alternatives. Then compare your list of descriptive alternatives with those of others in the class.

go   throw   exercise
see   take   study
say   drink   sleep

Suggested Writing Assignments

1. Consider the following photograph of the Taj Mahal. What is your dominant impression of it? What details in the photograph come together to create this dominant impression for you? You may wish to supplement your observations about and impressions of the Taj Mahal with a brief Internet search. Finally, write a description of the Taj Mahal that captures the dominant impression you identified above.

2. What is your favorite city, and what are your favorite historic, political, religious, or social landmarks in that city? For example, if Washington, D.C., were your favorite city, the Capitol, White House, National Gallery, Washington Monument, Lincoln Memorial, National Cathedral, Vietnam War Memorial, and National Zoo might be among the landmarks that most impress or inspire you. Make a list of the famous landmarks in your favorite city, and then write an essay in which you describe one of these places.

Process Analysis

When you give someone directions to your home, tell how to make ice cream, or explain how a president is elected, you are using **process analysis.** Process analysis usually arranges a series of events in order and relates them to one another, as narration and cause and effect do, but process analysis has a different emphasis. Whereas narration tells mainly *what* happens and cause and effect focuses on *why* it happens, process analysis tries to explain—in detail—*how* it happens.

There are two types of process analysis—directional and informational. The *directional* type provides instructions on how to do something. These instructions can be as brief as the directions for making instant coffee printed on the label or as complex as the directions in a manual for assembling a new gas grill. The purpose of directional process analysis is to give the reader directions to follow that will lead to the desired results.

Consider these directions for sharpening a knife:

> If you have never done any whittling or wood carving before, the first skill to learn is how to sharpen your knife. You may be surprised to learn that even a brand-new knife needs sharpening. Knives are never sold honed (finely sharpened), although some gouges and chisels are. It is essential to learn the firm stroke on the stone that will keep your blades sharp. The sharpening stone must be fixed in place on the table, so that it will not move around. You can do this by placing a piece of rubber inner tube or a thin piece of foam rubber under it. Or you can tack four strips of wood, if you have a rough worktable, to frame the stone and hold it in place. Put a generous puddle of oil on the stone—this will soon disappear into the surface of a new stone, and you will need to keep adding more oil. Press the knife blade flat against the stone in the puddle of oil, using your index finger. Whichever way the cutting edge of the knife faces is the side of the blade that should get a little more

pressure. Move the blade around three or four times in a narrow oval about the size of your fingernail, going *counterclockwise* when the sharp edge is facing right. Now turn the blade over in the same spot on the stone, press hard, and move it around the small oval *clockwise,* with more pressure on the cutting edge that faces left. Repeat the ovals, flipping the knife blade over six or seven times, and applying lighter pressure to the blade the last two times. Wipe the blade clean with a piece of rag or tissue and rub it flat on the piece of leather strop at least twice on each side. Stroke *away* from the cutting edge to remove the little burr of metal that may be left on the blade.

–Florence H. Pettit

After first establishing her context and purpose, Pettit presents step-by-step directions for sharpening a knife, selecting details that a novice would understand.

After explaining in two previous paragraphs the first two steps involved in learning how to juggle, a student writer moves to the important third step. Notice here how he explains the third step, offers advice on what to do if things go wrong, and encourages your efforts—all useful in directional process writing:

Step three is merely a continuum of "the exchange" with the addition of the third ball. Don't worry if you are confused—I will explain. Hold two balls in your right hand and one in your left. Make a perfect toss with one of your balls in your right hand and then an exchange with the one in your left hand. The ball coming from your left hand should now be exchanged with the, as of now, unused ball in your right hand. This process should be continued until you find yourself reaching under nearby chairs for bouncing tennis balls. It is true that many persons' backs and legs become sore when learning how to juggle because they've been picking up balls that they've inadvertently tossed around the room. Try practicing over a bed; you won't have to reach down so far. Don't get too upset if things aren't going well; you're probably keeping the same pace as everyone else at this stage.

–William Peterson, student

The *informational* type of process analysis, on the other hand, tells how something works, how something is made, or how something occurs. You would use informational process analysis if you wanted to explain how the human heart functions, how an atomic bomb

Graphic by Nigel Holmes.

works, how hailstones are formed, how you selected the college you are attending, or how the polio vaccine was developed. Rather than giving specific directions, informational process analysis explains and informs.

In the illustration by Nigel Holmes on page 425, Jim Collins uses informational process analysis to explain a basic legislative procedure—how a bill becomes a law.

Clarity is crucial for successful process analysis. The most effective way to explain a process is to divide it into steps and to present those steps in a clear (usually chronological) sequence. Transitional words and phrases such as *first, next, after,* and *before* help to connect steps to one another. Naturally, you must be sure that no step is omitted or given out of order. Also, you may sometimes have to explain *why* a certain step is necessary, especially if it is not obvious. With intricate, abstract, or particularly difficult steps, you might use analogy or comparison to clarify the steps for your reader.

The Principles of Poor Writing

◼ Paul W. Merrill

Paul Willard Merrill (1887–1961) was a noted astronomer whose specialty was spectroscopy—the measurement of a quantity as a function of either wavelength or frequency. Merrill earned his AB at Stanford University in 1908 and his PhD at the University of California in 1913. After spending three years at the University of Michigan, Merrill went to work at the National Bureau of Standards, concentrating on aerial photography in the visible and infrared. He was the first to propose doing infrared astronomy from airplanes. In 1919, he joined the Mt. Wilson Observatory, located near Pasadena, California, where he spent more than three decades researching peculiar stars, especially long-period variables. He is the recipient of the Bruce Medal and the Henry Draper Medal, has an asteroid and a lunar crater named after him, and is the author of four books: The Nature of Variable Stars *(1938),* Spectra of Long-Period Variable Stars *(1940),* Lines of the Chemical Elements in Astronomical Spectra *(1956), and* Space Chemistry *(1963).*

As Merrill writes in the beginning of his essay, "Poor writing is so common that every educated person ought to know something about it." As a scientist, he thinks that other scientists write poorly but more by ear than by a set of principles, which he freely offers in his essay. This essay first appeared in the January 1947 issue of Scientific Monthly.

Reflecting on What You Know

Describe your three most serious failings when it comes to writing. What do you think you can do to remedy each one?

Books and articles on good writing are numerous, but where can   1
you find sound, practical advice on how to write poorly? Poor writing is so common that every educated person ought to know

something about it. Many scientists actually do write poorly, but they probably perform by ear without perceiving clearly how their results are achieved. An article on the principles of poor writing might help. The author considers himself well qualified to prepare such an article; he can write poorly without half trying.

The average student finds it surprisingly easy to acquire the usual   2
tricks of poor writing. To do a consistently poor job, however, one must grasp a few essential principles:

1. Ignore the reader.
2. Be verbose, vague, and pompous.
3. Do not revise.

Ignore the Reader

The world is divided into two great camps: yourself and others. A little   3
obscurity or indirection in writing will keep the others at a safe distance. Write as if for a diary. Keep your mind on a direct course between yourself and the subject; don't think of the reader—he makes a bad triangle. This is fundamental. Constant and alert consideration of the probable reaction of the reader is a serious menace to poor writing; moreover, it requires mental effort. A logical argument is that if you write poorly enough, your readers will be too few to merit any attention whatever.

Ignore the reader wherever possible. If the proposed title, for   4
example, means something to you, stop right there; think no further. If the title baffles or misleads the reader, you have won the first round. Similarly, all the way through you must write for yourself, not for the reader. Practice a dead-pan technique, keeping your facts and ideas all on the same level of emphasis with no telltale hints of relative importance or logical sequence. Use long sentences containing many ideas loosely strung together. *And* is the connective most frequently employed in poor writing because it does not indicate cause and effect, nor does it distinguish major ideas from subordinate ones. *Because* seldom appears in poor writing, nor does the semicolon—both are replaced by *and*.

Camouflage transitions in thought. Avoid such connectives as   5
moreover, nevertheless, on the other hand. If unable to resist the temptation to give some signal for a change in thought, use *however*. A poor sentence may well begin with *however* because to the reader, with no idea what comes next, *however* is too vague to be useful. A good sentence begins with the subject or with a phrase that needs emphasis.

The "hidden antecedent" is a common trick of poor writing. Use 6
a pronoun to refer to a noun a long way back, or to one decidedly
subordinate in thought or syntax; or the pronoun may refer to something not directly expressed. If you wish to play a little game with the
reader, offer him the wrong antecedent as bait; you may be astonished how easy it is to catch the poor fish.

In ignoring the reader, avoid parallel constructions which give the 7
thought away too easily. I need not elaborate, for you probably employ
inversion frequently. It must have been a naive soul who said, "When
the thought is parallel, let the phrases be parallel."

In every technical paper omit a few items that most readers need 8
to know. You had to discover these things the hard way; why make it
easy for the reader? Avoid defining symbols: never specify the units in
which data are presented. Of course it will be beneath your dignity to
give numerical values of constants in formulae. With these omissions,
some papers may be too short; lengthen them by explaining things
that do not need explaining. In describing tables, give special attention
to self-explanatory headings; let the reader hunt for the meaning of *Pr*.

Be Verbose, Vague, and Pompous

The cardinal sin of poor writing is to be concise and simple. Avoid 9
being specific: it ties you down. Use plenty of deadwood: include
many superfluous words and phrases. Wishful thinking suggests to a
writer that verbosity somehow serves as a cloak or even as a mystic
halo by which an idea may be glorified. A cloud of words may conceal
defects in observation or analysis, either by opacity or by diverting the
reader's attention. Introduce abstract nouns at the drop of a hat—even
in those cases where the magnitude of the motion in a downward
direction is inconsiderable. Make frequent use of the words *case, character, condition, former* and *latter, nature, such, very.*

Poor writing, like good football, is strong on razzle-dazzle, weak 10
on information. Adjectives are frequently used to bewilder the reader.
It isn't much trouble to make them gaudy or hyperbolic; at least they
can be flowery and inexact.

BIBLE: Render to Caesar the things that are Caesar's.

POOR: In the case of Caesar it might well be considered
              appropriate from a moral or ethical point of view
              to render to that potentate all of those goods and

materials of whatever character or quality which can be shown to have had their original source in any portion of the domain of the latter.

SHAKESPEARE: I am no orator as Brutus is.

POOR: The speaker is not, what might be termed as adept in the profession of public speaking, as might be properly stated of Mr. Brutus. (Example from P. W. Swain. *Amer. J. Physics,* 13, 318, 1945.)

CONCISE: The dates of several observations are in doubt.

POOR: It should be mentioned that in the case of several observations there is room for considerable doubt concerning the correctness of the dates on which they were made.

REASONABLE: Exceptionally rapid changes occur in the spectrum.

POOR: There occur in the spectrum changes which are quite exceptional in respect to the rapidity of their advent.

REASONABLE: Formidable difficulties, both mathematical and observational, stand in the way.

POOR: There are formidable difficulties of both a mathematical and an observational nature that stand in the way.

Case

REASONABLE: Two sunspots changed rapidly.

POOR: There are two cases where sunspots changed with considerable rapidity.

REASONABLE: Three stars are red.

POOR: In three cases the stars are red in color.

Razzle-Dazzle

Immaculate precision of observation and extremely delicate calculations . . .

It would prove at once a world imponderable, etherealized. Our actions would grow gradific.

Well for us that the pulsing energy of the great life giving dynamo in the sky never ceases. Well, too, that we are at a safe distance from the flame-licked whirlpools into which our earth might drop like a pellet of waste fluff shaken into the live coals of a grate fire.

Do Not Revise

Write hurriedly, preferably when tired. Have no plan; write down items as they occur to you. The article will thus be spontaneous and poor. Hand in your manuscript the moment it is finished. Rereading a few days later might lead to revision—which seldom, if ever, makes the writing worse. If you submit your manuscript to colleagues (a bad practice), pay no attention to their criticisms or comments. Later, resist firmly any editorial suggestion. Be strong and infallible; don't let anyone break down your personality. The critic may be trying to help you or he may have an ulterior motive, but the chance of his causing improvement in your writing is so great that you must be on guard.

11

Thinking Critically about This Reading

Why do you think Merrill might have written "The Principles of Poor Writing"? What special motivation do you think his career as a scientist might have provided him? Explain.

Questions for Study and Discussion

1. *Irony* is the use of words to suggest something different from their meaning. At what point in the essay did you realize that Merrill is being ironic? (Glossary: *Irony*) Did his title, introduction, or actual advice tip you off? Explain.

2. Is the author's process analysis the directional type or the informational type? What leads you to this conclusion?

3. Why has Merrill ordered his three process steps in this particular way? Could he have used a different order? (Glossary: *Organization*) Explain.

4. How helpful are the author's examples in helping you understand his principles? Do you agree with all his examples? (Glossary: *Example*) Explain.

5. Why do you suppose Merrill used irony to show his readers that they needed to improve their writing? (Glossary: *Irony*) What do

you see as the potential advantages and disadvantages to such a strategy?

6. In what types of writing situations is irony especially useful?

Classroom Activity Using Process Analysis

Most do-it-yourself jobs require that you follow a set process to achieve results. Make a list of the steps involved in doing one of the following household activities:

cleaning windows
repotting a plant
making burritos
changing a flat tire
unclogging a drain
doing laundry

Have at least one other person read your list of steps, checking for both the order of the steps and any omitted steps.

Suggested Writing Assignments

1. Write a process analysis in which you explain the steps you usually follow when deciding to make a purchase of some importance or expense to you. Hint: It's best to analyze your process with a specific product in mind. Do you compare brands, store prices, and so on? What are your priorities—that the item be stylish or durable, offer good overall value, or give high performance?

2. Try writing a process analysis essay in which you are ironic about the steps that need to be followed. For example, in an essay on how to lose weight by changing your diet or increasing your exercise, you might cast in a positive light all the things that absolutely should not be done. These might include parking as close as you can to your destination to avoid walking or buying a half gallon of your favorite ice cream instead of a pint because the half gallons are on sale.

How to Make Chocolate Sauce

■ **Nicholson Baker**

Nicholson Baker is a writer of both fiction and nonfiction. Born in 1957 in New York City, he grew up in Rochester, New York, where in 1975 he attended the Eastman School of Music. A 1979 graduate of Haverford College, Pennsylvania, with a BA in philosophy, Baker now makes his home in South Berwick, Maine. The author is most noted for creating in his first novel Mezzanine
(1988) a subgenre of fiction that focuses intensely on the minute details of his characters' and narrators' stream-of-consciousness storytelling, an approach that has gained him both supporters and detractors—the former praising his elevation of the minutiae of life to the level of art, the latter decrying the accompanying lack of narrative action. The novel is replete with long footnotes. In this same vein are two other works: Room Temperature *(1990), a follow-up to* Mezzanine *in which Baker concentrates on just a few minutes in his narrator's life, and* U and I *(1991), a work of nonfiction that explores the dynamics of how we read. Among Baker's other works are* Vox *(1992),* The Fermata *(1994),* Checkpoint *(2004),* Human Smoke: The Beginnings of World War II, The End of Civilization *(2008), and* The Anthologist *(2009).*

The following selection is taken from Baker's The Size of Thoughts: Essays and Other Lumber *(1997), a collection of pieces about various aspects of daily life—from thoughts on a toenail clipper to the act of changing your mind rather than making decisions, building model airplanes, and the literary history of the word* lumber. *Originally titled "Recipe," this brief directional process was provided to the Monroe (Michigan) County Library System to be included in a book of recipes by noteworthy authors.*

Reflecting on What You Know

Why make chocolate sauce from scratch when you can just as easily buy a jar of prepared sauce, heat it, and pour it over your ice cream? What are the advantages and disadvantages of making the sauce yourself?

The Monroe County Library System, of Monroe, Michigan, asked for a recipe to include in a collection of "Favorite Recipes by Favorite Authors," entitled *Read 'em and Eat*.

Take one ingot of unsweetened Baker's chocolate, remove the   1
paper, and drop it in a tiny saucepan settled over an adjustable heat-source. Then unfold one end of a brand-new silver bar of unsalted Land O Lakes butter and cut a chunk off roughly comparable to the piece of Baker's chocolate, which has by this time begun to smear slightly. (An old stick of butter has too much refrigerator flavor in its exposed end.) The butter will melt faster than the chocolate. Entertain yourself by breaking the ingot of chocolate into its two halves and pushing the halves and the subsiding chunk of butter around with the tip of the butter knife. Then abandon the butter knife and switch to a spoon. When the unmelted chocolate is no more than a small soft shape difficult to locate in the larger velouté, shake some drifts of confectioners' sugar into the liquid. You're aiming for a bittersweet taste, a taste quite a bit less sweet than ice cream—so sprinkle accordingly. But you'll find that a surprising amount of sugar is necessary. Stir idly. If the mixture becomes thick and paste-like, add another three-eighth-inch sliver of butter; to your relief, all will effortlessly reliquefy. Avoid bubbling or burning the mixture, which can now be called sauce. Turn off the heat, or turn it down so low that you don't have to worry about it. Spoon out some premium plain vanilla ice cream. Lately this has become hard to find—crowded out by low-fat premiums and Fragonard flavors. But you want the very best vanilla ice cream available in your area; you have to have that high butterfat content for it to be compatible with the chocolate sauce. Spoon the sauce over the ice cream. It will harden. This is what you have been working for. Once cooled, it will make a nice sound when you tap it with a spoon. If you want more tappable chocolate sauce and you have already covered your scoop or scoops of ice cream with a complete trelliswork,

simply turn over one of the scoops and dribble more over the exposed underside. Eat with haste, because premium vanilla ice cream melts fast. Refrigerate the unused sauce right in the original saucepan, covered with tinfoil, with the spoon resting in it; that way, when you put it back on the heat-source, you'll be able to brandish the whole solidified disk of chocolate merely by lifting the spoon. It looks like a metal detector.

Thinking Critically about This Reading

Baker's recipe is not formatted as we are accustomed to seeing most recipes presented. What's different? Why do you suppose Baker chose to present his recipe as he did? What advantages and disadvantages do you see in his particular format?

Questions for Study and Discussion

1. Evaluate Baker's recipe for its adherence to the principles of a well-written directional process analysis. As you read it, are there steps left out or directions that are unclear? What changes, if any, would you suggest?

2. How easy would Baker's recipe be to follow if you were actually making his chocolate sauce? Would his style of recipe writing be appropriate in all instances of recipe writing? Explain. (Glossary: *Style*)

3. Baker has built a reputation as a writer who places extreme importance on details. Why is his style particularly suited to recipe writing? (Glossary: *Details*)

4. Cite several examples of the descriptive language Baker uses in his recipe. In your opinion, how helpful is his descriptive language in accomplishing his purpose? (Glossary: *Description*)

5. Baker uses several words you might not be familiar with: velouté and Fragonard. What does each term mean? Are they technical cooking terms? Explain.

6. What is Baker's tone in this selection? How has he established that tone? How appropriate is that tone to the task at hand? Explain. (Glossary: *Tone*)

Suggested Writing Assignments

1. Using the illustration on page 425 as a preliminary outline of how a bill becomes law, research the topic more thoroughly through reading. If possible, discuss the process with a political science instructor at your school. The illustration ends with the question, "Does it *ever* go as smoothly as this?" and the answer, "Nope." What kinds of situations can and often do alter the process?

2. Think about a familiar process that you believe needs improvement. After choosing your topic, do some background research. In your own words, write a process analysis in which you argue for a revision of the existing process. (Glossary: *Argumentation*) For example, are you happy with the process for dealing with recyclables where you live, the process for registering for classes, or the way dorm rooms are assigned on campus?

Classroom Activity Using Process Analysis

An airfoil is a device that provides reactive force (e.g., lift) when in motion relative to the surrounding air. Carefully read the following directions for constructing an astro tube—a cylindrical airfoil made from a sheet of heavy writing paper. Now construct your own astro tube, and fly it. How far, if at all, did your astro tube fly? How helpful did you find the illustrations that accompany the written instructions? Based on your results, what revisions to the instructions would you make? Why?

Making an Astro Tube

Start with an 8.5-inch by 11-inch sheet of heavy writing paper. (Never use newspaper in making paper models because it isn't strongly bonded and can't hold a crease.) Follow these numbered steps, corresponding to the illustrations.

1. With the long side of the sheet toward you, fold up one third of the paper.
2. Fold the doubled section in half.
3. Fold the section in half once more and crease well.
4. Unfold preceding crease.
5. Curve the ends together to form a tube, as shown in the illustration.

6. Insert the right end inside the left end between the single outer layer and the doubled layers. Overlap the ends about an inch and a half. (This makes a tube for right-handers, to be used with an underhand throw. For an overhand tube, or an underhand version to be thrown by a lefty, reverse the directions, and insert the left end inside the right end at this step.)

7. Hold the tube at the seam with one hand, where shown by the dot in the illustration, and turn the rim inward along the crease made in step 3. Start turning in at the seam and roll the rim under, moving around the circumference in a circular manner. Then round out the rim.

8. Fold the fin to the left, as shown, then raise it so that it's perpendicular to the tube. Be careful not to tear the paper at the front.

9. Hold the tube from above, near the rim. Hold it between the thumb and fingers. The rim end should be forward, with the fin on the bottom. Throw the tube underhanded, with a motion like throwing a bowling ball, letting it spin off the fingers as it is released. The tube will float through the air, spinning as it goes. Indoor flights of 30 feet or more are easy. With practice you can achieve remarkable accuracy.

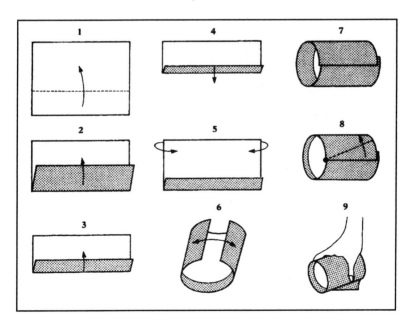

Why Leaves Turn Color in the Fall

■ Diane Ackerman

Born in Waukegan, Illinois, in 1948, Diane Ackerman received degrees from Pennsylvania State University and Cornell University. She has written several books of poetry, a prose memoir, a play, and several collections of essays, including The Moon by Whale Light, and Other Adventures among Bats, Penguins, Crocodilians, and Whales *(1991);* A Natural History of Love *(1994);* The Rarest of the Rare: Vanishing Animals, Timeless Worlds *(1995);* The Curious Naturalist *(1998);* Deep Play *(1999);* Cultivating Delight *(2002);* An Alchemy of Mind: The Marvel and Mystery of the Brain *(2004);* The Zookeeper's Wife: A War Story *(2007);* Dawn Light: Dancing with Cranes and Other Ways to Start the Day *(2009); and* One Hundred Names for Love: A Stroke, a Marriage, and the Language of Healing *(2011). Ackerman has worked as a writer-in-residence at several major universities, has directed the Writers' Program at Washington University in St. Louis, and has been a staff writer at the* New Yorker. *Currently she lives in upstate New York.*

Every October, residents of the northeastern United States are dazzled by a spectacular color show that sets them to wondering, "Where do the colors come from?" In the following selection, from Ackerman's acclaimed A Natural History of the Senses *(1990), she lets us in on one of nature's secrets. Notice the way Ackerman shares her enthusiasm for the natural world as she explains the process by which autumn leaves assume their brilliant colors.*

Reflecting on What You Know

What is your favorite season? What about this season makes it your favorite—the weather, the activities and memories, the time of year, or a combination of these and other factors?

The stealth of autumn catches one unaware. Was that a goldfinch 1
perching in the early September woods, or just the first turning
leaf? A red-winged blackbird or a sugar maple closing up shop for the
winter? Keen-eyed as leopards, we stand still and squint hard, looking
for signs of movement. Early-morning frost sits heavily on the grass,
and turns barbed wire into a string of stars. On a distant hill, a small
square of yellow appears to be a lighted stage. At last the truth dawns
on us: Fall is staggering in, right on schedule, with its baggage of chilly
nights, macabre holidays, and spectacular, heart-stoppingly beautiful
leaves. Soon the leaves will start cringing on the trees, and roll up in
clenched fists before they actually fall off. Dry seedpods will rattle like
tiny gourds. But first there will be weeks of gushing color so bright, so
pastel, so confetti like, that people will travel up and down the East
Coast just to stare at it—a whole season of leaves.

Where do the colors come from? Sunlight rules most living 2
things with its golden edicts. When the days begin to shorten, soon
after the summer solstice on June 21, a tree reconsiders its leaves. All
summer it feeds them so they can process sunlight, but in the dog
days of summer the tree begins pulling nutrients back into its trunk
and roots, pares down, and gradually chokes off its leaves. A corky
layer of cells forms at the leaves' slender petioles, then scars over.
Undernourished, the leaves stop producing the pigment chlorophyll,
and photosynthesis ceases. Animals can migrate, hibernate, or store
food to prepare for winter. But where can a tree go? It survives by
dropping its leaves, and by the end of autumn only a few fragile
threads of fluid-carrying xylem hold leaves to their stems.

A turning leaf stays partly green at first, then reveals splotches 3
of yellow and red as the chlorophyll gradually breaks down. Dark
green seems to stay longest in the veins, outlining and defining them.
During the summer, chlorophyll dissolves in the heat and light, but it
is also being steadily replaced. In the fall, on the other hand, no new
pigment is produced, and so we notice the other colors that were always there, right in the leaf, although chlorophyll's shocking green
hid them from view. With their camouflage gone, we see these colors
for the first time all year, and marvel, but they were always there, hidden like a vivid secret beneath the hot glowing greens of summer.

The most spectacular range of fall foliage occurs in the north- 4
eastern United States and in eastern China, where the leaves are ro-
bustly colored, thanks in part to a rich climate. European maples
don't achieve the same flaming reds as their American relatives,

which thrive on cold nights and sunny days. In Europe, the warm, humid weather turns the leaves brown or mildly yellow. Anthocyanin, the pigment that gives apples their red and turns leaves red or red-violet, is produced by sugars that remain in the leaf after the supply of nutrients dwindles. Unlike the carotenoids, which color carrots, squash, and corn, and turn leaves orange and yellow, anthocyanin varies from year to year, depending on the temperature and amount of sunlight. The fiercest colors occur in years when the fall sunlight is strongest and the nights are cool and dry (a state of grace scientists find vexing to forecast). This is also why leaves appear dizzyingly bright and clear on a sunny fall day: The anthocyanin flashes like a marquee.

Not all leaves turn the same colors. Elms, weeping willows, 5 and the ancient ginkgo all grow radiant yellow, along with hickories, aspens, bottlebrush buckeyes, cottonweeds, and tall, keening poplars. Basswood turns bronze, birches bright gold. Water-loving maples put on a symphonic display of scarlets. Sumacs turn red, too, as do flowering dogwoods, black gums, and sweet gums. Though some oaks yellow, most turn a pinkish brown. The farmlands also change color, as tepees of cornstalks and bales of shredded-wheat-textured hay stand drying in the fields. In some spots, one slope of a hill may be green and the other already in bright color, because the hillside facing south gets more sun and heat than the northern one.

An odd feature of the colors is that they don't seem to have any 6 special purpose. We are predisposed to respond to their beauty, of course. They shimmer with the colors of sunset, spring flowers, the tawny buff of a colt's pretty rump, the shuddering pink of a blush. Animals and flowers color for a reason—adaptation to their environment—but there is no adaptive reason for leaves to color so beautifully in the fall any more than there is for the sky or ocean to be blue. It's just one of the haphazard marvels the planet bestows every year. We find the sizzling colors thrilling, and in a sense they dupe us. Colored like living things, they signal death and disintegration. In time, they will become fragile and, like the body, return to dust. They are as we hope our own fate will be when we die: Not to vanish, just to sublime from one beautiful state into another. Though leaves lose their green life, they bloom with urgent colors, as the woods grow mummified day by day, and Nature becomes more carnal, mute, and radiant.

We call the season "fall," from the Old English *feallan*, to fall, which leads back through time to the Indo-European *phol*, which also means to fall. So the word and the idea are both extremely ancient, and haven't really changed since the first of our kind needed a name for fall's leafy abundance. As we say the word, we're reminded of that other Fall, in the garden of Eden, when fig leaves never withered and scales fell from our eyes. Fall is the time when leaves fall from the trees, just as spring is when flowers spring up, summer is when we simmer, and winter is when we whine from the cold. 7

Children love to play in piles of leaves, hurling them into the air like confetti, leaping into soft unruly mattresses of them. For children, leaf fall is just one of the odder figments of Nature, like hailstones or snowflakes. Walk down a lane overhung with trees in the never-never land of autumn, and you will forget about time and death, lost in the sheer delicious spill of color. Adam and Eve concealed their nakedness with leaves, remember? Leaves have always hidden our awkward secrets. 8

But how do the colored leaves fall? As a leaf ages, the growth hormone, auxin, fades, and cells at the base of the petiole divide. Two or three rows of small cells, lying at right angles to the axis of the petiole, react with water, then come apart, leaving the petioles hanging on by only a few threads of xylem. A light breeze, and the leaves are airborne. They glide and swoop, rocking in invisible cradles. They are all wing and may flutter from yard to yard on small whirlwinds or updrafts, swiveling as they go. Firmly tethered to earth, we love to see things rise up and fly—soap bubbles, balloons, birds, fall leaves. They remind us that the end of a season is capricious, as is the end of life. We especially like the way leaves rock, careen, and swoop as they fall. Everyone knows the motion. Pilots sometimes do a maneuver called a "falling leaf," in which the plane loses altitude quickly and on purpose, by slipping first to the right, then to the left. The machine weighs a ton or more, but in one pilot's mind it is a weightless thing, a falling leaf. She has seen the motion before, in the Vermont woods where she played as a child. Below her the trees radiate gold, copper, and red. Leaves are falling, although she can't see them fall, as she falls, swooping down for a closer view. 9

At last the leaves leave. But first they turn color and thrill us for weeks on end. Then they crunch and crackle underfoot. They *shush*, as children drag their small feet through leaves heaped along the curb. Dark, slimy mats of leaves cling to one's heels after a rain. 10

A damp, stuccolike mortar of semidecayed leaves protects the tender shoots with a roof until spring, and makes a rich humus. An occasional bulge or ripple in the leafy mounds signals a shrew or a field mouse tunneling out of sight. Sometimes one finds in fossil stones the imprint of a leaf, long since disintegrated, whose outlines remind us how detailed, vibrant, and alive are the things of this earth that perish.

Thinking Critically about This Reading

In paragraphs 2 and 6 Ackerman attributes some human qualities to Nature and to the trees. What effect does her personification have on you as a reader? Why do you think she chose to use these figures of speech in a process analysis essay? (Glossary: *Figures of Speech*)

Questions for Study and Discussion

1. According to Ackerman, exactly what causes leaves to change color? What particular conditions cause the brightest colors in autumn leaves?

2. Briefly summarize the steps of the process by which leaves change color in autumn.

3. Not only does Ackerman describe the process by which leaves change color, she includes other information as well. For example, she uses cause-and-effect analysis to explain what causes leaves to be particularly bright some years, to explain why trees turn color at different rates, and to explain why leaves lose their grip and fall from the trees. (Glossary: *Cause and Effect*) Did you find this information useful? What, if anything, did it add to your appreciation of Ackerman's process analysis?

4. How has Ackerman organized her essay? (Glossary: *Organization*) Explain why this organization seems most appropriate for her subject.

5. Identify several figures of speech—simile, metaphor, and personification—that Ackerman uses, and explain how each functions in the context of her essay. (Glossary: *Figure of Speech*)

6. Reread Ackerman's concluding sentence. What does she mean? Why do you suppose she has chosen to end her essay in this way?

In what ways, if any, is it a particularly appropriate ending for her essay? (Glossary: *Beginnings and Endings*)

Classroom Activity Using Process Analysis

To give another person clear directions about how to do something, you need to have a thorough understanding of the process yourself. Analyze one of the following activities by listing any materials you might need and the steps you would follow in completing it:

studying for an exam

determining miles per gallon for an automobile

finding a person's name and address (or e-mail address) on the Internet

beginning an exercise program

getting from where your writing class meets to where you normally have lunch

installing new software on your computer

writing an essay

buying a DVD player on the Internet

adding or dropping a class from your course schedule

Have at least one other person read your list of materials and the steps involved, checking for anything you may have omitted.

Suggested Writing Assignments

1. Our world is filled with hundreds of natural processes—for example, the cycle of the moon, the "rising" and "setting" of the sun, the germination of a seed, the movement of the tides, the formation of a tornado, the transformation of a caterpillar into a butterfly or moth, and the flowering of a tree. Using Ackerman's essay as a model, write an informational process analysis explaining one such natural process.

2. Select one of the tasks listed in the Classroom Activity, and write a brief essay in which you give directions for successfully performing the task.

Definition

Definition allows you to communicate precisely what you want to say. At its most basic level, you will frequently need to define key words. Your reader needs to know just what you mean when you use unfamiliar words (such as *accoutrement*), words that are open to various interpretations (such as *liberal*), or familiar words that are used in a particular sense. Important terms that are not defined or that are defined inaccurately confuse readers and hamper communication.

Consider the opening paragraph from a student essay titled "Secular Mantras":

> Remember *The Little Engine That Could*? That's the story about the tiny locomotive that hauled the train over the mountain when the big, rugged locomotives wouldn't. Remember how the Little Engine strained and heaved and chugged, "I think I can—I think I can—I think I can" until she reached the top of the mountain? That's a perfect example of a secular mantra in action. You probably have used a secular mantra (pronounce it "mantruh") already today. It's any word or group of words that helps you use your energy when you consciously repeat it to yourself. You must understand two qualities about secular mantras to be able to recognize one.
>
> –Keith Eldred, student

Eldred engages his readers with the story of the Little Engine and then uses that example to lead into a definition of *secular mantra*. He concludes the paragraph with a sentence that tells readers what is coming next.

There are three basic ways to define a word, and each is useful in its own way. The first method is to give a *synonym*—that is, use a word that has nearly the same meaning as the word you wish to define (*face* for *countenance*, *nervousness* for *anxiety*). No two words have exactly the same meaning, but you can nevertheless pair an unfamiliar word with a familiar one and thereby clarify your meaning.

Another way to define a word quickly, often within a single sentence, is to give a *formal definition*—that is, place the term in a general class and then distinguish it from other members of that class by describing its particular characteristics. For example:

Word	*Class*	*Characteristics*
A watch	is a mechanical device	that is used for telling time and is usually carried or worn.
Semantics	is an area of linguistics	that is concerned with the study of the meaning of words.

The third method of defining a word is to give an *extended definition*—that is, to use one or more paragraphs (or even an entire essay) to define a new or difficult term or to rescue a controversial word from misconceptions that may obscure its meaning. In an essay-length extended definition, you provide your readers with information about the meaning of a single word, a concept, or an object. You must consider what your readers already know, or think they know, about your topic. Are there popular misconceptions that need to be corrected? Are some aspects of the topic seldom considered? Have particular experiences helped you understand the topic? You can use synonyms or formal definitions in an extended definition, but you must convince readers to accept your particular understanding of it.

In the following four-paragraph sequence, the writers provide an extended definition of *freedom,* an important but elusive concept:

> Choosing between negative alternatives often seems like no choice at all. Take the case of a woman trying to decide whether to stay married to her inconsiderate, incompetent husband, or get a divorce. She doesn't want to stay with him, but she feels divorce is a sign of failure and will stigmatize her socially. Or think of the decision faced by many young men [more than forty] years ago, when they were forced to choose between leaving their country and family or being sent to Vietnam.
>
> When we face decisions involving only alternatives we see as negatives, we feel so little freedom that we twist and turn searching for another choice with some positive characteristics.
>
> Freedom is a popular word. Individuals talk about how they feel free with one person and not with another, or how their bosses

encourage or discourage freedom on the job. We hear about civil wars and revolutions being fought for greater freedom, with both sides righteously making the claim. The feeling of freedom is so important that people say they're ready to die for it, and supposedly have.

Still, most people have trouble coming up with a precise definition of freedom. They give answers describing specific situations — "Freedom means doing what I want to do, not what the Government wants me to do," or "Freedom means not having my mother tell me when to come home from a party" — rather than a general definition covering many situations. The idea they seem to be expressing is that freedom is associated with making decisions, and that other people sometimes limit the number of alternatives from which they can select.

–Jerald M. Jellison and John H. Harvey

Another term that illustrates the need for extended definition is *obscene*. What is obscene? Books that are banned in one school system are considered perfectly acceptable in another. Movies that are shown in one town cannot be shown in a neighboring town. The meaning of *obscene* has been clouded by contrasting personal opinions as well as by conflicting social norms. Therefore, if you use the term *obscene* (and especially if you tackle the issue of obscenity itself), you must define clearly and thoroughly what you mean by that term—that is, you have to give an extended definition. There are a number of methods you might use to develop such a definition. You could define *obscene* by explaining what it does not mean. You could also make your meaning clear by narrating an experience, by comparing and contrasting it to related terms (such as *pornographic* or *exotic*), by citing specific examples, or by classifying the various types of obscenity. Any of these methods could help you develop an effective definition.

What Is Crime?

■ Lawrence M. Friedman

Born in 1930 in Chicago, Lawrence M. Friedman is currently Marion Rice Kirkwood Professor of Law at Stanford University. He earned his undergraduate degree in 1948 and his law degree in 1951, both from the University of Chicago. After serving a two-year stint in the military, he practiced law in Chicago before embarking on his long and distinguished teaching and writing career. He taught law at St. Louis University and the University of Wisconsin before settling at Stanford in 1968. *A prize-winning expert on U.S. legal history, Friedman is perhaps best known for his* A History of American Law *(1973) and its sequel,* American Law in the Twentieth Century *(2002). His other books include* The Republic of Choice: Law, Authority, and Culture *(1990),* The Horizontal Society *(1999), and* Law in America: A Short History *(2002). In 2003, he wrote* Legal Culture in the Age of Globalization: Latin America and Latin Europe *with Rogelio Perez Perdomo. He has been president of the American Society for Legal History, the Law and Society Association, and the Research Committee on Sociology of Law.*

The following selection is taken from the introduction to Crime and Punishment in American History *(1993), a book in which Friedman traces the response to crime throughout U.S. history. Here he explains what it takes for a certain behavior or act to be considered a crime.*

Reflecting on What You Know

How would you answer the question "What is crime?" For you, what makes some acts criminal and others not? Explain.

There is no real answer to the question, What is crime? There are   1
popular ideas about crime: crime is bad behavior, antisocial behavior, blameworthy acts, and the like. But in a very basic sense, crime is a *legal* concept: what makes some conduct criminal, and

other conduct not, is the fact that some, but not others, are "against the law." *

Crimes, then, are forbidden acts. But they are forbidden in a special way. We are not supposed to break contracts, drive carelessly, slander people, or infringe copyrights; but these are not (usually) criminal acts. The distinction between a *civil* and a *criminal* case is fundamental in our legal system. A civil case has a life cycle entirely different from that of a criminal case. If I slander somebody, I might be dragged into court, and I might have to open my checkbook and pay damages; but I cannot be put in prison or executed, and if I lose the case, I do not get a criminal "record." Also, in a slander case (or a negligence case, or a copyright-infringement case), the injured party pays for, runs, and manages the case herself. He or she makes the decisions and hires the lawyers. The case is entirely voluntary. Nobody forces anybody to sue. I can have a good claim, a valid claim, and simply forget it, if I want.

In a criminal case, in theory at least, society is the victim, along with the "real" victim—the person robbed or assaulted or cheated. The crime may be punished without the victim's approval (though, practically speaking, the complaining witness often has a crucial role to play). In "victimless crimes" (gambling, drug dealing, certain sex offenses), there is nobody to complain; both parties are equally guilty (or innocent). Here the machine most definitely has a mind of its own. In criminal cases, moreover, the state pays the bills. It should be pointed out, however, that the further back in history one goes, the more this pat[1] distinction between "civil" and "criminal" tends to blur. In some older cultures, the line between private vengeance and public prosecution was indistinct or completely absent. Even in our own history, we shall see some evidence that the cleavage between "public" and "private" enforcement was not always deep and pervasive.

All sorts of nasty acts and evil deeds are not against the law, and thus not crimes. These include most of the daily events that anger or irritate us, even those we might consider totally outrageous. Ordinary lying is not a crime; cheating on a wife or husband is not a crime in

---

*Most criminologists, but not all, would agree with this general formulation; for an exception see Michael R. Gottfredson and Travis Hirschi, *A General Theory of Crime* (1990). [Friedman's note]
[1]*pat:* seemingly precise.

most states (at one time it was, almost everywhere); charging a huge markup at a restaurant or store is not, in general, a crime; psychological abuse is (mostly) not a crime.

Before some act can be isolated and labeled as a crime, there must be   5
a special, solemn, social, and *political* decision. In our society, Congress, a state legislature, or a city government has to pass a law or enact an ordinance adding the behavior to the list of crimes. Then this behavior, like a bottle of poison, carries the proper label and can be turned over to the heavy artillery of law for possible enforcement.

We repeat: crime is a *legal* concept. This point, however, can lead   6
to a misunderstanding. The law, in a sense, "creates" the crimes it punishes; but what creates criminal law? Behind the law, and above it, enveloping it, is society; before the law made the crime a crime, some aspect of social reality transformed the behavior, culturally speaking, into a crime; and it is the social context that gives the act, and the legal responses, their real meaning. Justice is supposed to be blind, which is to say impartial. This may or may not be so, but justice is blind in one fundamental sense: justice is an abstraction.[2] It cannot see or act on its own. It cannot generate its own norms, principles, and rules. Everything depends on society. Behind every *legal* judgment of criminality is a more powerful, more basic *social* judgment; a judgment that this behavior, whatever it is, deserves to be outlawed and punished.

Thinking Critically about This Reading

What does Friedman mean when he states, "Behind every *legal* judgment of criminality is a more powerful, more basic *social* judgment; a judgment that this behavior, whatever it is, deserves to be outlawed and punished" (paragraph 6)? According to Friedman, what must happen before any offensive behavior can be deemed criminal?

Questions for Study and Discussion

1. What general definition of *crime* do most criminologists agree on, according to Friedman?
2. What are the major differences between a criminal case and a civil case? Why does Friedman make this distinction? Explain.

---

[2]*abstraction:* a theoretical concept.

3. In what sense is society the "victim" in a criminal case (3)? Do you believe that it is important for society to join with the "real victim" in prosecuting the criminal case? Explain.

4. Friedman states that "all sorts of nasty acts and evil deeds are not against the law, and thus not crimes" (4). What examples does he provide to illustrate this point? (Glossary: *Example*) Do any of his examples surprise you? Explain.

5. What does Friedman mean by "crime is a *legal* concept" (1)? Why do you think that he repeats the statement in paragraph 6? According to the writer, what misunderstanding can the statement lead to?

Classroom Activity Using Definition

Define one of the following terms formally by putting it in a class and then differentiating it from other words in the class. (See p. 445.)

potato chips	tenor saxophone	sociology	Monopoly (the game)
love	physical therapy	chickadee	Buddhism

Suggested Writing Assignments

1. Write an essay recounting a time when you were the victim of somebody's outrageous behavior. What were the circumstances of the incident? How did you respond at the time? What action, if any, did you take at a later time? According to Friedman's definition, was the behavior criminal?

2. Some of the most pressing social issues in American life today are further complicated by imprecise definitions of critical terms. Various medical cases, for example, have brought worldwide attention to the legal and medical definitions of the word *death*. Debates continue about the meanings of other controversial words. Using one of the following controversial terms or another of your choosing, write an essay in which you discuss its definition and the problems that are associated with defining it.

minority (ethnic)	theft	equality
monopoly (business)	lying	success
morality	addiction	pornography
cheating	life	marriage

The Company Man

■ **Ellen Goodman**

Ellen Goodman, American journalist and Pulitzer Prize–winning columnist, was born in Boston in 1941. After graduating cum laude from Radcliffe College in 1963, she worked as a reporter and researcher for Newsweek. *In 1967, she began working at the* Boston Globe *and in 1974 became a full-time columnist. Her regular column, "At Large," was syndicated by the* Washington Post's Writer's *Group and appeared in nearly four hundred newspapers across the country. She wrote her last column on January 1, 2010. In addition, her writing has appeared in* McCall's, Harper's Bazaar, *and* Family Circle, *and her commentaries have been broadcast on radio and television. Several collections of Goodman's columns have been published as books, including* Close to Home *(1979),* At Large *(1981),* Keeping in Touch *(1985),* Value Judgments *(1995),* Making Sense *(1999), and* Paper Trail: Common Sense in Uncommon Times *(2004).*

In the following essay, taken from Close to Home, *Goodman defines* workaholic *by offering a poignant example.*

Reflecting on What You Know

Many jobs have regular hours, but some—like journalism, medicine, and high-level management—are less predictable and may require far more time. Think about your career goals. Do you think that you will emphasize your work life more than your home life? How much time beyond the standard thirty-five work hours per week are you willing to spend to advance your career or support your family? Has this issue influenced your choice of career in any way, or do you anticipate that it will? Explain.

He worked himself to death, finally and precisely, at 3:00 A.M.   1
Sunday morning.

The obituary didn't say that, of course. It said that he died of a 2
coronary thrombosis—I think that was it—but everyone among his
friends and acquaintances knew it instantly. He was a perfect Type A,
a workaholic, a classic, they said to each other and shook their
heads—and thought for five or ten minutes about the way they lived.

This man who worked himself to death finally and precisely at 3
3:00 A.M. Sunday morning—on his day off—was fifty-one years old
and a vice-president. He was, however, one of six vice-presidents, and
one of three who might conceivably—if the president died or retired
soon enough—have moved to the top spot. Phil knew that.

He worked six days a week, five of them until eight or nine at night, 4
during a time when his own company had begun the four-day week
for everyone but the executives. He worked like the Important People.
He had no outside "extracurricular interests," unless, of course, you
think about a monthly golf game that way. To Phil, it was work. He
always ate egg salad sandwiches at his desk. He was, of course, overweight, by twenty or twenty-five pounds. He thought it was okay,
though, because he didn't smoke.

On Saturdays, Phil wore a sports jacket to the office instead of a 5
suit, because it was the weekend.

He had a lot of people working for him, maybe sixty, and most 6
of them liked him most of the time. Three of them will be seriously
considered for his job. The obituary didn't mention that.

But it did list his "survivors" quite accurately. He is survived by 7
his wife, Helen, forty-eight years old, a good woman of no particular
marketable skills, who worked in an office before marrying and
mothering. She had, according to her daughter, given up trying to
compete with his work years ago, when the children were small.
A company friend said, "I know how much you will miss him." And
she answered, "I already have."

"Missing him all these years," she must have given up part of 8
herself which had cared too much for the man. She would be "well
taken care of."

His "dearly beloved" eldest of the "dearly beloved" children is a 9
hard-working executive in a manufacturing firm down South. In the
day and a half before the funeral, he went around the neighborhood
researching his father, asking the neighbors what he was like. They
were embarrassed.

His second child is a girl, who is twenty-four and newly married. 10
She lives near her mother and they are close, but whenever she was

alone with her father, in a car driving somewhere, they had nothing to say to each other.

The youngest is twenty, a boy, a high-school graduate who has   11
spent the last couple of years, like a lot of his friends, doing enough odd jobs to stay in grass and food. He was the one who tried to grab at his father, and tried to mean enough to him to keep the man at home. He was his father's favorite. Over the last two years, Phil stayed up nights worrying about the boy.

The boy once said, "My father and I only board here."   12

At the funeral, the sixty-year-old company president told the   13
forty-eight-year-old widow that the fifty-one-year-old deceased had meant much to the company and would be missed and would be hard to replace. The widow didn't look him in the eye. She was afraid he would read her bitterness and, after all, she would need him to straighten out the finances—the stock options and all that.

Phil was overweight and nervous and worked too hard. If he wasn't   14
at the office, he was worried about it. Phil was a Type A, a heart-attack natural. You could have picked him out in a minute from a lineup.

So when he finally worked himself to death, at precisely 3:00 A.M.   15
Sunday morning, no one was really surprised.

By 5:00 P.M. the afternoon of the funeral, the company president   16
had begun, discreetly of course, with care and taste, to make inquiries about his replacement. One of three men. He asked around: "Who's been working the hardest?"

Thinking Critically about This Reading

What is the significance of Phil's youngest son's statement, "My father and I only board here" (paragraph 12)? What does it convey about Phil's relationship with his family?

Questions for Study and Discussion

1. After reading Goodman's essay, how would you define *company man*? As you define the term, consider what such a man is not, as well as what he is. Is *company man* synonymous with *workaholic*? Explain.

2. In paragraph 4, Goodman says that Phil worked like "the Important People." How would you define that term in the context of the essay?

3. What is Goodman's purpose? (Glossary: *Purpose*) Explain.

4. Do you think Goodman's unemotional tone is appropriate for her purpose? (Glossary: *Tone; Purpose*) Why or why not?

5. Goodman repeats the day and time that Phil worked himself to death. Why are those facts important enough to bear repetition? What about them is ironic? (Glossary: *Irony*)

Classroom Activity Using Definition

The connotation of the term *workaholic* depends on the context. For Phil's employers—and at his workplace in general—the term had a positive connotation. For those who knew Phil outside the workplace, it had a negative one. Choose one of the terms below, and provide two definitions, one positive and one negative, that could apply to the term in different contexts.

go-getter   overachiever

party animal   mover and shaker

Suggested Writing Assignments

1. A procrastinator—a person who continually puts off responsibilities—is very different from a workaholic. Write an essay, modeled on Goodman's, using an extended example to define this personality type.

2. One issue Goodman does not raise is how a person becomes a workaholic. Write an essay in which you speculate about how someone might develop workaholism. How does a desirable trait like a strong work ethic begin to affect someone adversely? How might workaholism be avoided?

3. The cartoon on page 455 depicts one "businessdog" talking with another about job benefits. What is your reaction to the idea that a company will put workers "to sleep at its own expense"? What insights does the cartoon give you into Goodman's essay about work in the corporate world? Write an essay in which you describe the ideal employee-management relationship. For support, use examples from Goodman's essay, the cartoon, or your own work experiences and observations.

"*And when the time comes the company will put you to sleep at its own expense.*"

What Happiness Is

■ **Eduardo Porter**

Eduardo Porter was born in Phoenix, Arizona, in 1963, of a Mexican mother and an American father. When he was six, his family moved to Mexico City, where he lived until he graduated from the Universidad Nacional Autonoma de Mexico in 1987 with a degree in physics. Later he earned an MSc from the Imperial College of Science and Technology in London, England. Porter started his career in journalism at Notimex, *a Mexican news agency, where he wrote mostly in Spanish about the stock market and the financial world. From 1996 to 2000, he worked for* America Economia, *a business magazine for Latin America. In 2000, he moved to the Los Angeles bureau of the* Wall Street Journal, *where he covered issues related to the Hispanic community. Porter joined the* New York Times *in 2004, first as an economics writer in the newsroom and later as a member of the editorial board. Once at the* Times, *he had the opportunity to explore his long-standing interest in the ubiquity of prices. "Slowly," he shared, "the broader idea that prices are involved in every one of our decisions, that economics affect people's behavior gelled for me." His research resulted in* The Price of Everything: Solving the Mystery of Why We Pay What We Do, *published in 2011.*

In the following selection, taken from the "The Price of Happiness" chapter in The Price of Everything, *Porter sheds some light on the "slippery concept" of happiness. As you read his essay, notice how Porter explores many different perspectives—from Gandhi, Lincoln, and Kennedy to Freud and even Snoopy—on the meaning of happiness, the pursuit of which is guaranteed in the U.S. Constitution, before settling upon a broad definition from the world of economics.*

Reflecting on What You Know

What makes you happy? A good relationship? A delicious meal? Satisfying or rewarding work? Money? Is *happiness* a term that's easy for you to define, or do you find it somewhat elusive? Explain.

Happiness is a slippery concept, a bundle of meanings with no pre-   1
cise, stable definition. Lots of thinkers have taken a shot at it.
"Happiness is when what you think, what you say, and what you do
are in harmony," proposed Gandhi. Abraham Lincoln argued "most
people are about as happy as they make up their minds to be." Snoopy,
the beagle-philosopher in *Peanuts*, took what was to my mind the most
precise stab at the underlying epistemological problem. "My life has no
purpose, no direction, no aim, no meaning, and yet I'm happy. I can't
figure it out. What am I doing right?"

Most psychologists and economists who study happiness agree   2
that what they prefer to call "subjective well-being" comprises three
parts: satisfaction, meant to capture how people judge their lives
measured up against their aspirations; positive feelings like joy; and
the absence of negative feelings like anger.

It does exist. It relates directly to objective measures of people's   3
quality of life. Countries whose citizens are happier on average report
lower levels of hypertension in the population. Happier people are
less likely to come down with a cold. And if they get one, they recover more quickly. People who are wounded heal more quickly if
they are satisfied with their lives. People who say they are happier
smile more often, sleep better, report themselves to be in better health,
and have happier relatives. And some research suggests happiness
and suicide rates move in opposite directions. Happy people don't
want to die.

Still, this conceptual mélange[1] can be difficult to measure. Just   4
ask yourself how happy you are, say, on a scale of one to three, as
used by the General Social Survey. Then ask yourself what you mean
by that. Answers wander when people are confronted with these
questions. We entangle gut reactions with thoughtful analysis, and
confound sensations of immediate pleasure with evaluations of how
life meshes with our long-term aspirations. We might say we know
what will make us happy in the future—fame, fortune, or maybe a
partner. But when we get to the future, it rarely does. While we do
seem to know how to tell the difference between lifelong satisfaction
and immediate well-being, the immediate tends to contaminate the
ontological.

During an experiment in the 1980s, people who found a dime on   5
top of a Xerox machine before responding to a happiness survey

---

[1]*mélange:* a mixture often of incongruous elements.

reported a much higher sense of satisfaction with life than those who didn't. Another study found that giving people a chocolate bar improved their satisfaction with their lives. One might expect that our satisfaction with the entire span of our existence would be a fairly stable quantity—impervious to day-to-day joys and frustrations. Yet people often give a substantially different answer to the same question about lifetime happiness if it is asked again one month later.

Sigmund Freud argued that people "strive after happiness; they want to become happy and to remain so." Translating happiness into the language of economics as "utility," most economists would agree. This simple proposition gives them a powerful tool to resist Bobby Kennedy's proposal to measure not income but something else. For if happiness is what people strive for, one needn't waste time trying to figure out what makes people happy. One must only look at what people do. The fact of the matter is that people mostly choose to work and make money. Under this optic, economic growth is the outcome of our pursuit of well-being. It is what makes us happy.   6

This approach has limitations. We often make puzzling choices that do not make us consistently happier. We smoke despite knowing about cancer and emphysema. We gorge on chocolate despite knowing it will make us unhappy ten pounds down the road. Almost two thirds of Americans say they are overweight, according to a recent Gallup poll. But only a quarter say they are seriously trying to lose weight. In the 1980s a new discipline called Prospect Theory—also known as behavioral economics—deployed the tools of psychology to analyze economic behavior. It found all sorts of peculiar behaviors that don't fit economics' standard understanding of what makes us happy. For instance, losing something reduces our happiness more than winning the same thing increases it—a quirk known as loss aversion. We are unable to distinguish between choices that have slightly different odds of making us happy. We extrapolate from a few experiences to arrive at broad, mostly wrong conclusions. We herd, imitating successful behaviors around us.   7

Still, it remains generally true that we pursue what we think makes us happy—and though some of our choices may not make us happy, some will. Legend has it that Abraham Lincoln was riding in a carriage one rainy evening, telling a friend that he agreed with economists' theory that people strove to maximize their happiness, when he caught sight of a pig stuck in a muddy riverbank. He ordered the carriage to stop, got out, and pulled the pig out of the muck to safety.   8

When the friend pointed out to a mud-caked Lincoln that he had just disproved his statement by putting himself through great discomfort to save a pig, Lincoln retorted: "What I did was perfectly consistent with my theory. If I hadn't saved that pig I would have felt terrible."

So perhaps the proper response to Bobby Kennedy's angst is to 9 agree that pursuing economic growth often has negative side effects—carbon emissions, environmental degradation—that are likely to make us unhappy down the road. Still, it remains true that American citizens—and the citizens of much of the world—expend enormous amounts of time and energy pursuing more money and a bigger GDP because they think it will improve their well-being. And that will make them happy.

Thinking Critically about This Reading

What do you think that Porter means when he says, "While we do seem to know how to tell the difference between lifelong satisfaction and immediate well-being, the immediate tends to contaminate the ontological" (paragraph 4). Do you agree with Porter?

Questions for Study and Discussion

1. Porter opens his essay with the statement, "Happiness is a slippery concept, a bundle of meanings with no precise, stable definition." How does he illustrate this generalization? (Glossary: *Example*) How effective did you find this beginning? (Glossary: *Beginnings and Endings*)

2. According to Porter, what are the three parts of what psychologists and economists call "subjective well-being" (2)? Why is it useful to have this information when discussing the meaning of happiness? Explain.

3. In what ways is happiness related to a person's "quality of life" (3)? What character traits, according to Porter, do happy people possess?

4. What point does Porter make with the story about Abraham Lincoln and the pig?

5. How does Porter use economics to explain what he thinks that happiness is? What are the limitations, if any, of his economic model?

Classroom Activity Using Definition

Definitions often depend on perspective, as Porter illustrates in his essay with the word *happiness*. Discuss with your classmates other words or terms (such as *competition, wealth, success, jerk, superstar, failure, poverty, luxury, beauty*) whose definitions depend on one's perspective. Choose several of these words, and write brief definitions for each of them from your perspective. Share your definitions with your classmates, and discuss how perspective affects the way we all define things in our world differently.

Suggested Writing Assignments

1. Using Porter's essay or Asimov's "Intelligence" (pp. 49–51) as a model, write a short essay in which you define one of the following abstract terms or another similar term of your own choosing. Before beginning to write, you may find it helpful to review what you and your classmates discovered in the Classroom Activity for this selection.

friendship	freedom	trust
commitment	love	hate
peace	liberty	charm
success	failure	beauty

2. How much stock do you put in Porter's claim that "people mostly choose to work and make money. . . . It is what makes us happy" (6)? Or do you side with Bobby Kennedy's "proposal to measure not income but something else"? Write an essay in which you present your position in this debate on what happiness is.

Division and Classification

A writer practices **division** by separating a class of things or ideas into categories following a clear principle or basis. In the following paragraph, journalist Robert MacNeil establishes categories of speech according to their level of formality:

> It fascinates me how differently we all speak in different circumstances. We have levels of formality, as in our clothing. There are very formal occasions, often requiring written English: the job application or the letter to the editor—the darksuit, serious-tie language, with everything pressed and the lint brushed off. There is our less formal out-in-the-world language—a more comfortable suit, but still respectable. There is language for close friends in the evenings, on weekends—bluejeans-and-sweat-shirt language, when it's good to get the tie off. There is family language, even more relaxed, full of grammatical short cuts, family slang, echoes of old jokes that have become intimate shorthand—the language of pajamas and uncombed hair. Finally, there is the language with no clothes on; the talk of couples—murmurs, sighs, grunts—language at its least self-conscious, open, vulnerable, and primitive.
>
> –Robert MacNeil

With **classification,** on the other hand, a writer groups individual objects or ideas into already established categories. Division and classification can operate separately but often accompany each other. Here, for example, is a passage about levers in which the writer first discusses generally how levers work. In the second paragraph, the writer uses division to establish three categories of levers and then uses classification to group individual levers into those categories:

> Every lever has one fixed point called the "fulcrum" and is acted on by two forces—the "effort" (exertion of hand muscles) and the "weight" (object's resistance). Levers work according to a

simple formula: the effort (how hard you push or pull) multiplied by its distance from the fulcrum (effort arm) equals the weight multiplied by its distance from the fulcrum (weight arm). Thus two pounds of effort exerted at a distance of four feet from the fulcrum will raise eight pounds located one foot from the fulcrum.

There are three types of levers, conventionally called "first kind," "second kind," and "third kind." Levers of the first kind have the fulcrum located between the effort and the weight. Examples are a pump handle, an oar, a crowbar, a weighing balance, a pair of scissors, and a pair of pliers. Levers of the second kind have the weight in the middle and magnify the effort. Examples are the handcar crank and doors. Levers of the third kind, such as a power shovel or a baseball batter's forearm, have the effort in the middle and always magnify the distance.

The following paragraph introduces a classification of the kinds of decisions one has to make when purchasing a mobile phone:

> When you buy a mobile phone you have a great number of options in phone technology and business offerings from which to choose; for example, plan type, coverage, minutes, data usage, voice communications, battery life, design, size, and weight. In just the area of design alone, there are even more options, each with its own advantages and disadvantages: flip, candy-bar, clamshell, slider, and swivel or twist open (with single or dual screens) styles.
>
> –Freddy Chessa, student

In writing, division and classification are affected directly by the writer's practical purpose—what the writer wants to explain or prove. That purpose determines the class of things or ideas being divided and classified. For instance, a writer might divide television programs according to their audiences (adults, families, or children) and then classify individual programs into each category to show that television networks value certain audiences more than others. A writer who is concerned about violence in television programming would divide programs into those with and without fights and murders and then would classify several programs into those categories. Other writers with different purposes might divide television programs differently (by the day and time of broadcast, for example, or by the number of women featured in prominent roles) and then would classify individual programs accordingly.

Another example may help clarify how division and classification work hand in hand in writing. Suppose a sociologist wants to determine whether income level influences voting behavior in a particular neighborhood. The sociologist chooses as her subject the 15 families living on Maple Street. Her goal then becomes to group these families in a way that is relevant to her purpose. She knows that she wants to divide the neighborhood in two ways—according to (1) income level (low, middle, and high) and (2) voting behavior (voters and nonvoters)—but her process of division won't be complete until she can classify the 15 families into her five groupings.

In confidential interviews with each family, the sociologist learns what the family's income is and whether any member of the household voted in a state or federal election in the last four years. Based on this information, she classifies each family according to her established categories and at the same time divides the neighborhood into the subclasses that are crucial to her study. Her work leads her to construct the following diagram of her divisions and classifications.

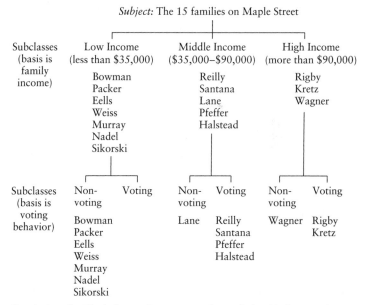

Purpose: To group 15 families according to income and voting behavior and to study the relationships between the two.

Subject: The 15 families on Maple Street

Subclasses (basis is family income)	Low Income (less than $35,000)	Middle Income ($35,000–$90,000)	High Income (more than $90,000)
	Bowman Packer Eells Weiss Murray Nadel Sikorski	Reilly Santana Lane Pfeffer Halstead	Rigby Kretz Wagner

Subclasses (basis is voting behavior)	Non-voting	Voting	Non-voting	Voting	Non-voting	Voting
	Bowman Packer Eells Weiss Murray Nadel Sikorski		Lane	Reilly Santana Pfeffer Halstead	Wagner	Rigby Kretz

Conclusion: On Maple Street, there seems to be a relationship between income level and voting behavior: the low-income families are nonvoters.

The diagram on page 463 allows the sociologist to visualize her division and classification system and its essential components—subject, basis or principle of division, subclasses or categories, and conclusion. Her ultimate conclusion depends on her ability to work back and forth among divisions, subclasses, and the actual families to be classified.

The following guidelines can help you use division and classification in your writing:

1. *Identify a clear purpose, and use a principle of division that is appropriate to that purpose.* If you want to examine the common characteristics of four-year athletic scholarship recipients at your college or university, you might consider the following principles of division—program of study, sport, place of origin, or gender. In this case, it would not be useful to divide students on the basis of their favorite type of music because that seems irrelevant to your purpose.

2. *Divide your subject into unique categories.* An item can belong to only one category. For example, don't divide students as men, women, and athletes.

3. *Make your division and classification complete.* Your categories should account for all items in a subject class. In dividing students on the basis of geographic origin, for example, don't consider only the United States because such a division does not account for foreign students. For your classification to be complete, every student must be placed in one of the established categories.

4. *State the conclusion that your division and classification lead you to draw.* For example, after conducting your division and classification of athletic scholarship recipients, you might conclude that the majority of male athletes with athletic scholarships come from the western United States.

The Ways of Meeting Oppression

■ Martin Luther King Jr.

Martin Luther King Jr. (1929–1968) was the leading spokesman for the rights of African Americans during the 1950s and 1960s before his assassination in 1968. He established the Southern Christian Leadership Conference, organized many civil rights demonstrations, and opposed the Vietnam War and the draft. In 1964, he was awarded the Nobel Peace Prize.

In the following essay, taken from his book Strive toward Freedom *(1958), King classifies the three ways that oppressed people throughout history have reacted to their oppressors. As you read, pay particular attention to how King orders his discussion of the three types of oppression to support his argument and the conclusion he presents in paragraph 8.*

Reflecting on What You Know

Isaac Asimov once said, "Violence is the last refuge of the incompetent." What are your thoughts on the reasons for violent behavior on either a personal or a national level? Is violence ever justified? If so, under what circumstances?

Oppressed people deal with their oppression in three characteristic 1
ways. One way is acquiescence: the oppressed resign themselves to their doom. They tacitly adjust themselves to oppression, and thereby become conditioned to it. In every movement toward freedom some of the oppressed prefer to remain oppressed. Almost 2800 years ago Moses[1] set out to lead the children of Israel from the slavery of Egypt to the freedom of the promised land. He soon discovered that slaves

---

[1]*Moses:* a Hebrew prophet, teacher, and leader in the fourteenth to thirteenth centuries B.C.E.

do not always welcome their deliverers. They become accustomed to being slaves. They would rather bear those ills they have, as Shakespeare pointed out, than flee to others that they know not of. They prefer the "fleshpots of Egypt" to the ordeals of emancipation.

There is such a thing as the freedom of exhaustion. Some people are so worn down by the yoke of oppression that they give up. A few years ago in the slum areas of Atlanta, a Negro guitarist used to sing almost daily: "Been down so long that down don't bother me."[2] This is the type of negative freedom and resignation that often engulfs the life of the oppressed.

But this is not the way out. To accept passively an unjust system is to cooperate with that system; thereby the oppressed become as evil as the oppressor. Noncooperation with evil is as much a moral obligation as is cooperation with good. The oppressed must never allow the conscience of the oppressor to slumber. Religion reminds every man that he is his brother's keeper. To accept injustice or segregation passively is to say to the oppressor that his actions are morally right. It is a way of allowing his conscience to fall asleep. At this moment the oppressed fails to be his brother's keeper. So acquiescence—while often the easier way—is not the moral way. It is the way of the coward. The Negro cannot win the respect of his oppressor by acquiescing; he merely increases the oppressor's arrogance and contempt. Acquiescence is interpreted as proof of the Negro's inferiority. The Negro cannot win the respect of the white people of the South or the peoples of the world if he is willing to sell the future of his children for his personal and immediate comfort and safety.

A second way that oppressed people sometimes deal with oppression is to resort to physical violence and corroding hatred. Violence often brings about momentary results. Nations have frequently won their independence in battle. But in spite of temporary victories, violence never brings permanent peace. It solves no social problem; it merely creates new and more complicated ones.

Violence as a way of achieving racial justice is both impractical and immoral. It is impractical because it is a descending spiral ending in destruction for all. The old law of an eye for an eye leaves everybody blind. It is immoral because it seeks to humiliate the opponent rather than win his understanding; it seeks to annihilate rather than

---

[2] *"Been down . . . bother me"*: lyric possibly adapted from "Stormy Blues" by American jazz singer Billie Holiday (1915–1959).

to convert. Violence is immoral because it thrives on hatred rather than love. It destroys community and makes brotherhood impossible. It leaves society in monologue rather than dialogue. Violence ends by defeating itself. It creates bitterness in the survivors and brutality in the destroyers. A voice echoes through time saying to every potential Peter, "Put up your sword."[3] History is cluttered with the wreckage of nations that failed to follow this command.

If the American Negro and other victims of oppression succumb   6
to the temptation of using violence in the struggle for freedom, future generations will be the recipients of a desolate night of bitterness, and our chief legacy to them will be an endless reign of meaningless chaos. Violence is not the way.

The third way open to oppressed people in their quest for free-   7
dom is the way of nonviolent resistance. Like the synthesis in Hegelian[4] philosophy, the principle of nonviolent resistance seeks to reconcile the truths of two opposites — acquiescence and violence — while avoiding the extremes and immoralities of both. The nonviolent resister agrees with the person who acquiesces that one should not be physically aggressive toward his opponent; but he balances the equation by agreeing with the person of violence that evil must be resisted. He avoids the nonresistance of the former and the violent resistance of the latter. With nonviolent resistance, no individual or group need submit to any wrong, nor need anyone resort to violence in order to right a wrong.

It seems to me that this is the method that must guide the actions   8
of the Negro in the present crisis in race relations. Through nonviolent resistance the Negro will be able to rise to the noble height of opposing the unjust system while loving the perpetrators of the system. The Negro must work passionately and unrelentingly for full stature as a citizen, but he must not use inferior methods to gain it. He must never come to terms with falsehood, malice, hate, or destruction.

Nonviolent resistance makes it possible for the Negro to remain   9
in the South and struggle for his rights. The Negro's problem will not be solved by running away. He cannot listen to the glib suggestion of those who would urge him to migrate en masse to other sections of

---

[3] *"Put up your sword":* the apostle Peter had drawn his sword to defend Jesus from arrest; the voice was Jesus's, who surrendered himself for trial and crucifixion (John 18:11).
[4] *Georg Wilhelm Friedrich Hegel* (1770–1831): German philosopher.

the country. By grasping his great opportunity in the South he can make a lasting contribution to the moral strength of the nation and set a sublime example of courage for generations yet unborn.

By nonviolent resistance, the Negro can also enlist all men of good will in his struggle for equality. The problem is not a purely racial one, with Negroes set against whites. In the end, it is not a struggle between people at all, but a tension between justice and injustice. Nonviolent resistance is not aimed against oppressors but against oppression. Under its banner consciences, not racial groups, are enlisted.

Thinking Critically about This Reading

King states "There is such a thing as the freedom of exhaustion" (paragraph 2). Why, according to King, is this type of freedom "negative"?

Questions for Study and Discussion

1. What is King's thesis? (Glossary: *Thesis*)
2. How does classifying the three types of resistance to oppression help him develop his thesis?
3. Why do you suppose King discusses acquiescence, violence, and nonviolent resistance in that order? What organizational principle does he use to rank them?
4. How does King's organizational pattern help him build his argument and support his thesis? Would his argument work as well if he changed the order of his discussion? Why or why not?
5. King states that he favors nonviolent resistance over the other two ways of meeting oppression. What disadvantages does he see in meeting oppression with acquiescence or with violence?

Classroom Activity Using Division and Classification

Be prepared to discuss in class why you believe that division and classification are important ways of thinking about everyday life. Give examples of how you use the two complementary strategies when you use a computer search engine, shop for DVDs on the Web, select items in your local supermarket, or look for textbooks in your college bookstore.

Suggested Writing Assignments

1. Using King's essay as a model, write an essay on various solutions to a current social or personal problem. Organize your ideas according to a rational scheme relying on the principles of division and classification. Be sure that you have a clear thesis statement and that the division and classification you employ to develop your essay help convince your reader of your ideas and beliefs.

2. King's use of division and classification in "The Ways of Meeting Oppression" is simple, logical, and natural. He knows that the oppressed can't give in to their oppressors, can't answer violence with violence, and therefore must take a third path of nonviolent resistance to rise above their enemies. Using King's essay as model, write an essay in which you discuss how to respond to prejudice, hatred, competition, greed, aggression, or some other social force that we all find difficult to overcome.

What Are Friends For?

■ Marion Winik

Marion Winik is a poet, freelance writer, radio commentator, and writer of essays. She was born in 1958 in New York City and grew up on the New Jersey shore. A graduate of Brown University in 1978, she earned her MFA from Brooklyn College in 1983. Her first literary efforts were two books of poetry published by small presses: Nonstop *(1981)* and BoyCrazy *(1986). After being contacted by a literary agent, Winik published* Telling *(1994), her first collection of essays, some of which were previously published in* Texas Quarterly, Parenting, American Way, *the* Austin Chronicle, *and the* Houston Chronicle. *She wrote about her marriage to her husband, Tony, who died of AIDS in* First Comes Love *(1996), which became a* New York Times Notable Book *for that year. She followed it with an account of life as a single mom,* The Lunch-Box Chronicles: Notes from the Parenting Underground *(1998), and a book of advice,* Rules for the Unruly: Living an Unconventional Life *(2001). Her last two books are another collection of her essays,* Above Us the Sky *(2005), and a book of very short essays in which she remembers people important in her life,* The Glen Rock Book of the Dead *(2008).*

In the following essay, first published in Telling *(1994), Winik classifies her friends, among them Buddies, Relative Friends, Faraway Friends, Friends You Love to Hate, and Hero Friends.*

Reflecting on What You Know

Think about your friends. Do you regard them all in the same light? Would you group them in any way? If so, on what basis would you group them?

I was thinking about how everybody can't be everything to each other, but some people can be something to each other, thank God, from the ones whose shoulder you cry on to the ones whose half-slips you borrow to the nameless ones you chat with in the grocery line.

Buddies, for example, are the workhorses of the friendship 2
world, the people out there on the front lines, defending you from
loneliness and boredom. They call you up, they listen to your complaints, they celebrate your successes and curse your misfortunes,
and you do the same for them in return. They hold out through in-
numerable crises before concluding that the person you're dating is
no good, and even then understand if you ignore their good coun-
sel. They accompany you to a movie with subtitles or to see the diving pig at Aquarena Springs. They feed your cat when you are out
of town and pick you up from the airport when you get back. They
come over to help you decide what to wear on a date. Even if it is
with that creep.

What about family members? Most of them are people you just 3
got stuck with, and though you love them, you may not have very
much in common. But there is that rare exception, the Relative
Friend. It is your cousin, your brother, maybe even your aunt. The
two of you share the same views of the other family members. Meg
never should have divorced Martin. He was the best thing that ever
happened to her. You can confirm each other's memories of things
that happened a long time ago. Don't you remember when Uncle
Hank and Daddy had that awful fight in the middle of Thanksgiving
dinner? Grandma always hated Grandpa's stamp collection; she
probably left the window open during the hurricane on purpose.

While so many family relationships are tinged with guilt and ob- 4
ligation, a relationship with a Relative Friend is relatively worry-free.
You don't even have to hide your vices from this delightful person.
When you slip out Aunt Joan's back door for a cigarette, she is
already there.

Then there is that special guy at work. Like all the other people 5
at the job site, at first he's just part of the scenery. But gradually he
starts to stand out from the crowd. Your friendship is cemented by
jokes about co-workers and thoughtful favors around the office. Did
you see Ryan's hair? Want half my bagel? Soon you know the names
of his turtles, what he did last Friday night, exactly which model CD
player he wants for his birthday. His handwriting is as familiar to you
as your own.

Though you invite each other to parties, you somehow don't 6
quite fit into each other's outside lives. For this reason, the friendship may not survive a job change. Company gossip, once an infallible source of entertainment, soon awkwardly accentuates the

distance between you. But wait. Like School Friends, Work Friends share certain memories which acquire a nostalgic glow after about a decade.

A Faraway Friend is someone you grew up with or went to school   7
with or lived in the same town as until one of you moved away. Without a Faraway Friend, you would never get any mail addressed in handwriting. A Faraway Friend calls late at night, invites you to her wedding, always says she is coming to visit but rarely shows up. An actual visit from a Faraway Friend is a cause for celebration and binges of all kinds. Cigarettes, Chips Ahoy, bottles of tequila.

Faraway Friends go through phases of intense communication,   8
then may be out of touch for many months. Either way, the connection is always there. A conversation with your Faraway Friend always helps to put your life in perspective: when you feel you've hit a dead end, come to a confusing fork in the road, or gotten lost in some crackerbox subdivision of your life, the advice of the Faraway Friend—who has the big picture, who is so well acquainted with the route that brought you to this place—is indispensable.

Another useful function of the Faraway Friend is to help you re-   9
member things from a long time ago, like the name of your seventh-grade history teacher, what was in that really good stir-fry, or exactly what happened that night on the boat with the guys from Florida.

Ah, the Former Friend. A sad thing. At best a wistful memory, at   10
worst a dangerous enemy who is in possession of many of your deepest secrets. But what was it that drove you apart? A misunderstanding, a betrayed confidence, an unrepaid loan, an ill-conceived flirtation. A poor choice of spouse can do in a friendship just like that. Going into business together can be a serious mistake. Time, money, distance, cult religions: all noted friendship killers. . . .

And lest we forget, there are the Friends You Love to Hate. They   11
call at inopportune times. They say stupid things. They butt in, they boss you around, they embarrass you in public. They invite themselves over. They take advantage. You've done the best you can, but they need professional help. On top of all this, they love you to death and are convinced they're your best friend on the planet.

So why do you continue to be involved with these people? Why   12
do you tolerate them? On the contrary, the real question is, What would you do without them? Without Friends You Love to Hate, there would be nothing to talk about with your other friends. Their problems and their irritating stunts provide a reliable source of

conversation for everyone they know. What's more, Friends You Love to Hate make you feel good about yourself, since you are obviously in so much better shape than they are. No matter what these people do, you will never get rid of them. As much as they need you, you need them too.

At the other end of the spectrum are Hero Friends. These people 13 are better than the rest of us, that's all there is to it. Their career is something you wanted to be when you grew up—painter, forest ranger, tireless doer of good. They have beautiful homes filled with special handmade things presented to them by villagers in the remote areas they have visited in their extensive travels. Yet they are modest. They never gossip. They are always helping others, especially those who have suffered a death in the family or an illness. You would think people like this would just make you sick, but somehow they don't.

A New Friend is a tonic unlike any other. Say you meet her at a 14 party. In your bowling league. At a Japanese conversation class, perhaps. Wherever, whenever, there's that spark of recognition. The first time you talk, you can't believe how much you have in common. Suddenly, your life story is interesting again, your insights fresh, your opinion valued. Your various shortcomings are as yet completely invisible.

It's almost like falling in love. 15

Thinking Critically about This Reading

Is Winik talking about classifying both female and male friends in her essay, is she speaking only of female friends, or is it difficult to determine whom her subjects are? Support your answer with evidence from the essay.

Questions for Study and Discussion

1. How does Winik's opening paragraph set up her division and classification? (Glossary: *Beginnings and Endings*)
2. What is Winik's purpose in this essay? (Glossary: *Purpose*)
3. How does Winik illustrate the types of friends she presents? (Glossary: *Illustration*)
4. Why do Friends You Love to Hate need you as much as you need them?

5. What are the special virtues of a New Friend?

6. What is Winik's tone in this essay? Is it appropriate to her purpose? Explain. (Glossary: *Tone*)

Classroom Activity Using Division and Classification

The drawing on page 475 is a basic exercise in classification. By determining the features the figures have in common, establish the general class to which they belong. Next, establish subclasses by determining the distinctive features that distinguish one subclass from another. Finally, place each figure in an appropriate subclass within your classification system. You may wish to compare your system with those developed by other members of your class and to discuss any differences that exist.

Suggested Writing Assignments

1. Review the categories of friends Winik establishes in her essay. Do the categories apply to your friends? What new categories would you create? Write an essay in which you explain the types of friends in your life.

2. In her essay, Winik appears to focus on the types of friendships between women. (Glossary: *Focus*) What about friendships between men, one of which is represented in the cartoon on page 476? What statement does the cartoon make about the nature of men's friendships? (Glossary: *Comparison and Contrast*) Using Winik's essay as a model, write an essay in which you divide and classify the friendships that you as a man have with other men or that you observe men to have. Interview others, if you find it necessary.

3. Music can be classified into many different types (such as jazz, country, pop, rock, soul, rap, classical, big band, western, blues, gospel). Each of these large classifications has a lot of variety within it. Write an essay in which you identify your favorite type of music as well as at least three subclassifications of that music. Explain the characteristics of each category, and use two or three artists and their songs as examples.

A friend will give up his life for you.
A *real* friend will help you move.

Doubts about Doublespeak

■ William Lutz

William Lutz is a professor of English at Rutgers University–Camden and was the editor of the Quarterly Review of Doublespeak *for 14 years. Born in Racine, Wisconsin, in 1940, Lutz is best known for* Doublespeak: From Revenue Enhancement to Terminal Living *(1990) and* The New Doublespeak: Why No One Knows What Anyone's Saying Anymore *(1996). His book* Doublespeak Defined: Cut through the Bull**** and Get to the Point *was published in 1999. (The term* doublespeak *was coined by George Orwell in his novel* Nineteen Eighty-Four. *It refers to speech or writing that presents two or more contradictory ideas in a way that deceives an unsuspecting audience.) As chair of the National Council of Teachers of English's Committee on Public Doublespeak, Lutz has been a watchdog of public officials who use language to "mislead, distort, deceive, inflate, circumvent, and obfuscate." Each year, the committee presents the Orwell Awards to recognize outrageous uses of doublespeak in government and business.*

The following essay first appeared in the July 1993 issue of State Government News. *As you read, notice how Lutz organizes his essay by naming and defining four categories of doublespeak, describing each one's function or consequences, and giving examples of each type. This organizational pattern is simple, practical, and easy to follow.*

Reflecting on What You Know

Imagine that you work for a manufacturing plant in your town and that your boss has just told you that you are on the list of people who will be "dehired" or that you are part of a program of "negative employee retention." What would you think was happening to you? Would you be happy about it? What would you think of the language that your boss used to describe your situation?

During the past year, we learned that we can shop at a "unique   1
retail biosphere" instead of a farmers' market, where we can buy
items made of "synthetic glass" instead of plastic, or purchase a "high
velocity, multipurpose air circulator," or electric fan. A "waste-water
conveyance facility" may "exceed the odor threshold" from time to
time due to the presence of "regulated human nutrients," but that is
not to be confused with a sewage plant that stinks up the neighborhood with sewage sludge. Nor should we confuse a "resource development park" with a dump. Thus does doublespeak continue to spread.

Doublespeak is language which pretends to communicate but   2
doesn't. It is language which makes the bad seem good, the negative
seem positive, the unpleasant seem attractive, or at least tolerable. It
is language which avoids, shifts, or denies responsibility; language
which is at variance with its real or purported meaning. It is language
which conceals or prevents thought.

Doublespeak is all around us. We are asked to check our packages   3
at the desk "for our convenience" when it's not for our convenience at
all but for someone else's convenience. We see advertisements for "pre-
owned," "experienced," or "previously distinguished" cars, not used
cars, and for "genuine imitation leather," "virgin vinyl," or "real coun-
terfeit diamonds." Television offers not reruns but "encore telecasts."
There are no slums or ghettos, just the "inner city" or "substandard
housing" where the "disadvantaged" or "economically nonaffluent"
live and where there might be a problem with "substance abuse."
Nonprofit organizations don't make a profit, they have "negative defi-
cits" or experience "revenue excesses." With doublespeak it's not dying
but "terminal living" or "negative patient care outcome."

There are four kinds of doublespeak. The first kind is the euphe-   4
mism, a word or phrase designed to avoid a harsh or distasteful reality.
Used to mislead or deceive, the euphemism becomes doublespeak. In
1984 the U.S. State Department's annual reports on the status of human
rights around the world ceased using the word "killing." Instead the
State Department used the phrase "unlawful or arbitrary deprivation of
life," thus avoiding the embarrassing situation of government-sanctioned
killing in countries supported by the United States.

A second kind of doublespeak is jargon, the specialized language   5
of a trade, profession, or similar group, such as doctors, lawyers,
plumbers, or car mechanics. Legitimately used, jargon allows members of a group to communicate with each other clearly, efficiently,
and quickly. Lawyers and tax accountants speak to each other of an

"involuntary conversion" of property, a legal term that means the loss or destruction of property through theft, accident, or condemnation. But when lawyers or tax accountants use unfamiliar terms to speak to others, then the jargon becomes doublespeak.

In 1978 a commercial 727 crashed on takeoff, killing three   6 passengers, injuring twenty-one others, and destroying the airplane. The insured value of the airplane was greater than its book value, so the airline made a profit of $1.7 million, creating two problems: the airline didn't want to talk about one of its airplanes crashing, yet it had to account for that $1.7 million profit in its annual report to its stockholders. The airline solved both problems by inserting a footnote in its annual report which explained that the $1.7 million was due to "the involuntary conversion of a 727."

A third kind of doublespeak is gobbledygook or bureaucratese.   7 Such doublespeak is simply a matter of overwhelming the audience with words—the more the better. Alan Greenspan, a polished practitioner of bureaucratese, once testified before a Senate committee that "it is a tricky problem to find the particular calibration in timing that would be appropriate to stem the acceleration in risk premiums created by falling incomes without prematurely aborting the decline in the inflation-generated risk premiums."

The fourth kind of doublespeak is inflated language, which is   8 designed to make the ordinary seem extraordinary, to make everyday things seem impressive, to give an air of importance to people or situations, to make the simple seem complex. Thus do car mechanics become "automotive internists," elevator operators become "members of the vertical transportation corps," grocery store checkout clerks become "career associate scanning professionals," and smelling something becomes "organoleptic analysis."

Doublespeak is not the product of careless language or sloppy   9 thinking. Quite the opposite. Doublespeak is language carefully designed and constructed to appear to communicate when in fact it doesn't. It is language designed not to lead but mislead. Thus, it's not a tax increase but "revenue enhancement" or "tax-base broadening." So how can you complain about higher taxes? Those aren't useless, billion dollar pork barrel projects; they're really "congressional projects of national significance," so don't complain about wasteful government spending. That isn't the Mafia in Atlantic City; those are just "members of a career-offender cartel," so don't worry about the influence of organized crime in the city.

New doublespeak is created every day. The Environmental 10
Protection Agency once called acid rain "poorly-buffered precipitation," then dropped that term in favor of "atmospheric deposition of anthropogenically-derived acidic substances," but recently decided that acid rain should be called "wet deposition." The Pentagon, which has in the past given us such classic doublespeak as "hexiform rotatable surface compression unit" for steel nut, just published a pamphlet warning soldiers that exposure to nerve gas will lead to "immediate permanent incapacitation." That's almost as good as the Pentagon's official term "servicing the target," meaning to kill the enemy. Meanwhile, the Department of Energy wants to establish a "monitored retrievable storage site," a place once known as a dump for spent nuclear fuel.

Bad economic times give rise to lots of new doublespeak designed 11
to avoid some very unpleasant economic realities. As the "contained depression" continues so does the corporate policy of making up even more new terms to avoid the simple, and easily understandable, term "layoff." So it is that corporations "reposition," "restructure," "reshape," or "realign" the company and "reduce duplication" through "release of resources" that involves a "permanent downsizing" or a "payroll adjustment" that results in a number of employees being "involuntarily terminated."

Other countries regularly contribute to doublespeak. In Japan, 12
where baldness is called "hair disadvantaged," the economy is undergoing a "severe adjustment process," while in Canada there is an "involuntary downward development" of the work force. For some government agencies in Canada, wastepaper baskets have become "user friendly, space effective, flexible, deskside sortation units." Politicians in Canada may engage in "reality augmentation," but they never lie. As part of their new freedom, the people of Moscow can visit "intimacy salons," or sex shops as they're known in other countries. When dealing with the bureaucracy in Russia, people know that they should show officials "normal gratitude," or give them a bribe.

The worst doublespeak is the doublespeak of death. It is the lan- 13
guage, wrote George Orwell in 1946, that is "largely the defense of the indefensible . . . designed to make lies sound truthful and murder respectable, and to give an appearance of solidity to pure wind." In the doublespeak of death, Orwell continued, "defenseless villages are bombarded from the air, the inhabitants driven out into the countryside, the cattle machine-gunned, the huts set on fire with incendiary bullets. This is called pacification. Millions of peasants are

robbed of their farms and sent trudging along the roads with no more than they can carry. This is called transfer of population or rectification of frontiers." Today, in a country once called Yugoslavia, this is called "ethnic cleansing."[1]

It's easy to laugh off doublespeak. After all, we all know what's 14 going on, so what's the harm? But we don't always know what's going on, and when that happens, doublespeak accomplishes its ends. It alters our perception of reality. It deprives us of the tools we need to develop, advance, and preserve our society, our culture, our civilization. It breeds suspicion, cynicism, distrust, and, ultimately, hostility. It delivers us into the hands of those who do not have our interests at heart. As Samuel Johnson[2] noted in eighteenth-century England, even the devils in hell do not lie to one another, since the society of hell could not subsist without the truth, any more than any other society.

Thinking Critically about This Reading

According to Lutz, doublespeak "alters our perception of reality. . . . It breeds suspicion, cynicism, distrust, and, ultimately, hostility" (paragraph 14). What is Lutz's plan for combating doublespeak and its negative effects?

Questions for Study and Discussion

1. What is Lutz's thesis? (Glossary: *Thesis*)
2. The author divides doublespeak into four categories. What are they?
3. For what purpose has Lutz used division and classification? (Glossary: *Purpose*)
4. Why might Lutz have ordered the categories as he has? (Glossary: *Organization*)
5. Are Lutz's illustrative examples good ones? (Glossary: *Example*) Why or why not? Should he have used fewer examples? More examples? Explain.
6. Could the order of Lutz's first two paragraphs be reversed? (Glossary: *Beginnings and Endings*) What would be gained or lost if they were?

---

[1] *"ethnic cleansing":* Lutz is referring to the breakup of the Federal Republic of Yugoslavia in the Balkan region of southeastern Europe in the early 1990s and the 1992–1995 genocide centered in the cities of Sarajevo and Srebrenica.
[2] *Samuel Johnson (1709–1784):* an important English writer.

7. Reread Lutz's last paragraph, where he makes some serious claims about the importance of doublespeak. Is such seriousness on his part justified by what he has written about doublespeak in the body of his essay? Why or why not?

Classroom Activity Using Division and Classification

Examine the following lists of hobbies, books, and buildings. Determine at least three principles that could be used to divide the items listed in each group. Finally, classify the items in each group according to one of the principles you have established.

Hobbies

watching sports on TV   surfing the Web

stamp collecting   hiking

scuba diving   dancing

Books

The Adventures of   *Guinness Book of*
Huckleberry Finn   *World Records*

American Heritage Dictionary   *To Kill a Mockingbird*

The Joy of Cooking   *Gone with the Wind*

Buildings

Empire State Building   Taj Mahal

White House   Library of Congress

The Alamo   Buckingham Palace

Suggested Writing Assignments

1. Write an essay in which you consider the effects of doublespeak. Is it always a form of lying? Is it harmful to our society, and if so, how? How can we measure its effects? Be sure to cite instances of doublespeak that are not included in Lutz's essay. You can uncover these through your reading, Web browsing, or library research.

2. College is a time of stress for many students. In an essay, use division and classification to discuss the different kinds of pressure students experience at your school.

Comparison and Contrast

A **comparison** points out the ways that two or more people, places, or things are alike. A **contrast** points out how they differ. The subjects of a comparison or contrast should be in the same class or general category; if they have nothing in common, there is no good reason for setting them side by side.

The function of any comparison or contrast is to clarify and explain. The writer's purpose may be simply to inform or to make readers aware of similarities or differences that are interesting and significant in themselves. Or the writer may explain something unfamiliar by comparing it with something very familiar, perhaps explaining the game of squash by comparing it with tennis. Finally, the writer can point out the superiority of one thing by contrasting it with another—for example, showing that one product is the best by contrasting it with all its competitors.

As a writer, you have two main options for organizing a comparison or contrast: the subject-by-subject pattern or the point-by-point pattern. For a short essay comparing and contrasting the cities of Philadelphia, Pennsylvania, and San Diego, California, as vacation destinations, you would probably follow the *subject-by-subject* pattern of organization. With this pattern, you first discuss the points you wish to make about one city and then discuss the corresponding points for the other city. An outline of the body of your essay might look like this:

Subject-by-Subject Pattern

   I. Philadelphia
      A. Climate
      B. Public transportation
      C. Tourist attractions (museums, zoos, theme parks)
      D. Accommodations

II. San Diego
   A. Climate
   B. Public transportation
   C. Tourist attractions (museums, zoos, theme parks)
   D. Accommodations

The subject-by-subject pattern presents a unified discussion of each city by emphasizing the cities and not the four points of comparison. Because these points are relatively few, readers should easily remember what was said about Philadelphia's climate when you later discuss San Diego's climate and should be able to make the appropriate connections between them.

For a somewhat longer essay comparing and contrasting solar energy and wind energy, however, you should consider the *point-by-point* pattern of organization. With this pattern, your essay is organized according to the various points of comparison. Discussion alternates between solar and wind energy for each point of comparison. An outline of the body of your essay might look like this:

Point-by-Point Pattern

I. Installation expenses	IV. Convenience
A. Solar	A. Solar
B. Wind	B. Wind
II. Efficiency	V. Maintenance
A. Solar	A. Solar
B. Wind	B. Wind
III. Operating costs	VI. Safety
A. Solar	A. Solar
B. Wind	B. Wind

With the point-by-point pattern, the writer makes immediate comparisons between solar and wind energy so that readers can consider each similarity and difference separately.

Each organizational pattern has its advantages. In general, the subject-by-subject pattern is useful in short essays where few points are to be considered, and the point-by-point pattern is preferable in long essays where numerous points are under consideration.

A good essay of comparison and contrast tells readers something significant that they do not already know—that is, it must do more than merely point out the obvious. As a rule, therefore, writers tend to draw contrasts between things that are usually perceived as being similar or comparisons between things usually perceived as being different. In fact, comparison and contrast often go together. For example, an essay about the twin cities of Minneapolis and St. Paul might begin by showing how much they are alike but end with a series of contrasts revealing how much they differ. A consumer magazine might report the contrasting claims made by six car manufacturers and then go on to demonstrate that the cars all actually do much the same thing in the same way.

The following student essay about hunting and photography explores the increasing popularity of photographic safaris. After first pointing out the obvious differences between hunting with a gun and hunting with a camera, the writer focuses on the similarities between the two activities that make many hunters "willing to trade their guns for cameras." Notice how she successfully uses the subject-by-subject organizational plan in the body of her essay to explore three key similarities between hunters and photographers.

Guns and Cameras

The hunter has a deep interest in the apparatus he uses to kill his prey. He carries various types of guns, different kinds of ammunition, and special sights and telescopes to increase his chances of success. He knows the mechanics of his guns and understands how and why they work. This fascination with the hardware of his sport is practical—it helps him achieve his goal—but it frequently becomes an end, almost a hobby in itself.

Not until the very end of the long process of stalking an animal does a game hunter use his gun. First he enters into the animal's world. He studies his prey, its habitat, its daily habits, its watering holes and feeding areas, its migration patterns, its enemies and allies, its diet and food chain. Eventually the hunter himself becomes animal-like, instinctively sensing the habits and moves of his prey. Of course, this instinct gives the hunter a better chance of killing the animal; he knows where and when he will get the best shot. But it gives him more than that. Hunting is not just pulling the trigger and killing the prey. Much of it is a multifaceted and ritualistic identification with nature.

After the kill, the hunter can do a number of things with his trophy. He can sell the meat or eat it himself. He can hang the animal's head on the wall or lay its hide on the floor or even sell these objects. But any of these uses is a luxury, and its cost is high. An animal has been destroyed; a life has been eliminated.

Like the hunter, the photographer has a great interest in the tools he uses. He carries various types of cameras, lenses, and film to help him get the picture he wants. He understands the way cameras work, the uses of telephoto and micro lenses, and often the technical procedures of printing and developing. Of course, the time and interest a photographer invests in these mechanical aspects of his art allow him to capture and produce the image he wants. But as with the hunter, these mechanics can and often do become fascinating in themselves.

The wildlife photographer also needs to stalk his "prey" with knowledge and skill in order to get an accurate "shot." Like the hunter, he has to understand the animal's patterns, characteristics, and habitat; he must become animal-like in order to succeed. And like the hunter's, his pursuit is much more prolonged and complicated than the shot itself. The stalking processes are almost identical and give many of the same satisfactions.

The successful photographer also has something tangible to show for his efforts. A still picture of an animal can be displayed in a home, a gallery, a shop; it can be printed in a publication, as a postcard, or as a poster. In fact, a single photograph can be used in all these ways at once; it can be reproduced countless times. And despite all these ways of using his "trophies," the photographer continues to preserve his prey.

–Barbara Bowman, student

Analogy is a special form of comparison. When a subject is unobservable, complex, or abstract—when it is so unfamiliar that readers may have trouble understanding it—analogy can be effective. By pointing out certain similarities between a difficult subject and a more familiar or concrete subject, writers can help their readers grasp a difficult subject. Unlike a true comparison, though, which analyzes items that belong to the same class (breeds of dogs or types of engines), analogy pairs things from different classes that have nothing in common except through the imagination of the writer. In addition, whereas comparison seeks to illuminate specific features of both subjects, the primary purpose of analogy is to clarify the one subject that is complex or unfamiliar. For example, to explore the similarities (and differences) between short stories and novels (two forms of fiction), you probably would choose comparison. Short stories and novels belong to the same class (fiction), and your purpose is to reveal something about both. If, however, your purpose is to explain the craft of fiction writing, you might note its similarities to the craft of carpentry. Then you would be drawing an analogy because the two subjects clearly belong to different classes. Carpentry is the more concrete subject and the one more people will have direct experience with. If you use your imagination, you will easily see many ways that the tangible work of the carpenter can be used to help readers understand the abstract work of the novelist. For an example of an essay built on an analogy, see Audrey Schulman's "Fahrenheit 59: What a Child's Fever Might Tell Us about Climate Change" on page 131.

Depending on its purpose, an analogy can be made in a sentence or in several paragraphs to clarify a particular aspect of the larger topic being discussed, as in the following example, or it can provide the organizational strategy for an entire essay:

> It has long struck me that the familiar metaphor of "climbing the ladder" for describing the ascent to success or fulfillment in any field is inappropriate and misleading. There are no ladders that lead to success, although there may be some escalators for those lucky enough to follow in a family's fortunes.
>
> A ladder proceeds vertically, rung by rung, with each rung evenly spaced, and with the whole apparatus leaning against a relatively flat and even surface. A child can climb a ladder as easily as an adult, and perhaps with a surer footing.
>
> Making the ascent in one's vocation or profession is far less like ladder climbing than mountain climbing, and here the analogy is a very real one. Going up a mountain requires a variety of skills, and includes a diversity of dangers, that are in no way involved in mounting a ladder.
>
> Young people starting out should be told this, both to dampen their expectations and to allay their disappointments. A mountain is rough and precipitous, with uncertain footing and a predictable number of falls and scrapes, and sometimes one has to take the long way around to reach the shortest distance.
>
> –Sydney J. Harris

Two Ways of Seeing a River

■ **Mark Twain**

Samuel L. Clemens (1835–1910), who wrote under the pen name of Mark Twain, was born in Florida, Missouri, and raised in Hannibal, Missouri. He wrote the novels Tom Sawyer *(1876),* The Prince and the Pauper *(1882),* Huckleberry Finn *(1884), and* A Connecticut Yankee in King Arthur's Court *(1889), as well as many other works of fiction and nonfiction. One of America's most popular writers, Twain is generally regarded as the most important practitioner of the realistic school of writing, a style that emphasizes observable details.*

The following passage is taken from Life on the Mississippi *(1883), Twain's study of the great river and his account of his early experiences learning to be a river steamboat pilot. As you read the passage, notice how Twain makes use of figurative language in describing two quite different ways of seeing the Mississippi River.*

Reflecting on What You Know

As we age and gain experience, our interpretation of the same memory—or how we view the same scene—can change. For example, the way we view our own appearance changes all the time, and photos from our childhood or teenage years may surprise us in the decades that follow. Perhaps something we found amusing in our younger days may make us feel uncomfortable or embarrassed now, or perhaps the house we grew up in later seems smaller or less appealing than it used to. Write about a memory that has changed for you over the years. How does your interpretation of it now contrast with how you experienced it at the time?

Now when I had mastered the language of this water and had come   1
to know every trifling feature that bordered the great river as familiarly as I knew the letters of the alphabet, I had made a valuable acquisition. But I had lost something, too. I had lost something which

could never be restored to me while I lived. All the grace, the beauty, the poetry, had gone out of the majestic river! I still kept in mind a certain wonderful sunset which I witnessed when steamboating was new to me. A broad expanse of the river was turned to blood; in the middle distance the red hue brightened into gold, through which a solitary log came floating, black and conspicuous; in one place a long, slanting mark lay sparkling upon the water; in another the surface was broken by boiling, tumbling rings that were as many tinted as an opal;[1] where the ruddy flush was faintest was a smooth spot that was covered with graceful circles and radiating lines, ever so delicately traced; the shore on our left was densely wooded, and the somber shadow that fell from this forest was broken in one place by a long, ruffled trail that shone like silver; and high above the forest wall a clean-stemmed dead tree waved a single leafy bough that glowed like a flame in the unobstructed splendor that was flowing from the sun. There were graceful curves, reflected images, woody heights, soft distances, and over the whole scene, far and near, the dissolving lights drifted steadily, enriching it every passing moment with new marvels of coloring.

I stood like one bewitched. I drank it in, in a speechless rapture. 2
The world was new to me and I had never seen anything like this at home. But as I have said, a day came when I began to cease from noting the glories and the charms which the moon and the sun and the twilight wrought upon the river's face; another day came when I ceased altogether to note them. Then, if that sunset scene had been repeated, I should have looked upon it without rapture and should have commented upon it inwardly after this fashion: "This sun means that we are going to have wind tomorrow; that floating log means that the river is rising, small thanks to it; that slanting mark on the water refers to a bluff reef which is going to kill somebody's steamboat one of these nights, if it keeps on stretching out like that; those tumbling 'boils' show a dissolving bar and a changing channel there; the lines and circles in the slick water over yonder are a warning that that troublesome place is shoaling up dangerously; that silver streak in the shadow of the forest is the 'break' from a new snag and he has located himself in the very best place he could have found to fish for steamboats; that tall dead tree, with a single living branch, is not going to last long, and then how is a body ever going to get through this blind place at night without the friendly old landmark?"

---

[1]*opal:* a multicolored, iridescent gemstone.

No, the romance and beauty were all gone from the river. All the   3
value any feature of it had for me now was the amount of usefulness
it could furnish toward compassing the safe piloting of a steamboat.
Since those days, I have pitied doctors from my heart. What does the
lovely flush in a beauty's cheek mean to a doctor but a "break" that
ripples above some deadly disease? Are not all her visible charms
sown thick with what are to him the signs and symbols of hidden
decay? Does he ever see her beauty at all, or doesn't he simply view
her professionally and comment upon her unwholesome condition all
to himself? And doesn't he sometimes wonder whether he has gained
most or lost most by learning his trade?

Thinking Critically about This Reading

In the opening paragraph, Twain exclaims, "All the grace, the beauty,
the poetry, had gone out of the majestic river!" What is "the poetry,"
and why was it lost for him?

Questions for Study and Discussion

1. What method of organization does Twain use in this selection?
   (Glossary: *Organization*) What alternative methods might he have
   used? What would have been gained or lost?
2. Explain the analogy Twain uses in paragraph 3. (Glossary:
   Analogy) What is his purpose in using this analogy?
3. Twain uses a number of similes and metaphors in this selection.
   (Glossary: *Figure of Speech*) Identify three of each, and explain
   what Twain is comparing in each case. What do these figures of
   speech add to Twain's writing?
4. Now that he has learned the trade of steamboating, does Twain
   believe that he has "gained most or lost most" (3)? What has he
   gained, and what has he lost?
5. Twain points to a change of attitude he underwent as a result of
   seeing the river from a new perspective, that of a steamboat pilot.
   What role does knowledge play in Twain's inability to see the
   river as he once did?

Classroom Activity Using Comparison and Contrast

Using the sample outlines on pages 483–84 as models, prepare both subject-by-subject and point-by-point outlines for one of the following topics:

dogs and cats as pets

Facebook and Twitter

an economy car and a luxury car

your local newspaper and the *New York Times* or *USA Today*

a high school–level course and a college-level course

the Boston Celtics and the Miami Heat basketball teams

Before starting your outline, determine the key points you wish to compare and contrast. Be prepared to explain any advantages that you see of one organizational plan over the other.

Suggested Writing Assignments

1. Twain's essay contrasts the perception of one person before and after acquiring a particular body of knowledge. Different people also usually perceive the same scene or event differently, even if they are experiencing it simultaneously. To use an example from Twain's writing, a poet and a doctor might perceive a rosy-cheeked young woman in entirely different ways. Write a comparison and contrast essay in which you show how two people with different experiences might perceive the same subject. It can be a case of profound difference (such as a musician and an electrician at the same pyrotechnic rock music concert) or more subtle (such as a novelist and a screenwriter seeing the same lovers' quarrel in a restaurant). Add a short postscript in which you explain your choice of subject-by-subject comparison or point-by-point comparison in your essay.

2. Learning how to drive a car may not be as involved as learning how to pilot a steamboat on the Mississippi River, but it has a tremendous effect on how we function and on how we perceive our surroundings. Write an essay about short trips you took as a passenger and as a driver. Compare and contrast your perceptions and actions. What is most important to you as a passenger?

What is most important to you as a driver? How do your perceptions shift between the two roles? What changes in what you notice around you and in the way you notice it?

3. What perspective does the following cartoon give you on Twain's point about his different views of the Mississippi River? Is it possible for two people to have two completely different views of something? How might experience or perspective change how they view something? Write an essay modeled on Twain's in which you offer two different views of an event. You might consider a reporter's view compared with a victim's view, a teacher's view compared with a student's view, or a customer's view compared with a salesperson's view.

"By George, you're right! I <u>thought</u> there was something familiar about it."

Two Ways to Belong in America

■ **Bharati Mukherjee**

Prominent Indian American writer and university professor Bharati Mukherjee was born into an aristocratic family in Calcutta (now Kolkata), India, in 1940. After her family relocated to England because of her father's work, she earned both her bachelor's and master's degrees from the University of Calcutta. In 1961, she pursued her long-held desire to become a writer by earning an MFA at the University of Iowa and eventually a PhD in English and comparative literature. *After marrying the American Clark Blaise, she and her husband moved to Canada, where they lived for 14 years until legislation against South Asians led them to move back to the United States. Before joining the faculty at the University of California, Berkeley, Mukherjee taught at McGill University, Skidmore College, Queens College, and City University of New York. Currently her work centers on writing and the themes of immigration, particularly concerning women, immigration policy, and cultural alienation. With her husband, she has authored* Days and Nights in Calcutta *(1977) and* The Sorrow and the Terror: The Haunting Legacy of the Air India Tragedy *(1987). In addition, she has published seven novels, including* The Tiger's Daughter *(1971),* Wife *(1975),* Jasmine *(1989),* The Holder of the World *(1993), and* The Tree Bride *(2004); two collections of short stories,* Darkness *(1985) and* The Middleman and Other Stories *(1988), for which she won the National Book Critics Circle Award; and two works of nonfiction,* Political Culture and Leadership in India *(1991) and* Regionalism in Indian Perspective *(1992).*

The following essay was first published in the New York Times *in 1996 in response to new legislation championed by then vice president Al Gore that gave expedited citizenship for legal immigrants living in the United States. As you read Mukherjee's essay, notice the way she has organized her presentation of the different views that she and her sister have toward the various aspects of living as either a legal immigrant or a citizen.*

Reflecting on What You Know

The word *immigrant* has many connotations. If you have moved to the United States from another country, what associations does the word have for you and your family? If you were born in the United States, what associations does the word have for you? Discuss the word *immigrant* with your classmates. How does one's perspective affect the associations that this word has for them? Explain.

This is a tale of two sisters from Calcutta, Mira and Bharati, who 1 have lived in the United States for some thirty-five years, but who find themselves on different sides in the current debate over the status of immigrants. I am an American citizen and she is not. I am moved that thousands of long-term residents are finally taking the oath of citizenship. She is not.

Mira arrived in Detroit in 1960 to study child psychology and 2 preschool education. I followed her a year later to study creative writing at the University of Iowa. When we left India, we were almost identical in appearance and attitude. We dressed alike, in saris; we expressed identical views on politics, social issues, love and marriage in the same Calcutta convent-school accent. We would endure our two years in America, secure our degrees, then return to India to marry the grooms of our father's choosing.

Instead, Mira married an Indian student in 1962 who was getting 3 his business administration degree at Wayne State University. They soon acquired the labor certifications necessary for the green card of hassle-free residence and employment.

Mira still lives in Detroit, works in the Southfield, Michigan, school 4 system, and has become nationally recognized for her contributions in the fields of preschool education and parent-teacher relationships. After thirty-six years as a legal immigrant in this country, she clings passionately to her Indian citizenship and hopes to go home to India when she retires.

In Iowa City in 1963, I married a fellow student, an American of 5 Canadian parentage. Because of the accident of his North Dakota birth, I bypassed labor-certification requirements and the race-related "quota" system that favored the applicant's country of origin over his or her merit. I was prepared for (and even welcomed) the emotional strain that came with marrying outside my ethnic community. In thirty-three years of marriage, we have lived in every part of North America. By choosing a husband who was not my father's selection, I was opting for fluidity, self-invention, blue jeans and T-shirts, and renouncing three thousand years (at least) of caste-observant, "pure culture" marriage in the Mukherjee family. My books have often been read as unapologetic (and in some quarters overenthusiastic) texts for cultural and psychological "mongrelization." It's a word I celebrate.

Mira and I have stayed sisterly close by phone. In our regular Sunday morning conversations, we are unguardedly affectionate. I am her only blood relative on this continent. We expect to see each other through the looming crises of aging and ill health without being asked. Long before Vice President Gore's "Citizenship USA" drive, we'd had our polite arguments over the ethics of retaining an overseas citizenship while expecting the permanent protection and economic benefits that come with living and working in America.   6

Like well-raised sisters, we never said what was really on our minds, but we probably pitied one another. She, for the lack of structure in my life, the erasure of Indianness, the absence of an unvarying daily core. I, for the narrowness of her perspective, her uninvolvement with the mythic depths or the superficial pop culture of this society. But, now, with the scapegoating of "aliens" (documented or illegal) on the increase, and the targeting of long-term legal immigrants like Mira for new scrutiny and new self-consciousness, she and I find ourselves unable to maintain the same polite discretion. We were always unacknowledged adversaries, and we are now, more than ever, sisters.   7

"I feel used," Mira raged on the phone the other night. "I feel manipulated and discarded. This is such an unfair way to treat a person who was invited to stay and work here because of her talent. My employer went to the INS and petitioned for the labor certification. For over thirty years, I've invested my creativity and professional skills into the improvement of *this* country's preschool system. I've obeyed all the rules, I've paid my taxes, I love my work, I love my students, I love the friends I've made. How dare America now change its rules in midstream? If America wants to make new rules curtailing benefits of legal immigrants, they should apply only to immigrants who arrive after those rules are already in place."   8

To my ears, it sounded like the description of a long-enduring, comfortable yet loveless marriage, without risk or recklessness. Have we the right to demand, and to expect, that we be loved? (That, to me, is the subtext of the arguments by immigration advocates.) My sister is an expatriate, professionally generous and creative, socially courteous and gracious, and that's as far as her Americanization can go. She is here to maintain an identity, not to transform it. 9

I asked her if she would follow the example of others who have decided to become citizens because of the anti-immigration bills in Congress. And here, she surprised me. "If America wants to play the manipulative game, I'll play it too," she snapped. "I'll become a U.S. citizen for now, then change back to Indian when I'm ready to go home. I feel some kind of irrational attachment to India that I don't to America. Until all this hysteria against legal immigrants, I was totally happy. Having my green card meant I could visit any place in the world I wanted to and then come back to a job that's satisfying and that I do very well." 10

In one family, from two sisters alike as peas in a pod, there could not be a wider divergence of immigrant experience. America spoke to me—I married it—I embraced the demotion from expatriate aristocrat to immigrant nobody, surrendering those thousands of years of "pure culture," the saris, the delightfully accented English. She retained them all. Which of us is the freak? 11

Mira's voice, I realize, is the voice not just of the immigrant South Asian community but of an immigrant community of the millions who have stayed rooted in one job, one city, one house, one ancestral culture, one cuisine, for the entirety of their productive years. She speaks for greater numbers than I possibly can. Only the fluency of her English and the anger, rather than fear, born of confidence from her education, differentiate her from the seamstresses, the domestics, the technicians, the shop owners, the millions of hardworking but effectively silenced documented immigrants as well as their less fortunate "illegal" brothers and sisters. 12

Nearly twenty years ago, when I was living in my husband's ancestral homeland of Canada, I was always well-employed but never allowed to feel part of the local Quebec or larger Canadian society. Then, through a Green Paper that invited a national referendum on the unwanted side effects of "nontraditional" immigration, the Government officially turned against its immigrant communities, particularly those from South Asia. 13

I felt then the same sense of betrayal that Mira feels now. I will 14
never forget the pain of that sudden turning, and the casual racist
outbursts the Green Paper elicited. That sense of betrayal had its desired effect and drove me, and thousands like me, from the country.

Mira and I differ, however, in the ways in which we hope to inter- 15
act with the country that we have chosen to live in. She is happier to
live in America as an expatriate Indian than as an immigrant American.
I need to feel like a part of the community I have adopted (as I tried to
feel in Canada as well). I need to put roots down, to vote and make the
difference that I can. The price that the immigrant willingly pays, and
that the exile avoids, is the trauma of self-transformation.

Thinking Critically about This Reading

What do you think that Mukherjee's sister means when she says in
paragraph 10, "If America wants to play the manipulative game, I'll
play it too"? How do you react to her decision and her possible plans
if and when she eventually returns to India?

Questions for Study and Discussion

1. What is Mukherjee's thesis? (Glossary: *Thesis*)
2. Mukherjee has used comparison and contrast as her organizing
   principle. What type of comparison and contrast has she used?
3. Why is the pattern of organization that Mukherjee used appropriate for her subject and her purpose?
4. Why might Mukherjee have ordered her points of discussion in
   the way that she has? Explain.
5. What arguments does Mukherjee make for becoming a U.S. citizen? What arguments does her sister make for retaining her Indian
   citizenship?
6. Why does Mukherjee's sister feel "used" by attempts to change
   U.S. laws regarding social security benefits for noncitizens?
7. What does Mukherjee mean when she says in paragraph 15, "The
   price that the immigrant willingly pays, and that the exile avoids,
   is the trauma of self-transformation"?

Classroom Activity Using Comparison and Contrast

In preparation for writing an essay of comparison and contrast on two world leaders (or popular singers, actors, or sports figures), write out answers to the following questions:

Who could I compare and contrast?

What is my purpose?

Are their similarities or differences more interesting?

What specific points should I discuss?

What organizational pattern will best suit my purpose: subject-by-subject or point-by-point?

Suggested Writing Assignments

1. Mukherjee writes about the relationship she had with her sister in paragraph 7 by saying that "we never said what was really on our minds, but we probably pitied one another." These types of differences are played out on a larger scale when immigrants who have transformed themselves into Americans are confronted by those who have chosen to retain their ethnic identity, and these tensions often lead to name-calling and aggressive prejudice. Similar situations also exist within the Latino, African American, and Southeast Asian American communities and perhaps among all immigrant groups. Write an essay comparing and contrasting the choices of lifestyle that members of an ethnic or cultural community you are familiar with make as they try to find a comfortable place in American society.

2. Mukherjee presents her sister's reasons for not becoming a citizen and supports them with statements that her sister has made. Imagine that you are Mira Mukherjee. Write a counterargument to the one presented by your sister that gives your reasons for remaining an Indian citizen. Consider that you have already broken with tradition by marrying a man not of your father's choosing but also that the "trauma of self-transformation" that your sister raises in the conclusion of her essay is much deeper and more complicated than she has represented it. Can you say that you are holding to tradition when you are not? Can you engage in a challenging self-transformation if it is not genuinely motivated?

That Lean and Hungry Look

■ Suzanne Britt

Born in Winston-Salem, North Carolina, Suzanne Britt now makes her home in Raleigh. She graduated from Salem College and Washington University, where she received her MA in English. A poet and essayist, Britt has been a columnist for the Raleigh News and Observer *and* Stars and Stripes, European edition. *Her work appears regularly in* North Carolina Gardens and Homes, *the* New York Times, Newsweek, *and the* Boston Globe. *Her essays have been collected in two books,* Skinny People Are Dull and Crunchy Like Carrots *(1982) and* Show and Tell *(1982). She is the author of* A Writer's Rhetoric *(1988), a college writing textbook, and* Images: A Centennial Journey *(1991), a history of Meredith College, a small, independent women's college in Raleigh where she teaches English and continues to write.*

The following essay first appeared in Newsweek *and later became the basis for her book* Skinny People Are Dull and Crunchy Like Carrots, *titled after a line in this essay. In this selection, mingling humor with a touch of seriousness, Britt examines the differences between fat and thin people and gives us some insights about several important personality traits. Notice how she has organized the points of her contrast.*

Reflecting on What You Know

What are your thoughts about fat people and thin people? Into which category would you place yourself? How do you feel about being fat or thin? In talking about a person's body shape or size, what words other than *fat* and *thin* could you use? What difference, if any, would these words make? Explain.

Caesar was right. Thin people need watching. I've been watching   1
them for most of my adult life, and I don't like what I see. When these narrow fellows spring at me, I quiver to my toes. Thin people

come in all personalities, most of them menacing. You've got your "together" thin person, your mechanical thin person, your condescending thin person, your tsk-tsk thin person, your efficiency-expert thin person. All of them are dangerous.

In the first place, thin people aren't fun. They don't know how to goof off, at least in the best, fat sense of the word. They've always got to be adoing. Give them a coffee break, and they'll jog around the block. Supply them with a quiet evening at home, and they'll fix the screen door and lick S&H green stamps.[1] They say things like "there aren't enough hours in the day." Fat people never say that. Fat people think the day is too damn long already.

Thin people make me tired. They've got speedy little metabolisms that cause them to bustle briskly. They're forever rubbing their bony hands together and eyeing new problems to "tackle." I like to surround myself with sluggish, inert, easygoing fat people, the kind who believe that if you clean it up today, it'll just get dirty again tomorrow.

Some people say the business about the jolly fat person is a myth, that all of us chubbies are neurotic, sick, sad people. I disagree. Fat people may not be chortling all day long, but they're a hell of a lot *nicer* than the wizened and shriveled. Thin people turn surly, mean, and hard at a young age because they never learn the value of a hot-fudge sundae for easing tension. Thin people don't like gooey soft things because they themselves are neither gooey nor soft. They are crunchy and dull, like carrots. They go straight to the heart of the matter while fat people let things stay all blurry and hazy and vague, the way things actually are. Thin people want to face the truth. Fat people know there is no truth. One of my thin friends is always staring at complex, unsolvable problems and saying, "The key thing is . . ." Fat people never say that. They know there isn't any such thing as the key thing about anything.

Thin people believe in logic. Fat people see all sides. The sides fat people see are rounded blobs, usually gray, always nebulous and truly not worth worrying about. But the thin person persists. "If you consume more calories than you burn," says one of my thin friends, "you will gain weight. It's that simple." Fat people always grin when they hear statements like that. They know better.

---

[1]*S&H green stamps:* popular trading stamps distributed to retail shoppers as part of a rewards program starting in the 1930s and running through the 1980s. Stamps could be redeemed for products.

Fat people realize that life is illogical and unfair. They know very   6
well that God is not in his heaven and all is not right with the world.
If God was up there, fat people could have two doughnuts and a big
orange drink anytime they wanted it.

Thin people have a long list of logical things they are always spout-   7
ing off to me. They hold up one finger at a time as they reel off these
things, so I won't lose track. They speak slowly as if to a young child.
The list is long and full of holes. It contains tidbits like "get a grip on
yourself," "cigarettes kill," "cholesterol clogs," "fit as a fiddle," "ducks
in a row," "organize," and "sound fiscal management." Phrases like that.

They think these 2,000-point plans lead to happiness. Fat people   8
know happiness is elusive at best and even if they could get the kind
thin people talk about, they wouldn't want it. Wisely, fat people see
that such programs are too dull, too hard, too off the mark. They are
never better than a whole cheesecake.

Fat people know all about the mystery of life. They are the ones   9
acquainted with the night, with luck, with fate, with playing it by ear.
One thin person I know once suggested that we arrange all the parts
of a jigsaw puzzle into groups according to size, shape, and color. He
figured this would cut the time needed to complete the puzzle by at
least 50 percent. I said I wouldn't do it. One, I like to muddle
through. Two, what good would it do to finish early? Three, the jigsaw puzzle isn't the important thing. The important thing is the fun
of four people (one thin person included) sitting around a card table,
working a jigsaw puzzle. My thin friend had no use for my list.
Instead of joining us, he went outside and mulched the boxwoods.
The three remaining fat people finished the puzzle and made chocolate, double-fudged brownies to celebrate.

The main problem with thin people is they oppress. Their good   10
intentions, bony torsos, tight ships, neat corners, cerebral machina-
tions, and pat solutions loom like dark clouds over the loose, comfortable, spread-out, soft world of the fat. Long after fat people have
removed their coats and shoes and put their feet up on the coffee
table, thin people are still sitting on the edge of the sofa, looking neat
as a pin, discussing rutabagas. Fat people are heavily into fits of
laughter, slapping their thighs and whooping it up, while thin people
are still politely waiting for the punch line.

Thin people are downers. They like math and morality and rea-   11
soned evaluation of the limitations of human beings. They have their
skinny little acts together. They expound, prognose, probe, and prick.

Fat people are convivial. They will like you even if you're irregu-   12
lar and have acne. They will come up with a good reason why you
never wrote the great American novel. They will cry in your beer with
you. They will put your name in the pot. They will let you off the
hook. Fat people will gab, giggle, guffaw, gallumph, gyrate, and gossip. They are generous, giving, and gallant. They are gluttonous and
goodly and great. What you want when you're down is soft and jig-
gly, not muscled and stable. Fat people know this. Fat people have
plenty of room. Fat people will take you in.

Thinking Critically about This Reading

What does Britt seem to have against thin people? Why does she consider thin people "dangerous" (paragraph 1)? What do you think Britt
herself looks like? What in her essay led you to this conclusion?

Questions for Study and Discussion

1. Does Britt use a subject-by-subject or a point-by-point pattern of
   organization to contrast fat people and thin people? Explain.
   What specific points of contrast does Britt discuss?
2. How does Britt characterize thin people? Fat people?
3. What is Britt's purpose in this essay? (Glossary: *Purpose*) Is she
   serious, partially serious, mostly humorous? Are fat and thin
   people really her subject? Explain.
4. Britt makes effective use of the short sentence. Identify examples
   of sentences with three or fewer words, and explain what function each serves.
5. Britt uses many clichés in her essay. Identify at least a dozen
   examples. What do you suppose is her purpose in using them?
   (Glossary: *Cliché*)
6. It is somewhat unusual for an essayist to use alliteration (the repetition of initial consonant sounds), a technique more commonly
   found in poetry. Where has Britt used alliteration, and why do
   you suppose she has used this particular technique?

Classroom Activity Using Comparison and Contrast

Carefully read and analyze the following paragraphs in which the late
Stephen E. Ambrose compares and contrasts Chief Crazy Horse and

General George Armstrong Custer. The passage is taken from Ambrose's book *Crazy Horse and Custer: The Parallel Lives of Two American Warriors* (1975). Then answer the questions that follow.

> It was bravery, above and beyond all other qualities, that Custer and Crazy Horse had in common. Each man was an outstanding warrior in war-mad societies. Thousands upon thousands of Custer's fellow whites had as much opportunity as he did to demonstrate their courage, just as all of Crazy Horse's associates had countless opportunities to show that they equaled him in bravery. But no white warrior, save his younger brother, Tom, could outdo Custer, just as no Indian warrior, save his younger brother, Little Hawk, could outdo Crazy Horse. And for both white and red societies, no masculine virtue was more admired than bravery. To survive, both societies felt they had to have men willing to put their lives on the line. For men who were willing to do so, no reward was too great, even though there were vast differences in the way each society honored its heroes.
>
> Beyond their bravery, Custer and Crazy Horse were individualists, each standing out from the crowd in his separate way. Custer wore outlandish uniforms, let his hair fall in long, flowing golden locks across his shoulders, surrounded himself with pet animals and admirers, and in general did all he could to draw attention to himself. Crazy Horse's individualism pushed him in the opposite direction—he wore a single feather in his hair when going into battle, rather than a war bonnet. Custer's vast energy set him apart from most of his fellows; the Sioux distinguished Crazy Horse from other warriors because of Crazy Horse's quietness and introspection. Both men lived in societies in which drugs, especially alcohol, were widely used, but neither Custer nor Crazy Horse drank. Most of all, of course, each man stood out in battle as a great risk taker.
>
> –Stephen E. Ambrose

What is Ambrose's point in these two paragraphs? How does he use comparison and contrast to make this point? How has he organized his paragraphs? How else might he have organized them? Explain.

Suggested Writing Assignments

1. Using Britt's argument against thin people as a model, write a counterargument in favor of thin people. Before beginning to write, make a list of the favorable points you would want to

make about thin people. How would you counter Britt's points about fat people?

2. Reread paragraphs 3 through 6, paying careful attention to how these paragraphs are developed by contrasting the features of thin people and fat people. Now, select two specific examples from one of the following categories—people, products, events, institutions, places—and make a list of their contrasting features. For example, you could select Bill Clinton and Barack Obama, Raisin Bran and Rice Krispies, the Statue of Liberty and the Washington Monument, or the Grand Canyon and Yellowstone National Park. Finally, write an essay modeled after Britt's in which you use the contrasting features on your list.

Who Says a Woman Can't Be Einstein?

■ Amanda Ripley

Longtime writer on terrorism, natural disas-ters, education, human behavior, and risk-taking, Amanda Ripley was born in 1975 in Yokahama, Japan, and grew up in New Orleans. Ripley graduated Phi Beta Kappa from Cornell University in 1996 with a major in government and launched her ca-reer in journalism in Washington, D.C., where she covered the court system for the Washington City Paper *and the legislature for* Congressional Quarterly. *At* Time *magazine, Ripley has written extensively about human behavior and public policy, always interested in not just what we do, but why. Her stories on Hurricane Katrina and the events leading up to the storm helped* Time *win two National Magazine Awards. Her award-winning book,* The Unthinkable: Who Survives When Disaster Strikes—and Why *(2008), explains how the human brain functions when con-fronted with a catastrophe like a hurricane, earthquake, heat wave, or terrorist attack. She is a frequent contributor to the* New York Times Magazine, Slate, *the* Atlantic, *and* Washington Monthly. *Ripley is a Bernard L. Schwartz fellow at the New America Foundation, where she is studying public education in the United States and abroad. An article that grew out of her studies, "What Makes a Great Teacher?" appeared in the* Atlantic *in February 2010.*

The following selection first appeared in the February 2005 issue of Time *magazine, and it reflects Ripley's long-standing in-terest in how the human brain works. Intrigued by the provoca-tive remarks about gender and aptitude made by Larry Summers, at the time president of Harvard University, Ripley explores what the research reveals about the differences and similarities between the brains of men and women to determine just how much truth there was in Summers "pet theory."*

Reflecting on What You Know

What differences, if any, have you observed between men and women when it comes to aptitude or intelligence? Do women seem to be better at some things, and men better at others? What are your own strengths? How do they align with others who share your gender?

There was something self-destructive about Harvard University President Larry Summers' speech on gender disparities in January. In his first sentence, he said his goal was "provocation" (rarely a wise strategy at a diversity conference). He called for "rigorous and careful" thinking to explain the gender gap among top-tier tenured science professors. But he described his pet theory with something less than prudence. The most likely explanations, he said, are that 1) women are just not so interested as men in making the sacrifices required by high-powered jobs, 2) men may have more "intrinsic aptitude" for high-level science and 3) women may be victims of old-fashioned discrimination. "In my own view, their importance probably ranks in exactly the order that I just described," he announced.

Cue the hysteria. The comments about aptitude in particular lingered, like food poisoning, long after the conference ended. For weeks, pundits and professors spouted outrage and praise, all of which added up to very little. Then came the tedious analysis of faculty-lounge politics at Harvard, as if anyone outside Cambridge really cared.

The rest of us were left with a nagging question: What is the latest science on the differences between men's and women's aptitudes, anyway? Is it true, even a little bit, that men are better equipped for scientific genius? Or is it ridiculous—even pernicious—to ask such a question in the year 2005?

It's always perilous to use science to resolve festering public debates. Everyone sees something different—like 100 people finding shapes in clouds. By the time they make up their minds, the clouds have drifted beyond the horizon. But scientists who have spent their lives studying sex differences in the brain (some of whom defend Summers and some of whom dismiss him as an ignoramus) generally concede that he was not entirely wrong. Thanks to new brain-imaging technology, we know there are indeed real differences between the male and the female brain, more differences than we would have imagined a decade ago. "The brain is a sex organ," says Sandra Witelson, a neuroscientist who became famous in the 1990s for her study of Albert Einstein's brain. "In the last dozen years, there has been an exponential increase in the number of studies that have found differences in the brain. It's very exciting."

But that's just the beginning of the conversation. It turns out that   5
many of those differences don't seem to change our behavior. Others do—in ways we might not expect. Some of the most dramatic differences are not just in our brains but also in our eyes, noses, and ears—which feed information to our brains. Still, almost none of those differences are static. The brain is constantly changing in response to hormones, encouragement, practice, diet, and drugs. Brain patterns fluctuate within the same person, in fact, depending on age and time of day. So while Summers was also right that more men than women make up the extreme high—and low—scorers in science and math tests, it's absurd to conclude that the difference is primarily because of biology—or environment. The two interact from the time of conception, which only makes life more interesting.

Any simplistic theory is "doomed to fail," says Yu Xie, a sociol-   6
ogy professor at the University of Michigan. Xie's research on women in the sciences was cited by Summers in his statement, and Xie has spent every day since trying to explain the intricacy of human behavior to reporters. "I don't exclude biology as an explanation," he says. "But I know biological factors would not play a role unless they interacted with social conditions."

Unless one appreciates that complexity, it would be all too easy   7
to look at the latest research on the brain and conclude, say, that men may not in fact make the best university presidents. For example, studies show that men are slightly more likely to say things without realizing how their actions will affect others. And as men age, they tend to lose more tissue from a part of the brain located just behind the forehead that concerns itself with consequences and self-control. Generally speaking, the brain of a female is more interlinked and—if one assumes that a basic requirement of the post is to avoid dividing the faculty into two sweaty mobs—may be better suited for the kind of cautious diplomacy required of a high-profile university leader. Of course, to borrow a line from Summers, "I would prefer to believe otherwise."

Now that scientists are finally starting to map the brain with   8
some accuracy, the challenge is figuring out what to do with that

knowledge. The possibilities for applying it to the classroom, workplace, and doctor's office are tantalizing. "If something is genetic, it means it must be biological. If we can figure out the biology, then we should be able to tweak the biology," says Richard Haier, a psychology professor who studies intelligence at the University of California at Irvine. Maybe Summers' failure was not one of sensitivity but one of imagination.

Lesson 1: Function over Form

Scientists have been looking for sex differences in the brain since they have been looking at the brain. Many bold decrees have been issued. In the 19th century, the corpus callosum, a bundle of nerve fibers that connects the two hemispheres of the brain, was considered key to intellectual development. Accordingly, it was said to have a greater surface area in men. Then, in the 1980s, we were told that no, it is larger in women—and that explains why the emotional right side of women's brains is more in touch with the analytical left side. Aha. That theory has since been discredited, and scientists remain at odds over who has the biggest and what it might mean. Stay tuned for more breaking news.   9

But most studies agree that men's brains are about 10 percent bigger than women's brains overall. Even when the comparison is adjusted for the fact that men are, on average, 8 percent taller than women, men's brains are still slightly bigger. But size does not predict intellectual performance, as was once thought. Men and women perform similarly on IQ tests. And most scientists still cannot tell male and female brains apart just by looking at them.   10

Recently, scientists have begun to move away from the obsession with size. Thanks to new brain-imaging technology, researchers can get a good look at the living brain as it functions and grows. Earlier studies relied on autopsies or X-rays—and no one wanted to expose children or women, who might be pregnant, to regular doses of radiation.   11

The deeper you probe, the more interesting the differences. Women appear to have more connections between the two brain hemispheres. In certain regions, their brain is more densely packed with neurons. And women tend to use more parts of their brain to accomplish certain tasks. That might explain why they often recover better from a stroke, since the healthy parts of their mind compensate for the injured regions. Men do their thinking in more focused   12 regions of the brain, whether they are solving a math problem, reading a book or feeling a wave of anger or sadness.

Indeed, men and women seem to handle emotions quite differently. While both sexes use a part of the brain called the amygdala, which is located deep within the organ, women seem to have stronger connections between the amygdala and regions of the brain that handle language and other higher-level functions. That may explain why women are, on average, more likely to talk about their emotions and men tend to compartmentalize their worries and carry on. Or, of course, it may not. 13

"Men and women have different brain architectures, and we don't know what they mean," says Haier. By administering IQ tests to a group of college students and then analyzing scans of their brain structure, Haier's team recently discovered that the parts of the brain that are related to intelligence are different in men and women. "That is in some ways a major observation, because one of the assumptions of psychology has been that all human brains pretty much work the same way," he says. Now that we know they don't, we can try to understand why some brains react differently to, say, Alzheimer's, many medications, and even teaching techniques, Haier says. 14

Even more interesting than the brain's adult anatomy might be the journey it takes to get there. For 13 years, psychiatrist Jay Giedd has been compiling one of the world's largest libraries of brain growth. Every Tuesday evening, from 5 o'clock until midnight, a string of children files into the National Institutes of Health outside Washington to have their brains scanned. Giedd and his team ease the kids through the MRI procedure, and then he gives them a brain tour of their pictures—gently pointing out the spinal cord and the corpus callosum, before offering them a copy to take to show-and-tell. 15

Most of the kids are all business. Rowena Avery, 6, of Sparks, Nevada, arrived last week with a stuffed animal named Sidewalk and stoically disappeared into the machine while her mom, dad, and little sister watched. In preparation, she had practiced at home by lying very still in the bathtub. Her picture came out crystal clear. "The youngest ones are the best at lying still. It's kind of surprising," Giedd says. "It must be because they are used to hiding in kitchen cabinets and things like that." 16

Among the girls in Giedd's study, brain size peaks around age 11½. For the boys, the peak comes three years later. "For kids, that's a long time," Giedd says. His research shows that most parts of the 17 brain mature faster in girls. But in a 1999 study of 508 boys and girls, Virginia Tech researcher Harriet Hanlon found that some areas mature faster in boys. Specifically, some of the regions involved in mechanical reasoning, visual targeting, and spatial reasoning appeared to mature four to eight years earlier in boys. The parts that handle verbal fluency, handwriting, and recognizing familiar faces matured several years earlier in girls.

Monkeys are among our most trusted substitutes in brain   18
research. This week a study in the journal *Behavioral Neuroscience* shows that stage of life is also important in male and female rhesus monkeys. In a sort of shell game, young male monkeys proved better at finding food after they saw it hidden on a tray—suggesting better spatial memory. But they peaked early. By old age, male and female monkeys performed equally well, according to the study, which was led by Agnès Lacreuse at the Yerkes National Primate Research Center. All of which suggests that certain aptitudes may not be that different between males and females. It just depends on when you test them. (We'll have more to say about those monkeys in just a bit.)

Lesson 2: The Segregation of the Senses

So how do we explain why, in study after study, boys and men are   19
still on average better at rotating 3-D objects in their minds? As for girls and women, how do we explain why they tend to have better verbal skills and social sensitivities?

The most surprising differences may be outside the brain. "If you   20
have a man and a woman looking at the same landscape, they see totally different things," asserts Leonard Sax, a physician and psychologist whose book *Why Gender Matters* came out last month. "Women can see colors and textures that men cannot see. They hear things men cannot hear, and they smell things men cannot smell." Since the eyes, ears, and nose are portals to the brain, they directly affect brain development from birth on.

In rats, for example, we know that the male retina has more cells   21
designed to detect motion. In females, the retina has more cells built to gather information on color and texture. If the same is true in humans, as Sax suspects, that may explain why, in an experiment in England four years ago, newborn boys were much more likely than girls to stare at a mobile turning above their cribs. It may also help explain why boys prefer to play with moving toys like trucks while

girls favor richly textured dolls and tend to draw with a wider range of colors, Sax says.

Likewise, women's ears are more sensitive to some noises. Baby 22 girls hear certain ranges of sound better. And the divergence gets even bigger in adults. As for smell, a study published in the journal *Nature Neuroscience* in 2002 showed that women of childbearing age were many times more sensitive than men to several smells upon repeated exposure. (Another study has found that heterosexual women have the most sensitive smell and homosexual men have the least.)

Rest assured, Sax says: none of that means women are, overall, 23 better than men at perception. It just means the species is internally diverse, making it more likely to survive. "The female will remember the color and texture of a particular plant and be able to warn people if it's poisonous. A man looking at the same thing will be more alert to what is moving in the periphery," he says. "Which is better? You need both."

Lesson 3: Never Underestimate the Brain

Until recently, there have been two groups of people: those who argue 24 sex differences are innate and should be embraced and those who insist that they are learned and should be eliminated by changing the environment. Sax is one of the few in the middle—convinced that boys and girls are innately different and that we must change the environment so differences don't become limitations.

At a restaurant near his practice in Montgomery County, Maryland, 25 Sax spreads out dozens of papers and meticulously makes his case. He is a fanatic, but a smart, patient one. In the early 1990s, he says, he grew alarmed by the "parade" of parents coming into his office wondering whether their sons had attention-deficit/hyperactivity disorder. Sax evaluated them and found that, indeed, the boys were not paying attention in school. But the more he studied brain differences, the more he became convinced that the problem was with the schools. Sometimes the solution was simple: some of the boys didn't hear as well as the girls and so needed to be moved into the front row. Other times, the solution was more complex.

Eventually, Sax concluded that very young boys and girls would 26 be better off in separate classrooms altogether. "[Previously], as far as I was concerned, single-sex education was an old-fashioned leftover. I thought of boys wearing suits and talking with British accents," he says. But coed schools do more harm than good, he decided, when they teach boys and girls as if their brains mature at the same time. "If you ask a child to do something not developmentally appropriate for him, he will, number 1, fail. Number 2, he will develop an aversion to the subject," he says. "By age 12, you will have girls who don't like science and boys who don't like reading." And they won't ever go back, he says. "The reason women are underrepresented in computer science and engineering is not because they can't do it. It's because of the way they're taught."

So far, studies about girls' and boys' achievements in same-sex grammar schools are inconclusive. But if it turns out that targeting sex differences through education is helpful, there are certainly many ways to carry it out. Says Giedd: "The ability for change is phenomenal. That's what the brain does best." A small but charming 2004 study published in *Nature* found that people who learned how to juggle increased the gray matter in their brains in certain locations. When they stopped juggling, the new gray matter vanished. A similar structural change appears to occur in people who learn a second language. Remember that new research on spatial memory in rhesus monkeys? The young females dramatically improved their performance through simple training, wiping out the gender gap altogether.   27

In a recent experiment with humans at Temple University, women showed substantial progress in spatial reasoning after spending a couple of hours a week for 10 weeks playing Tetris, of all things. The males improved with weeks of practice too, says Nora Newcombe, a Temple psychologist who specializes in spatial cognition, and so the gender gap remained. But the improvement for both sexes was "massively greater" than the gender difference. "This means that if the males didn't train, the females would outstrip them," she says.   28

Of course, we already manipulate the brain through drugs— many of which, doctors now realize, have dramatically different effects on different brains. Drugs for improving intelligence are in the works, says Haier, in the quest to find medication for Alzheimer's. "We're going to get a lot better at manipulating genetic biology. We may even be better at manipulating genetic biology than manipulating the environment."   29

Until then, one solution to overcoming biological tendencies is to consciously override them, to say to yourself, "O.K., I may have a hard time with this task, but I'm going to will myself to conquer it." Some experiments show that baby girls, when faced with failure, tend   30 to give up and cry relatively quickly, while baby boys get angry and persist, says Witelson at Ontario's Michael G. DeGroote School of Medicine at McMaster University. "What we don't know is whether that pattern persists into adulthood," she says. But in her experience in academia, she says she knows of at least a couple of brilliant women who never realized their potential in science because they stopped trying when they didn't get grants or encountered some other obstacle. "It's much better," she says, "for people to understand what the differences are, act on their advantages, and be prepared for their disadvantages."

Lesson 4: Expectations Matter

We have a tendency to make too much of test-score differences 31 between the sexes (which are actually very small compared with the differences between, say, poor and affluent students). And regardless of what happens in school, personality and discipline can better predict success when it comes to highly competitive jobs.

One thing we know about the brain is that it is vulnerable to 32 the power of suggestion. There is plenty of evidence that when young women are motivated and encouraged, they excel at science. For most of the 1800s, for example, physics, astronomy, chemistry, and botany were considered gender-appropriate subjects for middle- and upper-class American girls. By the 1890s, girls outnumbered boys in public high school science courses across the country, according to *The Science Education of American Girls*, a 2003 book by Kim Tolley. Records from top schools in Boston show that girls outperformed boys in physics in the mid-19th century. Latin and Greek, meanwhile, were considered the province of gentlemen—until the 20th century, when lucrative opportunities began to open up in the sciences.

Today, in Iceland and Sweden, girls consistently outperform boys 33 in math and physics. . . . In Sweden the gap is widest in the remote regions in the north. That may be because women want to move to the big cities farther south, where they would need to compete in high-tech economies, while men are focused on local hunting, fishing, and forestry opportunities, says Niels Egelund, a professor of educational psychology at the Danish University of Education. The phenomenon even has a name, the Jokkmokk effect, a reference to an isolated town in Swedish Lapland.

Back in the States, the achievement gap in the sciences is closing, 34
albeit slowly. Female professors have been catching up with male professors in their publishing output. Today half of chemistry and almost
60 percent of biology bachelor of science degrees go to females.
Patience is required.

Next, Summers may want to take up the male question. In all 35
seriousness. Why do so many more boys than girls have learning disorders, autism, attention-deficit problems, and schizophrenia? Why are
young men now less likely to go to college than women are? And what
to make of a 2003 survey that found eighth-grade girls outperforming
boys in algebra in 22 countries, with boys outscoring girls in only
three nations? If we're not careful, the next Einstein could find herself
working as a high-powered lawyer who does wonders with estate-tax
calculations instead of discovering what the universe is made of.

Thinking Critically about This Reading

Ripley believes that it is "absurd to conclude that the difference
[between male and female brains] is primarily because of biology — or
environment" (paragraph 5). In light of the research on the brain that
Ripley presents, why is it important for us to appreciate the complexity of human behavior and to resist drawing overly simplistic
conclusions?

Questions for Study and Discussion

1. How does Ripley use Summers remarks in January 2005 to
   introduce the subject of the differences between male and female brains? Did you find her beginning effective? (Glossary:
   Beginnings and Endings) Explain why or why not.

2. Ripley organizes her essay into four parts, or "lessons." In your
   own words, summarize the key point(s) of each part. Why do
   you think that she presents the four parts in the order she does?
   Did you find this organizational plan helpful? Explain.

3. What key differences between men's and women's brains does
   Ripley note in the section titled "Lesson 1: Function over Form"?

4. Ripley begins the section "Lesson 2: The Segregation of the
   Senses" with two questions (19). How do these questions func-
   tion in the context of her essay? (Glossary: *Rhetorical Question*)
   How does Ripley answer these questions?

5. According to Ripley, what insights does animal research—namely with rhesus monkeys and rats—give us into possible gender differences in the workings of the human brain?

6. Ripley references a number of expert sources in her essay. How does she integrate each of these sources into her essay? (Glossary: *Signal Phrase*) For what purpose does she quote Professor Yu Xie in paragraph 6 and Professor Richard Haier in paragraphs 8 and 14?

7. What is physician and psychologist Leonard Sax's position in the debate between those who believe that sex differences are "innate" and those who believe that they are "learned"? In what ways does he believe that environments can be changed so that "differences don't become limitations" (24)?

Classroom Activity Using Comparison and Contrast

When flu season is upon us, it is helpful to know the difference between normal cold symptoms and flu symptoms. Consider the point-by-point comparison of the common cold and the H1N1 flu on page 516. What are the most important differences in symptoms between a cold and the H1N1 flu? Why do you think that people often confuse a cold with the flu? Do you find this chart to be helpful? What, if anything, do you think could be done to enhance the chart's effectiveness? Explain.

Suggested Writing Assignments

1. Based on what he has learned from brain studies on boys and girls and the ways their brains develop, Leonard Sax has come to believe that "very young boys and girls would be better off in separate classrooms altogether" (26). What are your thoughts about single-sex education? Write an essay in which you compare and contrast the advantages and disadvantages of single-sex education with education in coed schools. You may find it helpful to research the topic in your college library or on the Internet before beginning to write.

2. In paragraph 6, Ripley quotes Yu Xie, a University of Michigan sociology professor, who says, "I don't exclude biology as an explanation. But I know biological factors would not play a role unless they interacted with social conditions." In the next paragraph, Ripley uses the example of university presidents to illustrate the point Xie is making. What other examples can you

think of that would validate Xie's point? Write an essay in which you explain why it is important—if not essential—for each one of us to appreciate the complexity of how biology and environment interact on the workings of each person's brain. You may find it helpful to review your answer to the "Thinking Critically about This Reading" prompt for this essay.

Point-by-Point Comparison of Common Cold and H1N1 Flu

Symptom	Cold	H1N1 Flu
Fever	Fever is rare with a cold.	Fever is usually present with the flu in up to 80% of all flu cases. A temperature of 100°F or higher for 3 to 4 days is associated with the flu.
Coughing	A hacking, productive (mucus-producing) cough is often present with a cold.	A nonproductive (non-mucus-producing) cough is usually present with the flu (sometimes referred to as dry cough).
Aches	Slight body aches and pains can be part of a cold.	Severe aches and pains are common with the flu.
Stuffy Nose	Stuffy nose is commonly present with a cold and typically resolves spontaneously within a week.	Stuffy nose is not commonly present with the flu.
Chills	Chills are uncommon with a cold.	Sixty percent of people who have the flu experience chills.
Tiredness	Tiredness is fairly mild with a cold.	Tiredness is moderate to severe with the flu.
Sneezing	Sneezing is commonly present with a cold.	Sneezing is not common with the flu.
Sudden Symptoms	Cold symptoms tend to develop over a few days.	The flu has a rapid onset within 3–6 hours. The flu hits hard and includes sudden symptoms like high fever, aches, and pains.
Headache	A headache is fairly uncommon with a cold.	A headache is very common with the flu, present in 80% of flu cases.
Sore Throat	Sore throat is commonly present with a cold.	Sore throat is not commonly present with the flu.
Chest Discomfort	Chest discomfort is mild to moderate with a cold.	Chest discomfort is often severe with the flu.

Cause and Effect

Every time you answer a question that asks *why*, you engage in the process of *causal analysis*—that is, you try to determine a *cause* or series of causes for a particular *effect*. When you answer a question that asks *what if*, you try to determine what *effect* will result from a particular *cause*. You will have many opportunities to use **cause and effect** in the writing you will do in college. For example, in history, you might be asked to determine the causes for the 1991 breakup of the former Soviet Union; in political science, you might be asked to determine the critical issues in the 2008 presidential election; in sociology, you might be asked to analyze the effects that the AIDS epidemic has had on sexual-behavior patterns among Americans; and in economics, you might be asked to predict what will happen to our country if we enact large tax cuts.

Fascinated by the effects that private real estate development was having on his neighborhood, a student writer decided to find out what was happening in the older sections of cities across the country. In his first paragraph, Kevin Cunningham describes three possible effects (or fates) of a city's aging. In his second paragraph, he singles out one effect, redevelopment, and discusses in detail the effect it has had on Hoboken, New Jersey.

Effect: decay

Effect: urban renewal

Effect: redevelopment

Effects of redevelopment

One of three fates awaits the aging neighborhood. Decay may continue until the neighborhood becomes a slum. It may face urban renewal, with old buildings being razed and ugly new apartment houses taking their place. Or it may undergo redevelopment, in which government encourages the upgrading of existing housing stock by offering low-interest loans or outright grants; thus, the original character of the neighborhood may be retained or restored, allowing the city to keep part of its identity.

An example of redevelopment at its best is Hoboken, New Jersey. In the early 1970s Hoboken was a dying city, with rundown housing and many abandoned buildings. However, low-interest loans enabled some younger residents to refurbish their homes, and soon the area began to show signs of renewed vigor. Even outsiders moved in and rebuilt some of the abandoned houses. Today, whole blocks have been restored, and neighborhood life is active again. The city does well, too, because property values are higher and so are property taxes.

–Kevin Cunningham, student

In the following example, popular author Bill Bryson explains why the transition from being hunter-gatherers to farmers and city dwellers did not have a beneficial effect on us as humans:

It is not as if farming brought a great improvement in living standards either. A typical hunter-gatherer enjoyed a more varied diet and consumed more protein and calories than settled people, and took in five times as much vitamin C as the average person today. Even in the bitterest depths of the ice ages, we now know, nomadic people ate surprisingly well—and surprisingly healthily. Settled people, by contrast, became reliant on a much smaller range of foods, which all but ensured dietary insufficiencies. The three great domesticated crops of prehistory were rice, wheat, and maize, but all had significant drawbacks as staples. As the journalist John Lanchester explains: "Rice inhibits the activity of Vitamin A; wheat has a chemical that impedes the action of zinc and can lead to stunted growth; maize is deficient in essential amino acids and contains phytates, which prevent the absorption of iron." The average height of people actually fell by almost six inches in the early days of farming in the Near East. Even on Orkney, where prehistoric life was probably as good as it could get, an analysis of 340 ancient skeletons showed that hardly any people lived beyond their twenties.

What killed the Orcadians was not dietary deficiency but disease. People living together are vastly more likely to spread illness from household to household, and the close exposure to animals through domestication meant that flu (from pigs or fowl), smallpox and measles (from cows and sheep), and anthrax (from horses and goats, among others) could become part of the human condition, too. As far as we can tell, virtually all of the infectious diseases have become endemic only since people took to living together. Settling down also brought a huge increase in "human commensals"—mice, rats, and other creatures that live with and off us—and these all too often acted as disease vectors.

So sedentism meant poorer diets, more illness, lots of toothache and gum disease, and earlier deaths. What is truly extraordinary is that these are all still factors in our lives today. Out of the thirty thousand types of edible plants thought to exist on Earth, just eleven—corn, rice, wheat, potatoes, cassava, sorghum, millet, beans, barley, rye, and oats—account for 93 percent of all that humans eat, and every one of them was first cultivated by our Neolithic ancestors. Exactly the same is true of husbandry. The animals we raise for food today are eaten not because they are notably delectable or nutritious or a pleasure to be around, but because they were the ones first domesticated in the Stone Age.

We are, in the most fundamental way, Stone Age people ourselves. From a dietary point of view, the Neolithic period is still with us. We may sprinkle our dishes with bay leaves and chopped fennel, but underneath it all is Stone Age food. And when we get sick, it is Stone Age diseases we suffer.

—Bill Bryson

Determining causes and effects is usually a complex process. One reason is that *immediate causes* are readily apparent (because they are closest to the effect) and *ultimate causes* are not as apparent (because they are somewhat removed and even hidden). Furthermore, ultimate causes may bring about effects that themselves become immediate causes, thus creating a *causal chain*. Consider the following causal chain: Sally, a computer salesperson, prepared extensively for a meeting with an important client (ultimate cause), impressed the client (immediate cause), and made a very large sale (effect). The chain did not stop there: the large sale caused her to be promoted by her employer (effect). For a detailed example of a causal chain, read Barry Commoner's analysis of the near disaster at the Three Mile Island nuclear facility in Chapter 5 (pp. 120–21).

A second reason causal analysis can be complex is that an effect may have several possible or actual causes and a cause may have several possible or actual effects. An upset stomach may be caused by eating spoiled food, but it may also be caused by overeating, flu, allergy, nervousness, pregnancy, or any combination of factors. Similarly, the high cost of electricity may have multiple effects—higher profits for utility companies, fewer sales of electrical appliances, higher prices for other products, and the development of alternative sources of energy.

Sound reasoning and logic are present in all good writing, but they are central to any causal analysis. Writers of believable causal analysis examine their material objectively and develop their essays carefully. They examine methodically all causes and effects and evaluate them. They are convinced by their own examination of the material but are not afraid to admit that other causes and effects might exist. Above all, they do not let their own prejudices interfere with the logic of their analyses and presentations.

Because people are accustomed to thinking of causes with their effects, they sometimes commit an error in logic known as the "after this, therefore because of this" fallacy (in Latin, *post hoc, ergo propter hoc*). This **logical fallacy** leads people to believe that one event somehow caused a second event, just because the second event followed the first—that is, they sometimes make causal connections that are not proven. For example, if students perform better after a free breakfast program is instituted at their school, one cannot assume that the improvement was caused by the breakfast program. There could be any number of other causes for this effect, and a responsible writer would analyze and consider them all before suggesting the cause.

The Famine of Bengal

■ **Gita Mehta**

Gita Mehta is a novelist, essayist, journalist, and documentary filmmaker. She was born in Delhi, India, in 1943, the daughter of Biju Patnaik, the most prominent activist against British rule in the state of Orissa in the Bay of Bengal in eastern India. She was educated in India and the United Kingdom and graduated from Cambridge University. Mehta now divides her time among New York, London, and her native India, on which all her work is focused. Among her publications are two collections of essays: Karma Cola: Marketing the Mystic East *(1979) and* Snakes and Ladders: Glimpses of Modern India *(1997). She has also written two novels:* Raj: A Novel *(1989) and* A River Sutra *(1993). As a journalist, she has produced numerous documentaries on Indian culture and politics for the BBC and European networks, and she has been a television war correspondent for NBC.*

In the following essay, Mehta reports on the ironic turn of events that caused three million Indians to die of starvation just prior to her birth. The essay is taken from We Are What We Ate: 24 Memories of Food, *edited by Mark Winegardner.*

Reflecting on What You Know

There are various estimates of how many people go to bed hungry every night in the United States, but figures range from 10 million to 17 million. What do you think the cause is—a lack of food supplies, government policies, a lack of money to buy food, poor eating habits, or something else?

In 1942, after the Japanese armies had overrun Burma and Singapore and bombed several Indian ports, it was feared World War II would engulf India. Preparations were made for a defense of India by Allied armies rerouted from other theaters of war. To feed the expected armies, entire harvests were bought from Indian villagers who eagerly sold all their grain, even family supplies, in this once-in-a-lifetime opportunity to free themselves of debt.

When the Japanese attack did not materialize the food was re- 2 leased as rapidly as it had been acquired—into the hands of middlemen who controlled the black market. Throughout that winter of 1942 and into the spring of 1943, tons of food rotted away, hoarded by black marketers. And three million people starved to death, most of them on the streets of Calcutta.

As hungry peasants flooded into Calcutta in search of work for 3 food, restaurants did brisk business. One roadside stall offered three options to its customers:

A price to see the food.   4

A higher price to smell the food.   5

A third price to eat the food.   6

After all, there was no shortage of food in the Famine of Bengal.   7

It must be hard to be hungry when food is plentiful. Hard to look   8 at billboards advertising food, to smell cooking through the doorways of restaurants, to watch people eating on the street. Hard to see food and smell food and not be able to eat. It must be hard to be hungry, even in the U.S.A.

Thinking Critically about This Reading

Who ruled India during the time of "The Famine of Bengal"? The British Raj, or government? Local Indian governors? Both? Use the Internet to research both the context of the famine and the measures the ruling government or governments took to alleviate the famine. Could the famine have been prevented?

Questions for Study and Discussion

1. What is Mehta's purpose in this essay? (Glossary: *Purpose*) Where does Mehta most directly indicate her purpose?

2. What are the immediate causes of the starvation that Mehta discusses?

3. What are the ultimate causes of the starvation she discusses?

4. What is black marketeering? Who do you think allowed black marketers to operate in Calcutta in the winter of 1942 and the spring of 1943?

5. What is the meaning of Mehta's last sentence? Does Mehta think that we have a problem in the United States similar to the one India faced in 1942 and 1943? Explain.

Classroom Activity Using Cause and Effect

Determining causes and effects requires careful thought, and establishing a causal chain of events can help clarify complex issues. Consider the following example involving pollution and environmental stewardship:

Ultimate Cause	Industrial smokestack emissions
Immediate Cause	Smoke and acid rain damage
Effect	Clean air legislation
Effect	Improved air quality and forest growth

Develop a causal chain for each of the four following cause-and-effect pairs. Then create a new pair (for example, develop a causal chain for vacation/anxiety). Be prepared to discuss your answer with the class.

fire drill/fear	party/excitement
giving a speech/anxiety	vacation/relaxation

Suggested Writing Assignments

1. Mehta presents us with one perspective on the cause of the famine of Bengal. Might there be other causes? Has Mehta left out anything? Do some research in your library and on the Internet to determine if there are other causes, either sole causes or ones that are part of the cause she presents. Write an essay in which you share your findings. Be sure to document the sources of your information.

2. Write an essay about a recent achievement you have experienced or about an important achievement in your community. Before beginning to write the essay, list the causes of the achievement and its effects. Also explain how you determined the main cause of the causal chain that led to the achievement.

Why We Crave Horror Movies

■ Stephen King

Stephen King's name is synonymous with hor-
ror stories. Born in 1947, King is a 1970 grad-
uate of the University of Maine. He worked as
a janitor in a knitting mill, a laundry worker,
and a high school English teacher before he
struck it big with his writing. Many consider
King to be the most successful writer of mod-
ern horror fiction today. To date, he has writ-
ten dozens of novels, collections of short

stories and novellas, and screenplays, among other works. His
books have sold well over 250 million copies worldwide, and
many of his novels have been made into popular motion pictures,
including Stand by Me, Misery, The Green Mile, *and*
Dreamcatcher. *His books, starting with* Carrie *in 1974, include*
Salem's Lot *(1975),* The Shining *(1977),* The Dead Zone *(1979),*
Christine *(1983),* Pet Sematary *(1983),* The Dark Half *(1989),* The
Girl Who Loved Tom Gordon *(1999),* From a Buick 8 *(2002),* The
Colorado Kid *(2005),* Cell *(2006),* Lisey's Story *(2006),* Duma Key
(2008), Under the Dome *(2009), and* Everything's Eventual: Five
Dark Tales *(2002), a collection of short stories. Other works of his*
include Danse Macabre *(1980), a nonfiction look at horror in the*
media, and On Writing: A Memoir of the Craft *(2000). The wide-*
spread popularity of horror books and films shows that many
people share King's fascination with the macabre.

In the following selection, originally published in Playboy
in 1982, a variation on "The Horror Movie as Junk Food"
chapter in Danse Macabre, *King analyzes the reasons we flock*
to good horror movies.

Reflecting on What You Know

What movies have you seen recently? Do you prefer watching
any particular kind of movie—comedy, drama, science fiction,
or horror, for example—more than others? How do you explain
your preference?

I think that we're all mentally ill; those of us outside the asylums only 1
hide it a little better—and maybe not all that much better, after all.
We've all known people who talk to themselves, people who sometimes squinch their faces into horrible grimaces when they believe no one
is watching, people who have some hysterical fear—of snakes, the dark,
the tight place, the long drop . . . and, of course, those final worms and
grubs that are waiting so patiently underground.

When we pay our four or five bucks and seat ourselves at tenth-row 2
center in a theater showing a horror movie, we are daring the nightmare.

Why? Some of the reasons are simple and obvious. To show that 3
we can, that we are not afraid, that we can ride this roller coaster.
Which is not to say that a really good horror movie may not surprise
a scream out of us at some point, the way we may scream when a
roller coaster twists through a complete 360 or plows through a lake
at the bottom of the drop. And horror movies, like roller coasters,
have always been the special province of the young; by the time one
turns forty or fifty, one's appetite for double twists or 360-degree
loops may be considerably depleted.

We also go to reestablish our feelings of essential normality; the 4
horror movie is innately conservative, even reactionary. Freda
Jackson as the horrible melting woman in *Die, Monster, Die!* confirms for us that no matter how far we may be removed from the
beauty of a Robert Redford or a Diana Ross, we are still light-years
from true ugliness.

And we go to have fun. 5

Ah, but this is where the ground starts to slope away, isn't it? 6
Because this is a very peculiar sort of fun, indeed. The fun comes from
seeing others menaced—sometimes killed. One critic has suggested
that if pro football has become the voyeur's[1] version of combat, then
the horror film has become the modern version of the public lynching.

It is true that the mythic, "fairy-tale" horror film intends to take 7
away the shades of gray. . . . It urges us to put away our more civilized and adult penchant for analysis and to become children again,
seeing things in pure blacks and whites. It may be that horror movies
provide psychic relief on this level because this invitation to lapse into
simplicity, irrationality, and even outright madness is extended so
rarely. We are told we may allow our emotions a free rein . . . or no
rein at all.

---

[1]*voyeur:* one who observes from a distance.

If we are all insane, then sanity becomes a matter of degree. If your 8 insanity leads you to carve up women like Jack the Ripper or the Cleveland Torso Murderer,[2] we clap you away in the funny farm (but neither of those two amateur-night surgeons was ever caught, heh-heh-heh); if, on the other hand, your insanity leads you only to talk to yourself when you're under stress or to pick your nose on your morning bus, then you are left alone to go about your business . . . though it is doubtful that you will ever be invited to the best parties.

The potential lyncher is in almost all of us (excluding saints, past 9 and present; but then, most saints have been crazy in their own ways), and every now and then, he has to be let loose to scream and roll around in the grass. Our emotions and our fears form their own body, and we recognize that it demands its own exercise to maintain proper muscle tone. Certain of these emotional muscles are accepted—even exalted—in civilized society; they are, of course, the emotions that tend to maintain the status quo of civilization itself. Love, friendship, loyalty, kindness—these are all the emotions that we applaud, emotions that have been immortalized in the couplets of Hallmark cards and in the verses (I don't dare call it poetry) of Leonard Nimoy.[3]

When we exhibit these emotions, society showers us with positive 10 reinforcement; we learn this even before we get out of diapers. When, as children, we hug our rotten little puke of a sister and give her a kiss, all the aunts and uncles smile and twit and cry, "Isn't he the sweetest little thing?" Such coveted treats as chocolate-covered graham crackers often follow. But if we deliberately slam the rotten little puke of a sister's fingers in the door, sanctions follow—angry remonstrance from parents, aunts, and uncles; instead of a chocolate-covered graham cracker, a spanking.

But anticivilization emotions don't go away, and they demand 11 periodic exercise. We have such "sick" jokes as, "What's the difference between a truckload of bowling balls and a truckload of dead babies?" (You can't unload a truckload of bowling balls with a pitchfork . . . a joke, by the way, that I heard originally from a ten-year-old.) Such a joke may surprise a laugh or a grin out of us even as we recoil, a possibility that confirms the thesis: if we share a brotherhood of

---

[2]*Jack the Ripper or the Cleveland Torso Murderer:* serial murderers who were active in the 1880s and the 1930s, respectively.
[3]*Leonard Nimoy* (b. 1931): an actor famous for playing Mr. Spock on the U.S. television series *Star Trek*, which aired from1966 to 1969.

man, then we also share an insanity of man. None of which is intended as a defense of either the sick joke or insanity but merely as an explanation of why the best horror films, like the best fairy tales, manage to be reactionary, anarchistic,[4] and revolutionary all at the same time.

The mythic horror movie, like the sick joke, has a dirty job to do. It deliberately appeals to all that is worst in us. It is morbidity unchained, our most base instincts let free, our nastiest fantasies realized . . . and it all happens, fittingly enough, in the dark. For those reasons, good liberals often shy away from horror films. For myself, I like to see the most aggressive of them—*Dawn of the Dead,* for instance—as lifting a trap door in the civilized forebrain and throwing a basket of raw meat to the hungry alligators swimming around in that subterranean river beneath.   12

Why bother? Because it keeps them from getting out, man. It keeps them down there and me up here. It was Lennon and McCartney who said that all you need is love, and I would agree with that.   13

As long as you keep the gators fed.   14

Thinking Critically about This Reading

What does King mean when he states that "the horror movie is innately conservative, even reactionary" (paragraph 4)?

Questions for Study and Discussion

1. What, according to King, causes people to crave horror movies? What other reasons can you add to King's list?

2. Identify the analogy King uses in paragraph 3, and explain how it works. (Glossary: *Analogy*)

3. What emotions does society applaud? Why? Which ones does King label "anticivilization emotions" (11)?

4. In what ways is a horror movie like a sick joke? What is the "dirty job" or effect that the two have in common (12)?

5. King starts his essay with the attention-grabbing sentence, "I think that we're all mentally ill." How does he develop this idea of

---

[4]*anarchistic:* against any authority; anarchy.

insanity in his essay? What does King mean when he says, "The potential lyncher is in almost all of us" (9)? How does King's last line relate to the theme of mental illness?

6. What is King's tone? (Glossary: *Tone*) Point to particular words or sentences that lead you to this conclusion.

Classroom Activity Using Cause and Effect

Use the following test, developed by William V. Haney, to determine your ability to analyze accurately evidence that is presented to you. After completing Haney's test, discuss your answers with other members of your class.

The Uncritical Inference Test

Directions

1. You will read a brief story. Assume that all of the information presented in the story is definitely accurate and true. Read the story carefully. You may refer back to the story whenever you wish.

2. You will then read statements about the story. Answer them in numerical order. *Do not go back* to fill in answers or to change answers. This will only distort your test score.

3. After you read each statement carefully, determine whether the statement is:
    a. "T"—meaning: On the basis of the information presented in the story the statement is *definitely true.*
    b. "F"—meaning: On the basis of the information presented in the story the statement is *definitely false.*
    c. "?"—The statement *may* be true (or false) but on the basis of the information presented in the story you cannot be definitely certain. (If any part of the statement is doubtful, mark the statement "?".)

4. Indicate your answer by circling either "T" or "F" or "?" opposite the statement.

The Story

Babe Smith has been killed. Police have rounded up six suspects, all of whom are known gangsters. All of them are known to have been near the scene of the killing at the approximate time that it occurred. All had substantial motives for wanting Smith killed. However, one of these suspected gangsters, Slinky Sam, has positively been cleared of guilt.

Statements about the Story

1. Slinky Sam is known to have been near the scene of
   the killing of Babe Smith. T F ?

2. All six of the rounded-up gangsters were known to
   have been near the scene of the murder. T F ?

3. Only Slinky Sam has been cleared of guilt. T F ?

4. All six of the rounded-up suspects were near the
   scene of Smith's killing at the approximate time
   that it took place. T F ?

5. The police do not know who killed Smith. T F ?

6. All six suspects are known to have been near the
   scene of the foul deed. T F ?

7. Smith's murderer did not confess of his own
   free will. T F ?

8. Slinky Sam was not cleared of guilt. T F ?

9. It is known that the six suspects were in the
   vicinity of the cold-blooded assassination. T F ?

Suggested Writing Assignments

1. Write an essay in which you analyze, in light of King's remarks
   about the causes of our cravings for horror movies, a horror movie
   you've seen. In what ways did the movie satisfy your "anticivilization emotions" (11)? How did you feel before going to the theater? How did you feel when leaving?

2. Write an essay in which you analyze the most significant reasons
   or causes for your going to college. You may wish to discuss such
   matters as your high school experiences, people and events that
   influenced your decision, and your goals in college as well as in
   later life.

3. In the following film still from Alfred Hitchcock's 1960 thriller,
   Psycho, Marion Crane (Janet Leigh) screams in terror as Norman
   Bates (Anthony Perkins) opens the shower curtain and she realizes
   that he is about to kill her with a large kitchen knife. For many
   viewers, this scene is iconographic—an unforgettable symbol of
   the essence of terror. For many others, different scenes of terror,
   actual or artistically represented, have become similarly powerful.
   Write an essay examining a situation or scene that terrifies you,
   and examining the causes of your fright.

Why and When We Speak Spanish in Public

■ **Myriam Marquez**

An award-winning columnist for the Orlando Sentinel, *Myriam Marquez was born in Havana, Cuba, in 1954 and grew up in southern Florida. After graduating from the University of Maryland in 1983 with a degree in journalism and a minor in political science, she worked for United Press International in Washington, D.C., and in Maryland, covering the Maryland legislature as statehouse bureau chief. Marquez joined the editorial board of the* Sentinel *in 1987 and, beginning in 1990, wrote three weekly columns. Her commentaries focused on state and national politics, the human condition, civil liberties, and issues important to women and Hispanics. The Florida Society of Newspaper Editors awarded her its highest award for commentary in 2003. In 2005, she joined the* Miami Herald, *where she is currently the editorial page editor.*

Marquez grew up bilingual and recognizes that English is the "common language" in the United States but knows that being American has little if anything to do with what language one speaks. In this article, which first appeared in the Orlando Sentinel *on July 5, 1999, Marquez explains why she and her parents continue to speak Spanish when they are together, even though they have lived in the United States for many years.*

Reflecting on What You Know

When you are in public and hear people around you speaking a foreign language, what is your immediate reaction? Are you intrigued? Do you feel uncomfortable? How do you regard people who speak a language other than English in public? Why?

W hen I'm shopping with my mother or standing in line with my   1
stepdad to order fast food or anywhere else we might be together, we're going to speak to one another in Spanish.

That may appear rude to those who don't understand Spanish and   2
overhear us in public places.

Those around us may get the impression that we're talking about   3
them. They may wonder why we would insist on speaking in a foreign tongue, especially if they knew that my family has lived in the
United States for forty years and that my parents do understand
English and speak it, albeit with difficulty and a heavy accent.

Let me explain why we haven't adopted English as our official   4
family language. For me and most of the bilingual people I know, it's
a matter of respect for our parents and comfort in our cultural roots.

It's not meant to be rude to others. It's not meant to alienate any-   5
one or to Balkanize[1] America.

It's certainly not meant to be un-American—what constitutes an   6
"American" being defined by English speakers from North America.

Being an American has very little to do with what language we use   7
during our free time in a free country. From its inception,[2] this country
was careful not to promote a government-mandated official language.

We understand that English is the common language of this country   8
and the one most often heard in international business circles from Peru
to Norway. We know that, to get ahead here, one must learn English.

But that ought not mean that somehow we must stop speaking   9
in our native tongue whenever we're in a public area, as if we were
ashamed of who we are, where we're from. As if talking in Spanish—
or any other language, for that matter—is some sort of litmus test[3] used
to gauge American patriotism.

Throughout this nation's history, most immigrants—whether from   10
Poland or Finland or Italy or wherever else—kept their language
through the first generation and, often, the second. I suspect that they
spoke among themselves in their native tongue—in public. Pennsylvania even provided voting ballots written in German during much of
the 1800s for those who weren't fluent in English.

In this century, Latin American immigrants and others have fought   11
for this country in U.S.-led wars. They have participated fully in this

---

[1]*Balkanize:* to divide a region or territory into small, often hostile units.
[2]*inception:* the beginning of something.
[3]*litmus test:* a test that uses a single indicator to prompt a decision.

nation's democracy by voting, holding political office, and paying taxes. And they have watched their children and grandchildren become so "American" that they resist speaking in Spanish.

You know what's rude? 12

When there are two or more people who are bilingual and another 13 person who speaks only English and the bilingual folks all of a sudden start speaking Spanish, which effectively leaves out the English-only speaker. I don't tolerate that.

One thing's for sure. If I'm ever in a public place with my mom 14 or dad and bump into an acquaintance who doesn't speak Spanish, I will switch to English and introduce that person to my parents. They will respond in English, and do so with respect.

Thinking Critically about This Reading

Marquez states that "being an American has very little to do with what language we use during our free time in a free country" (paragraph 7). What activities does Marquez suggest truly make someone an American?

Questions for Study and Discussion

1. What is Marquez's thesis? (Glossary: *Thesis*)
2. Against what ideas does she seem to be arguing? How do you know?
3. Writers are often advised not to begin a paragraph with the word *but*. Why do you think Marquez ignores this rule in paragraph 9?
4. Is this essay one of causes, effects, or both? What details lead you to this conclusion?
5. Do you agree with Marquez that our patriotism should not be gauged by whether we speak English in public? Or do you think that people living in this country ought to affirm their patriotism by speaking only English in public? Explain.

Classroom Activity Using Cause and Effect

Develop a causal chain in which you examine the ramifications of an action you took in the past. Identify each part in the chain. For example, you decided that you wanted to do well in a course (ultimate cause), so you got started on a research project early (immediate cause), which enabled you to write several drafts of your paper (immediate cause), which earned you an A for the project (effect), which earned you an excellent grade for the class (effect), which enabled you to take the advanced seminar you wanted (effect).

Suggested Writing Assignments

1. Marquez's essay is set against the backdrop of a larger language-based controversy currently taking place in the United States called the English-only movement. Research the controversy in your school library or on the Internet, and write a cause-and-effect essay exploring why the movement began and what is keeping it alive.

2. There is often more than one cause for an event. List at least six possible causes for one of the following events:

   an upset victory in a competition   a change in your major
   an injury you suffered   a quarrel with a friend

   Examine your list, and identify the causes that seem most probable. Which of these are immediate causes, and which are ultimate causes? Using this material, write a short cause-and-effect essay on one of the topics.

Stuck on the Couch

■ **Sanjay Gupta**

Sanjay Gupta is a practicing neurosurgeon at Grady Memorial Hospital in Atlanta, Georgia; is CNN's chief medical correspondent; and is a special correspondent for CBS News. An American of Indian descent, Gupta grew up in Novi, Michigan, and received both his undergraduate and medical degrees at the University of Michigan. As an embedded correspondent in the Iraq war in 2003, he witnessed the first surgical operation that was performed in the war and operated on a wounded Marine twice pronounced dead on the battlefield. Criticized for switching roles from correspondent to surgeon, Gupta said in Newsweek *magazine, "Medically and morally, it was the right thing to do." Author of numerous scholarly articles on neurosurgery, Gupta has also published* Chasing Life: New Discoveries in the Search for Immortality to Help You Age Less Today *(2007) and* Cheating Death: The Doctors and Medical Miracles That Are Saving Lives Against All Odds *(2009) for general audiences.*

In "Stuck on the Couch," first published in Time *on February 22, 2008, Gupta attempts to answer the puzzling question of why we don't exercise more when all the evidence supports the medical benefits of being active.*

Reflecting on What You Know

If you exercise regularly, you have also probably experienced periods of inactivity. What were your reasons for failing to maintain a regular exercise schedule?

As a doctor, I can give you a lot of useful advice about how to get healthy and stay that way, but one thing you don't need me to tell you is that exercise is good for you. By this point, it's not news to anyone that staying active can benefit the heart, the waistline, even the mind. Still, there's a real disconnect between what we know and what we do. More than 60 percent of American adults do not exercise regularly, and many are content to admit they don't exercise at all. More than 72 million are obese, and almost every one of them would like to shed the extra pounds. So if exercise is such a good idea, why don't more people do it?

The most paradoxical part of our sedentary nature is that we   2
don't start out that way. Even as I write this, I am watching my two-year-old run around in circles. In the last paragraph alone, she has made six circumnavigations of the house. Kids seem to be born in constant motion, but along the way that behavior gets hijacked.

According to kinesiologist Steven Bray at McMaster University in   3
Ontario, the slowdown occurs for many of us at around the time we start college. Bray followed 127 subjects and found that on the whole, first-year college students participate in significantly less exercise than they did just one year before. Academic demands and lack of organized sports are certainly part of the problem. A bigger part may be a curious human tendency to look at life changes as an occasion to blow up the old rules and not create new ones in their place. This is especially so when it comes to staying fit. "College is the first big transition in life," Bray says. "And it becomes an excuse not to exercise."

That's a pattern we repeat over and over. The demands of a new   4
job usually mean less time at the gym or on the jogging track. How about a new marriage? How many times have we seen newlyweds looking a lot plumper in first-anniversary photos than they did in the wedding pictures? And whatever exercise resolve that married couples have left can be wiped out when a new baby comes along. "A lot of people don't like to exercise," says Bray, "so it's the first thing to go when you get the opportunity to rearrange your schedule."

In a recent issue of *Observer,* the magazine of the Association for   5
Psychological Science, Ian Herbert, a journalist and triathlete, reported on numerous other studies that explain why we fall off the exercise wagon. Research by psychologist Roy Baumeister at Florida State University, for example, suggests that self-control is like a psychological muscle—one that can simply become exhausted. Spend your day trying to maintain your composure with a willful toddler or a demanding boss, and you may not have enough discipline left later to stick to your fitness routine. If that routine involves a diet, things can get even more complicated, as the effort you make to resist having a Snickers in the afternoon depletes your resolve to work out in the evening. "The more you use the self-control muscle," Herbert says, "the more tired it gets."

Not having a clearly defined exercise plan can hurt too. Investi- 6
gators at Berlin's Free University found that people who set general
goals, like "I will exercise in my free time," did a far worse job of
sticking to that plan than did people who made a firm commitment,
like "I will walk to my friend's house and back every Monday,
Wednesday, and Friday."

Even something that ought to help—having a personal trainer— 7
can hurt over time. Research at the University of Saskatchewan
shows that while a trainer may ensure that we stick to a fitness program, our resolve melts away once the training sessions end. In these
cases, we become so dependent on someone else to monitor our progress that we never develop what psychologists call the self-efficacy to
follow a plan on our own.

The good news is, there are solutions to all of these problems. 8
Baumeister thinks the self-control muscle may be strengthened and
trained—sometimes beginning with exercises as simple as remembering to sit straighter or drink enough water. Specific workout plans,
like scheduling a gym visit with friends, can turn a general desire to
exercise into a firm commitment. Trying to do without a trainer, or at
least tapering off slowly when you quit, can help you learn to be accountable only to you. We may never again have the stamina of a
two-year-old, but recapturing even a little of our early-life energy can
make our later lives a whole lot healthier.

Thinking Critically about This Reading

How helpful do you find Gupta's reasons for why we stop exercising?
Do you think that knowing why you stop will help you get started again
and maintain your commitment? Explain.

Questions for Study and Discussion

1. What is Gupta's purpose in this essay? (Glossary: *Purpose*)
2. Why do so many "first-year college students participate in significantly less exercise than they did just one year before," according
   to kinesiologist Steven Bray (paragraph 3)?
3. Gupta quotes journalist and triathlete Ian Herbert in paragraph 5
   as saying, "The more you use the self-control muscle, . . . the
   more tired it gets." What is "the self-control muscle," and what
   does he mean?

4. What has research shown about the benefits of a personal trainer over time? What suggestion does Gupta make about using a personal trainer?

5. What suggestions does the author offer for sticking with an exercise program?

6. Is Gupta's tone in this essay appropriate for his subject and audience, or do you think that he should be more forceful in his approach? (Glossary: *Tone*)

Classroom Activity Using Cause and Effect

In preparation for writing a cause-and-effect essay, list four effects (two on society and two on personal behavior) for one of the following items—television, cell phones, e-mail, microwave ovens, DVD technology, the Internet, or an item of your choice. For example, the automobile could be said to have had the following effects:

Society

A national highway system developed that is based on asphalt roads.
The petroleum and insurance industries expanded in size and influence.

Personal Behavior

People with cars can live far from public transportation.
Suburban and rural drivers walk less than urban dwellers.

Suggested Writing Assignments

1. Write an essay in which you assess the effects of the Internet. What do the capabilities of search engines allow us to do now that people could not do just a few years ago? Also consider negative effects that the ability to search the Internet has caused.

2. One way to think of ourselves is in terms of the influences that have caused us to be who we are. Write an essay in which you discuss two or three of the most important influences in your life. You may wish to consider the following areas as you plan your essay:

books or movies	coaches
parents	ethnic background
clergy	neighborhoods
teachers	friends
heroes	youth organizations

Argument

The word *argument* probably brings to mind a verbal disagreement of the sort that nearly everyone has participated in. Such disputes are satisfying when you convert someone to your point of view. More often, though, verbal arguments are inconclusive and frustrating because you might fail to make your position understood or may believe that your opponent has been stubborn and unreasonable. Because verbal arguments generally arise spontaneously, they cannot be thoughtfully planned or researched. Indeed, it is often not until later that the convincing piece of evidence or the forcefully phrased assertion finally comes to mind.

Also known as **argumentation**, written arguments share common goals with spoken ones: they attempt to convince a reader to agree with a particular point of view, to make a particular decision, or to pursue a particular course of action. Written arguments, however, involve the presentation of well-chosen evidence and the artful control of language. Writers of arguments must imagine their probable audience and predict the sorts of objections that may be raised. Writers must choose in advance a specific, sufficiently detailed thesis or proposition. There is a greater need to be organized, to choose the most effective types of evidence from all that is available, and to determine the strategies of rhetoric, language, and style that will best suit the argument's subject, purpose, and thesis and ensure its effect on the intended audience. In the end, such work can be far more satisfying than spontaneous oral argument.

Most people who specialize in the study of arguments identify two essential categories—persuasion and logic. *Persuasive appeals* are directed at readers' emotions, at their subconscious, even at their biases and prejudices. These appeals involve diction, slanting, figurative language, analogy, rhythmic patterns of speech, and the establishment of a tone that will encourage a positive response. Persuasion very often attempts to get the audience to take action. Examples of persuasive argument are found in the exaggerated claims of advertisers and the speech making of political and social activists.

Logical appeals, on the other hand, are directed primarily at the audience's intellectual faculties, understanding, and knowledge. Such appeals depend on the reasoned movement from assertion to evidence to conclusion and on an almost mathematical system of proof and counterproof. Logical argument, unlike persuasion, does not normally impel its audience to action. Logical argument is commonly found in scientific or philosophical articles, legal decisions, and technical proposals.

Most arguments are neither purely persuasive nor purely logical. A well-written editorial, for example, will present a logical arrangement of assertions and evidence, but it will also employ striking diction and other persuasive patterns of language to reinforce its effectiveness. Thus the kinds of appeals a writer emphasizes depend on the nature of the topic, the thesis or proposition of the argument, the writer's purpose, the various kinds of support (evidence, opinions, examples, facts, statistics) offered, and a thoughtful consideration of the audience. Knowing the differences between persuasive and logical appeals is essential in learning both to read and to write arguments.

True arguments make assertions about which there is a legitimate and recognized difference of opinion. Readers probably do not need to be convinced that falling in love is a beautiful and intense experience, that crime rates should be reduced, or that computers are changing the world; most everyone would agree with such assertions. But not everyone would agree that women experience love more intensely than men, that the death penalty reduces the incidence of crime, or that computers are changing the world for the worse; these assertions are arguable and admit of differing perspectives. Similarly, a leading heart specialist might argue in a popular magazine that too many doctors are advising patients to have pacemakers implanted when the devices are not necessary; the editorial writer for a small-town newspaper could write urging that a local agency supplying food to poor families be given a larger percentage of the town's budget; in a long and complex book, a foreign-policy specialist might attempt to prove that the current administration exhibits no consistent policy in its relationship with other countries and that the Department of State needs to be overhauled. No matter what its forum or its structure, an argument has as its chief purpose the detailed setting forth of a particular point of view and the rebuttal of any opposing views.

Argumentation frequently uses the other rhetorical strategies covered in Chapters 13 to 20. In your efforts to argue convincingly, you may find it necessary to define, to compare and contrast, to analyze causes and effects, to classify, to describe, or to narrate. Nevertheless, it is the writer's attempt to convince, not explain, that is of primary importance in an argumentative essay. In this respect, it is helpful to keep in mind that there are two basic patterns of thinking and presenting our thoughts that are followed in argumentation—**induction** and **deduction.**

Inductive reasoning, the more common type of reasoning, moves from a set of specific examples to a general statement. In doing so, the writer makes an *inductive leap* from the evidence to the generalization. For example, after examining enrollment statistics, we can conclude that students do not like to take courses offered early in the morning or late in the afternoon.

Deductive reasoning, in contrast, moves from a general statement to a specific conclusion. It works on the model of the **syllogism,** a three-part argument that consists of a major premise, a minor premise, and a conclusion, as in the following example:

a. All women are mortal. *(Major premise)*

b. Jeanne is a woman. *(Minor premise)*

c. Jeanne is mortal. *(Conclusion)*

A syllogism will fail to work if either of the premises is untrue:

a. All living creatures are mammals. *(Major premise)*

b. A butterfly is a living creature. *(Minor premise)*

c. A butterfly is a mammal. *(Conclusion)*

The problem is immediately apparent. The major premise is false: Many living creatures are not mammals, and a butterfly happens to be one of the nonmammals. Consequently, the conclusion is invalid.

■ WRITING ARGUMENTS

Writing an argument is a challenging assignment that can be very rewarding. By nature, an argument must be carefully reasoned and thoughtfully structured to have maximum effect. Therefore, allow yourself enough time to think about your thesis, to gather the evidence you need, and to draft, revise, edit, and proofread your essay. Fuzzy thinking, confused expression, and poor organization will be immediately evident to your reader and will diminish your chances for completing the assignment successfully. The following seven steps will remind you of some key features of arguments and help you sequence your activities as you research and write.

1. Determine the Thesis or Proposition

Begin by deciding on a topic that interests you and that has some significant differences of opinion or some points that you have questions about. Find out what's in the news about your topic, what people are saying about it, and what authors and instructors are emphasizing as important intellectual arguments. As you pursue your research, consider what assertion or assertions you can make about the topic you choose. The more specific you make this thesis or proposition, the more directed your research can become and the more focused your ultimate argument will be. Don't hesitate to modify or even reject an initial thesis as your research warrants.

A thesis can be placed anywhere in an argument, but while learning to write arguments, you should place the statement of your controlling idea near the beginning of your composition. Explain the importance of the thesis, and make clear to your reader that you share a common concern or interest in this issue. State your central assertion directly in your first or second paragraph so that your reader will have no doubt or confusion about your position. You may also wish to lead off with a striking piece of evidence to capture your reader's interest.

2. Take Account of Your Audience

In no other type of writing is the question of audience more important than in argumentation. The tone you establish, the type of diction you choose, the kinds of evidence you select to buttress your assertions, and the organizational pattern you follow can influence your audience to trust you and believe your assertions. If you judge the nature of your audience accurately, respect its knowledge of the subject, and correctly envision whether it is likely to be hostile, neutral, complacent, or receptive, you will be able to tailor the various aspects of your argument appropriately. (For more on audience, refer to the discussion of ethos, pathos, and logos on pp. 545–46.)

3. Gather the Necessary Supporting Evidence

For each point of your argument, be sure to provide appropriate and sufficient evidence—verifiable facts and statistics, illustrative examples and narratives, or quotations from authorities. Don't overwhelm your reader with evidence, but don't skimp either. Demonstrate your command of the topic and control of the thesis by choosing carefully from all the evidence at your disposal.

4. Settle on an Organizational Pattern

Once you think that you have sufficient evidence to make your assertion convincing, consider how best to organize your argument. To some extent, your organization will depend on your method of reasoning—inductive, deductive, or a combination of the two. For example, is it necessary to establish a major premise before moving on to discuss a minor premise? Should most of your evidence precede your direct statement of an assertion or follow it? Will induction work better with the particular audience you have targeted? As you present your primary points, you may find it effective to move from least important to most important or from most familiar to least familiar. A scratch outline can help, but often a writer's most crucial revisions in an argument involve rearranging its components into a sharper, more coherent order. Often it is difficult to tell what that order should be until the revision stage of the writing process.

5. Consider Refutations to Your Argument

As you proceed with your argument, you may wish to take into account well-known and significant opposing arguments. To ignore opposing views would be to suggest to your readers any one of the following: you don't know about the opposing views, you know about them and are obviously and unfairly weighting the arguments in your favor, or you know about them and have no reasonable answers for them. Grant the validity of opposing arguments or refute them, but respect your reader's intelligence by addressing the objections to your assertion. Your readers will in turn respect you for doing so.

Logical Fallacies

Oversimplification: A drastically simple solution to what is clearly a complex problem: *We have a balance-of-trade deficit because foreigners make better products than we do.*

Hasty generalization: In inductive reasoning, a generalization that is based on too little evidence or on evidence that is not representative: *My grandparents eat bran flakes for breakfast, just as most older folks do.*

Post hoc, ergo propter hoc: "After this, therefore because of this." Confusing chance or coincidence with causation. One event coming after another does not necessarily mean that the first event caused the second: *I went to the hockey game last night. The next thing I knew I had a cold.*

Begging the question: Assuming in a premise something that needs to be proven: *Lying is wrong because people should always tell the truth.*

False analogy: Making a misleading analogy between logically unconnected ideas: *If we can clone mammals, we should be able to find a cure for cancer.*

Either/or thinking: Seeing only two alternatives when there may in fact be other possibilities: *Either you love your job, or you hate it.*

Non sequitur: "It does not follow." An inference or conclusion that is not clearly related to the established premises or evidence: *She is very sincere. She must know what she's talking about.*

---

6. Avoid Faulty Reasoning

Have someone read your argument for errors in judgment and for faulty reasoning. Sometimes others can see easily what you can't see because you are so intimately tied to your assertion. These errors are typically called **logical fallacies.** Review the Logical Fallacies box above, making sure that you have not committed any of these errors in reasoning.

7. Conclude Forcefully

In the conclusion of your essay, be sure to restate your position in new language, at least briefly. Besides persuading your reader to accept your point of view, you may also want to encourage some specific course of action. Above all, your conclusion should not introduce new information that may surprise your reader. It should seem to follow naturally, almost seamlessly, from the series of points that you have carefully established in the body of the essay. Don't overstate your case, but at the same time don't qualify your conclusion with the use of too many words or phrases like *I think, in my opinion, maybe, sometimes,* and *probably.* These words can make you sound indecisive and fuzzy-headed rather than rational and sensible.

■ THINKING CRITICALLY ABOUT ARGUMENT

Take a Stand

Even though you have chosen a topic, gathered information about it, and established a thesis statement or proposition, you need to take a stand—to fully commit yourself to your beliefs and ideas about the issue before you. Your writing will show if you attempt to work with a thesis that you have not clearly thought through or are confused about or if you take a position you do not fully believe in or care about. Your willingness to research, to dig up evidence, to find the most effective organizational pattern for your material, to construct strong paragraphs and sentences, and to find just the right diction to convey your argument is a direct reflection of just how strongly you take a stand and how much you believe in that stand. With a strong stand, you can argue vigorously and convincingly.

Consider Ethos, Pathos, and Logos

Classical thinkers believed that there are three key components in all rhetorical communication—the *speaker* (or writer) who comments on a *subject* to an *audience.* For purposes of discussion, we can isolate each of these entities, but in actual rhetorical situations they are inseparable, and each inextricably influences the other two. The ancients also recognized the importance of three elements of argumentation—ethos, which is related to the speaker/writer; logos, which is related to the subject; and pathos, which is related to the audience.

Ethos (the Greek word for "character") has to do with the authority, credibility, and, to a certain extent, morals of the speaker/writer. The classical rhetoricians believed that it was important for the speaker/ writer to be credible and to argue for a worthwhile cause. Putting one's argumentative skills in the service of a questionable cause was simply not acceptable. But how does one establish credibility? Sometimes it is gained through achievements outside the rhetorical arena — that is, the speaker has had experience with an issue, has argued the subject before, and has been judged to be honest and sincere. In the case of your own writing, establishing such credentials is not always possible, so you will need to be more concerned than usual with presenting your argument reasonably, sincerely, and in language untainted by excessive emotionalism. Finally, you should always respect your audience in your writing.

Logos (Greek for "word") is related to the subject and is the effective presentation of the argument itself. Is the thesis or claim worthwhile? Is it logical, consistent, and well buttressed by supporting evidence? Is the evidence itself factual, reliable, and convincing? Finally, is the argument so thoughtfully organized and clearly presented that it will affect the audience? This aspect of argumentation is at once the most difficult to accomplish and the most rewarding.

Pathos (Greek for "emotion") has most to do with the audience. How does the speaker/writer present an argument to maximize its appeal for a given audience? One way is through artful and strategic use of well-crafted language. Certain buzzwords, slanted diction, or loaded language may become either rallying cries or causes of resentment in an argument. Remember that audiences can range from friendly and sympathetic to hostile and resistant, with myriad possibilities in between. A friendly audience will welcome new information and support your position; a hostile audience will look for flaws in your logic and examples of dishonest manipulation. Caution, subtlety, and critical thinking must be applied to an uncommitted audience.

The Declaration of Independence

■ Thomas Jefferson

President, governor, statesman, lawyer, architect, philosopher, and writer, Thomas Jefferson (1743–1826) is one of the most important figures in U.S. history. He was born in Albemarle County, Virginia, in 1743 and attended the College of William and Mary. After being admitted to law practice in 1767, he began a long and illustrious career of public service to the colonies and, later, the  *new republic. In 1809, after two terms as president, Jefferson retired to Monticello, a home he had designed and helped build. Ten years later, he founded the University of Virginia. Jefferson died at Monticello on July 4, 1826, the fiftieth anniversary of the signing of the Declaration of Independence.*

Jefferson drafted the Declaration in 1776. Although it was revised by Benjamin Franklin and his colleagues at the Continental Congress, the Declaration retains in its sound logic and forceful, direct style the unmistakable qualities of Jefferson's prose.

Reflecting on What You Know

In your mind, what is the meaning of democracy? Where do your ideas about democracy come from?

W hen in the course of human events, it becomes necessary for one people to dissolve the political bands which have connected them with another, and to assume among the Powers of the earth, the separate and equal station to which the Laws of Nature and of Nature's God entitle them, a decent respect to the opinions of mankind requires that they should declare the causes which impel them to the separation.   1

We hold these truths to be self-evident, that all men are created equal, that they are endowed by their Creator with certain unalienable   2

Rights, that among these are Life, Liberty and the pursuit of Happiness. That to secure these rights, Governments are instituted among Men deriving their just powers from the consent of the governed. That whenever any Form of Government becomes destructive of these ends, it is the Right of the People to alter or to abolish it, and to institute new Government, laying its foundation on such principles and organizing its powers in such form, as to them shall seem most likely to effect their Safety and Happiness. Prudence, indeed, will dictate that Governments long established should not be changed for light and transient[1] causes; and accordingly all experience hath shown, that mankind are more disposed to suffer, while evils are sufferable, than to right themselves by abolishing the forms to which they are accustomed. But when a long train of abuses and usurpations pursuing invariably the same Object evinces a design to reduce them under absolute Despotism, it is their right, it is their duty, to throw off such government, and to provide new Guards for their future security. Such has been the patient sufferance of these Colonies; and such is now the necessity which constrains them to alter their former Systems of Government. The history of the present King of Great Britain[2] is a history of repeated injuries and usurpations, all having in direct object the establishment of an absolute Tyranny over these States. To prove this, let Facts be submitted to a candid world.

He has refused his Assent to Laws, the most wholesome and necessary for the public good.   3

He has forbidden his Governors to pass Laws of immediate and pressing importance, unless suspended in their operation till his Assent should be obtained; and when so suspended, he has utterly neglected to attend to them.   4

He has refused to pass other Laws for the accommodation of large districts of people, unless those people would relinquish the right of Representation in the Legislature, a right inestimable to them and formidable to tyrants only.   5

He has called together legislative bodies at places unusual, uncomfortable, and distant from the depository of their Public Records, for the sole purpose of fatiguing them into compliance with his measures.   6

He has dissolved Representative Houses repeatedly, for opposing with manly firmness his invasions on the rights of the people.   7

---

[1]*transient:* not lasting; not permanent.
[2]*King of Great Britain:* King George III (1738–1820), who ruled the British empire from 1760 to 1820.

He has refused for a long time, after such dissolutions, to cause 8
others to be elected; whereby the Legislative Powers, incapable of
Annihilation, have returned to the People at large for their exercise;
the State remaining in the mean time exposed to all the dangers of
invasion from without, and convulsions within.

He has endeavoured to prevent the population of these States; for 9
that purpose obstructing the Laws of Naturalization of Foreigners;
refusing to pass others to encourage their migration hither, and raising
the conditions of new Appropriations of Lands.

He has obstructed the Administration of Justice, by refusing his 10
Assent to Laws for establishing Judiciary Powers.

He has made Judges dependent on his Will alone, for the tenure of 11
their offices, and the amount and payment of their salaries.

He has erected a multitude of New Offices, and sent hither swarms 12
of Officers to harass our People, and eat out their substance.

He has kept among us, in time of peace, Standing Armies without 13
the Consent of our Legislature.

He has affected to render the Military independent of and superior 14
to the Civil Power.

He has combined with others to subject us to jurisdictions foreign 15
to our constitution, and unacknowledged by our laws; giving his Assent
to their acts of pretended Legislation:

For quartering large bodies of armed troops among us: 16

For protecting them, by a mock Trial, from Punishment for 17
any Murders which they should commit on the Inhabitants of these
States:

For cutting off our Trade with all parts of the world: 18

For imposing Taxes on us without our Consent: 19

For depriving us in many cases, of the benefits of Trial by Jury: 20

For transporting us beyond Seas to be tried for pretended offenses: 21

For abolishing the free System of English Laws in a Neighbouring 22
Province, establishing therein an Arbitrary government, and enlarging
its boundaries so as to render it at once an example and fit instrument
for introducing the same absolute rule into these Colonies:

For taking away our Charters, abolishing our most valuable Laws, 23
and altering fundamentally the Forms of our Governments:

For suspending our own Legislatures, and declaring themselves 24
invested with Power to legislate for us in all cases whatsoever.

He has abdicated Government here, by declaring us out of his 25
Protection and waging War against us.

He has plundered our seas, ravaged our Coasts, burnt our towns 26 and destroyed the Lives of our people.

He is at this time transporting large Armies of foreign Mercenaries 27 to compleat works of death, desolation and tyranny, already begun with circumstances of Cruelty & perfidy scarcely paralleled in the most barbarous ages, and totally unworthy the Head of a civilized nation.

He has constrained our fellow Citizens taken Captive on the high 28 Seas to bear Arms against their Country, to become the executioners of their friends and Brethren, or to fall themselves by their Hands.

He has excited domestic insurrections amongst us, and has endeav- 29 oured to bring on the inhabitants of our frontiers, the merciless Indian Savages, whose known rule of warfare, is an undistinguished destruction of all ages, sexes and conditions.

In every stage of these Oppressions We Have Petitioned for Redress 30 in the most humble terms: Our repeated petitions have been answered only by repeated injury. A Prince, whose character is thus marked by every act which may define a Tyrant, is unfit to be the ruler of a free People.

Nor have We been wanting in attention to our British brethren. We 31 have warned them from time to time of attempts by their legislature to extend an unwarrantable jurisdiction over us. We have reminded them of the circumstances of our emigration and settlement here. We have appealed to their native justice and magnanimity[3] and we have conjured them by the ties of our common kindred to disavow these usurpations, which would inevitably interrupt our connections and correspondence. They too have been deaf to the voice of justice and of consanguinity. We must, therefore acquiesce[4] in the necessity, which denounces our Separation, and hold them, as we hold the rest of mankind, Enemies in War, in Peace Friends.

We, therefore, the Representatives of the United States of America, 32 in General Congress, Assembled, appealing to the Supreme Judge of the world for the rectitude of our intentions, do, in the Name, and by Authority of the good People of these Colonies, solemnly publish and declare, That these United Colonies are, and of Right ought to be Free and Independent States; that they are Absolved from all Allegiance to the British Crown, and that all political connection between them and the State of Great Britain, is and ought to be totally dissolved; and that

---

[3]*magnanimity:* quality of being calm, generous, upstanding.
[4]*acquiesce:* comply; accept.

as Free and Independent States, they have full power to levy War, conclude Peace, contract Alliances, establish Commerce, and to do all other Acts and Things which Independent States may of right do. And for the support of this Declaration, with a firm reliance on the protection of Divine Providence, we mutually pledge to each other our lives, our Fortunes and our sacred Honor.

Thinking Critically about This Reading

What, according to the Declaration of Independence, is the purpose of government?

Questions for Study and Discussion

1. In paragraph 2, Jefferson presents certain "self-evident" truths. What are these truths, and how are they related to his argument? Do you consider them self-evident?

2. The Declaration of Independence is a deductive argument; therefore, it can be presented in the form of a syllogism. (Glossary: *Syllogism*) What are the major premise, the minor premise, and the conclusion of Jefferson's argument?

3. The list of charges against the king is given as evidence in support of Jefferson's minor premise. (Glossary: *Evidence*) Does Jefferson offer any evidence in support of his major premise?

4. How does Jefferson refute the possible charge that the colonists should have tried to solve their problems by less drastic means?

5. Where in the Declaration does Jefferson use parallel structure? (Glossary: *Parallelism*) What does he achieve by using it?

6. Although the basic structure of the Declaration reflects sound deductive reasoning, Jefferson's language, particularly when he lists the charges against the king, tends to be emotional. (Glossary: *Diction*) Identify as many examples of this emotional language as you can, and discuss possible reasons for why Jefferson uses this kind of language.

Classroom Activity Using Argument

Choose one of the following controversial subjects, and think about how you would write an argument for or against it. Write three sentences that summarize three important points, two based on logic and one based on persuasion/emotion. Then write one sentence that acknowledges the opposing point of view. For example, if you were to argue for stricter enforcement of a leash law and waste pickup ordinance for dog owners in your town, you might write the following:

Logic	Dogs allowed to run free can be a menace to joggers and local wildlife.
Logic	Dog waste poses a health risk, particularly in areas where children play.
Emotion	How would you feel if you hit an unleashed dog with your car?
Counterargument	Dogs need fresh air and exercise, too.

Gun control
Tobacco restrictions
Cutting taxes and social programs
Paying college athletes
Assisted suicide for the terminally ill
Widespread legalization of gambling

Suggested Writing Assignments

1. The issue of human rights is often discussed. Review the arguments for and against the U.S. government's active and outspoken promotion of the human rights issue as reported in the press. Then write an argument of your own in favor of a continued strong human rights policy on the part of leaders of the United States.

2. Using one of the subjects listed below, develop a thesis, and then write an essay in which you argue in support of that thesis:

Minimum wage	Welfare
Social Security	Separation of church and state
Capital punishment	First Amendment rights
Erosion of individual rights	

I Have a Dream

■ Martin Luther King Jr.

Civil rights leader Martin Luther King Jr. (1929–1968) was the son of a Baptist minister in Atlanta, Georgia. Ordained at the age of eighteen, King went on to earn academic degrees from Morehouse College, Crozer Theological Seminary, Boston University, and Chicago Theological Seminary. He came to prominence in 1955 in Montgomery, Alabama, when he led a successful boycott against the  *city's segregated bus system. The first president of the Southern Christian Leadership Conference, King became the leading spokesman for the civil rights movement during the 1950s and 1960s, espousing a consistent philosophy of nonviolent resistance to racial injustice. He also championed women's rights and protested the Vietnam War. Named* Time *magazine's Man of the Year in 1963, King was awarded the Nobel Peace Prize in 1964. King was assassinated in April 1968 after speaking at a rally in Memphis, Tennessee.*

"I Have a Dream," the keynote address for the March on Washington in 1963, has become one of the most renowned and recognized speeches of the twentieth century. Notice how King uses allusions and parallelism to give life to his argument.

Reflecting on What You Know

Most Americans have seen film clips of King delivering the "I Have a Dream" speech. What do you know of the speech? What do you know of the events and conditions under which King presented it almost fifty years ago?

Five score years ago, a great American, in whose symbolic shadow we stand, signed the Emancipation Proclamation.[1] This momentous decree came as a great beacon light of hope to millions of Negro slaves

1

---

[1]*Emancipation Proclamation:* a decree enacted by President Abraham Lincoln (1809–1865) in 1863 that freed the slaves in the southern states.

who had been seared in the flames of withering injustice. It came as a joyous daybreak to end the long night of captivity.

But one hundred years later, we must face the tragic fact that the Negro is still not free. One hundred years later, the life of the Negro is still sadly crippled by the manacles of segregation and the chains of discrimination. One hundred years later, the Negro lives on a lonely island of poverty in the midst of a vast ocean of material prosperity. One hundred years later, the Negro is still languishing in the corners of American society and finds himself an exile in his own land. So we have come here today to dramatize an appalling condition.

In a sense we have come to our nation's Capitol to cash a check. When the architects of our republic wrote the magnificent words of the Constitution and the Declaration of Independence, they were signing a promissory note to which every American was to fall heir. This note was a promise that all men would be guaranteed the unalienable rights of life, liberty, and the pursuit of happiness.

It is obvious today that America has defaulted on this promissory note insofar as her citizens of color are concerned. Instead of honoring this sacred obligation, America has given the Negro people a bad check; a check which has come back marked "insufficient funds." But we refuse to believe that the bank of justice is bankrupt. We refuse to believe that there are insufficient funds in the great vaults of opportunity of this nation. So we have come to cash this check—a check that will give us upon demand the riches of freedom and the security of justice. We have also come to this hallowed spot to remind America of the fierce urgency of *now*. This is no time to engage in the luxury of cooling off or to take the tranquilizing drug of gradualism. *Now* is the time to make real the promises of Democracy. *Now* is the time to rise from the dark and desolate valley of segregation to the sunlit path of racial justice. *Now* is the time to open the doors of opportunity to all of God's children. *Now* is the time to lift our nation from the quicksands of racial injustice to the solid rock of brotherhood.

It would be fatal for the nation to overlook the urgency of the moment and to underestimate the determination of the Negro. This sweltering summer of the Negro's legitimate discontent will not pass until there is an invigorating autumn of freedom and equality. 1963 is not an end, but a beginning. Those who hope that the Negro needed to blow off steam and will now be content will have a rude awakening if the nation returns to business as usual. There will be neither rest nor tranquility in America until the Negro is granted his citizenship rights. The whirlwinds of revolt will continue to shake the foundations of our nation until the bright day of justice emerges.

But there is something I must say to my people who stand on the warm threshold which leads into the palace of justice. In the process of gaining our rightful place we must not be guilty of wrongful deeds. Let us not seek to satisfy our thirst for freedom by drinking from the cup of bitterness and hatred. We must forever conduct our struggle on the high plane of dignity and discipline. We must not allow our creative protest to degenerate into physical violence. Again and again we must rise to the majestic heights of meeting physical force with soul force. The marvelous new militancy which has engulfed the Negro community must not lead us to a distrust of all white people, for many of our white brothers, as evidenced by their presence here today, have come to realize that their destiny is tied up with our destiny and their freedom is inextricably bound to our freedom. We cannot walk alone.

6

And as we walk, we must make the pledge that we shall march ahead. We cannot turn back. There are those who are asking the devotees of civil rights, "When will you be satisfied?" We can never be satisfied as long as the Negro is the victim of the unspeakable horrors of police brutality. We can never be satisfied as long as our bodies, heavy with the fatigue of travel, cannot gain lodging in the motels of the highways and the hotels of the cities. We cannot be satisfied as long as the Negro's basic mobility is from a smaller ghetto to a larger one. We can never be satisfied as long as a Negro in Mississippi cannot vote and a Negro in New York believes he has nothing for which to vote. No, no, we are not satisfied, and we will not be satisfied until justice rolls down like waters and righteousness like a mighty stream.

7

I am not unmindful that some of you have come here out of great trials and tribulations. Some of you have come fresh from narrow jail cells. Some of you have come from areas where your quest for freedom left you battered by the storms of persecution and staggered by the winds of police brutality. You have been the veterans of creative suffering. Continue to work with the faith that unearned suffering is redemptive.

8

Go back to Mississippi, go back to Alabama, go back to South Carolina, go back to Georgia, go back to Louisiana, go back to the slums and ghettoes of our northern cities, knowing that somehow this situation can and will be changed. Let us not wallow in the valley of despair.

9

I say to you today, my friends, that in spite of the difficulties and frustrations of the moment I still have a dream. It is a dream deeply rooted in the American dream.

10

I have a dream that one day this nation will rise up and live out the 11
true meaning of its creed: "We hold these truths to be self-evident; that
all men are created equal."[2]

I have a dream that one day on the red hills of Georgia the sons 12
of former slaves and the sons of former slaveowners will be able to sit
down together at the table of brotherhood.

I have a dream that the state of Mississippi, a desert state sweltering 13
with the heat of injustice and oppression, will be transformed into an
oasis of freedom and justice.

I have a dream that my four little children will one day live in a 14
nation where they will not be judged by the color of their skin but by
the content of their character.

I have a dream today. 15

I have a dream that the state of Alabama, whose governor's[3] lips 16
are presently dripping with the words of interposition and nullification,[4] will be transformed into a situation where little black boys and
black girls will be able to join hands with little white boys and white
girls and walk together as sisters and brothers.

I have a dream today. 17

I have a dream that one day every valley shall be exalted, every 18
hill and mountain shall be made low, the rough places will be made
plain, and the crooked places will be made straight, and the glory of
the Lord shall be revealed, and all flesh shall see it together.

This is our hope. This is the faith with which I return to the 19
South. With this faith we will be able to hew out of the mountain
of despair a stone of hope. With this faith we will be able to
transform the jangling discords of our nation into a beautiful symphony of brotherhood. With this faith we will be able to work together, to pray together, to struggle together, to go to jail together,
to stand up for freedom together, knowing that we will be free
one day.

This will be the day when all of God's children will be able to sing 20
with new meaning.

---

[2]"*We hold . . . created equal*": a phrase from the Declaration of Independence by
Thomas Jefferson (1743–1826) (see p. 547).
[3]*Alabama . . . governor:* George Wallace (1919–1998), a segregationist in 1963 who
later changed his views and received integrated political support.
[4]*nullification:* a state's refusal to recognize or enforce within its borders U.S. federal
law.

> My country, 'tis of thee
> Sweet land of liberty,
> Of thee I sing:
> Land where my fathers died,
> Land of the pilgrims' pride,
> From every mountainside
> Let freedom ring.

And if America is to be a great nation this must become true. So 21 let freedom ring from the prodigious hilltops of New Hampshire. Let freedom ring from the mighty mountains of New York. Let freedom ring from the heightening Alleghenies of Pennsylvania!

Let freedom ring from the snowcapped Rockies of Colorado! 22

Let freedom ring from the curvaceous peaks of California! 23

But not only that; let freedom ring from Stone Mountain of 24 Georgia!

Let freedom ring from Lookout Mountain of Tennessee! 25

Let freedom ring from every hill and molehill of Mississippi. From 26 every mountainside, let freedom ring.

When we let freedom ring, when we let it ring from every village 27 and every hamlet, from every state and every city, we will be able to speed up that day when all of God's children, black men and white men, Jews and Gentiles, Protestants and Catholics, will be able to join hands and sing in the words of the old Negro spiritual, "Free at last! free at last! thank God almighty, we are free at last!"

Thinking Critically about This Reading

What does King mean when he says, "In the process of gaining our rightful place [in society] we must not be guilty of wrongful deeds" (paragraph 6)? Why is this issue so important to him?

Questions for Study and Discussion

1. What is King's thesis? (Glossary: *Thesis*) How has the United States "defaulted" on its promise?
2. King delivered his speech to two audiences—the huge audience that listened to him in person and another, larger audience. (Glossary: *Audience*) What is that larger audience? How does King's speech catch the audience's attention and deliver his point?

3. Examine the speech to determine how King organizes his presentation. (Glossary: *Organization*) What are the main sections of the speech, and what is the purpose of each? How does the organization serve King's overall purpose? (Glossary: *Purpose*)

4. King uses parallel constructions and repetitions throughout his speech. (Glossary: *Parallelism*) Identify the phrases and words that he emphasizes. Explain what these techniques add to the persuasiveness of his argument.

5. Explain King's choice for the title. (Glossary: *Title*) Why is the title particularly appropriate given the context in which the speech was delivered? What other titles might he have used?

Classroom Activity Using Argument

Write a paragraph that argues that people should compliment one another more. Use *one* of the following quotes to support your argument:

> "Compliments are the high point of a person's day," said self-help author Melodie Bronson. "Without compliments, anyone's life is sure to be much more difficult."

> "Compliments have been proven to lower blood pressure and increase endorphin production to the brain," said Dr. Ruth West of the Holistic Medicine Committee. "A compliment a day may lengthen your life span by as much as a year."

> "Compliments are a special way people communicate with each other," said Bill Goodbody, therapist at the Good Feeling Institute. "Ninety percent of our patients report happier relationships or marriages after they begin compliment therapy."

Explain why you chose the quote you did. How did you integrate it into your paragraph?

Suggested Writing Assignments

1. King's language is powerful, and his imagery is vivid, but the effectiveness of any speech depends partially on its delivery. If read in monotone, King's use of repetition and parallel language would sound almost redundant rather than inspiring. (Glossary: *Parallelism*) Keeping presentation in mind, write a short speech

that argues a point of view about which you feel strongly. Using King's speech as a model, incorporate imagery, repetition, and metaphor to communicate your point. (Glossary: *Figure of Speech*) Read your speech aloud to a friend to see how it flows and how effective your use of language is. Refine your presentation—both your text and how you deliver it—before presenting the speech in class.

2. Using King's assessment of the condition of African Americans in 1963 as a foundation, research the changes that have occurred in the years following King's speech. How have laws changed? How have demographics changed? Present your information in an essay that assesses what still needs to be done to fulfill King's dream for the United States. Where does the country still fall short of the racial equality envisioned by King? What are the prospects for the future?

What Pro Sports Owners Owe Us

■ Dave Zirin

Dave Zirin, a sportswriter whose column "Edge of Sports" is a part of Sports Illustrated's *Web site, is the only writer in the history of* The Nation *to contribute a sports column to that magazine. Zirin focuses on the politics of sports and has been a strong voice in support of non-sports-related political views. For example, in 2010 he called for a boycott of Arizona sports teams, especially the* Diamondbacks *baseball team, in protest over Arizona's Support Our Law Enforcement and Safe Neighborhoods Act, otherwise known as the Arizona immigration bill. Among his books are the following:* What's My Name, Fool? Sports and Resistance in the United States *(2005);* Welcome to the Terrordome: The Pain, Politics, and Promise of Sports *(2007);* Muhammad Ali Handbook *(2007);* A People's History of Sports: From Bull-Baiting to Barry Bonds *(2008); and* Bad Sports: How Owners Are Ruining the Games We Love *(2010). His work has also appeared in the* Los Angeles Times, Washington Post, New York Daily News, Baltimore Sun, The Source, Pittsburgh Courier, *and* New York Newsday, *among other publications.*

In the following essay, which first appeared in the August 2010 issue of The Progressive, *Zirin argues that the owners of sports franchises are treating their fans harshly and are only attuned to their own selfish interests.*

Reflecting on What You Know

If you have attended a major sporting event recently, how did you feel about the way you were treated as a fan? What about the cost of your ticket and refreshments? How does the cost of attending a sporting event affect your enjoyment of the game?

I once had a coach who could spit tobacco hard enough to break a   1
window. He smelled like an old hamper, and only wore pants that
came with an elastic waist. Still, every last one of us loved the guy. He
always said, "Sports is like a hammer, gents. And you can use a hammer for all kinds of things. You can use it to build a house, or you
can use it to bash somebody's head. Choose wisely."

In the twenty-first century, the heads of far too many sports fans   2
have been bashed by far too many hammers. Our collective migraine
comes from the idea that we are loving something that just doesn't
love us back. If sports was once like a playful puppy you would
wrestle on the floor, it's now like a housecat demanding to be stroked
and giving nothing in return.

Sports fans are fed up.   3

It's the extra commercials tacked onto a broadcast, as companies   4
attempt to use the games to brand our subconscious. It's when you decide to finally take the trip to the park, look up the ticket prices, and
decide immediately to do something—anything—else with your time.

And so you go a year without making it to the ballpark and fail   5
to even notice. Or you don't feel the same urgency to watch every
minute of every game for fear you might miss something magical.

If a car's brakes failed, you wouldn't blame the driver. You'd   6
blame the manufacturer. And when we feel bludgeoned by the state
of professional sports, it's the owners who need to answer for this
sorry state of affairs.

Players play.   7

Fans watch.   8

Owners are uniquely charged with being the stewards of the game.   9
It's a task that they have failed to perform in spectacular fashion.

In fact, with barely a sliver of scrutiny, they are wrecking the   10
world of sports. The old model of the paternalistic owner caring for a
community has become as outdated as the typewriter. Because of
publicly funded stadium construction, luxury box licenses, sweet-
heart cable deals, globalized merchandising plans, and other "revenue
streams," the need for owners to cater to a local working- and middle-
class fan base has shrunk dramatically.

Fans have become scenery for television broadcasts.   11

Mike Lupica of the *New York Daily News* once wrote, "You are   12
owed nothing in sports, no matter how much you care. You are owed
nothing, no matter how long you've rooted or how much you've paid
to do it."

I couldn't disagree more. We are owed plenty by the world of 13
sports.

We are owed loyalty. 14

We are owed accessibility. 15

We are owed a return on our massive civic investment. 16

And more than anything, we are owed respect 17

We aren't owed this respect because it's the kind or human thing 18
to do.

We aren't owed any love because we cheered ourselves hoarse 19
and passed the precious rooting tradition down to our children.

We are owed it because the teams are ours as much as they are 20
theirs. Literally.

By calling for and receiving public funds, owners have sacrificed 21
their moral, if not financial, claim of ownership. Cities and city coun-
cils that allow their funds to be used by private franchises should, in
turn, have some say in the relationship between team and fan.

That means lower ticket prices. 22

That means an end to the $8 beer. 23

As sports fans, we have to accept that we do in fact deserve bet- 24
ter, but as the great abolitionist Frederick Douglass said, "Power concedes nothing without a demand."

If we aren't making demands, we have no one to blame but ourselves. 25

Thinking Critically about This Reading

There are two sides to every question. In fact, there are often many
sides to every question. Assume you are the owner of a sports franchise;
what problems might you be facing that Zirin needs to understand.

Questions for Study and Discussion

1. What is Zirin's thesis? (Glossary: *Thesis*) What evidence does he
   use to support his thesis, and how effective is it? (Glossary:
   Evidence)
2. Zirin begins his essay with a description of a former coach and a
   quote by him. How do the description and the quotation serve to
   establish Zirin's thesis and purpose in writing? (Glossary:
   Beginnings and Endings)
3. Why do you suppose Zirin uses very short paragraphs? Do you
   find them effective? Why or why not?

4. In paragraph 12, Zirin quotes sportswriter Mike Lupica. Why do you suppose Lupica said what he did? How does Zirin refute this counterargument to his own?

5. Cite several examples of Zirin's use of figurative language, and explain how they work and what they add to his style. (Glossary: *Figure of Speech*)

Classroom Activity Using Argumentation

An excellent way to gain some experience in formulating an argumentative position on an issue and establishing your own thesis is to engage in a debate with someone who is on the other side of the question. When we listen to arguments and think of refutations and counterarguments, we have a chance to rehearse and revise our position before we put it in written form.

To try this exercise, use Zirin's argument against sports owners as the subject of your debate. Divide the class into pro and con sides. Each side should elect a spokesperson to present that group's argument before the class. Finally, have the class make some estimate of the success of each side in (1) articulating its position, (2) presenting ideas and evidence to support that position, and (3) convincing the audience of its position. The exercise should give you a good idea of the kind of work involved in preparing a written argument.

Suggested Writing Assignments

1. If you are a fan of a major sports team, what do you know about the relationship of your team to local government? Did your community help finance an arena or stadium for the franchise? If so, what obligations did that deal entail for both the franchise and the community? How happy are both parties with the arrangement? If there is tension between the parties, what can be done to alleviate ill feelings? How well is the partnership working?

2. Write an essay in which you argue for the ideal sports franchise. Here are some questions you might consider: What would characterize the organization? How would an ideal owner treat fans, players, and business associates? How would the ideal owner finance the franchise? How would the owner treat the community? What would be the community's involvement and responsibility toward the team and the team's toward the community?

In Praise of the F Word

■ **Mary Sherry**

Mary Sherry was born in Bay City, Michigan, and received her bachelor's degree from Rosary College in River Forest, Illinois. She owns her own research and publishing company specializing in information for economic and development organizations. Sherry also teaches in adult-literacy programs and has written essays on educational problems for various newspapers, including the Wall Street Journal *and* Newsday.

In the following essay, originally published in Newsweek *in 1991, Sherry takes a provocative stance—that the threat of flunking is a "positive teaching tool." She believes students would be better off if they had a "healthy fear of failure," and she marshals a series of logical appeals to both clarify and support her argument.*

Reflecting on What You Know

Comment on what you see as the relationship between learning and grades. Do teachers and students pay too much attention to grades at the expense of learning? Or are grades not seen as that important?

Tens of thousands of eighteen-year-olds will graduate this year and   1
be handed meaningless diplomas. These diplomas won't look any different from those awarded their luckier classmates. Their validity will be questioned only when their employers discover that these graduates are semiliterate.

Eventually a fortunate few will find their way into educational-   2
repair shops—adult-literacy programs, such as the one where I teach basic grammar and writing. There, high-school graduates and high-school dropouts pursuing graduate-equivalency certificates will learn the skills they should have learned in school. They will also discover they have been cheated by our educational system.

As I teach, I learn a lot about our schools. Early in each session   3
I ask my students to write about an unpleasant experience they had in school. No writers' block here! "I wish someone would have made

me stop doing drugs and made me study." "I liked to party and no one seemed to care." "I was a good kid and didn't cause any trouble, so they just passed me along even though I didn't read well and couldn't write." And so on.

I am your basic do-gooder, and prior to teaching this class I blamed   4
the poor academic skills our kids have today on drugs, divorce, and other impediments to concentration necessary for doing well in school. But, as I rediscover each time I walk into the classroom, before a teacher can expect students to concentrate, he has to get their attention, no matter what distractions may be at hand. There are many ways to do this, and they have much to do with teaching style. However, if style alone won't do it, there is another way to show who holds the winning hand in the classroom. That is to reveal the trump card[1] of failure.

I will never forget a teacher who played that card to get the at-   5
tention of one of my children. Our youngest, a world-class charmer, did little to develop his intellectual talents but always got by. Until Mrs. Stifter.

Our son was a high-school senior when he had her for English.   6
"He sits in the back of the room talking to his friends," she told me. "Why don't you move him to the front row?" I urged, believing the embarrassment would get him to settle down. Mrs. Stifter looked at me steely-eyed over her glasses. "I don't move seniors," she said. "I flunk them." I was flustered. Our son's academic life flashed before my eyes. No teacher had ever threatened him with that before. I regained my composure and managed to say that I thought she was right. By the time I got home I was feeling pretty good about this. It was a radical approach for these times, but, well, why not? "She's going to flunk you," I told my son. I did not discuss it any further. Suddenly English became a priority in his life. He finished out the semester with an A.

I know one example doesn't make a case, but at night I see a   7
parade of students who are angry and resentful for having been passed along until they could no longer even pretend to keep up. Of average intelligence or better, they eventually quit school, concluding they were too dumb to finish. "I should have been held back" is a comment I hear frequently. Even sadder are those students who are high-school graduates who say to me after a few weeks of class, "I don't know how I ever got a high-school diploma."

---

[1]*trump card:* a secret weapon; hidden advantage.

Passing students who have not mastered the work cheats them and 8
the employers who expect graduates to have basic skills. We excuse this
dishonest behavior by saying kids can't learn if they come from terrible environments. No one seems to stop to think that—no matter
what environments they come from—most kids don't put school first
on their list unless they perceive something is at stake. They'd rather
be sailing.

Many students I see at night could give expert testimony on unem- 9
ployment, chemical dependency, abusive relationships. In spite of these
difficulties, they have decided to make education a priority. They are
motivated by the desire for a better job or the need to hang on to
the one they've got. They have a healthy fear of failure.

People of all ages can rise above their problems, but they need to 10
have a reason to do so. Young people generally don't have the maturity
to value education in the same way my adult students value it. But
fear of failure, whether economic or academic, can motivate both.

Flunking as a regular policy has just as much merit today as it did 11
two generations ago. We must review the threat of flunking and see it as
it really is—a positive teaching tool. It is an expression of confidence by
both teachers and parents that the students have the ability to learn the
material presented to them. However, making it work again would take
a dedicated, caring conspiracy between teachers and parents. It would
mean facing the tough reality that passing kids who haven't learned the
material—while it might save them grief for the short term—dooms
them to long-term illiteracy. It would mean that teachers would have
to follow through on their threats, and parents would have to stand
behind them, knowing their children's best interests are indeed at
stake. This means no more doing Scott's assignments for him because
he might fail. No more passing Jodi because she's such a nice kid.

This is a policy that worked in the past and can work today. A wise 12
teacher, with the support of his parents, gave our son the opportunity
to succeed—or fail. It's time we return this choice to all students.

Thinking Critically about This Reading

According to Sherry, "We must review the threat of flunking and see it
as it really is—a positive teaching tool. It is an expression of confidence by both teachers and parents that the students have the ability
to learn the material presented to them" (paragraph 11). How can
flunking students be "an expression of confidence" in them?

Questions for Study and Discussion

1. What is Sherry's *thesis?* (Glossary: *Thesis*) What evidence does she use to support her argument?

2. Sherry uses dismissive terms to characterize objections to flunking—*cheats* and *excuses*. In your opinion, does she do enough to acknowledge the other side of the argument? Explain.

3. What is the "F word" discussed in the essay? Does referring to it as the "F word" increase the effectiveness of the essay? Why?

4. Who is Sherry's audience? (Glossary: *Audience*) Is it receptive to the "F word"? Explain your answer.

5. In what way is Sherry qualified to comment on the potential benefits of flunking students? Do you think her induction is accurate?

Classroom Activity Using Argument

A first-year composition student, Marco Schmidt, is preparing to write an essay in which he will argue that music should be a required course for all public high school students. He has compiled the following pieces of evidence:

- Informal interviews with four classmates. Three of the classmates stated that they would have enjoyed and benefited from taking a music course in high school, and the fourth stated that she would not have been interested in taking music.

- An article from a professional journal for teachers comparing the study habits of students who were involved in music and those who were not. The author, a psychologist, found that students who play an instrument or sing regularly have better study habits than students who do not.

- A brief article from a national newsmagazine praising an inner-city high school's experimental curriculum, in which music classes play a prominent part.

- The personal Web site of a high school music teacher who posts information about the successes and achievements of her former students.

Discuss these pieces of evidence with your classmates. Which are most convincing? Which provide the least support for Marco's argument?

Why? What other types of evidence might Marco find to support his argument?

Suggested Writing Assignments

1. Write an essay in which you argue against Sherry's thesis. (Glossary: *Thesis*) In what ways is flunking bad for students? Are there techniques more positive than a "fear of failure" that can be used to motivate students?

2. Think of something that involves short-term pain or sacrifice but that can be beneficial in the long run. For example, exercising requires exertion, but it may help prevent health problems. Studying and writing papers when you'd rather be having fun or even sleeping may seem painful, but earning a college degree leads to personal growth and development. Even if the benefits are obvious, imagine a skeptical audience, and write an argument in favor of the short-term sacrifice over the long-term consequences of avoiding it. (Glossary: *Audience*)

Condemn the Crime, Not the Person

■ June Tangney

Psychology educator and researcher June Tangney was born in Buffalo, New York, in 1958. After graduating from the State University of New York at Buffalo in 1979, she attended the University of California–Los Angeles, where she earned a master's degree in 1981 and a doctorate in 1985. Tangney taught briefly at Bryn Mawr College and held a research position at the Regional Center for Infants and Young Children in Rockville, Maryland. Since 1988 she has been a professor of psychology at George Mason University, where she was recognized with a Teaching Excellence Award. She is the co-author of five books—Self-Conscious Emotions: The Psychology of Shame, Guilt, Embarrassment, and Pride (1995), with Kurt W. Fisher; Shame and Guilt (2002), with Rhonda L. Dearing; Handbook of Self and Identity (2005), with Mark R. Leary; Social Psychological Foundations of Clinical Psychology (2010), with James E. Maddux; and Shame in the Therapy Hour (2011), with Rhonda L. Dearing—and is an associate editor of the journal Self and Identity.*

In the following essay, first published in the Boston Globe *on August 5, 2001, Tangney argues against the use of public humiliation as punishment. She bases her position on recent scientific evidence, much of which comes from her own work on shame and guilt.*

Reflecting on What You Know

For you, what is the difference between *shame* and *guilt*? Provide an example from your own experience to illustrate your understanding of each concept.

As the costs of incarceration mount and evidence of its failure as a deterrent grows, judges understandably have begun to search for creative alternatives to traditional sentences. One recent trend is the use of "shaming" sentences—sanctions explicitly designed to induce feelings of shame. 1

Judges across the country are sentencing offenders to parade around in public carrying signs broadcasting their crimes, to post signs on their front lawns warning neighbors of their vices, and to display "drunk driver" bumper stickers on their cars. 2

A number of social commentators have urged America to embrace public shaming and stigmatization as cheaper and effective alternatives for curbing a broad range of nonviolent crimes. Punishments aimed at public humiliation certainly appeal to our sense of moral righteousness. They do indeed appear fiscally attractive when contrasted with the escalating costs of incarceration. 3

But recent scientific evidence suggests that such attempts at social control are misguided. Rather than fostering constructive change, shame often makes a bad situation worse. 4

The crux[1] of the matter lies in the distinction between shame and guilt. Recent research has shown that shame and guilt are distinct emotions with very different implications for subsequent moral and interpersonal behavior. Feelings of shame involve a painful focus on the self—the humiliating sense that "I am a bad person." 5

Such humiliation is typically accompanied by a sense of shrinking, of being small, worthless, and powerless, and by a sense of being exposed. Ironically, research has shown that such painful and debilitating feelings of shame do not motivate constructive changes in behavior. 6

Shamed individuals are no less likely to repeat their transgressions (often more so), and they are no more likely to attempt reparation[2] (often less so). Instead, because shame is so intolerable, people in the midst of the experience often resort to any one of a number of defensive tactics. 7

---

[1]*crux:* the essential or deciding point.
[2]*reparation:* a making of amends; repayment.

They may seek to hide or escape the shameful feeling, denying 8
responsibility. They may seek to shift the blame outside, holding
others responsible for their dilemma. And not infrequently, they become irrationally angry with others, sometimes resorting to overtly aggressive and destructive actions. In short, shame serves to escalate the
very destructive patterns of behavior we aim to curb.

Contrast this with feelings of guilt which involve a focus on a spe- 9
cific behavior—the sense that "I did a bad thing" rather than "I am a
bad person."

Feelings of guilt involve a sense of tension, remorse, and regret over 10
the "bad thing done."

Research has shown that this sense of tension and regret typically 11
motivates reparative action (confessing, apologizing, or somehow repairing the damage done) without engendering[3] all the defensive and re-
taliative responses that are the hallmark of shame.

Most important, feelings of guilt are much more likely to foster 12
constructive changes in future behavior because what is at issue is not
a bad, defective self, but a bad, defective behavior. And, as anyone
knows, it is easier to change a bad behavior (drunken driving, slumlord-
ing, thievery) than to change a bad, defective self.

How can we foster constructive feelings of guilt among America's 13
offenders? Well, one way is to force offenders to focus on the negative
consequences of their behavior, particularly on the painful negative consequences for others.

Community service sentences can do much to promote constructive 14
guilt when they are tailored to the nature of the crime. What is needed
are imposed activities that underscore the tangible destruction caused
by the offense and that provide a path to redemption by ameliorating[4]
similar human misery.

Drunk drivers, for example, could be sentenced to help clear 15
sites of road accidents and to assist with campaigns to reduce
drunken driving. Slumlords could be sentenced to assist with nuts
and bolts repairs in low-income housing units. In this way, offenders are forced to see, first-hand, the potential or actual destructiveness of their infractions and they become actively involved in
constructive solutions.

Some critics have rejected community service as an alternative to in- 16
carceration, suggesting that such community-based sentences somehow

---

[3]*engendering*: causing or producing.
[4]*ameliorating*: improving or making better.

cheapen an otherwise honorable volunteer activity while at the same time not adequately underscoring the criminal's disgrace.

Scientific research, however, clearly indicates that public shaming 17 and humiliation is not the path of choice. Such efforts are doomed to provoke all sorts of unintended negative consequences.

In contrast, thoughtfully constructed guilt-oriented community 18 service sentences are more likely to foster changes in offenders' future behaviors, while contributing to the larger societal good. My guess is that any honorable community service volunteer would welcome such constructive changes.

Thinking Critically about This Reading

Tangney states, "A number of social commentators have urged America to embrace public shaming and stigmatization as cheaper and effective alternatives for curbing a broad range of nonviolent crimes" (paragraph 3). What evidence does she present to counter these arguments?

Questions for Study and Discussion

1. What is a "shaming" sentence (1)? According to Tangney, why do judges use such sentences in place of more traditional ones?
2. What is Tangney's position on using sentences intended to shame offenders? Briefly state her thesis in your own words. (Glossary: *Thesis*)
3. What for Tangney is the key difference between *shame* and *guilt*? Why does she believe that guilt works better than shame as a form of punishment?
4. Paragraph 13 begins with a rhetorical question: "How can we foster constructive feelings of guilt among America's offenders?" (Glossary: *Rhetorical Question*) How does Tangney answer this question? What suggestions would you add to her solution?
5. How does Tangney counter the critics of community service? Do you find her counterarguments convincing? Why or why not?

Classroom Activity Using Argument

The effectiveness of a writer's argument depends in large part on the writer's awareness of audience. For example, a writer arguing that there is too much violence portrayed on television might present different kinds of evidence, reasoning, and diction for different audiences, such as parents, lawmakers, or television producers and writers.

Review several of the argument essays you have read in this chapter. In your opinion, for what primary audience is each essay intended? List the evidence you found in each essay that helped you to determine your answers. (Glossary: *Evidence*)

Suggested Writing Assignments

1. Write an essay in which you tell the story of a childhood punishment that you received or witnessed. (Glossary: *Narration*) How did you feel about the punishment? Was it justified? Appropriate? Effective? Why or why not? In retrospect, did the punishment shame or humiliate you, or did it bring out feelings of guilt? What did you learn from this experience? Before starting to write, read or review Dick Gregory's "Shame" (pp. 288–93).

2. Tangney writes, "As the costs of incarceration mount and evidence of its failure as a deterrent grows, judges understandably have begun to search for creative alternatives to traditional sentences" (1). Ideally, knowing what the punishment will be should deter people from doing the wrong thing in the first place, but do punishments really act as deterrents? Are certain punishments more effective as deterrents than others? What are the deterrent benefits of both shame and guilt punishments? Conduct library and Internet research to answer these questions, and then report your findings and conclusions in an essay. To begin your research online, go to **bedfordstmartins.com/models** and click on "Argument Links."

Shame Is Worth a Try

■ Dan M. Kahan

*Dan M. Kahan was born in 1963 and gradu-
ated from Middlebury College in 1986 and
Harvard Law School in 1989, where he served
as president of the* Harvard Law Review. He
*clerked for Judge Harry Edwards of the U.S.
Court of Appeals for the District of Columbia
circuit in 1989–1990 and for Justice Thurgood
Marshall of the U.S. Supreme Court in 1990–
1991. After practicing law for two years in*
*Washington, D.C., Kahan launched his teaching career, first at the
University of Chicago Law School and later at Yale Law School,
where since 2003 he has been the Elizabeth K. Dollard Professor
of Law. His teaching and research interests include criminal law,
risk perception, punishment, and evidence. Kahan, who has written widely in legal journals on current social issues including gun
control, is coauthor, with Tracey Meares, of* Urgent Times:
Policing and Rights in Inner-City Communities *(1999). From
2005 to 2006, he was deputy dean of Yale Law School.*

In the following essay, first published in the Boston Globe
*on August 5, 2001, Kahan argues in favor of the use of shame as a
punishment that is "an effective, cheap, and humane alternative
to imprisonment."*

Reflecting on What You Know

Think about the times you were punished as a child. Who punished you—parents, teachers, or other authority figures? What
kinds of bad behavior were you punished for? What type of punishment worked best to deter you from behaving badly later on?
Explain.

Is shame an appropriate criminal punishment? Many courts and legis-   1
lators around the country think so. Steal from your employer in
Wisconsin and you might be ordered to wear a sandwich board
proclaiming your offense. Drive drunk in Florida or Texas and you

might be required to place a conspicuous "DUI" bumper sticker on your car. Refuse to make your child-support payments in Virginia and you will find that your vehicle has been immobilized with an appropriately colored boot (pink if the abandoned child is a girl, blue if a boy).

Many experts, however, are skeptical of these new shaming punishments. Some question their effectiveness as a deterrent. Others worry that the new punishments are demeaning and cruel.   2

Who's right? As is usually the case, both sides have their points. But what the shame proponents seem to be getting, and the critics ignoring, is the potential of shame as an effective, cheap, and humane alternative to imprisonment.   3

There's obviously no alternative to imprisonment for murderers, rapists, and other violent criminals. But they make up less than half the American prison population.   4

Liberal and conservative reformers alike have long believed that the remainder can be effectively punished with less severe "alternative sanctions," like fines and community service. These sanctions are much cheaper than jail. They also allow the offender to continue earning an income so he can compensate his victim, meet his child-support obligations, and the like.   5

Nevertheless, courts and legislators have resisted alternative sanctions—not so much because they won't work, but because they fail to express appropriate moral condemnation of crime. Fines seem to say that offenders may buy the privilege of breaking the law; and we can't very well condemn someone for purchasing what we are willing to sell.   6

Nor do we condemn offenders to educate the retarded, install smoke detectors in nursing homes, restore dilapidated low income housing, and the like. Indeed, saying that such community service is punishment for criminals insults both those who perform such services voluntarily and those whom the services are supposed to benefit.   7

There's no confusion about the law's intent to condemn, however, when judges resort to public shaming. As a result, judges, legislators, and the public at large generally do accept shame as a morally appropriate punishment for drunken driving, nonaggravated assaults, embezzlement,[1] small-scale drug distribution, larceny,[2] toxic waste dumping, perjury, and a host of other offenses that ordinarily would result in a short jail term.   8

---

[1]*embezzlement:* stealing money or goods entrusted to one's care.
[2]*larceny:* theft.

The critics' anxieties about shame, moreover, seem overstated.   9
Clearly, shame hurts. People value their reputations for both emotional
and financial reasons. In fact, a series of studies by Harold Grasmick,
a sociologist at the University of Oklahoma, suggests that the prospect
of public disgrace exerts greater pressure to comply with the law than
does the threat of imprisonment and other formal punishments.

There's every reason to believe, then, that shaming penalties will be   10
an effective deterrent, at least for nonviolent crimes. Indeed, preliminary
reports suggest that certain shaming punishments, including those
directed at deadbeat dads, are extraordinarily effective.

At the same time, shame clearly doesn't hurt as much as imprison-   11
ment. Individuals who go to jail end up just as disgraced as those who
are shamed, and lose their liberty to boot. Those who've served prison
time are also a lot less likely to regain the respect and trust of their law-
abiding neighbors — essential ingredients of rehabilitation. Given all
this, it's hard to see shame as cruel.

Consider the case of a Florida mother sentenced to take out a   12
newspaper ad proclaiming "I purchased marijuana with my kids in
the car."

The prospect that her neighbors would see the ad surely caused   13
her substantial embarrassment. But the alternative was a jail sentence,
which would not only have humiliated her more but could also have
caused her to lose custody of her children. Not surprisingly, the woman
voluntarily accepted the shaming sanction in lieu of[3] jail time, as nearly
all offenders do.

Shame, like any other type of criminal punishment, can definitely   14
be abused. Some forms of it, like the public floggings imposed by au-
thoritarian states abroad, are pointlessly degrading.

In addition, using shame as a supplement rather than a substitute   15
for imprisonment only makes punishment more expensive for society
and destructive for the offender. Accordingly, requiring sex offenders to
register with local authorities is harder to defend than are other types
of shaming punishments, which are true substitutes for jail.

These legitimate points, however, are a reason to insist that sham-   16
ing be carried out appropriately, not to oppose it across the board.

In short, shame is cheap and effective and frees up scarce prison   17
space for the more serious offenses. Why not at least give it a try?

---

[3]*in lieu of:* in place of; instead of.

Thinking Critically about This Reading

What does Kahan mean when he states that "requiring sex offenders to register with local authorities is harder to defend than are other types of shaming punishments" (paragraph 15)?

Questions for Study and Discussion

1. What is Kahan's thesis? (Glossary: *Thesis*) Where does he state it most clearly?
2. What examples of shaming punishments does Kahan provide? For you, do these punishments seem to fit the crime? Explain.
3. How does Kahan handle the opposition argument that public shaming is cruel?
4. According to Kahan, why have courts and legislators resisted alternative punishments such as fines and community service?
5. What evidence does Kahan present to show that shaming punishments work? (Glossary: *Evidence*)
6. How convincing is Kahan's argument? What is the strongest part of his argument? The weakest part? Explain.

Classroom Activity Using Argument

Can killing ever be justified? If so, under what circumstances? Have six members of the class, three on each side of the question, volunteer to hold a debate. Team members should assign themselves different aspects of their position and then do library and Internet research to develop ideas and evidence. The teams should be allowed equal time to present their assertions and the evidence they have to support them. Finally, the rest of the class should be prepared to discuss the effectiveness of the presentations on both sides of the question.

Suggested Writing Assignments

1. Write an essay in which you argue your position on the issue of using public shaming as a punishment. Is public shaming appropriate for some or all offenses that would otherwise result in a short jail term? Explain. Support your argument with evidence from Kahan's essay, June Tangney's "Condemn the Crime, Not the

Person" (pp. 569–72), and your own experiences and observations. (Glossary: *Evidence*) You may find it helpful to review your journal response for this selection.

2. Identify several current problems at your college or university involving violations of campus rules for parking, cheating on exams, plagiarizing papers, recycling waste, using drugs or alcohol, defacing school property, and so on. Select *one* problem, and write a proposal to treat violators with a shaming punishment of your own design. Address your proposal to your school's student government organization or administration office.

3. What is your position on the issue of whether convicted sex offenders should be required to register with local authorities? Should registration be required even though they have already served their sentences in prison? Should people have the right to know the identity of any sex offenders living in their neighborhoods, or is this an invasion of privacy? Conduct library and Internet research on the subject of sex offender registration, and write an essay arguing for or against such measures. To begin your research online, go to **bedfordstmartins.com/models** and click on "Argument Links."

Petty Crime, Outrageous Punishment

■ Carl M. Cannon

Veteran journalist Carl M. Cannon was born in San Francisco and attended the University of Colorado, where he majored in journalism. For 20 years, he worked on a number of newspapers covering local and state politics, education, crime, and race relations. His reporting was instrumental in securing the freedom of a mentally impaired man in Georgia who had been wrongfully sentenced to prison after being influenced by police into confessing to murders he did not commit. In the 1980s, Cannon was similarly heroic in getting a California man pardoned who had been wrongfully convicted of a murder. On vacation in 1989, Cannon found himself covering the Loma Prieta earthquake in the San Francisco Bay area, which caused dozens of fires and a great deal of structural damage to commercial buildings. His reporting on that event for the San Jose Mercury *won him a Pulitzer Prize. In 1998, Cannon joined the staff of the prestigious* National Journal, *a weekly journal, where he is now White House correspondent. In early 2003, Cannon published* Boy Genius *(with Lou Dubose and Jan Reid), a biography of top Bush advisor Karl Rove. Later in 2003, he published* The Pursuit of Happiness in Times of War, *a book that examines the meaning of Thomas Jefferson's influential and quintessentially American phrase and traces it through U.S. history. In 2010, Cannon and Patrick Dillon published* Circle of Greed: The Spectacular Rise and Fall of America's Most Feared and Loathed Lawyer, *a book about William S. Lerach.*

The following essay first appeared in the October 2005 edition of Reader's Digest. *Here Cannon argues against the severity, both in personal terms and in the cost to the state, of the "three strikes and you're out" laws passed by many states starting in the 1990s.*

Reflecting on What You Know

What is your opinion of the criminal justice system in the United States? In general, do you think it's fair? As far as you know, does the punishment fit the crime in most cases?

There was nothing honorable about it, nothing particularly heinous, either, when Leandro Andrade, a 37-year-old Army veteran with three kids and a drug habit, walked into a Kmart store in Ontario, California, stuffed five videos into his waistband and tried to leave without paying. Security guards stopped him, but two weeks later, Andrade went to another Kmart and tried to steal four more videos. The police were called, and he was tried and convicted.

That was ten years ago, and Leandro Andrade is still behind bars. He figures to be there a lot longer: He came out of the courtroom with a sentence of 50 years to life.

If you find that stunningly harsh, you're in good company. The Andrade case went all the way to the U.S. Supreme Court, where Justice David Souter wrote that the punishment was "grossly disproportionate" to the crime.

So why is Andrade still serving a virtual life sentence? For the same reason that, across the country, thousands of others are behind bars serving extraordinarily long terms for a variety of low-level, nonviolent crimes. It's the result of well-intentioned anticrime laws that have gone terribly wrong.

Convinced that too many judges were going easy on violent recidivists. Congress enacted federal "mandatory minimum" sentences two decades ago, mainly targeting drug crimes. Throughout the 1990s, state legislatures and Congress kept upping the ante, passing new mandatory minimums, including "three strikes and you're out" laws. The upshot was a mosaic of sentencing statutes that all but eliminated judicial discretion, mercy, or even common sense.

Now we are living with the fallout. California came down hard on Andrade because he'd committed a petty theft in 1990 that allowed prosecutors to classify the video thefts as felonies, triggering the three-strikes law.

The videos that Andrade stole were kids' movies, such as *Casper* and *Snow White*—Christmas presents, he said, for nieces and nephews. A pre-sentence report theorized he was swiping the videos to feed a heroin habit. Their retail value: $84.70 for the first batch and $68.84 for the second.

When Andrade's case went before the Supreme Court, a bare majority upheld his sentence. But rather than try to defend the three-strikes law, the opinion merely said the Court should not function as a super-legislature.   8

Andrade will languish in prison, then, serving a much longer state sentence for his nonviolent crimes than most first offenders or even second-timers convicted of sexual assault or manslaughter.   9

Politicians saw harsh sentences as one way to satisfy voters fed up with the rising crime rates of the '70s and '80s, and the violence associated with crack cocaine and other drugs. And most would agree that strict sentencing laws have played a key role in lowering the crime rate for violent and property crimes.   10

Last June, Florida Governor Jeb Bush celebrated his state's 13th straight year of declining crime rates, thanks in part to tough sentencing statutes he enacted. "If violent habitual offenders are in prison," Bush said, "they're not going to be committing crimes on innocent people."   11

California, in particular, has seen a stark drop in crime since passing its toughest-in-the-nation three-strikes law more than ten years ago. Mike Reynolds, who pushed for the legislation after his 18-year-old daughter was murdered by two career criminals, says that under three-strikes, "those who can get their lives turned around, will. Those who can't have two choices—leave California or go to prison. The one thing we cannot allow is another victim to be part of their criminal therapy."   12

But putting thousands behind bars comes at a price—a cool $750 million in California alone. That's the annual cost to the state of incarcerating the nonviolent offenders sentenced under three-strikes. Add up all the years these inmates will serve on average and, according to the Justice Policy Institute, California's taxpayers will eventually shell out more than $6 billion. For a state with a battered economy, that's a pile of money to spend on sweeping up petty crooks.   13

The law also falls hardest on minorities. African Americans are imprisoned under three-strikes at ten times the rate of whites, and Latinos at nearly double the white rate. While crime rates are higher for these   14 minorities than for whites, the incarceration gap is disproportionately wide under three-strikes largely because of drug-related convictions.

Arkansas Governor Mike Huckabee is blunt when it comes to the three-strikes approach to justice: "It's the dumbest piece of public-policy legislation in a long time. We don't have a massive crime problem; we have a massive drug problem. And you don't treat that by locking drug addicts up. We're putting away people we're mad at, instead of the people we're afraid of." 15

There are some telling figures. In 1985 about 750,000 Americans were incarcerated on a variety of pending charges and convictions in federal and state prisons and local jails. The number of inmates is now about 2.1 million, of which some 440,000 were convicted on drug charges. A significant portion of the rest are there because drug addiction led them to rob and steal. 16

Early on there were signs that mandatory minimum laws— especially three-strikes statutes—had gone too far. Just a few months after Washington State passed the nation's first three-strikes law in 1993, a 29-year old named Paul Rivers was sentenced to life for stealing $337 from an espresso stand. Rivers had pretended he had a gun in his pocket, and the theft came after earlier convictions for second-degree robbery and assault. A prison term was appropriate. But life behind bars, without the possibility of parole? If Rivers had been packing a gun—and shot the espresso stand owner—he wouldn't have gotten any more time. 17

Just a few weeks after California's three-strikes law took effect, Brian A. Smith, a 30-year-old recovering crack addict, was charged with aiding and abetting two female shoplifters who took bed sheets from Robinsons-May department store in Los Cerritos Shopping Center. Smith got 25 years to life. 18

As a younger man, his first two strikes were for unarmed robbery and for burglarizing an unoccupied residence. Was Brian Smith really the kind of criminal whom California voters had in mind when they approved their three-strikes measure? Proponents sold the measure by saying it would keep murderers, rapists, and child molesters behind bars where they belong. Instead, the law locked Smith away for his petty crime until at least 2020, and probably longer—at a cost to the state of more than $750,000. 19

His case is not an aberration. By the end of last year, 2,344 of the 7,574 three-strikers in the state's penal system got their third strike 20 for a property offense. Scott Benscoter struck out after stealing a pair of running shoes, and is serving 25 years to life. His prior offenses were for residential burglaries that, according to the public defender's office, did not involve violence. Gregory Taylor, a homeless man in Los Angeles, was trying to jimmy a screen open to get into the kitchen of a church where he had previously been given food. But he had two prior offenses from more than a decade before: one for snatching a purse and the other for attempted robbery without a weapon. He's also doing 25 years to life.

One reason the pendulum has swung so far is that politicians love   21 to get behind popular slogans, even if they lead to bad social policy.

Few California lawmakers, for example, could resist the "use a   22 gun, go to prison" law, a concept so catchy that it swept the nation, and is now codified in one form or another in many state statutes and in federal law. It began as a sensible idea: Make our streets safer by discouraging drug dealers and the like from packing guns during their crimes. But the law needs to be more flexible than some rigid slogan. Ask Monica Clyburn. You can't, really, because she's been in prison these past ten years. Her crime? Well, that's hard to figure out.

A Florida welfare mom, Clyburn accompanied her boyfriend to a   23 pawnshop to sell his .22-caliber pistol. She provided her ID because her boyfriend didn't bring his own, and the couple got $30 for the gun. But Clyburn had a previous criminal record for minor drug charges, and when federal authorities ran a routine check of the pawnshop's records, they produced a "hit" — a felon in possession of a firearm. That's automatically 15 years in federal prison, which is exactly what Clyburn got. "I never even held the gun," she noted in an interview from prison.

No one is more appalled than H. Jay Stevens, the former federal   24 public defender for the middle district of Florida. "Everyone I've described this case to says, 'This can't have happened.' [But] it's happening five days a week all over this country."

Several years ago, a prominent Congressman, Representative   25 Dan Rostenkowski of Illinois, was sent to prison on mail-fraud charges. It was only then that he learned what he'd been voting for all those years when anticrime legislation came up and he cast the safe "aye" vote. Rostenkowski told of being stunned at how many young, low-level drug offenders were doing 15- and 20-year stretches in federal prison.

"The waste of these lives is a loss to the entire community," 26
Rostenkowski said. "I was swept along by the rhetoric about getting tough on crime. Frankly, I lacked both expertise and perspective on these issues."

Former Michigan Governor William G. Milliken signed into 27
law his state's mandatory minimums for drug cases, but after leaving office he lobbied the state legislature to rescind them. "I have since come to realize that the provisions of the law have led to terrible injustices," Milliken wrote in 2002. Soon after, Governor John Engler signed legislation doing away with most of Michigan's mandatory sentences.

On the federal level, judges have been expressing their anger 28
with Congress for preventing them from exercising discretion and mercy. U.S. District Court Judge John S. Martin, Jr., appointed by the first President Bush, announced his retirement from the bench rather than remain part of "a sentencing system that is unnecessarily cruel and rigid."

While the U.S. Supreme Court has yet to strike down mandatory 29
minimums, one justice at least has signaled his opposition to them. Justice Anthony M. Kennedy said in a speech at the 2003 American Bar Association meeting that he accepted neither the "necessity" nor "wisdom" of mandatory minimums.

"One day in prison is longer than almost any day you and I have 30
had to endure," Justice Kennedy told the nation's lawyers. "When the door is locked against the prisoner, we do not think about what is behind it. To be sure, the prisoner must be punished to vindicate the law, to acknowledge the suffering of the victim, and to deter future crimes. Still, the prisoner is a person. Still, he or she is part of the family of humankind."

Thinking Critically about This Reading

There are countless versions of the following idea throughout history, but it was the English jurist William Blackstone who perhaps said it most memorably: "It is better that ten guilty persons escape than that one innocent suffer." Cannon is not protesting the guilt of the people in his examples of what seems unjust punishment, but he is arguing that "three-strikes and you're out" laws demand that judges hand down sentences that are too severe. What, in your opinion, is the solution?

Questions for Study and Discussion

1. What is Cannon's thesis in this essay? (Glossary: *Thesis*)

2. Does Cannon say what, if anything, he would like to see happen as a result of his argument? If so, where does he make his wishes clear?

3. How and where in his essay does Cannon use illustration, cause and effect, and narration to develop his argument? (Glossary: *Illustration; Cause and Effect; Narration*)

4. In paragraph 7, Cannon writes, "The videos that Andrade stole were kids' movies, such as *Casper* and *Snow White*—Christmas presents, he said, for nieces and nephews." Why do you think that Cannon includes this information? Does it matter to you what the videos were or why Andrade stole them? Did it matter to the court? Explain.

5. *Reader's Digest* does not usually require that their writers document their sources in print, but the magazine has a well-known reputation for making sure that those sources are nonetheless accurate. Would you have liked to have seen Cannon's sources cited in the article? Why or why not? Does the magazine's and the writer's reputation for accuracy matter in this regard? Explain.

6. Cannon's subject is very serious. Is his tone always equally serious? Do you notice what some might consider inappropriate tonal lapses? If so, cite some examples. (Glossary: *Tone*)

Classroom Activity Using Argument

Identify the fallacy in each of the following statements. (For more information on logical fallacies, see the box on p. 544.)

a. Oversimplification
b. Hasty generalization
c. *Post hoc, ergo propter hoc*
d. Begging the question

e. False analogy
f. Either/or thinking
g. *Non sequitur*

1. America: Love it or leave it! _____

2. Two of my best friends who are overweight don't exercise at all. Overweight people are simply not getting enough exercise. _____

3. If we use less gasoline, the price of gasoline will fall. _____

4. Life is precious because we want to protect it at all costs. _____
5. Randy is a good mechanic, so he'll be a good race car driver. _____
6. Susan drank hot lemonade, and her cold went away. _____
7. Students do poorly in college because they do too much surfing on the Web. _____
8. If we can eliminate pollution, we can cure cancer. _____
9. Such actions are illegal because they are prohibited by law. _____
10. Every time I have something important to do on my computer, it crashes. _____
11. We should either raise taxes or cut social programs. _____
12. Education ought to be managed just as a good business is managed. _____

Suggested Writing Assignments

1. If you believe, as does Cannon, that politicians and legislators overreacted to the high incidence of drug crimes and that "the upshot was a mosaic of sentencing statutes that all but eliminated judicial discretion, mercy, or even common sense" (paragraph 5), write your own argument in favor of a revision of those federal and state mandates. You are not writing with the same authority as Cannon or *Reader's Digest*, so you would be well-advised to include a set of formal citations for your sources. Your readers may want to reference your sources for accuracy and as a basis for their own arguments either in support or in refutation of your own. Finally, consider sending your argument to your state and federal representatives for their responses.

2. Has the imposition of "three strikes and you're out" laws reduced the rate of recidivism with respect to serious drug-related crimes? In other words, have proponents achieved their purpose? What do the statistics tell us? Depending on the data you collect and the evidence you can bring to bear on the question, write an argument putting forth your views on the subject as to whether or not these laws should be kept on the books.

The Piracy of Privacy: Why Marketers Must Bare Our Souls

■ **Allen D. Kanner**

Allen D. Kanner was born in 1952 on an air force base in Recife, Brazil, and grew up in Redwood City, California. He is a child, family, and adult psychologist now working in the San Francisco Bay area. He earned both his AB (1974) and his PhD (1981) in psychology from the University of California, Berkeley; has been in private practice as a psychotherapist; and has held teaching and clinical appointments in a number of institutions, most notably Harvard University and Stanford University. Kanner is co-founder of the Campaign for a Commercial-Free Childhood and a coeditor with Tim Kasser of Psychology Consumer Culture: The Struggle for a Good Life in a Materialistic World *(2003) and with Theodore Roszak and Mary E. Gomes of* Ecopsychology: Restoring the Earth, Healing the Mind *(1995), an early work that helped formulate the ecopsychology movement. In 1997, Kanner was named by* UTNE Reader *as one of the nation's top ten activists in the field of psychotherapy.*

"The Piracy of Privacy: Why Marketers Must Bare Our Souls," was first published in the July-August 2009 issue of Tikkun. *The magazine's title is derived from the Hebrew phrase* Tikkun olam, *or "repairing the world." In his essay, Kanner argues that the increasingly sophisticated high-tech tools and strategies that marketers employ to gain sales are methods that are having a profound effect on our psychological well-being.*

Reflecting on What You Know

What effects do you think corporatized advertising techniques are having on your buying habits? Have you ever wondered, after the fact, why you bought something? Do you always feel in control of yourself when you make purchases? How has being a consumer changed you, if at all?

When The Police sang their famous lines, "Every breath you take, every move you make, . . . I'll be watching you," they may have had an obsessed stalker in mind or even a government run by Big Brother. They probably were not thinking of the exponentially expanding world of high-tech marketing. Yet corporate advertising constitutes the greatest threat to privacy in human history. It is a threat, moreover, that has arisen as a byproduct of an economic system so single-mindedly bent on increasing profits that it is only vaguely aware of what it is actually doing. 1

The corporate capacity to scrutinize people's private lives has made great leaps forward in the last five years, with further advances on the horizon. To remain competitive, corporations are now compelled to probe more intimately and thoroughly than ever before. Consider the following developments. 2

Every Step You Take

Using built-in links to the global positioning system (GPS), smartphones such as the iPhone and Blackberry can now track individuals down to the street corner on which they stand. This enables marketers to send ads, say, for a nearby restaurant as someone emerges from a movie theater. In a similar vein, AisleCaster is a GPS-linked mobile phone program that offers shoppers specials based on their precise location in a supermarket or mall. 3

Further, some mobile phones collect and store an average of twenty pieces of information per customer, including the person's age, gender, race, income, health, travel patterns, interests, purchasing history, and whether she or he has children. Using these data, smartphones can customize commercials to a particular customer. Thus, different people receive different ads. 4

In 2006, Google CEO Eric Schmidt predicted that within several years, highly personalized car ads will be sent based on an individual's GPS location. Schmidt has described privacy as passé. 5

Quividi and TruMedia are companies that produce digital bill-   6
boards with tiny cameras that gather information from passersby,
such as their gender, age, race, and length of time looking at the
billboard, and tailor their display ads accordingly. With the rapid
spread of digital screens to stores, gyms, doctor's offices, elevators,
taxicabs, the sides of buildings, and elsewhere, these miniature snoop-
ing cameras have a bright future.

It is well known that marketers monitor online activity. But the   7
amount of information collected is staggering. According to a study
commissioned by the *New York Times* (see Louise Story's article "To
Aim Ads, Web Is Keeping Closer Eye on You" from March 10, 2008),
in December 2007, Yahoo, Google, Microsoft, AOL, and MySpace
recorded 336 billion transmissions in which the consumer's data were
sent back to the Web companies' servers. Advertisers are now choosing where to place their ads not so much on the size of a site's audience as on how much the site knows about its visitors.

In the public sphere, marketers are constantly achieving new levels   8
of intrusiveness. Ads are appearing on supermarket eggs, airline
motion sickness bags, and paper liners in pediatricians' offices. A picture of Adidas sneakers placed in a subway station bursts into a whirl
of flying shoes when someone walks past it. "Got Milk?" billboards
have emitted chocolate chip cookie odors in bus stops, a practice that
was halted due to complaints. Some shopping carts at Jewel-Osco
grocery stores are equipped with two screens, one that advertises to
parents as they pass by specific products and another that plays TV
shows for the children in the cart.

Neuromarketing is a growing area of research that uses brain-   9
imaging techniques, such as MRIs, to monitor neural activity while
people view commercials. In one recent study, investigators were
able to predict whether a product would be bought by examining
shoppers' neuronal firing patterns as they evaluated products on
computer screens. A Harvard University study sponsored by Jack
Daniels compared scans of teenagers, twenty-year-olds, and older
men in various drinking situations. The results were used to refine a
whiskey advertising campaign. Other investigators are measuring
eye blink rates in children to determine what types of images keep
them glued to the screen.

The ongoing integration of various media such as television,   10
computers, cell phones, and iPods means that information collected
through one media is automatically transferred to another. Soon the

electronic media will function like a giant octopus, with each tentacle monitoring our lives.

The Larger Structure

Does the invasion of privacy really matter? Imagine five years from now that you are undergoing a divorce and that you are the father of a young boy. A toy company's marketing division has flagged your situation; its research indicates you're likely worried about the relationship with your son. The marketers also know that you've just been paid and that the boy's birthday is next week. The ad they send on your smartphone—showing an ecstatic boy receiving an expensive video game from his loving father—has been electronically tweaked so the boy looks a little like your child. You order the game on the spot. 11

Your love for your son has been subtly altered during this process. Instead of paying close attention to his true needs, perhaps for more time with you, your attention has been shifted at a vulnerable moment toward making him happy through buying him gifts. You might work extra hours to afford the video game, time you could have spent with him. 12

By exposing people to thousands of such exquisitely personalized ads, corporate marketing could surreptitiously mold the most meaningful episodes of our lives. Our greatest passions, anxieties, dreams, and losses would be distorted and redirected to serve the consumer culture. 13

Yet the intersection of corporate capitalism with modern communication technology necessitates the sacrifice of privacy. The reason is simple; the more advertisers know about their customers, the greater their chances of making a sale. Knowledge is power. But as each new area of privacy is transgressed, it soon becomes saturated with commercial messages. Competition among marketers guarantees that the industry maintains its trajectory toward a more complete inner invasion and outer immersion, a total marketing envelopment of our being. 14

Of course, once personal information is gathered, it can be used for purposes other than selling products. We saw this recently with the Bush administration's requisitioning of phone company information to spy on American citizens. Since corporations are profit-driven, their valuable data banks will not remain within the confines of their sales departments. 15

Just to be clear, corporations do believe in privacy—for themselves. Their privacy is called proprietary information or trade secrets. 16

The possible revelation of trade secrets is routinely, and successfully, used as an argument against regulation.

Similar to environmental destruction or the exploitation of labor, the corporate violation of privacy reflects fundamental structural flaws in corporate capitalism that transcend the type of product or service being sold. In each of these instances, the damage wrought is an inevitable byproduct of the economic system. Corporations do not destroy nature because their charters demand it, nor exploit labor because they have a mandate to see working people suffer, nor intrude upon privacy because they wish to embarrass and expose people. Rather, the manipulations necessary to increase sales require drastic interventions with side effects that rain ruin upon the world and ravage the psyche. 17

The long-term answer is not more regulation. There is something deeply amiss about a perennial battle between marketers and regulators over corporate access to our inner and outer lives. We must escape from the battle itself. This will require an economic system that cherishes the planet and its people, and does not compel its businesses to demolish our privacy for their quarterly profits. 18

Thinking Critically about This Reading

Is Kanner's argument inductive, deductive, or a combination of both models of argumentation? Explain.

Questions for Study and Discussion

1. What is Kanner's thesis in this essay, and where does he state it most clearly? (Glossary: *Thesis*)
2. What is Kanner's purpose in writing this essay? (Glossary: *Purpose*) Does he want us to do anything? Explain.
3. What types of evidence does Kanner use to support his thesis? (Glossary: *Evidence*) Is it reliable and valid, in your opinion?
4. What issue does Kanner raise with respect to regulation? What does he say are the pros and cons of regulation with respect to high-tech marketing?
5. How does Kanner make use of the three elements of argumentation: ethos, pathos, and logos? Explain.

6. For what audience do you think Kanner is writing: those who are like-minded, those who are potentially like-minded, or those who might be difficult to convince? (Glossary: *Audience*) Why is the question an important one for Kanner to consider?

Classroom Activity Using Argument

We asked Kanner what prompted him to write "The Piracy of Privacy." As a class, discuss the implications of the following explanation he offered in response:

> In my work as a psychologist I witness daily the undiagnosed but enormous emotional damage caused by capitalism. When capitalism undermines privacy, it destroys a precious right that is essential to our mental health. The trust and sense of safety that is necessary for healing in my work, but impossible without privacy, is but one example of this. Yet we give up this right so tamely when that sacred cow, the free marketplace, demands it. This article is intended to illustrate one of the many ways that an economic system built on the assumption that people are fundamentally selfish, materialistic, and competitive is inevitably anti-life.

Here are some questions you may find useful in starting your discussion:

1. Are we able to assess the validity of Kanner's findings and analysis? Explain.
2. If we believe that the problem he addresses is real, what can we as consumers do to help the situation?
3. What can corporations do to lessen or eliminate assaults on privacy through their marketing analyses?
4. Is American business "anti-life"?

Suggested Writing Assignments

1. Write an essay in which you argue that although he is correct, Kanner is fighting a useless battle because average citizens have long ago lost the battle for privacy. In fact, he cites Eric Schmidt of Google as describing "privacy as passé" (paragraph 5). Don't we already have surveillance cameras everywhere we go, hasn't Google already captured the street where we live and maybe even

our place of residence, isn't our GPS being used to track us, and haven't we willingly given up our privacy on Facebook, Twitter, MySpace, LinkedIn, Blogger, YouTube, and other social, business, and professional networking sites? How do we weigh the advantages and disadvantages of technological innovations?

2. Argue that Kanner is correct and that high-tech technology not only invades our privacy but actually causes us to modify our behavior. He cites the example of the divorced dad who receives an ad on his smartphone, buys his son an expensive video game, and in the process subtly alters his relationship with the boy. If you or your friends have your own examples of how the intrusions of high-tech marketing strategies, not the communications channels of the old media, have affected you and your personal relationships and "bared your soul," use them to support your argument.

3. At the end of his essay Kanner writes: "There is something deeply amiss about a perennial battle between marketers and regulators over corporate access to our inner and outer lives. We must escape from the battle itself. This will require an economic system that cherishes the planet and its people, and does not compel its businesses to demolish our privacy for their quarterly profits." Write an essay in which you argue for the kind of economic system you think that Kanner envisions.

Marketing Ate Our Culture—But It Doesn't Have To

■ **Terry O'Reilly**

Terry O'Reilly is the coproducer and writer of The Age of Persuasion, *the hit CBC radio show about the business of advertising, what its goals are, how it is created, and how it affects society. O'Reilly, born in 1959 in Sudbury, Ontario, began his career as an advertising copywriter and then in 1990 started his own radio and television production company, Pirate Radio & Television, based in New York and Toronto. He was the host of the highly successful CBC Radio One series* O'Reilly on Advertising *before creating* The Age of Persuasion. *The winner of more than 400 awards for writing and directing, O'Reilly hosts sold-out radio workshops for those in the advertising business and, with Mike Tennant, published* The Age of Persuasion: How Marketing Ate Our Culture *(2009).*

In the following essay, which appeared in AlterNet *on October 10, 2010, O'Reilly presents the intriguing argument that rather than running to the bathroom or kitchen when the commercials come on, we have an obligation to watch those commercials. One might expect this argument from an advertising guru, after all, but still you might find his reasoning worth your time.*

Reflecting on What You Know

What are your thoughts about the commercials you see on television? Do they annoy you because there are far too many of them and bore you because they are dull and repetitive? Or do you watch them because they are informative and occasionally creative and funny? Do you record the programs you watch so that you can skip the commercials?

What if I told you that you should be watching more commercials? Yes, I'm an adman. And yes, you'd expect me to say that. But you just might have a moral obligation to watch more commercials. Let me explain.

A few decades back, Texan Claudia Alta Taylor Johnson gazed down the highway and didn't like what she saw. Billboards blocked her view of the plains, of the distant hills, and of her beloved wildflowers. So she complained to her husband. He had a fairly influential job. He was President of the United States. Like all good husbands, Lyndon Baines Johnson knew what was good for him, and prompted Congress to pass the Highway Beautification Act, which placed limits on the spread of posters—or billboards as they're popularly known—and preserved the views that Ladybird Johnson loved so much.

The new restrictions drew rave reviews, particularly from one British ex-pat, who later wrote: "As a private person, I have a passion for landscape, and have never seen one improved by a billboard. Where every prospect pleases, man is at his vilest when he erects a billboard. When I retire, I am going to start a secret society of masked vigilantes who will travel around the world on silent motor bicycles, chopping down posters at the dark of the moon. How many juries will convict us when we are caught in these acts of beneficent citizenship?"

It's a remarkable manifesto considering its author is the legendary advertising mogul David Ogilvy, he of Ogilvy & Mather advertising agency fame. Throughout his career, he railed at large outdoor posters, even though his advertising agency created hundreds, if not thousands, of them for their various blue-chip clients.

Let's stick a bookmark in here for a moment, and go back in time a bit further. At the beginning of the 20th century, one of the most powerful advertising agencies in America was Lord & Thomas, headed by the most influential, albeit most forgotten adman ever to stride purposefully down Madison Avenue (even though he was based in Chicago, but stay with me). Inspired one day by Canadian copywriter John E. Kennedy's famous insight that advertising really was "salesmanship on paper" and not just "news," Lasker took that seemingly obvious tidbit and built Lord & Thomas into one of the world's largest advertising empires.

Radio was just coming out of its wrapping back then, and Lasker initially paid little attention to the medium as it struggled for the economic model that would sustain it. What he couldn't ignore, however, was the success of radio advertising pioneers such as Bernard Gimbel, of Gimbel's department stores and Saks Fifth Avenue. Even harder to ignore was Lasker's client David Sarnoff of RCA, who also happened to be the founder of the NBC radio network in 1926. Eventually, Lasker decided to experiment with radio advertising and asked his New York office to create a program based on some sort of Broadway entertainment as a vehicle for Palmolive.

Meanwhile, NBC president Merlin Aylesworth didn't believe in radio advertising as you hear it today, but preferred that sponsors (a word not yet invented in the late twenties) be mentioned before and after a program with a passing phrase like, "The following program comes to you through the courtesy of Lucky Strike." Clearly, he hadn't met Albert Lasker. But he was about to. The locomotive that was Albert Lasker had a completely different point of view: He reckoned that in exchange for underwriting a broadcast, brands should be offered an opportunity to present the sort of "reason why" advertising they did in print, but adapted for sound. Instead of parcels of space, they would occupy parcels of time. And that is how the broadcast "commercial," as it came to be known, was born. Merlin, meet Albert.   7

In no time, Lasker was basking in the success of sponsored radio programs, like *Amos 'n' Andy* and *The Pepsodent Show Starring Bob Hope,* and quickly embraced the new medium on behalf of other clients. In solving a problem for his clients, Lasker provided the economic model radio had been struggling to find: big-name advertisers could provide big money to underwrite high-caliber entertainment for a mass audience. The bigger the audience, the greater the value to advertisers, and theoretically, the more they would pay for production. Radio would provide top-rank entertainment, but it would not be free.   8

Listeners would pay by allowing themselves to be exposed to a commercial. It seemed just the right fit in a world of compromise. You want to go camping? You tolerate mosquitoes. You want to fly? You tolerate removing your belt at airports. You want Groucho Marx in your living room? No problem, provided the nation's three thousand Plymouth-DeSoto dealers could tag along. And there it was: The Great Unwritten Contract. Sponsors funded programming, and in return, they took some of the listener's time and attention.   9

And it was good.   10

When television took off in the 1950s, it suffered few of the birth-   11
ing pains that radio had; Albert Lasker had provided a readymade
economic template. At the same time, the postwar economic boom
gave consumers enough cash to buy television sets, and as TV viewer-
ship grew, the value of its audience became increasingly attractive to
advertisers. Sponsors lined up to pour fresh buckets of money into the
new medium.

A large part of the attraction was the "mass audience" experi-   12
ence of the new medium; like radio, it drew millions of people to the
same event during the same time span. The morning after a broadcast, it seemed that the talk was all about what "everyone" had been
watching the night before: Ralph and Norton's latest get-rich-quick
scheme or which dress Uncle Miltie wore on *Texaco Star Theatre*. It
was the shared experience, as much as the programs themselves that
caused a buzz around the broadcasts. There was a thrill in knowing
that millions of others were watching the same show at the same moment. Sponsors' ads were a small price to pay.

OK, back to the bookmark. Here's the point, and even Ogilvy   13
agreed with this: Advertising has to uphold its end of the Great
Unwritten Contract. Put simply, advertising has to give you something
back in exchange for your time. At the low end of that transaction,
the ads themselves have to at least be entertaining, or informative, or
dramatically interesting. In other words, the advertiser has to reward
you with a smile or a bit of information that you didn't know before.
That's motherhood in this debate.

At the high end, the advertising has to give you something sub-   14
stantive back in exchange for your attention. Advertising should
underwrite the entertainment. The ad revenue should be plowed
back into creative production. So when CBS makes $271M
per year from advertising revenue on *Late Night With David
Letterman,* a big chunk of it goes to making more David Letterman
shows. The ads in news programs fund the travel and salaries of
the news gatherers around the world. The ads in a magazine fund
the magazine content. Ads in a newspaper pay the reporter's salaries. Paid keyword searches fund that wonderful little thing you
call Google.

That's the basis of the Great Unwritten Contract. The ads under-   15
write the programs or content you love, you sit through the ads in
return. It was and is a good deal.

When advertising breaks that contract, trouble brews. I truly be-   16
lieve that you can chart the start of ad-induced bathroom runs to
when advertising started to take but not give. When the ads themselves stopped being interesting, and became repetitive and relentless
and unrewarding, people started getting annoyed with them. When
1950s ad gurus like Rosser Reeves believed that high repetition of
kindergarten-like ad propositions (Anacin relieves headaches! Anacin
relieves headaches!! Anacin relieves headaches!!!) were the path to big
sales, he and admen like him, broke the contract. When one of his
own clients asked Reeves whether the ice-pick-to-the-forehead strategy wasn't turning people off, Reeves answered with a famous question: "Do you want to be liked, or do you want to be rich?"

I dislike telemarketing not just because it's annoying, but also be-   17
cause it breaks the contract, disrespecting the customer and interrupt-
ing without apology. It breaks all the rules of good marketing, which
is to say it isn't pleasantly surprising or polite or humorous or meaningful. Telemarketers make no attempt to build a relationship with
their clients, nor do they try to live up to the Contract: offering something in exchange for the customer's time. Telemarketers don't give
you anything. They just call to take, and leave you with a cold bucket
of the Colonel's chicken.

Let's talk cinema advertising. Unless I'm very wrong, ticket prices   18
didn't come down when ads went up. These days, the moviegoer has
been demoted from welcome guest to mere chattel, whose time and attention are commodified and sold to a growing number of advertisers.

And for this you pay them.   19

Billboards have to figure out a way to give back. Ladybird was sim-   20
ply reacting to the fissure in the Contract. She didn't know it then, but
she was. Where was the giveback? Where was the reciprocity? Cut to Mr.
Johnson having to introduce billboard legislation to keep the Mrs. happy
while juggling civil rights and Viet Nam. No one said marriage was easy.

By now, you must think this is quite a rant for an adman. Followed   21
by the question—will he ever work again?

Yet I believe in the Contract. Wholeheartedly. But here's the thing: 22
Every contract has two sides. A contract isn't a contract until two
people shake hands. Which means, if you have some favorite television
programs like the *Letterman* show, or *Survivor,* or *60 Minutes,* you
should be honoring your side of the Contract, and watching the commercials embedded in those programs.

Because if you're not, you're breaking the Contract. You are in 23 breach.

Every time you leave the room to go to the fridge, or to the bath- 24 room during a commercial break, or fast-forward through the ads with your TiVo, you are quietly, surreptitiously, covertly, violating the Contract.

You get away with it because it's not enforceable by law. If a 25 roofing contractor took your money, and didn't replace your roof, you'd be outraged. If your dentist sent you a bill but didn't fill the cavity, you'd bounce off all four walls.

So how do you justify not watching the commercials that under- 26 write the programs you watch and religiously record?

Screw 'em, I hear you say. The commercials they put out are crap, 27 most are barely watchable. But there are also scores of good commercials. Just like there are good and bad movies, books and songs. As a matter of fact, the United States constantly ranks first or second internationally every year when it comes to creative advertising. It's a verifiable fact.

So here we are at that rarely talked about impasse. Advertisers 28 break the contract with bad commercials, you avoid their commercials to punish them, but still take the programs. It's like a Quentin Tarrantino standoff, where everyone has a gun.

So here's an idea: Stop buying from advertisers that send you bad 29 commercials. Every time you buy from those advertisers, they come to people like me and ask for more bad commercials. When I protest, they just point to their sales results, and the air goes out of my argument. They believe that bad ads work, because you, the consuming public, are enablers. Instead, only buy from the advertisers that assume intelligence, that make you smile, that give you advertising that tells you something you didn't know 30 seconds ago, advertisers that respect you.

Then, stop the TiVo when you see one of their ads go whizzing 30 by, rewind the machine, and watch the commercial. Don't punch that button on your car radio when a good commercial comes on, listen to it. Read that interesting ad across from the story you're devouring in *Vanity Fair*. Don't answer the phone when a 1-800 number shows up on the readout.

Patronize the advertisers holding up their end of the Contact. 31 And do the honorable thing: hold up your end.

Thinking Critically about This Reading

O'Reilly writes, "Billboards have to figure out a way to give back" (paragraph 20). Whether or not you like billboards and whether or not you think that they have a right to exist, what imaginative ideas do you have to make them more reciprocal, to pay us back for our attention to them and maybe even our loyalty in supporting the products and services they advertise?

Questions for Study and Discussion

1. What is O'Reilly's thesis? Where does he state it? (Glossary: *Thesis*)
2. Explain how O'Reilly uses narration to develop his argument. (Glossary: *Narration*)
3. O'Reilly uses a number of analogies in his essay to focus the points he makes. Identify several of those analogies, and explain how effective you think that they are. (Glossary: *Analogy*)
4. O'Reilly uses a "bookmark" device in paragraph 5. To what end does he use it? Where in his essay does he return to it? Is it, in your opinion, an effective rhetorical device? Explain.
5. What point does O'Reilly make about the importance of a "mass audience" for radio (12)? How does he use that point to further develop his argument?
6. What is the Great Unwritten Contract O'Reilly refers to in paragraphs 13 and 14? Do you think that there is such a contract? Explain.
7. Who do you think that O'Reilly had in mind as an audience for his argument? (Glossary: *Audience*) What does he want his readers to do as a consequence of reading his essay? Will you follow his advice? Why or why not?

Classroom Activity Using Argument

Lady Bird Johnson began the movement to eliminate billboards from U.S. highways, and in 1965 the Highway Beautification Act was signed into law. Now four states have antibillboard laws: Vermont, Alaska, Hawaii, and Maine. Are billboards necessary? Would they be missed if banned? As a class, generate the ideas, information, and arguments necessary to write a strong essay in favor of banning billboards. Instructors should allow a few days' notice so that students can gather the information they need from books, articles, and the Internet. One source of information can be gained by searching the legislative history of the four states that have already banned billboards. Be sure to be ready to refute arguments in favor of billboards. For example, can states do without the rental income they may derive from advertisers? If everyone agrees, students may later want to use the information and ideas gathered by the class to write their own essays arguing against billboards, and perhaps even send them to a state legislative body in charge of such matters.

Suggested Writing Assignments

1. In his essay "The Piracy of Privacy" on pages 587–91, Allen Kanner argues, on the basis of the problems he sees with patients in his psychotherapy practice, that advertisers are increasingly using high-tech strategies and techniques to rob us of our privacy and destabilize our mental well-being. On the other hand, Terry O'Reilly, in "Marketing Ate Our Culture — But It Doesn't Have To," says that we have to uphold our end of an unwritten contract that requires us to watch commercials, so as to increase the sale of products that support the programming we enjoy. Who's right? Write an argumentative essay in which you put forth your own views on whether advertising should have a bigger or smaller role in our lives.

2. Most of us have problems with the commercials we see on television. What's wrong with them? How do they fail in most cases to inform and entertain us? Write an essay in which you argue for more creativity and inspiration on the parts of the producers and writers of television commercials. Be sure to support your argument with expert testimony and with examples that illustrate both what you find wrong and what you find that is heading in the right direction.

Generation E. A.: Ethnically Ambiguous

■ **Ruth La Ferla**

Ruth La Ferla is a journalist who for more than 30 years has worked in the fast-paced, dynamic world of fashion. Based at the center of one of the world's great fashion capitals, Seventh Avenue in New York City, La Ferla has been identifying what's about to appear, what has already appeared, and what has gone around again and again and been reinvented. Since 2000, she has been a styles  *reporter for the* New York Times, *where she has written articles covering such diverse topics as Bill Blass, Fashion Week in New York City, the return to the 1950s in fashion (it happens every ten years), the vampire trend, brides who chose to wear less and less to the altar, shopping for the latest looks in jewelry, and, more recently, discovering what J. Crew's new bridal shop is all about, as well as the influence of the movie* Black Swan *on fashion. Before writing for the* New York Times, *La Ferla was an editor and writer at* Elle Magazine, Mirabella, Women's Wear Daily, *and* W.

In the following article, which was first published in the New York Times *in 2003, La Ferla was one of the first reporters to argue that a new trend in fashion advertising was developing, one using models of indeterminate ethnic and racial origin, an approach to image-making that remains popular today.*

Reflecting on What You Know

Think about the advertising models, both men and women, who appear in the magazines you read and the commercials for your favorite programs on television. Do they resemble your friends in age, appearance, body language, and dress? Might you encounter them at a campus hangout, local eatery, or coffee shop? Explain.

Each week, Leo Jimenez, a 25-year-old New Yorker, sifts 1
through a mound of invitations, pulling out the handful that
seem most promising. On back-to-back nights earlier this month,
he dropped in to Lotus on West 14th Street for the unveiling of
a new fashion line, and turned up at the opening of Crobar, a
dance club in Chelsea, mingling with stars like Rosie Perez, long-
stemmed models and middle-aged roués[1] trussed in dinner jackets.
Wherever he goes, Mr. Jimenez himself is an object of fascination.
"You get the buttonhole," he said. "You get the table, you get the
attention."

Mr. Jimenez, a model, has appeared in ads for Levi's, DKNY, 2
are EAs and Aldo, but he is anything but a conventional pretty
face. His steeply raked cheekbones, dreadlocks, and jet-colored
eyes suggest a background that might be Mongolian, American
Indian, or Chinese. In fact he is Colombian by birth, a product of
that country's mixed racial heritage, and he fits right in with the
melting-pot aesthetic of the downtown scene. It is also a look that
is reflected in the latest youth marketing trend: using faces that are
ethnically ambiguous.

Ad campaigns for Louis Vuitton, YSL Beauty, and H&M stores 3
have all purposely highlighted models with racially indeterminate features. Or consider the careers of movie stars like Vin Diesel, Lisa
Bonet, and Jessica Alba, whose popularity with young audiences
seems due in part to the tease over whether they are black, white,
Hispanic, American Indian, or some combination.

"Today what's ethnically neutral, diverse, or ambiguous has tre- 4
mendous appeal," said Ron Berger, the chief executive of Euro RSCG
MVBMS Partners in New York, an advertising agency and trend research company whose clients include Polaroid and Yahoo. "Both in
the mainstream and at the high end of the marketplace, what is perceived as good, desirable, successful is often a face whose heritage is
hard to pin down."

Ambiguity is chic, especially among the under-25 members of 5
Generation Y, the most racially diverse population in the nation's history. *Teen People*'s current issue, devoted to beauty, features make-
overs of girls whose backgrounds are identified on full-page head
shots as "Puerto Rican and Italian-American" and "Finnish-German-
Irish- and Scotch-American."

---

[1]*roué:* one devoted to a life of sensual pleasure.

"We're seeing more of a desire for the exotic, left-of-center   6
beauty that transcends race or class," Amy Barnett, the magazine's
managing editor, said. It "represents the new reality of America,
which includes considerable mixing," she added. "It is changing the
face of American beauty."

Nearly seven million Americans identified themselves as members   7
of more than one race in the 2000 census, the first time respondents
were able to check more than one category. In addition, more than
14 million Latinos—about 42 percent of Latino respondents—ignored
the census boxes for black or white and checked "some other race,"
an indication, experts said, of the mixed-race heritage of many
Hispanics—with black, white, and indigenous Indian strains in the mix.

The increasingly multiracial American population, demogra-   8
phers say, is due to intermarriage and waves of immigration. Mixed-
race Americans tend to be young—those younger than 18 were
twice as likely as adults to identify themselves as multiracial on the
census.

"The younger the age group, the more diverse the population,"   9
said Gregory Spencer, who heads the Census Bureau's population
projections branch.

It is no surprise that the acceptance of a melting-pot chic is   10
greater in places like downtown New York, where immigrants and
young people flood in. On a recent evening Pedro Freyre, 26, an artist of French, Mexican, and Spanish heritage, was strolling there with
his cap tilted to accentuate his cheekbones. "We are the new mix,"
Mr. Freyre said, borrowing the language of the DJ booth. "We are the
remix."

Mr. Jimenez, the model, said that being perceived as a racial hy-   11
brid "has definitely opened doors for me." He added, "suddenly
there is a demand for my kind of face."

Ahmed Akkad, 44, a New York artist who is Turkish and   12
Albanian, said that being an ethnic composite "sometimes gives you
an edge, a certain sexual appeal."

But some multiracial 20-somethings view their waxing popularity   13
with skepticism. "Back home in Minneapolis, I sometimes feel like a
trophy," said Ryoji Suguro, a 28-year-old lighting director of Sri
Lankan and Japanese descent. "When you're introduced, it's sometimes like, 'Oh, here is my exotic friend,'" said Mr. Suguro, who
shared cocktails with his girlfriend, who is Korean and Caucasian, at
Max Fish on the Lower East Side.

Carrie Hazelwood, 30, an art dealer's assistant who is Welsh, 14
Swedish, and American Indian, is put off by advertisers' efforts to
exploit mixed ethnicity. "They are just trying to cover their
bases—casting as if they were solving a math problem," she said.

Mr. Diesel, 36, the star of action-adventure films like *The Fast* 15
and the Furious, once downplayed his multiracial heritage, saying in
public only that his mother is Irish and his father's background was
unknown. But in more recent interviews he has acknowledged that his
mixed background has been an asset, allowing him to play all types
of roles and ethnicities.

Among art directors, magazine editors, and casting agents, there 16
is a growing sense that the demand is weakening for P&G (Procter &
Gamble), industry code for blond-haired, blue-eyed models.

"People think blond-haired, blue-eyed kids are getting all the 17
work, but these days they are working the least," said Elise Koseff,
vice president of J. Mitchell Management in New York, which represents children and teenagers for ads and television. Instead, Ms.
Koseff said, actors like Miles Thompson, 13, who is Jamaican, Native
American, and Eastern European, are in demand. Miles has appeared
on the television show *Third Watch* and will be in ads for Microsoft's
Xbox video game player.

As evidence of the trend, Ms. Koseff exhibited a selection of 18
"casting breakdowns," descriptions from television producers of
roles to be filled. "Sarah, 16 to 18 years old. Light complexioned
African-American. Could be part Brazilian or Dominican," read
one request from CBS for its daytime serial *As the World Turns*.
"Zach, 12 to 14, African-American. Zach's father is Caucasian,"
stated another, from the producers of "Unfabulous," a pilot for
Nickelodeon.

Ethnically ambiguous casting has been slower to make inroads in 19
the fashion world. The casting of multiracial models "is just beginning," said Nian Fish, the creative director of KCD in New York,
which produces fashion shows. "Fashion is taking its lead from
Hollywood."

One who typifies the trend is Ujjwala, a model from India and 20
the new face of YSL Beauty, a prestigious cosmetics brand. "Ujjwala
is a woman of color," said Ivan Bart, the director of IMG Models,
which represents her, "but look at her and begin to play a guessing
game: Is she Mexican, Spanish, Russian? The fact you can't be sure is
part of her seductiveness."

Such is the power of ethnic ambiguity that even megastars like   21
Jennifer Lopez, Christina Aguilera, and Beyoncé Knowles have, from
time to time, deliberately tweaked their looks, borrowing from
diverse cultures and ethnic backgrounds. Thus, Beyoncé, an African-
American, sometimes wears her hair blond; Ms. Lopez, who is Puerto
Rican, takes on the identity of a Latina-Asian princess in the latest
Louis Vuitton ads, and Christina Aguilera, who is half Ecuadorean,
poses as a Bollywood goddess on the cover of the January *Allure*,
which arrives on newsstands this week.

Their willful masquerade reflects a current fascination with the   22
racial hybrid, according to Linda Wells, *Allure*'s editor in chief, a
fascination the magazine does not hesitate to exploit. "Five years
ago, about 80 percent of our covers featured fair-haired, blue-eyed
women, even though they represented a minority," Ms. Wells said.
Today such covers are a rarity. "Uniformity just isn't appealing anymore," she said.

Global marketers like H&M, the cheap chic clothing chain with   23
stores in 18 countries, increasingly highlight models with racially indeterminate features. "For us the models must be inspiring and attractive and at the same time, neutral," said Anna Bergare, the
company's Stockholm-based spokeswoman. The campaigns contrast
notably with the original marketing strategy of Benetton, another
global clothing chain, whose path-breaking 1980's ads highlighted
models of many races, each very distinct. These days even Benetton's
billboards play up the multiracial theme. In a typical campaign, a
young man with Asian features and an Afro hairdo is posed beside a
blue-eyed woman with incongruously tawny skin and brown hair
with the texture of yarn.

Such a transition—from racial diversity portrayed as a beautiful   24
mosaic to a melting pot—is in line with the currently fashionable argument that race itself is a fiction. This theory has been advanced by
prominent scholars like K. Anthony Appiah, professor of philosophy
at Princeton, and Evelyn Hammond, a professor of the history of science and Afro-American studies at Harvard. In a PBS broadcast last
spring, Ms. Hammond said race is a human contrivance, a "concept
we invented to categorize the perceived biological, social, and cultural
differences between human groups."

More and more, that kind of thinking is echoed by the profes-   25
sional image makers. "Some of us are just now beginning to recognize that many cultures and races are assimilating," said John Partilla,

the chief executive of Brand Buzz, a marketing agency owned by the WPP group. "If what you're seeing now is our focus on trying to reflect the blending of individuals, it reflects a societal trend, not a marketing trend."

"For once," Mr. Partilla added, "it's about art imitating life."   26

Thinking Critically about This Reading

What are the melting pot and mosaic concepts of assimilation to which La Ferla refers? How much do you know about the history of the melting pot idea in the United States and the mosaic concept in Canada?

Questions for Study and Discussion

1. What is La Ferla's thesis, and where does she state it most clearly? (Glossary: *Thesis*)
2. What kinds of evidence does La Ferla use to document her thesis? (Glossary: *Evidence*)
3. How, according to La Ferla, does the 2000 census help explain what characterizes the evolving racial and ethnic makeup of the United States?
4. Does La Ferla's documentation of the trend toward ethnic ambiguity have any larger significance than it being simply a fashion trend? Explain.
5. How does ethnic ambiguity relate to recent demographic trends in the United States and perhaps the world?
6. Explain the meaning of the quotation by John Partilla in La Ferla's last sentence.

Classroom Activity Using Argument

In "U.S. Not Speeding Toward 'Ethnic Ambiguity,'" first published in lodinews.com on February 7, 2004, and then picked up by AmericanRenaissance.com, writer Joe Guzzardi critiques Ruth La Ferla's *New York Times* article. Read Guzzardi's article. Be prepared to summarize his points and offer your response to them in a class discussion.

Suggested Writing Assignments

1. Write an essay in which you analyze a series of print and electronic advertisements for a product you use or might use, arguing that the ads for the product either support or contradict La Ferla's argument that advertisers were, and perhaps still are, leaning toward the use of ethnically ambiguous models.

2. Write an essay in which you argue that advertisers' use of ethnically ambiguous models (1) reflects the "remix" of ethnicities and races that we see in our society, (2) makes it easier for people of various backgrounds to interact more comfortably and without fear of society's disapproval, or (3) both reflects and promotes greater human appreciation and understanding among a diverse population. Be sure to draw on as many examples of models as you can from both print and electronic media to support the thesis you choose.

Intensify/Downplay

■ HUGH RANK

In 1976, the Committee on Public Doublespeak (a committee of the National Council of Teachers of English) gave Professor Hugh Rank (1932–2010) of Governors State University in Illinois its Orwell Award for the Intensify/Downplay schema he developed to help people analyze public persuasion. As Rank explains, "All people *intensify* (commonly by *repetition, association, composition*) and *downplay* (commonly by *omission, diversion, confusion*) as they communicate in words, gestures, numbers, etc. But, 'professional persuaders' have more training, technology, money, and media access than the average citizen. Individuals can better cope with organized persuasion by recognizing the common ways that communication is intensified or downplayed, and by considering who is saying what to whom, with what intent and what result." Look closely at Rank's schema on pages 610–11, listing questions you can ask yourself about any type of advertisement.

Use Rank's schema to analyze the advertisements on pages 612–15. Find examples of intensifying and downplaying in each. In the advertisement that begins with Gay, for example, how is the ad composed? Does the ad remind you of a dictionary entry? What might the creators of the ad want to reinforce by that association? What effect does reversing the black and white of traditional text have on you? What is the mind/body connection that Acics want to reinforce in their ad? How does repetition work in the ad? What main objective do you think the creator of the ad has? Did you notice the fine print at the bottom of the ad? What's the intent? What's left out of the Join the Navy advertisement? Why doesn't the Navy produce ads like this anymore? Are we too smart for them? How so? These are only a few of the questions that you as a critical thinker might ask yourself in becoming a more astute consumer of advertising. Hugh Rank's intention in "Intensify/Downplay" is to empower you, to free you from being merely a passive receiver of advertisement, and to help you understand how others may be trying to manipulate you and keep you from making decisions in your own best interest rather than theirs. It's a good set of tools to have on your side.

INTENSIFY

Repetition

How often have you seen the ad? On TV? In print? Do you recognize the **brand name? trademark? logo? company? package?** What key words or images repeated within ad? Any repetition patterns (*alliteration, anaphora, rhyme*) used? Any **slogan?** Can you hum or sing the **musical theme** or **jingle?** How long has this ad been running? How old were you when you first heard it? (For information on frequency, duration, and costs of ad campaigns, see *Advertising Age.*)

Association

What **"good things"** - already loved or desired by the intended audience - are associated with the product? Any links with basic needs (*food, activity, sex, security*)? With an appeal to save or gain money? With desire for certitude or outside approval (from *religion, science,* or the *"best," "most,"* or *"average" people*)? With desire for a sense of space (*neighborhood, nation, nature*)? With desire for love and belonging (*intimacy, family, groups*)? With other human desires (*esteem, play, generosity, curiosity, creativity, completion*)? Are **"bad things"** - things already hated or feared - stressed, as in a **"scare-and-sell"** ad? Are *problems* presented, with products as *solutions*? Are the speakers (models, endorsers) **authority figures:** people you respect, admire? Or **friend figures:** people you'd like as friends, identify with, or would like to be?

Composition

Look for the basic strategy of "the pitch": Hi . . . TRUST ME . . . YOU NEED . . . HURRY . . . BUY. What are the **attention-getting (HI)** words, images, devices? What are the **confidence-building (TRUST ME)** techniques: words, images, smiles, endorsers, brand names? Is the main **desire-stimulation (YOU NEED)** appeal focused on our benefit-seeking *to get* or *to keep* a "good," or *to avoid* or *to get rid of* a "bad"? Are you the **"target audience"?** If not, who is? Are you part of an unintended audience ? When and where did the ads appear? Are **product claims** made for: *superiority, quantity, beauty, efficiency, scarcity, novelty, stability, reliability, simplicity, utility, rapidity,* or *safety*? Are any **"added values"** suggested or implied by using any of the association techniques (see above)? Is there any **urgency-stressing (HURRY)** by words, movement, pace? Or is a "soft sell" conditioning for *later* purchase? Are there specific **response-triggering (BUY):** to buy, to do, to call? Or is it conditioning (image building or public relations) to make us *"feel good"* about the company, to get favorable public opinion on *its* side (*against government regulations. laws, taxes*)? **Persuaders seek some kind of response!**

Omission

What "bad" aspects, disadvantages, drawbacks, hazards, have been **omitted** from the ad? Are there some unspoken assumptions? An unsaid story? Are some things implied or suggested, but not explicitly stated? Are there concealed problems concerning the **maker**, the **materials**, the **design**, the **use**, or the **purpose of the product? Are there any unwanted or harmful side effects:** *unsafe, unhealthy, uneconomical, inefficient, unneeded?* Does any **"disclosure law"** exist (or is needed) requiring public warning about a concealed hazard? In the ad, what gets less time, less attention, smaller print? *(Most ads are true, but incomplete.)*

Diversion

What benefits (low cost, high speed, etc.) get high priority in the ad's claim and promises? Are these **your** priorities? Significant, important to you? Is there any **"bait-and-switch"**? *(Ad stresses* low cost, *but the actual seller switches buyer's priority to* high quality.) Does ad divert focus from **key issues,** important things *(e.g., nutrition, health, safety)*? Does ad focus on **side-issues,** unmeaningful trivia *(common in parity products)*? Does ad divert attention from your other choices, other options: buy something else, use less, use less often, rent, borrow, share, do without? *(Ads need not show other choices, but you should know them.)*

Confusion

Are the words clear or ambiguous? Specific or vague? Are claims and promises absolute, or are there qualifying words *("may help," "some")*? Is the claim measurable? Or is it **"puffery"**? *(Laws permit most "sellers's talk" of such general praise and subjective opinions.)* Are the words common, understandable, familiar? Uncommon? Jargon? Any parts difficult to "translate" or explain to others? Are analogies clear? Are comparisons within the same kind? Are examples related? Typical? Adequate? Enough examples? Any contradictions? Inconsistencies? Errors? Are there frequent changes, variations, revisions *(in size, price, options, extras, contents, packaging)*? Is it too complex: too much, too many? Disorganized? Incoherent? Unsorted? Any confusing statistics? Numbers? Do you know exact costs? Benefits? Risks? Are **your own goals,** priorities, and desires clear or vague? Fixed or shifting? Simple or complex? *(Confusion can also exist within us as well as within an ad. If any confusion exists: slow down, take care.)*

DOWNPLAY

The Truth about Torture

■ Charles Krauthammer

Pulitzer Prize–winning columnist and commentator Charles Krauthammer was born in 1950 in New York City to parents of French citizenship. He grew up in Montreal, Canada, and graduated from McGill University in 1970. The following year he continued his studies in political science as a Commonwealth Scholar at Balliol College, Oxford. In 1972, he moved to the United States and enrolled in Harvard University Medical School, earning his MD in psychiatry in 1975. In 1978, he joined President Jimmy Carter's administration to direct planning in psychiatric research; he later served as speechwriter for Vice President Walter Mondale and as senior editor at the New Republic. *As a journalist, Krauthammer quickly gained a reputation for his clear prose and sound arguments. He is widely recognized for his political and social columns, which have appeared regularly in the* Washington Post, Time, New Republic, *and* The Weekly Standard. *In 1985, he published* Cutting Edges: Making Sense of the Eighties, *a collection of his essays. One critic commented that "Krauthammer is at his best when he writes not so much about 'hard' politics as about political culture . . . and beyond that about the contemporary social climate in general."*

In the following essay, first published in The Weekly Standard *on December 5, 2005, Krauthammer presents the case for the very limited use of torture under controlled circumstances in potentially dangerous situations. Andrew Sullivan's essay "The Abolition of Torture," first published soon after in* The New Republic *on December 19, 2005, argues against Krauthammer's position and makes references to it; thus, we present Sullivan's essay second as a rebuttal to Krauthammer's.*

Reflecting on What You Know

You would not want to be tortured, nor would you want to torture others. The argument over whether the government should engage in such activity, however, has been before the American people for some time. Have you heard about the incidents at Abu Ghraib Prison in Baghdad and at Guantanamo Prison? What do you know about the arguments on both sides of the torture question?

During the last few weeks in Washington the pieties about torture have lain so thick in the air that it has been impossible to have a reasoned discussion. The McCain amendment that would ban "cruel, inhuman, or degrading" treatment of any prisoner by any agent of the United States sailed through the Senate by a vote of 90–9. The Washington establishment remains stunned that nine such retrograde, morally inert persons—let alone senators—could be found in this noble capital.

Now, John McCain has great moral authority on this issue, having heroically borne torture at the hands of the North Vietnamese. McCain has made fine arguments in defense of his position. And McCain is acting out of the deep and honorable conviction that what he is proposing is not only right but is in the best interest of the United States. His position deserves respect. But that does not mean, as seems to be the assumption in Washington today, that a critical analysis of his "no torture, ever" policy is beyond the pale.

Let's begin with a few analytic distinctions. For the purpose of torture and prisoner maltreatment, there are three kinds of war prisoners:

First, there is the ordinary soldier caught on the field of battle. There is no question that he is entitled to humane treatment. Indeed, we have no right to disturb a hair on his head. His detention has but a single purpose: to keep him hors de combat. The proof of that proposition is that if there were a better way to keep him off the battlefield that did not require his detention, we would let him go. Indeed, during one year of the Civil War, the two sides did try an alternative. They mutually "paroled" captured enemy soldiers, i.e., released them to return home on the pledge that they would not take up arms again. (The experiment failed for a foreseeable reason: cheating. Grant found that some paroled Confederates had reenlisted.)

Because the only purpose of detention in these circumstances is to prevent the prisoner from becoming a combatant again, he is entitled to all the protections and dignity of an ordinary domestic prisoner—indeed, more privileges, because, unlike the domestic prisoner, he has committed no crime. He merely had the misfortune to enlist on the other side of a legitimate war. He is therefore entitled to many of the privileges enjoyed by an ordinary citizen—the right to send correspondence, to engage in athletic activity and intellectual pursuits, to receive allowances from relatives—except, of course, for the freedom to leave the prison.

Second, there is the captured terrorist. A terrorist is by profession, indeed by definition, an unlawful combatant: He lives outside the laws of war because he does not wear a uniform, he hides among civilians, and he deliberately targets innocents. He is entitled to no protections whatsoever. People seem to think that the postwar Geneva Conventions were written only to protect detainees. In fact, their deeper purpose was to provide a deterrent to the kind of barbaric treatment of civilians that had become so horribly apparent during the first half of the 20th century, and in particular, during the Second World War. The idea was to deter the abuse of civilians by promising combatants who treated noncombatants well that they themselves would be treated according to a code of dignity if captured—and, crucially, that they would be denied the protections of that code if they broke the laws of war and abused civilians themselves. 6

Breaking the laws of war and abusing civilians are what, to understate the matter vastly, terrorists do for a living. They are entitled, therefore, to nothing. Anyone who blows up a car bomb in a market deserves to spend the rest of his life roasting on a spit over an open fire. But we don't do that because we do not descend to the level of our enemy. We don't do that because, unlike him, we are civilized. Even though terrorists are entitled to no humane treatment, we give it to them because it is in our nature as a moral and humane people. And when on rare occasions we fail to do that, as has occurred in several of the fronts of the war on terror, we are duly disgraced. 7

The norm, however, is how the majority of prisoners at Guantanamo have been treated. We give them three meals a day, superior medical care, and provision to pray five times a day. Our scrupulousness extends even to providing them with their own Korans, which is the only reason alleged abuses of the Koran at Guantanamo ever became an issue. That we should have provided those who kill innocents in the name of Islam with precisely the document that inspires their barbarism is a sign of the absurd lengths to which we often go in extending undeserved humanity to terrorist prisoners. 8

Third, there is the terrorist with information. Here the issue of   9
torture gets complicated and the easy pieties don't so easily apply.
Let's take the textbook case. Ethics 101: A terrorist has planted a nuclear bomb in New York City. It will go off in one hour. A million
people will die. You capture the terrorist. He knows where it is. He's
not talking.

Question: If you have the slightest belief that hanging this man   10
by his thumbs will get you the information to save a million people,
are you permitted to do it?

Now, on most issues regarding torture, I confess tentativeness   11
and uncertainty. But on this issue, there can be no uncertainty: Not
only is it permissible to hang this miscreant by his thumbs. It is a
moral duty.

Yes, you say, but that's an extreme and very hypothetical case.   12
Well, not as hypothetical as you think. Sure, the (nuclear) scale is hypothetical, but in the age of the car- and suicide-bomber, terrorists are
often captured who have just set a car bomb to go off or sent a suicide bomber out to a coffee shop, and you only have minutes to find
out where the attack is to take place. This "hypothetical" is common
enough that the Israelis have a term for precisely that situation: the
ticking time bomb problem.

And even if the example I gave were entirely hypothetical, the   13
conclusion—yes, in this case even torture is permissible—is telling
because it establishes the principle: Torture is not always impermissible. However rare the cases, there are circumstances in which, by any
rational moral calculus, torture not only would be permissible but
would be required (to acquire life-saving information). And once
you've established the principle, to paraphrase George Bernard Shaw,
all that's left to haggle about is the price. In the case of torture, that
means that the argument is not whether torture is ever permissible,
but when—i.e., under what obviously stringent circumstances: how
big, how imminent, how preventable the ticking time bomb.

That is why the McCain amendment, which by mandating "tor-   14
ture never" refuses even to recognize the legitimacy of any moral calculus, cannot be right. There must be exceptions. The real argument
should be over what constitutes a legitimate exception.

Let's take an example that is far from hypothetical. You capture   15
Khalid Sheikh Mohammed in Pakistan. He not only has already killed
innocents, he is deeply involved in the planning for the present and future killing of innocents. He not only was the architect of the 9/11

attack that killed nearly three thousand people in one day, most of them dying a terrible, agonizing, indeed tortured death. But as the top al Qaeda planner and logistical expert he also knows a lot about terror attacks to come. He knows plans, identities, contacts, materials, cell locations, safe houses, cased targets, etc. What do you do with him?

We have recently learned that since 9/11 the United States has maintained a series of "black sites" around the world, secret detention centers where presumably high-level terrorists like Khalid Sheikh Mohammed have been imprisoned. The world is scandalized. Black sites? Secret detention? Jimmy Carter calls this "a profound and radical change in the . . . moral values of our country." The Council of Europe demands an investigation, calling the claims "extremely worrying." Its human rights commissioner declares "such practices" to constitute "a serious human rights violation, and further proof of the crisis of values" that has engulfed the war on terror. The gnashing of teeth and rending of garments has been considerable. 16

I myself have not gnashed a single tooth. My garments remain entirely unrent. Indeed, I feel reassured. It would be a gross dereliction of duty for any government not to keep Khalid Sheikh Mohammed isolated, disoriented, alone, despairing, cold and sleepless, in some godforsaken hidden location in order to find out what he knew about plans for future mass murder. What are we supposed to do? Give him a nice cell in a warm Manhattan prison, complete with Miranda rights, a mellifluent lawyer, and his own website? Are not those the kinds of courtesies we extended to the 1993 World Trade Center bombers, then congratulated ourselves on how we "brought to justice" those responsible for an attack that barely failed to kill tens of thousands of Americans, only to discover a decade later that we had accomplished nothing—indeed, that some of the disclosures at the trial had helped Osama bin Laden avoid U.S. surveillance? 17

Have we learned nothing from 9/11? Are we prepared to go back with complete amnesia to the domestic-crime model of dealing with terrorists, which allowed us to sleepwalk through the nineties while al Qaeda incubated and grew and metastasized unmolested until on 9/11 it finished what the first World Trade Center bombers had begun? 18

Let's assume (and hope) that Khalid Sheikh Mohammed has been kept in one of these black sites, say, a cell somewhere in Romania, held entirely incommunicado and subjected to the kind of "coercive interrogation" that I described above. McCain has been going around praising the Israelis as the model of how to deal 19 with terrorism and prevent terrorist attacks. He does so because in 1999 the Israeli Supreme Court outlawed all torture in the course of interrogation. But in reality, the Israeli case is far more complicated. And the complications reflect precisely the dilemmas regarding all coercive interrogation, the weighing of the lesser of two evils: the undeniable inhumanity of torture versus the abdication of the duty to protect the victims of a potentially preventable mass murder.

In a summary of Israel's policies, Glenn Frankel of the *Washington*   20
Post, noted that the 1999 Supreme Court ruling struck down secret guidelines established 12 years earlier that allowed interrogators to use the kind of physical and psychological pressure I described in imagining how KSM might be treated in America's "black sites."

"But after the second Palestinian uprising broke out a year later,   21
and especially after a devastating series of suicide bombings of passenger buses, cafes, and other civilian targets," writes Frankel, citing human rights lawyers and detainees, "Israel's internal security service, known as the Shin Bet or the Shabak, returned to physical coercion as a standard practice." Not only do the techniques used "command widespread support from the Israeli public," but "Israeli prime ministers and justice ministers with a variety of political views," including the most conciliatory and liberal, have defended these techniques "as a last resort in preventing terrorist attacks."

Which makes McCain's position on torture incoherent. If this   22
kind of coercive interrogation were imposed on any inmate in the American prison system, it would immediately be declared cruel and unusual, and outlawed. How can he oppose these practices, which the Israelis use, and yet hold up Israel as a model for dealing with terrorists? Or does he countenance this kind of interrogation in extreme circumstances—in which case, what is left of his categorical opposition to inhuman treatment of any kind?

But let us push further into even more unpleasant territory, the   23
territory that lies beyond mere coercive interrogation and beyond McCain's self-contradictions. How far are we willing to go?

This "going beyond" need not be cinematic and ghoulish. (Jay   24
Leno once suggested "duct tape" for Khalid Sheikh Mohammed.) Consider, for example, injection with sodium pentathol. (Colloquially known as "truth serum," it is nothing of the sort. It is a barbiturate whose purpose is to sedate. Its effects are much like that of alcohol: disinhibiting the higher brain centers to make someone more likely to

disclose information or thoughts that might otherwise be guarded.) Forcible sedation is a clear violation of bodily integrity. In a civilian context it would be considered assault. It is certainly impermissible under any prohibition of cruel, inhuman, or degrading treatment.

Let's posit that during the interrogation of Khalid Sheikh 25 Mohammed, perhaps early on, we got intelligence about an imminent al Qaeda attack. And we had a very good reason to believe he knew about it. And if we knew what he knew, we could stop it. If we thought we could glean a critical piece of information by use of sodium pentathol, would we be permitted to do so?

Less hypothetically, there is waterboarding, a terrifying and 26 deeply shocking torture technique in which the prisoner has his face exposed to water in a way that gives the feeling of drowning. According to CIA sources cited by ABC News, Khalid Sheikh Mohammed "was able to last between two and 2½ minutes before begging to confess." Should we regret having done that? Should we abolish by law that practice, so that it could never be used on the next Khalid Sheikh Mohammed having thus gotten his confession?

And what if he possessed information with less imminent impli- 27 cations? Say we had information about a cell that he had helped found or direct, and that cell was planning some major attack and we needed information about the identity and location of its members. A rational moral calculus might not permit measures as extreme as the nuke-in-Manhattan scenario, but would surely permit measures beyond mere psychological pressure.

Such a determination would not be made with an untroubled 28 conscience. It would be troubled because there is no denying the monstrous evil that is any form of torture. And there is no denying how corrupting it can be to the individuals and society that practice it. But elected leaders, responsible above all for the protection of their citizens, have the obligation to tolerate their own sleepless nights by doing what is necessary—and only what is necessary, nothing more—to get information that could prevent mass murder.

Given the gravity of the decision, if we indeed cross the 29 Rubicon[1]—as we must—we need rules. The problem with the McCain

---

[1]*Crossing the Rubicon:* a metaphor for deliberately crossing a "point of no return." The term originated when Julius Caesar illegally crossed the river into Ancient Rome with his army.

amendment is that once you have gone public with a blanket ban on all forms of coercion, it is going to be very difficult to publicly carve out exceptions. The Bush administration is to be faulted for having attempted such a codification with the kind of secrecy, lack of coherence, and lack of strict enforcement that led us to the McCain reaction.

What to do at this late date? Begin, as McCain does, by ban- 30 ning all forms of coercion or inhuman treatment by anyone serving in the military—an absolute ban on torture by all military personnel everywhere. We do not want a private somewhere making these fine distinctions about ticking and slow-fuse time bombs. We don't even want colonels or generals making them. It would be best for the morale, discipline, and honor of the Armed Forces for the United States to maintain an absolute prohibition, both to simplify their task in making decisions and to offer them whatever reciprocal treatment they might receive from those who capture them—although I have no illusion that any anti-torture provision will soften the heart of a single jihadist holding a knife to the throat of a captured American soldier. We would impose this restriction on ourselves for our own reasons of military discipline and military honor.

Outside the military, however, I would propose, contra McCain, 31 a ban against all forms of torture, coercive interrogation, and inhuman treatment, except in two contingencies: (1) the ticking time bomb and (2) the slower-fuse high-level terrorist (such as KSM). Each contingency would have its own set of rules. In the case of the ticking time bomb, the rules would be relatively simple: Nothing rationally related to getting accurate information would be ruled out. The case of the high-value suspect with slow-fuse information is more complicated. The principle would be that the level of inhumanity of the measures used (moral honesty is essential here—we would be using measures that are by definition inhumane) would be proportional to the need and value of the information. Interrogators would be constrained to use the least inhumane treatment necessary relative to the magnitude and imminence of the evil being prevented and the importance of the knowledge being obtained.

These exceptions to the no-torture rule would not be granted to 32 just any nonmilitary interrogators, or anyone with CIA credentials. They would be reserved for highly specialized agents who are experts and experienced in interrogation, and who are known not to abuse it for the satisfaction of a kind of sick sadomasochism Lynndie England

and her cohorts indulged in at Abu Ghraib. Nor would they be acting on their own. They would be required to obtain written permission for such interrogations from the highest political authorities in the country (cabinet level) or from a quasi-judicial body modeled on the Foreign Intelligence Surveillance Court (which permits what would ordinarily be illegal searches and seizures in the war on terror). Or, if the bomb was truly ticking and there was no time, the interrogators would be allowed to act on their own, but would require post facto authorization within, say, 24 hours of their interrogation, so that they knew that whatever they did would be subject to review by others and be justified only under the most stringent terms.

One of the purposes of these justifications would be to estab- 33 lish that whatever extreme measures are used are for reasons of nothing but information. Historically, the torture of prisoners has been done for a variety of reasons apart from information, most prominently reasons of justice or revenge. We do not do that. We should not do that. Ever. Khalid Sheikh Mohammed, murderer of 2,973 innocents, is surely deserving of the most extreme suffering day and night for the rest of his life. But it is neither our role nor our right to be the agents of that suffering. Vengeance is mine, sayeth the Lord. His, not ours. Torture is a terrible and monstrous thing, as degrading and morally corrupting to those who practice it as any conceivable human activity including its moral twin, capital punishment.

If Khalid Sheikh Mohammed knew nothing, or if we had reached 34 the point where his knowledge had been exhausted, I'd be perfectly prepared to throw him into a nice, comfortable Manhattan cell and give him a trial to determine what would be fit and just punishment. But as long as he had useful information, things would be different.

Very different. And it simply will not do to take refuge in the 35 claim that all of the above discussion is superfluous because torture never works anyway. Would that this were true. Unfortunately, on its face, this is nonsense. Is one to believe that in the entire history of human warfare, no combatant has ever received useful information by the use of pressure, torture, or any other kind of inhuman treatment? It may indeed be true that torture is not a reliable tool. But that is very different from saying that it is never useful.

The monstrous thing about torture is that sometimes it does 36 work. In 1994, 19-year-old Israeli corporal Nachshon Waxman was kidnapped by Palestinian terrorists. The Israelis captured the driver of the car used in the kidnapping and tortured him in order to find where Waxman was being held. Yitzhak Rabin, prime minister and peacemaker, admitted that they tortured him in a way that went even beyond the '87 guidelines for "coercive interrogation" later struck down by the Israeli Supreme Court as too harsh. The driver talked. His information was accurate. The Israelis found Waxman. "If we'd been so careful to follow the ['87] Landau Commission [which allowed coercive interrogation]," explained Rabin, "we would never have found out where Waxman was being held."

In the Waxman case, I would have done precisely what Rabin 37
did. (The fact that Waxman's Palestinian captors killed him during the Israeli rescue raid makes the case doubly tragic, but changes nothing of the moral calculus.) Faced with a similar choice, an American president would have a similar obligation. To do otherwise—to give up the chance to find your soldier lest you sully yourself by authorizing torture of the person who possesses potentially lifesaving information—is a deeply immoral betrayal of a soldier and countryman. Not as cosmically immoral as permitting a city of one's countrymen to perish, as in the Ethics 101 case. But it remains, nonetheless, a case of moral abdication—of a kind rather parallel to that of the principled pacifist. There is much to admire in those who refuse on principle ever to take up arms under any conditions. But that does not make pure pacifism, like no-torture absolutism, any less a form of moral foolishness, tinged with moral vanity. Not reprehensible, only deeply reproachable and supremely impracticable. People who hold such beliefs are deserving of a certain respect. But they are not to be put in positions of authority. One should be grateful for the saintly among us. And one should be vigilant that they not get to make the decisions upon which the lives of others depend.

Which brings us to the greatest irony of all in the torture debate. 38
I have just made what will be characterized as the pro-torture case contra McCain by proposing two major exceptions carved out of any no-torture rule: the ticking time bomb and the slow-fuse high-value terrorist. McCain supposedly is being hailed for defending all that is good and right and just in America by standing foursquare against any inhuman treatment. Or is he?

According to *Newsweek*, in the ticking time bomb case McCain 39
says that the president should disobey the very law that McCain seeks

to pass—under the justification that "you do what you have to do. But you take responsibility for it." But if torturing the ticking time bomb suspect is "what you have to do," then why has McCain been going around arguing that such things must never be done?

As for exception number two, the high-level terrorist with   40
slow-fuse information, Stuart Taylor, the superb legal correspondent for *National Journal,* argues that with appropriate legal interpretation, the "cruel, inhuman, or degrading" standard, "though vague, is said by experts to codify . . . the commonsense principle that the toughness of interrogation techniques should be calibrated to the importance and urgency of the information likely to be obtained." That would permit "some very aggressive techniques . . . on that small percentage of detainees who seem especially likely to have potentially life-saving information." Or as Evan Thomas and Michael Hirsh put it in the *Newsweek* report on McCain and torture, the McCain standard would "presumably allow for a sliding scale" of torture or torture-lite or other coercive techniques, thus permitting "for a very small percentage—those High Value Targets like Khalid Sheikh Mohammed—some pretty rough treatment."

But if that is the case, then McCain embraces the same excep-   41
tions I do, but prefers to pretend he does not. If that is the case, then his much-touted and endlessly repeated absolutism on inhumane treatment is merely for show. If that is the case, then the moral preening and the phony arguments can stop now, and we can all agree that in this real world of astonishingly murderous enemies, in two very circumscribed circumstances, we must all be prepared to torture. Having established that, we can then begin to work together to codify rules of interrogation for the two very unpleasant but very real cases in which we are morally permitted—indeed morally compelled—to do terrible things.

Thinking Critically about This Reading

By John McCain's own admission, torture worked when he gave up sensitive military information that he was not required to provide his captors when he was held as a prisoner of war in North Vietnam. Speculate on whether or not the issue could be so emotionally sensitive that it drove McCain into what Krauthammer sees as an inconsistent position with regard to the use of torture.

Questions for Study and Discussion

1. What is Krauthammer's thesis in this essay? (Glossary: *Thesis*)
2. What is Krauthammer's purpose in writing? (Glossary: *Purpose*) What does he hope to accomplish in developing his argument?
3. Explain the importance of Krauthammer's classification in paragraphs 3–9. How does the classification help him develop his argument? (Glossary: *Classification*)
4. Who is Khalid Sheik Mohammed, and why does Krauthammer use that case to support points he makes in his argument?
5. Why does Krauthammer believe that McCain's "no-torture" position is merely for show? Is his argument in that respect convincing? Why or why not?
6. Krauthammer's argument is a fairly long one. If you believe that the length is justified, explain why. If you believe that the argument could have been shorter, explain why and how.

Classroom Activity Using Argument

No one except a sadist wants to see another human being suffer, so it's safe to say that we're all against torture. If that's so, why is there an argument about whether or not to use it? What facts and situations, some of which have already been discussed by Krauthammer, complicate the issue and turn it into an argument?

Suggested Writing Assignments

1. On May 16, 2004, Michael Slackman wrote the following in the *New York Times* in reference to the use of torture: "In the face of a dangerous, implacable enemy, such methods, and perhaps others still more extreme, may easily come to seem more acceptable. As Richard A. Posner, a judge of the United States Court of Appeals for the Seventh Circuit, wrote in *The New Republic* in September 2002, in a review of Mr. Dershowitz's book, *Why Terrorism Works: Understanding the Threat, Responding to the Challenge:* 'If torture is the only means of obtaining the information necessary to prevent the detonation of a nuclear bomb in Times Square, torture should be used—and will be used—to obtain the information.'" If you support Posner's statement, write

an essay in which you argue that any absolute prohibition against torture, such as the one McCain has espoused, is wrong. Gather more information as necessary from books and articles from your library and additional information from the Internet to support your view.

2. Here are two possibilities for argument essays: On the one hand, you can argue that if we are going to use torture, we should, at least, be up front about it. On the other hand, you can argue that if we say that we are not going to use torture, we should mean it and prosecute anyone who engages in it. Think about ideas you will need to develop your argument as well as the kinds of evidence you will need to support your position and where you might find that evidence.

The Abolition of Torture

■ Andrew Sullivan

Andrew Sullivan was born in 1963 in South Godstone, Surrey, England, to Irish parents. He earned his BA in modern history at Magdalene College, Oxford, and his master's degree and PhD at Harvard University in government. Sullivan began his career in journalism at The New Republic *and later wrote for the* New York Times Magazine*. A gay, Catholic, conservative, and often controversial commentator, Sullivan has made history as a blogger. His* The Daily Dish *became very popular post 9/11 and was by the middle of 2003 receiving about 300,000 visits a month. By 2005, it was receiving more than 50,000 hits a day, and his nearly five years of blogging and writing of books and articles caused him to take a break from his feverish journalism activity. In 2007, he accepted an editorial position with* The Atlantic. *Sullivan has written several books:* Virtually Normal: An Argument about Homosexuality *(1995);* Love Undetectable: Notes on Friendship, Sex and Survival *(1998); and* The Conservative Soul: How We Lost It, How to Get It Back *(2006).*

In "The Abolition of Torture," first published in The New Republic *on December 19, 2005, Sullivan takes issue with Charles Krauthammer's advocacy of the limited use of torture (see previous selection). He argues that the United States cannot engage in torture if it is to rise above its enemies and hold true to the very ideals that represent the country and that the United States stands for around the world.*

Reflecting on What You Know

Torture and the pain it has caused throughout history form an ugly chronicle of the depths to which humans will sometimes go to dominate one another. Why is the torture perpetrated by Americans and the U.S. military, particularly in Abu Ghraib Prison and at Guantanamo Bay, particularly ironic?

Why is torture wrong? It may seem like an obvious question, or 1
even one beneath discussion. But it is now inescapably before
us, with the introduction of the McCain Amendment banning all
"cruel, inhuman, and degrading treatment" of detainees by American
soldiers and CIA operatives anywhere in the world. The amendment
lies in legislative limbo. It passed the Senate in October by a vote of
90 to nine, but President Bush has vowed to veto any such blanket
ban on torture, or abuse; Vice President Cheney has prevailed upon
enough senators and congressmen to prevent the amendment—and
the defense appropriations bill to which it is attached—from moving
out of conference; and my friend Charles Krauthammer, one of the
most respected conservative intellectuals in Washington (and a *New
Republic* contributing editor) has written a widely praised cover essay
for *The Weekly Standard* endorsing the legalization of full-fledged
torture by the United States under strictly curtailed conditions. We
stand on the brink of an enormously important choice—one that is
critical, morally as well as strategically, to get right.

This debate takes place after three years in which the Bush ad- 2
ministration has defined "torture" in the narrowest terms and has
permitted coercive, physical abuse of enemy combatants if "military
necessity" demands it. It comes also after several internal Pentagon
reports found widespread and severe abuse of detainees in
Afghanistan, Iraq, and elsewhere that has led to at least two dozen
deaths during interrogation. Journalistic accounts and reports by the
International Committee of the Red Cross paint an even darker picture of secret torture sites in Eastern Europe and innocent detainees
being murdered. Behind all this, the grim images of Abu Ghraib—the
worst of which have yet to be released—linger in the public consciousness.

In this inevitably emotional debate, perhaps the greatest failing of 3
those of us who have been arguing against all torture and "cruel, inhuman, and degrading treatment" of detainees is that we have assumed the reasons why torture is always a moral evil, rather than
explicating them. But, when you fully ponder them, I think it becomes
clearer why, contrary to Krauthammer's argument, torture, in any
form and under any circumstances, is both antithetical to the most
basic principles for which the United States stands and a profound im-
pediment to winning a wider war that we cannot afford to lose.

Torture is the polar opposite of freedom. It is the banishment of 4
all freedom from a human body and soul, insofar as that is possible.

As human beings, we all inhabit bodies and have minds, souls, and reflexes that are designed in part to protect those bodies: to resist or flinch from pain, to protect the psyche from disintegration, and to maintain a sense of selfhood that is the basis for the concept of personal liberty. What torture does is use these involuntary, self-protective, self-defining resources of human beings against the integrity of the human being himself. It takes what is most involuntary in a person and uses it to break that person's will. It takes what is animal in us and deploys it against what makes us human. As an American commander wrote in an August 2003 e-mail about his instructions to torture prisoners at Abu Ghraib, "The gloves are coming off gentlemen regarding these detainees, Col. Boltz has made it clear that we want these individuals broken."

What does it mean to "break" an individual? As the French essayist Michel de Montaigne once commented, and Shakespeare echoed, even the greatest philosophers have difficulty thinking clearly when they have a toothache. These wise men were describing the inescapable frailty of the human experience, mocking the claims of some seers to be above basic human feelings and bodily needs. If that frailty is exposed by a toothache, it is beyond dispute in the case of torture. The infliction of physical pain on a person with no means of defending himself is designed to render that person completely subservient to his torturers. It is designed to extirpate his autonomy as a human being, to render his control as an individual beyond his own reach. That is why the term "break" is instructive. Something broken can be put back together, but it will never regain the status of being unbroken—of having integrity. When you break a human being, you turn him into something subhuman. You enslave him. This is why the Romans reserved torture for slaves, not citizens, and why slavery and torture were inextricably linked in the antebellum South.

What you see in the relationship between torturer and tortured is the absolute darkness of totalitarianism. You see one individual granted the most complete power he can ever hold over another. Not just confinement of his mobility—the abolition of his very agency. Torture uses a person's body to remove from his own control his conscience, his thoughts, his faith, his selfhood. The CIA's definition of "waterboarding"—recently leaked to ABC News—describes that process in plain English: "The prisoner is bound to an inclined board, feet raised and head slightly below the feet. Cellophane is wrapped over the prisoner's face and water is poured over him. Unavoidably, the gag reflex kicks in and a terrifying fear of drowning leads to al-most instant pleas to bring the treatment to a halt." The ABC report then noted, "According to the sources, CIA officers who subjected themselves to the waterboarding technique lasted an average of 14 seconds before caving in. They said Al Qaeda's toughest prisoner, Khalid Sheikh Mohammed, won the admiration of interrogators when he was able to last between two and two and a half minutes before begging to confess."

Before the Bush administration, two documented cases of the U.S. Armed Forces using "waterboarding" resulted in courts-martial for the soldiers implicated. In Donald Rumsfeld's post-September 11 Pentagon, the technique is approved and, we recently learned, has been used on at least eleven detainees, possibly many more. What you see here is the deployment of a very basic and inescapable human reflex—the desire not to drown and suffocate—in order to destroy a person's autonomy. Even the most hardened fanatic can only endure two and a half minutes. After that, he is indeed "broken." 7

The entire structure of Western freedom grew in part out of the searing experience of state-sanctioned torture. The use of torture in Europe's religious wars of the sixteenth and seventeenth centuries is still etched in our communal consciousness, as it should be. Then, governments deployed torture not only to uncover perceived threats to their faith-based autocracies, but also to "save" the victim's soul. Torturers understood that religious conversion was a difficult thing, because it necessitated a shift in the deepest recesses of the human soul. The only way to reach those depths was to deploy physical ter-ror in the hopes of completely destroying the heretic's autonomy. They would, in other words, destroy a human being's soul in order to save it. That is what burning at the stake was—an indescribably ago-nizing act of torture that could be ended at a moment's notice if the victim recanted. In a state where theological doctrine always trumped individual liberty, this was a natural tactic. 8

Indeed, the very concept of Western liberty sprung in part from an understanding that, if the state has the power to reach that deep into a person's soul and can do that much damage to a human being's per-son, then the state has extinguished all oxygen necessary for freedom to survive. That is why, in George Orwell's totalitarian nightmare, the final ordeal is, of course, torture. Any polity that endorses torture has incorporated into its own DNA a totalitarian mutation. If the point of the U.S. Constitution is the preservation of liberty, the formal 9 incorporation into U.S. law of the state's right to torture—by legally codifying physical coercion, abuse, and even, in Krauthammer's case, full-fledged torture of detainees by the CIA—would effectively end the American experiment of a political society based on inalienable human freedom protected not by the good graces of the executive, but by the rule of law.

The founders understood this argument. Its preeminent propo- 10 nent was George Washington himself. As historian David Hackett Fischer memorably recounts in his 2004 book, *Washington's Crossing*: "Always some dark spirits wished to visit the same cruelties on the British and Hessians that had been inflicted on American captives. But Washington's example carried growing weight, more so than his written orders and prohibitions. He often reminded his men that they were an army of liberty and freedom, and that the rights of humanity for which they were fighting should extend even to their ene-mies. . . . Even in the most urgent moments of the war, these men were concerned about ethical questions in the Revolution."

Krauthammer has described Washington's convictions concern- 11 ing torture as "pieties" that can be dispensed with today. He doesn't argue that torture is not evil. Indeed, he denounces it in unequivocal moral terms: "[T]orture is a terrible and monstrous thing, as de-grading and morally corrupting to those who practice it as any con-ceivable human activity including its moral twin, capital punishment." But he maintains that the nature of the Islamofascist enemy after September 11 radically altered our interrogative options and that we are now not only permitted, but actually "morally com-pelled," to torture.

This is a radical and daring idea: that we must extinguish human 12 freedom in a few cases in order to maintain it for everyone else. It goes beyond even the Bush administration's own formal position, which states that the United States will not endorse torture but merely "coercive interrogation techniques." (Such techniques, in the adminis-tration's elaborate definition, are those that employ physical force short of threatening immediate death or major organ failure.) And it is based on a premise that deserves further examination: that our en-emies actually deserve torture; that some human beings are so de-praved that, in Krauthammer's words, they "are entitled to no humane treatment."

Let me state for the record that I am second to none in decry- 13 ing, loathing, and desiring to defeat those who wish to replace freedom with religious tyranny of the most brutal kind—and who have murdered countless innocent civilians in cold blood. Their acts are monstrous and barbaric. But I differ from Krauthammer by believing that monsters remain human beings. In fact, to reduce them to a subhuman level is to exonerate them of their acts of terrorism and mass murder—just as animals are not deemed morally responsible for killing. Insisting on the humanity of terrorists is, in fact, critical to maintaining their profound responsibility for the evil they commit.

And, if they are human, then they must necessarily not be treated   14
in an inhuman fashion. You cannot lower the moral baseline of a terrorist to the subhuman without betraying a fundamental value. That is why the Geneva Conventions have a very basic ban on "cruel treatment and torture," and "outrages upon personal dignity, in particular humiliating and degrading treatment"—even when dealing with illegal combatants like terrorists. That is why the Declaration of Independence did not restrict its endorsement of freedom merely to those lucky enough to find themselves on U.S. soil—but extended it to all human beings, wherever they are in the world, simply because they are human.

Nevertheless, it is important to address Krauthammer's practical   15
points. He is asking us to steel ourselves and accept that, whether we like it or not, torture and abuse may be essential in a war where our very survival may be at stake. He presents two scenarios in which he believes torture is permissible. The first is the "ticking bomb" scenario, a hypothetical rarity in which the following conditions apply: a) a terrorist cell has planted a nuclear weapon or something nearly as devastating in a major city; b) we have captured someone in this cell; c) we know for a fact that he knows where the bomb is. In practice, of course, the likelihood of such a scenario is extraordinarily remote. Uncovering a terrorist plot is hard enough; capturing a conspirator involved in that plot is even harder; and realizing in advance that the person knows the whereabouts of the bomb is nearly impossible. (Remember, in the war on terrorism, we have already detained—and even killed—many innocents. Pentagon reports have acknowledged that up to 90 percent of the prisoners at Abu Ghraib, many of whom were abused and tortured, were not guilty of anything.) But let us assume, for the sake of argument, that all of Krauthammer's conditions apply. Do we have a right to torture our hypothetical detainee?

According to Krauthammer, of course we do. No responsible 16
public official put in that position would refuse to sanction torture if
he believed it could save thousands of lives. And, if it's necessary,
Krauthammer argues, it should be made legal. If you have conceded
that torture may be justified in one case, Krauthammer believes, you
have conceded that it may be justified in many more. In his words,
"Once you've established the principle, to paraphrase George
Bernard Shaw, all that's left to haggle about is the price."

But this is too easy and too glib a formulation. It is possible to 17
concede that, in an extremely rare circumstance, torture may be used
without conceding that it should be legalized. One imperfect but instructive analogy is civil disobedience. In that case, laws are indeed
broken, but that does not establish that the laws should be broken. In
fact, civil disobedience implies precisely that laws should not be broken, and protesters who engage in it present themselves promptly for
imprisonment and legal sanction on exactly those grounds. They do
so for demonstrative reasons. They are not saying that laws don't
matter. They are saying that laws do matter, that they should be en-
forced, but that their conscience in this instance demands that they
disobey them.

In extremis, a rough parallel can be drawn for a president faced 18
with the kind of horrendous decision on which Krauthammer rests
his entire case. What should a president do? The answer is simple: He
may have to break the law. In the Krauthammer scenario, a president
might well decide that, if the survival of the nation is at stake,
he must make an exception. At the same time, he must subject
himself—and so must those assigned to conduct the torture—to the
consequences of an illegal act. Those guilty of torturing another
human being must be punished—or pardoned ex-post-facto.[1] If the
torture is revealed to be useless, if the tortured man is shown to have
been innocent or ignorant of the information he was tortured to reveal, then those responsible must face the full brunt of the law for, in
Krauthammer's words, such a "terrible and monstrous thing." In
Michael Walzer's formulation, if we are to have dirty hands, it is essential that we show them to be dirty.

What Krauthammer is proposing, however, is not this compromise, 19
which allows us to retain our soul as a free republic while protecting us

---

[1]*ex-post-facto:* Latin for "a thing done afterward." The expression refers to a statute that
makes an act punishable as crime when such an act was not an offense when committed.

from catastrophe in an extremely rare case. He is proposing something very different: that our "dirty hands" be wiped legally clean before and after the fact. That is a Rubicon we should not cross, because it marks the boundary between a free country and an unfree one.

Krauthammer, moreover, misses a key lesson learned these past 20 few years. What the hundreds of abuse and torture incidents have shown is that, once you permit torture for someone somewhere, it has a habit of spreading. Remember that torture was originally sanctioned in administration memos only for use against illegal combatants in rare cases. Within months of that decision, abuse and torture had become endemic throughout Iraq, a theater of war in which, even Bush officials agree, the Geneva Conventions apply. The extremely coercive interrogation tactics used at Guantanamo Bay "migrated" to Abu Ghraib. In fact, General Geoffrey Miller was sent to Abu Ghraib specifically to replicate Guantanamo's techniques. According to former Brigadier General Janis Karpinski, who had original responsibility for the prison, Miller ordered her to treat all detainees "like dogs." When Captain Ian Fishback, a West Point graduate and member of the 82nd Airborne, witnessed routine beatings and abuse of detainees at detention facilities in Iraq and Afghanistan, often for sport, he tried to stop it. It took him a year and a half to get any response from the military command, and he had to go to Senator John McCain to make his case.

In short, what was originally supposed to be safe, sanctioned, 21 and rare became endemic, disorganized, and brutal. The lesson is that it is impossible to quarantine torture in a hermetic box; it will inevitably contaminate the military as a whole. Once you have declared that some enemies are subhuman, you have told every soldier that every potential detainee he comes across might be exactly that kind of prisoner—and that anything can therefore be done to him. That is what the disgrace at Abu Ghraib proved. And Abu Ghraib produced a tiny fraction of the number of abuse, torture, and murder cases that have been subsequently revealed. The only way to control torture is to ban it outright. Everywhere. Even then, in wartime, some "bad apples" will always commit abuse. But at least we will have done all we can to constrain it.

Krauthammer's second case for torture is equally unpersuasive. 22 For "slow-fuse" detainees—high-level prisoners like Khalid Sheikh Mohammed with potentially, if not immediately, useful intelligence— Krauthammer again takes the most extreme case and uses it to establish a general rule. He concedes that torture, according to almost every careful student and expert, yields highly unreliable information. Anyone can see that. If you are screaming for relief after a few seconds of waterboarding, you're likely to tell your captors anything, true or untrue, to stop the agony and terror. But Krauthammer then argues that, unless you can prove that torture never works, it should always be retained as an option. "It may indeed be true that torture is not a reliable tool," he argues. "But that is very different from saying that it is never useful." And if it cannot be deemed always useless, it must be permitted—even when an imminent threat is not in the picture.

The problem here is an obvious one. You have made the extreme   23 exception the basis for a new rule. You have said that, if you cannot absolutely rule out torture as effective in every single case, it should be ruled in as an option for many. Moreover, if allowing torture even in the "ticking bomb" scenario makes the migration of torture throughout the military likely, this loophole blows the doors wide open. And how do we tell good intelligence from bad intelligence in such torture-infested interrogation? The short answer is: We cannot. By allowing torture for "slow-fuse" detainees, you sacrifice a vital principle for intelligence that is uniformly corrupted at best and useless at worst.

In fact, the use of torture and coercive interrogation by U.S.   24 forces in this war may have contributed to a profound worsening of our actionable intelligence. The key to intelligence in Iraq and, indeed, in Muslim enclaves in the West, is gaining the support and trust of those who give terrorists cover but who are not terrorists themselves. We need human intelligence from Muslims and Arabs prepared to spy on and inform on their neighbors and friends and even family and tribe members. The only way they will do that is if they perceive the gains of America's intervention as greater than the costs, if they see clearly that cooperating with the West will lead to a better life and a freer world rather than more of the same.

What our practical endorsement of torture has done is to remove   25 that clear boundary between the Islamists and the West and make the two equivalent in the Muslim mind. Saddam Hussein used Abu Ghraib to torture innocents; so did the Americans. Yes, what Saddam did was exponentially worse. But, in doing what we did, we blurred the critical, bright line between the Arab past and what we are proposing as the Arab future. We gave Al Qaeda an enormous propaganda coup, as we have done with Guantanamo and Bagram, the "Salt Pit" torture chambers in Afghanistan, and the secret torture sites in Eastern Europe. In World War II, American soldiers were often tortured by the Japanese when captured. But FDR refused to reciprocate. Why? Because he knew that the goal of the war was not just Japan's defeat but Japan's transformation into a democracy. He knew that, if the beacon of democracy—the United States of America—had succumbed to the hallmark of totalitarianism, then the chance for democratization would be deeply compromised in the wake of victory.

No one should ever underestimate the profound impact that the   26 conduct of American troops in World War II had on the citizens of the eventually defeated Axis powers. Germans saw the difference between being liberated by the Anglo-Americans and being liberated by the Red Army. If you saw an American or British uniform, you were safe. If you didn't, the terror would continue in different ways. Ask any German or Japanese of the generation that built democracy in those countries, and they will remind you of American values—not trumpeted by presidents in front of handpicked audiences, but demonstrated by the conduct of the U.S. military during occupation. I grew up in Great Britain, a country with similar memories. In the dark days of the cold war, I was taught that America, for all its faults, was still America. And that America did not, and constitutively could not, torture anyone.

If American conduct was important in Japan and Germany, how   27 much more important is it in Iraq and Afghanistan. The entire point of the war on terrorism, according to the president, is to advance freedom and democracy in the Arab world. In Iraq, we had a chance not just to tell but to show the Iraqi people how a democracy acts. And, tragically, in one critical respect, we failed. That failure undoubtedly contributed to the increased legitimacy of the insurgency and illegitimacy of the occupation, and it made collaboration between informed Sunnis and U.S. forces far less likely. What minuscule intelligence we might have plausibly gained from torturing and abusing detainees is vastly outweighed by the intelligence we have forfeited by alienating many otherwise sympathetic Iraqis and Afghans, by deepening the divide between the democracies, and by sullying the West's reputation in the Middle East. Ask yourself: Why does Al Qaeda tell its detainees to claim torture regardless of what happens to them in U.S. custody? Because Al Qaeda knows that one of America's greatest weapons in this war is its reputation as a repository of freedom and decency. Our policy of permissible torture has handed Al Qaeda this weapon—to use against us. It is not just a moral tragedy. It is a pragmatic disaster. Why compound these crimes and errors by subsequently legalizing them, as Krauthammer (explicitly) and the president (implicitly) are proposing?

Will a ban on all "cruel, inhuman, and degrading treatment" render interrogations useless? By no means. There are many techniques for gaining intelligence from detainees other than using their bodies against their souls. You can start with the 17 that appear in the Army Field Manual, tested by decades of armed conflict only to be discarded by this administration with barely the blink of an eye. Isolation, psychological disorientation, intense questioning, and any number of other creative techniques are possible. Some of the most productive may well be those in which interrogators are so versed in Islamic theology and Islamist subcultures that they win the confidence of prisoners and pry information out of them—something the United States, with its dearth of Arabic speakers, is unfortunately ill-equipped to do.   28

Enemy combatants need not be accorded every privilege granted legitimate prisoners of war; but they must be treated as human beings. This means that, in addition to physical torture, wanton abuse of their religious faith is out of bounds. No human freedom is meaningful without religious freedom. The fact that Koran abuse has been documented at Guantanamo; that one prisoner at Abu Ghraib was forced to eat pork and drink liquor; that fake menstrual blood was used to disorient a strict Muslim prisoner at Guantanamo—these make winning the hearts and minds of moderate Muslims far harder. Such tactics have resulted in hunger strikes at Guantanamo—perhaps the ultimate sign that the coercive and abusive attempts to gain the cooperation of detainees has completely failed to achieve the desired results.   29

The war on terrorism is, after all, a religious war in many senses. It is a war to defend the separation of church and state as critical to the existence of freedom, including religious freedom. It is a war to persuade the silent majority of Muslims that the West offers a better way—more decency, freedom, and humanity than the autocracies they live under and the totalitarian theocracies waiting in the wings. By endorsing torture—on anyone, anywhere, for any reason—we help obliterate the very values we are trying to promote. You can see this contradiction in Krauthammer's own words: We are "morally   30 compelled" to commit "a terrible and monstrous thing." We are obliged to destroy the village in order to save it. We have to extinguish the most basic principle that defines America in order to save America.

No, we don't. In order to retain fundamental American values, 31 we have to banish from the United States the totalitarian impulse that is integral to every act of torture. We have to ensure that the virus of tyranny is never given an opening to infect the Constitution and replicate into something that corrupts as deeply as it wounds. We should mark the words of Ian Fishback, one of the heroes of this war: "Will we confront danger and adversity in order to preserve our ideals, or will our courage and commitment to individual rights wither at the prospect of sacrifice? My response is simple. If we abandon our ideals in the face of adversity and aggression, then those ideals were never really in our possession. I would rather die fighting than give up even the smallest part of the idea that is 'America.'" If we legalize torture, even under constrained conditions, we will have given up a large part of the idea that is America. We will have lost the war before we have given ourselves the chance to win it.

Thinking Critically about This Reading

As a class, discuss Ian Fishback's statement about torture in the final paragraph of Sullivan's essay. How well does Fishback's statement, (particularly when he says, "If we abandon our ideals in the face of adversity and aggression, then those ideals were never really in our possession") encapsulate the central point of Sullivan's essay?

Questions for Study and Discussion

1. What is Sullivan's thesis? (Glossary: *Thesis*) Where in his essay does he offer the clearest statement of his thesis?

2. Review Sullivan's essay starting with paragraph 15. How does Sullivan counter the arguments that Krauthammer makes, particularly those starting with paragraph 15, that he deems "practical points"? Do you find Sullivan's counterarguments convincing? Why or why not?

3. Sullivan says in paragraph 3 that the debate is "inevitably emotional." Does that mean that it is without logos or ethos? Explain.

4. Is Sullivan soft on terrorism? How do you know?

5. Explain how Sullivan uses definition in his essay. (Glossary: *Definition*) Why is it important for him to define *torture* and *break*, for example?

6. Evaluate the effectiveness of the way that Sullivan opens and closes his essay. (Glossary: *Beginnings and Endings*)

Classroom Activity Using Argument

Read the following passages. What type of logical fallacy does each represent? See page 544.

1. He'll be an excellent windsurfer. He won several skateboarding competitions when he was a student.

2. Ever since 1985, the year people in the United States started to eat more fish, the average height of ten-year-olds has increased each year.

3. Stressful jobs with long hours are the reason the divorce rate is going up.

4. This breed of dog is very loyal, so it's a good choice for people with small apartments.

5. The Internet is growing at a phenomenal rate. Other methods of communication will soon become obsolete.

Suggested Writing Assignments

1. In "Torture for Dummies," published in the December 13, 2005, issue of the online magazine *Slate*, journalist Michael Kinsley, like Andrew Sullivan, takes issue with some aspects of Krauthammer's argument advocating the limited use of torture. Read Kinsley's essay on the Internet (http://www.slate.com/id/2132195/), and write an argument in which you support or take issue with his position.

2. Krauthammer's essay (pp. 616) was published on December 5, 2005, and Sullivan's was published on December 19, 2005. In preparation for an argument of your own on the subject of whether or not the United States should engage in torture, consider whether or not these two writers have articulated the basic arguments on the subject. Or have more and better arguments been put forth? What is the law as it stands now?

A Brief Guide to
Writing a Research Paper

The research paper is an important part of a college education—and for good reason. In writing a research paper, you acquire a number of indispensable skills that you can adapt to other college assignments and to situations after graduation.

The real value of writing a research paper, however, goes beyond acquiring basic skills; it is a unique hands-on learning experience. The purpose of a research paper is not to present a collection of quotations that show you can report what others have said about your topic. Rather, your goal is to analyze, evaluate, and synthesize the materials you research and thereby learn how to do so with any topic. You learn how to view the results of research from your own perspective and to arrive at an informed opinion of a topic.

Writing a researched essay is not very different from the other writing you will be doing in your college writing course. You will find yourself drawing heavily on what you learned from the four student papers in the first two chapters of this text. First you determine what you want to write about. Then you decide on a purpose, consider your audience, develop a thesis, collect your evidence, write a first draft, revise and edit, and prepare a final copy. What differentiates the research paper from other kinds of papers is your use of outside sources and how you acknowledge them. Your library research will involve working with print and electronic sources. Your aim is to select the most appropriate sources for your research from the many that are available on your topic. (See also Chapter 10, Writing with Sources.)

In this chapter, you will learn some valuable research techniques:

- How to establish a realistic schedule for your research project
- How to conduct research on the Internet using directory and keyword searches
- How to evaluate sources

- How to analyze sources
- How to develop a working bibliography
- How to take useful notes
- How to acknowledge your sources using Modern Language Association (MLA) style in-text citations and a list of works cited
- How to present/format your research paper

■ ESTABLISHING A REALISTIC SCHEDULE

A research project easily spans several weeks. To avoid losing track of time and finding yourself facing an impossible deadline at the last moment, establish a realistic schedule for completing key tasks. By thinking of the research paper as a multistage process, you avoid becoming overwhelmed by the size of the whole undertaking.

Your schedule should allow at least a few days to accommodate unforeseen needs and delays. Use the following template, which lists the essential steps in writing a research paper, to plan your own research schedule.

Research Paper Schedule	
Task	**Completion Date**
1. Choose a research topic, and pose a worthwhile question.	___/___/___
2. Locate print and electronic sources.	___/___/___
3. Develop a working bibliography.	___/___/___
4. Evaluate and analyze your sources.	___/___/___
5. Read your sources, taking complete and accurate notes.	___/___/___
6. Develop a preliminary thesis, and make a working outline.	___/___/___
7. Write a draft of your paper, including sources that you have summarized, paraphrased, and quoted.	___/___/___
8. Visit your college writing center for help with your revision.	___/___/___
9. Decide on a final thesis, and modify your outline.	___/___/___
10. Revise your paper, and properly cite all borrowed materials.	___/___/___
11. Prepare a list of works cited.	___/___/___
12. Prepare the final manuscript, and proofread.	___/___/___
13. Submit your research paper.	___/___/___

■ FINDING AND USING SOURCES

You should use materials found through a search of your school library's holdings — including books, newspapers, journals, magazines, encyclopedias, pamphlets, brochures, and government documents — as your primary tools for research. Print sources, unlike many Internet sources, are often reviewed by experts in the field before they are published, are generally overseen by a reputable publishing company or organization, and are examined by editors and fact checkers for accuracy and reliability. Unless you are instructed otherwise, you should try to use print sources in your research.

The best place to start any search for print and online sources is your college library's home page (see p. 645). There you will find links to the computerized catalog of book holdings, online reference works, periodical databases, and electronic journals as well as a list of full-text databases. You'll also find links for subject study guides and for help conducting your research.

To get started, decide on some likely search terms and try them out. You might have to try a number of different terms related to your topic to generate the best results. (For tips on refining your searches, see pp. 645–47.) Your goal is to create a preliminary listing of books, magazine and newspaper articles, public documents and reports, and other sources that may be helpful in exploring your topic. At this early stage, it is better to err on the side of listing too many sources so that, later on, you will not have to relocate sources you discarded too hastily.

You will find that Internet sources can be informative and valuable additions to your research. The Internet is especially useful in providing recent data, stories, and reports. For example, you might find a just-published article from a university laboratory or a news story in your local newspaper's online archives. Generally, however, Internet sources should be used alongside other sources and not as a replacement for them. The Internet offers a vast number of useful and carefully maintained resources, but it also contains much unreliable information. It is your responsibility to determine whether a given Internet source should be trusted. (For advice on evaluating sources, see pp. 648–50.)

If you need more instruction on conducting Internet searches, go to your campus computer center, or consult one of the many books written for Internet beginners. You can also access valuable

Library Home Page

information for searching the Internet at Diana Hacker's Research and Documentation Online at **bedfordstmartins.com/resdoc**.

■ CONDUCTING KEYWORD SEARCHES

When searching for sources about your topic in an electronic database, in the library's computerized catalog, or on the Internet, you should start with a keyword search. To make the most efficient use of your time, you will want to know how to conduct a keyword search that is likely to yield solid sources and leads for your research project. As obvious or simple as it may sound, the key to a successful keyword search is the quality of the keywords you generate about your topic.

You might find it helpful to start a list of potential keywords as you begin your search and add to it as your work proceeds. Often you will discover meaningful combinations of keywords that will lead you directly to the sources you need.

Databases and library catalogs index sources by author, title, year of publication, and subject headings (which are assigned by a cataloger who has previewed the source). The object here is to find a keyword that matches one of the subject headings. Once you begin to locate sources that are on your topic, be sure to note the subject headings that are listed for each source. You can use these subject headings as keywords to lead you to additional book sources. They can also lead you to articles that are gathered in full-text databases (such as *InfoTrac, LexisNexis, Expanded Academic ASAP,* and *JSTOR*) to which your library subscribes.

The keyword search process is somewhat different—more wide open—when you are searching on the Internet. It is always a good idea to look for search tips on the help screens or advanced search

---

Refining Keyword Searches on the Web

Command terms and characters vary somewhat among electronic databases and popular Internet search engines, but the following functions are almost universally accepted. You can click on the site's "Help" or "Advanced Search" links to ask questions about refining your keyword search.

- Use quotation marks or parentheses when you are searching for words in exact sequence—for example, "whooping cough"; (Supreme Court).
- Use AND or a plus sign (+) between words to narrow your search by specifying that all words need to appear in a document—for example, tobacco AND cancer; Shakespeare + sonnet.
- Use NOT or a minus sign (−) between words to narrow your search by eliminating unwanted words—for example, monopoly NOT game; cowboys−Dallas.
- Use an asterisk (*) to indicate that you will accept variations of a term—for example, "food label*" for food labels, food labeling, and so forth.

instructions for the search engine you are using before initiating a keyword search. When you type a keyword in the "Search" box on a search engine's home page, the search engine electronically scans Internet sites to match your keyword to titles and texts. On the Internet, the quality of the search terms (the keywords) is determined by the relevance of the hits on the first page that comes up. A search on the Internet might yield a million hits, but the search engine's algorithm puts the best sources up front. After you scan the first couple of pages of results, you can decide whether these sites seem on topic. If they seem off topic, you will need to refine your search terms to narrow or broaden your search (for tips, see p. 646).

■ USING SUBJECT DIRECTORIES TO DEFINE AND DEVELOP YOUR RESEARCH TOPIC

If you do not know exactly what you want to write about, the subject directories on the home pages of search engines make it easy to browse the Web by various subjects and topics for ideas that interest you. Subject directories are also helpful if you have a topic but need an exact research question or if you want to know if you'll be able to supplement your research work with enough print sources. Once you choose a subject area in the directory, you can select specialized subdirectories and eventually arrive at a list of sites that are closely related to your topic.

The most common question students have at this stage of a Web search is, "How can I tell that I'm looking in the right place?" There is no simple answer to this question. If more than one subject area sounds plausible, you will have to dig more deeply into each of their subdirectories, using logic and the process of elimination to determine which one is likely to produce the best leads for your topic. In most cases, it takes just one or two clicks to figure out whether you're searching in the right subject area. If you click on a subject area and the topics in its subdirectories do not relate to your research topic, try a different subject area. As you browse through various subject directories and subdirectories, keep a running list of keywords that are associated with your topic so that you can use them in subsequent keyword searches.

■ EVALUATING YOUR PRINT AND ONLINE SOURCES

You will not have to spend much time in the library to realize that you cannot read every print and online source that appears relevant. Given the abundance of print and Internet sources, the key to successful research is identifying those books, articles, Web sites, and other online sources that will help you most. You must evaluate your potential sources to determine which materials you will read, which you will skim, and which you will simply eliminate. Here are some evaluation strategies and questions to assist you in identifying your most promising sources.

Strategies for Evaluating Print and Online Sources

Evaluating a Book
- Read the dust jacket or cover copy for insights into the book's coverage, its currency, and the author's expertise.
- Scan the table of contents, and identify any promising chapters.
- Read the author's preface, looking for his or her thesis and purpose.
- Check the index for key words or key phrases related to your research topic.
- Read the opening and concluding paragraphs of any promising chapters. If you are unsure about its usefulness, skim the whole chapter.
- Ask yourself: Does the author have a discernable bias? If so, you must be aware that this bias will color his or her claims and evidence. (See Analyzing Your Sources, pp. 650–51.)

Evaluating an Article
- Ask yourself what you know about the journal or magazine publishing the article:
  - Is the publication scholarly or popular? Scholarly journals (*American Economic Review, Journal of Marriage and the Family,* and *Wilson Quarterly,* for example) publish articles representing original research written by authorities in the field. Such articles always cite their sources in footnotes or bibliographies, which means that you can check their accuracy and delve deeper into the topic by locating these sources. Popular news and general-interest magazines (*National Geographic, Smithsonian, Time,* and *Ebony,* for example), on the other hand, publish informative, entertaining, and easy-to-read articles written by editorial staff or freelance writers. Popular essays sometimes cite sources but often do not, making them somewhat less authoritative and less helpful in terms of extending your own research.
  - What is the reputation of the journal or magazine? Determine the publisher or sponsor. Is it an academic institution, a commercial

enterprise, or an individual? Does the publisher or publication have a reputation for accuracy and objectivity?
  • Who are the readers of this journal or magazine?
• Try to determine the author's credentials. Is he or she an expert on the topic?
• Consider the title or headline of the article, the opening paragraph or two, and the conclusion. Does the source appear to be too general or too technical for your needs and audience?
• For articles in journals, read the abstract (a summary of the main points), if there is one.
• Examine any photographs, charts, graphs, or other illustrations that accompany the article. Determine how useful they might be for your research purposes.

Evaluating a Web Site
• Consider the type of Web site. Is this site a personal blog or professional publication? Often the URL, especially the top-level domain name, can give you a clue about the kinds of information provided and the type of organization behind the site. Common suffixes include:
  .com — business, commercial, or personal
  .edu — educational institution
  .gov — government sponsored
  .net — various types of networks
  .org — nonprofit organization, but also some commercial or personal
  Be advised that *.org* is not regulated like *.edu* and *.gov*, for example. Most nonprofits use *.org*, but many commercial and personal sites do as well.
• Examine the home page of the cite:
  • Does the content appear to be related to your research topic?
  • Is the home page well maintained and professional in appearance?
  • Is there an *About* link on the home page that takes you to background information on the site's sponsor? Is there a mission statement, history, or statement of philosophy? Can you verify whether the site is official; that is, is it actually sanctioned by the organization or company?
• Identify the author of the site. What are the author's qualifications for writing on this subject?
• Determine whether a print equivalent is available. If so, is the Web version identical to the print version, or is it altered in some way?
• Determine when the site was last updated. Is the content current enough for your purposes?

You can also find sources on the Internet itself that offer useful guidelines for evaluating electronic sources. One excellent example was created by reference librarians at the Wolfgram Memorial Library of Widener University. Type *Wolfgram evaluate web pages* into a search engine to access that site. For additional guidance, go to <bedfordstmartins.com/researchroom> and click on "How to Evaluate Sources" or "Evaluating Online Sources: A Tutorial."

On the basis of your evaluation, select the most promising books, articles, and Web sites to pursue in depth for your research project.

■ ANALYZING YOUR PRINT AND ONLINE SOURCES

Before beginning to take notes, analyze your sources for their relevance, bias, overall argument, and reliability in helping you explore your topic. Look for the writers' main ideas, key examples, strongest arguments, and conclusions. Read critically: It is easy to become absorbed in sources that support your beliefs, but always seek out several sources with opposing viewpoints, if only to test your own position. Look for information about the authors themselves—information that will help you determine their authority and perspective or bias on the issues. You should also know the reputation and special interests of book publishers and magazines because you are likely to get different views—conservative, liberal, international, feminist—on the same topic, depending on the publication you read. Use the accompanying checklist to assist you in analyzing your print and online sources.

Checklist for Analyzing Print and Online Sources

- What is the writer's thesis or claim?
- How does the writer support this thesis? Does the evidence seem reasonable and ample, or is it mainly anecdotal?
- Does the writer consider opposing viewpoints?
- Does the writer have any obvious political or religious biases? Is the writer associated with a special-interest group such as Planned Parenthood, Greenpeace, Amnesty International, or the National Rifle Association?
- Is the writer an expert on the subject? Do other writers mention this author in their work?
- Does the publisher or publication have a reputation for accuracy and objectivity?

- Is important information documented in footnotes or links so that it can be verified or corroborated in other sources?
- Is the author's purpose to inform? Or is it to argue for a particular position or action?
- Do the writer's thesis and purpose clearly relate to your topic?
- Does the source appear to be too general or too technical for your needs and audience?
- Does the source reflect current thinking and research in the field?

■ DEVELOPING A WORKING BIBLIOGRAPHY FOR YOUR SOURCES

As you discover books, journal and magazine articles, newspaper stories, and Web sites that you think might be helpful for writing your paper, you need to start maintaining a record of important information about each source. This record, called a *working bibliography,* will enable you to know where sources are located when it comes time to consult and acknowledge them in your paper and list of works cited (see pp. 656–67). In all likelihood, your working bibliography will contain more sources than you actually consult and include in your list of works cited.

You may find it easy to make a separate bibliography card, using a 3-inch by 5-inch index card, for each work that you think might be helpful to your research. As your collection of cards grows, alphabetize them by the authors' last names. By using a separate card for each book, article, or Web site, you can continually edit your working bibliography, dropping sources that do not prove helpful and adding new ones.

With the computerization of most library resources, you can copy bibliographic information from the library computer catalog and periodical indexes or from the Internet and paste it into a document on your computer. Then you can edit, add, delete, and search these sources throughout the research process. You can also track your project online with a citation manager like the Bedford Bibliographer <bedfordstmartins.com/bibliographer>. One advantage of the copy/paste option over the index card method is accuracy, especially in punctuation, spelling, and capitalization, details that are essential in accessing Internet sites.

Checklist for a Working Bibliography

For Books
Library call number
Names of all authors, editors, and translators
Title and subtitle
Publication data:
Place of publication (city and state)
Publisher's name
Date of publication
Edition number (if not the first) and volume number (if applicable)

For Periodical Articles
Names of all authors
Title and subtitle of article
Title of journal, magazine, or newspaper
Publication data:
Volume number and issue number
Date of issue
Page numbers

For Internet Sources
Names of all authors, editors, compilers, or sponsoring agents
Title and subtitle of the document
Title of the longer work to which the document belongs
(if applicable)
Title of the site or discussion list name
Author, editor, or compiler of the Web site or online database
Date of release, online posting, or latest revision
Name and vendor of database or name of online service or network
Medium (online, CD-ROM, etc.)
Format of online source (Web page, e-mail, etc.)
Date of access
Electronic address (URL or network path)

For Other Sources
Name of author, government agency, organization, company,
recording artist, personality, etc.
Title of the work

> Format (pamphlet, unpublished diary, interview, television broadcast, etc.)
> Publication or production data:
>> Name of publisher or producer
>> Date of publication, production, or release
>> Identifying codes or numbers (if applicable)

■ TAKING NOTES

As you read, take notes. You're looking for ideas, facts, opinions, statistics, examples, and other evidence that you think will be useful as you write your paper. As you read through books and articles, look for recurring themes, and notice where writers are in agreement and where they differ. Try to remember that the effectiveness of your paper is largely determined by the quality—not necessarily the quantity—of your notes. Your purpose is not to present a collection of quotes that show that you've read all the material and know what others have said about your topic. Your goal is to analyze, evaluate, and synthesize the information you collect—in other words, to enter into the discussion of the issues and thereby take ownership of your topic. You want to view the results of your research from your own perspective and arrive at an informed opinion of your topic. (For more on writing with sources, see Chapter 10.)

Now for some practical advice on taking notes. First, be systematic in your note taking. As a rule, write one note on a card and include the author's full name, the complete title of the source, and a page number indicating the origin of the note. Use cards of uniform size, preferably 4-inch by 6-inch cards because they are large enough to accommodate even a long note on a single card and yet small enough to be easily handled and conveniently carried. If you keep notes electronically, consider creating a separate file for each topic or source, or using an electronic research manager like Zotero **<zotero .org>**. If you keep your notes organized, when you get to the planning and writing stage you will be able to sequence them according to the plan you have envisioned for your paper. Furthermore, should you decide to alter your organizational plan, you can easily reorder your notes to reflect those revisions.

Second, try not to take too many notes. One good way to control your note taking is to ask yourself, "How exactly does this material help prove or disprove my thesis?" Try to envision where in your paper you could use the information. If it does not seem relevant to your thesis, don't bother to take a note.

Once you decide to take a note, you must decide whether to summarize, paraphrase, or quote directly. The approach you take should be determined by the content of the passage and the way you plan to use it in your paper. For detailed advice on summaries, paraphrases, and quotations, see Chapter 10, pages 241–45.

■ DOCUMENTING SOURCES

Whenever you summarize, paraphrase, or quote a person's thoughts and ideas and whenever you use facts or statistics that are not commonly known or believed, you must properly acknowledge the source of your information. If you do not properly acknowledge ideas and information created by someone else, you are guilty of *plagiarism,* of using someone else's material but making it look as if it were your own (see pp. 251–54). You must document the source of your information whenever you do the following:

- Quote a source word for word
- Refer to information and ideas from another source that you present in your own words as either a paraphrase or a summary
- Cite statistics, tables, charts, or graphs

You do not need to document these types of information:

- Your own observations, experiences, and ideas
- Factual information available in a number of reference works (known as "common knowledge")
- Proverbs, sayings, and familiar quotations

A reference to the source of your borrowed information is called a *citation.* There are many systems for making citations, and your citations must consistently follow one of these systems. The documentation style recommended by the Modern Language Association is commonly used in English and the humanities and is the style used throughout this book. Another common system is the American Psychological Association (APA) style, which is generally used in the social sciences. Your instructor will probably tell you which style to use. For more information on documentation styles, consult the appropriate manual or handbook, or go to Diana Hacker's Research and Documentation Online at **bedfordstmartins.com/resdoc**.

There are two components of documentation. *In-text citations* are placed in the body of your paper, and the *list of works cited* provides complete publication data for your in-text citations and is placed at the end of your paper. Both of these components are necessary for complete documentation.

In-Text Citations

In-text citations, also known as *parenthetical citations,* give the reader citation information immediately, at the point at which it is most meaningful. Rather than having to find a footnote or an endnote, the reader sees the citation as a part of the writer's text.

Most in-text citations consist of only the author's last name and a page reference. Usually the author's name is given in an introductory or signal phrase at the beginning of the borrowed material, and the page reference is given in parentheses at the end. If the author's name is not given at the beginning, put it in parentheses along with the page reference. When you borrow material from two or more works by the same author, you must include the title of the work in the signal phrase or parenthetically at the end. (See pp. 671 and 672 for examples.) The parenthetical reference signals the end of the borrowed material and directs your readers to the list of works cited should they want to pursue a particular source. Treat electronic sources as you do print sources, keeping in mind that some electronic sources use paragraph numbers instead of page numbers. Consider the following examples of in-text citations, taken from the opening paragraph of student Charley Horton's paper "How Humans Affect Our Global Environment."

In-Text Citations (MLA Style)

Controversy has always shadowed public discussions of our environment and environmental policy. In her book *Silent Spring* (1962), Rachel Carson first warned Americans about the dire consequences of the irresponsible use of herbicides and insecticides. She clearly saw that "a grim specter has crept upon us almost unnoticed" (54). First decried as an alarmist, Carson is now revered as an early leader in the ecology movement. Today the debate is not limited to pesticides where controversy still swirls around the use of certain lawn care products and their commercial agricultural counterparts. It has expanded to include often uncivil discussions about the causes of climate change. Audrey Schulman has written extensively on severe climatic events, and she concludes that human behavior has had a direct impact on global climate change. She knows that while "some human cultures, through their agriculture and hunting, have respected and adapted to ecological limits" (134), others have not. Like her predecessor Rachel Carson, Schulman believes that Americans must act to avoid an ecological tragedy: "We have the ability to shape our destiny" (134).

List of Works Cited (MLA Style)

Carson, Rachel. "Fable for Tomorrow." *Models for Writers.* 11th ed. Eds. Alfred Rosa and Paul Eschholz. Boston: Bedford, 2012. 52–54. Print.

Schulman, Audrey. "Fahrenheit 59: What a Child's Fever Might Tell Us about Climate Change." *Models for Writers.* 11th Ed. Eds. Alfred Rosa and Paul Eschholz. Boston: Bedford, 2012. 131–34. Print.

In the preceding example, the student followed MLA style guidelines for his Works Cited list. When constructing the list of works cited page for your paper, consult the following MLA guidelines, based on the *MLA Handbook for Writers of Research Papers*, 7th edition (2009), where you will find model entries for periodical print publications, nonperiodical print publications, Web publications, and other common sources.

List of Works Cited

In this section, you will find general MLA guidelines for creating a works cited list followed by sample entries that cover the citation situations you will encounter most often. Make sure that you follow the formats as they appear on the following pages. If you would like to compile your list of works cited online, go to **bedfordstmartins.com/bibliographer**.

Guidelines for Constructing Your Works Cited Page

1. Begin the list on a fresh page following the last page of text.
2. Center the title *Works Cited* at the top of the page.
3. Double space both within and between entries on your list.
4. Alphabetize your sources by the authors' last names. If you have two or more authors with the same last name, alphabetize first by last names and then by first names.
5. If you have two or more works by the same author, alphabetize by the first word of the titles, not counting *A, An,* or *The.* Use the author's name in the first entry and three unspaced hyphens followed by a period in subsequent entries:

    Quart, Alissa. *Branded: The Buying and Selling of Teenagers.* New York: Perseus, 2003. Print.

    ---. "Welcome to (Company Name Here) High (TM)." *New York Times* 1 July 2003, late ed.: A19. Print.

6. If no author is known, alphabetize by title.
7. Begin each entry at the left margin. If the entry is longer than one line, indent the second and subsequent lines five spaces or one-half inch.
8. Italicize the titles of books, journals, magazines, and newspapers. Use quotation marks with titles of periodical articles, chapters and essays within books, short stories, and poems.
9. Provide the medium of the source (Print, Web, Film, Television, Performance).

Periodical Print Publications: Journals, Magazines, and Newspapers

ARTICLE IN A SCHOLARLY JOURNAL

For all scholarly journals—whether they paginate continuously throughout a given year or not—provide the volume number, the issue number, the year, the page numbers, and the medium. Separate the volume number and the issue number with a period.

McGlone, Matthew S. "Quoted Out of Context: Contextomy and Its Consequences." *Journal of Communication* 55.2 (2005): 330-46. Print.

ARTICLE IN A MAGAZINE

When citing a weekly or biweekly magazine, give the complete date (day, month, year).

Brokaw, Tom. "Walter Cronkite: The Most Trusted Man in America." *Time* 3
   Aug. 2009: 20-21. Print.

When citing a magazine published every month or every two months, provide the month or months and year. If an article in a magazine is not printed on consecutive pages—for example, an article might begin on page 45 and then skip to 48—include only the first page followed by a plus sign.

Mascarelli, Amanda Leigh. "Fall Guys." *Audubon* Nov.-Dec. 2009: 44+. Print.

ARTICLE IN A NEWSPAPER

Wheeler, Ginger. "Weighing in on Chubby Kids: Smart Strategies to Curb
   Obesity." *Chicago Tribune* 9 Mar. 2004, final ed.: C11+. Print.

REVIEW (BOOK/FILM)

Ruta, Suzanne. "Midnight Minus One." Rev. of *The Point of Return*, by
   Siddhartha Deb. *New York Times Book Review* 23 Mar. 2003: 13. Print.

Lane, Anthony. "Under Pressure." Rev. of *K-19: The Widowmaker*, dir. Kathryn
   Bigelow. *New Yorker* 29 July 2002: 92-93. Print.

If the review has no title, simply begin with *Rev.* after the author's name. If there is neither title nor author, begin with *Rev.* and alphabetize by the title of the book or film being reviewed.

ANONYMOUS ARTICLE

When no author's name is given, begin the entry with the title.

"Pompeii: Will the City Go from Dust to Dust? *Newsweek* 1 Sept. 1997: 8. Print.

EDITORIAL (SIGNED/UNSIGNED)

Jackson, Derrick Z. "The Winner: Hypocrisy." Editorial. *Boston Globe* 6 Feb.
   2004, 3rd ed.: A19. Print.

"A Real Schedule for Ground Zero." Editorial. *New York Times* 18 June 2008,
   national ed.: A22. Print.

LETTER TO THE EDITOR

Echevarria-Leary, Cheers. Letter. *Newsweek* 14 Sept. 2009: 4. Print.

Nonperiodical Print Publications: Books, Brochures, and Pamphlets

BOOK BY A SINGLE AUTHOR

Nathan, Rebekah. *My Freshman Year: What a Professor Learned by Becoming a Student*. Ithaca: Cornell UP, 2005. Print.

Feel free to use a shortened version of the publisher's name—for example, *Houghton* for Houghton Mifflin, or *Cambridge UP* for Cambridge University Press.

ANTHOLOGY

Eggers, Dave, ed. *The Best American Nonrequired Reading, 2002*. New York: Houghton, 2002. Print.

BOOK BY TWO OR MORE AUTHORS

For a book by two or three authors, list the authors in the order in which they appear on the title page.

Douglas, Susan, and Meredith Michaels. *The Mammy Myth: The Idealization of Motherhood and How It Has Undermined Women*. New York: Free, 2004. Print.

For a book by four or more authors, list the first author in the same way for a single-author book, followed by a comma and the abbreviation *et al.* ("and others").

Beardsley, John, et al. *Gee's Bend: The Women and Their Quilts*. Atlanta: Tinwood, 2002. Print.

BOOK BY A CORPORATE AUTHOR

Carnegie Foundation for the Advancement of Teaching. *Campus Life: In Search of Community*. Princeton: Princeton UP, 1990. Print.

WORK IN AN ANTHOLOGY

Smith, Seaton. "'Jiving' with Your Teen." *The Best American Nonrequired Reading, 2002*. Ed. Dave Eggers. New York: Houghton, 2002. 217-20. Print.

ARTICLE IN A REFERENCE BOOK

Preuss, Harry G. "Nutrition." *The Encyclopedia Americana*. 2004 ed. Print.

If an article is unsigned, begin with the title.

"Dostoyevsky, Fyodor Mikhailovich." *Benet's Reader's Encyclopedia*. 5th ed. 2008. Print.

INTRODUCTION, PREFACE, FOREWORD, OR AFTERWORD TO A BOOK

Wirzba, Norman. Introduction. *The Art of the Commonplace: The Agrarian Essays of Wendell Berry*. By Wendell Berry. Washington: Shoemaker & Hoard, 2002. vii-xx. Print.

ANONYMOUS BOOK

Children of the Dragon: The Story of Tiananmen Square. New York: Collier-Macmillan, 1990. Print.

TRANSLATION

Basho, Matsuo. *Basho's Journey: The Literary Prose of Matsuo Basho*. Trans. David Landis Barnhill. Albany: State U of New York P, 2005. Print.

AN ILLUSTRATED BOOK OR GRAPHIC NOVEL

Clemens, Samuel L. *The Adventures of Huckleberry Finn*. Illus. Norman Rockwell. New York: Heritage, 1940. Print.

Neufield, Josh, writer and artist. *A.D.: New Orleans After the Deluge*. New York: Pantheon, 2009. Print.

BOOK PUBLISHED IN A SECOND OR SUBSEQUENT EDITION

Phillipson, David W. *African Archeology*. 3rd ed. New York: Cambridge UP, 2005. Print.

Modern Language Association of America. *MLA Handbook for Writers of Research Papers*. 7th ed. New York: MLA, 2009. Print.

BROCHURE/PAMPHLET

Clay County Department of Parks, Recreation & Historic Sites. *Jesse James Birth Place: Clay County, Missouri*. Liberty: Clay County Parks, 2004. Print.

GOVERNMENT PUBLICATION

United States. Dept. of Labor. *Child Care: A Workforce Issue*. Washington: GPO, 1988. Print.

Give the government, the agency, and the title with a period and a space after each. The publisher is the Government Printing Office (GPO).

Web Publications

The following guidelines and models for citing information retrieved from the World Wide Web have been adapted from the most recent advice of the MLA, as detailed in the *MLA Handbook for Writers of Research Papers*, 7th ed. (2009), and from the "MLA Style" section on the MLA's Web site <http://www.mla.org>. You will quickly notice that citations of Web publications have some common features with both print publications and reprinted works, broadcasts, and live performances. Standard information for all citations of online materials includes:

1. Name of the author, editor, or compiler of the work. The guidelines for print sources for works with more than one author, a corporate author, or an unnamed author apply. For anonymous works, begin your entry with the title of the work.
2. Title of the work. Italicize the title, unless it part of a larger work. Titles that are part of a larger work should be presented within quotation marks.
3. Title of the overall Web site in italics, if distinct from item 2.
4. Version or edition of the site, if relevant.
5. Publisher or sponsor of the site. This information is often found at the bottom of the Web page. If this information is not available, use *N.p.* (for *no publisher*).
6. Date of publication (day, month, and year, if available). If no date is given, use *n.d.*
7. Medium of publication. For online sources, the medium is *Web*.
8. Date of access (day, month, and year).

MLA style does not require you to include URLs in works cited entries. If your instructor wants you to include URLs in your citations or if you believe readers will not be able to locate the source without the URL, insert the URL as the last item in an entry, immediately after the date of access. Enclose the URL in angle brackets, followed by a period. Include the page number, if any, after the year of publication; if no page number is given, use *n. pag.* The following example illustrates an entry with the URL included:

Finley, Laura L. "How Can I Teach Peace When the Book Only Covers War?" *The Online Journal of Peace and Conflict Resolution* 5.1 (2003): n. pag. Web. 12 Feb. 2011. <http://www.trinstitute.org/ojpcr/5_1finley.htm>.

MLA style requires that you break URLs extending over more than one line only after a slash. Do *not* add spaces, hyphens, or any other punctuation to indicate the break.

Online Scholarly Journals

To cite an article, review, editorial, or letter to the editor in a scholarly journal existing only in electronic form on the Web, provide the author, the title of the article, the title of the journal, the volume and issue, and the date of issue, followed by the page numbers (if available), the medium, and the date of access.

ARTICLE IN AN ONLINE SCHOLARLY JOURNAL

Rist, Thomas. "Religion, Politics, Revenge: The Dead in Renaissance Drama." *Early Modern Literary Studies* 9.1 (2003): n. pag. Web. 28 Feb. 2011.

BOOK REVIEW IN AN ONLINE SCHOLARLY JOURNAL

Opongo, Elias Omondi. Rev. of *Responsibility to Protect: The Global Effort to End Mass Atrocities*, by Alex J. Bellamy. *Journal of Peace, Conflict, and Development* 14.14 (2009): n. pag. 7 Mar. 2011.

EDITORIAL IN AN ONLINE SCHOLARLY JOURNAL

"Writing Across the Curriculum and Writing Centers." Editorial. *Praxis: A Writing Center Journal* 6.2 (2009): n. pag. Web. 10 Jan. 2011.

Periodical Publications in Online Databases

Here are some model entries for periodical publications collected in online databases.

JOURNAL ARTICLE FROM AN ONLINE DATABASE OR SUBSCRIPTION SERVICE

Kauver, Elaine M. "Warring Desires: The Future of Jewish American Literature." *American Literary History* 21.4 (2009): 877-90. *Project Muse.* Web. 17 Feb. 2011.

MAGAZINE ARTICLE FROM AN ONLINE DATABASE OR SUBSCRIPTION SERVICE
Keizer, Garret. "Sound and Fury: The Politics of Noise in a Loud Society."
　　Harper's Magazine. Mar. 2001: 39-48. *Expanded Academic ASAP Plus*. Web.
　　27 Mar. 2011.

NEWSPAPER ARTICLE FROM AN ONLINE DATABASE OR SUBSCRIPTION SERVICE
Sanders, Joshunda. "Think Race Doesn't Matter? Listen to Eminem." *San
　　Francisco Chronicle* 20 July 2003. *LexisNexis*. Web. 18 Mar. 2011.

McEachern, William Ross. "Teaching and Learning in Bilingual Countries: The
　　Examples of Belgium and Canada." *Education* 123.1 (2002): 103. *Expanded
　　Academic ASAP Plus*. Web. 17 Mar. 2011.

Nonperiodical Web Publications

Nonperiodical Web publication include all Web-delivered content
that does not fit into one of the previous two categories—scholarly
journal Web publications and periodical publications in an online
database or subscription service.

ARTICLE IN AN ONLINE MAGAZINE
Lamott, Anne. "Because I'm a Mother." *Salon.com*. 4 July 2003. Web. 4 Jan.
　　2011.

Huang, Lily. "The Case of the Disappearing Rabbit." *Newsweek*. Newsweek, 25
　　July 2009. Web. 10 Jan. 2011.

ARTICLE IN AN ONLINE NEWSPAPER
Hanley, Charles J., and Jan M. Olsen. "Climate Drama Climax Looks Elusive in
　　Copenhagen." *Seattletimes.com*. Seattle Times, 5 Dec. 2009. Web. 28 Feb.
　　2011.

"Beyond Copenhagen." Editorial. *New York Times*. New York Times, 6 Dec. 2009.
　　Web. 7 Feb. 2011.

ARTICLE IN AN ONLINE SCHOLARLY PROJECT
Driscoll, Dana Lynn. "Irregular Verbs." Chart. *The OWL at Purdue*. Purdue U
　　Online Writing Lab, 13 May 2007. Web. 8 Mar. 2011.

BOOK OR PART OF A BOOK ACCESSED ONLINE

For a book available online, provide the author, the title, the editor (if any), original publication information, the name of the database or Web site, the medium (*Web*), and the date of access.

Hawthorne, Nathaniel. *The Blithedale Romance*. Intro. George Parsons Lathrop. Salem Edition. Boston, 1894. Web. 28 Feb. 2011.

If you are citing only part of an online book, include the title or name of the part directly after the author's name.

Woolf, Virginia. "Kew Gardens." *Monday or Tuesday*. New York: Harcourt, 1921. *Bartleby.com: Great Books Online*. Web. 15 Nov. 2010.

SPEECH, ESSAY, POEM, OR SHORT STORY FROM AN ONLINE SITE

Faulkner, William. "On Accepting the Nobel Prize." 10 Dec. 1950. *The History Place: Great Speeches Collection*. Web. 12 Mar. 2011.

ARTICLES AND STORIES FROM ONLINE NEWS SERVICES

Pressman, Gabe. "Eminent Domain: Let the Public Beware!" *NBCNewYork.com*. NBC New York, 5 Dec. 2009. Web. 6 Mar. 2011.

"Iran Police Clash with Protesters." *CNN.com*. Cable News Network, 7 Dec. 2009. Web. 7 Mar. 2011.

ARTICLE IN AN ONLINE ENCYCLOPEDIA OR OTHER REFERENCE WORK

"Chili Pepper." *Encyclopaedia Britannica Online*. Encyclopaedia Britannica, 2011. Web. 3 Mar. 2011.

"Blog." *Merriam-Webster Online Dictionary*. Merriam-Webster, 2011. Web. 3 Mar. 2011.

ONLINE ARTWORK, PHOTOGRAPHS, MAPS, CHARTS, AND OTHER IMAGES

da Vinci, Leonardo. *Mona Lisa*. 1503-06. Musee du Louvre, Paris. *WebMuseum*, 19 June 2006. Web. 22 Mar. 2011.

"West Hartford, Connecticut." Map. *Google Maps*. Google, 4 Mar. 2011. Web. 4 Mar. 2011.

ONLINE GOVERNMENT PUBLICATION

United States. Dept. of Treasury. Internal Revenue Service. *Your Rights as a Taxpayer*. May 2005. Web. 2 Apr. 2011.

HOME PAGE FOR AN ACADEMIC DEPARTMENT

Dept. of English. Home page. Arizona State U, n.d. Web. 29 Mar. 2011.

HOME PAGE FOR AN ACADEMIC COURSE

Magistrale, Tony. Home page. *Poe's Children*. Dept. of English. U of Vermont, 6 Nov. 2002. Web. 9 Mar. 2011.

WIKI ENTRY

"C. S. Lewis." *Wikipedia*. Wikimedia Foundation, 27 Feb. 2011. Web. 4 Mar. 2011.

No author is listed for a Wiki entry because the content is written collaboratively.

POSTING ON A BLOG

Broadway Bob. "Defining Home." *babblebob*. By Robert M. Armstrong, 24 Aug. 2009. Web. 10 Feb. 2011.

VIDEO RECORDING POSTED ONLINE

ManakinBird. "Manakin Bird." *YouTube*. YouTube, 12 Apr. 2008. Web. 12 Mar. 2011.

Additional Common Sources

TELEVISION OR RADIO BROADCAST

"Everyone's Waiting." *Six Feet Under*. Dir. Alan Ball. Perf. Peter Krause, Michael C. Hall, Frances Conroy, and Lauren Ambrose. Writ. Alan Ball. HBO. 21 Aug. 2005. Television.

SOUND RECORDING

Beethoven, Ludwig van. *The Complete Sonatas*. Perf. Richard Goode. Warner, 1993. CD.

FILM OR VIDEO RECORDING

Schindler's List. Dir. Steven Spielberg. Perf. Liam Neeson, Ralph Fiennes, and
     Ben Kingsley. 1993. Universal. 2004. DVD.

WORK OF VISUAL ART

Botticelli, Sandro. *Birth of Venus*. 1485-86? Tempura on panel. Uffizi Gallery.
     Florence.

If you use a reproduction of a piece of visual art, give the institution and city as well as the complete publication information for the
source, including the medium of reproduction.

Parks, Gordon. *Muhammad Ali*. 1970. Photograph. The Capital Group
     Foundation, Atlanta. *Bare Witness: Photographs by Gordon Parks*. Milan:
     Skira, 2007. Print.

INTERVIEW

Handke, Peter. Interview. *New York Times Magazine* 2 July 2006: 13. Print.

For interviews that you conduct, provide the name of the person
interviewed, the type of interview (personal, telephone, e-mail), and
the date.

Mosher, Howard Frank. Telephone interview. 30 Jan 2011.

CARTOON OR COMIC STRIP

Luckovich, Mike. Cartoon. *Atlanta Journal-Constitution* 24 Nov. 2009. Print.

ADVERTISEMENT

Sprint. Advertisement. *Newsweek* 7 Sept. 2009: 15. Print.

LECTURE, SPEECH, ADDRESS, READING

England, Paula. "Gender and Inequality: Trends and Causes." President's
     Distinguished Lecture Series. U of Vermont. Memorial Lounge, Burlington.
     22 Mar. 2004. Lecture.

LETTER, MEMO, OR E-MAIL MESSAGE

Proulx, E. Annie. Letter to the author. 22 Jan. 2011. MS.

Moore, Mallory. "Re: New Visual Options." Message to the author. 10 Feb. 2011.
     E-mail.

Indicate the medium using *MS* (handwritten manuscript), *TS* (typescript), or *E-mail*.

PUBLICATION ON CD-ROM OR DVD-ROM

Cite CD-ROMs published as a single edition as you would a book, being careful to add *CD-ROM* as the publication medium.

Shakespeare, William. *Macbeth*. Ed. A. R. Branmuller. New York: Voyager, 1994.
  CD-ROM.

Some CD-ROMs and DVD-ROMs are updated on a regular basis because they cover publications such as journals, magazines, and newspapers that are themselves published periodically. Start your entry with the author's name and the publication information for the print source, followed by the medium of publication, the title of the database (italicized), the name of the vendor, and the electronic publication date.

James, Caryn. "An Army Family as Strong as Its Weakest Link." *New York Times*
  16 Sept. 1994, late ed.: C8. CD-ROM. *New York Times Ondisc*. UMI-ProQuest,
  1994.

DIGITAL FILE

A number of different types of work can come to you as a digital file—a book, typescript, photograph, or sound recording. It is important that you record the format of the digital file (JPEG file, PDF file, Microsoft Word file, MP3 file) in the space reserved for medium of publication.

Dengle, Isabella. *Eben Peck Cabin*. ca. 1891. Wisconsin Historical Society,
  Madison. JPEG file.

Federman, Sarah. "An American in Paris: French Health Care." 2011. *Microsoft
  Word* file.

■ AN ANNOTATED STUDENT RESEARCH PAPER

Cori Schmidtbauer's assignment was to write an argument, and she was free to choose her own topic. After considering a number of possible topics and doing some preliminary research on several of them, she turned to the subject that she and her friends were debating, the pros and cons of social networking on such popular sites as Facebook, LinkedIn, and World of Warcraft. Cori and her friends were intrigued by some of the unexpected problems they were experiencing on these social networks as well as by the sometimes harsh criticism of networking they heard or read about in the press.

Schmitbauer began by brainstorming about her topic. She made lists of ideas, facts, issues, arguments, and opposing arguments. Once she was confident that she had amassed enough information to begin writing, she made a rough outline of an organizational plan that she thought she could follow. With this plan in mind, she wrote a first draft of her essay—a draft in which she tried to explore Facebook, LinkedIn, and World of Warcraft. After letting it set for a day or two, Cori went back and examined the draft carefully, assessing how it could be improved.

Quickly, she realized that she had taken on too much for her topic and needed to focus the scope of her paper. Instead of trying to cover all three social networking sites, Cori decided to focus her discussion on Facebook, the most popular and widely used of the three networks. With this new focus, she now realized what she wanted to say in her paper: When used responsibly, the benefits of Facebook and social networking outweigh the possible dangers. She saw that her organizational plan could be tweaked so as to emphasize three critical concerns that users had about Facebook. More important is that she realized that she could now use more examples about Facebook, examples that should be more specific than what she had in her first draft and that could better help her in making her argument. Armed with a new sense of direction and purpose, Schmidtbauer scoured her sources for material that best supported the points she wanted to make about user responsibility and Facebook. In particular, she looked for appropriate and memorable quotations to include in her paper. All the while, Cori was careful to take accurate notes and to keep a record of where she found each quotation, paraphrase, and summary.

The final draft of Schmidtbauer's research paper illustrates that she has learned how the parts of a well-researched and well-written essay fit together and how to make revisions that emulate some of the qualities of the model essays she had read and studied. The following is the final draft of her paper, and it demonstrates MLA-style documentation and format for research papers.

Schmidtbauer 1

Cori Schmidtbauer

Professor Moore

English Composition

20 March 2011

To Facebook or Not

Facebook and other social networks allow users to interact in an online environment to share common interests. In 2010, Facebook surpassed Google as the most visited Web site in the U.S., and its impact on daily life cannot be ignored (Daily Mail). There are many benefits to online social networking sites, such as the ability to interact even when you can't be face to face with other people. Social networks can break barriers of time and space, allowing individuals to connect with friends in different time zones and in different places. Yet, as popular as Facebook is, there have been concerns raised about this social networking site: privacy settings, cyber-bullying, and the potential hazards to personal relationships have all been presented as examples of the dangers of Facebook. But if used responsibly, the benefits of Facebook and social networking outweigh the detriments.

In the past year, Facebook's privacy settings, as noted by one digital journalist, have been criticized by many of its users. The main concern is that Facebook allows personal information to be seen and discovered through search engines by everyone (Fox). Many people are skeptical about creating a Facebook profile, and those who have profiles complain about Facebook's settings. These people are right to be skeptical, but they should also know that there are ways to control your privacy on the site, and if they make responsible, informed decisions about their privacy settings, the site is fairly secure. Under account settings on any Facebook profile, users have the ability to limit who sees their profile and photos and whether people can message them, users can even set whether people can search for their profile at all.

Writer's name, course information, and date—all double-spaced

Title centered

Writer introduces organizational plan—to address the three main concerns or criticisms of social networking on Facebook.

Writer presents her thesis.

Summary of source introduced with signal phrase and concluded with parenthetical citation.

Schmidtbauer 2

Writer uses personal example to dismiss concerns about privacy settings.

Privacy settings can be adapted to your level of comfort as well. I personally don't hide all of my information, and I allow people to search for my profile. Yes, knowing that anyone can find my Facebook profile, which displays my age, gender, and location, can be a little disconcerting, but it is necessary for Facebook to be a useful social networking site. For me, these aspects of Facebook have helped me reconnect with old friends from high school, and add new friends that I've met in college. What is useful about being able to view a person's gender, age, and location is that I am able to determine if it is the right person. There are so many people with the last name "Torres" or "Miller" that having specific information and pictures makes finding specific friends easier.

Quotation of Coursey introduced with signal phrase. No page number is given parenthetically at the end of the quotation as the source is an unnumbered Web page.

Users' concerns about privacy were heightened, according to technology commentator David Coursey, when Facebook started making changes to its privacy platform without warning: "Users began noticing that their Friends List had become public and could not be hidden. The list includes the identities of everyone the user has 'Friended' and some users don't want the information made public." Honestly, who cares who your friends are? They are your friends and other users or nonusers of Facebook should not judge you for being friends with specific people. Nor should users be ashamed of having Friended their friends on Facebook. This goes back to using the site responsibly; if you friend responsibly, only adding people that you know and are actually acquainted with, this would not be an issue. The only time these issues about security have any merit is when people

Writer emphasizes the need for user responsibility with regard to privacy settings.

are uninformed about their privacy settings or make bad decisions about who they add as a friend, which is the user's fault, not the site's. The site should not be blamed for the user's lapses in judgment. Users need to be aware if their profile is open to "Everyone," "Friends of Friends," or just "Friends."

These are options that are available to the user in the privacy settings, and they are the only way to make sure that you are only contacted by people you want to be contacted by.

Paraphrase of Lyons's Newsweek article introduced with a signal phrase. Parenthetical citation indicates which of Lyons's two articles is being referenced.

Some critics argue that Facebook is taking too many liberties with their privacy, however, and many who were concerned with recent privacy changes left the site altogether. In April 2010, Daniel Lyons, a senior editor at *Forbes* magazine, reported that many tech-savvy bloggers were (very publicly) deactivating their Facebook accounts because of the rapid changes made to the privacy settings. Now Facebook is going even further, Lyons believes, by insisting that unless you agree to make things like your hometown, interests, and friends' names public, then you can't list them at all. This change in privacy triggered a negative reaction from many users, but Facebook executives said it was all a misunderstanding, and that users were resistant to change ("Google's Orwell Moment"). The privacy settings have since been fixed and you can again make all your information private if you wish. It seems every time a problem like this arises, it is quickly remedied by Facebook. I don't mind having to change my privacy settings every once in a while when they are modified, and every once in a while I check the privacy settings to make sure they are exactly how I want them. There is an especially useful tool that allows you to see your profile as nonfriends see it, so you can easily tell if anything that you wish to be private isn't.

Writer uses examples of several of her friends to illustrate irresponsible use of Facebook.

Sometimes, though, Facebook users are not that responsible. The only times my friends have ever gotten in trouble with Facebook are when they do not have secure privacy settings. For example, one of my closest friends received what he called unnecessary comments from people he never met or wanted to meet during his early stages on Facebook. One day, he posted a status update that said: "Nobody dies a Virgin, Life f***s us all." Someone he did not know then commented on the

Schmidtbauer 4

Writer comments on friend's irresponsible behavior.

status, "Stop complaining and being lazy, and get a life!" (Gaines) What my friend wrote for his status update was not appropriate for public display, but his status was a phrase that epitomized his personality. Those who did not know him would not understand the humor behind the phrase. Even though I did not approve of this new status update, I did not respond with a rude or mean comment. Unfortunately, someone

Signal phrase marks beginning of information learned during personal interview. Parenthetical citation indicates the end.

else — someone who did not know my friend, but was a friend of another friend of his — decided to criticize and berate him. In this case, my friend acted irresponsibly in two ways: he didn't hide his profile from strangers, and he posted something that could be easily misconstrued by people who didn't know him. But this bad experience, as my friend told me, had a positive outcome: he was inspired to check his privacy settings and change them so he would not receive unwanted comments.

The writer indents a long quotation ten spaces, double spaces the text, and omits quotation marks.

Initially, he had his privacy settings set so "Everyone" could view his profile and make comments. Now that he has updated his privacy settings so that only "Friends" can view and comment on his profile, he does not have any problems (Gaines).

Some, like Daniel Lyons, worry that the privacy settings still are not clear enough. Lyons warns,

Citation in parentheses comes after the end punctuation. Short title indicates which of Lyons's two articles is being referenced.

> I also suspect that whatever Facebook has done so far to invade our privacy, it's only the beginning. Which is why I'm considering deactivating my account. Facebook is a handy site, but I'm freaked by the idea that my information is in the hands of people I don't trust. That's too high a price to pay. ("The High Price")

But every time a privacy setting is changed, Web sites like Gizmodo.com and Slate.com alert users to the changes. Viral copy and paste status updates start circulating on Facebook notifying users of the privacy changes, and you are able to make the necessary updates to your profile to stay

Schmidtbauer 5

secure. All of the criticisms Facebook is subjected to due to its evolution are overblown because users who are unsatisfied with their privacy settings can simply delete personal information from their profile, or routinely check their privacy settings like I do.

Writer begins discussion of second concern: cyberbullying on Facebook.

There are extreme instances of the misuse of Facebook, though, and these are also cited as examples of why Facebook is a dangerous site. In January 2011, six middle school students in Carson City, Nevada were arrested after they created a Facebook event called Attack a Teacher Day and invited 100 of their friends. They named specific teachers, and gave a time that the attacks would take place (Norton). This case is a perfect example

Writer summarizes scary event reported by F. T. Norton in a Nevada online newspaper.

of how Facebook can be dangerous, but only if it is used inappropriately. The girls who set the page up claimed that it was just a joke, and were unaware of the severity of posting something like this online (Norton). But their actions were irresponsible, and Facebook should not take the blame (or even the bad press they received) for these individuals' poor decisions.

Writer introduces quotation with signal phrase. No parenthetical citation is needed because the article is referenced in the text.

In the beginning Facebook was restricted to college students, but it is now open to everyone. In her article, "More Cyberbullying on Facebook, Social Sites than Rest of Web," Sarah Perez explains that these new, younger users "are still learning how to use the Web properly, often with adult supervision." She goes on to explain what can happen with irresponsible use on the part of these teens: "They learn sometimes the hard way why it's not appropriate to post every thought that pops into their heads. . . . They learn that over-sharing can have real-world consequences. And, unfortunately, they learn that, just like in the real world, not everyone is going to play nice."

Cyber-bullying is currently a hot-button issue for parents and teens, and in October 2010, *My Foxaustin.com*

Schmidtbauer 6

Writer introduces summary of online article with signal phrase. The parenthetical citation marks the end of the summary and the beginning of the writer's own observation.

posted an article, detailing one girl's experience being cyber-bullied. The subject of the article, Jessica Christopher, described the disturbing messages she received on Facebook, messages in which someone taunted her, called her names, and even threatened physical harm. Luckily, her father, David Christopher, noticed changes in her behavior after she received these messages and stepped in to protect his only daughter from further abuse by actively supervising and participating in his daughter's use of Facebook ("Parents Confront"). In the case of cyber-bullying, it is the parents' responsibility to monitor what their child is doing on Facebook, and if they do see anything that seems threatening, they need to step in, just like David Christopher did.

When users are old enough to make these decisions for themselves, there are still instances in which users' judgment can be impaired in an eagerness to share experiences. Just as my friend Brad Gaines learned the consequences of over-sharing his thoughts in an inappropriate status update, others have learned the negative reactions that sharing something personal online can cause. For example, Doyle Byrnes, a nursing student from Kansas City, recently discovered the severe consequences of over-sharing when she posted a picture of herself posing with a human placenta in a nursing class. Instead of receiving hurtful comments about her photo, she was expelled from the nursing program mere months away from graduation. Byrnes has since won a lawsuit that allowed her to be reinstated into the nursing program, but not before her education was jeopardized, as well as her potential career and livelihood. As a result of her experience, Byrnes closed her Facebook account, removing any temptation that hindered her better judgment (Campbell).

Writer introduces example of nursing student Doyle Byrnes.

Parenthetical citation identifies the source of the example.

As Doyle Byrnes's case illustrates, photo sharing on Facebook can be dangerous, which is why you need to be very

Writer stresses need for responsible sharing of photographs on Facebook.

careful about the images you share. But that doesn't mean that photo sharing is a bad thing. Facebook friends can share many new photos of each other without having to print them out or without having to send multiple emails. For college students, like me and my friends, who have to go to class everyday and work, Facebook proves useful since it allows us to see what our friends did over the weekend. These photos are a useful way of communicating with your friends and keeping up with their lives, even if you can not see them in person, and just like most things on Facebook, as long as you don't post anything inappropriate, you won't get into any trouble.

Topic sentence initiates discussion of third main concern with Facebook: hazards to personal relationships.

Writer uses source to illustrate potential relationship problems on Facebook.

While friendships may be enhanced by interaction on Facebook, there seems to be evidence that romantic relationships can be hurt by such interaction. This is so much a concern that many Internet sites have created guidelines on how to behave on Facebook so you do not get in trouble with your significant other. Marushka Mujic of *Mademan.com* wrote one such article entitled "13 Ways Facebook Can Ruin Your Relationship." From not updating your relationship status to poking someone you should not poke, the article cautions men not to make any mistakes on Facebook that might lead to their girlfriend breaking up with them (Mujic). All of the advice in the article, though, seems to be common sense, and some of the ways that Facebook is said to ruin relationships can be easily fixed so that the relationship can remain intact. Mujic says one of the ways relationships can be ruined is if users are posting and tagging embarrassing pictures of their partners (Mujic). This is easily avoidable — either do not post embarrassing pictures or post them but do not tag them. According to Mujic, men should also avoid spending too much time on electronic devices, such as their phone, checking Facebook updates. I could not agree more that watching my date on his Blackberry for more than a minute is a big turn-off,

Schmidtbauer 8

but again, that seems to be common sense. Couples should be paying attention to each other, not checking to see if they have new updates from friends. The solution: just don't do it. Anyone, man or woman, who does not spend enough time paying attention to their date offline is not worth dating. But even though there can be complications with dating a Facebook friend, there can also be some benefits: Facebook makes it possible to share photos and links with a partner, and it provides another outlet for communication when couples can not be together.

Writer begins to conclude with discussion of the benefits of Facebook when used responsibly.
Despite all the criticism Facebook faces, it continues to prove more beneficial than disadvantageous, as long as people use it intelligently. Businesses and companies can use the site to market their product to a specific demographic, celebrities can reach out to their fans and inform them of upcoming events. Relationships formed through Facebook can be expanded to offline interaction, as people meet up at designated places for a common cause, be it to attend a concert or help clean up a beach. Facebook simplifies communication and allows people to connect with both their friends that they see every day, and people that they have never met. The detrimental aspects of the site are completely in the hands of the user, and the site should not be held accountable. If Facebook users have so many concerns about using the social networking site, why keep a profile? Those who already have a profile made the choice of putting information online, where it can be openly viewed. Those who do not yet have a profile should do some research about the social networking site, so they are fully aware of both pros and cons of Facebook. Using the site responsibly will keep private information safe, and will ensure that you do not suffer any of the consequences that people who misuse the site suffer from. Some argue that this is not enough, and that the only way to be completely safe is to not have a profile at all. But where is the fun in that?

Schmidtbauer 9

Works Cited

Campbell, Matt. "Nursing Student, Ousted over Placenta Photo, Sues." *Appeal-Democrat* 1 Jan. 2011, final ed.: A5. Print.

Coursey, David. "After Criticism, Facebook Tweaks Friends List Privacy Options." *PCWorld.com*. PC World. 10 Dec. 2009. Web. 20 Nov. 2010.

Daily Mail Reporter. "Clash of the Titans: Facebook Passes Google as the Most Popular Website in the U.S." *www.dailymail.co.uk*. 2 Jan. 2011. Web. 9 Feb. 2011.

Fox, Gemma. "Facebook Faces Wide Criticism over Privacy Changes." *Digitaljournal.com*. Digital Journal. 10 Dec. 2009. Web. 20 Nov. 2010.

Gaines, Brad. Personal interview. 22 Nov. 2010.

Gonzalez, Maria. Personal interview. 22 Nov. 2010.

Lyons, Daniel. "The High Price of Facebook." *Newsweek.com*. 15 May 2010. Web. 8 Jan. 2011.

---. "Google's Orwell Moment: On the Web, Privacy Has Its Price." *Newsweek.com*. 17 Feb. 2010. Web. 8 Jan. 2011.

Mujic, Marushka. "13 Ways Facebook Ruins Your Relationship." *Mademan.com*. 30 Apr. 2010. Web. 22 Nov. 2010.

Norton, F. T. "Six Girls Arrested in Online Threats." *nevadaappeal.com*. The Nevada Appeal, 6 Jan. 2011. Web. 4 Feb. 2011.

Papacharissi, Zizi. "The Virtual Geographies of Social Networks: A Comparative Analysis of Facebook, LinkedIn and ASmallWorld. *New Media Society* (2009): 199-220. Web. 28 Oct. 2010.

"Parents Confront Problem of Cyberbullying." *Myfoxaustin.com*. 11 Oct. 2010.

Perez, Sarah. "More Cyberbullying on Facebook, Social Sites than Rest of Web." *Readwriteweb.com*. Read Write Web. 10 May 2010. Web. 20 Nov. 2010.

Reuters. "Study: Facebook Makes People More Social." *Foxbusiness.com*. Fox News. 24 Nov. 2010. Web. 26 Nov. 2010.

The heading Works Cited is centered at top of page.

Writer uses MLA style for her list of works cited.

The list begins on a new page. Entries are presented in alphabetical order. The first line of each entry begins at the left margin; subsequent lines are indented five spaces. Double space within entries as well as between entries.

The correct MLA forms for various other kinds of publications are given on pages 657–67.

Glossary of Useful Terms

Abstract See *Concrete/Abstract*.

Allusion An allusion is a passing reference to a familiar person, place, or thing, often drawn from history, the Bible, mythology, or literature. An allusion is an economical way for a writer to capture the essence of an idea, atmosphere, emotion, or historical era, as in "The scandal was his Watergate" or "He saw himself as a modern Job" or "The campaign ended not with a bang but a whimper." An allusion should be familiar to the reader; if it is not, it will add nothing to the meaning.

Analogy Analogy is a special form of comparison in which the writer explains something unfamiliar by comparing it to something familiar: "A transmission line is simply a pipeline for electricity. In the case of a water pipeline, more water will flow through the pipe as water pressure increases. The same is true of electricity in a transmission line."

Anecdote An anecdote is a short narrative about an amusing or interesting event. Writers often use anecdotes to begin essays as well as to illustrate certain points.

Argumentation To argue is to attempt to persuade the reader to agree with a point of view, to make a given decision, or to pursue a particular course of action. There are two basic types of argumentation: logical and persuasive. See the introduction to Chapter 21 (pp. 539–46) for a detailed discussion of argumentation.

Attitude A writer's attitude reflects his or her opinion of a subject. The writer can think very positively or very negatively about a subject or have an attitude that falls somewhere in between. See also *Tone*.

Audience An audience is the intended readership for a piece of writing. For example, the readers of a national weekly newsmagazine come from all walks of life and have diverse interests, opinions, and educational backgrounds. In contrast, the readership for an organic chemistry journal is made up of people whose interests and education are quite similar. The essays in *Models for Writers* are intended for general readers, intelligent people who may lack specific information about the subject being discussed.

Beginnings and Endings A beginning is the sentence, group of sentences, or section that introduces an essay. Good beginnings usually identify the thesis or controlling idea, attempt to interest readers, and establish a tone.

An ending is the sentence or group of sentences that brings an essay to a close. Good endings are purposeful and well planned. They can be a summary, a concluding example, an anecdote, or a quotation. Endings satisfy readers when they are the natural outgrowths of the essays themselves and give readers a sense of finality or completion. Good essays do not simply stop; they conclude. See the introduction to Chapter 6 (pp. 145–53) for a detailed discussion of beginnings and endings.

Cause and Effect Cause-and-effect analysis explains the reasons for an occurrence or the consequences of an action. See the introduction to Chapter 20 (pp. 517–20) for a detailed discussion of cause and effect.

Citation A reference to a published or unpublished work that indicates that the material being referenced is not original with the present author. A citation allows a reader to examine the referenced material to verify its authenticity, accuracy, and appropriateness.

Classification See *Division and Classification*.

Cliché A cliché is an expression that has become ineffective through overuse. Expressions such as *quick as a flash, jump for joy,* and *slow as molasses* are clichés. Writers normally avoid such trite expressions and seek instead to express themselves in fresh and forceful language. See also *Diction*.

Coherence Coherence is a quality of good writing that results when all sentences, paragraphs, and longer divisions of an essay are naturally connected. Coherent writing is achieved through (1) a logical sequence of ideas (arranged in chronological order, spatial order, order of importance, or some other appropriate order), (2) the purposeful repetition of key words and ideas, (3) a pace suitable for your topic and your reader, and (4) the use of transitional words and expressions. Coherence should not be confused with unity. (See *Unity*.) See also *Transition*.

Colloquial Expression   A colloquial expression is an expression that is characteristic of or appropriate to spoken language or to writing that seeks the effect of spoken language. Colloquial expressions are informal, as *chem, gym, come up with, be at wit's end, won't,* and *photo* illustrate. Thus, colloquial expressions are acceptable in formal writing only if they are used purposefully. See also *Diction*.

Combined Strategies   By combining rhetorical strategies, writers are able to develop their ideas in interesting ways. For example, in writing a cause-and-effect essay about a major oil spill, the writer might want to describe the damage the spill caused as well as explain the cleanup process step by step.

Comparison and Contrast   Comparison and contrast is used to point out the similarities and differences between two or more subjects in the same class or category. The function of any comparison and contrast is to clarify — to reach some conclusion about the items being compared and contrasted. See the introduction to Chapter 19 (pp. 483–87) for a detailed discussion of comparison and contrast.

Conclusions   See *Beginnings and Endings*.

Concrete/Abstract   A concrete word names a specific object, person, place, or action that can be directly perceived by the senses, such as *car, bread, building, book, John F. Kennedy, Chicago,* or *hiking*. An abstract word, in contrast, refers to general qualities, conditions, ideas, actions, or relationships that cannot be directly perceived by the senses, such as *bravery, dedication, excellence, anxiety, stress, thinking,* or *hatred*. See the introduction to Chapter 11 (pp. 283–87) for more on abstract and concrete words.

Connotation/Denotation   Both connotation and denotation refer to the meanings of words. Denotation is the dictionary meaning of a word, the literal meaning. Connotation, on the other hand, is the implied or suggested meaning of a word. For example, the denotation of *lamb* is "a young sheep." The connotations of *lamb* are numerous: *gentle, docile, weak, peaceful, blessed, sacrificial, blood, spring, frisky, pure, innocent,* and so on. See the introduction to Chapter 11 (pp. 283–87) for more on connotation and denotation.

Controlling Idea　See *Thesis*.

Coordination　Coordination is the joining of grammatical constructions of the same rank (e.g., words, phrases, clauses) to indicate that they are of equal importance. For example, *"They ate hot dogs,* and *we ate hamburgers."* See the introduction to Chapter 9 (pp. 217–21) for more on coordination. See also *Subordination*.

Deduction　Deduction is the process of reasoning from stated premises to a conclusion that follows necessarily. This form of reasoning moves from the general to the specific. See the introduction to Chapter 21 (pp. 539–46) for a discussion of deductive reasoning and its role in argumentation. See also *Syllogism*.

Definition　Definition is a rhetorical pattern. Definition is a statement of the meaning of a word. A definition may be either brief or extended, part of an essay or an entire essay itself. See the introduction to Chapter 17 (pp. 444–46) for a detailed discussion of definition.

Denotation　See *Connotation/Denotation*.

Description　Description tells how a person, place, or thing is perceived by the five senses. See the introduction to Chapter 15 (pp. 400–401) for a detailed discussion of description.

Details　Details are the small elements that collectively contribute to the overall impression of a person, place, thing, or idea. For example, in the sentence "The *organic, whole-grain* dog biscuits were *reddish brown, beef flavored,* and in the *shape of a bone,*" the italicized words are details.

Dialogue　Dialogue is the conversation of two or more people as represented in writing. Dialogue is what people say directly to one another.

Diction　Diction refers to a writer's choice and use of words. Good diction is precise and appropriate: The words mean exactly what the writer intends, and the words are well suited to the writer's subject, intended audience, and purpose in writing. The word-conscious writer knows that there are differences among *aged, old,* and *elderly; blue, navy,* and *azure;* and *disturbed, angry,* and *irritated.* Furthermore, this writer knows in which situation to use each word. See the introduction to Chapter 11 (pp. 283–87) for a detailed discussion of diction. See also *Cliché; Colloquial Expression; Connotation/Denotation; Jargon; Slang*.

Direct Quotation Material borrowed word for word that must be placed within quotation marks and properly cited.

Division and Classification Division and classification are rhetorical patterns used by the writer first to establish categories and then to arrange or sort people, places, or things into these categories according to their different characteristics, thus making them more manageable for the writer and more understandable and meaningful for the reader. See the introduction to Chapter 18 (pp. 461–64) for a detailed discussion of division and classification.

Documentation The act or the instance of supplying documents or references as to where they may be found.

Dominant Impression A dominant impression is the single mood, atmosphere, or quality a writer emphasizes in a piece of descriptive writing. The dominant impression is created through the careful selection of details and is, of course, influenced by the writer's subject, audience, and purpose. See the introduction to Chapter 15 (pp. 400–401) for more on dominant impression.

Emphasis Emphasis is the placement of important ideas and words within sentences and longer units of writing so that they have the greatest impact. In general, what comes at the end has the most impact, and at the beginning nearly as much; what comes in the middle gets the least emphasis.

Endings See *Beginnings and Endings.*

Evaluation An evaluation of a piece of writing is an assessment of its effectiveness or merit. In evaluating a piece of writing, one should ask the following questions: What is the writer's purpose? Is it a worthwhile purpose? Does the writer achieve the purpose? Is the writer's information sufficient and accurate? What are the strengths of the essay? What are its weaknesses? Depending on the type of writing and the purpose, more specific questions can also be asked. For example, with an argument one could ask: Does the writer follow the principles of logical thinking? Is the writer's evidence sufficient and convincing?

Evidence Evidence is the information on which a judgment or argument is based or by which proof or probability is established. Evidence usually takes the form of statistics, facts, names, examples or illustrations, and opinions of authorities.

Example   An example illustrates a larger idea or represents something of which it is a part. An example is a basic means of developing or clarifying an idea. Furthermore, examples enable writers to show and not simply to tell readers what they mean. See the introduction to Chapter 13 (pp. 339–42) for more on example.

Facts   Facts are pieces of information presented as having objective reality—that is, having actual existence. For example, water boils at 212°F, Katharine Hepburn died in 2003, and the USSR no longer exists—these are all facts.

Fallacy   See *Logical Fallacy.*

Figure of Speech   A figure of speech is a brief, imaginative comparison that highlights the similarities between things that are basically dissimilar. Figures of speech make writing vivid, interesting, and memorable. The most common figures of speech are:

> *Simile:* An explicit comparison introduced by *like* or *as.* "The fighter's hands were like stone."
> *Metaphor:* An implied comparison that makes one thing the equivalent of another. "All the world's a stage."
> *Personification:* A special kind of figure of speech in which human traits are assigned to ideas or objects. "The engine coughed and then stopped."

See the introduction to Chapter 12 (pp. 314–15) for a detailed discussion of figurative language.

Focus   Focus is the limitation a writer gives his or her subject. The writer's task is to select a manageable topic given the constraints of time, space, and purpose. For example, within the general subject of sports, a writer could focus on government support of amateur athletes or narrow the focus further to government support of Olympic athletes.

General   See *Specific/General.*

Idiom   An idiom is a word or phrase that is used habitually with special meaning. The meaning of an idiom is not always readily apparent to nonnative speakers of that language. For example, *catch cold, hold a job, make up your mind,* and *give them a hand* are all idioms in English.

Illustration   Illustration is the use of examples to explain, elucidate, or corroborate. Writers rely heavily on illustration to make their ideas both clear and concrete. See the introduction to Chapter 13 (pp. 339–42) for a detailed discussion of illustration.

Induction Induction is the process of reasoning to a conclusion about all members of a class through an examination of only a few members of the class. This form of reasoning moves from the particular to the general. See the introduction to Chapter 21 (pp. 539–46) for a discussion of inductive reasoning and its role in argumentation.

Inductive Leap An inductive leap is the point at which a writer of an argument, having presented sufficient evidence, moves to a generalization or conclusion. See also *Induction*.

Introduction See *Beginnings and Endings*.

Irony Irony is the use of words to suggest something different from their literal meaning. For example, when Jonathan Swift suggested in "A Modest Proposal" that Ireland's problems could be solved if the people of Ireland fattened their babies and sold them to the English landlords for food, he meant that almost any other solution would be preferable. A writer can use irony to establish a special relationship with the reader and to add an extra dimension or twist to the meaning. See the introduction to Chapter 11 (pp. 283–87) for more on irony.

Jargon Jargon, or technical language, is the special vocabulary of a trade, profession, or group. Doctors, construction workers, lawyers, and teachers, for example, all have a specialized vocabulary that they use on the job. See also *Diction*.

Logical Fallacy A logical fallacy is an error in reasoning that renders an argument invalid. See the introduction to Chapter 21 (pp. 539–46) for a discussion of common logical fallacies.

Metaphor See *Figure of Speech*.

Narration To narrate is to tell a story, to tell what happened. Although narration is most often used in fiction, it is also important in expository writing, either by itself or in conjunction with other types of prose. See the introduction to Chapter 14 (pp. 372–75) for a detailed discussion of narration.

Opinion An opinion is a belief or conclusion, which may or may not be substantiated by positive knowledge or proof. (If not substantiated, an opinion is a prejudice.) Even when based on evidence and sound reasoning, an opinion is personal and can be changed and is therefore less persuasive than facts and arguments.

Organization   Organization is the pattern or order the writer imposes on his or her material. Some often-used patterns of organization include time order, space order, and order of importance. See the introduction to Chapter 5 (pp. 119–23) for a detailed discussion of organization.

Paradox   A paradox is a seemingly contradictory statement that is nonetheless true. For example, "We little know what we have until we lose it" is a paradoxical statement.

Paragraph   The paragraph, the single most important unit of thought in an essay, is a series of closely related sentences. These sentences adequately develop the central or controlling idea of the paragraph. This central idea, usually stated in a topic sentence, is necessarily related to the purpose of the whole composition. A well-written paragraph has several distinguishing characteristics: a clearly stated or implied topic sentence, adequate development, unity, coherence, and an appropriate organizational strategy. See the introduction to Chapter 7 (pp. 172–75) for a detailed discussion of paragraphs.

Parallelism   Parallel structure is the repetition of word order or grammatical form either within a single sentence or in several sentences that develop the same central idea. As a rhetorical device, parallelism can aid coherence and add emphasis. Franklin Roosevelt's statement "I see one-third of a nation ill-housed, ill-clad, and ill-nourished" illustrates effective parallelism. See the introduction to Chapter 9 (pp. 217–21) for more on parallelism.

Paraphrase   A restatement of the information a writer is borrowing. A paraphrase closely parallels the presentation of ideas in the original, but it does not use the same words or sentence structure. See also *Direct Quotation, Plagiarism,* and *Summary.*

Perhapsing   To use speculative material when the facts necessary to develop a work of nonfiction are not known or available to the writer. See "Thinking Critically about This Reading" in Erin Murphy's "White Lies" (p. 383). For more discussion, see Lisa Knopp's brief explanation of how Maxine Hong Kingston uses the technique in *Woman Warrior* in "'Perhapsing': The Use of Speculation in Creative Nonfiction" in *Brevity: A Journal of Concise Literary Nonfiction* (http://www.creativenonfiction.org/brevity/craft/craft_knopp1_09.htm).

Personification   See *Figure of Speech*.

Persuasion   Persuasion, or persuasive argument, is an attempt to convince readers to agree with a point of view, to make a decision, or to pursue a particular course of action. Persuasion appeals strongly to the emotions, whereas logical argument does not.

Plagiarism   The use of someone else's ideas in their original form or in an altered form without proper documentation. Writers avoid plagiarism by (1) putting direct quotations within quotation marks and properly citing them and (2) documenting any idea, explanation, or argument that is borrowed and presented in a summary or paraphrase, making it clear where the borrowed material begins and ends. See also *Direct Quotation, Paraphrase,* and *Summary.*

Point of View   Point of view refers to the grammatical person in an essay. For example, the first-person point of view uses the pronoun *I* and is commonly found in autobiography and the personal essay; the third-person point of view uses the pronouns *he, she,* or *it* and is commonly found in objective writing. See the introduction to Chapter 14 (pp. 372–75) for a discussion of point of view in narration.

Process Analysis   Process analysis is a rhetorical strategy used to explain how something works or to give step-by-step directions for doing something. See the introduction to Chapter 16 (pp. 423–26) for a detailed discussion of process analysis.

Purpose   Purpose is what the writer wants to accomplish in a particular piece of writing. Purposeful writing seeks to *tell* (narration), to *describe* (description), to *explain* (process analysis, definition, classification, comparison and contrast, and cause and effect), or to *convince* (argumentation).

Rhetorical Modes   Spoken or written strategies for presenting subjects, the most common of which are argument, cause and effect, comparison and contrast, definition, description, division and classification, exemplification, narration, and process analysis.

Rhetorical Question   A rhetorical question is asked for its rhetorical effect but requires no answer from the reader. "When will nuclear proliferation end?" is such a question. Writers use rhetorical questions to introduce topics they plan to discuss or to emphasize important points. See the introduction to Chapter 6 (p. 150) for another example.

Sentence   A sentence is a grammatical unit that expresses a complete thought. It consists of at least a subject (a noun) and a predicate (a verb). See the introduction to Chapter 9 (pp. 217–21) for a detailed discussion of effective sentences.

Signal Phrase   A phrase alerting the reader that borrowed information follows. A signal phrase usually consists of an author's name and a verb (for example, "Coughlan argues" or "Yadav disagrees") and helps integrate direct quotations, paraphrases, and summaries into the flow of a paper. A signal phrase tells the reader who is speaking and indicates exactly where your ideas end and your source's begin.

Simile   See *Figure of Speech.*

Slang   Slang is the unconventional, informal language of particular subgroups in our culture. Slang terms, such as *bummed, sweat, dark,* and *cool,* are acceptable in formal writing only if used selectively for specific purposes.

Specific/General   General words name groups or classes of objects, qualities, or actions. Specific words, on the other hand, name individual objects, qualities, or actions within a class or group. To some extent the terms *general* and *specific* are relative. For example, *clothing* is a class of things. *Shirt,* however, is more specific than *clothing* but more general than *T-shirt.* See also *Diction.*

Strategy   A strategy is a means by which a writer achieves his or her purpose. Strategy includes the many rhetorical decisions the writer makes about organization, paragraph structure, sentence structure, and diction. In terms of the whole essay, strategy refers to the principal rhetorical mode a writer uses. If, for example, a writer wishes to explain how to make chocolate chip cookies, the most effective strategy would be process analysis. If it is the writer's purpose to analyze why sales of American cars have declined in recent years, the most effective strategy would be cause-and-effect analysis.

Style   Style is the individual manner in which a writer expresses his or her ideas. Style is created by the author's particular choice of words, construction of sentences, and arrangement of ideas.

Subordination   Subordination is the use of grammatical constructions to make one part of a sentence dependent on, rather than equal to, another. For example, the italicized clause in the following sentence is subordinate: "They all cheered *when I finished the race.*" See the introduction to Chapter 9 (pp. 217–21) for more on subordination. See also *Coordination.*

Summary A condensed form of the essential idea of a passage, article, or entire chapter. A summary is always shorter than the original. See also *Paraphrase, Plagiarism,* and *Direct Quotation.*

Supporting Evidence See *Evidence.*

Syllogism A syllogism is an argument that uses deductive reasoning and consists of a major premise, a minor premise, and a conclusion:

All trees that lose leaves are deciduous. (*Major premise*)
Maple trees lose their leaves. (*Minor premise*)
Therefore, maple trees are deciduous. (*Conclusion*)

See pages 541 and 543 in Chapter 21 for more on syllogisms. See also *Deduction.*

Symbol A symbol is a person, place, or thing that represents something beyond itself. For example, the bald eagle is a symbol of the United States, and the maple leaf is a symbol of Canada.

Syntax Syntax refers to the way in which words are arranged to form phrases, clauses, and sentences, as well as to the grammatical relationship among the words themselves.

Technical Language See *Jargon.*

Thesis The thesis, also known as the controlling idea, is the main idea of an essay. It may sometimes be implied rather than stated directly. See the introduction to Chapter 3 (pp. 81–83) for more on the thesis statement.

Title A title is a word or phrase set off at the beginning of an essay to identify the subject, to state the main idea of the essay, or to attract the reader's attention. A title may be explicit or suggestive. A subtitle, when used, explains or restricts the meaning of the main title.

Tone Tone is the manner in which a writer relates to an audience, the "tone of voice" used to address readers. Tone may be friendly, serious, distant, angry, humorous, cheerful, bitter, cynical, enthusiastic, morbid, resentful, warm, playful, and so forth. A particular tone results from a writer's diction, sentence structure, purpose, and attitude toward the subject. See the introduction to Chapter 11 (pp. 283–87) for several examples that display different tones.

Topic Sentence   The topic sentence states the central idea of a paragraph and thus limits the content of the paragraph. Although the topic sentence normally appears at the beginning of the paragraph, it may appear at any other point, particularly if the writer is trying to create a special effect. Not all paragraphs contain topic sentences. See also *Paragraph.*

Transition   A transition is a word or phrase that links sentences, paragraphs, and larger units of a composition to achieve coherence. Transitions include parallelism, pronoun references, conjunctions, and the repetition of key ideas, as well as the many conventional transitional expressions such as *moreover, on the other hand, in addition, in contrast,* and *therefore.* See the introduction to Chapter 8 (pp. 193–96) for a detailed discussion of transitions. See also *Coherence.*

Unity   Unity is that quality of oneness in an essay that results when all the words, sentences, and paragraphs contribute to the thesis. The elements of a unified essay do not distract the reader. Instead, they all harmoniously support a single idea or purpose. See the introduction to Chapter 4 (pp. 99–102) for a detailed discussion of unity.

Verb   Verbs can be classified as either strong verbs (*scream, pierce, gush, ravage,* and *amble*) or weak verbs (*be, has, get,* and *do*). Writers prefer to use strong verbs to make their writing more specific, more descriptive, and more action filled.

Voice   Verbs can be classified as being in either the active or the passive voice. In the *active voice,* the doer of the action is the grammatical subject. In the *passive voice,* the receiver of the action is the subject:

> *Active:* Glenda questioned all of the children.
> *Passive:* All the children were questioned by Glenda.

Writing Process   The writing process is the sequence of activities that most writers follow most of the time when composing a written work. It consists of four stages:

> *Prewriting:* The stage in the writing process in which you select your subject and topic, gather ideas and information, and determine the thesis and organization pattern or patterns of a written work.

Drafting: The process of creating the first version of your writing in which you lay out your ideas and information and through revision subsequently prepare more focused and polished versions referred to as second and third drafts, and more if necessary.

Revision: The stage in the writing process in which you reconsider and possibly change the large elements of your writing, such as thesis, purpose, content, organization, and paragraph structure.

Editing: The stage in the writing process in which you reconsider and possibly change the small elements of your writing, such as grammar, punctuation, mechanics, and spelling.

Acknowledgments

Diane Ackerman. "Why Leaves Turn Color in the Fall." Copyright © 1990 by Diane Ackerman. Reprinted by permission of William Morris Agency, LLC, on behalf of the author.

Maya Angelou, "Momma, the Dentist, and Me." From *I Know Why the Caged Bird Sings.* Copyright © 1969 and renewed 1997 by Maya Angelou. Used by permission of Random House, Inc.

Tina McElroy Ansa. "The Center of the Universe" by Tina McElroy Ansa. Copyright © 2003 by Tina McElroy Ansa. Reprinted by permission of the author.

Isaac Asimov. "What Is Intelligence, Anyway?" Published by the permission of the Asimov Estate c/o Ralph M. Vicinanza Ltd, via Trident Media Group, LLC. All rights reserved.

Nicholson Baker. "Recipe." Copyright © 1996 by Nicholson Baker. From *The Size of Thoughts* by Nicholson Baker. Used by permission of Random House, Inc. Copyright © 1996 by Nicolson Baker. From *The Size of Thoughts* (Random House). Reprinted with permission of Melanie Jackson Agency, LLC.

Russell Baker. "Becoming a Writer." Excerpt from Chapter 2 of *Growing Up.* Copyright © 1982 by Russell Baker. Reprinted with the permission of Don Congdon Associates, Inc.

Sharon Begley. "Praise the Humble Dung Beetle." From *Newsweek* (June 9, 2008). Copyright © 2008 by *Newsweek, Inc.* All rights reserved. Used by permission and protected by the Copyright Laws of the United States. The printing, copying, redistribution, or retransmission of the Material without express written permission is prohibited.

Suzanne Britt. "That Lean and Hungry Look." From *Newsweek*, October 9, 1978. Reprinted by permission of the author.

Carl Cannon. "Petty Crime, Outrageous Punishment" by Carl M. Cannon. Reprinted with permission from *Reader's Digest.* Copyright © 2005 by The Reader's Digest Association, Inc.

Rachel Carson. "Fable for Tomorrow." From *Silent Spring.* Copyright © 1962 by Rachel L. Carson. Copyright © renewed 1990 by Roger Christie. Used by permission of Houghton Mifflin Harcourt Publishing Company. All rights reserved.

Sandra Cisneros. From *The House on Mango Street.* Copyright © 1984 by Sandra Cisneros. Published by Vintage Books, a division of Random House, Inc., and in hardcover by Alfred A. Knopf in 1994. By permission of Susan Bergholz Literary Services, New York, NY, and Lamy, NM. All Rights Reserved.

Judith Ortiz Cofer. "Volar" is reprinted with permission from the publisher of *Riding Low on the Streets of Gold: Latino Literature for Young Adults* by Judith Ortiz Cofer. (© 2003 Arte Publico Press—University of Houston.)

James Lincoln Collier. "Anxiety: Challenge by Another Name." From *Reader's Digest* (December 1986). Reprinted with the permission of the author.

Brian Doyle. "Irreconcilable Dissonance" by Brian Doyle. *Oregon Humanities:* Summer 2009. Reprinted with the permission of the author and publisher *Oregon Humanities Magazine.*

Lawrence M. Friedman. "What Is Crime?" From *Crime and Punishment in American History.* Copyright © 1993 by Lawrence M. Friedman. Reprinted with the permission of Basic Books, a member of Perseus Books Group, LLC.

Thomas L. Friedman. "My Favorite Teacher." From *The New York Times* (January 9, 2001). Copyright © 2001 by *The New York Times Company.* All rights reserved. Used by permission and protected by the Copyright Laws of the United States. The printing, copying, redistribution, or retransmission of the Material without express written permission is prohibited.

Henry Louis Gates, Jr. "What's in a Name?" From *Dissent*, Volume 36, No. 4, Fall 1989. Reprinted with the permission of the Foundation for the Study of Independent Social Ideas.

Nancy Gibbs. "The Magic of the Family Meal." From *Time* (June 12, 2006). Copyright © 2006 by *Time, Inc.* Reprinted with permission.

Natalie Goldberg. "Be Specific." From *Writing Down the Bones: Freeing the Writer Within* by Natalie Goldberg. © Copyright 1986 by Natalie Goldberg. Reprinted by arrangement with Shambhala Publications, Inc., Boston, MA. www.shambhala.com.

Gita Mehta. "The Famine of Bengal." Copyright © 1998 by Gita Mehta. Reprinted with the permission of the author.

Paul W. Merrill. "The Principles of Poor Writing." From *The Scientific Monthly*, Vol. 64, No. 1 (Jan 1947). Reprinted with permission from SCIENCE/AAAS.

Kyoko Mori. "Yarn." From *The Harvard Review*, No. 24 (Spring, 2003). Copyright © Kyoko Mori. Reprint with the permission of the author and Harvard Review.

Bharati Mukherjee. "Two Ways to Belong in America" by Bharati Mukherjee. Copyright © 1996 by Bharati Mukherjee. Originally published in the *New York Times*. Reprinted by permission of the author.

Erin Murphy. "White Lies." From *Brevity33* (First appeared in May 2010 issue). Reprinted with the permission of the author.

Gloria Naylor. "The Meanings of a Word." From *The New York Times* (February 20, 1986). Copyright © 1986 by Gloria Naylor. Reprinted with the permission of SLL/Sterling Lord Literistic, Inc.

Terry O'Reilly. "Marketing Ate Our Culture—But It Doesn't Have To." From *AlterNet*. Copyright © 2010 Independent Media Institute. Reprinted with the permission of the author.

Gregory Pence. "Let's Think Outside the Box of Bad Cliches." From *Newsweek* (August 6, 2007). Copyright © 2007 by Newsweek, Inc. Used by permission and protected by the Copyright Laws of the United States. The printing, copying, redistribution, or retransmission of the Material without express written permission is prohibited.

Benjamin Percy. "Invasion" by Benjamin Percy. Copyright © 2010 by Benjamin Percy. First appeared in *Fugue*. Reprinted by permission of Curtis Brown, Ltd.

Steven Pinker. "In Defense of Dangerous Ideas." From *What Is Your Dangerous Idea?: Today's Leading Thinkers on the Unthinkable*, edited by John Brockman. Copyright © 2007 by Edge Foundation, Inc. Reprinted by permission of HarperCollins Publishers.

Eduardo Porter. From *The Price of Everything* by Eduardo Porter. Copyright © 2011 by Eduardo Porter. Used by permission of Portfolio, an imprint of Penguin Group (USA) Inc.

Sean Prentiss. "Buying a House." From *Sou'Wester*, Vol. 38, No. 2 (Spring 2010). Reprinted with the permission of the author.

Robert Ramirez. "The Barrio" (original title "The Woolen Serape"). From *Pain and Promise: The Chicano Today*, edited by Edward Simmens (New York: New American Library, 1972). Reprinted with the permission of the author.

David Raymond. "On Being 17, Bright, and Unable to Read." From *The New York Times* (April 25, 1976). Copyright © 1976 by The New York Times Company. Used by permission and protected by the Copyright Laws of the United States. The printing, copying, redistribution, or retransmission of the Material without express written permission is prohibited.

Amanda Ripley. "Who Says a Woman Can't Be Einstein?" *Time Magazine*, Sunday, Feb 27, 2005. Copyright TIME INC. Reprinted by permission. TIME is a registered trademark of Time Inc. All rights reserved.

Mike Rose. "I Just Wanna Be Average." From *Lives on the Boundary: Struggles and Achievements of America's Underprepared*. Copyright © 1989 by Mike Rose. Reprinted with the permission of The Free Press, a division of Simon & Schuster, Inc. All rights reserved.

Carl T. Rowan. "Unforgettable Miss Bessie." From *Reader's Digest*. Reprinted with permission from Reader's Digest. Copyright © 1985 by The Reader's Digest.

Salman Rushdie. "The Taj Mahal." From *Step Across the Line* by Salman Rushdie. Copyright © 2002 by Salman Rushdie. Used by permission of Random House, Inc.

Audrey Schulman. "Fahrenheit 59: What a Child's Fever Might Tell Us about Climate Change." Copyright by permission of the author.

David Sedaris. "Me Talk Pretty One Day." From *Me Talk Pretty One Day*. Copyright © 2000 by David Sedaris. Reprinted by permission of Little, Brown & Company and Don Congdon Associates, Inc. First published in *Esquire Magazine* and reprinted by permission of Don Congdon Associates, Inc. Copyright © 1999 David Sedaris.

Sherry, Mary. "In Praise of the F Word." From *Newsweek*, May 6, 1991. Copyright © 1991 by Mary Sherry. Reprinted by permission of the author.

Photo Credits

Page 208: Nancy Gibbs. Diana Walker/Getty Images.

Page 216: *Family Dinner*. © Michael Elins/CORBIS.

Page 222: Alice Walker. Noah Berger/AP Photo.

Page 228: Langston Hughes. CORBIS.

Page 233: Judith Ortiz Cofer. Miriam Berkley.

Page 255: Sharon Begley. Courtesy of Sharon Begley.

Page 260: *Beetle*. Mark Moffett/Minden.

Page 260: *Polar Bear*. Alfred Rosa.

Page 269: Terry Tempest Williams. Lyon Goldsmith/CORBIS.

Page 288: Dick Gregory. Ethan Miller/Getty Images.

Page 294: David Sedaris. Ralph Orlowski/Getty Images.

Page 301: *Cartoon*. ©David Sipress/The New Yorker Collection/CartoonBank.com.

Page 302: Tina McElroy Ansa. Courtesy of Jonee Ansa.

Page 308: Brian Doyle. ©László Bencze.

Page 316: Robert Ramirez. Courtesy of Robert Ramirez.

Page 322: *Barrio mural*. ©Peter Menzel/Stock Boston, Inc.

Page 323: Anne Lamott. Mark Richards.

Page 329: Benjamin Percy. Miriam Berkley.

Page 335: *House under construction*. ©Philip Wegener/Beateworks/CORBIS.

Page 354: *Cartoon*. ©Clive Goddard/CartoonStock.com.

Page 355: Verlyn Klinkenborg. Fred Conrad/Redux.

Page 361: Steven Pinker. David Levenson/Getty Images.

Page 376: Henry Louis Gates Jr. ©Marc Brasz/CORBIS.

Page 381: Erin Murphy. Courtesy of Erin Murphy.

Page 386: Maya Angelou. Syracuse Newspapers/The Image Works.

Page 395: Kate Chopin. The Granger Collection.

Page 402: Eudora Welty. Philip Gould/CORBIS.

Page 406: *Train Station*. Alfred Rosa.

Page 407: Joanne Lipman. Sipa/Newscom.

Page 412: Kyoko Mori. Miriam Berkley.

Page 419: Salman Rushdie. Eric Fougers/CORBIS.

Page 422: *Taj Mahal*. iStockphoto.com.

Page 425: *Bill graphic*. Nigel Holmes.

Page 427: Paul W. Merrill. Rick Friedman/CORBIS.

Page 433: Nicholson Baker. Bob Daemmrich/CORBIS.

Page 437: *Astro tube graphic*. ©Peter Steiner/The New Yorker Collection/CartoonBank.com.

Page 438: Diane Ackerman. Bob Daemmrich/CORBIS.

Page 447: Lawrence M. Friedman. Courtesy of Lawrence M. Friedman.

Page 451: Ellen Goodman. ©Bettmann/CORBIS.

Page 455: *Cartoon*. ©Charles Barsotti/The New Yorker Collection/CartoonBank.com.

Page 456: Eduardo Porter. Miriam Berkley.

Page 465: Martin Luther King Jr. ©Bettmann/CORBIS.

Index

a, basics of, 30–31
"The Abolition of Torture" (Sullivan),
629–40
abstract words, 284
academic departments/courses, online,
citation of, 665
academic writing, diction and tone for,
28–30
Ackerman, Diane, "Why Leaves Turn
Color in the Fall," 438–42
active reading, 43, 57–58. *See also* reading
active voice, 220
Addams, Charles, 492
addition, words and phrases for, 193
addresses, citation of, 666
advertisements, citation of, 666
"after this, therefore because of this"
fallacy, 520, 544
afterword, citation of, 660
Aldrich, Lance, 476
Allen, Woody, 286
Alvarado, Hilda, 341–42
Ambrose, Stephen E., *Crazy Horse and
Custer: The Parallel Lives of Two
American Warriors*, 502–3
American Psychological Association
(APA) style, 654
American Standard English, 28
an, basics of, 30–31
analogies
beginning with, 146–47
false, 544
understanding, 486–87
and
keyword searches and, 646
pronoun-antecedent agreement and,
25
anecdotes
beginning with, 146
as narration, 372
Angell, Roger, 121
Angelou, Maya, "Momma, the Dentist,
and Me," 386–93

angry tone, 286, 287
annotating text, 47–51
anonymous article, citation of, 658
anonymous book, citation of, 660
Ansa, Tina McElroy, "The Center of the
Universe," 302–6
antecedents, pronoun-antecedent
agreement and, 24–25
anthology, citation of, 659
"Anxiety: Challenge by Another Name"
(Collier), 1, 94–97
APA style, 654
apology, beginning with, 150
argument, 539–641
description of, 15
readings
"The Abolition of Torture"
(Sullivan), 629–40
"Condemn the Crime, Not the
Person" (Tangney), 569–72
"The Declaration of Independence"
(Jefferson), 547–51
"Generation E. A.: Ethnically
Ambiguous" (La Ferla), 602–7
"I Have a Dream" (King Jr.), 553–57
"In Praise of the F Word" (Sherry),
564–66
"Marketing Ate Our Culture—But
It Doesn't Have To" (O'Reilly),
594–99
"Petty Crime, Outrageous
Punishment" (Cannon), 579–84
"The Piracy of Privacy: Why
Marketers Must Bare Our Souls"
(Kanner), 587–91
"Shame Is Worth a Try" (Kahan),
574–76
"The Truth about Torture"
(Krauthammer), 616–26
"What Pro Sports Owners Owe Us"
(Zirin), 560–62
student example of, 73–77
thinking critically about, 545–46

argument (*contd.*)
 understanding, 539–41
 writing, 541–45
argumentation, 539. *See also* argument
argument synthesis, 248
articles. *See also* journal articles; magazine
  articles; newspaper articles
 evaluating, 648–49
 in working bibliography, 652
articles (*a, an, the*), basics of, 30–31
artwork, citation of, 664, 666
as
 parallelism and, 27
 similes and, 314
Asimov, Isaac, 465
 "Intelligence"
  annotation of, 49–51
  headnote for, 45–46
  writing prompt for, 46
assignment, understanding, 8–9
asterisk, keyword searches and, 646
audience
 argument and, 542
 determining, 14
 pathos and, 546
audio recording, citation of, 665
author
 in-text citation of, 655–56
 in signal phrases, 246–47

Bachman, Benjamin B., 314
Baker, Nicholson, "How to Make
  Chocolate Sauce," 433–35
Baker, Russell, "Becoming a Writer," 1,
  203–6
Bardeen, David P., 23
"The Barrio" (Ramirez), 316–20
Barsotti, Charles, 455
"Becoming a Writer" (Baker), 1, 203–6
begging the question, 544
beginnings, 145–71
 citation of, 660
 focusing on, 19–20
 readings
  "The Case for Short Words"
   (Lederer), 160–63
  "Of My Friend Hector and My
   Achilles Heel" (Kaufman), 154–57
  "Unforgettable Miss Bessie"
   (Rowan), 166–70
 understanding, 145–50

Begley, Sharon, "Praise the Humble Dung
  Beetle," 255–57
"Be Specific" (Goldberg), 90–92
bibliography, working, 651–53
biographical notes
 example of, 45
 getting information from, 44
blog postings, citation of, 665
Blue, Heather C., 286
book review, citation of, 658, 662
books
 citation of, 659, 660
 evaluating, 648
 online, citation of, 664
 in working bibliography, 652
Borland, Hal, 315
 "October," 327–28
both . . . and, parallelism and, 27
"A Bowl of Noodles" (Chu), 68–72
Bowman, Barbara, "Guns and Cameras,"
  485–86
braille alphabet, 88–89
brainstorming
 student example of, 33–34
 for titles, 19
 for topic ideas, 11
Brandeis, Louis, 371
Briggs, Will, 221
Britt, Suzanne, 149
 "That Lean and Hungry Look,"
  499–502
Britto, Marah, "The Qualities of Good
  Teachers," 248–49
brochure, citation of, 660
Bryson, Bill, 518–19
Bubany, Dan, 401
"Burdens of the Modern Beast" (Weeks),
  359–60
Burns, Betty, 99
Burrell, Leon F., *The Other America*, 267
"Buying a House" (Prentiss), 137–42

"Calvin and Hobbes" (Watterson),
  129, 130
Cannon, Carl M., "Petty Crime,
  Outrageous Punishment," 579–84
Carson, Rachel, 195
 "Fable for Tomorrow," 52–54
cartoons, citation of, 666
"The Case for Short Words" (Lederer),
  160–63, 242

"The Case of the Disappearing Rabbit"
(Huang), 239
categories, for division and classification,
464
Catton, Bruce, "Grant and Lee: A Study
in Contrasts," 252
causal analysis, 517. *See also* cause and effect
causal chain, 519–20
cause and effect, 517–38
description of, 15
readings
"The Famine of Bengal" (Mehta),
521–22
"Stuck on the Couch" (Gupta),
535–37
"Why and When We Speak Spanish
in Public" (Marquez), 531–33
"Why We Crave Horror Movies"
(King), 524–27
understanding, 517–20
words and phrases for, 193
CD-ROM, citation of, 667
"The Center of the Universe" (Ansa), 302–6
charts, online, citation of, 664
Chase, Stuart, "Overgeneralizing,"
100–101
Chessa, Freddy, 462
"Childhood" (Walker), 222–25
Chopin, Kate, "The Story of an Hour,"
395–98
chronological order, 119–21
Chu, Jennifer, "A Bowl of Noodles,"
67–72
Cisneros, Sandra, "My Name," 109–10
citation, 654. *See also* documenting
sources
citation manager, 651
claims, thesis statement as, 82
"The Clan of One-Breasted Women"
(Williams), 269–77
clarity, in process analysis, 426
classification, 461–82
description of, 15
readings
"Doubts about Doublespeak" (Lutz),
477–81
"The Ways of Meeting Oppression"
(King Jr.), 465–68
"What Are Friends For?" (Winik),
470–73
understanding, 461–65

clichés, 284–85
climactic order, 119
clustering
student example of, 34
for topic ideas, 11
Cofer, Judith Ortiz, "Volar," 233–35
coherence
within paragraph, 173, 174–75
transitions for, 195
Collier, James Lincoln, "Anxiety:
Challenge by Another Name,"
1, 94–97
Collins, Jim, 425, 426
.com, 649
comic strips, citation of, 666
comma splices, 21–22
Commoner, Barry, 120–21
common knowledge, documentation of,
251
"The Company Man" (Goodman),
451–53
comparison and contrast, 483–516
description of, 15
in "Fable for Tomorrow" (Carson),
55–56
readings
"That Lean and Hungry Look"
(Britt), 499–502
"Two Ways of Seeing a River"
(Twain), 488–90
"Two Ways to Belong in America"
(Mukherjee), 488–90
"Who Says a Woman Can't Be
Einstein?" (Ripley), 505–14
understanding, 483–87
comparisons. *See also* comparison and
contrast
beginning with, 146–47
words and phrases for, 193
complaint, beginning with, 150
complete thoughts, sentence fragments
and, 22–23
compound subjects, subject-verb
agreement and, 24
computer, proofreading with, 32
concession, words and phrases for, 193
conclusions. *See* endings
concrete words, 284
"Condemn the Crime, Not the Person"
(Tangney), 569–72
connotation, 283, 300

contrast. *See also* comparison and
    contrast
  definition of, 483
  words and phrases for, 193
Coontz, Stephanie, *The Way We Really
    Are: Coming to Terms with
    America's Changing Families*,
    240–41
coordinating conjunctions, 221
coordination, 221
"The Corner Store" (Welty), 402–5
corporate author, citation of, 659
Coughlan, Liz, 220
Council of Writing Program
    Administrators, on plagiarism, 251
counterarguments, 543
count nouns, 30–31
*Crazy Horse and Custer: The Parallel
    Lives of Two American Warriors*
    (Ambrose), 502–3
creative thinking, in prewriting process,
    11–12
credibility of author, argument and,
    545–46
A Crime of Compassion (Huttmann),
    343–46, 372
Cunningham, Kevin, 517–18

dangling modifiers, 26–27
databases
  documenting, 662–63
  keyword searches in, 646
Davis, Corey, 315
Davis, Flora, 82
"The Declaration of Independence"
    (Jefferson), 547–51
deductive reasoning, 541
definite articles, 30–31
definition, 444–60
  beginning with, 150
  description of, 15
  readings
    "The Company Man" (Goodman),
      451–53
    "What Happiness Is" (Porter),
      456–59
    "What Is Crime?" (Friedman),
      447–49
  understanding, 444–46
denotation, 283

dependent clauses, 218–19
description, 400–422
  description of, 15
  readings
    "The Corner Store" (Welty), 402–5
    "And the Orchestra Played On"
      (Lipman), 407–10
    "The Taj Mahal" (Rushdie), 419–21
    "Yarn" (Mori), 412–16
  understanding, 400–401
development, of paragraph, 173–74
dialogue, beginning with, 147–48
diction, 283–313
  academic, 28–30
  readings
    "The Center of the Universe" (Ansa),
      302–6
    "Irreconcilable Dissonance" (Doyle),
      308–11
    "Me Talk Pretty One Day" (Sedaris),
      294–99
    "Shame" (Gregory), 288–92
  understanding, 283–85
dictionary definition, beginning with, 150
digital files, citation of, 667
directional process analysis, 423–24
direct quotations
  avoiding plagiarism with, 254
  basics of, 241, 244–45
discipline-specific language, 29–30
division, 461–82
  description of, 15
  readings
    "Doubts about Doublespeak" (Lutz),
      477–81
    "The Ways of Meeting Oppression"
      (King Jr.), 465–68
    "What Are Friends For?" (Winik),
      470–73
  understanding, 461–65
documenting sources, 654–67
  in-text citations for, 655–56
  list of works cited for, 655, 656–67
    additional sources in, 665–67
    books, brochures and pamphlets in,
      659–61
    journals, magazines and newspapers
      in, 657–59
    web publications in, 661–65
dominant impression, 400

"Don't Let Stereotypes Warp Your
Judgments" (Heilbroner), 253, 267
"Doubts about Doublespeak" (Lutz),
477–81
Dove, Rita, "Loose Ends," 259
Doyle, Brian
on advice for aspiring writers, 312
"Irreconcilable Dissonance," 308–11
draft, first, writing, 18–20
dramatically short sentences, 220
Duffy, James, "One Dying Wish," 73–77
DVD-ROM, citation of, 667

editing, 21–31
for academic diction and tone, 28–30
for ESL concerns, 30–31
for faulty parallelism, 27
for misplaced and dangling modifiers,
26–27
for pronoun-antecedent agreement,
24–25
for run-on sentences, 21–22
for sentence fragments, 22–23
student example of, 37–38
for subject-verb agreement, 23–24
for verb tense shifts, 25–26
for weak nouns and verbs, 28
editorials, citation of, 658, 662
.edu, 649
effect, 517. *See also* cause and effect
either . . . or
parallelism and, 27
subject-verb agreement and, 24
either/or thinking, 544
Eldred, Keith, "Secular Mantras," 444
electronic research manager, 653
electronic sources. *See* Internet sources
Elins, Michael, 216
e-mails, citation of, 666–67
encyclopedia articles, online, citation of,
664
endings, 145–71
of argument, 544–45
in division and classification, 464
focusing on, 19–20
readings
"The Case for Short Words"
(Lederer), 160–63
"Of My Friend Hector and My
Achilles Heel" (Kaufman), 154–57

"Unforgettable Miss Bessie"
(Rowan), 166–70
understanding, 145, 151–53
English as Second Language, articles and
nouns and, 30–31
"The English-Only Movement: Can
America Proscribe Language with
a Clear Conscience?" (Jamieson),
261–66
Eschholz, Paul, 172–73
ESL concerns, articles and nouns and,
30–31
essays, online, citation of, 664
ethos, in argument, 545–46
evidence, in argument, 543
examples
in illustration, 339–42
words and phrases for, 193
"The Excuse 'Not To'" (Ockenga), 63–67
explanatory synthesis, 248
extended definitions, 445
extended metaphors, 315

"Fable for Tomorrow" (Carson), 52–54
facts
avoiding plagiarism and, 254
beginning with, 148
"The Fading Season," 327
"Fahrenheit 59: What a Child's Fever
Might Tell Us about Climate
Change" (Schulman), 131–34
false analogy, 544
"The Famine of Bengal" (Mehta),
521–22
faulty reasoning, in argument, 544
Federman, Sarah, 147–48
Fenton, Patrick, 286–87
Ferguson, Andrew, "How Marijuana Got
Mainstreamed," 239–40
figurative language, 314–35
readings
"The Barrio" (Ramirez), 316–20
"Invasion" (Percy), 329–33
"Polaroids" (Lamott), 323–26
understanding, 314–15
figures of speech. *See* figurative language
film, citation of, 666
film review, citation of, 658
first draft, writing, 18–20
first-person point of view, 373–74

first-person pronouns
  antecedents and, 25
  informal writing and, 29
flashback, 374–75
For All Mankind (Reinhert), 279
foreword, citation of, 660
formal definitions, of words, 445
formal diction, 285
formal writing, diction and tone for,
  28–39
fragments, 22–23
Friedman, Lawrence M., "What Is
  Crime?" 447–49
Friedman, Thomas L., "My Favorite
  Teacher," 103–5
fused sentences, 21–22

Garrison, Roger, 146–47
Gates Jr., Henry Louis, "What's in a
  Name?" 376–79
generalizations
  beginning with, 149
  hasty, 544
  illustration and, 340–41
general words, 284
"Generation E. A.: Ethnically
  Ambiguous" (La Ferla), 602–7
Gibbs, Nancy
  learning from writings of, 58
  "The Magic of the Family Meal,"
  208–13
Gladstone, Bernard
  "How to Build a Fire in a Fireplace,"
  111–12
  *The New York Times Complete Manual
  of Home Repair*, 201–2
Goddard, Clive, 237, 353–54
Goldberg, Natalie, "Be Specific," 90–92
"Golf: A Character Builder" (Olesky),
  38–42
Goodman, Ellen, "The Company Man,"
  451–53
good writing, characteristics of, 1
.gov, 649
government publications, citation of, 661,
  665
grammar, proofreading for, 32
"Grant and Lee: A Study in Contrasts"
  (Catton), 252
graphic novel, citation of, 660

Gregory, Dick, "Shame," 288–92
Guilbault, Rose Del Castillo, 151
"Guns and Cameras" (Bowman), 485–86
Gupta, Sanjay, "Stuck on the Couch,"
  535–37
Guthrie, Helen A., 82

Hall, Edward T., 339–40
Haney, William V., "The Uncritical
  Inference Test," 528–29
Harris, Sydney J., 487
Harvey, John H., 445–46
hasty generalizations, 544
he
  formal writing and, 28–39
  pronoun-antecedent agreement and, 25
headnote
  example of, 45
  getting information from, 44
Heilbroner, Robert L., "Don't Let
  Stereotypes Warp Your
  Judgments," 253, 267
Henderson, Lynne, "Shyness," 29–30
Hendrick, Richard, *The Voyage of the
  Mimi*, 278
Hitchcock, Alfred, *Psycho*, 529–30
Holmes, Nigel, 425, 426
Horton, Charley, "How Humans Affect
  Our Global Environment," 655–56
how, process analysis and, 423
"How Humans Affect Our Global
  Environment" (Horton), 655–56
"How Marijuana Got Mainstreamed"
  (Ferguson), 239–40
"How to Build a Fire in a Fireplace"
  (Gladstone), 111–12
"How to Make Chocolate Sauce" (Baker),
  433–35
Huang, Lily, "The Case of the
  Disappearing Rabbit," 239
Hughes, Langston, "Salvation," 228–30
humor, beginning with, 148–49
humorous tone, 286
Huttmann, Barbara, "A Crime of
  Compassion," 343–46, 372

I
  informal writing and, 29
  pronoun-antecedent agreement and, 25
  use of in narration, 18

ideas, getting for topic, 10–12
"I Have a Dream" (King Jr.), 553–57
"I Just Wanna Be Average" (Rose),
    183–86
illustrated book, citation of, 660
illustration, 339–71
    description of, 15
    readings
        "A Crime of Compassion"
            (Huttmann), 343–46
        "In Defense of Dangerous Ideas"
            (Pinker), 361–70
        "Let's Think Outside the Box of Bad
            Clichés" (Pence), 349–51
        "Our Vanishing Night"
            (Klinkenborg), 355–59
    understanding, 339–42
images, online, citation of, 664
immediate causes, 519
importance, order of, 121–23
"In Defense of Dangerous Ideas" (Pinker),
    361–70
indefinite articles, 30–31
indefinite pronouns, pronoun-antecedent
    agreement and, 25
inductive reasoning, 541
informal diction, 285
informal writing, diction and tone for, 29
information, collecting in prewriting
    process, 10–12
informational process analysis, 423,
    424–26
informational synthesis, 248
"In Praise of the F Word" (Sherry),
    564–66
"Intelligence" (Asimov)
    annotation of, 49–51
    headnote for, 45–46
    writing prompt for, 46
"Intensify/Downplay" (Rank), 609–11
Internet sources
    analyzing, 650–51
    documenting, 661–65
    evaluating, 648–50
    finding and using, 644–45
    keyword searches in, 646–47
    notes from, 245
    subject directories and, 647
    working bibliography for, 651–53
interviews, citation of, 666

in-text citations, 655–56
introductions. *See* beginnings
"Invasion" (Percy), 329–33
irony
    beginning with, 148–49
    in process analysis, 431
    as tone of writing, 287
"Irreconcilable Dissonance" (Doyle),
    308–11
Isley, Trena, 375
    "On the Sidelines," 59–62
"Is Your Jar Full?" 372–73
it
    formal writing and, 28–39
    pronoun-antecedent agreement and,
        25
"it does not follow" fallacy, 544

Jamieson, Jake, "The English-Only
    Movement: Can America
    Proscribe Language with a Clear
    Conscience?" 261–66
jargon, 285
Jarjosa, Jen, 152
Jefferson, Thomas, "The Declaration of
    Independence," 547–51
Jellison, Jerald M., 445–46
journal articles
    citation of, 657
    evaluating, 648–49
    online, citation of, 662
    in working bibliography, 652
journalistic writing, short paragraphs
    in, 175

Kahan, Dan M., "Shame Is Worth a Try,"
    575–76
Kanner, Allen D.
    "The Piracy of Privacy: Why Marketers
        Must Bare Our Souls," 587–91
    on purpose for writing, 592
Katz, Jon, 146
Kaufman, Michael T., "Of My Friend
    Hector and My Achilles Heel,"
    154–57
Keller, Helen
    braille alphabet and, 88–89
    "The Most Important Day," 84–87
Ketch, Tara, 83
keyword searches for sources, 645–47

King, Stephen, "Why We Crave Horror Movies," 524–27
King Jr., Martin Luther
  "I Have a Dream," 553–57
  learning from writings of, 58
  "The Ways of Meeting Oppression," 243, 465–68
Klinkenborg, Verlyn, "Our Vanishing Night," 355–59
Kosinski, Jerzy, 83
Kralovec, Etta, 149
Krauthammer, Charles, "The Truth about Torture," 616–26
Kuykendall, Danielle, 220

ladder of abstraction
  illustration and, 352–53
  using specific words and, 92–93
La Ferla, Ruth, "Generation E. A.: Ethnically Ambiguous," 602–7
Lamott, Anne, "Polaroids," 323–26
"The Last Shot" (Wolff), 189–91
lead. *See* beginnings
lectures, citation of, 666
Lederer, Richard, "The Case for Short Words," 160–63, 242
Lee, Laurie, 314
"Let's Think Outside the Box of Bad Clichés" (Pence), 349–51
letters, citation of, 666–67
letter to the editor, citation of, 659
library catalogs
  finding and using sources in, 644, 645
  keyword searches in, 646
like, similes and, 314
Lincoln, Abraham, 221
Lipman, Joanne, "And the Orchestra Played On," 407–10
list of works cited
  basics of, 655, 656–67
  student example of, 677
logic, in cause and effect, 520
logical appeals, 540
logical fallacies
  in argument, 544
  in cause and effect, 520
logical order
  basics of, 121–23
  in description, 401
logos, in argument, 545–46

"Loose Ends" (Dove), 259
loose sentences, 219
Lupica, Mike, 563
Lutz, William, "Doubts about Doublespeak," 477–81

MacNeil, Robert, 461
magazine articles
  citation of, 658
  evaluating, 648–49
  online, citation of, 663
  in working bibliography, 652
"The Magic of the Family Meal" (Gibbs), 208–13
main clauses
  placement of within sentence, 219
  subordination and, 218–19
main idea, of paragraph, 173–74. *See also* thesis
"Making an Astro Tube," 436–37
Mann, Thomas, 400
Mannes, Marya, 286
Mansfield, Stephanie, 172
mapping organization
  of essay, 17–18
  student example of, 35–36
maps, online, citation of, 664
marginal notes, annotating with, 47–48
"Marketing Ate Our Culture—But It Doesn't Have To" (O'Reilly), 594–99
Marquez, Myriam, "Why and When We Speak Spanish in Public," 531–33
McCarthy, Mary, 400–401
McCullough, David, 149
McDonald, Cherokee Paul, "A View from the Bridge," 124–27
"The Meanings of a Word" (Naylor), 113–16
Mehta, Gita, "The Famine of Bengal," 521–22
memos, citation of, 666–67
Merrill, Paul W., "The Principles of Poor Writing," 427–31
"Me Talk Pretty One Day" (Sedaris), 294–99
metaphors
  in description, 411
  understanding, 314–15

methods of development
  combining within essay, 3, 15–16
  determining in prewriting process,
    15–17
Minsky, Marvin, *The Society of Mind*,
    279
minus sign, keyword searches and, 646
misplaced modifiers, 26–27
*MLA Handbook for Writers of Research
    Papers*, 656, 661
MLA style
  in-text citations in, 655–56
  list of works cited in, 655, 656–67
Modern Language Association style. *See*
    MLA style
modifiers, misplaced and dangling, 26–27
"Momma, the Dentist, and Me"
    (Angelou), 386–93
Mori, Kyoko, "Yarn," 412–16
Morris, Willie, 373–74
"The Most Important Day" (Keller),
    84–87
Mukherjee, Bharati, "Two Ways to Belong
    in America," 493–97
Murphy, Erin, "White Lies," 381–83
"My Favorite Teacher" (Friedman), 103–5
"My Name" (Cisneros), 109–10

narration, 372–99
  description of, 15
  readings
    "Momma, the Dentist, and Me"
      (Angelou), 386–93
    "The Story of an Hour" (Chopin),
      395–98
    "What's in a Name?" (Gates Jr.),
      376–79
    "White Lies" (Murphy), 381–83
  student example of, 59–62
  understanding, 372–75
Naylor, Gloria, "The Meanings of a
    Word," 113–16
neither . . . nor
  parallelism and, 27
  subject-verb agreement and, 24
.net, 649
Newman, Judith, "What's Really Going
    On Inside Your Teen's Head," 240
newspaper articles
  citation of, 658

online, citation of, 663
  in working bibliography, 652
news services, online, citation of, 664
*The New York Times Complete Manual
    of Home Repair* (Gladstone),
    201–2
noncount nouns, 30–31
non sequitur fallacy, 544
Norvig, Peter, 150
nostalgic tone, 286
not, keyword searches and, 646
notebook, for annotating, 48
note cards
  for direct quotations, 244
  for note-taking, 653
  for paraphrasing, 243
  for summarizing, 242
  for summarizing with direct quotations,
    245
  for working bibliography, 651
note-taking, for research paper, 653–54
not only . . . but also
  parallelism and, 27
  subject-verb agreement and, 24
nouns
  basics of, 30–31
  weak versus strong and specific, 28
number
  pronoun-antecedent agreement in,
    24–25
  subject-verb agreement in, 23–24

obscene, defining, 446
Ockenga, Zoe, "The Excuse 'Not To',"
    62–67
"October" (Borland), 327–28
"Of My Friend Hector and My Achilles
    Heel" (Kaufman), 154–57
Olesky, Jeffrey
  "Golf: A Character Builder," 38–42
  writing process of, 33–38
"On Being 17, Bright, and Unable to
    Read" (Raymond), 197–200
"Once More to the Lake" (White),
    214–15
"Once Unique, Soon a Place Like Any
    Other" (Whaley), 244–45
"One Dying Wish" (Duffy), 73–77
online sources. *See* Internet sources
"On the Sidelines" (Isley), 59–62

On Writing Well (Zinsser), 180–82
opposing arguments, 543
"And the Orchestra Played On"
    (Lipman), 407–10
order of importance, 121–23
O'Reilly, Terry, "Marketing Ate Our
    Culture—But It Doesn't Have To,"
    594–99
.org, 649
organization, 119–44
  in description, 401
  readings
      "Buying a House" (Prentiss), 137–42
      "Fahrenheit 59: What a Child's
          Fever Might Tell Us about Climate
          Change" (Schulman), 131–34
      "A View from the Bridge"
          (McDonald), 124–27
  understanding, 119–23
organizational mapping
  student example of, 35–36
  in writing process, 17–18
organizational patterns
  in argument, 543
  combining within essay, 3, 15–16
  determining in prewriting process,
      15–17
Orwell, George, 148
  "Politics and the English Language,"
      351
The Other America (Walsh and Burrell),
    267
"Our Vanishing Night" (Klinkenborg),
    355–59
outlining
  to check organization, 123
  to organize essay, 17
  student example of, 35–36
"Overgeneralizing" (Chase), 100–101
oversimplification, 544

page reference, in-text citation of, 655–56
pamphlet, citation of, 660
paragraphs, 172–92
  readings
      "I Just Wanna Be Average" (Rose),
          183–86
      "The Last Shot" (Wolff), 189–91
      "Simplicity" (Zinsser), 176–79
  understanding, 172–75

parallelism, 221
  faulty, 27
paraphrasing sources, 241, 243–44
  avoiding plagiarism while, 254
  combining with direct quotations,
      244–45
  using own words and word order for,
      253–54
parentheses, keyword searches and, 646
parenthetical citations, 655–56
passive voice, 220
pathos, in argument, 545–46
Pence, Gregory, "Let's Think
    Outside the Box of Bad
    Clichés," 349–51
Percy, Benjamin, "Invasion," 329–33
perhapsing, 383–84
periodic sentences, 219
person, pronoun-antecedent agreement
    in, 24–25
personification, 315
persuasive appeals, 539–40
persuasive synthesis, 248
Peterson, William, 424
Pettit, Florence H., 423–24
"Petty Crime, Outrageous Punishment"
    (Cannon), 579–84
photographs, online, citation of, 664
Pinker, Steven, "In Defense of Dangerous
    Ideas," 361–70
"The Piracy of Privacy: Why Marketers
    Must Bare Our Souls" (Kanner),
    587–91
place, words and phrases for, 194
plagiarism, avoiding, 251–54, 654
platitudes, beginning with, 150
plural nouns, articles with, 30–31
plural pronouns/antecedents, 25
plural subjects/verbs, 23–24
plus sign, keyword searches and, 646
poems, online, citation of, 664
point-by-point comparison, 484
"Polaroids" (Lamott), 323–26
"Politics and the English Language"
    (Orwell), 351
Porter, Eduardo, "What Happiness Is,"
    456–59
Posner, Richard A., 627
post hoc, ergo propter hoc fallacy, 520,
    544

"Praise the Humble Dung Beetle"
(Begley), 255–57
preface, citation of, 660
Prentiss, Sean, "Buying a House," 137–42
prepositional phrases, subject-verb
agreement and, 23–24
prewriting, 7–18
choosing subject and, 9–10
collecting information and, 10–12
determining method of development
and, 15–17
establishing thesis and, 12–14
focusing on topic and, 9–10
getting ideas and, 10–12
knowing audience and, 14
mapping organization and, 17–18
understanding assignment and, 8–9
"The Principles of Poor Writing"
(Merrill), 427–31
print sources. *See* sources
process analysis, 423–43
description of, 15
readings
"How to Make Chocolate Sauce"
(Baker), 433–35
"The Principles of Poor Writing"
(Merrill), 427–31
"Why Leaves Turn Color in the Fall"
(Ackerman), 438–42
understanding, 423–26
pronoun-antecedent agreement, 24–25
pronoun references, making transitions
with, 194–95
proofreading, 32
propositions
of argument, 542
beginning with, 149
Psycho (Hitchcock), 529–30
publication information, 44, 45
purpose of written piece
in division and classification, 462, 463
organization and, 119
thesis statement and, 12

"The Qualities of Good Teachers"
(Britto), 248–49
questions, asking
for audience, 14
to avoid plagiarism, 254
for conclusions, 20

to develop thesis, 81, 87–88
for editing sentences, 31
for introductions, 20
in prewriting process, 10–11
for proofreading, 32
for revising, 21
rhetorical, beginning with, 150
for thesis, 14
while rereading text, 48–49
Quindlen, Anna, 148
quotation marks
avoiding plagiarism and, 251, 252–53
for direct quotations, 244, 245
keyword searches and, 646
quotations
avoiding plagiarism with, 254
basics of, 241, 244–45
beginning with, 147–48
signal phrases for, 246–47

radio broadcast, citation of, 665
Ramirez, Robert, "The Barrio," 316–20
Rank, Hugh, "Intensify/Downplay,"
609–11
rather . . . than, parallelism and, 27
Rathje, William L., "Rubbish!" 258–59
Raymond, David, "On Being 17, Bright,
and Unable to Read," 197–200
reading, 43–77
aloud, for revising, 20
analyzing with questions while, 48–49
annotating while, 47–48, 49–51
argument based on, 73–77
learning to write by, 1
narration based on, 59–62
preparing for, 44–46
prewriting and, 7
reflective essay based on, 67–72
and rereading, 47
response essay based on, 62–67
using in writing process, 57–59
readings, citation of, 666
reasoning, in cause and effect, 520
reference book, citation of, 660
reference work articles, online, citation
of, 664
reflection, before reading
example of, 46
purpose of, 44–45
reflective essay, student example of, 67–72

refutations to argument, 543
Reinhert, Al, *For All Mankind*, 279
relative pronouns, for subordination, 218
repetition, making transitions with,
194–95
rereading, 47
research, in prewriting process, 11
research paper, 642–77
setting schedule for, 643
sources for
analyzing, 650–51
documenting, 654–67
evaluating, 648–50
finding and using, 644–45
keyword searches for, 645–47
working bibliography for, 651–53
student example of, 667–77
subject directories for, 647
taking notes for, 653–54
resigned tone, 286
response essay, student example of, 62–67
restatement, words and phrases for, 194
review, citation of, 658
revising, 20–21
rhetorical highlights
example of, 45–46
getting information from, 44
rhetorical modes, combining within essay,
3, 15–16
rhetorical patterns, determining in
prewriting process, 15–17
rhetorical questions, beginning with, 150
Ripley, Amanda, "Who Says a Woman
Can't be Einstein?" 505–14
Rockwell, Norman, 215–16
Rosa, Alfred, 172–73
Rose, Mike, "I Just Wanna Be Average,"
183–86
Rowan, Carl T., "Unforgettable Miss
Bessie," 166–70
"Rubbish!" (Rathje), 258–59
Running, Steve, 239
run-on sentences, 21–22
Rushdie, Salman, "The Taj Mahal,"
419–21
Russell, Ruth, "The Wounds That Can't
Be Stitched Up," 247

Safire, William, 148–49
"Salvation" (Hughes), 228–30

Saturday Evening Post, 215–16
schedule for research paper, 643
Schmidt, Marco, 567–68
Schmidtbauer, Cori
"To Facebook or Not," 669–77
writing process of, 667–68
scholarly journal articles. *See* journal
articles
scholarly project article, online, citation
of, 663
Schulman, Audrey, "Fahrenheit 59: What
a Child's Fever Might Tell Us
about Climate Change," 131–34
second-person pronouns
academic writing and, 29
antecedents and, 25
"Secular Mantras" (Eldred), 444
Sedaris, David, "Me Talk Pretty One
Day," 294–99
sentence fragments, 22–23
sentences, 217–37
readings
"Childhood" (Walker), 222–25
"Salvation" (Hughes), 228–30
"Volar" (Cofer), 233–35
understanding, 217–21
variety of, 217–20
sequence, words and phrases for, 194
Shaffer, Charles, 162–63
"Shame" (Gregory), 288–92
"Shame Is Worth a Try" (Kahan),
575–76
she
formal writing and, 28–39
pronoun-antecedent agreement and, 25
Sherman, Bonnie, "Should Shame Be Used
as Punishment?" 249–50
Sherry, Mary, "In Praise of the F Word,"
564–66
short sentences, dramatically, 220
short stories, online, citation of, 664
"Should Shame Be Used as Punishment?"
(Sherman), 249–50
"Shyness" (Henderson and Zimbardo),
29–30
The Sierra Club, 287
signal phrase, 246–47
similes
in description, 411
understanding, 314

"Simplicity" (Zinsser), 176–79
  direct quotation note card for, 244
singular nouns, articles with, 30–31
singular pronouns/antecedents, 25
singular subjects/verbs, 23–24
Sipress, David, 301
Slackman, Michael, 627
The Society of Mind (Minsky), 279
sound recording, citation of, 665
sources, 238–79
  analyzing, 650–51
  avoiding plagiarism and, 251–54
  documenting, 654–67. *See also*
      documenting sources
  evaluating, 648–50
  finding and using, 644–45
  integrating material from, 246–47
  keyword searches for, 645–47
  paraphrasing, 241, 243–45
  quoting from, 241, 244–45
  readings
    "The Clan of One-Breasted Women"
        (Williams), 269–77
    "The English-Only Movement: Can
        America Proscribe Language with
        a Clear Conscience?" (Jamieson),
        261–66
    "Praise the Humble Dung Beetle"
        (Begley), 255–57
  subject directories and, 647
  summarizing, 241–42
  synthesizing, 247–50
  understanding, 238
  using, 238–41
  working bibliography for, 651–53
space order
  basics of, 121
  in description, 401
specific words, 284
speeches, citation of, 664, 666
spelling, proofreading for, 32
startling claim, beginning with, 149
statistics
  avoiding plagiarism and, 254
  beginning with, 148
Stevens, Paul, 151–52
stories, as narration, 372
"The Story of an Hour" (Chopin),
    395–98
"Strong School Leaders" (Wanner), 107–8

"Stuck on the Couch" (Gupta), 535–37
subject, choosing and narrowing, 9–10
subject-by-subject comparison, 483–84
subject directories, 647
subject-verb agreement, 23–24
subordinating conjunctions
  sentence fragments and, 22–23
  for subordination, 218
subordination, 218–19
subscription service, documenting, 662–63
Sullivan, Andrew
  "The Abolition of Torture," 629–40
  learning from writings of, 58
summarizing sources, 241–42
  avoiding plagiarism while, 254
  combining with direct quotations,
      244–45
  using own words and word order for,
      253–54
summary, words and phrases for, 194
surprise, beginning with, 149
syllogism, 541
synonyms
  connotation of words and, 283
  defining words with, 444–45
synthesis of sources, 247–50

"The Taj Mahal" (Rushdie), 419–21
Tangney, June, "Condemn the Crime,
    Not the Person," 569–72
Teale, Edwin Way, 340
technical language
  appropriate use of, 285
  discipline-specific, 29–30
television broadcast, citation of, 665
than, parallelism and, 27
"That Lean and Hungry Look" (Britt),
    499–502
the, basics of, 30–31
thesaurus, 28
thesis, 81–98. *See also* thesis statement
  of argument, 542
  beginnings and, 146
  establishing, 12–14
  readings
    "Anxiety: Challenge by Another
        Name" (Collier), 94–97
    "Be Specific" (Goldberg), 90–92
    "The Most Important Day" (Keller),
        84–87

thesis (*contd.*)
  understanding, 81–83
  unity with, 99–102
thesis-driven argument, student example
  of, 73–77
thesis statement. *See also* thesis
  student example of, 35, 36
  unity with, 100
  writing and revising, 12–14, 81–83
they
  formal writing and, 28–39
  pronoun-antecedent agreement and,
    25
third-person point of view, 373
third-person pronouns
  antecedents and, 25
  formal writing and, 28–39
time, words and phrases for, 194
time management, for research paper,
  643
time order, 119–21
title
  creating, 19
  getting information from, 44, 145
  reference to, beginning with, 150
"To Facebook or Not" (Schmidtbauer),
  669–77
tone, 283–313
  academic, 28–30
  readings
    "The Center of the Universe" (Ansa),
      302–6
    "Irreconcilable Dissonance" (Doyle),
      308–11
    "Me Talk Pretty One Day" (Sedaris),
      294–99
    "Shame" (Gregory), 288–92
  understanding, 285–87
topic, narrowing and focusing on, 9–10
topic sentences, of paragraphs, 172, 174
transitional words/phrases
  list of, 193–94
  within paragraphs, 174
  in process analysis, 426
  use of, 194–95
transitions, 193–216
  readings
    "Becoming a Writer" (Baker), 203–6
    "The Magic of the Family Meal"
      (Gibbs), 208–13

"On Being 17, Bright, and Unable to
  Read" (Raymond), 197–200
  understanding, 193–96
translation, citation of, 660
"The Truth about Torture"
  (Krauthammer), 616–26
Turple, Marcie, 13
Twain, Mark, 221, 283
  "Two Ways of Seeing a River," 488–90
"Two Ways of Seeing a River" (Twain),
  488–90
"Two Ways to Belong in America"
  (Mukherjee), 493–97

ultimate causes, 519
"The Uncritical Inference Test" (Haney),
  528–29
"Unforgettable Miss Bessie" (Rowan),
  166–70
unity, 99–118
  within paragraph, 172, 173, 174–75
  readings
    "The Meanings of a Word" (Naylor),
      113–16
    "My Favorite Teacher" (Friedman),
      103–5
    "My Name" (Cisneros), 109–10
  understanding, 99–102
Updike, John, 219, 314
URLs, in works cited, 661–62

Van Loon, Hendrick Willem, 121–22
verbs
  in description, 421–22
  for diction and tone, 293
  in signal phrases, 246–47
  subject-verb agreement and, 23–24
  weak versus strong and specific, 28
verb tense, shifts in, 25–26
video recordings, citation of, 665, 666
"A View from the Bridge" (McDonald),
  124–27
visual images, online, citation of, 664
"Volar" (Cofer), 233–35
The Voyage of the Mimi (Hendrick), 278

Wai, Grace Ming-Yee, 119–20
Walker, Alice, "Childhood," 222–25
Walsh, Robert L., *The Other America*,
  267

Wanner, Mark
"Strong School Leaders," 107–8
thesis statement of, 106
Ward, Jinsie, 122–23
Watterson, Bill, "Calvin and Hobbes,"
129, 130
"The Ways of Meeting Oppression"
(King Jr.), 465–68
*The Way We Really Are: Coming to
Terms with America's Changing
Families* (Coontz), 240–41
we
informal writing and, 29
pronoun-antecedent agreement and, 25
web sites, evaluating, 649. *See also*
Internet sources
Webster's dictionary, beginning with, 150
Weeks, Linton, "Burdens of the Modern
Beast," 359–60
Welty, Eudora, 314
"The Corner Store," 402–5
Whaley, Abe, "Once Unique, Soon a Place
Like Any Other," 244–45
"What Are Friends For?" (Winik), 470–73
"What Happiness Is" (Porter), 456–59
what if, effect and, 517
"What Is Crime?" (Friedman), 447–49
"What Pro Sports Owners Owe Us"
(Zirin), 560–62
"What's in a Name?" (Gates Jr.), 376–79
"What's Really Going On Inside Your
Teen's Head" (Newman), 240
White, Carrie , 99–100, 173
White, E. B., "Once More to the Lake,"
214–15
White, T. H., 315
"White Lies" (Murphy), 381–83
"Who Says a Woman Can't be Einstein?"
(Ripley), 505–14
why, causal analysis and, 517
"Why and When We Speak Spanish in
Public" (Marquez), 531–33
"Why Leaves Turn Color in the Fall"
(Ackerman), 438–42
"Why We Crave Horror Movies" (King),
524–27
wiki entries, citation of, 665

Williams, Terry Tempest, "The Clan of
One-Breasted Women," 269–77
Wilson-Libby, Mundy, 195–96
Winik, Marion, "What Are Friends For?"
470–73
Wise, David, 220
Wise, Gary, 476
Wolff, Tobias, "The Last Shot," 189–91
Wolfgram Memorial Library of Widener
University, 650
word processor, proofreading with, 32
working bibliography, 651–53
works cited
basics of, 655, 656–67
student example of, 677
works of art, citation of, 664, 666
World Wide Web sources. *See* Internet
sources
"The Wounds That Can't Be Stitched Up"
(Russell), 247
Wren, Celia, 163
writing, good, characteristics of, 1
writing process, 7–42
editing and, 21–31
first draft and, 18–20
prewriting and, 7–18
proofreading and, 32
revising and, 20–21
student example of, 33–42
writing prompt
example of, 46
getting information from, 44–45

"Yarn" (Mori), 412–16
you
academic writing and, 29
pronoun-antecedent agreement and,
25

Zimbardo, Philip, "Shyness," 29–30
Zimring, Franklin E., 82
Zinsser, William, 82, 315
"Simplicity," 176–79
direct quotation note card for, 244
On Writing Well, 180–82
Zirin, Dave, "What Pro Sports Owners
Owe Us," 560–62